International Relations

CANADIAN EDITION

JOSHUA S. GOLDSTEIN
American University, Washington, D.C.

Canadian Edition by **SANDRA WHITWORTH**
of York University, based on *International Relations*,
Fifth Edition, by Joshua S. Goldstein

PEARSON
Longman

Toronto

Library and Archives Canada Cataloguing in Publication

Goldstein, Joshua S., 1952–
        International relations / Joshua S. Goldstein, Sandra Whitworth.
— Canadian ed.

Includes bibliographical references and index.

ISBN 0-321-18880-2

        1. International relations. I. Whitworth, Sandra, 1959– II. Title.

JZ1242.G64 2005   327   C2004-904292-0

ISBN 0-321-18880-2

Vice President, Editorial Director: Michael J. Young
Executive Acquisitions Editor: Christine Cozens
Signing Representative: Patty Riediger
Marketing Manager: Ryan St. Peters
Developmental Editor: John Polanszky
Production Editor: Söğüt Y. Güleç
Copy Editor: Lisa Berland
Proofreader: Tara Tovell
Production Coordinator: Peggy Brown
Page Layout: Jansom
Photo Research: Sandy Cooke
Cover and Interior Design: Julia Hall
Cover Image: Getty Images / Peter Poulides

The credits appear on page 548. They should be considered an extension of the copyright page.

    3 4 5   09 08 07 06 05

Printed and bound in USA.

PEARSON
Longman

To my family

J.S.G.

To my students, who have taught me so much

S.W.

Brief Contents

Detailed Contents

---

*Note: Each chapter ends with questions on thinking critically,
a chapter summary, and a list of key terms and weblinks.*

Part Three International Organizations and International Political Economy

Note: Coloured reference maps appear at the back of the book after the Subject Index.

Preface

Canadians are in a unique and interesting position when confronting international relations (IR). Both the study and practice of IR in Canada has been conducted in the shadow of one of the world's superpowers—today's only superpower—the United States. Canada is not only a contiguous neighbour to the U.S. but shares many ideological and social commitments with that neighbour, as well as defence and security arrangements, a robust trading relationship, and important diplomatic ties. Likewise, Canadian students of international relations more commonly read U.S. texts and scholarly journals of IR than they will Canadian sources, for no other reason than that there are far *more* texts and journals that originate in the U.S. than in Canada.

Canada's relationship with the United States was once characterized by Prime Minister Pierre Elliot Trudeau as being like that of "a mouse in bed with an elephant." Nonetheless, Canada's engagements with global-level politics, in both practical and scholarly terms, have sometimes shared the U.S. position but at other times charted a very different course than that of its southern neighbour. Recently, in foreign policy terms, while Canada supported the U.S. after the horrific attacks of September 11, 2001, it later refused to participate in the invasion of Iraq in 2003. Canadian governments have long been committed to multilateralism and institutions like the United Nations, whereas the U.S. has been far more critical and considerably less enthusiastic about many of these institutions.

Likewise, while the U.S. has been reluctant to ratify some international human rights conventions (such as the Convention on the Elimination of Discrimination Against Women, or CEDAW), environmental protections (such as the Kyoto Accord), or disarmament agreements (like the 1999 Landmines Ban), Canada has often taken the lead in pursuing these kinds of instruments. Canadian and U.S. governments have long shared a commitment to freeing up trade and enhancing globalization, but they sometimes differ on the nuances of how this is to be accomplished.

In terms of scholarship, it is probably not unfair to describe the Canadian IR academic community as more heterogeneous in theoretical orientation than its counterpart in the United States. As will be described in later chapters, the study of IR has been dominated by an approach that is called "realism," and this has been particularly true in the United States. This does not mean that there are not many realist scholars of IR in Canada—indeed there are; nor does it mean that scholars working from theoretical perspectives other than realism do not exist in the United States—indeed they do. But in part because of the different practical orientation of decision-makers in Canada, and in part because of the particular contributions that some IR theorists in Canada have made, there is a greater tendency in Canadian university classrooms to ensure that students are exposed to the range of theoretical debate around questions of global politics, and that they come to appreciate that realism is one theoretical approach among many in IR.

It is for these reasons that IR textbooks written in the U.S. for American university students are not entirely appropriate for a Canadian audience. Those textbooks may be empirically rigorous and theoretically sound, but they "speak to" a different context than is found in Canada. This textbook takes one of the best introductory textbooks on IR available today, Joshua Goldstein's *International Relations*, and develops it for Canadian readers. This has been accomplished in two interrelated ways. First, examples of the role of Canada, and Canadians, in global-level politics have been introduced throughout the text. This has not meant eliminating information about the United States—as the world's only remaining superpower, the U.S. will always be an important part of the study of IR, and is treated as such in this edition. Rather it has meant the introduction of Canadian-relevant historical information, data, and policy concerns. What is clear in the Canadian edition of *International Relations* is that Canadian activity in the world, whether on the part of our politicians, policy-makers, diplomats, scholars, activists, or citizens, is an important element in the workings of global politics.

The second way in which this text has been written for Canadian students has been to develop some of the theoretical coverage, provide greater exposure to Canadian IR theorists (as well as theorists from other parts of the world), and in particular to make clear throughout the text the kinds of debates that take place between IR theorists on the variety of issues they engage, from war and peace to political economy, through international law, to development and underdevelopment and the environment. This is done in a variety of ways: through the "Thinking Theoretically" boxes and the "Changing World Order" boxes, as well as discussions in the text.

The rich complexity of international relationships—political, economic, social, and cultural—provides a fascinating puzzle for all students of IR to try to understand. The puzzle is not just intellectually challenging; it is also emotionally powerful. It contains human-scale stories in which the subject's grand themes—war and peace, tragedy and triumph, conflict, inequality, and community—are played out. International relations is also relevant to our daily lives as never before; today's students will graduate into a global economy in which no nation stands alone and in which their understanding of the world is more sophisticated than any generation that preceded them. This book links the conceptual apparatus of the field to the people who make up international relations and those whose lives are at stake.

Pedagogical Elements

This book's aim is to present the current state of knowledge in IR in a comprehensive and accessible way—to provide a map of the subject covering its various research communities in a logical order. This map is organized around the subfields of international security, international organizations and political economy, and North-South issues and the environment.

These subfields, although separated physically in this book, are integrated conceptually and overlap in many ways. No longer does one set of principles apply to military affairs, another set to economic relations, and a third to development issues, as was sometimes argued during the Cold War. This book connects the subfields of IR to the real world by using concrete examples to illustrate theories. Many people in the television generation find information—especially abstract concepts—easier to grasp when linked with pictures. Thus, the book uses photographs extensively to illustrate important points. Photo captions reinforce main themes from each section of the text and link them with the scenes pictured.

In a subject like IR, where knowledge is tentative and empirical developments can overtake theories, critical thinking is a key skill for university and college students to develop. At various points in the text, conclusions are left open-ended to let students reason their way through an issue. The questions at the end of each chapter are designed to engage students in thinking critically about the contents of the chapter.

The use of quantitative data also encourages critical thinking. Basic data, presented simply and appropriately at a global level, allow students to form their own judgments and to reason through the implications of different policies and theories. The text uses global-level data (showing the whole picture) and conveys information graphically where appropriate.

Many people come to the study of IR with little background in world geography and history. The first chapter of this book presents background material on these topics. A historical perspective places recent decades in the context of the evolution of the modern international system. The global orientation of the book reflects the diversity of IR experiences for different actors, including those in the global South.

Three levels of analysis—individual, domestic, and interstate—have often been used to sort out the multiple influences operating in international relations. This book adds a fourth, the global level. Global-level phenomena such as the United Nations, the world environment, the global political economy, and global telecommunications and culture receive special attention.

IR is a large subject that offers many directions for further exploration. The footnotes in this book suggest further reading on various topics; unless otherwise noted, they are not traditional source notes. Each chapter ends with questions on thinking critically, a chapter summary, a list of key terms, and a list of chapter-related weblinks.

Structure of the Book

The book is divided into four parts. In Part One, studying International Relations is examined, first (in Chapter 1) by conveying the state of the field of IR as well as its geographic and historical context. Chapter 2 then examines realist approaches to the study of IR, followed (in Chapter 3) by liberal and critical approaches. Parts Two, Three, and Four then follow substantive topics: international security in Part Two, international organizations and international political economy in Part Three, and North-South issues and the environment in Part Four. Parts Two, Three, and Four, although convenient for organization, overlap substantively and theoretically, as noted in several places.

The three chapters of Part Two begin with the foreign policy process and the roles of substate actors in Chapter 4. Chapter 5 introduces the main sources of international conflict, including ethnic, territorial, and economic conflicts, and terrorism. The conditions and manner in which such conflicts lead to the use of violence are discussed in Chapter 6, on military force.

Part Three begins with Chapter 7, which shows how international agreements, treaties, organizations, and law, and especially the United Nations, have evolved to become major influences in IR. Chapter 8 introduces again some of the theoretical concepts in political economy and discusses the most important topic in international political economy, namely, trade relations. Chapter 9 describes the politics of international money, banking, and multinational business operations. Chapter 10 explores the processes of international integration, telecommunications, and cultural exchange on both a regional scale—the European Union—and a global one.

Part Four opens with Chapter 11, which addresses global North-South relations, with particular attention to poverty in the global South. Chapter 12 then considers alternatives for economic development in the context of international business, debt, and foreign aid. Chapter 13 examines some of the most pressing issues of IR today: the environment and population growth. Chapter 14—a brief postscript—reflects on the book's central themes and encourages critical thinking about the future.

Supplements

Instructor's Manual/Test Item File This resource, available to instructors using this textbook, includes chapter overviews, learning objectives, lecture outlines, teaching suggestions, ideas for student projects, and key words, in addition to numerous multiple-choice, short answer, map, and essay questions.

Companion Website   Students are invited to use the learning resources at this book's Companion Website by visiting **www.pearsoned.ca/goldstein**. There you can find useful chapter overviews with learning objectives, take practice tests, follow hot links onto the Web, and explore the implications of the information revolution for international relations.

Acknowledgments

Thanks go first to Emily Saso for research assistance on the Canadian edition. Others who were very helpful in tracking down sources for me include Marshall Beier, Eric Helleiner, Keith Krause, Nicole LaViolette, Ananya Mukherjee-Reed, Leo Panitch, and Alejandra Roncallo. I would also like to thank Elizabeth Dauphinee, Tami Jacoby, and Cristina Masters for advice and suggestions. The team at Pearson Education Canada who assisted me with the book—Lori Will, Christine Cozens, John Polanszky, Söğüt Güleç, Lisa Berland, Tara Tovell, and others behind the scenes—both initiated this timely project and were enormously helpful in seeing it to completion. I have been encouraged by students for over some fifteen years to develop a textbook of IR; to them go my largest thanks. Among the many colleagues who contributed ideas that influenced this textbook, the following reviewers, in particular, made many useful suggestions:

Isabella Bakker, *York University*

Mark Baron, *University of Calgary*

Vincent Della Salla, *Carleton University*

Alistair D. Edgar, *Wilfrid Laurier University*

Nancy Kokaz, *University of Toronto*

Ed Lavalle, *Capilano College*

Logan Masilamani, *Simon Fraser University*

David Mutimer, *York University*

Julian Schofield, *Concordia University*

Yasmine Shamsie, *Wilfrid Laurier University*

Elliot Tepper, *Carleton University*

Sandra Whitworth

To the Student

The topics studied by scholars are like a landscape with many varied locations and terrains. This textbook is a map that can orient you to the main topics, debates, and issue areas in international relations. Scholars use specialized language to talk about their subjects. This text is also a phrase book that can translate such lingo and explain the terms and concepts that scholars use to talk about international relations. However, IR is filled with many voices speaking many tongues. The text translates some of those voices—of prime ministers and professors, free-traders and feminists—to help you sort out the contours of the subject and the state of knowledge about its various topics. But, ultimately, the synthesis presented in this book is the authors' own. Both you and your professor may disagree with many points. Thus, this book is only a starting point for conversations and debates.

With map and phrase book in hand, you are ready to explore a fascinating world. The great changes taking place in world politics have made the writing of this textbook an exciting project. May you enjoy your own explorations of this realm.

A Note on Nomenclature

In international relations, names are politically sensitive; different actors may call a territory or an event by different names. This book cannot resolve such conflicts; it has adopted the following naming conventions for the sake of consistency. The United Kingdom of Great Britain (England, Scotland, Wales) and Northern Ireland are usually called Britain. Burma, renamed Myanmar by its military government, is generally referred to as Burma or Burma/Myanmar. Cambodia, renamed Kampuchea by the Khmer Rouge in the 1970s, is called Cambodia. The 1991 U.S.-led multinational military campaign that retook Kuwait after Iraq's 1990 invasion is called the Gulf War. The war between Iran and Iraq in the 1980s is called the Iran-Iraq War (not the "Gulf War" as some called it at the time). The U.S. war against Iraq in 2003 is usually called the Iraq War. The country of Bosnia and Herzegovina is generally shortened to Bosnia (with apologies to Herzegovinians). The former Yugoslav Republic of Macedonia is called Macedonia. The People's Republic of China is referred to as China. The former Zaire is now Democratic Congo. Elsewhere, country names follow common usage, dropping formal designations such as "Republic of."

A Great Way to Learn and Instruct Online

The Pearson Education Canada Companion Website is easy to navigate and is organized to correspond to the chapters in this textbook. Whether you are a student in the classroom or a distance learner you will discover helpful resources for in-depth study and research that empower you in your quest for greater knowledge and maximize your potential for success in the course.

[www.pearsoned.ca/goldstein]

Jump to...   http://www.pearsoned.ca/goldstein   Home Search Help Profile

Home >

Companion Website

International Relations, Canadian Edition, by Goldstein and Whitworth

Student Resources

The modules in this section provide students with tools for learning course material. These modules include:

- Chapter Summary
- Multiple-Choice Quiz
- True/False Quiz
- Pattern Match
- Short Essay
- Long Essay
- Simulation
- Information Revolution
- Let's Debate the Issue
- Weblinks

In the quiz modules students can send answers to the grader and receive instant feedback on their progress through the Results Reporter.

Instructor Resources

A link to this book on the Pearson Education Canada online catalogue (vig.pearsoned.ca) provides instructors with additional teaching tools. Downloadable PowerPoint Presentations and an Instructor's Manual are just some of the materials that may be available. The catalogue is password protected. To get a password, simply contact your Pearson Education Canada Representative or call Faculty Sales and Services at 1-800-850-5813.

Introduction

A vote is taken at the UN Security Council.

THE STUDY OF IR

Our world is large and complex. International relations is a fascinating topic because it concerns peoples, institutions and cultures throughout the world. The scope and complexity of the interactions among these groups make international relations a challenging subject to master. There is always more to learn. This book is only the beginning of the story.

The field of **international relations (IR)** at one time concerned strictly the relationships among the world's governments. But this is no longer true today. Contemporary scholars and students of IR study international organizations, multinational corporations, social movements, nongovernmental organizations, individuals, as well as the world's governments. IR also is concerned with economics, culture, and domestic politics; issues of gender, race, ethnicity, and class; and geographical and historical factors that influence politics at the global level. IR is a large subject that overlaps several other fields.

The purpose of this book is to introduce the field of IR, to organize in a logical way what is known and theorized about IR, and to convey key concepts and ideas. This first chapter defines IR as a field of study, introduces the actors of interest, and reviews the geographical and historical contexts within which IR occurs.

international relations (IR)
The relationships among the world's state governments and the connection of those relationships with other actors (such as the United Nations, multinational corporations, and individuals), with other social relationships (including economics, culture, and domestic politics), and with geographic and historical influences.

IR and Daily Life

Sometimes international relations is portrayed as a distant and abstract ritual conducted by a small group of people such as prime ministers, generals, and diplomats. This picture is not

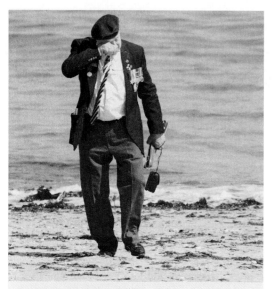

REFLECTIONS OF WAR
IR touches our lives in many ways. Canadian veterans mark the D-Day memorial in 2004.

an accurate one. Although leaders do play a major role in international affairs, many other people participate as well. University students and other citizens participate in international relations every time they vote in an election or work on a political campaign, every time they buy a product or service traded on world markets, and every time they watch the news. The choices we make in our daily lives ultimately affect the world we live in. Each person faces unique choices as an individual human being. Through those choices, every person makes a unique contribution, however small, to the world of international relations.

In turn, IR profoundly affects the daily lives of university students and other citizens. The prospects for getting jobs after graduation depend on the global economy and international economic competition. For middle-class Canadians with university degrees, those jobs also are more likely than ever to entail international travel or communication. And the rules of the world trading system affect the goods that students consume, from mobile phones to gasoline.

Although international economics pervades daily life, war dominates daily life only infrequently. Still, war casts a long shadow. In major wars, of course, students and their friends and families may go off to war and their lives change irreversibly. In Canada, people involved in the armed forces are more likely to be deployed on peacekeeping missions than to engage in battle, but this too has an enormous impact on their lives. Even in peacetime, war is among the most pervasive international influences in daily life. Children play with war toys; TV and films reproduce and multiply the images of war; and a sizeable sector of the world economy is structured around military production.

The internationalization of daily life is increasing rapidly. Better communication and transportation capabilities are constantly expanding the ordinary person's contact with people, products, and ideas from other countries. As technology advances, the world is thus shrinking year by year.

IR as a Field of Study

IR as a field of study, separate from the study of diplomatic history or economics or politics more generally, is a relatively recent enterprise. The very first Chair of International Relations was established at the University of Wales in Aberystwyth in 1919. Though IR as a field had its beginnings in the United Kingdom, by the post–World War II period it was in the United States that the study of IR really took hold—with the creation of programs, university departments, and research institutes all focused on developing expertise in the study of global level politics.[1] Today, universities around the world have courses and programs devoted to the study of IR.

IR as a field of study, whether it is taught in Canada, the U.K., Mexico, or Thailand, has always had uncertain boundaries.[2] As a part of political science, IR is about *politics at*

[1] Martin Hollis and Steve Smith, *Explaining and Understanding International Relations* (Oxford: Clarendon, 1991). Stanley Hoffmann, "An American Social Science: International Relations," *Daedalus*, 106.3 (1977), 41–60.

[2] Peter J. Katzenstein, Robert O. Keohane, and Stephen D. Krasner, eds., *Exploration and Contestation in the Study of World Politics* (Cambridge, MA: MIT P, 1999). John Macmillan and Andrew Linklater, eds., *Boundaries in Question: New Directions in International Relations* (London: Pinter, 1995).

the global level—the decisions of governments concerning their actions toward other governments, the activities of international institutions, global trade and armed conflict, protest movements, international financial institutions, environmental issues, global trafficking in minerals or people, and international human rights, to name but a few. Some universities offer separate degrees or departments for IR. Most, however, teach IR in political science classes.

One kind of politics that has an international character is not generally included in the field of IR: the domestic politics of foreign countries. That is a separate field of political science called *comparative politics*. Comparative politics overlaps with IR to the considerable extent that domestic politics influences foreign policy in many countries, and many actors at the global level (businesses, nongovernmental organizations, social movements) are involved in both local-level and global-level politics. Despite these overlaps, IR as a field tends to avoid issues that concern domestic politics in Canada, the United States, or other countries *except* to the extent that they affect politics at the global level.

The scope of the field of IR may also be defined by the *subfields* it encompasses. Traditionally, the study of IR has focused on questions of war and peace—the subfield of **international security** studies. The movements of armies and of diplomats, the crafting of treaties and alliances, the development and deployment of military capabilities—these are the subjects that dominated the study of IR in the past, especially in the 1950s and 1960s, and they continue to hold a central position in the field. In the 1990s, after the Cold War, the subfield of security studies broadened beyond its traditional focus on military forces and the superpower arms race. Regional conflicts began to receive more attention, and ethnic conflicts became more prominent. Scholars of foreign policy processes increasingly saw themselves as part of this broader security studies community. Meanwhile, interdisciplinary peace studies programs, which emerged in the 1980s at many universities, sought to broaden concepts of "security" further—as did feminist scholars. While the study of war, weapons, and military forces continues to be the core concern of international security studies, these trends have expanded the boundaries of the subfield.[3]

In the 1970s and 1980s, as economics became increasingly central to international relations, the subfield of **international political economy (IPE)** grew and became the counterpoint to international security studies as a second main subfield of IR. Scholars of IPE study trade relations and financial relations among nations, and the international institutions that support these relations, such as the World Trade Organization and the International Monetary Fund. Since the 1990s, growing attention has been paid also to global North-South relations between rich and poor nations (see pp. 14–22), including such topics as economic dependency, debt, foreign aid, and technology transfer. As the East-West confrontation of the Cold War recedes into history, North-South issues are becoming more salient. So are problems of international environmental management and of global telecommunications. The subfield of IPE is expanding accordingly. Of course, different professors see the scope and structure of the field of IR in different ways.

IR scholars now recognize the close connections of IPE with security (after decades of treating them as separate and different). The same principles and theories that help us understand international security (covered in Part Two) also help us to understand IPE (Part Three), and the environment and development. Economics is important in security

international security
A subfield of *international relations (IR)* that focuses on questions of war and peace.

international political economy (IPE) The study of the politics of trade, monetary, and other economic relations among nations, and their connection to other transnational forces.

---

[3] Stephen M. Walt, "The Renaissance of Security Studies," *International Studies Quarterly* 35.2 (1991): 211–40. Barry Buzan, *People, States and Fear: An Agenda for International Security Studies in the Post–Cold War Era*, 2nd ed. (Boulder, CO: Rienner, 1991). Keith Krause and Michael C. Williams, eds., *Critical Security Studies* (Minneapolis: U of Minnesota P, 1997). Ronnie D. Lipschutz, ed., *On Security* (NY: Columbia UP, 1995). Stuart Croft and Terry Terriff, eds., *Contemporary Security Policy: Critical Reflections on Twenty Years of Change* (Ilford, UK: Frank Cass, 2000).

affairs, and vice versa. The organization of this book may seem to create a divide between the subfields, but in reality they are interwoven.

Theories

IR scholars want to understand why and how international events occur in the way they do. Why did a certain war break out? Why did a certain trade agreement benefit one nation or group of people more than another? How have some countries come to be so much richer than others? These questions can be answered in several ways. One kind of answer results from tracing the immediate, short-term sequence of events and decisions that led to a particular outcome. For instance, the outbreak of war might be traced to a critical decision made by a particular leader. This kind of answer is largely *descriptive*—it seeks to describe how particular forces and actors operate to bring about a particular outcome.

Another kind of answer to these types of questions results from seeking general explanations and longer-term, more indirect causes. For example, the outbreak of a war might be seen as an instance of a general pattern in which arms races lead to war. Conversely, wars may occur because particular interests within a state see it as to their advantage to push their state to engage in armed conflict. These kinds of answers are *theoretical* because they place the particular event in the context of a more general pattern applicable across many cases.

Understanding IR requires both descriptive and theoretical knowledge. It would do little good only to describe events without being able to generalize or draw lessons from them. Nor would it do much good to formulate purely abstract theories without being able to apply them to the finely detailed and complex world in which we live.

IR has long been a rather practical discipline. There is a close connection between scholars in colleges, universities, and think-tanks and the policy-making community working in the government. This is especially true in the United States, but it also occurs in other countries. Some professors serve in the government (for instance, Professor Condoleezza Rice became U.S. President Bush's National Security Advisor in 2001). Sometimes when policy-makers retire from political life they turn to research and teaching (for instance, Canada's former Minister of Foreign Affairs and International Trade, Lloyd Axworthy, joined the University of British Columbia when he left politics in 2000 and then became president of the University of Winnipeg in 2004). Professors also publicize their ideas about global politics through newspaper columns or TV interviews. In many cases, they are seeking to influence their government's foreign policies or even just the opinion of average citizens.

IR is an unpredictable realm of turbulent processes and events that catch the experts by surprise, such as the fall of the Berlin Wall in 1989. Most IR scholars are modest about their ability to make accurate predictions—and with good reason. The best theories provide only a rough guide to understanding what actually occurs in IR or to predicting what will happen next.

Perhaps because of this complexity and unpredictability, IR scholars do not agree on a single set of theories to explain IR or even on a single set of concepts with which to discuss the field. Throughout these discussions, no single theoretical framework has the support of all IR scholars.[4]

---

[4] A. J. R. Groom and Margot Light, *Contemporary International Relations: A Guide to Theory* (NY: St. Martin's, 1994). Robert J. Art and Robert Jervis, eds., *International Politics: Enduring Concepts and Contemporary Issues*, 4th ed. (NY: Longman, 1996). James E. Dougherty, Jr., and Robert L. Pfaltzgraff, *Contending Theories of International Relations: A Comprehensive Survey* 4th ed. (NY: Longman, 1997). Michael W. Doyle, *Ways of War and Peace: Realism, Liberalism, and Socialism* (NY: Norton, 1997). Paul R. Viotti and Mark V. Kauppi, eds., *International Relations Theory: Realism, Pluralism, Globalism, and Beyond*, 3rd ed. (Needham Heights, MA: Allyn & Bacon, 1999).

One way to look at the variety of theories is to distinguish three broad theoretical perspectives, or paradigms: realist, liberal-pluralist, and critical. A paradigm, for our purposes here, means a group of theories which each: (1) shares a vision of what the world looks like; (2) shares some sense of what to study in that world (states? transnational organizations or businesses? social movements? economic classes?); and (3) shares certain values about the purpose or goal of theorizing about global-level politics. In some sense, each is a lens through which the world looks different and different things seem important. At the same time, the three perspectives can complement each other, and certainly theorists within each of the paradigms engage with one another and are sometimes influenced by each other. Each broad paradigm contains within it different specific theories, and debate and disagreement can take place within the paradigms as much as between them. But within each, there is a general shared consensus about what the world looks like, what we should study in that world, and what our purpose or goals are in making theory in IR.

The *realist* paradigm sees the world as characterized primarily by conflict. Realists believe that the most important actors in world politics are states and state decision-makers, and that the purpose of theorizing is to provide insights to help guide those decision-makers as they try to decide what they must do on the global stage. This paradigm generally values maintenance of the status quo and discounts the element of large-scale change in IR. It focuses on the laws of power politics, which are considered timeless and universal. Realist perspectives find their most fertile ground in the subfield of international security, with its logic of military power. Relative position with regard to other states is more important than the absolute condition of a state, because in the anarchic world with its ever-present possibility of war, winning and losing matter above all. Realist perspectives tend to see conflict, or the potential for conflict, as the natural order of things, a sometimes necessary evil for which one should always be prepared. They see international trade as a potential source of national power, a view expressed in IPE as *mercantilism* (the accumulation of national war chests, or the equivalent, through control of trade).

The *liberal-pluralist* paradigm sees the world as characterized more by cooperative relations than conflictual ones. Liberal pluralists believe we should look at the activities of states and the many other actors involved in global politics: individuals, multinational corporations, international institutions, and nongovernmental organizations. The purpose of theorizing, by this view, is to provide practical advice, but not simply to state decision-makers; rather, that advice can be provided to any of the actors in global politics: states, businesses, individual actors, and others. Liberal pluralists do not deny that conflicts occur, but they argue that cooperative relations among states and peoples and institutions far outnumber conflictual relations. This is harder to see in international relations partly because the drama of war and armed conflict captures our attention in a way that cooperative relations do not. But for liberal pluralists, we could not travel, communicate, or trade with people from other parts of the world if there were not an intricate web of agreements and institutions in place that allowed us to do so. The liberal-pluralist paradigm values reform of the status quo through an evolutionary process of incremental change. Theories that build on the liberal tradition often focus on the mutual benefits to be gained in IR through interdependence and reciprocity. Gaining wealth in absolute terms is more important from this perspective than gaining power relative to other countries. Liberal approaches find their most fertile ground in the IPE subfield because of the potentials for mutual gain in trade and exchange, with each nation exploiting its comparative advantage in particular products and services. Liberal approaches tend to value *freedom*, especially free trade and free exchange of ideas. They tend to see war not as a natural tendency but as a mistake, to be prevented or at least minimized by international agreements and organizations.

The *critical* paradigm sees the world as characterized primarily by inequalities: inequalities among states, peoples, races, genders, classes, ethnic groups, and others. Critical theorists believe we must look at those inequalities, and at the activities of the peoples, states, or groups who have been marginalized, in both the practice and study of IR. Those people are the most affected by international relations, but they have not been in a position to call the tune. For critical theorists, the purpose of theorizing about IR is to contribute to a transformation of global politics, in particular to transform those inequalities and make them more equal. Critical theorists may disagree on which inequalities are the most important: some focus on class inequality, others on inequalities of wealth between states, others on relations of inequality between genders or races. What they all share is a view of the world that does not take existing power relations for granted but rather asks, "How did this world come about and whose interests does it serve?"[5] These perspectives often focus on the unfair and exploitive aspects of international relationships, and on efforts to radically change those relationships. Critical approaches have found resonance in those areas of IR scholarship dealing with North-South relations and global development because of the evident injustice of grinding poverty suffered by a majority of the world's people. Critical approaches tend to value *justice*. They often see war as a product of underlying exploitative economic relationships, or as perpetrated to serve particular interests.

Although each of the paradigms has found more resonance, or been more influential, in different areas of IR (realism in international security, liberal pluralism in IPE, and critical theories in North-South relations and development issues), this does not mean that they are each silent about the issues that tend to be dominated by one or another of the paradigms. For example, critical theorists have a great deal to say about security and IPE issues, and liberal pluralism engages with questions of development and international security. Likewise, variants of realism engage with questions of IPE and North-South issues. Chapters 2 and 3 discuss the paradigms in more detail. In addition, throughout this textbook, the manner in which the different paradigms engage with specific substantive issues of IR will be highlighted, both in the text and in the "Thinking Theoretically" boxes.

The theoretical debates in the field of IR are fundamental, but unresolved. They leave IR scholarship in a turbulent condition, racing to try to make sense of a rapidly changing world in which old ideas work poorly. Students of global politics must begin to confront not only the various issues of IR, but to think through which—if any—of the theoretical paradigms within IR provides the most persuasive account of different events in world politics. In some cases, students may find that none of the theories answer their questions sufficiently; in other cases, students may find that part of each theory is useful. The goal of this book is to lay out the current state of knowledge without exaggerating the successes of the discipline or any particular approach.

ACTORS AND INFLUENCES

Who are the actors in IR? The international stage is crowded with actors large and small that are intimately interwoven within global level politics. These actors are governments and the people within them who make decisions about foreign policy. They are also individual leaders and citizens. They are bureaucratic agencies in foreign ministries. They are multinational corporations and terrorist groups. They are international institutions such as

---

[5] Cynthia Enloe, *Bananas, Beaches and Bases: Making Feminist Sense of International Politics* (Berkeley: U California P, 1990). Robert Cox, "Social Forces, States and World Orders: Beyond International Relations Theory," *Approaches to World Order*, R.W. Cox, with Timothy J. Sinclair (Cambridge UP, 1996).

Thinking Theoretically

Theories provide possible ways to understand events in IR. These boxes on "thinking theoretically" will encourage you to think of possible theoretical (generalizable) explanations for several prominent cases. For example, consider some of the biggest tests of response to aggression in the post–Cold War era—Kuwait, Rwanda, the former Yugoslavia, 9/11, nuclear tests in India and Pakistan, sabre-rattling in North Korea, and the U.S. invasion of Iraq. As you read about these cases throughout this text, ask yourself: What accounts for the different responses by various states to these events? How would each of the paradigms interpret these events? Whose views were included in the formal responses and whose were excluded?

Theoretical knowledge accumulates by a repeated cycle of generalizing and then testing or interpreting events. For a given puzzle, various theories can explain the result (though none perfectly) as a case of a more general principle or category. Each theory also logically predicts other outcomes, and some of these can be tested empirically. A laboratory science, controlling all but one variable, can test theoretical predictions efficiently. Obviously IR does not have this luxury and must untangle many variables and elements that operate simultaneously. Since knowledge of IR is tenuous in this way, it is especially important to think critically and creatively about IR events and consider several different theoretical explanations before deciding which (if any) provides the best explanation.

the United Nations and the International Monetary Fund, and the people who staff these organizations. They are women and men, ethnic groups, and social movement activists.

State Actors

A **state** is a territorial entity controlled by a government and inhabited by a population. A state government answers to no higher authority; it exercises *sovereignty* over its territory—to make and enforce laws, to collect taxes, and so forth. This sovereignty is recognized (acknowledged) by other states through diplomatic relations and usually by membership in the **United Nations (UN).** (The concepts of state sovereignty and territoriality are elaborated in Chapter 2.) The population inhabiting a state forms a *civil society* to the extent it has developed participatory institutions of social life. All or part of the population that shares a group identity may consider itself a *nation* (see "Nationalism, 1500–the Present" later in this chapter). The state's government is a *democracy* to the extent that the government is controlled by the members of the population rather than imposed on them.[6] (Note that the word *state* in IR does not mean a state in the United States.)

In political life, and to some extent in IR scholarship, the terms *state, nation,* and *country* are used imprecisely, usually to refer to the decisions of state governments. It is common to discuss states as if they were people, as in "France supports the UN resolution" or "the United States attacked Iraq." In reality, states take such actions as the result of complex internal processes and the alliances of various domestic groups and interests. Ultimately, only individual human beings are true actors making conscious decisions. But treating states like people makes it easier to describe and explain the relations among them.

With few exceptions, each state has a capital city—the seat of government from which it administers its territory—and often a single individual who acts in the name of the state. We may refer to this person simply as the "state leader." Often he or she is the *head of government* (such as a prime minister), or the *head of state* (such as a president or a

state An inhabited territorial entity controlled by a government that exercises sovereignty on its territory.

United Nations (UN) An organization of nearly all world states, created after World War II to promote collective security.

---

[6] Gianfranco Poggi, *The State: Its Nature, Development, and Prospects* (Palo Alto, CA: Stanford UP, 1991). Hendrik Spruyt, *The Sovereign State and Its Competitors: An Analysis of Systems Change* (Princeton, NJ: Princeton UP, 1994).

king or queen). In some countries, such as the United States, the same person is head of state and government. In other countries, such as Canada, the Queen and her representative (the Governor General) have become more figurehead or symbolic positions (though technically they can still be called upon in certain instances). In any case the most powerful political figure is the one we mean by "state leader," and these figures are important individual actors in IR, ever since the days when kings or queens ruled territories by decree. The state actor includes the individual leader as well as bureaucratic organizations (such as foreign ministries) that act in the name of the state.

The **international system** is the set of relationships among the world's states, structured according to certain rules and patterns of interaction. Some such rules are explicit, some implicit. They include who is considered a member of the system, what rights and responsibilities the members have, and what kinds of actions and responses normally occur between states. The international system is discussed in detail in Chapter 2.

The modern international system has existed for less than 500 years. Before then, people were organized into more mixed and overlapping political units such as city-states, empires, and feudal fiefs. In the past 200 years the idea has spread that nations—groups of people who share a sense of national identity, usually including a language and culture—should have their own states (see "Nationalism, 1500–the Present" later in this chapter). Most large states today are such **nation-states.** But since World War II, the decolonization process in much of Asia and Africa has added many new states, not all of which can be considered nation-states. A major source of conflict and war at present is the frequent mismatch between perceived nations and actual state borders (for example, in Sri Lanka or Democratic Republic of Congo). When people identify with a nationality that their state government does not represent, they may fight to form their own state and thus to gain sovereignty over their territory and affairs. This substate nationalism is only one of several growing trends that undermine the present-day system of states. Other such trends include the globalization of economic processes, the power of telecommunications, and the proliferation of ballistic missiles.

The independence of former colonies and, more recently, the breakup into smaller states of large multinational states (the Soviet Union, Yugoslavia, and Czechoslovakia) have increased the number of states in the world. The exact total depends on the status of a number of quasi-state political entities, and it keeps changing as political units split

international system The set of relationships among the world's states, structured by certain rules and patterns of interaction.

nation-states States whose populations share a sense of national identity, usually including a language and culture.

POWERS THAT BE
States are important actors in IR. Here, Canadian Prime Minister Paul Martin and U.S. President George W. Bush shake hands during a bilateral meeting at a G8 summit.

apart or merge. There were 191 members of the UN in 2004. Palestine is widely expected to gain formal statehood, although under restricted terms, in the coming years.

Some other political entities are often referred to as states or countries although they are not formally recognized as states. Taiwan is the most important of these. It operates independently in practice but is claimed by China (a claim recognized formally by outside powers and until recently by Taiwan itself), and is not a UN member. Formal colonies and possessions still exist; their status may change in the future. They include Puerto Rico (U.S.), Bermuda (British), Martinique (French), French Guiana, the Netherlands Antilles (Dutch), the Falkland Islands (British), and Guam (U.S.). Hong Kong reverted from British to Chinese rule in 1997, and retains a somewhat separate economic identity under China's "one country, two systems" formula. The smaller former Portuguese colony of Macau also recently reverted to Chinese rule. The status of the Vatican (Holy See) in Rome is ambiguous. Including these various territorial entities with states brings the world total to about 200 state or quasi-state actors.

There are also several would-be states (such as Kurdistan and Western Sahara) that do not fully control the territory they claim and are not universally recognized. Since smaller states may continue to split away from larger ones (for instance, if Québec were ever to separate from Canada), the number of states is likely to grow.

The size of the world's states varies dramatically, from China with more than 1 billion people to microstates with populations of less than 100 000. With the creation of many small states in recent decades, the majority of states now have fewer than 10 million people each, and more than half of the rest have 10 to 50 million each. Only 23 of the world's 200 states have more than 50 million people each. These 23 states contain three-quarters of the world's people. In decreasing order of population, they are China, India, the United States, Indonesia, Brazil, Pakistan, Russia, Bangladesh, Nigeria, Japan, Mexico, Germany, Vietnam, the Philippines, Turkey, Ethiopia, Egypt, Iran, Thailand, France, Britain, Italy, and Democratic Congo.

States also differ tremendously in the size of their total annual economic activity— **gross domestic product (GDP)**[7]—from the $10 trillion U.S. economy to the economies of tiny states such as the Pacific island of Vanuatu ($600 million). The world economy is dominated by a few states, just as world population is. The United States alone accounts for one-fifth of the world economy; together with six other great powers it accounts for more than half (see pp. 76–78). The world's 15 largest economies—which together make up three-quarters of the world economy—are the United States, China, Japan, India, Germany, France, Britain, Italy, Brazil, Russia, Canada, Mexico, Spain, South Korea, and Indonesia.

gross domestic product (GDP) The size of a state's total annual economic activity.

A few of these large states possess especially great military and economic strength and influence, and are sometimes called *great powers*. They are defined and discussed in Chapter 2. For realists, the *great-power system* may be defined as the set of relationships among great powers, with their rules and patterns of interaction (a subset of the international system). Great powers have special ways of behaving and of treating each other

---

[7] GDP is the total of goods and services produced by a nation; it is very close to the gross national product (GNP). Such data are difficult to compare across nations with different currencies, economic systems, and levels of development. In particular, comparisons of GDP in capitalist and socialist economies, or in rich and poor countries, should be treated cautiously. GDP data used in this book are mostly from the World Bank. GDP data are adjusted through time and across countries for "purchasing-power parity" (how much a given amount of money can buy). World total GDP is US$47 trillion by this method, but only US$32 trillion without it. See Robert Summers and Alan Heston, "The Penn World Table (Mark 5): An Expanded Set of International Comparisons, 1950–1988," *Quarterly Journal of Economics* 106.2 (1991): 327–68. GDP and population data are for 2002 unless otherwise noted.

that do not apply to other states. The most powerful of great powers, those with truly global influence, have been called *superpowers*. This term generally meant the United States and the Soviet Union during the Cold War, but most IR scholars now consider the United States to be the world's only superpower (if indeed it still is one). Countries such as Canada are sometimes described as middle powers: too small to be great powers, but too large to be marginal. Smaller and weaker states also are important in IR, but taken singly most of them do not affect the outcomes in IR nearly as much as the major states or middle powers do.

Nonstate Actors

nonstate actors Actors other than state governments that operate either below the level of the state (that is, within states) or across state borders.

National governments may be important actors in IR, but they are strongly conditioned, constrained, and influenced by a variety of actors that are not states. These **nonstate actors** may be grouped in several categories. First there are groups and interests within states that attempt to influence the state's foreign policy. These are *substate actors*. For instance, the American automobile industry and tobacco industry have distinct interests in American foreign economic policy (to sell cars or cigarettes abroad; to reduce imports of competing products made abroad). They are politically mobilized to influence those policies through political action committees, lobbying, and other means. Similarly, the Canadian fishing industry tries to influence the Canadian government to enforce fishing quotas against foreign fishers. They do not want to see their own conservation efforts lost to overfishing by other countries in, or near, Canadian waters.

The actions of substate economic actors—companies, consumers, workers, investors—help to create the context of economic activity in which international political events play out, and within which governments must operate. Day in and day out, people extract natural resources, produce and consume goods, buy and sell products and services. These activities of substate actors take place in what is now clearly a world economy—a global exchange of goods and services woven together by a worldwide network of communication and culture.

Increasingly, then, actors operating below the state level also operate across state borders, becoming *transnational actors*. Businesses that buy, sell, or invest in a variety of countries are a good example. The decision of a company to do business with or in another state changes the relationship between the two states, making them, especially from the perspective of liberal pluralists, more interdependent and creating a new context for the decisions the governments make about each other.

The thousands of multinational corporations (MNCs) are important transnational actors. The interests of a large company doing business globally do not correspond with any one state's interests. Such a company may sometimes even act against its home government's policies. MNCs often control greater resources, and operate internationally with greater efficiency, than many small states. MNCs may prop up (or even help to create) friendly foreign governments, as the United Fruit Company did in Guatemala in the 1950s and the International Telephone and Telegraph Company did in Chile in the early 1970s. But MNCs also provide poor states with much-needed foreign investment and tax revenues. MNCs in turn depend on states to provide protection, well-regulated markets, and a stable political environment. MNCs as international actors receive special attention in Chapters 9 and 13.

nongovernmental organizations (NGOs) Transnational groups or entities (such as the Catholic Church, Greenpeace, and the International Olympic Committee) that interact with states, multinational corporations (MNCs), other NGOs, and intergovernmental organizations (IGOs).

Another type of transnational actor is the **nongovernmental organization (NGO)**, thousands of which pull and tug at international relations every day. These private organizations, some of considerable size and resources, interact with states, MNCs, and other NGOs. Increasingly NGOs are being recognized, in the UN and other forums, as legitimate actors along with states, though not equal to them. Examples of NGOs include the Catholic Church, Greenpeace, and the International Olympic Committee. Some of these groups have a political purpose, some a humanitarian one, some an economic or technical one. Sometimes NGOs combine efforts through transnational advocacy networks.[8] There is no single pattern to NGOs.

Global social movements are also increasingly important actors in international relations. These include antiwar protesters, environmental activists, women's movements, human rights activists and the many elements associated with the antiglobalization protests that were seen in Seattle, Washington, Québec City, Prague, and Genoa. Social movements are not formally institutionalized in the way that NGOs are, although some social movements have transformed into formal NGOs (for example, Greenpeace had its roots in environmental activism). Social movements have a variety of goals; some are aimed at reforming current global practices, others at completely transforming the system. Social movement activists successfully shut down World Trade Organization talks in Seattle in 1999—a dramatic example of the impact such movements can have.

Contemporary *international terrorist networks* are not NGOs, or social movements, but they operate in similar ways—interacting both with states and directly with relevant populations and institutions. The spectacularly destructive attacks on the United States of September 11, 2001, demonstrated the increasing power that technology gives terrorists as nonstate actors. Just as Greenpeace can travel to remote locations and beam video of its environmental actions to the world, or social movements can organize thousands to arrive at world trade talks through email and websites, so too can the al Qaeda network place suicide bombers in U.S. cities, coordinate their operations and finances through the internet and global banking system, and reach a global audience with the videotaped exhortations of Osama bin Laden. "Global reach," once an exclusive capability of great powers, now is available to many others, for better and worse.

Finally, states often take actions through, within, or in the context of **intergovernmental organizations (IGOs)**—organizations whose members are national governments. The UN and its agencies are IGOs. So are most of the world's economic coordinating institutions, such as the World Bank and the International Monetary Fund (IMF). IGOs fulfill a variety of functions, and they vary in size from just a few states to virtually the whole UN membership. For example, the Organization of Petroleum Exporting Countries (OPEC) seeks to coordinate the production and pricing policies of its 11 member states. The World Trade Organization (WTO) sponsors negotiations on lowering trade barriers worldwide, and enforces trade rules.

Military alliances such as NATO and political groupings such as the African Union are also IGOs. The hundreds of IGOs now operating on the world scene (several times more than the number of states) all have been created by their member states to provide some function that those states find useful.

Together, IGOs and NGOs are referred to simply as international organizations (IOs). By one count there are now over 25 000 NGOs and over 5000 IGOs. In this world of interlaced connections, of substate actors and transnational actors, states are still important. But to some extent they are being gradually pushed aside as corporations, groups, and individuals deal ever more directly with each other across borders, and as the world economy becomes globally integrated (see Chapter 10).

global social movements
Non-state groups that organize transnationally, usually to protest around an issue or event (such as the environment, peace, women's issues, human rights, globalization).

intergovernmental organizations (IGOs) Organizations (such as the United Nations and its agencies) whose members are state governments.

---

[8] Margaret E. Keck and Kathryn Sikkink, *Activists Beyond Borders: Advocacy Networks in International Politics* (Ithaca, NY: Cornell UP, 1998). Ann M. Florini, ed., *The Third Force: The Rise of Transnational Civil Society* (Washington, DC: Carnegie Endowment for International Peace, 2000). Union of International Associations, *Yearbook of International Associations 2000–2001* (Munich: K.G. Saur Verlag).

The Information Revolution

Both state and nonstate actors are strongly affected by the revolution in information technologies now under way. The new information-intensive world promises to reshape international relations profoundly. Technological change dramatically affects actors' relative capabilities and even preferences. Nobody knows where those changes will take us. Already, information capabilities are the central motor of "globalization." Telecommunications and computerization allow economics, politics, and culture alike to operate on a global scale as never before. The ramifications of information technology for various facets of IR will be developed in each chapter of this book.

Levels of Analysis

The many actors involved at once in IR contribute to the complexity of competing explanations and theories. One way scholars of IR have sorted out this multiplicity of influences, actors, and processes is to categorize them into different *levels of analysis* (see Table 1.1). IR scholars have proposed various level-of-analysis schemes, most often with three main levels (and sometimes a few sublevels between) including the individual level, state level and system level.[9]

The *individual* level of analysis concerns the perceptions, choices, and actions of individual human beings. Great leaders influence the course of history, as do individual citizens, thinkers, soldiers, and voters. Without Lenin, it is said, there might well have been no Soviet Union. If a few more university students had voted for Nixon rather than Kennedy in the razor-close 1960 election, the Cuban Missile Crisis might have ended differently. United Nations peacekeeping may never have evolved without Canada's Lester B. Pearson. The study of foreign policy decision-making, which is discussed in Chapter 4, pays special attention to individual-level explanations of IR.

The *domestic* (or *state* or *societal*) level of analysis concerns the aggregations of individuals within states that influence state actions in the international arena. Such aggregations include interest groups, political organizations, and government agencies. These groups operate differently (with different international effects) in different kinds of societies and states. For instance, democracies and dictatorships may act differently from one another, and democracies may act differently in an election year from the way they act at other times. The politics of ethnic conflict and nationalism, bubbling up from within states,

IN THE ACTION
Nonstate actors participate in IR alongside states. Nongovernmental organizations (NGOs) such as the Catholic Church are becoming increasingly active in IR. Here, Pope John Paul II addresses bishops from North and South America at the Vatican, 1997.

The Information Revolution

In each chapter, these "information revolution" boxes pose critical-thinking questions about the impacts that rapid changes in information technology have on IR.

To explore the questions further, visit this book's Companion Website at www.pearsoned.ca/goldstein.

[9] J. David Singer, "The Level-of-Analysis Problem in International Relations," *World Politics* 14.1 (1961): 77–92. Kenneth Waltz, *Man, the State and War* (NY: Columbia UP, 1959).

Table 1.1 Levels of Analysis

Many influences affect the course of international relations. Levels of analysis provide a framework for categorizing these influences and thus for suggesting various explanations of international events. Examples include

Global Level

North-South gap	Technological change
World regions	Information revolution
European imperialism	Global telecommunications
UN	Worldwide scientific and business
World environment	communities

Interstate Level

Power	IGOs
Balance of power	Diplomacy
Alliance formation and dissolution	Summit meetings
Wars	Bargaining
Treaties	Reciprocity
Trade agreements	

Domestic Level

Nationalism	Political parties and elections
Ethnic conflict	Public opinion
Type of government	Gender
Democracy	Economic sectors and industries
Dictatorship	Military-industrial complex
Domestic coalitions	Foreign policy bureaucracies

Individual Level

Great leaders	Learning
Crazy leaders	Assassinations, accidents of history
Decision-making in crises	Citizens' participation (voting, rebelling,
Psychology of perception and decision	going to war, etc.)

plays an increasingly important role in the relations among states. Economic sectors within states, including the military-industrial sector, can influence their governments to take actions in the international arena that are good for business. Within governments, foreign policy agencies often fight bureaucratic battles over policy decisions.

The *interstate* (or *international* or *systemic*) level of analysis concerns the influence of the international system upon outcomes. This level of analysis therefore focuses on the interactions of states themselves, without regard to their internal makeup or the particular individuals who lead them. This level pays attention to the geographic locations of states and their relative power positions in the international system.

To these three levels can be added a fourth, the *global* level of analysis.[10] It seeks to explain international outcomes in terms of global trends and forces that transcend the interactions of states themselves. This level of analysis deserves particular attention because of the growing importance of global-level processes. The evolution of human technology, of the global political economy, of certain worldwide beliefs, and of humans' relationship to the natural environment are all processes at the global level that reach down to influence international relations. The global level is also increasingly the focus of IR scholars studying transnational integration through worldwide scientific, technical, and business communities (see Chapter 10). Another pervasive global influence is the lingering effect of historical European imperialism—Europe's conquest of Latin America, Asia, and Africa (see "Imperialism, 1500–the Present" later in this chapter).

Levels of analysis offer different sorts of explanations for international events. For example, there are many possible explanations for the 1999 Kosovo War between Serbia and NATO. At the individual level, the war might be attributed to the irrational gambles and mistaken judgments of Serbia's leader, Slobodan Milosevic. At the domestic level, the war might be attributed to the fragmentation of Yugoslavia's multiethnic federation, which left Kosovo—with a largely Albanian population—as a province of an aggressively nationalistic Serbia. At the interstate level, the war might be attributed to the balance-of-power process in which a state (Serbia) eventually galvanizes a countercoalition of states (NATO) to contain it. At the global level, the war might be attributed to the resistance of Serbia to its economic incorporation into Western capitalism, a process that had begun over a decade before with IMF austerity measures.[11]

Although IR scholars often focus their study mainly on one level of analysis, other levels bear on a problem simultaneously. There is no single correct level for a given question of global politics, and moreover, the levels usually overlap with each other. Levels of analysis help to suggest multiple explanations and approaches to consider in trying to explain a given event. They remind scholars and students to look beyond the immediate and superficial aspects of an event to explore the possible influences of more distant causes. IR is such a complex process that there is rarely any single cause that completely explains an outcome. Table 1.1 lists some of the processes operating on each level of analysis. Note that the processes at higher levels tend to operate more slowly than those on the lower levels. Individuals go in and out of office often; the structure of the international system, or the nature of global capitalism, changes more slowly.

Geography

International relations takes place in the context of geography. To highlight the insights afforded by a global level of analysis, this book uses a division of the world into nine regions. These *world regions* differ from each other in the number of states they contain and in each region's particular mix of cultures, geographical realities, and languages. But each represents a geographical corner of the world, and together they reflect the overall macrolevel divisions of the world. Later chapters refer back to these regions, especially in discussing the North-South gap (Chapters 12 and 13).

The global **North-South gap** between the relatively rich industrialized countries of the North and the relatively poor countries of the South is the most important geographical element at the global level of analysis. The regions used in this book have been

North-South gap The disparity in resources (income, wealth, and power) between the industrialized, relatively rich countries of the West (and the former Communist bloc) and the poorer countries of Africa, the Middle East, and much of Asia and Latin America.

[10] Robert C. North, War, *Peace, Survival: Global Politics and Conceptual Synthesis* (Boulder, CO: Westview, 1990).

[11] Paul Phillips, "Why Were We Bombing Yugoslavia?" *Studies in Political Economy*, 60 (Autumn 1999): 85–98.

drawn so as to separate (with a few exceptions) the rich countries from the poor ones. The North includes both the West (the rich countries of North America, Western Europe, and Japan) and the old East (the former Soviet Union and its bloc of allies).[12] The South includes Latin America, Africa, the Middle East, and much of Asia. The South is sometimes called the "Third World" (third after the so-called "first world" of the West and the "second world" of the former Communist bloc)—but this is a term that, although still used by many people, is considered problematic. Likewise, countries in the South are also referred to as "developing" countries or "less-developed" countries (LDCs), in contrast to the "developed" countries of the North. With each of these terms, the global South is described as "less than" the North (*"Third* World," *"less*-developed country"). This text book will use the terms global South and global North to describe these areas of the world.

Several criteria beyond income levels help distinguish major geographically contiguous regions. Countries with similar economic levels, cultures, and languages have been kept together where possible. States with a history of interaction, including historical empires or trading zones, are also placed together in a region. Finally, countries that might possibly unify in the future—notably South Korea with North Korea, and China with Taiwan—are kept in the same region. Of course, no scheme works perfectly, and some states are pulled toward two regions.

The overall world regions are shown in Figure 1.1. The global North is divided into *North America* (the United States and Canada); *Western Europe* (mainly European Union members); *Japan/Pacific* (mainly Japan, the Koreas, Australia, and New Zealand); and *Russia and Eastern Europe* (mainly the former Soviet bloc). The South is divided into *China* (including Hong Kong and Taiwan); the *Middle East* (from North Africa through Turkey and Iran); *Latin America* (Mexico, Central America, the Caribbean, and South America); *South Asia* (Afghanistan through Indonesia and the Philippines); and *Africa* (below the Sahara desert).

Most of these regions correspond with commonly used geographical names, but a few notes may help. *East Asia* refers to China, Japan, and Korea. *Southeast Asia* refers to countries from Burma through Indonesia and the Philippines. Russia is considered a European state, although a large section (Siberia) is in Asia. The *Pacific Rim* usually means East and Southeast Asia, Siberia, and the Pacific coast of North America and Latin America.[13] *South Asia* only sometimes includes parts of Southeast Asia. Narrow definitions of the *Middle East* exclude both North Africa and Turkey. The *Balkans* are the states of southeastern Europe, bounded by Slovenia, Romania, and Greece.

Table 1.2 (p. 17) shows the approximate population and economic size (GDP) of each region in relation to the world as a whole. As the table indicates, income levels per capita are, overall, about five times higher in the North than in the South. *The North contains only 20 percent of the world's people but 60 percent of its goods and services.* The other 80 percent of the world's people, in the South, have only 40 percent of the goods and services.

---

[12] Note that geographical designations such as the "West" and the "Middle East" are European-centred. From Korea, for example, China and Russia are to the west and Japan and the United States are to the east. On world-level geography, see Michael Kidron, Ronald Segal, and Angela Wilson, *The State of the World Atlas*, 5th ed. (NY: Penguin, 1995); Andrew Boyd, *An Atlas of World Affairs*, 9th ed. (NY: Routledge, 1994). On the synthesis of world-level geography and social and political phenomena, see Dan Smith, *The State of War and Peace Atlas* (Penguin, 1996); and Joni Seager, *The State of Women in the World Atlas* (Penguin, 1997).

[13] James C. Hsiung, ed., *Asia Pacific in the New World Politics* (Boulder, CO: Rienner, 1993). Gerald Segal, *Rethinking the Pacific* (NY: Oxford UP, 1991). Derek McDougall, *The International Politics of the New Asia Pacific* (Boulder, CO: Rienner, 1997). Fu-Chen Lo and Yue-man Yeung, eds., *Emerging World Cities in Pacific Asia* (Tokyo: UN University Press, 1997).

Figure 1.1 Nine Regions of the World

Table 1.2 Comparison of World Regions

Region	Population (Millions)	GDP (Trillion US$)	GDP per Capita (US Dollars)
The North			
North America	300	$10.5	$35 000
Western Europe	400	9.1	24 000
Japan/Pacific	200	4.7	21 000
Russia & E. Europe	400	2.7	7 000
The South			
China	1 300	5.2	4 000
Middle East	400	2.1	6 000
Latin America	500	3.7	7 000
South Asia	1 900	4.9	2 700
Africa	600	1.1	1 700
Total North	1 300 (22%)	27 (62%)	20 000
Total South	4 700 (78%)	17 (38%)	3 600
World Total	6 000	$44	$7 300

Note: Data adjusted for purchasing-power parity. 2000 GDP estimates (in 2000 U.S. dollars) are author's estimates based on World Bank; those for Russia and Eastern Europe, and for China, should be treated especially cautiously.

Within the global North, Russia and Eastern Europe lag behind in income levels, and suffered declines in the 1990s. In the global South, the Middle East, Latin America, and (more recently) China have achieved somewhat higher income levels than have Africa and South Asia, which remain extremely poor. Even in the higher-income regions, income is distributed quite unevenly and many people remain very poor. Some observers have noted that divisions like the "First World" and "Third World" tend to ignore the ways in which there are "Third Worlds" in otherwise "First World" countries, and vice versa.[14] Note that more than half of the world's population lives in the densely populated (and poor) regions of South Asia and China.

IR scholars have no single explanation of the tremendous North-South gap in wealth and poverty (see Chapter 12). Some see it as part of a natural process of uneven growth in the world economy. Others tie it to the history of imperialism by European states, as well as by Russia, the United States, and Japan. Some see the gap as a reflection of racism—the North is predominantly white whereas most of the South is nonwhite.

Using the nine world regions as an organizing framework, the world's states and territories are listed in Table 1.3, with an estimate of the total size of each state's economy (GDP). Reference maps with greater detail appear after the Subject Index.

Geographic divisions of the world, based on either territory or GDP, do not tell us everything there is to know about global politics. No single map or table would tell us all that we need to know, but different types of maps can signal different ways to think about how the world is configured. In Figure 1.2 (pp. 20–21), the representation of women in

---

[14] Chandra Talpade Mohanty, "Women Workers and Capitalist Scripts: Ideologies of Domination, Common Interests and the Politics of Solidarity," *Feminist Genealogies, Colonial Legacies, Democratic Futures*, ed. M. Jacqui Alexander and Chandra Talpade Mohanty, (New York: Routledge, 1997) 3–29.

Table 1.3 States and Territories with Estimated Total 2002 GDP
(In Billions of 2002 US Dollars)

North America

United States	10 000	Canada	900	Bahamas	5

Western Europe

Germany	2 000	Switzerland	200	Luxembourg	30
France	1 600	Austria	200	Iceland	8
Britain	1 500	Portugal	200	Malta	7
Italy	1 500	Greece	200	Andorra	1
Spain	900	Denmark	200	Monaco	1
Netherlands	400	Norway	200	Liechtenstein	1
Belgium	300	Finland	100	San Marino	1
Sweden	200	Ireland	100	Vatican City[a]	0

Japan/Pacific

Japan	3 300	Guam/Marianas[b]	3	Nauru	0
South Korea	800	Solomon Islands	1	Marshall Islands	0
Australia	500	Samoa	1	Palau	0
New Zealand	80	Vanuatu	1	Kiribati	0
North Korea	20	Tonga	1	Tuvalu	0
Papua New Guinea	10	Micronesia	0		
Fiji	4	American Samoa[b]	0		

Russia and Eastern Europe

Russia[c]	1 100	Uzbekistan[c]	40	Georgia[c]	10
Poland	400	Croatia	40	Albania	10
Ukraine[c]	200	Slovenia	40	Macedonia	10
Czech Republic	200	Lithuania	30	Armenia[c]	9
Romania	100	Azerbaijan[c]	30	Kyrgyzstan[c]	8
Hungary	100	Turkmenistan[c]	30	Moldova	6
Kazakhstan[c]	90	Serbia-Montenegro	20	Tajikistan[c]	6
Slovakia	70	Latvia	20	Mongolia	4
Belarus[c]	50	Estonia	20		
Bulgaria	50	Bosnia and Herzegovina	20		

China

China	5 700	Hong Kong[b]	200	Macau[b]	8
Taiwan[b]	400				

The Middle East

Turkey	400	Iraq	60	Lebanon	20
Iran	400	Tunisia	60	Jordan	20
Saudi Arabia	200	Syria	60	Qatar	20
Egypt	200	United Arab Emirates	50	Yemen	10
Algeria	200	Libya	50	Cyprus	10
Israel/Palestine	100	Kuwait	30	Bahrain	10
Morocco/W. Sahara	100	Oman	30		

Latin America

Brazil	1 300	El Salvador	30	Netherlands Antilles[b]	2
Mexico	900	Bolivia	20	Virgin Islands[b]	2
Argentina	400	Paraguay	20	Bermuda[b]	2
Colombia	300	Cuba	20	Suriname	2
Venezuela	100	Panama	20	French Guiana[b]	1
Chile	100	Honduras	20	St. Lucia	1
Peru	100	Trinidad & Tobago	10	Belize	1
Puerto Rico[b]	90	Jamaica	10	Antigua & Barbuda	1
Dominican Republic	50	Nicaragua	10	Grenada	1
Guatemala	50	Haiti	10	St. Vincent & Grenadines	1
Ecuador	40	Martinique[b]	4	St. Kitts & Nevis	0
Uruguay	40	Barbados	4	Dominica	0
Costa Rica	30	Guyana	3		

South Asia

India	2 700	Vietnam	200	Afghanistan	10
Indonesia	700	Singapore	100	Laos	9
Thailand	400	Sri Lanka	70	Brunei	5
Philippines	300	Burma (Myanmar)	60	Bhutan	1
Pakistan	300	Nepal	30	Maldives	1
Malaysia	200	Cambodia	20	East Timor	0
Bangladesh	200				

Africa

South Africa	400	Mauritius	10	Central African Republic	4
Nigeria	100	Botswana	10	Burundi	4
Sudan	60	Burkina Faso	10	Somalia	4
Ethiopia	50	Namibia	10	Eritea	4
Ghana	40	Equatorial Guinea	10	Reunion[b]	3
Democratic Congo	30	Mali	10	Congo Republic	3
Angola	30	Rwanda	10	Sierra Leone	3
Kenya	30	Niger	9	Liberia	2
Zimbabwe	30	Zambia	8	Gambia	2
Uganda	30	Gabon	8	Cape Verde	2
Cameroon	30	Chad	8	Guinea-Bissau	1
Côte d'Ivoire (Ivory Coast)	30	Togo	7	Djibouti	1
Tanzania	20	Benin	7	Comoros Islands	1
Mozambique	20	Malawi	6	Seychelles	1
Guinea	20	Swaziland	5	São Tomé & Principe	0
Senegal	20	Lesotho	5		
Madagascar	10	Mauritania	4		

[a] Nonmember of UN (independent state).

[b] Nonmember of UN (colony or territory).

[c] Commonwealth of Independent States (former USSR).

Note: GDP data are inexact by nature. Estimates for Russia and Eastern Europe, China, and other nonmarket or transitional economies are particularly suspect and should be used cautiously. Numbers below 0.5 are listed as 0.

Sources: Data are author's estimates based on World Bank. Data are at purchasing-power parity. See footnote 7 on p. 9.

Women in Government

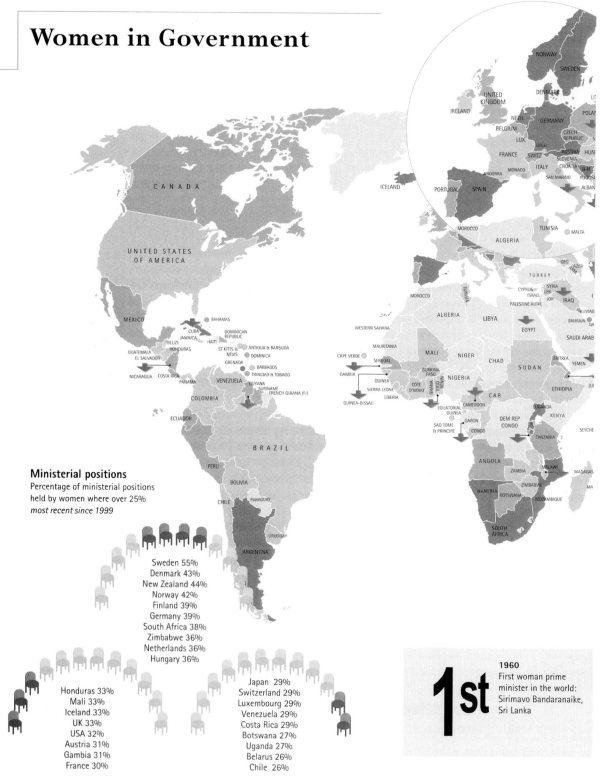

Ministerial positions
Percentage of ministerial positions
held by women where over 25%
most recent since 1999

Sweden 55%
Denmark 43%
New Zealand 44%
Norway 42%
Finland 39%
Germany 39%
South Africa 38%
Zimbabwe 36%
Netherlands 36%
Hungary 36%

Honduras 33%
Mali 33%
Iceland 33%
UK 33%
USA 32%
Austria 31%
Gambia 31%
France 30%

Japan 29%
Switzerland 29%
Luxembourg 29%
Venezuela 29%
Costa Rica 29%
Botswana 27%
Uganda 27%
Belarus 26%
Chile 26%

1st
1960
First woman prime
minister in the world:
Sirimavo Bandaranaike,
Sri Lanka

Figure 1.2 Women in Government, 2002

Source: Joni Seager, *The Penguin Atlas of Women in the World*, 3rd Edition, New York: Penguin Books 2003.

Women in government

As a proportion of elected officials *2002*
(in lower house if a two-house legislature)
world average: 14.5%

- 25% and over
- 15% – 24%
- 5% – 14%
- under 5%
- no women in government
- no data

Losses
proportion of women
in government
was *lower* in 2000
than in the late 1980s

East Timor
24 women represent 27% of the
transitional government elected in
2001, an 88-seat body that is charged
with drafting the country's new
constitution and paving the way for
elections of a national assembly.

Afghanistan
Building of a newly democratic government
in Afghanistan is occurring in several stages:
- 3 women participated in the Bonn meetings in
  November 2001 that established an interim
  post-Taliban government;
- 2 of the 30 Ministers in the 2001–2002 Interim Government
  were women;
- The Commission to convene the Loya Jirga included 3 women
  out of 21;
- The Loya Jirga, which met in 2002 to choose the government
  that will rule Afghanistan until national elections in 2004,
  included 160 women out of 1550.

1st
1975
First Black woman
prime minister of an
independent state:
Elisabeth Domitien,
Central African
Republic.

1st
1999
Sweden became the
first country to have
a majority of female
government ministers.

governments around the world, as of 2002, is depicted. This map is interesting for a number of reasons, not least because it challenges some of the assumptions that people living in the North may hold. Notice that many countries of the South have equal or better representation of women in government than do countries in the North. According to this map, for example, Botswana, Tanzania, Angola, and Peru all have more women in government than does the United States; Malawi, Mozambique, Uganda, Argentina, and Rwanda have more women in government than both the U.S. and Canada. Maps such as this one provide us with information about different parts of the world, and also confront stereotypes that are associated with some of the traditional geographic and economic divisions of the world.

Although geography provides one context in which IR takes place, history provides another. The world as we perceive it developed over many years, step by step. Of special interest in IR are the past 500 years, known as the "modern age." This has been the age of the international system that we know (sovereign states). The remainder of this chapter briefly reviews the historical development of that system and its context. Special attention is given to the relations between Europe and the rest of the world, in which are found the roots of the present North-South gap.

HISTORY

The turn of the century and millennium finds the world breaking free of the logic of the two world wars and the Cold War that dominated the twentieth century. New possibilities are emerging everywhere, some good and some bad. With so much change occurring, one might wonder whether history is still relevant to understanding the world. It is. The basic structures and principles of international relations, even in the current era, are deeply rooted in historical developments. Our discussion of these developments—necessarily only a series of brief sketches—begins with a long-term perspective and gradually focuses on more recent history.

World Civilizations to the Present Day

The present-day international system is the product of a particular civilization—Western civilization, centred in Europe. The international system as we know it developed among the European states of 300 to 500 years ago, was exported to the rest of the world, and has in the last century subsumed virtually all of the world's territory into sovereign states (see Figure 1.3). It is important to keep in mind that other civilizations existed in other world regions for centuries before Europeans ever arrived. These cultural traditions continue to exert an influence on IR, especially when the styles and expectations of these cultures come into play in international interactions.[15]

North American students should note that much of the world differs from North America in this regard. Before Europeans arrived, cultures in North America did not have extensive agriculture, large cities, irrigation, and the other trappings of "civilization." Its

---

[15] Isaac Asimov, *Asimov's Chronology of the World: The History of the World from the Big Bang to Modern Times* (NY: HarperCollins, 1991). Geoffrey Barraclough, ed., *The Times Atlas of World History* (Maplewood, NJ: Hammond, 1978). William Hardy McNeill, *The Pursuit of Power* (Chicago: U Chicago P, 1982). Janet Abu-Lughod, *Before European Hegemony: The World System, A.D. 1250–1350* (NY: Oxford UP, 1989). Marshall G. S. Hodgson, *The Venture of Islam: Conscience and History in a World Civilization* (Chicago: U Chicago P, 1974). Adda Bozeman, *Politics and Culture in International History* (Princeton, NJ: Princeton UP, 1960). Raymond Cohen and Raymond Westbrook, eds., *Amarna Diplomacy: The Beginnings of International Relations* (Baltimore: Johns Hopkins UP, 1999).

Region	Before A.D. 1000	A.D. 1000 – 1250	1250 – 1500	1500 – 1750	1750 – 2000
Japan	Korean and Chinese influences	samurai shoguns		Tokugawa isolation	Meiji restoration WW II prosperity
China	Dynasties; Great Wall begun; Taoism; Buddhism; paper, gunpowder	Sung dynasty	Mongol dynasty	Ming dynasty	Manchu dynasty European dominance People's Republic
S. Asia	Emergence of Hinduism, Buddhism; Ancient India; Arab conquest	Turkish period		Taj Mahal built	European colonialism → independence
Africa	Kingdom of Ghana	Yoruba, Mali, Benin (kingdoms)	Congo	slave trade Zimbabwe Buganda Ashanti	European colonialism independence
Middle East	Mesopotamia, Egypt, Persia; Jews, Christians; Greeks/Romans; Islam	Crusades — Arab empire		Ottoman Empire	Arab nationalism Islamic rev. European colonialism
W. Europe	Ancient Greece; Roman Empire; Vikings; Feudalism	"Dark Ages"	Venice	Renaissance Protestantism Empires	French Revolution German/Italian unifications loss of empires WW I/II
Russia & E. Europe	Khazars		Genghis Khan	Ivan the Terrible czars	Lenin USSR WW II CIS
N. America	(Preagricultural)			Columbus European colonization	War of 1812 BNA Act westward expansion WW II Cold War
Latin America	Mayans	Aztec & Inca Empires		Portuguese & Spanish conquest colonialism	European & U.S. interventions independence wars, debts, dictators, revolutions

Timeline scale: Before A.D. 1000 | A.D. 1000 | 1250 | 1500 | 1750 | 2000

Figure 1.3 World Civilizations, 1000–the Present

indigenous cultures were largely exterminated or pushed aside by European settlers. Today's North American population is overwhelmingly descended from immigrants. In other regions, however, the European conquest followed many centuries of advanced civilization—more advanced than that of Europe in the case of China, India, Japan, the Middle East, and Central America. In most of the world (especially in Africa and Asia), European empires incorporated rather than pushed aside indigenous populations. Today's populations are descended primarily from indigenous inhabitants, not immigrants. These populations are therefore more strongly rooted in their own cultural traditions and history than are most Canadians or Americans.

European civilization evolved from roots in the Eastern Mediterranean—Egypt, Mesopotamia (Iraq), and especially Greece. Of special importance for IR is the classical period of Greek city-states around 400 B.C., which exemplified some of the fundamental principles of interstate power politics (reflected in Thucydides's classic account of the Peloponnesian Wars between Athens and Sparta). By that time states were carrying out sophisticated trade relations and warfare with each other in a broad swath of the world from the Mediterranean through India to East Asia. Much of this area came under Greek influence with the conquests of Alexander the Great (around 300 B.C.), then under the Roman Empire (around A.D. 1), and then under an Arab empire (around A.D. 600).

China remained an independent civilization during all this time. In the "warring states" period, at about the same time as the Greek city-states, sophisticated states (organized as territorial political units) first used warfare as an instrument of power politics. This is described in the classic work *The Art of War*, by Sun Tzu.[16] By about A.D. 800, when Europe was in its "dark ages" and Arab civilization in its golden age, China under the T'ang dynasty was a highly advanced civilization quite independent of Western influence. Japan, strongly influenced by Chinese civilization, flowered on its own in the centuries leading up to the Shoguns (around A.D. 1200). Japan isolated itself from Western influence under the Tokugawa shogunate for several centuries, ending after 1850 when the Meiji restoration began Japanese industrialization and international trade. Latin America also had flourishing civilizations—the Mayans around A.D. 100 to 900 and the Aztecs and Incas around 1200—independent of Western influence until conquered by Spain around 1500. In Africa, the great kingdoms flowered after about A.D. 1000 (as early as A.D. 600 in Ghana) and were highly developed when the European slave traders arrived on the scene around 1500.

The Arab empire of about A.D. 600 to 1200 plays a special role in the international relations of the Middle East. Almost the whole of the region was once united in this empire, which arose and spread with the religion of Islam. European invasions—the Crusades—were driven out. In the sixteenth to nineteenth centuries, the eastern Mediterranean came under the Turkish-based Ottoman Empire, which gave relative autonomy to local cultures if they paid tribute. This history of empires continued to influence the region in the twentieth century. For example, *Pan-Arabism* (or Arab nationalism), especially strong in the 1950s and 1960s, saw the region as potentially one nation again, with a single religion, language, and identity. Iraq's Saddam Hussein during the Gulf War likened himself to the ruler who drove away Crusaders a thousand years ago. The strength of Islamic fundamentalism throughout the region today, as well as the emotions attached to the Arab-Israeli conflict, reflect the continuing importance of the historic Arab empire.

Europe itself began its rise to world dominance around 1500, after the Renaissance (when the Greek and Roman classics were rediscovered). The Italian city-states of the

---

[16] Sun Tzu, *The Art of War*, trans. Samuel B. Griffith (NY: Oxford UP, 1963).

period also rediscovered the rules of interstate power politics, as described by an adviser to Renaissance princes named Niccolò Machiavelli. Feudal units began to merge into large territorial nation-states under single authoritarian rulers (monarchs). The military revolution of the period created the first modern armies.[17] European monarchs put cannons on sailing ships and began to "discover" the world. The development of the international system, of imperialism, of trade and war, were all greatly accelerated by the *Industrial Revolution* after about 1750. Ultimately the European conquest of the world brought about a single world civilization, albeit with regional variants and subcultures.[18]

In recent decades, the world regions formerly dominated by Europe have gained independence, with their own sovereign states participating in the international system. Independence came earlier in the Americas (around 1800). In Latin America, most of the nineteenth century was absorbed with wars, border changes, the rise and fall of dictatorships and republics, a chronic foreign debt problem, revolutions, and recurrent military incursions by European powers and the United States to recover debts.

The Great-Power System, 1500–the Present

The modern state system is often dated (most particularly by realists) from the *Treaty of Westphalia* in 1648, which established the principles of independent, sovereign states that continue to shape the international system today. These rules of state relations did not, however, originate at Westphalia; they took form in Europe in the sixteenth century (see Figure 1.4). Key to this system was the ability of one state, or a coalition, to balance the power of another state so that it could not gobble up smaller units and create a universal empire.

This power-balancing system placed special importance on the handful of great powers with strong military capabilities, global interests and outlooks, and intense interactions with each other. (Great powers are defined and discussed on pp. 76–78.) A system of great-power relations has existed since around A.D. 1500, and the structure and rules of that system have remained fairly stable through time, although the particular members change. The structure is a balance of power among the six or so most powerful states, which form and break alliances, fight wars, and make peace, letting no single state conquer the others.

The most powerful states in sixteenth-century Europe were Britain (England), France, Austria-Hungary, and Spain. The Ottoman Empire (Turkey) recurrently fought with the European powers, especially with Austria-Hungary. Today, that historic conflict between the (Islamic) Ottoman Empire and (Christian) Austria-Hungary is a source of ethnic conflict in the former Yugoslavia (the edge of the old Ottoman Empire).

Within Europe, Austria-Hungary and Spain were allied under control of the Hapsburg family, which also owned the territory of the Netherlands. The Hapsburg countries (which were Catholic) were defeated by mostly Protestant countries in northern Europe—France, Britain, Sweden, and the newly independent Netherlands—in the

---

[17] Michael Howard, *War in European History* (NY: Oxford UP, 1976). Geoffrey Parker, *The Military Revolution: Military Innovation and the Rise of the West, 1500–1800*, 2nd ed. (NY: Cambridge UP, 1996). Jeremy Black, ed., *The Origins of War in Early Modern Europe* (Edinburgh: Donald, 1987). Janice E. Thomson, *Mercenaries, Pirates, and Sovereigns: State-Building and Extraterritorial Violence in Early Modern Europe* (Princeton, NJ: Princeton UP, 1994).

[18] Geoffrey Barraclough, *An Introduction to Contemporary History* (NY: Penguin, 1964). Carlo M. Cipolla, *Guns, Sails and Empires* (NY: Pantheon, 1965). Perry Anderson, *Lineages of the Absolutist State* (London: N.L.B., 1974). Fernand Braudel, *Civilization and Capitalism, 15th–18th Century*, 3 vols. (NY: Harper & Row, 1984). Hedley Bull and Adam Watson, eds., *The Expansion of International Society* (NY: Oxford UP, 1984).

	1500	1600	1700	1800	1900	2000
Wars		Spain conquers Portugal Spanish Armada	30 Years' War	War of the Spanish Succession	7 Years' War	Napoleonic Wars	Franco-Prussian War	World War I	World War II	Cold War
Major Alliances		Turkey (Muslim) vs. Europe (Christian)	Hapsburgs (Austria-Spain) vs. France, Britain, Netherlands, Sweden		France vs. Britain, Spain	France vs. Britain, Netherlands		Germany (& Japan) vs. Britain, France, Russia, United States, Canada, China	Russia vs. U.S., Canada, W. Eur., Japan
Rules & Norms		Nation-states (France, Austria)	Dutch independence **Treaty of Westphalia 1648** Grotius on int'l law		Treaty of Utrecht 1713	Congress of Vienna 1815 Kant on peace	Concert of Europe	League of Nations Geneva conventions Communism	UN Security Council 1945– Human rights
Rising Powers		Britain France	Russia	**Netherlands hegemony**	Prussia	United States Germany Japan Italy	**British hegemony**		**U.S. hegemony**	China
Declining Powers		Venice	Spain	Netherlands	Sweden Ottoman Empire			Britain France Austria Italy	Russia	U.S.?

Figure 1.4 The Great-Power System, 1500–the Present

Thirty Years' War of 1618–1648.[19] The 1648 Treaty of Westphalia established the basic rules that have defined the international system ever since—the sovereignty and territorial integrity of states as equal and independent members of an international system. Since then, states defeated in war might be stripped of some territories but were generally allowed to continue as independent states rather than being subsumed into the victorious state.

In the eighteenth century, the power of Britain increased as it industrialized, and Britain's great rival was France. Sweden, the Netherlands, and the Ottoman Empire all declined in power, but Russia and later Prussia (the forerunner of modern-day Germany) emerged as major players. In the *Napoleonic Wars* (1803–1815), which followed the French Revolution, France was defeated by a coalition of Britain, the Netherlands, Austria-Hungary, Spain, Russia, and Prussia. The *Congress of Vienna* (1815) ending that war reasserted the principles of state sovereignty in reaction to the challenges of the French Revolution and Napoleon's empire.[20] In the *Concert of Europe* that dominated the following decades, the five most powerful states tried, with some success, to cooperate on major issues to prevent war—a possible precedent for today's UN Security Council. In this period, Britain became a balancer, joining alliances against whatever state emerged as the most powerful in Europe.

By the outset of the twentieth century, three new rising powers had appeared on the scene: the United States (which had become the world's largest economy), Japan, and Italy. The great-power system became globalized instead of European. Powerful states were industrializing, extending the scope of their world activities and the might of their militaries. After Prussia defeated Austria and France in wars, a larger Germany emerged to challenge Britain's position.[21] In *World War I* (1914–1918), Germany and Austria-Hungary were defeated by a coalition that included Britain, France, Russia, Italy, and the United States. After a 20-year lull, Germany, Italy, and Japan were defeated in *World War II* (1939–1945) by a coalition of the United States, Britain, France, Russia (the Soviet Union), and China. Those five winners of World War II make up the permanent membership of today's UN Security Council.

After World War II, the United States and the Soviet Union, which had been allies in the war against Germany, became adversaries for 40 years in the Cold War. Europe was split into rival blocs—East and West—with Germany itself split into two states. The rest of the world became contested terrain where each bloc tried to gain allies or influence, often by sponsoring opposing sides in regional and civil wars. The end of the Cold War around 1990, when the Soviet Union collapsed, returned the international system to a more cooperative arrangement of the great powers somewhat similar to the Concert of Europe in the nineteenth century. However, new strains emerged among the European-American-Japanese "allies" once they no longer faced a common threat from the Soviet Union.[22] Some of those relations became particularly strained when the United States decided to invade Iraq in 2003, with the support of some of its allies (the U.K. and Japan, for example), but not others (Canada and France).

---

[19] Theodore K. Rabb,, ed., *The Thirty Years' War* (NY: UP of America, 1981).

[20] Henry A. Kissinger, *A World Restored* (1957; Boston: Houghton Mifflin, 1973).

[21] William L. Langer, *European Alliances and Alignments, 1871–1890* (NY: Knopf, 1931).

[22] Daniel Unger and Paul Blackburn, eds., *Japan's Emerging Global Role* (Boulder, CO: Rienner, 1993). Tsuneo Akaha and Frank Langdon, eds., *Japan in the Posthegemonic World* (Boulder, CO: Rienner, 1993). Takashi Inoguchi and Daniel I. Okimoto, eds., *The Political Economy of Japan.* Vol. 2: *The Changing International Context* (Palo Alto, CA: Stanford UP, 1988).

Imperialism, 1500–the Present

European imperialism (described more fully in Chapter 12) got its start in the fifteenth century with the development of oceangoing sailing ships in which a small crew could transport a sizeable cargo over a long distance (see Figure 1.5). Portugal pioneered the first voyages of exploration beyond Europe. Spain, France, and Britain soon followed. With superior military technology, Europeans gained control of coastal cities and of resupply outposts along major trade routes. Gradually this control extended further inland, first in Latin America, then in North America, and later throughout Asia and Africa.

In the sixteenth century, Spain and Portugal had extensive empires in Central America and Brazil, respectively. Britain and France had colonies in North America and the Caribbean. The imperialists bought slaves in Africa and shipped them to Mexico and Brazil, where they worked in tropical agriculture and in mining silver and gold. The wealth produced was exported to Europe, where monarchs used it to buy armies and build states.

These empires decimated indigenous populations and cultures, causing immense suffering. Over time, the economies of colonies developed with the creation of basic transportation and communication infrastructure, factories, and so forth. But these economies were often molded to the needs of the colonizers, not the local populations.

Decolonization began with the British colonists in the United States who declared independence in 1776. Most of Latin America gained independence a few decades later. The new states in North America and Latin America were, of course, still run by the descendants of Europeans, to the disadvantage of Native Americans and African slaves.

New colonies were still being acquired by Europe through the end of the nineteenth century, culminating in a scramble for colonies in Africa in the 1890s (resulting in arbitrary territorial divisions as competing European armies rushed inland from all sides). India became Britain's largest and most important colony in the nineteenth century. Latecomers such as Germany and Italy were frustrated to find few attractive territories remaining in the world when they tried to build overseas empires in the late nineteenth century. Ultimately, only a few non-European areas of the world retained their independence: Japan, most of China, Iran, Turkey, and a few other areas. Japan began building its own empire, as did the United States, at the end of the nineteenth century. China became weaker and its coastal regions fell under the domination, if not the formal control, of European powers.

In the wave of decolonization after World War II, it was not local colonists (as in the Americas) but indigenous populations in Asia and Africa who won independence. Decolonization continued through the mid-1970s until almost no European colonies remained. Most of the newly independent states have faced tremendous challenges and difficulties in the postcolonial era. Because long-established economic patterns continue despite political independence, some refer to the postcolonial era as being *neocolonial*. Although the global North no longer imports slave labour from the South, it continues to rely on the South for cheap labour, for energy and minerals, and for the products of tropical agriculture. However, the North in turn makes vital contributions to the South in capital investment, technology transfer, and foreign assistance (see Chapter 13).

The collapse of the Soviet Union and its bloc, which reduced Russia to its size of a century earlier, can be seen as an extension of the post–World War II wave of decolonization and self-determination. There, as in much of the global south, imperialism has left ethnic conflict in its wake, as new political units come to terms with territorial divisions created in distant imperial capitals.

Figure 1.5 Imperialism, 1500–the Present

Region	1500	1600	1700	1800	1900	2000
North America	Columbus	British & French colonization		U.S. independence · War of 1812	Canada →	
Latin America	Brazil (Portuguese) · Central & S. America (Spanish)			Independence	European & U.S. interventions · Mexican Revolution	
East Asia		Russian conquest of Siberia	(China)	Opium Wars · T'ai P'ing Rebellion	Taiwan & Korea (Japanese) · Boxer Rebellion · Japanese empire · Communist China · Korea split · Taiwan autonomous · Hong Kong to China	
South Asia	European explorers	Dutch East Indies Company · Indonesia (Dutch) →			India (British) · Philippines (U.S.) · Indian independence · Vietnam War	
Africa	Slave trade · Angola, Mozambique (Portuguese)				Scramble for colonies (Brit., Fr., Ger.) · Independence	
Middle East	Ottoman Empire				British & French mandates · Algerian (Palestine) independence	

Nationalism, 1500–the Present

nationalism The identification with and devotion to the interests of one's nation. It usually involves a large group of people who share a national identity and often a language, culture, or ancestry.

Many people consider **nationalism**—devotion to the interests of one's nation—to be the most important force in world politics in the last two centuries. A nation is a population that shares an identity, usually including a language and culture. For instance, most of the 60 million inhabitants of France speak French, eat French cuisine, learn French history in school, and are represented (for better or worse) by the national government in Paris. But nationality is a difficult concept to define precisely. To some extent, the extension of political control over large territories like France created the commonality necessary for nationhood—states created nations. At the same time, however, the perceived existence of a nation has often led to the creation of a corresponding state as a people win sovereignty over their own affairs—nations created states.

Around A.D. 1500, countries such as France and Austria began to bring entire nations together into single states. These new nation-states were very large and powerful; they overran smaller neighbours. Over time, many small territorial units were conquered and incorporated into nation-states.[23] Eventually the idea of nationalism itself became a powerful force and ultimately contributed to the disintegration of large, multinational states such as Austria-Hungary (in World War I), the Soviet Union, and Yugoslavia.

The principle of *self-determination* implies that people who identify as a nation should have the right to form a state and exercise sovereignty over their affairs. Self-determination is a widely praised principle in international affairs today (not historically). But it is generally secondary to the principles of sovereignty (noninterference in other states' internal affairs) and territorial integrity, with which it frequently conflicts. Self-determination does not give groups the right to change international borders, even those imposed arbitrarily by colonialism, in order to unify a group with a common national identity. Generally, though not always, self-determination has been achieved by violence. When the borders of (perceived) nations do not match those of states, conflicts almost inevitably arise. Today such conflicts are widespread—in Northern Ireland, Québec, Israel-Palestine, India-Pakistan, Sri Lanka, Tibet, Sudan, and many other places.[24] In some cases, these conflicts are addressed through democratic means; in others, through repression and violence.

The Netherlands helped to establish the principle of self-determination when it broke free of Spanish ownership around 1600 and set up a self-governing Dutch republic. The struggle over control of the Netherlands was a leading cause of the Thirty Years' War (1618–1648), and in that war states mobilized their populations for war in new ways. For instance, Sweden drafted one man out of ten for long-term military service, while the Netherlands used the wealth derived from global trade to finance a standing professional army.

This process of popular mobilization intensified greatly in the French Revolution and the subsequent Napoleonic Wars, when France instituted a universal draft and a centrally run "command" economy. Its motivated citizen armies, composed for the first time of Frenchmen rather than mercenaries, marched longer and faster. People participated in part because they were patriotic. Their nation-state embodied their aspirations, and brought them together in a common national identity.

---

[23] Ernest Gellner, *Nations and Nationalism* (Ithaca, NY: Cornell UP, 1983). Charles Tilly, *Coercion, Capital and European States, A.D. 990–1990* (Oxford: Blackwell, 1990). E. J. Hobsbawm, *Nations and Nationalism since 1780: Programme, Myth, Reality* (NY: Cambridge UP, 1990). James Mayall, *Nationalism and International Society* (NY: Cambridge UP, 1990). Liah Greenfeld, *Nationalism: Five Roads to Modernity* (Cambridge, MA: Harvard UP, 1992).

[24] David Carment and Patrick James, eds., *Wars in the Midst of Peace: The International Politics of Ethnic Conflict* (Pittsburgh: U Pittsburgh P, 1997).

The United States meanwhile had followed the example of the Netherlands by declaring independence from Britain in 1776. The U.S. nation held together in the Civil War of the 1860s and developed a surprisingly strong sense of nationalism, considering how large and diverse the country was. Latin American states gained independence early in the nineteenth century, and Germany and Italy unified their nations out of multiple political units (through war) later in that century. As a Dominion of Britain, Canada was expected to follow the British government particularly on matters of foreign affairs. It was only with the Statute of Westminster of 1931 that the Canadian government could sign its own treaties and act independently of the British House of Lords.[25]

Before World War I, socialist workers from different European countries had banded together as workers to fight for workers' rights. In that war, however, most abandoned such solidarity and instead fought for their own nation; nationalism proved a stronger force than socialism. Before World War II, nationalism helped Germany, Italy, and Japan to build political orders based on *fascism*—an extreme authoritarianism girded by national chauvinism. And in World War II it was nationalism and patriotism (not communism) that rallied the Soviet people in order to sacrifice by the millions to turn back Germany's invasion.

In the past 50 years nations by the dozens have gained independence and statehood. Jews worked persistently in the first half of the twentieth century to create the state of Israel, and Palestinians have aspired in the second half to create a Palestinian state. While multinational states such as the Soviet Union and Yugoslavia have fragmented in recent years, ethnic and territorial units such as Ukraine, Slovenia, and East Timor have established themselves as independent nation-states. Others, such as Kosovo and Kurdistan, are seeking to do so. The continuing influence of nationalism in today's world is evident. More than ever, it is a major factor in international conflict and war.

National identity is psychologically reinforced on a daily basis by symbols such as the national flag, by rituals such as singing the national anthem, and by other practices designed to reinforce the identification of a population with its nation and government. In truth, people have multiple identities, belonging to various circles from their immediate family through their town, ethnic or religious group, nation or state, and humanity as a whole (see pp. 173–176). Nationalism has been remarkably successful in establishing national identity as a people's primary affiliation in much of the world. (In many places a sense of local affiliation remains important, however.)

Nationalism harnesses the energies of large populations based on their patriotic feelings toward their nation. The feeling of "we the people" is hard to sustain if the people are excluded from participating in their government. This participation is so important that even authoritarian governments often go through the motions of holding elections (with one candidate or party). Democracy can be a force for peace, constraining the power of state leaders to commit their nations to war. But popular influence over governments can also increase conflict with other nations, especially when ethnic tensions erupt.

Over time, democratic participation has broadened to more countries and more people within those countries (nonlandowners, women, etc.). The trend toward democracy seems to be continuing in most regions of the world in recent years—in Russia and Eastern Europe, Africa, Latin America, and Asia. Both nationalism and democracy remain great historical forces exerting strong influences in IR.

---

[25] J. L. Granatstein, "Introduction," *Canadian Foreign Policy: Historical Readings*, ed. J. L. Granatstein (Toronto: Copp Clark Pitman, 1993) 1–4.

The World Economy, 1750–the Present

In 1750, Britain, the world's most advanced economy, had a GDP of about $1200 per capita (in today's U.S. dollars). That is less than the present level of most of the global South. However, today Britain produces more than 10 times that much per person (and with a much larger population than in 1750). This accomplishment was due to **industrialization**—the use of energy to drive machinery and the accumulation of such machinery along with the products created by it. The Industrial Revolution started in Britain in the eighteenth century (notably with the inventions of a new steam engine in 1769, a mechanized thread-spinner in 1770, and the cotton gin in America in 1794). It was tied to Britain's emerging leadership role in the world economy. Industrialization—a process at the world level of analysis—spread to the other advanced economies (see Figure 1.6).[26]

By around 1850, the wooden sailing ships of earlier centuries had been replaced by larger and faster coal-powered iron steamships. Coal-fuelled steam engines also drove factories producing textiles and other commodities. The great age of railroad building was taking off. These developments not only increased the volume of world production and trade, but also tied distant locations more closely together economically. The day trip across France by railroad contrasted with the same route a hundred years earlier, when it took three weeks to complete. In this period of mechanization, however, factory conditions were extremely harsh, especially for women and children operating machines.

Britain dominated world trade in this period. Because Britain's economy was the most technologically advanced in the world, its products were competitive worldwide. Thus British policy favoured **free trade.** In addition to its central role in world trade, Britain served as the financial capital of the world, managing an increasingly complex world market in goods and services in the nineteenth century. The British currency, pounds sterling (silver), became the world standard. International monetary relations were still based on the value of precious metals, as they had been in the sixteenth century when Spain bought its armies with Mexican silver and gold.

By the outset of the twentieth century, however, the world's largest and most advanced economy was no longer Britain but the United States. The industrialization of the U.S. economy was fuelled by territorial expansion throughout the nineteenth century, adding vast natural resources. The U.S. economy was attracting huge pools of immigrant labour from the poorer fringes of Europe as well. The United States led the world in converting from coal to oil and from horse-drawn transportation to motor vehicles. New technical innovations, from electricity to airplanes, also helped push the U.S. economy into a dominant world position.

In the 1930s, the Canadian and world economies suffered a severe setback in the Great Depression. The protectionist Hawley-Smoot Act adopted by the United States in 1930, which imposed tariffs on imports, contributed to the severity of the depression by provoking retaliation and reducing world trade.

Following World War II, the capitalist world economy was restructured under U.S. leadership. Today's international economic institutions, such as the World Bank and International Monetary Fund (IMF), date from this period. The United States provided massive assistance to resuscitate the Western European economies (through the Marshall Plan) as well as Japan's economy. World trade greatly expanded, and the world market

industrialization The use of fossil-fuel energy to drive machinery and the accumulation of such machinery along with the products created by it.

free trade The flow of goods and services across national boundaries unimpeded by tariffs or other restrictions; in principle (if not always in practice), free trade was a key aspect of Britain's policy after 1846 and of U.S. and Canadian policy after 1945.

---

[26] Douglass C. North, and Robert Paul Thomas, *The Rise of the Western World: A New Economic History* (NY: Cambridge UP, 1973). E. J. Hobsbawm, *Industry and Empire: From 1750 to the Present Day* (Harmondsworth, UK: Penguin-Pelican, 1969). James D. Tracy, ed., *The Political Economy of Merchant Empires: State Power and World Trade, 1350–1750* (NY: Cambridge UP, 1991).

	1750	1800	1850	1900	1950	2000
Production		industrialization →		WW I WW II world depression Soviet industrialization assembly line oil	postwar prosperity Cold War arms race Japanese & German growth	world recession Soviet collapse
Energy	coal →			oil →	nuclear power → nat. gas →	
Leading Sectors	steam engine cotton gin	iron & steam →	textiles →	steel → electricity → motor vehicles →	electronics → computers → plastics → biotech →	
Transportation	(wooden sailing ships)	iron steamships →	railroads → Suez Canal	airplanes → Trans-Siberian Railroad automobiles → Panama Canal	jets → freeways → high-speed rail →	
Trade		British dominance	(free trade)	protectionism U.S. dominance	GATT European integration	WTO NAFTA
Money			sterling (British) as world currency	post-WWI inflation	U.S. dollar as world currency IMF Bretton Woods Keynes Marshall Plan	U.S. drops gold standard Russia joins IMF debt crises
Communication			telegraph →	telephone invented transoceanic cables radio →	information revolution →	communication satellites internet fax, modem, cellular, etc.

Figure 1.6 The World Economy, 1750–the Present

became ever more closely woven together through air transportation and telecommunications. Electronics emerged as a new leading sector, and technological progress accelerated throughout the twentieth century.

Standing apart from this world capitalist economy in the years after World War II were the economies of the Soviet Union and Eastern Europe, organized on communist principles of central planning and state ownership. The Soviet economy had some notable successes in rapidly industrializing the country in the 1930s, surviving the German assault in the 1940s, and developing world-class aerospace and military production capability in the 1950s and 1960s. The Soviet Union launched the world's first satellite (*Sputnik*) in 1957, and in the early 1960s its leaders boasted that communist economies would outperform capitalist ones within decades. Instead, the Soviet bloc economies stagnated under the weight of bureaucracy, ideological rigidity, environmental destruction, corruption, and extremely high military spending. In the 1990s, the former Soviet republics and their Eastern European neighbours tried—with mixed success—to make a transition to some form of capitalist market economy, but found it difficult.

Today there is a single integrated world economy that almost no country can resist joining. At the same time, the imperfections and problems of that world economy are evident in the periodic crises and recessions of recent years—in Russia and Eastern Europe, Japan and other Asian economies, and even periodically in the mature industrialized countries of North America and Western Europe. Above all, the emergence of a global capitalist economy has sharpened disparities between the richest and poorest world regions. While countries such as Canada and the United States enjoy unprecedented prosperity, Africa's increasing poverty has created a human catastrophe on a continental scale.

Just as the world economy climbed out of previous depressions in the 1890s and 1930s, it appears that a new wave of technological innovation is pulling the advanced industrialized countries into a new phase of growth—possibly one that is more information-intensive and resource-efficient. Much less clear is whether technological change will bypass or empower the global South (see Chapters 12 and 13).

The Two World Wars, 1900–1950

World War I (1914–1918) and World War II (1939–1945) occupied only 10 years of the twentieth century (see Figure 1.7). But they shaped the character of the century. Nothing like those wars has happened since, and they remain a key reference point for the world in which we live today. With perhaps just two other cases in history—the Thirty Years' War and the Napoleonic Wars—the two world wars were global or hegemonic wars in which almost all major states participated in an all-out struggle over the future of the international system.[27]

For many people, World War I symbolizes the tragic irrationality of war. It fascinates scholars of IR because it was a catastrophic war that seems unnecessary and perhaps even accidental. After a century of relative peace, the great powers marched off to battle for no good reason. There was even a popular feeling that Europe would be uplifted and

[27] Michael Dockrill, *Atlas of Twentieth Century World History* (NY: HarperCollins, 1991). Niall Ferguson, *The Pity of War: Explaining World War I* (NY: Basic, 1999). John Keegan, ed., *The Times Atlas of the Second World War* (NY: HarperCollins, 1989). Gerhard L. Weinberg, *A World at Arms: A Global History of World War II* (NY: Cambridge UP, 1994).

Figure 1.7 The Two World Wars, 1900–1950

	1900	1910	1920	1930	1940	1950
Europe		mobilization plans developed; Balkan crises; Sarajevo; U.S. enters war *(World War I)*		Italy invades Ethiopia; Munich Agreement	U.S. enters war; D Day *(World War II)*	
Germany	naval arms race with Britain	Defeat; Weimar Republic	hyperinflation	Hitler wins power; rearmament; occupation of Austria, Czech.; invasion of Poland	The Holocaust; strategic bombing; occupation of Europe; Defeat; occupied by Allied forces	
Russia		Russian Revolution (civil war); USSR formed		(industrialization); pact with Hitler	German invasion; Victory	
Asia	U.S. in Philippines; Russo-Japanese War	Japan neutral in WW I		Japan occupies Manchuria (China); Japan invades China; Japan quits League of Nations	Pearl Harbor; Japan occupies S.E. Asia; island battles; Hiroshima; Occupied by U.S.	
International Norms & Law	Hague Peace Conferences		Versailles treaty; League of Nations; Washington Naval Treaty	U.S. isolationism	Nuremberg Tribunal; United Nations	
Technology	destroyers	trench warfare; chemical weapons; tanks; submarines		mechanized armour	air war; radar; nuclear weapons	

reinvigorated by a war—that young men could once again prove their manhood on the battlefield in a glorious adventure. Such ideas were soon crushed by the immense pain and evident pointlessness of the war.

The previous major war had been the Franco-Prussian war of 1870–1871, when Germany executed a swift offensive using railroads to rush forces to the front. That war had ended quickly, decisively, and with a clear winner (Germany). People expected that a new war would follow the same pattern. All the great powers made plans for a quick railroad-borne offensive and rapid victory—what has been called the *cult of the offensive*. Under these doctrines, one country's mobilization for war virtually forced its enemies to mobilize as well. The one to strike first would win, it was believed. Thus, when a Serbian nationalist assassinated Archduke Ferdinand of Austria in 1914 in Sarajevo, a minor crisis escalated and the mobilization plans pushed Europe to all-out war.[28]

Contrary to expectations, the war was neither short nor decisive, and certainly not glorious. It bogged down in *trench warfare* along a fixed front. For example, in 1917 at the Battle of Passchendaele (Belgium), the British in three months fired 4.5 tonnes of artillery shells per metre of front line, over an 18-kilometre-wide front, and then lost 400 000 men in a failed ground attack. The horrific conditions were worsened by chemical weapons and by the attempts of Britain and Germany to starve each other's population into surrender.

Russia was the first state to crumble. Revolution at home removed Russia from the war in 1917 (and led to the founding of the Soviet Union). But the entry of the United States into the war on the anti-German side that year quickly turned the tide. In the *Treaty of Versailles* of 1919, Germany was forced to give up territory, pay reparations, limit its future armaments, and admit guilt for the war. German resentment against the harsh terms of Versailles would contribute to Adolf Hitler's rise to power in the 1930s. After World War I, U.S. President Woodrow Wilson led the effort to create the **League of Nations**, a forerunner of today's UN. But the U.S. Senate would not approve U.S. participation, and the League did not prove effective. U.S. isolationism between the world wars, along with declining British power and Russia's withdrawal into revolution, left a power vacuum in world politics.

In the 1930s, Germany and Japan stepped into that vacuum, embarking on aggressive expansionism that ultimately led to World War II. Japan had already occupied Taiwan and Korea, after defeating China in 1895 and Russia in 1905. In World War I Japan gained some German colonies in Asia. In 1931, Japan occupied Manchuria (northeast China) and set up a puppet regime there. In 1937, Japan invaded the rest of China and began a brutal occupation that continues to haunt Chinese-Japanese relations. Japanese leaders planned a *coprosperity sphere* in which an industrialized Japan would control the natural resources of East and Southeast Asia.

Meanwhile, in Europe in the 1930s, Nazi Germany under Hitler had rearmed, intervened to help fascists win the Spanish Civil War, and grabbed territory from its neighbours under the rationale of reuniting ethnic Germans in those territories with their homeland. Hitler was emboldened by the weak response of the international community and League of Nations to aggression by fascist regimes in Italy and Spain. In an effort to appease German ambitions, Britain agreed in the **Munich Agreement** of 1938 to let Germany occupy part of Czechoslovakia. Appeasement has since had a negative

League of Nations
Established after World War I and a forerunner of today's United Nations, the organization achieved certain humanitarian and other successes but was weakened by the absence of U.S. membership and by its own lack of effectiveness in ensuring collective security. See also *collective security*.

Munich Agreement
A symbol of the failed policy of appeasement, this agreement, signed in 1938, allowed Nazi Germany to occupy a part of Czechoslovakia. Rather than appease German aspirations, it was followed by further German expansions, which triggered World War II.

---

[28] Stephen Van Evera, "The Cult of the Offensive and the Origins of the First World War," *International Security* 9 (1984): 58–107. Jack Lewis Snyder, *The Ideology of the Offensive: Military Decision Making and the Disasters of 1914* (Ithaca, NY: Cornell UP, 1984). Miles Kahler, "Rumors of War: The 1914 Analogy," *Foreign Affairs* 58.2 (1979/80): 374–96.

connotation in IR, because the Munich Agreement seemed only to encourage Hitler's further conquests.

In 1939, Germany invaded Poland, and Britain joined the war against Germany in response. World War II was an important turning point for Canada. In World War I, Britain declared war on Germany on behalf of Canada, but by World War II, Canada joined the war as a fully sovereign nation. By formally allying itself with Britain and France, Canada was engaging in war for the first time as an independent nation.[29]

Hitler signed a nonaggression pact with his archenemy Joseph Stalin of the Soviet Union and threw his full army against France, occupying most of it quickly. Hitler then double-crossed Stalin and invaded the Soviet Union in 1941. This offensive ultimately bogged down and was turned back after several years. But the Soviet Union took the brunt of the German attack and suffered by far the greatest share of the 60 million deaths caused by World War II. This trauma continues to be a powerful memory that shapes views of IR in Russia and Eastern Europe.

The United States joined World War II against Germany in 1942. The U.S. economy produced critically important weapons and supplies for allied armies. The United States played an important role with Britain in the strategic bombing of German cities—including the firebombing of Dresden in February 1945, which caused 100 000 civilian deaths. In 1944, after crossing the English Channel on June 6 (*D-Day*), British, American, and Canadian forces pushed into Germany from the west while the Soviets pushed from the east. A ruined Germany surrendered and was occupied by the allied powers.

At its peak, Nazi Germany and its allies occupied virtually all of Europe, except Britain and part of Russia. Under its fanatical policies of racial purity, Germany rounded up and exterminated 6 million Jews and millions of others, including homosexuals, Gypsies, and communists. The mass murders, now known as the Holocaust, along with the sheer scale of war unleashed by Nazi aggression, are considered among the greatest *crimes against humanity* in history. Responsible German officials faced justice in the *Nuremberg Tribunal* after the war (see pp. 283–288). The pledges of world leaders after that experience to "never again" allow **genocide**—the systematic extermination of a racial or religious group—have been found wanting as genocide recurred in the 1990s in Bosnia and Rwanda.

genocide The intentional and systematic attempt to destroy a national, ethnic, racial, or religious group, in whole or part. It was confirmed as a crime under international law by the UN Genocide Convention (1948). See also *crimes against humanity* and *dehumanization*.

While the war in Europe was raging, Japan fought a war over control of Southeast Asia with the United States and its allies. Japan's expansionism in the 1930s had only underscored the dependence on foreign resources that it was intended to solve: the United States punished Japan by cutting off U.S. oil exports. Japan then destroyed much of the U.S. Navy in a surprise attack at *Pearl Harbor* (Hawaii) in 1941, and seized desired territories (including Indonesia, whose oil replaced that of the United States). The United States, however, built vast new military forces and retook a series of Pacific islands in subsequent years. The strategic bombing of Japanese cities by the United States culminated in the only historical use of nuclear weapons in war—the destruction of the cities of *Hiroshima* and *Nagasaki* in August 1945—which triggered Japan's quick surrender.

The lessons of the two world wars seem contradictory. From the failure of the Munich Agreement in 1938 to appease Hitler, many people have concluded that only a hard-line foreign policy with preparedness for war will deter aggression and prevent war. Yet in 1914 it was just such hard-line policies that apparently led Europe into a disastrous war, which might have been avoided by appeasement. Evidently the best policy would be sometimes harsh and at other times conciliatory, but IR scholars have not discovered a simple formula for choosing (see "The Causes of War" in Chapter 5).

---

[29] D. W. Middlemiss and J. J Sokolsky, *Canadian Defence: Decisions and Determinants* (Toronto: Harcourt, 1988).

The Cold War, 1945–1990

The United States and the Soviet Union became the two superpowers of the post–World War II era.[30] Each had its ideological mission (capitalist democracy versus communism), its networks of alliances and client states in the global South, and its deadly arsenal of nuclear weapons. Europe was divided, with massive military forces of the United States and its *North Atlantic Treaty Organization (NATO)* allies on one side and massive forces of the Soviet Union and its *Warsaw Pact* allies on the other. Germany itself was split, with three-quarters of the country—and three-quarters of the capital city of Berlin—occupied by the United States, Britain, and France. The remainder, surrounding West Berlin, was occupied by the Soviet Union. Crises in Berlin in 1948 and 1961 led to armed confrontations but not war. In 1961, East Germany built the Berlin Wall separating East from West Berlin. It symbolized the division of Europe by what Winston Churchill had called the "iron curtain."

Cold War The hostile relations—punctuated by occasional periods of improvement, or détente—between the two superpowers, the U.S. and the U.S.S.R., from 1945 to 1990.

Despite the hostility of East-West relations during the **Cold War**, a relatively stable framework of relations emerged, and conflicts never escalated to all-out war (see Figure 1.8). At a U.S.-Soviet-British meeting at *Yalta* in 1945, when the defeat of Germany was imminent, the Western powers acknowledged the fact of the Soviet army's presence in Eastern Europe, allowing that area to remain under Soviet influence. Although the Soviet bloc did not join Western economic institutions such as the IMF, all the world's major states joined the UN. Signatories to the United Nations Charter pledged to try to save future generations from the scourge of war; to reaffirm faith in fundamental human rights; to establish conditions under which justice and respect for international law can be maintained; and to promote social progress. The United Nations (unlike the ill-fated League of Nations) managed to maintain almost universal membership and adherence to basic structures and rules throughout the Cold War era.

The central concern of the West during the Cold War was that the Soviet Union might gain control of Western Europe—either through outright invasion or through communists' taking power in war-weary and impoverished countries of Western Europe. This could have put the entire industrial base of the Eurasian landmass (from Europe to Siberia) under one state. The *Marshall Plan*—U.S. financial aid to rebuild European economies—responded to these fears, as did the creation of the NATO alliance. Half of the entire world's military spending was devoted to the European standoff. Much spending was also devoted to a superpower nuclear arms race, in which each superpower produced tens of thousands of nuclear weapons (see pp. 226–228).

containment A policy adopted in the late 1940s by which the United States sought to halt the global expansion of Soviet influence on several levels—military, political, ideological, and economic.

Through the policy of **containment**, adopted in the late 1940s, the United States sought to halt the expansion of Soviet influence globally on several levels at once—military, political, ideological, economic. The United States maintained an extensive network of military bases and alliances worldwide. Virtually all of U.S. foreign policy in subsequent decades, from foreign aid and technology transfer to military intervention and diplomacy, came to serve the goal of containment.

Sino-Soviet split A rift in the 1960s between the communist powers of the Soviet Union and China, fuelled by China's opposition to Soviet moves toward peaceful coexistence with the United States.

The *Chinese communist revolution* in 1949 led to a Sino-Soviet alliance (*Sino* means "Chinese"). But China became fiercely independent in the 1960s following the **Sino-Soviet split**, when China opposed Soviet moves toward *peaceful coexistence* with the

[30] John Lewis Gaddis, *We Now Know: Rethinking Cold War History* (NY: Oxford UP, 1997). Vladislav Zubok and Constantine Pleshakov, *Inside the Kremlin's Cold War: From Stalin to Krushchev* (Cambridge, MA: Harvard UP, 1996). Raymond Garthoff, *Détente and Confrontation: American-Soviet Relations from Nixon to Reagan* (Washington, DC: Brookings, 1985). Deborah Welch Larson, *Anatomy of Mistrust: U.S.-Soviet Relations during the Cold War* (Ithaca, NY: Cornell UP, 1997). Marc Trachtenberg, *A Constructed Peace: The Making of the European Settlement, 1945–1963* (Princeton, NJ: Princeton UP, 1999).

Figure 1.8 The Cold War, 1945–1990

Time axis: 1940 — 1950 — 1960 — 1970 — 1980 — 1990

Soviet Union (leaders: Stalin | Khrushchev | Brezhnev | Andropov | Chernenko | Gorbachev)
A-bomb · Warsaw Pact → · Sputnik · nuclear arms race → · nuclear parity with U.S. · military buildup · reforms (perestroika, glasnost)

United States (presidents: F. D. Roosevelt | Truman | Eisenhower | Kennedy | Johnson | Nixon | Ford | Carter | Reagan | Bush)
(WW II alliance) · NATO → · containment policy → · (nuclear superiority over USSR) · human rights → · military buildup · (Iran crisis) · "Star Wars" (SDI)

China
civil war (Nationalists-Communists) · Sino-Soviet alliance · People's Republic (Taiwan nationalist) · Taiwan Straits crises (vs. U.S.) → · Sino-Soviet split · A-bomb · Cultural Revolution · Soviet border clashes · U.S.-China rapprochement · death of Mao · joins UN · neutral to pro-U.S.

Confrontations
Berlin crisis · Korean War · Soviet invasion of Hungary · U-2 incident · Berlin Wall · Berlin crisis · **Cuban Missile Crisis** · **Vietnam War** · USSR invades Czechoslovakia · **Afghanistan War** · U.S. invasion of Grenada

Proxy Wars
Greek civil war · Suez crisis · Cuban revolution · Indonesia · Arab-Israeli wars · Chile coup · Somalia vs. Ethiopia · Cambodia → · Nicaragua → · El Salvador → · Angola →

Co-operation
Yalta summit · Geneva summit · Limited Test Ban Treaty · Non-Proliferation Treaty · SALT I · détente · SALT II · start talks · Paris summit (CFE) · INF treaty

Figure 1.8 The Cold War, 1945–1990

United States.[31] In the late 1960s, young radicals, opposed to both superpowers, ran China during the chaotic and destructive *Cultural Revolution*. But feeling threatened by Soviet power, China's leaders developed a growing affiliation with the United States during the 1970s, starting with a dramatic visit to China by U.S. President Nixon in 1972. This visit led to U.S.-Chinese diplomatic relations in 1979, and ended a decades-long argument in the U.S. foreign policy establishment about "who lost China" to communism in 1949. During the Cold War, China generally tried to play a balancer role against whichever superpower seemed most threatening at the time.

In 1950, the *Korean War* broke out when communist North Korea attacked and overran most of U.S.-allied South Korea. The United States and its allies (under UN authority obtained after the Soviets walked out of the Security Council in protest) counterattacked and overran most of North Korea. China sent masses of "volunteers" to help North Korea, and the war bogged down near the original border until a 1953 truce ended the fighting. The Korean War hardened U.S. attitudes toward communism and set a negative tone for future East-West relations, especially for U.S.-Chinese relations in the 1950s. U.S. leaders considered using nuclear weapons during the Korean War, but decided not to do so.

The Cold War thawed temporarily after Stalin died in 1953 and Eisenhower was elected promising to bring an end to the Korean conflict. The first **summit meeting** between superpower leaders took place in Geneva in 1955. But the Soviet Union sent tanks to crush a popular uprising in Hungary in 1956 (an action it repeated in 1968 in Czechoslovakia), and the Soviet missile program that orbited *Sputnik* in 1957 alarmed the United States. The shooting down of a U.S. spy plane (the *U-2*) over the Soviet Union in 1960 scuttled a summit meeting between superpower leaders Nikita Khrushchev and Dwight D. Eisenhower. Meanwhile in Cuba, after Fidel Castro's communist revolution in 1959, the United States attempted a counterrevolution in the botched 1961 *Bay of Pigs* invasion.

These hostilities culminated in the **Cuban Missile Crisis** of 1962, when the Soviet Union installed medium-range nuclear missiles in Cuba. The Soviet aims were to reduce the Soviet Union's strategic nuclear inferiority, to counter the deployment of U.S. missiles on Soviet borders in Turkey, and to deter another U.S. invasion of Cuba. U.S. leaders, however, considered the missiles threatening and provocative. As historical documents revealed years later, nuclear war was quite possible. Some U.S. policy-makers favoured military strikes before the missiles became operational, when in fact some nuclear weapons in Cuba were already operational and commanders were authorized to use them in the event of a U.S. attack.[32] Instead, President John F. Kennedy imposed a naval blockade to force their removal. The Soviet Union backed down on the missiles, and the United States promised not to invade Cuba in the future. Leaders on both sides were shaken, however, by the possibility of nuclear war. They signed the *Limited Test Ban Treaty* in 1963, prohibiting atmospheric nuclear tests, and began to cooperate in cultural exchanges, space exploration, aviation, and other areas.

Despite these moments of tension, the Cold War was described by some observers as a "long peace" because war never did break out between the United States and Soviet Union. However, the two superpowers often jockeyed for position in the global South, supporting **proxy wars** in which they typically supplied and advised opposing factions in

summit meeting A meeting between heads of state, often referring to leaders of great powers, as in the Cold War superpower summits between the United States and the Soviet Union or today's meetings of the Group of Eight on economic coordination.

Cuban Missile Crisis (1962) A superpower crisis, sparked by the Soviet Union's installation of medium-range nuclear missiles in Cuba, that marks the moment when the United States and the Soviet Union came closest to nuclear war.

proxy wars Wars in the global South—often civil wars—in which the United States and the Soviet Union jockeyed for position by supplying and advising opposing factions.

---

[31] David Allan Mayers, *Cracking the Monolith: U.S. Policy Against the Sino-Soviet Alliance, 1949–1955* (Baton Rouge: Louisiana State UP, 1986). Ilpyong J. Kim, ed., *Beyond the Strategic Triangle* (NY: Paragon, 1992).

[32] James A. Nathan, ed., *The Cuban Missile Crisis Revisited* (NY: St. Martin's, 1992). Ernest May and Philip Zelikow, eds., *The Kennedy Tapes: Inside the White House During the Cuban Missile Crisis* (Cambridge, MA: Harvard UP, 1997).

civil wars. The alignments were often arbitrary. For instance, the United States backed the Ethiopian government and the Soviets backed next-door rival Somalia in the 1970s; when an Ethiopian revolution caused the new government to seek Soviet help, the United States switched to support Somalia instead. The Cold War may have been a period of relative peace for the superpowers, but it was a period of profound violence for many states and peoples of the South.[33]

One flaw of U.S. policy in the Cold War period was to see regional conflicts through East-West lenses. Its preoccupation with communism led the United States to support unpopular pro-Western governments in a number of poor countries, nowhere more disastrously than during the *Vietnam War* in the 1960s. The war in Vietnam divided U.S. citizens and ultimately failed to prevent a communist takeover. The fall of South Vietnam in 1975 appeared to signal U.S. weakness, especially combined with U.S. setbacks in the Middle East—the 1973 Arab oil embargo against the United States and the 1979 overthrow of the U.S.-backed Shah of Iran by Islamic fundamentalists.

In this period of apparent U.S. weakness, the Soviet Union invaded Afghanistan in 1979. But, like the United States in Vietnam, the Soviet Union could not suppress rebel armies supplied by the opposing superpower. The Soviets ultimately withdrew after almost a decade of war that considerably weakened the Soviet Union. Meanwhile, President Ronald Reagan built up U.S. military forces to record levels and supported rebel armies in the Soviet-allied states of Nicaragua and Angola (and one faction in Cambodia) as well as Afghanistan. Superpower relations slowly improved after Mikhail Gorbachev, a reformer, took power in the Soviet Union in 1985. But some of the global South battlegrounds (notably Afghanistan and Angola) continued to suffer from brutal civil wars (fought with leftover Cold War arms) into the new century.

In retrospect, it seems that both superpowers exaggerated Soviet strength. In the early years of the nuclear arms race, U.S. military superiority was absolute, especially in nuclear weapons. The Soviets managed to match the United States over time, from A-bombs to H-bombs to multiple-warhead missiles. By the 1970s the Soviets had achieved strategic parity, meaning that neither side could prevent its own destruction in a nuclear war. But behind this military parity lay a Soviet Union lagging far behind the West in everything else—sheer wealth, technology, infrastructure, and citizen/worker motivation.

In June 1989, massive pro-democracy demonstrations in China's capital of Beijing (Tiananmen Square) were put down violently by the communist government. Hundreds were shot dead in the streets. Around 1990, as the Soviet Union stood by, one after another Eastern European country replaced its communist government under pressure of mass demonstrations. The toppling of the Berlin Wall in late 1989 symbolized the end of the Cold War division of Europe. Germany formally reunified in 1990. The Soviet leader, Gorbachev, allowed these losses of external power (and more) in hopes of concentrating on Soviet domestic restructuring under his policies of *perestroika* (economic reform) and *glasnost* (openness in political discussion). In 1991, however, the Soviet Union itself broke apart. Russia and many of the other former republics struggled throughout the 1990s against economic and financial collapse, inflation, corruption, war, and military weakness, although they remained political democracies. China remained a communist, authoritarian government but liberalized its economy and avoided military conflicts. In contrast to the Cold War era, China developed close ties with both the United States and Russia, and joined the world's liberal trading regime.

---

[33] Amitav Acharya, "Beyond Anarchy: Third World Instability and International Order after the Cold War," *International Relations Theory and the Third World*, ed. Stephanie G. Neuman (NY: St. Martin's, 1998) 159–211.

Scholars do not agree on the important question of why the Cold War ended.[34] One view is that U.S. military strength under President Reagan forced the Soviet Union into bankruptcy as it tried to keep up in the arms race. A different position is that the Soviet Union suffered from internal stagnation over decades and ultimately imploded because of weaknesses in its system of governance that had little to do with external pressure. Indeed, some scholars think the Soviet Union might have fallen apart earlier without the United States as a foreign enemy to bolster the Soviet government's legitimacy with its own people.

The Early Post–Cold War Era, 1990–

The post–Cold War era began with a bang, while the Soviet Union was still disintegrating. In 1990, perhaps believing that the end of the Cold War had left a power vacuum in its region, Iraq occupied its neighbour Kuwait in an aggressive grab for control of Middle East oil. Western powers were alarmed—both about the example that such aggression, if unpunished, could set in a new era, and about the direct threat to energy supplies for the world economy. The United States mobilized a coalition of the world's major countries (with almost no opposition) to oppose Iraq. Working through the UN, the U.S.-led coalition applied escalating sanctions against Iraq—from condemnation, to embargoing Iraq's oil exports, to threats and ultimatums. President Bush received authorization from the U.S. Congress to use force against Iraq.

When Iraq did not withdraw from Kuwait by the UN's deadline, the United States and its allies easily smashed Iraq's military and evicted its army from Kuwait in the *Gulf War*. But the coalition did not occupy Iraq or overthrow its government. The costs of the Gulf War were shared among the participants in the coalition, with Britain and France making military commitments while Japan and Germany made substantial financial contributions. The pass-the-hat financing for this war was an innovation, one that worked fairly well.[35]

The final collapse of the Soviet Union followed only months after the Gulf War. The 15 republics of the Union—of which Russia under President Boris Yeltsin was just one—had begun taking power from a weakened central government, declaring themselves as sovereign states. This process, which is still working itself out, raised complex problems ranging from issues of national self-determination to the reallocation of property. The Baltic republics (Estonia, Latvia, and Lithuania), which had been incorporated into the Soviet Union only in the 1940s, were leaders in breaking away. The others held long negotiations under Gorbachev's leadership to restructure their confederation, with stronger republics and a weaker centre.

The *Union Treaty* outlining this new structure provoked hard-liners in the old central government to try to seize control of the Soviet Union in a military coup in 1991.[36] The failure of the coup—and the prominent role of Russian President Yeltsin in opposing it—accelerated the collapse of the Soviet Union. The Communist party was banned, and soon both capitalism and democracy were adopted as the basis of the economies and polit-

---

[34] Rey Koslowski and Friedrich Kratochwil, "Understanding Change in International Politics: The Soviet Empire's Demise and the International System," *International Organization* 48.2 (1994): 215–48. Stephen G. Brooks and William C. Wohlforth, "Power, Globalization, and the End of the Cold War: Reevaluating a Landmark Case for Ideas," *International Security* 25.3 (2000/2001): 5–53. Karin Fierke, *Changing Games, Changing Strategies: Critical Reflections in Security* (Manchester, UK: Manchester UP, 1998).

[35] Lawrence Freedman and Efraim Karsh, *The Gulf Conflict: 1990–1991* (Princeton, NJ: Princeton UP, 1993).

ical systems of the former Soviet states. (In reality, the daily workings of society change somewhat more slowly; the old guard tends to retain power wearing new hats.) The republics became independent states and formed a loose coordinating structure—the **Commonwealth of Independent States (CIS)**—whose future, if any, is still unclear. Of the former Soviet republics, only the three small Baltic states are not members. Russia and Belarus formed a quasi-union in 2000.

Western relations with Russia and the other republics have been mixed since the 1990s. Because of their own economic problems, and because of a sense that Russia needed internal reform more than external aid, Western countries provided only limited aid for the region's harsh economic transition, which had drastically reduced living standards. Russia's brutal suppression of its secessionist province of Chechnya in 1995 and 1999 provoked Western fears of an expansionist, aggressive Russian nationalism, especially after success of ultranationalists in Russian parliamentary elections earlier in the decade. Russian leaders feared that NATO expansion into Eastern Europe would place threatening Western military forces on Russia's borders, creating a new division of Europe. Russian President Yeltsin warned of a "Cold Peace." Meanwhile, Japan and Russia could not resolve a lingering, mostly symbolic, territorial dispute.[37]

Despite these problems, the world's great powers overall increased their cooperation after the Cold War. Russia was accepted as the successor state to the Soviet Union and took its seat on the Security Council. Russia and the United States agreed to major reductions in their nuclear weapons, and carried them out in the 1990s.

U.S. leaders had hoped that the Gulf War would set valuable precedents for the future—the punishment of aggression, the reaffirmation of sovereignty and territorial integrity (of both Kuwait and Iraq), the utility of the UN Security Council, and the willingness of the United States to lead the post–Cold War order, which President George H. W. Bush named the "New World Order." The prime architect of the "New World Order" of the early 1990s was, in many ways, Franklin D. Roosevelt—the U.S. president during most of World War II in the 1940s. His vision was of a great power collaboration through a new United Nations after the defeat of Germany and Japan in the war. Included would be the winners of the war—the United States, the Soviet Union, and Britain, along with France and (for the first time) China. The five would hold permanent seats on the UN Security Council. Germany and Japan would be reconstructed as democracies, and the United States would take a strong leadership role in world affairs. Roosevelt's vision was delayed by 40 years while the Soviet Union and United States contested the world order. But then, surprisingly, it came into existence in the early 1990s in something close to the original vision.

Hopes for a "New World Order" after the Gulf War quickly collided with less pleasant realities, however. In Bosnia-Herzegovina (hereafter called Bosnia for short), the UN mounted its largest peacekeeping mission, yet the gap between the international community's words and deeds took years to close. Just after the Gulf War in 1991, the former

Commonwealth of Independent States (CIS)
The loose coordinating structure linking the former republics of the Soviet Union (except the Baltic states) since 1991.

---

[36] Michael McFaul, *Russia's Unfinished Revolution: Political Change from Gorbachev to Putin* (Ithaca, NY: Cornell UP, 2001). James H. Billington, *Russia Transformed: Breakthrough to Hope: Moscow, August 1991* (NY: Free Press, 1992). Marshall I. Goldman, *What Went Wrong with Perestroika* (NY: Norton, 1994).

[37] G. John Ikenberry, *After Victory* (Princeton, NJ: Princeton UP, 2000). Raymond L. Garthoff, *The Great Transition: American-Soviet Relations and the End of the Cold War* (Washington, DC: Brookings, 1994). John Lewis Gaddis, *The United States and the End of the Cold War: Implications, Reconsiderations, Provocations* (NY: Oxford UP, 1992). Robert Jervis and Seweryn Bialer, eds., *Soviet-American Relations after the Cold War* (Durham, NC: Duke UP, 1991). Bennett Ramberg, ed., *Arms Control without Negotiation: From the Cold War to the New World Order* (Boulder, CO: Rienner, 1993). Francis Fukuyama, *The End of History and the Last Man* (NY: Free Press, 1992).

Yugoslavia broke apart, with several of its republics declaring independence. Ethnic Serbs, who were minorities in Croatia and Bosnia, seized about a third of Croatia and two-thirds of Bosnia as territory to form a "Greater Serbia" with the neighbouring republic of Serbia. In those territories, with help from Serbia, which controlled the Yugoslav army, the Serb forces massacred hundreds of thousands of non-Serb Bosnians and Croatians and expelled millions more, to create an ethnically pure state. Croatian militias in Bosnia emulated these tactics, though on a smaller scale.

The international community recognized the independence of Croatia and Bosnia, admitting them to the UN and passing dozens of Security Council resolutions to protect their territorial integrity and their civilian populations. But in contrast to the Gulf War, the great powers showed no willingness to bear major costs to protect Bosnia. Instead they tried to contain the conflict by assuming a neutral role as peacekeeper and intermediary, offering a variety of peace plans, economic sanctions and rewards, and other inducements, none of which convinced Serb forces to withdraw from the territory they occupied. International "neutrality" included an arms embargo imposed on unarmed Bosnia and heavily armed Serbia alike, despite the UN resolutions declaring Serbia the aggressor. The UN sent almost 40 000 peacekeepers to Bosnia and Croatia, at a cost of more than $1 billion per year. NATO threatened military actions repeatedly, only to back down when costs appeared too high, as when Serb forces took peacekeepers hostage and threatened to kill them if NATO attacked.[38]

By 1995, the international community's Bosnia policy was in shambles. The Serbian forces overran two UN-designated "safe areas" in eastern Bosnia, expelling the women and slaughtering thousands of the men, but then the tide of battle turned and Serb forces lost ground. Fears of a widening war, along with the pressures of an upcoming U.S. presidential election, finally triggered a more assertive international policy in Bosnia. Two weeks of NATO air strikes (the alliance's first-ever military engagement) induced Serb forces to come to terms. U.S. negotiators pushed through the *Dayton Agreement*, which formally held Bosnia together as a single country, but granted Serb forces great autonomy on half of Bosnia's territory (the other half being controlled by a federation of Muslim, Croatian, and multiethnic parties). Sixty thousand heavily armed troops, mostly from NATO, went to Bosnia and established a stable ceasefire. Provisions on refugees' return to their homes, and on the arrest of war criminals, were not implemented, however. The international forces extended their mission year after year (gradually shrinking it), for fear that withdrawal would spark renewed war. As of June 2004, some 7000 troops remained in Bosnia as part of the NATO mission. More than 40 000 Canadians served in Bosnia in either the UN or NATO missions since 1992, and 24 Canadians lost their lives serving in Bosnia.

In contrast to their indecision early in the Bosnia crisis, the Western powers acted with dispatch in 1999 when Serbian forces carried out "ethnic-cleansing" actions in the Serbian province of Kosovo, where ethnic Albanians made up 90 percent of the population. The guerrilla Kosovo Liberation Army had been conducting a violent campaign for independence, and Serbian forces had responded with massacres and the forced displacement of hundreds of thousands of Albanians. After a Western-sponsored peace initiative collapsed, NATO launched an air war against Serbia. The air campaign escalated over 10 weeks as the Serbian government intensified its campaign in Kosovo. In response,

[38] James Gow, *Triumph of the Lack of Will: International Diplomacy and the Yugoslav War* (NY: Columbia UP, 1997). David Rieff, *Slaughterhouse: Bosnia and the Failure of the West* (NY: Simon & Schuster, 1995). Noel Malcolm, *Bosnia: A Short History* (NY: New York UP, 1994). Roy Gutman, *A Witness to Genocide* (NY: Macmillan, 1993). Steven L. Burg and Paul S. Shoup, *The War in Bosnia-Herzegovina: Ethnic Conflict and International Intervention* (Armonk, NY: Sharpe, 1999).

Serbian strongman Slobodan Milosevic was indicted for war crimes by the UN tribunal for the former Yugoslavia, and eventually delivered to the tribunal in 2001, after losing power.[39]

NATO came under criticism—notably from Russia and China—for acting without explicit UN authorization and interfering in Serbia's internal affairs. (The international community and the UN considered Kosovo, unlike Bosnia, to be a part of Serbia.) Critics also faulted NATO for relying on air-only tactics in response to atrocities on the ground. Although smart bombs kept civilian casualties relatively low as compared with previous wars, mistakes in bombing killed dozens of Serbian civilians in several instances. NATO blamed a targeting error for its bombing of the Chinese embassy in Yugoslavia, which triggered nationalistic anti-American demonstrations in China.

In the end, Serbian forces withdrew from Kosovo and were replaced by a UN-authorized, NATO-led international force. Most refugees returned home, although much of the Serbian minority then fled Kosovo in the face of Albanian reprisals. The province's destiny, and the debate about the limits of air warfare, remain unsettled.

Other Western military intervention decisions since 1990—outside the strategically important locations of the Persian Gulf and former Yugoslavia—do not easily map onto a "New World Order." In Cambodia, the United Nations launched one of its largest multidimensional peacekeeping missions to literally rebuild the Cambodian state, only to see one of the Cambodian political parties launch a coup and then conduct a highly questionable set of elections several years later. In Somalia, a U.S.-led coalition sent tens of thousands of troops to suppress factional fighting and deliver relief supplies to a large population that was starving. However, when those forces were drawn into the fighting and sustained casualties, the United States abruptly pulled out, with the UN following by 1995.[40] In Rwanda in 1994, the genocide of more than half a million civilians—massacred in just a few weeks—was virtually ignored by the international community, despite the efforts of the Canadian force commander of the UN mission, Lieutenant-General Roméo Dallaire, to draw the world's attention to the horrors that were taking place there. The great powers, burned by failures in Somalia and Bosnia, decided that their vital interests were not at stake. In 1997, the Rwanda conflict spilled into neighbouring Zaire (now the Democratic Republic of Congo), where rebels overthrew a corrupt dictator. Neighbouring countries were drawn into the fighting but the international community steered clear even as living conditions worsened and millions of civilians died. The U.S. military intervened in Haiti to restore the elected president, but the situation there remained bleak for years afterwards. In 2004, rebels forced Aristide from office and U.S., French, and Canadian forces moved in to provide stability under a United Nations–authorized mission.

Yeltsin resigned at the end of 1999 and his designated successor, prime minister Vladimir Putin, took office and was elected president a few months later, while Putin's war against Chechen rebels was still popular with Russians. Despite the leadership change, Russian-American relations faced the continuing challenges of conflicting interests in multiple areas. Not only has the U.S. provided precious little aid, in Russia's perspective, but it is pushing NATO's boundaries eastward. It is promoting new pipelines to bypass Russian territory in moving oil from former Soviet republics to Western consumers. Prior

---

[39] Andrew J. Bacevich and Eliot A. Cohen, *War over Kosovo* (NY: Columbia UP, 2002). Peter R. Prifti, *Confrontation in Kosovo: The Albanian-Serb Struggle, 1969–1998* (NY: Columbia UP, 1999). Julie A. Mertus, *Kosovo: How Myths and Truths Started a War* (Berkeley: U California P, 1999). Miranda Vickers, *Between Serb and Albanian: A History of Kosovo* (NY: Columbia UP, 1998).

[40] Walter S. Clarke and Jeffrey I. Herbst, eds., *Learning from Somalia: The Lessons of Armed Humanitarian Intervention* (Boulder, CO: Westview, 1997). Helen Fogarassy, *Mission Improbable: The World Community on a UN Compound in Somalia* (Lanham, MD: UP America, 1999).

to September 2001, it criticized the conduct of the war in Chechnya, a province of Russia, yet conducts its own military attacks around the world unilaterally when it so chooses. In 2001, conflicts intensified over U.S. plans to rapidly deploy ballistic missile defenses and withdraw from the ABM Treaty (see p. 273).

While these U.S.-Russian conflicts reflect lingering problems from earlier times, new rifts opened in 2001 between the United States and both China and Europe—possibly signalling a realignment against U.S. predominance in world affairs. In President George W. Bush's first year, the United States stood nearly alone against the rest of the international community on a range of issues—on the one hand supporting missile defences, and on the other opposing the Kyoto treaty on global warming, a treaty to enforce the prohibition on biological weapons, a proposal to curb international small-arms sales, a proposed International Criminal Court (to replace the ad hoc war-crimes tribunals of the 1990s), and a proposal to curb tobacco marketing in poor countries. Signalling aspects of this shifting alignment, Russia and China signed a treaty of friendship in 2001, and European countries helped vote the United States off two important UN commissions.

These divisive issues receded for a time, however, when the United States was attacked by terrorists on September 11, 2001. The attack destroyed the World Trade Center in New York and a wing of the Pentagon in Washington, killing thousands of Americans and citizens of about 60 other countries. The attacks mobilized support for the United States by a very broad coalition of states, not only out of sympathy but out of a realization that terrorism threatens the interstate system itself. President Bush declared a "war on terrorism" that was expected to last years and span continents, employing both conventional and unconventional means. In late 2001, U.S., Canadian, and British forces and their Afghan allies ousted the Taliban regime in Afghanistan, which the United States claimed had harboured and supported the al Qaeda network (led by Osama bin Laden) responsible for attacks on the United States.

Then in 2003 the United States and the United Kingdom invaded Iraq based on the belief that President Saddam Hussein had been amassing weapons of mass destruction, which he intended to use against the U.S., Israel, or other allies. The attack on Iraq went ahead without United Nations approval, and without the support of many of America and Britain's allies, including Canada, France, and Germany. No weapons of mass destruction were ever uncovered, and though the original offensive to oust Saddam Hussein went relatively smoothly for the United States, the continued occupation of Iraq over the course of the next year resulted in numerous casualties, for both Coalition forces and Iraqi citizens. The revelation in 2004 that U.S. personnel had abused Iraqi prisoners at Abu Ghraib prison outside of Baghdad, inflamed anti-U.S. sentiments even further, especially throughout the Muslim world.

The post–Cold War era may seem a conflict-prone period in which savage wars flare up with unexpected intensity around the world, in places such as Bosnia and Rwanda—even New York City. It is true that the era is complex and unpredictable, leaving some policy-makers and

CHANGE IN THE AIR
Peaceful trends mark the post–Cold War era, but war and terrorism continue. Here, women begin to remove the burqa covering after the liberation of Kabul, Afghanistan, December 2001.

IR theorists susceptible to Cold War nostalgia—longing for a time when world politics followed simpler rules based on a bipolar world order. Despite these new complexities, however, *the post–Cold War era has been more peaceful than the Cold War*. World military spending decreased by about one-third from its peak in the 1980s, although it has risen again since 2001. Old wars have ended faster than new ones have begun. Latin America and Russia/Eastern Europe have nearly extinguished significant interstate war in their regions, joining a zone of peace already encompassing North America, Western Europe, Japan/Pacific, and China.

Warfare is diminishing worldwide but remains "hot" in an arc of conflict from Africa through the Middle East to South Asia. Long, bloody wars in South Africa, Mozambique, Angola, Sudan, and Ethiopia-Eritrea are over or ending. The Israeli-Palestinian conflict saw rising expectations of peace in the 1990s, although the conflict worsened again in 2000 after a proposed deal fell through. Although war drags on in Democratic Republic of the Congo, Cambodia's has nearly died out. Peace agreements ended long-standing wars in several countries. The Serbian ultranationalism that undermined world order in the 1990s was put down by international action and then decisively repudiated by Serbs themselves.

At the same time, however, the United States and the United Kingdom remained embroiled in Iraq, and terrorist actions against the United Nations in Iraq, and any state seen to support the U.S.—even if they had not contributed troops to the Iraqi invasion, such as Turkey—were on the rise. In some cases, such as in Spain, governments that had supported the United States were democratically removed after terrorist attacks against Spanish citizens. The government of North Korea, meanwhile, restarted its nuclear weapons program and apparently produced a half-dozen nuclear bombs in 2003.

In international economic relations, the post–Cold War era is one of globalization. Countries worldwide are integrating into a world market, for better or worse. New hubs of economic growth are emerging, notably in parts of Asia that racked up remarkable economic growth in the 1990s (notwithstanding a sharp setback in 1997). At the same time, disparities between the rich and poor are growing, both globally and within individual countries (including Canada). Globalization has created backlashes among people who are adversely affected or who believe their identities are threatened by foreign influences. The resurgence of nationalism and ethnic-religious conflict—occasionally in extremely brutal form—results partly from that backlash. So does the growing protest movement against capitalist-led globalization, such as at the failed 1999 Seattle meeting of the World Trade Organization and great-power summit meetings in Québec (2000) and Genoa, Italy (2001).

China is becoming more central to world politics as the twenty-first century begins. Its size and rapid growth make China a rising power—a situation that some scholars liken to Germany's rise a century earlier. Historically, such shifts in power relations have caused instability in the international system. China is the only great power that is not a democracy. Its poor record on human rights—symbolized dramatically by the killing of hundreds of peaceful demonstrators in Tiananmen Square (Beijing) in 1989—makes it a frequent target of Western criticism from both governments and NGOs. With the transfer of Hong Kong from Britain in 1997, China acquired a valuable asset and turned to hopes of someday reintegrating Taiwan as well, under the Hong Kong formula of "one country, two systems."

The issues of Taiwan and human rights are central to China's relations with the international community, but other issues matter as well: China holds (but seldom uses) veto power in the UN Security Council, and it has a credible nuclear arsenal. China adjoins several regional conflict areas (Korea, Southeast Asia, India, and Central Asia) and affects the global proliferation of missiles and nuclear weapons. It claims disputed territory in the resource-rich South China Sea, but has not fought a military battle in 25 years. China also claims the mountainous country of Tibet, though many people around the

The Changing World Order

A New Era?

"World order" refers to the rules that govern—albeit in a messy and ambiguous way—the most important relationships of the interstate system in general and the world's great powers in particular. Aspects include balance of power, spheres of influence, shared beliefs, key treaties and institutions, principles like sovereignty, practices like free trade, and so forth. Historically, transformations of the world order and the rise of new guiding principles have occurred after terrible great-power wars. However, the end of the Cold War (1945–1990) brought a more peaceful transition in world order.

In the 1990s, world order lacked a strong direction or guiding principle—notwithstanding the attempt by President Bush (senior) to codify a "new world order." State and nonstate actors adapted incrementally to changing relationships and technologies. The world seemed to pick its way through the world-order challenges of the 1990s, from the Gulf to former Yugoslavia, a falling Russia and a rising China, learning by trial and error what worked. The idea of "human security" emerged, a notion promoted in particular by Canada. Overall, the reduced warfare and more stable great-power relations of the 1990s—along with the stable cheap oil prices that resulted partly from the Gulf War—underwrote a period of unprecedented prosperity in North America, Europe, and China.

At the same time, however, in the late 1990s southeast Asia experienced one of the worst financial crises since the Depression, and this had an impact on economies around the world. Although Yugoslavia had descended into hellish war, Russia and the rest of Eastern Europe hung on through a long depression without imploding. Western military interventions, following a painful learning curve, suppressed ultranationalism in Yugoslavia before it spread as a model. Indeed, democracy was the growing model in the 1990s. Unprecedented world trade and technical integration fuelled prosperity in Canada and other Western economies.

In 2001 the United States suffered the worst foreign attack on U.S. territory in history. The destruction of the World Trade Center—prominent symbol of American wealth and power, and defining feature of New York's skyline—caused direct and indirect damage estimated on the order of magnitude of $100 billion. The attack came as a U.S. recession was already underway after the collapse of a speculative bubble in internet stocks.

World Trade Center, New York, September 2001.

The terrorist attacks altered international relationships. Tensions between the great powers eased for a time, and unprecedented cooperation began. Borders became tighter—a security asset but an economic liability and an infringement on civil liberties, with racial profiling used to target people of Muslim heritage. The U.S. military became more active in more countries, and began operating from Central Asian military bases. In Afghanistan, the might of a technologically advanced superpower turned the tide of a low-tech war, sweeping out terrorists and their collaborators. As the war began to wane in Afghanistan, a new apparent threat emerged in Iraq. On the assumption that Saddam Hussein was amassing weapons of mass destruction, the U.S. formed a new coalition (this time with less widespread and less enthusiastic support from its allies) and invaded Iraq in 2003. By mid-2004, cheap oil had all but disappeared, and economists debated whether this signalled a looming recession or merely a period of short-term adjustment.

Do these changes mean a new world order? Were the 1990s just an unstable interim that ended as abruptly as it began? Or were the 2001 attacks a temporary aberration in the world order as it had evolved over the prior decade? Is a new order taking shape only slowly as various episodes take us along a long learning curve—September 11 being only one in a series of good and bad experiences? As the new world order does take form, what are its salient features? Its winners and losers? The prospects for war and peace? "The Changing World Order" boxes throughout the book will take up these questions.

world dispute that claim. In 2004, Canadian Prime Minister Paul Martin rankled Chinese authorities by agreeing to meet with the Dalai Lama, the spiritual leader of Tibet.

China is the only great power from the global South. Its population size and rapid industrialization from a low level make China a big factor in the future of global environmental trends such as global warming. All these elements make China an important actor in the coming decades of international relations. Western policy-makers argue about whether a harsh policy of containment or a mild policy of engagement will best get China to cooperate on a range of issues such as trade, human rights, weapons sales, and intellectual property rights.

It remains to be seen whether, in the coming years, the international system can provide China with appropriate status and respect to reflect its rising power and historical importance, and whether China in turn can come to conform with international rules and norms. The decision to hold the 2008 Olympic games in Beijing, which was greeted with tremendous popular enthusiasm when announced in 2001, may affect these long-term processes. So will the Chinese leadership's decisions about whether to encourage or discourage the rising tide of nationalism among China's young people as communist ideology loses its hold.

The post–Cold War era has barely begun. The transition into this era has been a turbulent time, full of international changes and new possibilities (both good and bad).[41] It is likely, however, that basic rules and principles of IR—those that scholars have long struggled to understand—will continue to apply even though their contexts and outcomes may change. Most central to sorting through these changing contexts and outcomes is to understand first the different theoretical approaches to the study of International Relations, to which we now turn.

Thinking Critically

1. Pick a current area in which interesting international events are taking place. Can you think of possible explanations for those events from each of the four levels of analysis? (See Table 1.1, p. 13.) Do explanations from different levels provide insights into different aspects of the events?

2. For a given nation-state that was once a *colony,* can you think of ways in which the state's current foreign policies might be influenced by its history of having been a colony?

3. For a state that was once a *colonizer,* can you think of ways in which its experience as colonizer might influence its current foreign policies?

4. Given the contradictory lessons of World Wars I and II, can you think of situations in today's world where appeasement (a conciliatory policy) would be the best course? Situations where hard-line containment policies would be best? Why?

5. What do you expect will be the character of the twenty-first century? Peaceful? War-prone? Orderly? Chaotic? Why do you have the expectations you do, and what clues from the unfolding of events in the world might tell you whether your guesses were correct?

---

[41] Max Singer and Aaron B. Wildavsky, *The Real World Order: Zones of Peace, Zones of Turmoil* (Chatham, NJ: Chatham House, 1996). Stanley Hoffmann, *World Disorders: Troubled Peace in the Post–Cold War Era* (Lanham, MD: Rowman & Littlefield, 1998).

Chapter Summary

- IR affects daily life profoundly; we all participate in IR.

- IR is a field of political science, concerned mainly with explaining and understanding political outcomes in international security affairs and international political economy.

- Theories complement descriptive narratives in explaining international events and outcomes, but scholars do not agree on a single set of theories or methods to use in studying IR.

- States are important actors in IR; the international system is based on the sovereignty of (about 200) independent territorial states.

- States vary greatly in size of population and economy, from tiny microstates to great powers.

- Nonstate actors such as multinational corporations (MNCs), nongovernmental organizations (NGOs), global social movements, and intergovernmental organizations (IGOs) exert a growing influence on international relations.

- The worldwide revolution in information technologies will profoundly reshape the capabilities and preferences of actors in IR, in ways that we do not yet understand.

- Four levels of analysis—individual, domestic, interstate, and global—suggest multiple explanations (operating simultaneously) for outcomes observed in IR.

- The global level of analysis draws attention especially to technological change and the global gap in wealth between the industrialized North and the South.

- A variety of world civilizations were conquered by Europeans over several centuries and forcefully absorbed into a single global international system initially centred in Europe.

- The great-power system, an idea particularly important for realists, is made up of about half a dozen states (with membership changing over time as state power rises and falls).

- Great powers have restructured world order through recurrent wars, alliances, and the reign of hegemons (states that temporarily gain a preponderance of power in the international system). The most important wars have been the Thirty Years' War, the Napoleonic Wars, World War I, and World War II. Periods of hegemony include Britain in the nineteenth century and the United States after World War II.

- European states colonized most of the rest of the world during the past five centuries. Latin American countries gained independence shortly after the United States did (about 200 years ago), while those in Africa, Asia, and the Middle East became independent states only in the decades after World War II.

- Nationalism strongly influences IR; conflict often results from the perception of nationhood leading to demands for statehood or for the adjustment of state borders.

- Democracy is a force of growing importance: more states are becoming democratically governed, and democracies rarely fight each other in wars.

- The world economy has generated wealth at an accelerating pace in the past two centuries and is increasingly integrated on a global scale, although with huge inequalities.

- World Wars I and II dominated the twentieth century, yet they seem to offer contradictory lessons about the utility of hard-line or conciliatory foreign policies.

- For most of the 50 years since World War II, world politics revolved around the East-West rivalry of the Cold War. This bipolar standoff created stability and avoided great-power wars, including nuclear war, but it had harmful consequences for states of the global South that became proxy battlegrounds.

- The post–Cold War era that began in the 1990s held hope of general great-power cooperation despite the appearance of new ethnic and regional conflicts.

- A "war on terrorism"—with broad international support but uncertain scope and duration—began in 2001 after terrorist attacks on the United States.

- The United States and Britain, without the support of the UN and key allies such as Canada, France, and Germany, invaded Iraq in 2003 to oust Iraqi leader Saddam Hussein

Key Terms

international relations (IR)   1
international security   3
international political economy
    (IPE)   3
state   7
United Nations (UN)   7
international system   8
nation-states   8
gross domestic product (GDP)   9
nonstate actors   10
nongovernmental organizations
    (NGOs)   10
global social movements   11
intergovernmental organizations
    (IGOs)   11

North-South gap   14
nationalism   30
industrialization   32
free trade   32
League of Nations   36
Munich Agreement   36
genocide   37
Cold War   38
containment   38
Sino-Soviet split   38
summit meeting   40
Cuban Missile Crisis   40
proxy wars   40
Commonwealth of Independent States
    (CIS)   43

Weblinks

One way to get a sense of both events going on in the world and different perspectives on those events is to visit media and news outlets from around the world. Here are a few you should bookmark and visit now and again as you go through the text. You can find media outlets for numerous other countries through an internet search. Do these media sources cover the same news items, and in the same way, as your own local media?

Africa News Service:
http://allafrica.com

Aljazeera English Language Site:
http://english.aljazeera.net/HomePage

Bangkok Post:
http://www.bangkokpost.net

BBC World News Service:
http://news.bbc.co.uk

Japan Times:
http://www.japantimes.co.jp

The Jerusalem Post:
http://www.jpost.com

The Mail and Guardian (South Africa):
http://www.mg.co.za

The New York Times:
http://www.nytimes.com

The People's Daily (China):
http://fpeng.peopledaily.com.cn

Phnom Penh Post:
http://www.PhnomPenhPost.com

Pravda (Russia):
http://english.pravda.ru

Times of India:
http://timesofindia.indiatimes.com

Realist Approaches

2

THEORETICAL APPROACHES IN INTERNATIONAL RELATIONS

REALISM

POWER
Defining Power
Estimating Power
Elements of Power

BARGAINING
Bargaining and Leverage
Strategies
Reciprocity, Deterrence, and Arms Races
Rationality
Game Theory

THE INTERNATIONAL SYSTEM
Anarchy and Sovereignty
Balance of Power
Great Powers and Middle Powers
Power Distribution
Hegemony

THE ECONOMIC VARIANT OF REALISM

U.S. tanks on Iraq's border, February 2003.

THEORETICAL APPROACHES IN INTERNATIONAL RELATIONS

Engaging with theoretical approaches in international relations is both indispensable and difficult. It is indispensable because everyone in IR operates from a theoretical perspective (or some combination of perspectives). Every academic book or article, media report, policy-maker, or student, is commenting or writing from the position of a theoretical perspective. No one is just presenting "the facts"; rather, they are interpreting what those facts mean through the lens of a theoretical approach. Part of the job of studying IR is to become familiar with the different theoretical perspectives that observers of IR use, and to be aware of the different implications of adopting one perspective over another. Students also need to think through, in an analytical way, the reasons they do, or do not, find arguments made in IR persuasive. Having a sense of the theoretical perspective in which an argument is based is one part of that analytical investigation.

But becoming familiar with and identifying the different paradigms is also difficult. Not everyone makes their theoretical perspective(s) explicit, and some people may even be unaware that their point of view has a basis in a theoretical approach. Some observers of international relations use different theoretical approaches to explain or understand different events; others may try to combine elements of the different approaches into a single new theory (this is difficult to accomplish without becoming contradictory). Many theoretical approaches are also quite fluid: they are adapted and modified by the people who use them, often in an effort to respond to criticisms, some of which come from competing paradigms.

There are many more theories of IR than can be covered here. What is offered in these chapters is an introduction to some of the main approaches to the study of IR. This text organizes those approaches into three main paradigms: realist, liberal-pluralist, and critical theories (see Chapters 2 and 3). These paradigms, or categories, group together theories that share some broad agreement about what the world looks like, how we should study the world, and what the purpose of theory should be.

But even categorizing *where* one specific theory should go is sometimes debated (some actual theorists of IR, for example, may consider themselves critical theorists and find that they are described here as falling within the liberal approaches, or vice versa). The approach that students should take toward the study of theory in IR is that they need to become familiar with the different perspectives and begin to think through which perspective, if any, they find most convincing. They also need to know that this is at best an inexact science, and debate exists in IR as much about the theories themselves as the issues the theories seek to address.

REALISM

realism (political realism)
A broad intellectual tradition that explains international relations mainly in terms of power.

Realism (or *political realism*) is a school of thought that explains international relations in terms of power (see "Defining Power," pp. 56–57). The exercise of power by states toward each other is sometimes called *realpolitik*, or just *power politics*. Realism has a long history, and it dominated the study of IR from the end of World War II until the early 1970s when alternative approaches began to emerge. Even as other theoretical approaches were developed, realism has remained very important to the study of international relations. Some schools of international relations or political science continue to teach IR as though it is still the only theoretical approach. This is particularly true in the United States, where realist thought first developed and had an important impact on both scholarship and policy-making.

idealism An approach that emphasizes international law, morality, and international organization, rather than power alone, as key influences on international relations.

Realism as we know it developed in reaction to a tradition that realists called **idealism** (of course, idealists themselves do not consider their approach unrealistic). Idealism emphasizes international law, morality, and international organization, rather than power alone, as key influences on international events. Idealists think that human nature is basically good. With good habits, education, and appropriate international structures, human nature can become the basis of peaceful and cooperative international relationships. Idealists see the international system as one based on a community of states with the potential to work together to overcome mutual problems (see Chapter 3).

For idealists, the principles of IR must flow from morality. More than 2000 years ago the Chinese writer Mo Ti pointed out that everyone "knows that [murder] is unrighteous," yet "when murder is committed in attacking a country it is not considered wrong; it is applauded and called righteous." For Mo Ti, this made no sense. "If a man calls black black if it is seen on a small scale, but calls black white when it is seen on a large scale, then he is one who cannot tell black from white."[1] Idealists were particularly active in the period between World Wars I and II, following the painful experience of World War I. U.S. President Woodrow Wilson and other idealists placed their hopes for peace in the League of Nations as a formal structure for the community of nations.

Those hopes were dashed when that structure proved helpless to stop German and Japanese aggression in the 1930s. Since World War II, realists have blamed idealists for looking too much at how the world *ought* to be instead of how it *really* is. Sobered by the

---

[1] Sun Tzu, *The Art of War*, trans. Samuel B. Griffith (NY: Oxford UP, 1963) 22.

experiences of World War II, realists set out to understand the principles of power politics without succumbing to wishful thinking. Realism provided a theoretical foundation for the Cold War policies of containment and the determination of U.S. policy-makers not to appease the Soviet Union and China.

Realists ground themselves in a long tradition. The Chinese strategist *Sun Tzu*, who lived two thousand years ago, at the time of Mo Ti, advised the rulers of states how to survive in an era when war had become a systematic instrument of power for the first time (the "warring states" period). Sun Tzu argued that moral reasoning was not very useful to the state rulers of the day, faced with armed and dangerous neighbours. Sun Tzu showed rulers how to use power to advance their interests and protect their survival.

At roughly the same time, in Greece, *Thucydides* wrote an account of the Peloponnesian War (431–404 B.C.) focusing on relative power among the Greek city-states. He stated that "the strong do what they have the power to do and the weak accept what they have to accept."[2] Much later, in Renaissance Italy (around 1500), *Niccolò Machiavelli* urged princes to concentrate on expedient actions to stay in power and to pay attention to war above all else. Today the adjective *Machiavellian* refers to excessively manipulative power manoeuvres.[3]

English philosopher *Thomas Hobbes* in the seventeenth century discussed the free-for-all that exists when government is absent and people seek their own self-interest. He called it the "state of nature" or "state of war" (in contrast to what we would now call the rule of law). Hobbes favoured a strong monarchy to prevent the condition, but in international affairs, according to realists, there is no such central authority (see pp. 71–74).

In the nineteenth century, the German military strategist *Karl von Clausewitz* said that "war is a continuation of politics by other means." U.S. admiral *Alfred Mahan* promoted naval power as the key means of achieving national political and economic interests. Realists see in these historical figures evidence that the importance of power politics is timeless and cross-cultural.

After World War II, scholar *Hans Morgenthau* argued that international politics is governed by objective, universal laws based on national interest defined as power (not on psychological motives of decision-makers). He reasoned that no nation had "God on its side" (a universal morality) and that all nations had to base their actions on prudence and practicality.

Realists tend to treat political power as separate from, and predominant over, morality, ideology, and other social and economic aspects of life. For realists, ideologies do not matter much, nor do religions or other cultural factors with which states may explain their actions. Realists see states with very different religions or ideologies or economic systems as quite similar in their actions with regard to national power.[4]

Today realists share several assumptions about how IR works. They assume that IR can be best (though not exclusively) explained by the choices of states operating as autonomous actors rationally pursuing their own interests in a system of sovereign states. Sometimes the realist framework is summarized in three propositions: (1) *states* are the

---

[2] Thucydides, *History of the Peloponnesian War*, trans. R. Warner (NY: Penguin, 1972) 402.

[3] Niccolò Machiavelli, *The Prince, and the Discourses*, trans. Luigi Ricci, revised by E. R. P. Vincent (NY: Modern Library, 1950). Friedrich Meinecke, *Machiavellism: The Doctrine of Raison d'État and Its Place in Modern History*, trans. D. Scott (New Haven, CT: Yale UP, 1957).

[4] Hans J. Morgenthau and Kenneth W. Thompson, *Politics among Nations: The Struggle for Power and Peace*, 6th ed. (NY: Knopf, 1985). Edward Hallett Carr, *The Twenty Years' Crisis, 1919–1939: An Introduction to the Study of International Relations* (1939; London: Macmillan, 1974). Raymond Aron, *Peace and War: A Theory of International Relations*, trans. R. Howard and A. B. Fox (NY: Doubleday, 1966).

most important actors (the state-centric assumption); (2) they act as *rational* individuals in pursuing power; pursuing power is in the national interest (the unitary rational-actor assumption); and (3) they act in the context of an international system lacking central government (the *anarchy* assumption).

POWER

Power is a central concept in international relations—the central one for realists—but one that is surprisingly difficult to define or measure.

Defining Power

power The ability or potential to influence others' behaviour, as measured by the possession of certain tangible and intangible characteristics.

Power is often defined as the ability to get another actor to do what it would not otherwise have done (or not to do what it would have done).[5] A variation on this idea is that actors are powerful to the extent that they affect others more than others affect them.[6] These definitions treat power as influence. If actors get their way a lot, they must be powerful.

One problem with this definition is that we seldom know what a second actor would have done in the absence of the first actor's power. There is a danger of circular logic: power explains influence, and influence measures power. Thus it is hard to use power to explain why international events occur (the aim of realism). A related problem is that common usage treats power as a thing rather than a process: states "have" power.

These problems are resolved if we recall that power is not influence itself, but the ability or potential to influence others. IR scholars believe that such potential is based on specific (tangible and intangible) characteristics or possessions of states—such as their sizes, levels of income, armed forces, and so forth. This is *power as capability*. Capabilities are easier to measure than influence and less circular in logic.

Measuring capabilities to explain how one nation influences another is not simple, however. It requires summing up various kinds of potentials. States possess varying amounts of population, territory, military forces, and so forth. Some realists consider the best single indicator of a state's power may be its total GDP, which combines overall size, technological level, and wealth. But even GDP is at best a rough indicator.

Furthermore, beyond tangible capabilities, power depends on intangible elements. Capabilities give a state the potential to influence others only to the extent that political leaders can mobilize and deploy them effectively and strategically. This depends on national will, on diplomatic skill, on popular support for the government (its legitimacy), and so forth. Some scholars emphasize the *power of ideas*—the ability to maximize the influence of capabilities through a psychological process. This process includes the domestic mobilization of capabilities—often through religion, ideology, or (especially) nationalism. International influence is also gained by being the one to form rules of behaviour, to change how others see their own national interests. If a state's own values become widely shared among other states, it will easily influence others. For example, the United States has influenced many other states to accept the value of free markets and free trade. Canada often has sought to influence other states to support diplomacy and international organizations. This has been called *soft power*.[7]

---

[5] Robert A. Dahl, *Modern Political Analysis*, 2nd ed. (Englewood Cliffs, NJ: Prentice Hall, 1970).

[6] Kenneth N. Waltz, *Theory of International Politics* (Reading, MA: Addison-Wesley, 1979).

[7] Joseph S. Nye, Jr., *Bound to Lead: The Changing Nature of American Power* (NY: Basic Books, 1990). See also Lloyd Axworthy, *Navigating a New World—Canada's Global Future* (Toronto: Knopf, 2004).

A state can have power only relative to other states. *Relative power* is the ratio of the power that two states can bring to bear against each other. It matters little to realists whether a state's capabilities are rising or declining in absolute terms, only whether they are falling behind or overtaking the capabilities of rival states.

Even realists recognize the limits to explanations based on power. At best, power provides a general understanding of typical or average outcomes. In actual IR there are many other elements at work, including an element of accident or luck. The more powerful actor does not always prevail. Power provides only a partial explanation.[8]

Estimating Power

Sun Tzu's first chapter advises rulers to accurately estimate their own power—ranging from money to territory to popular domestic support—and that of their potential enemies. "Know the enemy and know yourself," he wrote. Any estimate of an actor's overall power must combine diverse elements and will therefore be inexact. But such estimates are nonetheless very useful. Consider two examples in which states went to war: Iraq and Iran in 1980, and the United States and Vietnam in 1965. The logic of power suggests that in wars the more powerful state will generally prevail. Thus, estimates of the relative power of the two antagonists should help explain the outcome of each war. These estimates could take into account the nations' relative military capabilities and the popular support for each one's government, among other factors. It would also take into account the total size of each nation's economy—the total GDP—which reflects both population size and the level of income per person (per capita). With a healthy enough economy, a state can buy a large army, buy popular support (by providing consumer goods), and even buy allies.

When Iraq attacked its neighbour Iran in 1980, the two countries appeared roughly equal in power. Both were oil-producing countries with middle-range income levels. Both could use oil income to buy arms on world markets, and both had relatively large and advanced military forces. Iran's military had been developed under the Shah in alliance with the United States; Iraq's had been largely supplied by the Soviet Union. Iran's population of 38 million was three times as large as Iraq's but its total GDP was less than double Iraq's.

Counterbalancing Iran's modest advantage in GDP was its short-term internal disorder. The Shah had been overthrown. Much of the military could be expected to offer little support, and perhaps active opposition, to Ayatollah Khomeini and the other new leaders who had overthrown the Shah. It seemed that the new government would be unable to mobilize its potential power. By contrast, Saddam Hussein had recently taken absolute power as leader of Iraq and could count on a loyal military. He invaded Iran, hoping for a quick victory and the installation of a friendly government there.

The key element on which Saddam Hussein's plan depended was Iran's low internal cohesion, which would counteract Iran's advantage in size. But he miscalculated this element. The Iranian military pulled together under Khomeini to put up a spirited defence, and its population proved more willing than Iraq's to die for its cause. The tide soon turned against Iraq, which then looked to allies in the Arab world. These, with the tacit support

---

[8] John M. Rothgeb, Jr., *Defining Power: Influence and Force in the Contemporary International System* (NY: St. Martin's, 1992). Ralph Pettman, *International Politics: Balance of Power, Balance of Productivity, Balance of Ideologies* (Boulder, CO: Rienner, 1991). Robert W. Cox, *Production, Power, and World Order: Social Forces in the Making of History* (NY: Columbia UP, 1987). George Liska, *The Ways of Power: Patterns and Meaning in World Politics* (Cambridge, UK: Blackwell, 1990). Richard Stoll and Michael D. Ward, eds., *Power in World Politics* (Boulder, CO: Rienner, 1988). Michael P. Sullivan, *Power in Contemporary International Politics* (Columbia, SC: U South Carolina P, 1990).

of all the great powers, provided enough aid to keep Iraq from losing (which would expand Iran's power) but not enough to win (which would expand Iraq's power). Thus the two sides were roughly equal in the power they could bring to bear. The war dragged on for 10 years, killing a million people, before its end was negotiated with no winner.

The second example could hardly be more different. When the United States decided under President Lyndon Johnson to expand its decade-long involvement in Vietnam by sending troops in support of South Vietnam, any analysis of the power differences between the U.S. and North Vietnam would anticipate a certain and swift U.S. victory. The power disparity was striking. The United States, by almost any measure, held an overwhelming advantage in GDP, population, size, and technological capabilities of its military. Though the United States always treated the war in Vietnam as a "limited war" (and, for that matter, an undeclared war), it nonetheless devoted considerable resources to its engagement in Vietnam. At its height, the United States deployed over half a million troops and was involved in a massive bombing campaign that included not only North and South Vietnam but neighbouring Cambodia and Laos as well.

The U.S. did not win the war in Vietnam but withdrew in 1973 under the terms of the Paris Peace Plan, leaving the South, which fell in 1975, to defend itself against the North. Although victorious, Vietnam suffered enormous losses: by some estimates, one million Vietnamese combatants and four million civilians were killed; the use of Agent Orange, a defoliation agent used by the U.S. to make bombing Vietnamese targets easier, resulted in long-term environmental and health effects; and unexploded bombs continue to injure and kill people to this day. Losses to the United States were also substantial: some 58 000 Americans were killed, over 300 000 wounded, at an estimated cost of $150 billion to the United States.

The Vietnam war also precipitated a crisis within American society more generally. For many it was a humiliating, unthinkable defeat. Revelations also emerged of the undeclared bombing campaign in both Laos and Cambodia; U.S. students protesting the war were killed by the Ohio National Guard at Kent State University in 1970; and Americans learned in the late 1960s that the Johnson Administration had exaggerated details of a 1964 Vietnamese attack against U.S. ships in the Gulf of Tonkin—the very event that had triggered the United State's escalating involvement in Vietnam. The war thus made many American citizens question their government and some suggested the cynicism associated with "the Vietnam syndrome" affected the U.S. national psyche for decades.

As the U.S. war against Vietnam illustrates, GDP may be a good indicator of a country's power, but it provides no prediction of who will win a war, or what kind of impact a war may have on an otherwise powerful country.

Elements of Power

State power is a mix of many ingredients, such as natural resources, industrial capacity, moral legitimacy, military preparedness, and popular support of government. All these elements contribute to an actor's power, but most realists acknowledge that there is no precise equation to determine which combination of these elements produces the greatest measure of power.

Power resources are elements that an actor can draw on over the *long term*. The power measure used earlier—total GDP—is in this category. So are population, territory, geography, and natural resources. These attributes change only slowly. Less tangible long-term power resources include political culture, patriotism, education of the population, and strength of the scientific and technological base. The credibility of its commitments (reputation for keeping its word) is also a power resource that a state can nurture over time.

So is the ability of one state's culture and values to consistently shape the thinking of other states (the power of ideas). Power resources shape an actor's potential power.

The importance of long-term power resources was illustrated after the Japanese surprise attack on the U.S. fleet at Pearl Harbor in 1941, which decimated U.S. naval capabilities in the Pacific. In the short term, Japan had superior military power and was able to occupy territories in Southeast Asia while driving U.S. forces from the region. In the longer term, the United States had greater power resources due to its underlying economic potential. It built up military capabilities over the next few years that gradually matched and then overwhelmed those of Japan in the Pacific.

Power capabilities allow actors to exercise influence in the *short term*. Military forces are such a capability—perhaps the most important kind. The size, composition, and preparedness of two states' military forces matter more in a short-term military confrontation than do their respective economies or natural resources. Another capability is the military-industrial capacity to quickly produce tanks, fighter planes, and other weapons. The quality of a state's bureaucracy is another type of capability, allowing the state to gather information, regulate international trade, or participate in international conferences.

As with power resources, some power capabilities are intangible. The *support* and *legitimacy* that an actor commands in the short term from constituents and allies are capabilities that the actor can use to gain influence. The *loyalty* of a nation's army and politicians to its leader (in the

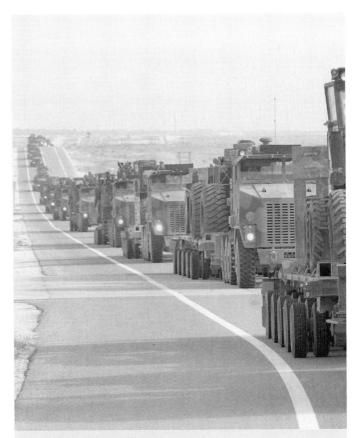

THE ECONOMICS OF POWER
Military power such as tanks rests on economic strength, roughly measured by GDP. The large U.S. economy supports U.S. military predominance. In the 2003 Iraq War, the United States could afford to send a large and technologically advanced military force to the Middle East. Here, U.S. forces enter Iraq, March 2003.

short term) is in effect a capability available to the leader. Although capabilities come into play more quickly than power resources, they are narrower in scope. In particular, military capabilities are useful only when military power can be effective in gaining influence. Likewise, economic capabilities are of little use in situations dominated by a military component.

Given the limited resources that any actor commands, there are always trade-offs among possible capabilities. Building up military forces diverts resources that might be put into foreign aid, for instance. Or buying a population's loyalty with consumer goods reduces resources available for building up military capabilities. To the extent that one element of power can be converted into another, it is *fungible*. Generally money is the most fungible capability because it can buy other capabilities.

Realists tend to see *military force* as the most important element of national power in the short term, and they see other elements such as economic strength or diplomatic skill or moral legitimacy as being important to the extent that they are fungible into military power. Such fungibility of nonmilitary elements of power into military ones is considerable, at least in the long term. Well-paid soldiers fight better, as do soldiers imbued with moral fervour for their cause, or soldiers using higher-technology weapons. Skilled diplomats can avoid unfavourable military confrontations or provoke favourable ones. Moral foreign policies can help sway public opinion in foreign countries and cement alliances that increase military strength. Realists tend to treat these dimensions of power as important mainly because of their potential military impact. Chairman Mao Zedong of China said: "All power grows out of the barrel of a gun."

The different types of power capabilities can be contrasted by considering the choice to possess tanks or gold. One standard power capability that states want is battle tanks. In land warfare to control territory, the tank is arguably the most powerful instrument available, and the leading defence against it is another tank. One can assess power on this dimension by counting the size and quality of a state's tank force (an imprecise but not impossible exercise). A different power capability of time-honoured value is the stockpile of *gold* (or its modern-day equivalent in hard currency reserves; see Chapter 9). Gold represents economic power and is a power resource, whereas tanks represent military power and are a power capability.

In the long term, the gold is better because one can always turn gold into tanks (it is fungible), but it might be hard to turn tanks into gold. However, in the short term the tanks might be better because if an enemy tank force invades one's territory, gold will not stop them; indeed they will soon take the gold for themselves. For example, in 1990 Iraq (which had gone for tanks) invaded its neighbour Kuwait (which had gone for gold). In the short term, Iraq proved much more powerful: it occupied Kuwait and plundered it.

Morality can contribute to power, by increasing the will to use power and by attracting allies. States have long clothed their actions, however aggressive, in rhetoric about their peaceful and defensive intentions. For instance, the 1989 U.S. invasion of Panama was named "Operation Just Cause." Military capabilities are most effective in the context of justifications that make state actions seem moral. Of course, if a state overuses moralistic rhetoric to cloak self-interest too often, it loses credibility even with its own population.

geopolitics The use of geography as an element of power, and the ideas about it held by political leaders and scholars.

The use of geography as an element of power is called **geopolitics**. It is often tied to the logistical requirements of military forces (see Chapter 6). Frequently, state leaders use maps in thinking about international power positions and alignments. In geopolitics, as in real estate, the three most important considerations are location, location, location. States increase their power to the extent they can use geography to enhance their military capabilities, such as by securing allies and bases close to a rival power or along strategic trade routes, or by controlling key natural resources. In general, power declines as a function of distance from a home state, although technology seems to be making this decline less steep.

A recurrent geopolitical theme for centrally located, largely land-locked states such as Germany and Russia is the threat of being surrounded. In the 1840s, British politician Lord Palmerston warned that "Russia has a basic drive for warm water ports" (free of ice year-round). The 1979 Soviet invasion of Afghanistan was seen by some Western leaders as a step toward Soviet expansion southward to the Indian Ocean, driven by such a motive. Militarily, centrally located states often face a *two-front problem*. Germany had to fight France to the west and Russia to the east simultaneously in World War I—a problem reduced early in World War II by Hitler's pact with Stalin (until Hitler's disastrous decision to invade the Soviet Union).

---

[9] Ludwig Dehio, *The Precarious Balance: Four Centuries of the European Power Struggle*, trans. Charles Fullman (Germany: 1948; NY: Vintage Books, 1962). George Modelski and William R. Thompson, *Seapower in Global Politics, 1494–1993* (Seattle: U Washington P, 1988). Joshua S. Goldstein and David P. Rapkin, "After Insularity: Hegemony and the Future World Order," *Futures* 23.9 (1991): 935–59.

For states less centrally located, such as Britain or the United States, different geopolitical problems appear. These states have been called "insular" in that bodies of water protect them against land attacks.[9] Their geopolitical problem in the event of war is to move soldiers and supplies over long distances to reach the scene of battle.

BARGAINING

The exercise of power involves two or more parties, each trying to influence the other more than it is itself influenced. The mutual attempts to influence others constitute a bargaining process. Bargaining is important in various theoretical perspectives (not just realism), though different theories emphasize different motivations, tactics, and outcomes.

Bargaining and Leverage

Bargaining may be defined as tacit or direct communication in an attempt to reach agreement on an exchange of value—that is, of tangible or intangible items that one or both parties value. Bargaining need not be explicit. Sometimes the content is communicated through actions rather than an exchange of words.[10]

A bargaining process has two or more *participants* and sometimes has *mediators* whose participation is nominally neutral. Participants have a direct stake in the outcome; mediators do not. There are one or more *issues* on which each participant hopes to reach agreement on terms favourable to itself, but the participants' *interests* diverge on these issues, creating conflicts. These conflicts define a *bargaining space*—one or more dimensions, each of which represents a distance between the positions of two participants concerning their preferred outcomes. The bargaining process disposes of these conflicts by achieving agreement on the distribution of the various items of value that are at stake. The end result is a position arrived at in the bargaining space.

Such agreements do not necessarily represent a *fair* exchange of value; many agreements are manifestly one-sided and unfair. But in a broad sense, bargains whether fair or unfair contain an element of *mutual gain*. This is possible because the items of value being exchanged have different value to the different parties. To take a clearly unfair example, an armed robber values a victim's wallet more than the victim does, and the victim values his or her own life more than the robber does. The robber "gives" the victim life and the victim "gives" the robber money—so both gain. As this example illustrates, the mutual gains in bargaining are relative to other possible outcomes, not necessarily to the status quo before the bargain.

Participants bring different means of *leverage* to the bargaining process.[11] Leverage derives from power capabilities that allow one actor to influence the other to reach agreements more favourable to the first actor's interests. Leverage may operate on any of three dimensions of power: the *promise* of positive sanctions (rewards) if the other actor gives one what one wants; the *threat* of negative sanctions (damage to valued items) if not; or

bargaining Tacit or direct communication that is used in an attempt to reach agreement on an exchange of value.

---

[10] Glenn H. Synder and Paul Diesing, *Conflict among Nations: Bargaining, Decision Making, and System Structure in International Crises* (Princeton, NJ: Princeton UP, 1977). T. Clifton Morgan, *Untying the Knot of War: A Bargaining Theory of International Crises* (Ann Arbor: U Michigan P, 1994). Shibley Telhami, *Power and Leadership in International Bargaining: The Path to the Camp David Accords* (NY: Columbia UP, 1990). William Mark Habeeb, *Power and Tactics in International Negotiation: How Weak Nations Bargain with Strong Nations* (Baltimore: Johns Hopkins UP, 1988). I. William Zartman, ed., *Elusive Peace: Negotiating an End to Civil Wars* (Washington, DC: Brookings, 1995).

[11] Robert C. North, *War, Peace, Survival: Global Politics and Conceptual Synthesis* (see footnote 10 in Chapter 1).

an *appeal* to the other's feeling of love, friendship, sympathy, or respect for oneself.[12] For instance, Cuba during the Cold War could obtain Soviet oil by purchasing the oil with hard currency, by threatening to cut its alliance with the Soviet Union unless given the oil at subsidized prices, or by appealing to the Soviet leaders' sense of socialist solidarity.

Bringing a bargaining leverage into play generally opens up a new dimension in the bargaining space, allowing outcomes along this new dimension to be traded off against those on the original dimension (the main issue at stake). Leverage thus helps to get deals done—albeit not always fair ones. One-sided agreements typically result when one side has a preponderance of leverage relative to the other.

The use of violence can be a means of settling conflicts. The application of violent negative leverage can force an agreement that ends a conflict. (Again, the agreement may not be fair.) Because such violence may also create new sources of conflict, agreements reached through violence may not last. Nonetheless, from a realist perspective violence is just another leverage—an extension of politics by other means. Politics itself has been described as the process of deciding "who gets what, when, how."[13]

The same principles of bargaining apply to both international security affairs and international political economy. In both cases power and leverage matter. Also in both cases structures and institutions have been designed to aid the bargaining process. Economic markets serve this purpose, from the New York or Toronto Stock Exchanges to the local supermarket. In international security such institutions as diplomatic missions and international organizations facilitate the bargaining process. Realists studying international security focus on political-military bargaining more than economic bargaining because they consider it more important. The economic framework will be elaborated in Chapter 8.

negotiation The process of formal bargaining, usually with the parties talking back and forth across a table.

Bargaining that takes place formally—usually at a table with back-and-forth dialogue—is called **negotiation**. Because the issues in IR are important and the actors are usually sophisticated players in a game with long-established rules and traditions, most issues of contention reach a negotiating table sooner or later. Often bargaining takes place simultaneously at the negotiating table and in the world (often on the battlefield). The participants talk in the negotiation hall while manipulating instruments of leverage outside it.

Negotiating styles vary from one culture or individual to another. In international negotiations on major political and military issues, problems of cultural difference may become serious obstacles. For example, straight-talking Canadians or Americans might misunderstand negotiators from Japan, where saying "no" is rude and is therefore replaced by phrases such as "that would be difficult." A good negotiator will take time to understand the other party's culture and bargaining style, as well as its interests and available means of leverage.

Strategies

Power strategies are plans actors use to develop and deploy power capabilities to achieve goals. A key aspect of strategy is choosing the kinds of capabilities to develop, given limited resources, in order to maximize international influence. This requires foresight because the capabilities required to manage a situation may need to be developed years before that situation presents itself. Yet the capabilities chosen often will not be fungible in the short term. Central to this dilemma is what kind of standing military forces to maintain in peacetime—enough to prevent a quick defeat if war breaks out, but not so

---

[12] Kenneth E. Boulding, *Three Faces of Power* (Newbury Park, CA: Sage, 1990).

[13] Harold D. Lasswell, *Politics: Who Gets What, When, How* (NY: Meridian, 1958).

much as to overburden one's economy (see pp. 199–205). Strategies also include choices about how capabilities are used in situations—sequences of actions designed for maximum effect; the creation of alliances; the use of contingency plans; and so forth. Depending on the situation, most power strategies mix economic instruments (trade, aid, loans, investment, boycotts) with military ones. (In the short term, within a given situation such plans are called *tactics*.)

Strategies include whether (and in which situations) a state is willing to use its power capabilities. For example, in the Vietnam War the United States had overall power capabilities far superior to those of the Vietnamese communists but lost the war because it was unwilling or unable to commit the resources necessary or use them effectively. The *will* of a nation or leader is hard to estimate. Even if leaders make explicit their intention to fight over an issue, they might be bluffing.

The strategic actions of China in recent years exemplify the concept of strategy as rational deployment of power capabilities. China's central foreign policy goal is to prevent the independence of Taiwan, which China considers an integral part of its territory (as does the United Nations and, to large extent, Canada). Taiwan's government was set up to represent all of China in 1949, when the nationalists took refuge there after losing to the communists in China's civil war. Since 1949, Taiwan has operated more and more independently, and many Taiwanese favour independence. China does not have the military power to invade Taiwan successfully, but it has declared repeatedly that it will go to war if Taiwan declares independence. So far, even though such a war might be irrational on China's part, the threat has deterred Taiwan from formally declaring independence. China might lose such a war, but would certainly inflict immense damage on Taiwan. In 1996, China held war games near Taiwan, firing missiles over the sea. The United States sent two aircraft carriers to signal to China that its exercises must not go too far.

Not risking war by declaring independence, Taiwan instead has engaged in diplomacy to gain influence in the world. It lobbies governments, asks for admission to the UN and other world organizations, and grants foreign aid to countries that recognize Taiwan's government (26 mostly small states as of 2004). In 1999, Taiwan's president declared that relations with China should be on a "state-to-state" basis, edging closer to declaring independence, and in 2004 he successfully ran for re-election on a platform promising a referendum on independence.

China has used its own diplomacy to counter these moves. It breaks diplomatic relations with countries that recognize Taiwan, and it punishes any moves in the direction of Taiwanese independence. China has tried to counter Taiwanese ties with countries that recognize Taiwan by manipulating various positive and negative leverages. For example, in Panama, where China is a major user of the Panama Canal (which reverted to Panama from U.S. ownership in 1999), Taiwan has cultivated close relations, invested in a container port, and suggested hiring guest workers from Panama in Taiwan. But China has implicitly threatened to restrict Panama's access to Hong Kong,

BARGAINING PROCESS Bargaining includes both indirect moves and explicit negotiations.

AMPLIFYING POWER
Coherent strategy can help a state to make the most of its power.
China's foreign policy is generally directed toward its most important
regional interests, above all preventing Taiwan's formal independence.
Despite conflicts with a number of its neighbours, China has had no mil-
itary engagements for two decades. Here, China uses its veto in the UN
Security Council for only the fifth time ever, to end a peacekeeping mis-
sion in Macedonia, which had just established ties with Taiwan (1999).

or to reregister China's many Panamanian-registered ships in the Bahamas instead. (Bahamas broke with Taiwan in 1997 after a Hong Kong conglomerate, now part of China, promised to invest in a Bahamian container port.)

Two of the five vetoes China has ever used in the UN Security Council were to block peacekeeping forces in countries that extended recognition to Taiwan. These vetoes demonstrate that if China believes its Taiwan interests are threatened, it can play a spoiler role on the Security Council. When the former Yugoslav republic of Macedonia recognized Taiwan in 1999 (in exchange for $1 billion in aid), China vetoed a UN peacekeeping mission there at a time of great instability in next-door Kosovo. By contrast, when its Taiwan interests are secure, China cooperates on issues of world order. For example, although China opposed the 1991 Gulf War, it did not veto the UN resolution authorizing it.

These Chinese strategies mobilize various capabilities, from missiles to diplomats to industrial conglomerates, in a coherent effort to influence the outcome of China's most important international issue. Strategy thus amplifies China's power. Similarly, during the Cold War China used strategy to amplify power, by playing a balancer role between two superpowers and by playing up the importance of the global South, which it claimed to lead.[14]

Some individual actors too are better than others at using their capabilities strategically. For instance, U.S. President Jimmy Carter in the 1970s used the great-power capabilities available to him, but his own strategic and interpersonal skills seem to have been the key to success in the Camp David agreements (which achieved the U.S. foreign policy goal of an Egyptian-Israeli treaty). Good strategies bring together power capabilities for maximum effect, but poor strategies make inefficient use of available capabilities. Of course, even the most skillful leader never has total control of an international situation, but can make best use of the opportunities available while minimizing the effects of bad luck.

[14] *Current History* 96.611 (Sept. 1997), spec. issue on China. Larry Rohter, "Taiwan and Beijing Duel for Recognition in Central America," *New York Times* 5 Aug. 1997: A7. Quansheng Zhao, *Interpreting Chinese Foreign Policy: The Micro-Macro Linkage Approach* (NY: Oxford UP, 1996). Chih-yu Shih, *China's Just World: The Morality of Chinese Foreign Policy* (Boulder, CO: Rienner, 1992). Paul M. Evans and B. Michael Frolic, eds., *Reluctant Adversaries: Canada and the People's Republic of China, 1949–1970* (Toronto: U Toronto P, 1991).

In the context of bargaining, actors use various strategies to employ leverage in an effort to move the final agreement point closer to their own positions. One common bargaining strategy is to start with extreme demands and then gradually compromise them in an effort to end up close to one's true (but concealed) position. Another strategy is to "drive a hard bargain" by sticking closely to one's original position in the belief that the other participant will eventually accept it.

Another common bargaining strategy is *fractionation*—splitting up a complex issue into a number of small components so that progress may be sought on solvable pieces. For instance, the Arab-Israeli negotiations that began in 1991 had many sets of talks concurrently working on various pieces of the problem. The opposite approach, which some bargainers prefer, is to lump together diverse issues—called *linkage*—so that compromises on one can be traded off against another in a grand deal. This was the case, for instance, in the Yalta negotiations of 1945 among Britain, the United States, and the Soviet Union. On the table simultaneously were such matters as the terms of occupation of Germany, the Soviet presence in Eastern Europe, the strategy for defeating Japan, and the creation of the United Nations.

Reciprocity, Deterrence, and Arms Races

To have the best effect, strategic bargaining over IR outcomes should take into account the other actor's own goals and strategies. Only then can one predict which forms of leverage may induce the other actor to take the actions one desires. But this can be a problem: often states do not know each others' true intentions but can only observe each others' actions and statements (which may be lies).

One very effective strategy for influencing another actor whose plans are not known is **reciprocity**—a response in kind to the other's actions.[15] A strategy of reciprocity uses positive forms of leverage as promises of rewards (if the actor does what one wants); simultaneously it uses negative forms of leverage as threats of punishment (if the actor does not refrain from doing what one does not want). Reciprocity is effective because it is easy to understand. After one has demonstrated one's ability and willingness to reciprocate—gaining a reputation for consistency of response—the other actor can easily calculate the costs of failing to cooperate or the benefits of cooperating.

reciprocity A response in kind to another's actions; a strategy of reciprocity uses positive forms of leverage to promise rewards and negative forms of leverage to threaten punishment.

Reciprocity can be an effective strategy for achieving cooperation in a situation of conflicting interests. If one side expresses willingness to cooperate and promises to reciprocate the other's cooperative and conflictual actions, the other side has great incentive to work out a cooperative bargain. And because reciprocity is relatively easy to interpret, the vow of future reciprocity often need not be stated explicitly.[16]

---

[15] Robert O. Keohane, "Reciprocity in International Relations," *International Organization* 40.1 (1986): 1–27. Deborah Welch Larson, "The Psychology of Reciprocity in International Relations," *Negotiation Journal* 4 (1988): 281–301. Robert Jervis, "Security Regimes," *International Regimes*, Stephen D. Krasner, ed. (Ithaca, NY: Cornell UP, 1983). Stephen R. Rock, *Why Peace Breaks Out: Great Power Rapprochement in Historical Perspective* (Chapel Hill, NC: U North Carolina P, 1989). George W. Downs and David M. Rocke, *Optimal Imperfection? Domestic Uncertainty and Institutions in International Relations* (Princeton, NJ: Princeton UP, 1995).

[16] Joshua S. Goldstein and John R. Freeman, *Three-Way Street: Strategic Reciprocity in World Politics* (Chicago: U Chicago P, 1990). Joshua S. Goldstein, "Great-Power Cooperation under Conditions of Limited Reciprocity: From Empirical to Formal Analysis," *International Studies Quarterly* 39.4 (1995): 453–77. Joshua S. Goldstein and Jon C. Pevehouse, "Reciprocity, Bullying, and International Cooperation: Time-Series Analysis of the Bosnia Conflict," *American Political Science Review* 91.3 (1997): 515–29.

deterrence The threat to punish another actor if it takes a certain negative action (especially attacking one's own state or one's allies). The term has a somewhat more specific meaning in the context of the nuclear balance between the superpowers during the Cold War. See also *mutually assured destruction (MAD)*.

compellence The use of force to make another actor take some action (rather than, as in *deterrence*, refrain from taking an action).

Reciprocity can also help achieve cooperation in the sense of refraining from an undesired action. This is the intent of the strategy of **deterrence**—the threat to punish another actor if it takes a certain negative action (especially attacking one's own state or one's allies). The slogan "peace through strength" reflects this approach. If deterrence works, its effects are almost invisible; its success is measured in attacks that did not occur.[17] Nuclear deterrence is the threat to use nuclear weapons if another state does so.

Generally, advocates of deterrence believe that conflicts are more likely to escalate into war when one party to the conflict is weak. In this view, building up military capabilities usually convinces the stronger party that a resort to military leverage would not succeed, so conflicts are less likely to escalate into violence. A strategy of **compellence**, sometimes used after deterrence fails, refers to the use of force to make another actor take some action (rather than refrain from taking an action).[18] Generally it is harder to get another state to change course (the purpose of compellence) than it is to get it to refrain from changing course (the purpose of deterrence).

One strategy used to try to compel compliance by another state is *escalation*—a series of negative sanctions of increasing severity applied in order to induce another actor to take some action. In theory, the less severe actions establish credibility—showing the first actor's willingness to exert its power on the issue—and the pattern of escalation establishes the high costs of future sanctions if the second actor does not cooperate. These should induce the second actor to comply, assuming that it finds the potential costs of the escalating punishments to be greater than the costs of compliance.

Escalation can be quite dangerous (especially when dealing with an adversary not as easily defeated). During the Cold War, many IR scholars worried that a conventional war could lead to nuclear war if the superpowers tried to apply escalation strategies. In fact, side by side with the potential for eliciting cooperation, reciprocity in general contains a danger of runaway hostility. When two sides both reciprocate but never manage to put relations on a cooperative footing, the result can be a drawn-out, nasty, tit-for-tat exchange of punishments. This characterizes Israeli relations with Islamic guerrillas in southern Lebanon, for instance.

arms race A reciprocal process in which two (or more) states build up military capabilities in response to each other.

An **arms race,** for realists, is a reciprocal process in which two (or more) states build up military capabilities in response to each other. Since each wants to act prudently against a threat (often a bit overblown in the leaders' perceptions), the attempt to reciprocate leads to a runaway production of weapons by both sides. The mutual escalation of threats erodes confidence, reduces cooperation, and makes it more likely that a crisis (or accident) could cause one side to strike first and start a war rather than wait for the other side to strike. The arms race process was illustrated vividly in the U.S.-Soviet nuclear arms race, which created arsenals of tens of thousands of nuclear weapons on each side.[19]

---

[17] Frank C. Zagare, *Perfect Deterrence* (NY: Cambridge UP, 2000). Avery Goldstein, *Deterrence and Security in the 21st Century* (Palo Alto, CA: Stanford UP, 2000). Ted Hopf, *Peripheral Visions: Deterrence Theory and American Foreign Policy in the Third World, 1965–1990* (Ann Arbor: U Michigan P, 1994). Paul K. Huth, *Extended Deterrence and the Prevention of War* (New Haven, CT: Yale UP, 1988). Robert Jervis, Richard Ned Lebow, and Janice Gross Stein, *Psychology and Deterrence* (Baltimore: Johns Hopkins UP, 1985). Alexander L. George and Richard Smoke, *Deterrence in American Foreign Policy: Theory and Practice* (NY: Columbia UP, 1974).

[18] Thomas C. Schelling, *The Strategy of Conflict* (Cambridge, MA: Harvard UP, 1960).

[19] Walter Isard and Charles H. Anderton, "Arms Race Models: A Survey and Synthesis," *Conflict Management and Peace Science* 8 (1985): 27–98. S. Plous, "Perceptual Illusions and Military Realities: The Nuclear Arms Race," *The Journal of Conflict Resolution* 29.3 (1985): 363–90. Michael D. McGinnis and John T. Williams, "Stability and Change in Superpower Rivalry," *American Political Science Review* 83 (1989): 1101–24.

INTERNAL DIVISIONS
The unitary actor assumption holds that states make important decisions as though they were single individuals able to act in the national interest. In truth, factions and organizations with differing interests put conflicting pressures on state leaders. Iran's government is badly split between reformers, led by President Khatami, and conservative ayatollahs who barred reformist candidates for parliament in 2004. This news kiosk in Tehran, in 2002, sells a postcard of Khatami (below soccer players, top centre) along with other political and sports figures.

Rationality

Consistent with the bargaining framework just outlined, most realists (and many non-realists) assume that those who wield power behave as **rational actors** in their efforts to influence others.[20]

> First, this rationality implies that the actor exercising power is a single entity that can "think" about its actions coherently and make choices. This is called the *unitary actor* assumption, or sometimes the *strong leader* assumption, and it is used to describe the nature of states as international actors. Although useful, this simplification does not capture the complexity of how states actually arrive at decisions (see Chapter 4).

> Second, the assumption of rationality implies that states and other international actors can identify their interests and put priorities on various interests. Realists assume that the exercise of power attempts to advance the **national interest**—the interests of the state itself. Again, the assumption is a simplification, because the interests of particular politicians, parties, economic sectors, or regions of a country often conflict.

rational actors Actors conceived as single entities that can "think" about their actions coherently, make choices, identify their interests, and rank the interests in terms of priority.

national interest The interests of a state overall (as opposed to particular parties or factions within the state).

[20] Michael E. Brown, Owen R. Coté, Jr., Sean M. Lynn-Jones, and Steven E. Miller, eds., *Rational Choice and Security Studies* (Cambridge, MA: MIT P, 2000). David A. Lake and Robert Powell, eds., *Strategic Choice and International Relations* (Princeton, CT: Princeton UP, 1999.) Michael Nicholson, *Rationality and the Analysis of International Conflict* (NY: Cambridge UP, 1992). Jeffrey Friedman, ed., *The Rational Choice Controversy: Economic Models of Politics Reconsidered* (New Haven, CT: Yale UP, 1996).

What are the interests of a state? Are they the interests of domestic groups (see Chapter 4)? The need to prevail in conflicts with other states (see Chapter 5)? The need to cooperate with the international community for mutual benefit (see Chapter 7)? There is no simple answer. Some realists simply define the national interest as maximizing power—a debatable assumption.

Third, rationality implies that actors are able to perform a **cost-benefit analysis**—calculating the costs incurred by a possible action and the benefits it is likely to bring. Applying power incurs costs and should produce commensurate gains. As in the problem of estimating power, one has to add up different dimensions in such a calculation. For instance, states presumably do not initiate wars that they expect to lose, except in cases where they stand to gain political benefits, domestic or international, that outweigh the costs of losing the war. But it is not easy to tally intangible political benefits against the tangible costs of a war. Even victory in a war may not be worth the costs paid. Rational actors can miscalculate costs and benefits, especially when using faulty information. Finally, human behaviour and luck can be unpredictable.

The ancient realist Sun Tzu advised that the best general was not the most courageous or aggressive one, but the one who could coolly calculate the costs and benefits of alternative courses of action. The best war was a short one, in Sun Tzu's view, because wars are costly. Better yet was to take another state intact without fighting—by intimidation, deception, and the disruption of enemy alliances. Capturing an enemy army was better than fighting it. If fighting was necessary, it should occur on another state's territory so the army could live off the land. Attacking cities was too destructive and thus reduced the benefits of war.

These three assumptions about rationality—that states are unitary actors, that they have coherent interests, and that they can make cost-benefit calculations—are simplifications that not all IR scholars accept. But realists consider these simplifications useful because they allow scholars to explain in a general way the actions of diverse actors. Power in IR has been compared with money in economics, as a universal measure. In this view, just as firms compete for money in economic markets, states compete for power in the international system.[21]

In order to provide a general explanation of state actions, realism makes a fourth assumption, implicit in the parallel to economics. This is the assumption that all states (or their leaders) have basically the same values and interests—*intersubjective preferences*. (The outcomes valued by an actor are called preferences or *utility*.) Economists assume that everyone prefers more money to less. Realists assume that all states prefer more power to less.

This assumption has been criticized. If a state leader prefers upholding his or her honour by fighting a losing war rather than being dictated to, such an action is rational in terms of the leader's own preferences—even though a Canadian university student or European prime minister might find it inexplicable in terms of Western cultural norms. Similarly, the suicidal charges of Iranian teenagers against Iraqi positions in the Iran-Iraq war were rational for the teenagers, who believed that as martyrs they would go directly to heaven. But such preferences are hardly universal.

Despite these criticisms, realists argue that rational-actor models capture not all but the most important aspects of IR. These simplified models provide the foundations for a large body of IR research that represents international bargaining relationships mathematically. By accepting the limitations of the four assumptions of rationality, IR scholars can build very general and abstract models of international relationships.

cost-benefit analysis A calculation of the costs incurred by a possible action and the benefits it is likely to bring.

Game Theory

Game theory is a branch of mathematics concerned with predicting bargaining outcomes. A game is a setting in which two or more players choose among alternative moves, either once or repeatedly. Each combination of moves (by all players) results in a set of payoffs (utility) to each player. The payoffs can be tangible items such as money or any intangible items of value. Game theory aims to deduce likely outcomes (what moves players will make), given the players' preferences and the possible moves open to them. Games are sometimes called formal models.

Game theory was first used extensively in IR in the 1950s and 1960s by scholars trying to understand U.S.-Soviet nuclear war contingencies. Moves were decisions to use nuclear weapons in certain ways, and payoffs were outcomes of the war. The use of game theory to study international interactions has become more extensive among IR scholars in recent years, especially among realists, who accept the assumptions about rationality. To analyze a game mathematically, one assumes that each player chooses a move rationally, to maximize its payoff.

Different kinds of situations are represented by different classes of games, as defined by the number of players and the structure of the payoffs. One basic distinction is between **zero-sum games,** in which one player's gain is by definition equal to the other's loss, and *non-zero-sum games*, in which it is possible for both players to gain (or lose). In a zero-sum game there is no point in communication or cooperation between the players because their interests are diametrically opposed. But in a non-zero-sum game, coordination of moves can maximize the total payoff to the players, although each may still manoeuvre to gain a greater share of that total payoff.

A *two-person game* has only two players; because it is simple and easy to analyze mathematically, this is the most common type of game studied. An *N-person* game has more than two players, and the moves typically result in coalitions of players, with the members of the winning coalition dividing the payoff among themselves in some manner. In most games, all the players make a move simultaneously. They may do so repeatedly, in a *repeated game* (or an *iterated game*, a *sequential game*, or a *supergame*). In a few games, the players alternate moves so each knows the other's move before deciding on its own.

Analysis of a game entails searching for a *solution*—a set of moves by all the players such that no player can increase its payoff by changing its move. It is the outcome at which rational players will arrive. Some simple games have one solution, but many games have multiple solutions or no stable solution.

A category of games with a given structure—in terms of the relationships between moves and payoffs—is sometimes given a name that evokes a story or metaphor representing the nature of the game. Each such game yields an insight or lesson regarding a category of international bargaining situations.[22]

The game called *Prisoner's Dilemma (PD)* is the one most commonly studied. It is a situation in which rational players will choose moves that produce an outcome in which all players are worse off than under a different set of moves. They all could do better, but as individual rational actors they are unable to achieve this outcome. How can this be?

game theory A branch of mathematics concerned with predicting bargaining outcomes. Games such as Prisoner's Dilemma and Chicken have been used to analyze various sorts of international interactions.

zero-sum games A situation in which one actor's gain is by definition equal to the other's loss, as opposed to a non-zero-sum game, in which it is possible for both actors to gain (or lose).

---

[22] Barry O'Neill, "A Survey of Game Theory Models on Peace and War," *Handbook of Game Theory*, R. Aumann and S. Hart, eds., vol. 2 (Amsterdam: North-Holland, 1994). Robert Powell, *In the Shadow of Power: States and Strategies in International Politics* (Princeton, NJ: Princeton UP, 1999). James D. Morrow, *Game Theory for Political Scientists* (Princeton, NJ: Princeton UP, 1995). Roger B. Myerson, *Game Theory: Analysis of Conflict* (Cambridge, MA: Harvard UP, 1991). Steven J. Brams, *Superpower Games: Applying Game Theory to Superpower Conflict* (New Haven, CT: Yale UP, 1985).

Thinking Theoretically

For game theorists, the Prisoner's Dilemma represents some of the basic elements of world politics as faced by state leaders: high risks and the imperative to make decisions quickly in situations of uncertainty. The one-shot PD game (a game played only once, not unlike the decision demanded of the prisoners themselves) is thought to best represent the realist vision of IR.

However, game theorists have shown that in an *iterated* PD game (one played repeatedly with the same players), the possibility of reciprocity can make it rational to cooperate. Now the players reason that they will meet one another in future games and a cooperative move in the present may be reciprocated by an opponent in future. Some suggest that this represents more of a liberal view of the world: states and other actors interact with one another repeatedly, and can learn from each other's behaviour and adjust their own behaviour accordingly.

Critical theorists are unlikely to be involved in elaborating upon game theory, but they would still have questions to pose of game theorists. Some might be, Who decides the rules of the game? Who determines the payoff matrix?

The original story tells of two prisoners questioned separately by a prosecutor. The prosecutor knows they committed a bank robbery but has only enough evidence to convict them of illegal possession of a gun unless one of them confesses. The prosecutor tells each prisoner that if he confesses and his partner doesn't confess, he will go free. If his partner confesses and he doesn't, he will get a long prison term for bank robbery (while the partner goes free). If both confess, they will get a somewhat reduced term. If neither confesses, they will be convicted on the gun charge and serve a short sentence. The story assumes that neither prisoner will have a chance to retaliate later, that only the immediate outcomes matter, and that each prisoner cares only about himself.

This game has a single solution: both prisoners will confess. Each will reason as follows: "If my partner is going to confess, then I should confess too, because I will get a slightly shorter sentence that way. If my partner is not going to confess, then I should still confess because I will go free that way instead of serving a short sentence." The other prisoner follows the same reasoning. The dilemma is that by following their individually rational choices both prisoners will end up serving a fairly long sentence when they could have both served a short one by cooperating (keeping their mouths shut).

In IR, the PD game has been used to gain insight into arms races. Consider the decisions of India and Pakistan about whether to build sizeable nuclear weapons arsenals. Both have the ability to do so. In 1998, when India detonated underground nuclear explosions to test weapons designs, Pakistan promptly followed suit. Now, neither side can know whether the other is secretly building up an arsenal, unless they reach an arms control agreement with strict verification provisions. To analyze the game, we assign values to each possible outcome—often called a *preference ordering*—for each player. This is not simple: if we misjudge the value a player puts on a particular outcome, we may draw wrong conclusions from the game.

The following preferences regarding possible outcomes are plausible: the best outcome would be that oneself but not the other player had a nuclear arsenal (the expense of building nuclear weapons would be worth it because one could then use them as leverage); second best would be for neither to go nuclear (no leverage, but no expense); third best would be for both to develop nuclear arsenals (a major expense without gaining leverage); worst would be to forgo nuclear weapons oneself while the other player developed them (and thus be subject to blackmail).

The game can be summarized in a *payoff matrix* (see Table 2.1). The first number in each cell is India's payoff, and the second number is Pakistan's. To keep things simple,

Table 2.1 Payoff Matrix in India-Pakistan PD Game

		Pakistan	
		Cooperate	Defect
India	Cooperate	(3,3)	(1,4)
	Defect	(4,1)	(2,2)

Note: First number in each group is India's payoff, second is Pakistan's. The number 4 is highest payoff, 1 lowest.

4 indicates the highest payoff, and 1 the lowest. As is conventional, a decision to refrain from building nuclear weapons is called "cooperation," and a decision to proceed with nuclear weapons is called "defection." The dilemma here parallels that of the prisoners just discussed. Each state's leader reasons: "If they go nuclear, we must; if they don't, we'd be crazy not to." The model seems to predict an inevitable Indian-Pakistani nuclear arms race, although both states would do better to avoid one. And, indeed, a costly and dangerous arms race is currently underway.

IR scholars have analyzed many other games beyond PD. For example, *Chicken* represents two male teenagers speeding toward a head-on collision. The first to swerve is "chicken." Each reasons: "If he doesn't swerve, I must; but if he swerves, I won't." The player who first commits irrevocably not to swerve ("throwing away the steering wheel") will win. Similarly, in the 1962 Cuban Missile Crisis, some scholars argued that President Kennedy "won" by seeming ready to risk nuclear war if Khrushchev did not back down and remove Soviet missiles from Cuba. (There are, however, alternative explanations of the outcome of the crisis.)

Through analysis of these and other games, IR researchers try to predict what rational actors would do in various types of situations. Games can capture and simplify the fundamental dynamics of various bargaining situations. However, a game-theoretic analysis is only as good as the assumptions that go into it. In particular, the results of the analysis depend on the preferences that players are assumed to have about outcomes. And it is difficult to test either the assumptions or the predictions of a formal model against the realities of IR, which are so much more complex in practice.

THE INTERNATIONAL SYSTEM

For realists, states interact within a set of well-defined and long-established "rules of the game" governing what is considered a state and how states treat each other. Together these rules shape the international system as we know it.[23]

Anarchy and Sovereignty

Realists emphasize that the rules of the international system create **anarchy**—a term that implies not complete chaos or absence of structure and rules, but rather the lack of a

anarchy In IR theory, the term implies not complete chaos but the lack of a central government that can enforce rules.

---

[23] Barry Buzan and Richard Little, *International Systems in World History: Remaking the Study of International Relations* (Oxford: Oxford UP, 2000). Evan Luard, *Conflict and Peace in the Modern International System: A Study of the Principles of International Order* (London: Macmillan, 1988). Martin Wight, *Systems of States* (Leicester: U Leicester P, 1977).

central government that can enforce rules.[24] In domestic society within states, governments can enforce contracts, deter participants from breaking rules, and use their monopoly on legally sanctioned violence to enforce a system of law. Both democracies and dictatorships provide central government enforcement of a system of rules. Lack of such a government among states is what realists mean by anarchy. No central authority enforces rules and ensures compliance with norms of conduct. The power of one state is countered only by the power of other states. States must rely on *self-help*, which they supplement with allies and the (sometimes) constraining power of international norms.

Some people think that only a world government can solve this problem. Others think that adequate order can be provided by international organizations and agreements, short of world government (see Chapter 7). But most realists think that IR cannot escape from a state of anarchy and will continue to be dangerous as a result.[25] In this anarchic world, realists emphasize prudence as a great virtue in foreign policy. States should pay attention not to the intentions of other states but rather to their capabilities. As Sun Tzu advised, do not assume that other states will not attack but rather be ready if they do.

Despite its anarchy, the international system is far from chaotic. The great majority of state interactions closely adhere to **norms** of behaviour—shared expectations about what behaviour is considered proper.[26] Norms change over time, slowly, but the most basic norms of the international system have changed little in recent centuries.

Sovereignty—traditionally the most important norm—means that a government has the right, at least in principle, to do whatever it wants in its own territory. States are separate, are autonomous, and answer to no higher authority (due to anarchy). In principle, all states are equal in status if not in power. Sovereignty also means that states are not supposed to interfere in the internal affairs of other states. Although states do try to influence each other (exert power) on matters of trade, alliances, war, and so on, they are not supposed to meddle in the internal politics and decision processes of other states. For example, it would be inappropriate for Russia or the United States to endorse a candidate for Canadian prime minister. (This rule is often bent in practice.)[27]

The principles of state sovereignty were exemplified during the era of South Africa's apartheid regime—a regime that excluded the majority of South Africa's population, blacks, from any political, social, or economic rights within South Africa. Many Western states claimed to be opposed to apartheid but insisted that they could do nothing because it was an "internal affair." During the 1980s many people around the world called for sanctions to be imposed on South Africa, a call that many countries resisted because it would have been a violation of South Africa's sovereignty. For defenders of sovereignty, change in South Africa would have to come from within, not be imposed from without.

In practice, states have a harder and harder time warding off interference in their affairs. Such "internal" matters as human rights or self-determination are, increasingly,

norms (of behaviour) The shared expectations about what behaviour is considered proper.

sovereignty A state's right, at least in principle, to do whatever it wants within its own territory; traditionally sovereignty is the most important international norm.

---

[24] Hedley Bull, *The Anarchical Society: A Study of Order in World Politics* (NY: Columbia UP, 1977). Michael Taylor, *Anarchy and Cooperation* (NY: Wiley, 1976). Harvey Starr, *Anarchy, Order, and Integration: How to Manage Interdependence?* (Ann Arbor: U Michigan P, 1997).

[25] John J. Mearsheimer, *The Tragedy of Great Power Politics* (NY: Norton, 2001).

[26] Dorothy Jones, *Code of Peace: Ethics and Security in the World of the Warlord States* (Chicago: U Chicago P, 1991. Thomas M. Franck, *The Power of Legitimacy among Nations* (NY: Oxford UP, 1990).

[27] Stephen D. Krasner, *Sovereignty: Organized Hypocrisy* (Princeton, NJ: Princeton UP, 1999). Charles W. Kegley, Jr. and Gregory A Raymond, *Exorcising the Ghost of Westphalia: Building World Order in the New Millennium* (Upper Saddle River, NJ: Prentice Hall, 2002). Gene M. Lyons and Michael Mastanduno, eds., *Beyond Westphalia: State Sovereignty and International Intervention* (Baltimore: Johns Hopkins UP, 1995).

seen as concerns for the international community. In the Helsinki agreements that codi-fied East-West détente in the Cold War, the Soviet Union and Eastern Europe promised to respect human rights within their own borders (an internal affair). When the inter-national community failed to respond to the 1994 Rwandan genocide, many viewed this as a horrifying and catastrophic failure, one for which President Bill Clinton subsequently personally apologized. Also, the integration of global economic markets and telecom-munications makes it easier than ever for ideas to penetrate state borders.

States are based on territory. Respect for the territorial integrity of all states, within recognized borders, is an important principle of IR. Many of today's borders are the result of past wars (in which winners took territory from losers), or were imposed arbitrarily by third parties such as colonizers. These borders therefore create many problems—the splitting of nations or ethnic groups into different states, the creation of oddly shaped states that may lack resources or access to ports, and so forth (see pp. 160–168). Despite these imperfections, the international system places the highest value on respect for internationally recognized borders. Almost all of the world's land territory falls under the sovereign control of existing states; very little is considered "up for grabs" (high seas are outside any state's territory; see Chapter 11).

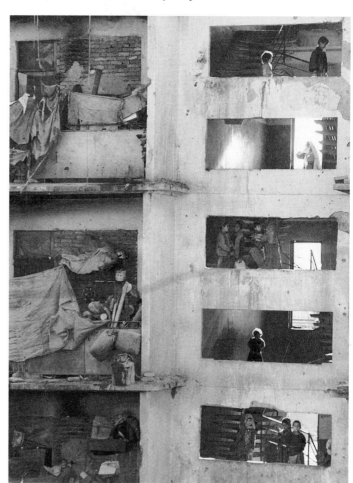

The territorial nature of the interstate sys-tem reflects the origins of that system in an age when agrarian societies relied on agriculture to generate wealth. In today's world, where trade and technology rather than land create wealth, the territorial state may be less important. Information-based economies are linked across borders instantly, and the idea of the state as having a hard shell now seems archaic. The accelerating revolution in information tech-nologies may dramatically affect the territorial state system in the coming years.

Membership in the international system rests on general recognition (by other states) of a government's sovereignty within its territory. This recognition is extended formally through diplomatic relations and by membership in the UN. It does not imply that a government has popular support but only that it controls the state's territory and agrees to assume its obliga-tions in the international system—to accept internationally recognized borders, to assume the international debts of the previous govern-ment, and to refrain from interfering in other states' internal affairs.

States have developed norms of diplomacy to facilitate their interactions. An embassy is con-sidered to be territory of the home state, not the country where it is located (see pp. 280–283).

STILL SOVEREIGN TERRITORY
Sovereignty and territorial integrity are central norms governing the behaviour of states. They give states control within estab-lished borders. Embassies are considered the home country's territory. Here, the ruined Russian Embassy grounds in the capital of Afghanistan become a refuge to 15 000 people displaced by war (2002).

Diplomatic norms recognize that states try to spy on each other. It is up to each state to keep others from successfully spying on it. In 2002, China discovered that its new presidential aircraft—a Boeing 767 refurbished in Texas—was riddled with sophisticated listening devices. But China did not make an issue of it (the plane had not gone into service), and a U.S.-China summit the next month went forward.

security dilemma A situation in which states' actions taken to assure their own security (such as deploying more military forces) are perceived as threats to the security of other states.

Realists acknowledge that the rules of IR often create a **security dilemma**—a situation in which states' actions taken to assure their own security (such as deploying more military forces) tend to threaten the security of other states.[28] The responses of those other states (such as deploying more of their own military forces) in turn threaten the first state. The dilemma parallels the Prisoner's Dilemma game discussed earlier. It is a prime cause of arms races in which states waste large sums of money on mutually threatening weapons that do not ultimately provide security. The current debate over developing U.S. missile defences hinges in part on whether such defences would cause a worried China or Russia to deploy more nuclear weapons against the United States—another case of a security dilemma.

The security dilemma is a negative consequence of anarchy in the international system. Realists tend to see the dilemma as unsolvable, whereas liberals think it can be solved through the development of norms and institutions (see Chapters 3 and 7).

As we shall see in later chapters, changes in technology and in norms are undermining the traditional principles of territorial integrity and state autonomy in IR. Some IR scholars find states to be practically obsolete as the main actors in world politics, as some integrate into larger entities and others fragment into smaller units.[29] Other scholars find the international system quite enduring in its structure and state units.[30] For realists, one of its most enduring features is the balance of power.

Balance of Power

balance of power The general concept of one or more states' power being used to balance that of another state or group of states. The term can refer to (1) any ratio of power capabilities between states or alliances, (2) a relatively equal ratio, or (3) the process by which counterbalancing coalitions have repeatedly formed to prevent one state from conquering an entire region.

In the anarchy of the international system, the most reliable brake on the power of one state is the power of other states. The term **balance of power** refers to the general concept of one or more states' power being used to balance that of another state or group of states. The term is used in several ways and is imprecisely defined. Balance of power can refer to any ratio of power capabilities between states or alliances; or it can mean only a relatively equal ratio. Alternatively, balance of power can refer to the process by which counterbalancing coalitions have repeatedly formed in history to prevent one state from conquering an entire region.[31]

The theory of balance of power argues that such counterbalancing occurs regularly and maintains the stability of the international system. The system is stable in that its rules and principles stay the same: state sovereignty does not collapse into a universal empire. This

---

[28] Robert. Jervis, "Cooperation under the Security Dilemma," *World Politics* 30.2 (1978): 167–214.

[29] James N. Rosenau, *Along the Domestic-Foreign Frontier: Exploring Governance in a Turbulent World* (NY: Cambridge UP, 1997). Yale H. Ferguson and Richard W. Mansbach, *Polities: Authority, Identities, and Change* (Columbia, SC: U South Carolina P, 1996).

[30] Daniel Drache, *Borders Matter: Homeland Security and the Search for North America* (Halifax: Fernwood, 2004). Robert Gilpin, *War and Change in World Politics* (NY: Cambridge UP, 1981).

[31] Edward V. Gulick, *Europe's Classical Balance of Power* (Ithaca, NY: Cornell UP, 1955). Emerson M. S. Niou, Peter C. Ordeshook, and Gregory F. Rose, *The Balance of Power: Stability and Instability in International Systems* (NY: Cambridge UP, 1989). Thomas R. Cusack and Richard J. Stoll, *Exploring Realpolitik: Probing International Relations Theory with Computer Simulation* (Boulder, CO: Rienner, 1990).

stability does not, however, imply peace; it is rather a stability maintained by means of recurring wars that adjust power relations.

Alliances (see Chapter 7) play a key role in the balance of power. Building up one's own capabilities against a rival is a form of power balancing, but forming an alliance against a threatening state is often quicker, cheaper, and more effective. When such a counterbalancing coalition has a geopolitical element—physically hemming in the threatening state—the power-balancing strategy is called *containment*. In the Cold War, the United States encircled the Soviet Union with military and political alliances to prevent Soviet territorial expansion.

The Information Revolution
Cyberspace versus Sovereignty?

The interstate system is based on states' sovereignty within their territories. In the 1990s, the astounding growth of the internet and World Wide Web created "cyberspace." It is a world of business relationships and communities with shared personal interests, in which geography is irrelevant. How is the growth of cyberspace changing state sovereignty?

To explore this question, go to www.pearsoned.ca/goldstein.

Sometimes a particular state deliberately becomes a balancer (in its region or the world), shifting its support to oppose whatever state or alliance is strongest at the moment. Britain played this role on the European continent for centuries, and China played it in the Cold War. But states do not always balance against the strongest actor. Sometimes smaller states "jump on the bandwagon" of the most powerful state; this has been called *bandwagoning* as opposed to balancing. For instance, after World War II a broad coalition did not form to contain U.S. power; rather most major states, including Canada, joined the U.S. bloc. States may seek to balance threats rather than raw power; U.S. power was greater than Soviet power but was less threatening to Europe and Japan (and later to China as well).[32] Furthermore, small states create variations on power-balancing themes when they play off rival great powers against each other. For instance, Cuba during the Cold War received massive Soviet subsidies by putting itself in the middle of the U.S.-Soviet rivalry.

In the post–Cold War era of U.S. dominance, balance-of-power theory would predict closer relations among Russia, China, and even France—great powers that are not close U.S. military allies. These predictions appear to be on the mark. Russian-Chinese relations have improved dramatically in such areas as arms trade and demilitarization of the border. France contested U.S. positions vigorously in global trade negotiations and discussions of NATO's command structure, and sometimes sided with Russia and China in the UN Security Council, notably before the 2003 Iraq War. French leaders have complained repeatedly of U.S. "hyperpower." Europe and Japan opposed U.S. positions on a range of proposed treaties in 2001, on such subjects as missile defence, biological weapons, small arms trade, and global warming. (Public opinion in European countries disapproved of Bush Administration international policies by large majorities in mid-2001.)[33] Only the appearance of a common enemy—international terrorists—brought the great powers back together in September 2001.

But the 2003 Iraq War brought back a power-balancing coalition of great powers (except Britain)—along with most other countries and world public opinion—against U.S. predominance. In 2003, as the United States used military force in Iraq, world public opinion revealed widespread anti-U.S. sentiment. In Indonesia, Pakistan, Turkey, and

[32] Stephen M. Walt, *The Origins of Alliances* (Ithaca, NY: Cornell UP, 1987).

[33] *New York Times* 24 Apr.1997: A3. "Going It Alone," *Washington Post* 4 Aug. 2001: A15. Adam Clymer, "Surveys Find European Public Critical of Bush Policies," *New York Times* 16 Aug. 2001: A6.

Nigeria—which contain half of all the world's Muslims—more than 70 percent worried that the United States could become a threat to their own country, a worry shared by 71 percent of Russians. In Indonesia, Pakistan, Turkey, and Jordan, less than a quarter of the population supported the U.S. war on terrorism. A survey of 38 000 people in 44 nations showed a dramatic drop in support for the United States from 2002 to 2003.

Great Powers and Middle Powers

Power, of course, varies greatly from one state to another. The *most powerful* states in the system exert most of the influence on international events and therefore get the most attention from IR scholars. By almost any measure of power, a handful of states possess the majority of the world's power resources. At most a few dozen states have any real influence beyond their immediate locality. These are called the great powers and middle powers in the international system.

great powers Generally, the half dozen or so most powerful states; the great-power club was exclusively European until the twentieth century. See also *middle powers.*

Although there is no firm dividing line, **great powers** are generally considered the half dozen or so most powerful states. Until the past century the great power club was exclusively European. Sometimes great powers' status is formally recognized in an inter-

---

The Changing World Order

The Bush Doctrine

The events of September 11, according to some observers, changed the world forever. Many realists might disagree with that statement. They would argue that the world is still characterized by conflict, insecurity, and uncertainty. While it is true that the sources of insecurity have shifted to nonstate actors (terrorists), those actors still rely on states for support. This is one reason the United States' response to September 11 emphasized that "states are responsible for what goes on inside their borders." Any states harbouring terrorists would be targeted themselves. This has been described as the "Bush Doctrine."

Even states that do not harbour terrorists have been subjected to greater scrutiny by the U.S., and this has been particularly true of Canada. The world's "longest undefended border" is one that terrorists could use to gain access to U.S. territory, and initial reports after the September 11 attacks suggested that the hijackers had entered the United States through Canada (this later proved to be untrue). U.S. policy-makers also worry about Canada's apparently more open immigration policy. Meanwhile, during the post–Cold War era, the Canadian government had allowed its military to shrink significantly and had shifted its emphasis to peacebuilding missions rather than the continental defence of North America.

Realist commentators on Canadian foreign policy have argued that while the world may not have changed

as a result of September 11, U.S. foreign policy has been transformed because of its heightened insecurity. The United States is the single most powerful state in the world today, so this means that Canada should adapt itself to a changing world order informed by this fact. By this view, Canadians need to recognize that on most issues, Canada's interests are the same as the U.S., and so Canada should work with, rather than against, the United States. This would mean, among other things, that Canada should refrain from open expressions of criticism against the U.S. and use "quiet diplomacy" instead; it should expand its armed forces; it should direct foreign aid more narrowly than it has in the past, and in particular in support of countries that are important to Canada's national security interests; and, though Canada should continue to promote international institutions, it should see those institutions as instruments to achieve national interests, not as ends in themselves.[*]

Are these realist suggestions the best responses for Canada as it negotiates the changing world order? Can you think of other responses? What would your arguments be in support of one or another set of policy options?

* Denis Stairs, David J. Bercuson, Mark Entwistle, J. L. Granatstein, Kim Richard Nossal, and Gordon S. Smith, *In the National Interest: Canadian Foreign Policy in an Insecure World* (Canadian Defence and Foreign Affairs Institute, 2003).

national structure such as the nineteenth-century Concert of Europe or the UN Security Council. In general, great powers may be distinguished by the criterion that they can be defeated militarily only by another great power. Great powers also tend to share a global outlook based on national interests far from their home territories.[34]

The great powers generally have the world's strongest military forces and the strongest economies to pay for military forces and for other power capabilities. These large economies in turn rest on some combination of large populations, plentiful natural resources, advanced technology, and educated labour forces. Because power is based on these underlying resources, membership in the great-power system changes slowly. Only rarely does a great power—even one defeated in a massive war—lose its status as a great power, because its size and long-term economic potential change slowly. Thus Germany and Japan, decimated in World War II, are powerful today, and Russia, after gaining and then losing the rest of the Soviet Union, is still considered a great power.

What states are great powers today? Although definitions vary, seven states appear to meet the criteria. Certainly the United States is one. In total GDP, a measure of potential power, the United States ranks highest by far at almost US$10 trillion per year (2002 data). Because of its historical role of world leadership (especially in and after World War II), and its predominant military might, the United States is considered the world's only superpower.

China, with a total GDP of nearly US$6 trillion, is or soon will be the world's second largest economy. China's GDP is especially hard to estimate, and another method would put it below US$2 trillion. In any case, China's sheer size (more than 1 billion people) and its rapid economic growth (10 percent annually in the 1990s and then around 8 percent) make it a powerful state. China has a large but not a very modern military, and its orientation is regional rather than global. But, with a credible nuclear arsenal and a seat on the UN Security Council, China qualifies as a great power. It is expected to play a central role in world politics in the twenty-first century. Japan ranks third (or perhaps second), with a GDP of US$3 trillion. Along with Germany (US$2 trillion GDP), Japan is an economic great power, but both countries' military roles in international security affairs have been curtailed since World War II. Nonetheless, both Japan and Germany have very large and capable military forces, and both have been edging toward using military forces beyond their own territories or regions.

Russia, even after the breakup of the Soviet Union, has a GDP above US$1 trillion—again a hard one to estimate—and very large (though run-down) military forces including a massive nuclear arsenal. France and Britain finish out the list at around US$1.5 trillion GDP each. With Russia, they were winners in World War II and have been active military powers since then. Although much reduced in stature from their colonial heydays, they still qualify as great powers by most standards.

The great powers thus include the five permanent members of the UN Security Council—the United States, Russia, France, Britain, and China. The same five states are also the members of the "club" possessing large nuclear weapons arsenals (there are also several recent smaller-scale nuclear states). In world political and economic affairs, Germany and Japan are also great powers (they would like Security Council seats, too; see p. 258).

These seven great powers account for about half of the world's total GDP—and hence, presumably, about half of the total power in the world. This concentration of power is especially strong in practice because the remaining half of the world's power is split up among nearly 200 other states.

---

[34] Jack S. Levy, *War in the Modern Great Power System, 1495–1975* (Lexington: UP Kentucky, 1983).

The slow change in great-power status is evident. Britain and France have been great powers for 500 years, Russia and Germany for more than 250 years, the United States and Japan for about 100 years, and China for 50 years. Only six other states were ever (but no longer are) considered great powers: Italy, Austria (Austria-Hungary), Spain, Turkey (the Ottoman Empire), Sweden, and the Netherlands.

Middle powers rank somewhat below the great powers in terms of their influence on world affairs. Some are large but not highly industrialized; others have specialized capabilities but are small. Some aspire to regional dominance, and many have considerable influence in their regions. Even more than with great powers, it is hard to establish a bottom criterion for distinguishing middle powers.

The top rungs of middle powers are easier to identify. India (US$2.7 trillion) and Brazil (US$1.3 trillion) are both regional giants that some scholars see as rising powers and possible new great powers in this century. In terms of total GDP, Italy and Canada are just below the range of France and Britain and some would consider them great powers. Both states belong to the Group of Eight (G8) economic powers (along with the United States, Germany, Japan, France, Britain, and Russia, which joined in 1998). Mexico, Indonesia, South Korea, Australia, and Spain all have GDPs greater than half a trillion dollars, and are active middle powers. Below this level, GDP estimates become more closely bunched and the order of national economies becomes much harder to sort out.

A list of middle powers (not everyone would agree on it) might include the following states. The first tier would include large states with substantial economic activity, fairly strong military forces, and considerable regional political influence: Canada, Italy, India, Brazil, Mexico, South Korea, Australia, Iran, and Turkey. A second tier could include important regional actors with somewhat smaller economies or with strong capabilities on specific dimensions of power: Taiwan, Indonesia, Spain, Ukraine, Argentina, Israel, Saudi Arabia, Egypt, Pakistan, South Africa, and Kazakhstan. A third tier might include smaller rich states along with middle-sized, middle-income ones and regional "activists" that exercise power beyond their size: the Netherlands, Belgium, Sweden, Greece, Poland, Nigeria, Venezuela, Vietnam, Syria, Iraq, Serbia, and North Korea.

Middle powers have not received as much attention in IR as have great powers. These states do, however, often come into play in specific regional conflicts or as mediators on various issues. A number of realist scholars argued during the Cold War that some middle powers, in particular Canada, should be termed a "principal power." Principal powers, they argued, were states at the top of the international hierarchy, closer in status to countries like France or Germany than true middle powers like Australia or Brazil. In part, the idea of Canada as a principal power came out of the observation in the Cold War's declining decade that power was becoming more diffuse and nonhegemonic, thus making room for important states such as Canada to take a more prominent role in international relations. It is less clear in the post–Cold War period, in which the United States has established itself as the preponderant global power, whether the idea of Canada as a principal power applies any longer (if it ever did).[35]

Smaller, weaker states (not even of middle-power strength) also are often at the centre of specific conflicts and crises. But their own actions have only minor influence on world politics; the actions of great powers and middle powers in those conflicts and crises have more impact.

middle powers States that rank somewhat below the great powers in terms of their influence on world affairs (for example, Canada, Brazil, and India). See also *great powers*.

[35] David Dewitt and John Kirton, *Canada as a Principal Power* (Toronto: Wiley, 1983). See also David R. Black and Heather A. Smith, "Notable Exceptions? New and Arrested Direction in Canadian Foreign Policy Literature," *Canadian Journal of Political Science* 26.4. (Dec. 1993).

Power Distribution

With each state's power balanced by other states, the most important characteristic of an international system in the view of many realists is the *distribution* of power among states in an international system. Power distribution as a concept can apply to all the states in the world or to just one region, but most often it refers to the great-power system (with most of the world's total power capabilities).

Neorealists (so called because they have adopted and refined realism) try to explain patterns of international events in terms of the system structure—the international distribution of power—rather than the internal makeup of individual states.[36] **Neorealism** is thus also called structural realism. Neorealists often use game theory and related models in such analyses.[37] Compared to traditional realism, neorealism is more scientific in the sense of proposing general laws to account for many complex elements (geography, willpower, diplomacy, etc.).

Sometimes an international power distribution (world or regional) is described in terms of polarity (a term adopted from physics), which refers to the number of independent power centres in the system. This concept encompasses both the underlying power of various participants and their alliance groupings.

In a **multipolar system** there are typically five or six centres of power, which are not grouped into alliances. Each state participates independently and on relatively equal terms with the others. They may form a coalition of the whole for mutual security through coordination of efforts. Some IR researchers think that multipolarity provides a context for smooth interaction. There are always enough actors present to prevent one from predominating. But to other IR scholars a multipolar system is particularly dangerous, lacking the discipline that predominant states or alliance blocs impose. In a sense, both are correct: In the classical multipolar balance of power, the great-power system itself was stable but wars were frequently used as power-adjusting mechanisms.

At the other extreme, a unipolar system has a single centre of power around which all others revolve. This is called hegemony, and will be discussed shortly. The predominance of a single state tends to reduce the incidence of war; the hegemonic state performs some of the functions of a government, somewhat reducing anarchy in the international system.

A bipolar system has two predominant states or two great rival alliance blocs. Tight bipolar systems, such as the East-West standoff in the 1950s, may be distinguished from looser ones such as developed when China and (to a lesser extent) France split off from their alliance blocs in the 1960s. IR scholars do not agree about whether bipolar systems are relatively peaceful or warlike. The U.S.-Soviet standoff seemed to provide stability and peace to great-power relations, but rival blocs in Europe before World War I did not.

In a tripolar system there are three great centres of power. Such a configuration is fairly rare; there is a tendency for a two-against-one alliance to form. Aspects of tripolarity can be found in the "strategic triangle" of the United States, the Soviet Union, and China during the 1960s and 1970s.[38] Some scholars imagine that in the coming decades a tripolar world will emerge, with rival power centres in North America, Europe, and East Asia.

neorealism A version of realist theory that emphasizes the influence on state behaviour of the system's structure, especially the international distribution of power. See also *realism*.

multipolar system An international system with typically five or six centres of power that are not grouped into alliances.

---

[36] Waltz, *Theory of International Politics* (see footnote 6 in this chapter).

[37] Robert O. Keohane, ed., *Neorealism and Its Critics* (NY: Columbia UP, 1986). Barry Buzan, Charles Jones, and Richard Little, *The Logic of Anarchy: Neorealism to Structural Realism* (NY: Columbia UP, 1993). Frank W. Wayman and Paul F. Diehl, eds., *Reconstructing Realpolitik* (Ann Arbor: U Michigan P, 1994).

[38] Randall Schweller, *Deadly Imbalances: Tripolarity and Hitler's Strategy of World Conquest* (NY: Columbia UP, 1998). Gerald Segal, *The Great Power Triangle* (NY: St. Martin's, 1982).

These various polarities can be conceptualized as a pyramid or hierarchy of power in an international system. At the top is the most powerful state, with other great powers and middle powers arrayed below. Such a pyramid is similar to the dominance (or status) hierarchies that many animals use to regulate access to valuable resources such as food. (We often call this a "pecking order.") A multipolar system, then, is one with a relatively flat pyramid—relative equality of status among actors. A unipolar system has a relatively steep pyramid with unequal status. The steepness of the pyramid represents the concentration of power in the international system.

Some IR scholars have argued that peace is best preserved by a relatively equal power distribution (multipolarity) because then no country has an opportunity to win easily. The empirical evidence for this theory, however, is not strong. The opposite proposition has more support: peace is best preserved by hegemony, and next best by bipolarity.

Such is the thrust of power transition theory.[39] This theory holds that the largest wars result from challenges to the top position in the status hierarchy, when a rising power is surpassing (or threatening to surpass) the most powerful state. At such times, power is relatively equally distributed, and these are the most dangerous times for major wars. Status quo powers that are doing well under the old rules will try to maintain them, whereas challengers that feel locked out by the old rules may try to change them.[40] Status disequilibrium refers to a difference between a rising power's status (formal position in the hierarchy) and its actual power. In such a situation, the rising power may suffer from relative deprivation—the feeling that it is not doing as well as others or as well as it deserves, even though its position may be improving in absolute terms. The classic example is Germany's rise in the nineteenth century, which gave it great-power capabilities even though it was left out of colonial territories and other signs of status.

If the challenger does not start a war to displace the top power, the latter may provoke a "preventive" war to stop the rise of the challenger before it becomes too great a threat.[41] Germany's intensive arms race with Britain (the top power) led to increasing hostility and the outbreak of World War I. After the war there was again a disparity between Germany's actual power (still considerable) and its harsh treatment under the terms of the Versailles Treaty. That disparity may have contributed to World War II.

According to power transition theory, then, peace among great powers results when one state is firmly in the top position, and the positions of others in the hierarchy are clearly defined and correspond with their actual underlying power. Such a situation usually results only from a great war, when one state predominates in power because its rivals and allies alike have been drained. Even then, the different rates of growth among great powers lead to a slow equalization of power and eventually the emergence of challengers: the system becomes more multipolar.

Hegemony

hegemony The holding by one state of a preponderance of power in the international system, so that it can single-handedly dominate the rules and arrangements by which international political and economic relations are conducted. See also *hegemonic stability theory.*

Hegemony is the holding by one state of a preponderance of power in the international system, so that it can single-handedly dominate the rules and arrangements by which

---

[39] A. F. K. Organski, *World Politics* (NY: Knopf, 1958). A. F. K. Organski and Jacek Kugler, *The War Ledger* (Chicago: U Chicago P, 1980). Jacek Kugler and Douglas Lemke, eds., *Parity and War: Evaluations and Extensions of the War Ledger* (Ann Arbor: U Michigan P, 1996).

[40] Edward D. Mansfield, "The Concentration of Capabilities and the Onset of War," *Journal of Conflict Resolution* 36.1 (1992): 3–24. William R. Thompson and Karen Rasler, "War and Systemic Capability Reconcentration," *Journal of Conflict Resolution* 32.2 (1988): 335–66. Charles F. Doran, *Systems in Crisis: New Imperatives of High Politics at Century's End* (NY: Cambridge UP, 1991).

[41] Jack S. Levy, "Declining Power and the Preventive Motivation for War," *World Politics* 40.1 (1987): 82–107.

international political and economic relations are conducted.[42] Such a state is called a *hegemon*. (Usually hegemony means domination of the world, but sometimes it refers to regional domination.) From a distinctly nonrealist perspective, the Italian Marxist theorist Antonio Gramsci used "hegemony" to refer not simply to dominance, but to the complex of ideas that rulers use to gain consent for their legitimacy and keep subjects in line.[43] By extension, such a meaning in IR refers to the hegemony of ideas such as democracy and capitalism, and to the global predominance of U.S. culture (see pp. 393–395).

Most studies of hegemony point to two examples: Britain in the nineteenth century and the United States after World War II. Britain's predominance followed the defeat of its archrival France in the Napoleonic Wars. Both world trade and naval capabilities were firmly in British hands, as "Britannia ruled the waves." U.S. predominance followed the defeat of Germany and Japan (and the exhaustion of the Soviet Union, France, Britain, and China in the effort). In the late 1940s, the U.S. GDP was more than half the world's total; U.S. vessels carried the majority of the world's shipping; the U.S. military could single-handedly defeat any other state or combination of states; and only the United States had nuclear weapons. U.S. industry led the world in technology and productivity, and U.S. citizens enjoyed the world's highest standard of living.

As the extreme power disparities resulting from major wars slowly diminish (states rebuild over years and decades), hegemonic decline may occur, particularly when hegemons have overextended themselves with costly military commitments. IR scholars do not agree about whether U.S. hegemony is in decline, or becoming more entrenched.[44] And beyond the U.S. and British cases, IR scholars do not agree on which historical cases were instances of hegemony. Some see the Netherlands in the early seventeenth century, or Spain in the sixteenth, as cases of hegemony.

The theory of hegemonic stability (see pp. 93–95) holds that hegemony provides some order in the international system, reducing anarchy, and provides some functions similar to a central government—deterring aggression, promoting free trade, and providing a hard currency that can be used as a world standard. Hegemons can help to resolve or at least keep in check conflicts among middle powers or small states.

From the perspective of less powerful states, of course, such hegemony may seem an infringement of state sovereignty, and the order it creates may seem unjust or illegitimate. For instance, China chafed under U.S.-imposed economic sanctions for 20 years after 1949, feeling itself encircled by U.S. military bases and hostile alliances led by the United States. To this day, Chinese leaders use the term *hegemony* as an insult, and the theory of hegemonic stability does not impress them.

Even in the United States itself there is considerable ambivalence about U.S. hegemony. U.S. foreign policy has historically alternated between *internationalist* and *isolationist* moods.[45] It was founded as a breakaway from the European-based international system,

---

[42] Ethan B. Kapstein and Michael Mastanduno, *Unipolar Politics* (NY: Columbia UP, 1999). Mark Rupert, *Producing Hegemony: The Politics of Mass Production and American Global Power* (NY: Cambridge UP, 1995). Lea Brilmayer, *American Hegemony: Political Morality in a One-Superpower World* (New Haven, CT: Yale UP, 1994). David P. Rapkin, ed., *World Leadership and Hegemony* (Boulder, CO: Rienner, 1990).

[43] Antonio Gramsci, *The Modern Prince and Other Writings* (NY: International, 1959). Stephen Gill, ed., *Gramsci, Historical Materialism and International Relations* (NY: Cambridge UP, 1993).

[44] Paul Kennedy, *The Rise and Fall of the Great Powers: Economic Change and Military Conflict from 1500–2000* (NY: Random House, 1987). W. R. Mead, *Mortal Splendor: The American Empire in Transition* (Boston: Houghton Mifflin, 1987). Bruce Russett, "The Mysterious Case of Vanishing Hegemony," *International Organization* 39.2 (1985): 207–31.

[45] Frank L. Klingberg, "The Historical Alternation of Moods in American Foreign Policy," *World Politics* 4.2 (1952): 239–73. Fareed Zakaria, *From Wealth to Power: The Unusual Origins of America's World Role* (Princeton, NJ: Princeton UP, 1998).

and its growth in the nineteenth century was based on industrialization and expansion within North America. The United States acquired overseas colonies in the Philippines and Puerto Rico but did not relish a role as an imperial power. In World War I, the country waited three years to weigh in—and refused to join the League of Nations afterward. U.S. isolationism peaked in the 1930s; public opinion polls late in that decade showed 95 percent of the U.S. public opposed to participation in a future great European war, and about 70 percent opposed to joining the League of Nations or joining with other nations to stop aggression.[46]

Internationalists, such as Presidents Theodore Roosevelt and Woodrow Wilson, favoured U.S. leadership and activism in world affairs. These views seemed vindicated by the failure of isolationism to prevent World War II (or to allow the United States to stay out of it). U.S. leaders after the war became alarmed by the threat of Soviet (and then Chinese) communism and drummed up U.S. public opinion to favour a strong internationalism during the Cold War. The United States became an activist, global superpower. Despite an inward-looking period after the Vietnam War, the United States has largely continued this internationalist stance ever since. That commitment became only stronger after the attacks on the World Trade Center and Pentagon in September 2001.[47]

A second area of U.S. ambivalence is *unilateralism* versus *multilateralism* in U.S. internationalism. Multilateral approaches—working through international institutions—augment U.S. power and reduce costs, but they limit U.S. freedom of action. For example, the United States cannot always get the UN to do what it wants. Polls in the 1990s showed that a majority of U.S. citizens supported working through the UN and other multilateral institutions.[48] However, members of the U.S. Congress, skeptical of the UN and international agencies, often favoured a more unilateralist approach, in which the United States dictated terms and expected the world to comply. In the 1990s, Congress slipped

PRICE OF WAGING WAR IN IRAQ

The United States is the world's most powerful single actor. Its ability and willingness to assume a role as hegemon—as after World War II—are important factors that will shape world order, but the U.S. role is still uncertain. U.S. willingness to absorb casualties will affect its role. Here soldiers return from Afghanistan, 2004.

more than US$1 billion behind in paying U.S. dues to the UN. Similarly, in the late 1990s Congress passed the *Helms-Burton Act*, which provides for sanctions against countries that do business in Cuba, and the *Iran-Libya Sanctions Act*, which imposes sanctions on countries that invest in Iran or Libya. These unilateralist U.S. policies, naturally, have been resisted by European states and Canada. In 2001, the new Bush Administration declined to participate in such international efforts as a treaty on global warming (see

---

[46] Lloyd A. Free and Hadley Cantril, *The Political Beliefs of Americans* (Piscataway, NJ: Rutgers UP, 1967).

[47] Michael E. Brown, Owen R. Cote, Jr., Sean M. Lynn-Jones, and Steven E. Miller, eds., *America's Strategic Choices*, rev. ed. (Cambridge, MA: MIT P, 2000). Richard N. Haass, *The Reluctant Sheriff: The United States after the Cold War* (Washington, DC: Brookings, 1997). John G. Ruggie, *Winning the Peace* (NY: Columbia UP, 1996). Kenneth A. Oye, Robert J. Lieber, and Donald Rothchild, eds., *Eagle in a New World: American Grand Strategy in the Post–Cold War Era* (NY: HarperCollins, 1992).

[48] Steven Kull and I. M. Destler, *Misreading the Public: The Myth of a New Isolationism* (Washington, DC: Brookings, 1999).

pp. 495–497), a conference on racism, and the International Criminal Court (see p. 283). The international community's united front against terrorism pushed these disputes to the back burner for a time, but disagreements over the 2003 Iraq War saw them re-emerge.

THE ECONOMIC VARIANT OF REALISM

This chapter has focused on realist analyses of questions of international security. Indeed, this is where realism seems to exhibit its greatest strength. But realism also offers an analysis of economic issues. **Mercantilism** (or economic nationalism) is the economic variant of realism. Mercantilism shares with realism most of its central assumptions: states are the most important actors in IR, and they act rationally in the pursuit of power in an anarchic international system. For mercantilists, the economy should always be subservient to politics, and economic relations are important only insofar as they contribute to the wealth (and therefore power) of the state. Mercantilists thus are concerned about trading relations with other states: increasing interdependence between states can produce vulnerabilities and make one country dependent on another for important goods. Mercantilists tend to recommend policies of self-sufficiency over interdependence.[49] Mercantilism will be discussed more fully in Chapter 8.

> **mercantilism** An economic theory and a political ideology opposed to free trade; it shares with *realism* the belief that each state must protect its own interests without seeking mutual gains through international organizations. See also *liberalism*.

This chapter has focused on realism and some of its concerns, such as the interests of states, distribution of power among states, and bargaining between states. Consistent with the realist framework, the chapter has treated states as unitary actors, much as one would analyze the interactions of individual people. The actions of state leaders have been treated as more or less rational in terms of pursuing definable interests through coherent bargaining strategies.

But realism is not the only way to frame the major issues of international security. Chapter 3 re-examines these themes, from liberal and critical theoretical perspectives.

Thinking Critically

1. Using Table 1.3 on pp. 18–19 (with GDP as a measure of power) and the maps at the back of the book, pick a state and speculate about what coalition of nearby states might form with sufficient power to oppose the state if it became aggressive.

2. Choose a recent international event and list the power capabilities that participants used as leverage in the episode. Which capabilities were effective, and which were not? Why?

3. Given the distinction between zero-sum and non-zero-sum games, can you think of a current international situation that is a zero-sum conflict? One that is non-zero-sum?

4. If you were the leader of a small state in Africa, bargaining with a great power about an issue where your interests diverged, what leverage and strategies could you bring into play to improve the outcome for your state?

5. Given recent changes in international power distribution and the end of the Cold War order, where do you think the threats to peace will come from in the future? Through what means could states respond to those threats?

6. The modern international system came into being at a time when agrarian societies relied primarily on farmland to create wealth. Now that most wealth is no longer created through farming, is the territorial nature of states obsolete? How might the diminishing economic value of territory change the ways in which states interact?

---

[49] Robert Gilpin, *Global Political Economy: Understanding the International Economic Order* (Princeton, NJ: Princeton UP, 2001).

Chapter Summary

- Realism explains international relations in terms of power.

- Realists and idealists differ in their assumptions about human nature, international order, and the potential for peace.

- Power can be conceptualized as influence or as capabilities that can create influence.

- The most important single indicator of a state's power is its GDP.

- Short-term power capabilities depend on long-term resources, both tangible and intangible.

- Realists consider military force the most important power capability.

- International affairs can be seen as a series of bargaining interactions in which states use power capabilities as leverage to influence the outcomes.

- Bargaining outcomes depend not only on raw power but also on strategies and luck.

- Reciprocity can be an effective strategy for reaching cooperation in ongoing relationships but carries a danger of turning into runaway hostility or arms races.

- Rational-actor approaches treat states as though they were individuals acting to maximize their own interests. These simplifications are debatable but allow realists to develop concise and general models and explanations.

- Game theory draws insights from simplified models of bargaining situations.

- International anarchy—the absence of world government—means that each state is a sovereign and autonomous actor pursuing its own national interests.

- The international system traditionally places great emphasis on the sovereignty of states, their right to control affairs in their own territory, and their responsibility to respect internationally recognized borders.

- Seven great powers account for half of the world's GDP as well as the great majority of military forces and other power capabilities.

- Power transition theory says that wars often result from shifts in relative power distribution in the international system.

- Hegemony—the predominance of one state in the international system—can help provide stability and peace in international relations, but with some drawbacks.

- The economic variant of realism, mercantilism, shares many of realism's central assumptions (in particular about primacy of states, power and anarchy) and applies them to economic issues.

- Mercantilists tend to suggest policies of economic nationalism.

Key Terms

realism   54
idealism   54
power   56
geopolitics   60
bargaining   61
negotiation   62
reciprocity   65
deterrence   66
compellence   66
arms race   66
rational actors   67
national interest   67
cost-benefit analysis   68

game theory   69
zero-sum games   69
anarchy   71
norms (of behaviour)   72
sovereignty   72
security dilemma   74
balance of power   74
great powers   76
middle powers   78
neorealism   79
multipolar system   79
hegemony   80
mercantilism   83

Weblinks

In addition to reading this text, you can read many scholarly journals of international relations. You should become familiar with some of these journals, either online or through your library. These links bring you to the home page of a number of relevant journals, but your university library may also have electronic subscriptions to some or all of these (which would give you access to all of the articles in the journal), so you should also ask at your library or explore your library's website.

Foreign Affairs:
http://www.foreignaffairs.org

International Journal of the Canadian Institute of International Affairs:
http://www.ciia.org/ij.htm

International Security Program at the Belfer Center for Science and International Affairs:
http://bcsia.ksg.harvard.edu/publications.cfm?program=ISP

International Studies Quarterly:
http://www.isq.unt.edu

Journal of Military and Strategic Studies:
http://www.jmss.org

Bahraini voter in 2003 in first elections since 1975.

ALTERNATIVES TO REALISM

Although realism has tended to dominate the study of international relations, especially in the U.S., it is not the only approach to the study of IR. Many alternatives exist, some with very different visions of what the world looks like, how the world should be studied, and what the purpose of theory is. The many different alternative theories that exist will be grouped here under two paradigms: liberal pluralism and critical theory.

Realism is the most *homogeneous* of the three paradigms. This does not mean that there is no debate among realists as they elaborate upon their theory and its application to particular issues or events. There is, and it is sometimes quite heated debate. But realists tend to identify as either realist or neorealist (or the economic variant, mercantilist), and most realists share the same basic assumptions of realism regarding the primacy of the state, the pursuit of power, and the anarchy of international relations.

Liberal pluralists are less homogeneous than realists. They may self-identify using a number of terms, such as liberal, pluralist, liberal pluralist, liberal internationalist, neoliberal, peace researcher, economic liberal, and others. Depending on what elements of liberalism are emphasized, there are also more potential contradictions between some liberals. For example, on questions of the environment, an economic liberal might argue that market forces should determine responses to industrial pollutants. If an industry is allowed to become profitable, its own research and entrepreneurship will eventually develop and implement pollution controls. A neoliberal internationalist, by contrast, would have more faith in establishing rules and regulations through international institutions. They would promote accords and other mechanisms to be administered through organizations like the UN in an effort to address industrial pollutants sooner rather than later. The theories and theorists grouped within the liberal-pluralist paradigm do share a number of assumptions, but this paradigm contains a more diverse group of theories than that found within realism.

Critical theory is the most *heterogeneous* paradigm of the three. It includes Marxists, Critical Theorists, Gramscian theorists, dependency theorists, world system theorists, neo-Marxists, socialists, feminists, poststructuralists, anti-racist scholars, postmodernists, queer theorists, postcolonial scholars, and others. Critical theorists do not share a view of what the world looks like so much as a disposition toward it. Each asks, "How did the world come about, and whose interests does it serve?" Many focus on the way in which the more mainstream approaches to IR preclude asking certain questions, and direct us to a view of the world that is taken as "given" or "natural." Most emphasize in one way or another the relations of inequality that characterize the world and our study of it (though they may not all use terms like "inequality"). Moreover, they often disagree about which inequalities matter the most. Orthodox Marxists, for example, may resist theories that draw attention away from a class analysis of contemporary capitalism and global politics, while anti-racist and feminist scholars may balk at a Marxist's insistence that class form the starting point for analysis. Many of the theorists within this paradigm also, of course, attempt to build bridges between these different forms of analysis, and try to understand the various ways relations of inequality, in all its guises, are mutually sustaining.[1]

LIBERAL PLURALISM

In the broadest terms, liberal pluralism differs from realism in a number of important respects. It suggests that while states are important actors in IR, there are also many more actors that operate in the global system. These include individuals, institutions, multinational corporations, NGOs, and social movements. Liberals also emphasize the cooperative features of global interaction over the conflictual. Finally, liberals are interested in producing policy-relevant advice, but may provide that advice to these many other actors, not simply states alone.

Traditional Liberal Critiques

Since the time of Mo Ti and Sun Tzu in ancient China, idealism (an early precursor to liberal pluralism) has provided a counterpoint to realism. This long tradition of idealism in IR holds that morality, law, and international organization can form the basis for relations among states; human nature is not evil; peaceful and cooperative relations among states are possible; and states can operate as a community rather than merely as autonomous self-interested agents.[2]

Traditionally, liberals have offered four major lines of criticism against thee key assumptions of realism. First, the assumption of international *anarchy* is no more than a partial truth. Of course, international interactions are structured by power relations, by

---

[1] For a more detailed review of theoretical approaches in IR, see Jill Steans and Lloyd Pettiford, *International Relations: Perspectives and Themes* (UK: Pearson Education, 2001). Scott Burchill, Richard Devetak, Andrew Linklater, Matthew Paterson, Christian Reus-Smit, and Jacqui True, eds., *Theories of International Relations* (NY: Palgrave, 2001).

[2] Terry Nardin, and David R. Mapel, eds., *Traditions of International Ethics* (NY: Cambridge UP, 1992). David Long and Peter Wilson, eds., *Thinkers of the Twenty Years' Crisis: Inter-War Idealism Reassessed* (NY: Oxford UP, 1995).

the distribution of power in the international system—whether a predominant power in the system (hegemony) or a multipolar "concert" of great powers. Realists can accept that anarchy includes international order structured by power. But order also evolves through norms and institutions based on reciprocity and cooperation, even on law. Realists have a harder time reconciling the ever-expanding scope of international interdependence and cooperation with the assumptions of anarchy, of the inevitability of security dilemmas, and of the primacy of military leverage.

Second, liberals criticize the notion of states as *unitary actors*, each with a single set of coherent interests. As the study of foreign policy reveals (Chapter 4), state actions often do not reflect a single individual set of preferences. Rather, state behaviour is shaped by internal bargaining among and within bureaucracies, interest groups, and other actors with divergent goals and interests. Nonstate actors—individuals, NGOs, IGOs, and ethnic groups, among others—further confound the idea that IR can be reduced to the interactions of a small number of well-defined state actors pursuing national interests.

Third, the concept of *rationality* is problematic. If states are single actors with coherent interests, they often seem to do a poor job in maximizing those interests. Of course, it is hard to tell from an actor's unexpected behaviour whether the actor was irrational or merely pursued a goal, interest, or value that *we* would not consider normal or productive. And the evident importance in ethnic conflicts of emotions such as hatred (see Chapter 5) also calls into question the more simplistic realist interpretations of such conflicts as rational bargaining moves by the participating actors.

Finally, *military force* as a form of leverage does not seem nearly as all-important as realism implies. It is a costly way to influence other actors (see Chapter 6), as compared with diplomacy, conflict resolution, peacekeeping, and other nonmilitary means. International organizations, laws, and norms create stable contexts for bargaining, making nonmilitary leverage increasingly effective as international organization develops (see Chapter 7). This criticism of realism applies even more to international political economy (Chapters 8 through 13) than to security affairs.

In addition to these general criticisms of realism, some liberals have argued that changes in the way IR works have made realist assumptions obsolete. Realism may once have been "realistic," when European kings and queens played war and traded territories as property. But states are now interconnected, a reality contradicting the assumptions of autonomy and sovereignty. Borders are becoming fluid, making territorial integrity increasingly untenable. The evolution of norms regarding the use of force has substantially changed the ways in which military force contributes to international power. This line of argument has been prominent in liberal interdependence approaches to IR since the 1970s.

What Is Rationality?

At the core of the liberal approach is a concept of *rationality* that differs sharply from the realist concept. Realists see rationality as an individual actor's attempt to maximize its own short-term interests. Liberals believe that rational actors are capable of forgoing short-term individual interests in order to further the long-term well-being of a community to which they belong. Such actions are rational because they contribute to the actor's individual well-being, indirectly or over the long term. The German philosopher Immanuel Kant argued, 200 years ago, that states, although autonomous, could join a worldwide federation like today's UN and respect its principles even at the cost of forgoing certain short-term individual gains. To Kant, international cooperation was a more rational option for states than resorting to war. Thus, in realist conceptions of rationality, war and violence appear rational (because they often advance short-term state interests), but liberals tend to see war and violence as irrational deviations that result from defective reasoning and that harm the (collective, long-term) well-being of states.[3]

This disagreement is particularly acute when it comes to nuclear weapons.[4] Liberals find it absurd to spend money building weapons that could destroy the world or to claim (as realists do) that there is a rational logic behind their deployment. Furthermore, many realists argue that nuclear deterrence will *prevent* the world from being destroyed— because the state actors owning nuclear weapons are rational. Liberals, however, because they see war as a breakdown in rationality, fear that nuclear weapons would be used, with tragic consequences.

Liberal and realist approaches to *power* reflect the distinction between rationality as seeking narrow self-interest and rationality as seeking to share in long-term collective benefits. Realists define power as the ability to get another actor to do something—or as the capabilities required to so influence an actor (see pp. 56–57). This is power *over* others—a concept that some liberals con-

HAPPY FAMILY
Liberals emphasize the potential for rivalries to evolve into cooperative relationships as states recognize that achieving mutual benefits is most cost-effective in the long run. The cooperation between U.S. and Soviet/Russian space programs starting in the 1960s is an example. Here, U.S. shuttle astronaut greets commander of Russian space station Mir, 1997.

sider inherently oppressive, rooted in a need to control or dominate other people. This is the power of the bully, to make others comply. But are bullies really the most powerful actors? Do they achieve the best outcomes? And do we really live in an international world populated by bullies?

An alternative definition of power is based not on power over others but on power to accomplish desirable ends. This kind of power often derives from capitalizing on common interests rather than gaining an edge in bargaining over conflicting interests. Such empowerment often entails the formation of coalitions and partnerships, or the mobilization of the resources of multiple actors for a common purpose. For many liberals, this is a truer, more useful concept of power.

Neoliberalism

In the 1980s, a new liberal critique of realism emerged. The approach stressed the importance of international institutions in reducing the inherent conflict that realists assume in an international system. The reasoning is based on the core liberal idea that seeking long-

---

[3] Norman Angell, *The Foundations of International Polity* (London: Heinemann, 1914).

[4] Scott D. Sagan and Kenneth N. Waltz, *The Spread of Nuclear Weapons: A Debate* (NY: Norton, 1995). Robert Jay Lifton and Richard Falk, *Indefensible Weapons: The Political and Psychological Case against Nuclearism* (NY: Basic, 1982).

neoliberalism Shorthand for "neoliberal institutionalism," an approach that stresses the importance of international institutions in reducing the inherent conflict that realists assume in an international system; the reasoning is based on the core liberal idea that seeking long-term mutual gains is often more rational than maximizing individual short-term gains. See also *liberalism*.

term mutual gains is often more rational than maximizing individual short-term gains. The approach became known as "neoliberal institutionalism" or **neoliberalism** for short.

The neoliberal approach differs from earlier liberal approaches in that it concedes to realism several important assumptions—among them, that states are unitary actors rationally pursuing their self-interests. Neoliberals say to realists, "Even if we grant your assumptions about the nature of states and their motives, your pessimistic conclusions do not follow." States achieve cooperation fairly often because it is in their interest to do so, and they can learn to use institutions to ease the pursuit of mutual gains and the reduction of possibilities for cheating or taking advantage of another state.

Despite the many sources of conflict in IR, states do cooperate most of the time. Neoliberal scholars ask how this is possible in an anarchic world.[5] They try to show that even in a world of unitary rational states the neorealists' pessimism about international cooperation is not valid. States can create mutual rules, expectations, and institutions to promote behaviour that enhances (or at least doesn't destroy) the possibilities for mutual gain.

Neoliberals use the *Prisoner's Dilemma (PD)* game (see pp. 69–71) to illustrate their argument that cooperation is possible. Each actor can gain by individually defecting, but both lose when both defect. The narrow, self-serving behaviour of each player leads to a bad outcome for both, one they could have improved by cooperation. Similarly, in IR states often have a mix of conflicting interests and mutual interests. The dilemma can be resolved if the game is played over and over again—an accurate model of IR, where states deal with each other in repeated interactions.

tit for tat A strategy of strict reciprocity (matching the other player's response) after an initial cooperative move; it can bring about mutual cooperation in a repeated Prisoner's Dilemma game, since it ensures that defection will not pay.

A strategy of strict reciprocity after an initial cooperative move (nicknamed **tit for tat**) can bring about mutual cooperation in a repeated PD game, because the other player must conclude that any defection will merely provoke a like defection in response.[6] The strategy parallels just war doctrine (see pp. 287–288), which calls for states never to initiate war but to use war in response to war. In international trade, such a strategy calls for opening one's markets but selectively closing them in response to another state's closing its markets (see pp. 319–320).

Reciprocity is an important principle in IR that helps international cooperation emerge despite the absence of central authority. Through reciprocity, not a world government, norms and rules are enforced. In international security, reciprocity underlies the gradual improvement of relations sought by arms control agreements and peacekeeping missions. In international political economy (IPE), where cooperation can create great benefits through trade, the threat to restrict trade in retaliation for unfair practices is a strong incentive to comply with rules and norms.

Although reciprocity is an important norm, it is just one among many norms that mediate states' interactions. For example, diplomatic practices and participation in international organizations (IOs) are both strongly governed by shared expectations about the

---

[5] David A. Baldwin, ed., *Neorealism and Neoliberalism: The Contemporary Debate* (NY: Columbia UP, 1993). Charles W. Kegley, Jr., ed., *Controversies in International Relations Theory: Realism and the Neoliberal Challenge* (NY: St. Martin's, 1995). Joseph S. Nye, Jr., rev. of Neorealism and Neoliberalism, *World Politics* 40.2 (1988): 235–51. John Gerard Ruggie, ed., *Multilateralism Matters: The Theory and Praxis of an Institutional Forum* (NY: Columbia UP, 1993). Helen Milner, rev. of *International Theories of Cooperation among Nations: Strengths and Weaknesses*, *World Politics* 44.3 (1992): 466–94. Kenneth A. Oye, ed., *Cooperation under Anarchy* (Princeton, NJ: Princeton UP, 1986).

[6] Robert Axelrod, *The Evolution of Cooperation* (NY: Basic, 1984). Robert Axelrod and Robert O. Keohane, "Achieving Cooperation under Anarchy: Strategies and Institutions," *Cooperation under Anarchy*, ed. Oye (see previous footnote) 226–54. Robert Axelrod, *The Complexity of Cooperation: Agent-Based Models of Competition and Collaboration* (Princeton, NJ: Princeton UP, 1997).

rules of correct behaviour. As dilemmas such as the Prisoner's Dilemma crop up in IR, states rely on a context of rules, norms, habits, and institutions that make it rational for all sides to avoid the self-defeating outcomes that would result from pursuing narrow, short-term self-interest. Neoliberals study historical and contemporary cases in IR to see how institutions and norms affected the possibilities for overcoming dilemmas and achieving international cooperation. Thus, for neoliberals the emergence of international institutions is key to understanding how states achieve a superior type of rationality that includes long-term self-interest and not just immediate self-interest.

Collective Goods

The problem of the security dilemma (p. 74), which helps explain costly arms races, is an example of a PD-like dilemma in international security. Such examples are even more common in IPE, where protectionism and other forms of economic nationalism attempt to increase national wealth (relative to other states), at some cost to global wealth (see Chapter 8). The overall efficiency of the world economy is reduced, but the distribution of gains from trade shifts toward one's own state or groups within it. The problem is that if other states take similar actions, global efficiency decreases and the distribution of benefits remains about the same. So all states end up worse off than they could be.

All these situations are examples of the **collective goods problem.** A collective good is a tangible or intangible good, created by members of a group, that is available to all group members, regardless of their individual contributions. As in the security dilemma or Prisoner's Dilemma, participants can gain by lowering their own contribution to the collective good, but if too many participants do so the good cannot be provided.

For example, it costs less to drive a polluting car than to pay for emission controls, and the air that the car owner breathes is hardly affected by his or her own car. The air quality is a collective good. If too many car owners pollute, all will breathe dirty air. But if just a few pollute, they will breathe fairly clean air; the few who pollute are **free riders,** because they benefit from someone else's provision of the collective good. These important concepts in IPE come up again in later chapters, especially in discussions of the global environment (Chapter 11) and of international organization and law (Chapter 7).

Within domestic society, many collective goods problems are solved by governments, which enforce rules for the common good. Governments can punish free riders who are tempted to avoid contributing. Governments can pass laws against polluting cars or force citizens to pay taxes to support collective goods such as national defence, highways, or schools. In the anarchic international system, the absence of central government sharpens the difficulties created by collective goods. It is difficult to maintain multilateral cooperation when each government is tempted by its own possibility of free riding.

In general, collective goods are easier to provide in small groups than in large ones.[7] In a small group, the defection (free riding) of one member is harder to conceal, has a greater impact on the overall collective good, and is easier to punish. The advantage of small groups helps explain the importance of the great-power system in international security affairs. And it is one reason why the G8 (Group of Eight) industrialized countries have frequent meetings to try to coordinate their economic policies, instead of relying only on groups such as the World Bank or WTO (each of which has more than a hundred member states). Small groups do not solve the problem entirely, however. Whether in small groups or large, the world's states lack a government to enforce contributions to collective goods; states must look elsewhere.

collective goods problem
A collective good is a tangible or intangible good, created by the members of a group, that is available to all group members regardless of their individual contributions; participants can gain by lowering their own contribution to the collective good, yet if too many participants do so, the good cannot be provided.

free riders Those who benefit from someone else's provision of a collective good without paying their share of costs.

---

[7] Mancur Olson, *The Logic of Collective Action* (1965; Cambridge, MA: Harvard UP, 1971).

International Regimes

Because of the contradictory interpretations that parties to a conflict usually have, it is difficult to resolve such conflicts without a third party to arbitrate or an overall framework to set common expectations for all parties. These considerations underlie the creation of IOs in the international security field (see Chapter 7). Norms of behaviour are at least as important in international economics as in international security because of the great gains to be realized from maintaining a stable framework for smoothly carrying on large economic transactions.

international regime A set of rules, norms, and procedures around which the expectations of actors converge in a certain international issue area (such as oceans or monetary policy).

An **international regime** is a set of rules, norms, and procedures around which the expectations of actors converge in a certain issue area (whether arms control, international trade, or Antarctic exploration).[8] The convergence of expectations means that participants in the international system have similar ideas about what rules will govern their mutual participation: each expects to play by the same rules. (This meaning of regime is not the same as that referring to the domestic governments of states, especially governments considered illegitimate or in power for only a short time.)

Regimes can help solve collective goods problems by increasing transparency—because everyone knows what everyone is doing, cheating is more costly. The current revolution in information technologies is strengthening regimes particularly in this aspect. Also, with better international communication, states can identify conflicts and negotiate solutions through regimes more effectively.

Regimes are an important and widespread phenomenon in IR. Several will be discussed in the remaining chapters on international security. For example, the Missile Technology Control Regime (see p. 229) is a set of rules and expectations governing the international trade in missiles. In IPE, regimes are even more central. The frameworks within which states carry on trade-monetary relations, communications, and environmental protection policies are key to realizing the benefits of mutual cooperation in these areas.

IR scholars conceive of regimes in several different ways, and the concept has been criticized as too vague. But the most common conception of regimes combines elements of realism and liberalism. States are considered the important actors, and states are seen as autonomous units maximizing their own interests in an anarchic context. Regimes do not play a role in issues where states can realize their interests directly through unilateral applications of leverage. Rather, regimes come into existence to overcome collective goods dilemmas by coordinating the behaviours of individual states. Although states continue to seek their own interests, they create frameworks to coordinate their actions with those of other states if and when such coordination is necessary to realize self-interest (that is, in collective goods dilemmas). Thus, regimes help make cooperation possible even within an international system based on anarchy—exactly the point neoliberals focus on.

Regimes do not substitute for the basic calculations of costs and benefits by states; they just open up new possibilities with more favourable benefit-cost ratios. Regimes do not constrain states, except in a very narrow and short-term sense. Rather they facilitate and empower national governments faced with issues where collective goods problems would otherwise prevent governments from achieving their ends. Regimes can be seen as *intervening variables* between the basic causal forces at work in IR—for realists, the relative power of state actors—and the outcomes such as international cooperation (or lack thereof).

---

[8] Stephen D. Krasner, ed., *International Regimes* (Ithaca, NY: Cornell UP, 1983). Charles Lipson, "Why Are Some International Agreements Informal?" *International Organization* 45.4 (1991): 495–538. Andreas Hasenclever, Peter Mayer, and Volker Rittberger, *Theories of International Regimes* (NY: Cambridge UP, 1997).

Regimes do not negate the effects of power: more often they codify and normalize existing power relations. For example, the ballistic missile regime just mentioned (see p. 229) protects the status quo in which only a few states have such missiles. If the regime works, it will keep less-powerful states from gaining leverage they could use against more-powerful states.

Hegemonic Stability

Since regimes depend on state power for their enforcement, some IR scholars argue that regimes are most effective when power in the international system is most concentrated—

> ## The Information Revolution
> ## Empowering Regimes?
>
> Liberal international regimes codify norms and help solve collective goods problems. "Transparency" reduces cheating or free riding (such as on a treaty, alliance, or cartel) because all states know what the others are doing. As evolving information technologies "illuminate" the world, will international regimes be strengthened and work better, or will information technologies become primarily an instrument of power in states' hands, as realists might argue?
>
> **To explore this question, go to www.pearsoned.ca/goldstein.**

when there is a hegemon to keep order (see "Hegemony" on pp. 80–83). This theory is known as **hegemonic stability theory.**[9] When one state's power is predominant, it can enforce rules and norms unilaterally, avoiding the collective goods problem. In particular, hegemons can maintain global free trade and promote world economic growth, in this view.

hegemonic stability theory
The argument that regimes are most effective when power in the international system is most concentrated. See also *hegemony*.

This theory attributes the peace and prosperity of the decades after World War II to U.S. hegemony, which created and maintained a global framework of economic relations supporting relatively stable and free international trade, as well as a security framework that prevented great-power wars. By contrast, the Great Depression of the 1930s and the outbreak of World War II have been attributed to the power vacuum in the international system at that time—Britain was no longer able to act as hegemon, and the United States was unwilling to begin doing so.[10]

Why should a hegemon care about enforcing rules for the international economy that are in the common good? According to hegemonic stability theory, a hegemon has the same interests as the common good of all states. Hegemons as the largest international traders have an inherent interest in the promotion of integrated world markets (where the hegemons will tend to dominate). As the most advanced state in productivity and technology, a hegemon does not fear competition from industries in other states; it fears only that its own superior goods will be excluded from competing in other states. Thus hegemons favour free trade and use their power to achieve free trade. Hegemony, then, provides both the ability and the motivation to maintain regimes that provide a stable political framework for free international trade, according to hegemonic stability theory. This theory is not, however, accepted by all IR scholars.[11]

---

[9] Robert O. Keohane, "The Theory of Hegemonic Stability and Change in International Economic Regimes, 1967–1977," *Change in the International System*, ed. Ole R. Holsti, R. M. Siverson, and A. L. George (Boulder, CO: Westview, 1980). Timothy J. McKeown, "Hegemonic Stability Theory and 19th Century Tariff Levels in Europe," *International Organization* 37.1 (1983): 73–91.

[10] Charles P. Kindleberger, *The World in Depression, 1929–1939* (Berkeley: U California P, 1973). David A. Lake, *Power, Protection, and Free Trade: International Sources of U.S. Commercial Strategy, 1887–1939* (Ithaca, NY: Cornell UP, 1988).

[11] Lloyd Gruber, *Ruling the World: Power Politics and the Rise of Supranational Institutions* (Princeton, NJ: Princeton UP, 2000). Joanne Gowa, "Rational Hegemons, Excludable Goods, and Small Groups: An Epitaph for Hegemonic Stability Theory?" *World Politics* 41.3 (1989): 307–24. Duncan Snidal, "The Limits of Hegemonic Stability Theory," *International Organization* 39.4 (1985): 580–614.

The Changing World Order
Hegemony, Stability, and the Study of IR

Most observers of international relations would acknowledge that the post–September 11 world is dominated by U.S. power more than at any previous time, and the United States appears much more willing to use its power internationally than it has in recent years. The international system has become unipolar.

For liberals and realists who have developed the idea of hegemonic stability theory, the rise of a strong hegemonic power will increase stability and peace in the world order. This seemed to be true after World War II when the United States was similarly dominant, and during the nineteenth century when Britain dominated. Of course, the prospect that a self-interested United States could impose its will on others without restraint makes other great powers nervous. But the theory is that the United States as a great trading power has a strong interest in a stable and peaceful international system where participants play by the rules. Ultimately, U.S. promotion of such a world order is also in other countries' interests. If this prediction holds true, the peaceful trends of the 1990s (see pp. 46–47) would accelerate in the 2000s.

Critical theorists, and some liberals, would dispute this view and argue instead that the increasing power of the United States has led to a very limited understanding of world politics and a tendency to see the world through a distinctly U.S. lens. We see this in both the dominant approach to the study of IR and the foreign policies being adopted by the U.S. and its allies. Such views privilege militarized responses to current events and seek to abandon (whenever they are not useful) the international institutions that were created in the post–World War II period. These responses, according to this more critical view, will only result in more rather than less violence.*

These are two decidedly different views of the changing world order. One sees U.S. predominance as something that will lead to greater stability and order, the other that it will result instead in more violence. Think through a number of contemporary events taking place in international relations. Which view do they support?

* Steve Smith, "The United States and the Discipline of International Relations: 'Hegemonic Country, Hegemonic Discipline,' " *International Studies Review* 4.2 (2002): 67–85.

What happens to regimes when hegemons lose power and decline? Regimes do not always decline with the power of hegemons that created them. Rather, they may take on a life of their own. Although hegemony may be crucial in *establishing* regimes, it is not necessary for *maintaining* them.[12] Once actors' expectations converge around the rules embodied in a regime, the actors realize that the regime serves their own interests. Working through the regime becomes a habit, and national leaders may not give serious consideration to breaking out of the established rules.

This persistence of regimes was demonstrated in the 1970s, when U.S. power declined following the decades of U.S. hegemony since 1945. Diminished U.S. power was evident in the loss of the Vietnam War, the rise of OPEC, and the malaise of the U.S. economy. Some IR scholars expected that the entire framework of international trade and monetary relations established after World War II would collapse once the United States was no longer able to enforce the rules of that regime. But that did not happen. The international economic regimes adjusted somewhat and survived.

In part, that survival is attributable to the embedding of regimes in permanent *institutions* such as the UN, NATO, and the International Monetary Fund. As the rules of the game persist over time and become habitual, institutions develop around them. These institutions become the tangible manifestation of shared expectations as well as the

---

[12] Robert O. Keohane, *After Hegemony: Cooperation and Discord in the World Political Economy* (Ithaca, NY: Princeton UP, 1984). Joanne Gowa, "Bipolarity, Multipolarity, and Free Trade," *American Political Science Review* 83.4 (1989): 1227–44.

machinery for coordinating international actions based on those expectations. In international security affairs, the UN, NATO and other IOs provide a stable framework for resolving disputes (Chapter 7). IPE is even more institutionalized, again because of the heavier volume of activity and the wealth that can be realized from cooperation.[13]

Economic Liberalism

The economic variant of liberal pluralism is called *economic liberalism*. Economic liberals are interested in the institutions and regimes that establish the rules of the game in IPE (such as the IMF, World Bank, and World Trade Organization), but economic liberals are most interested in the institution of the market. For economic liberals (unlike mercantilists, discussed in Chapter 2 and Chapter 8), the state should allow markets to function freely. In other words, states should seek to open up trading relations and financial markets rather than restrict them to serve political ends. For economic liberals, when institutions like the IMF and WTO seek to accomplish these ends (and by most accounts, they do), they are important elements of the global political economy. But when institutions interfere with the market, they detract from growth and efficiency and can even impact on the peaceful relations between states. The economic liberal argument will be discussed in greater detail in Chapter 8.

Collective Security

A major application of liberal conceptions of international security affairs is the concept of **collective security**—the formation of a broad alliance of most major actors in an international system for the purpose of jointly opposing aggression by any actor. The rationale for this approach was laid out by Immanuel Kant. Since past treaties ending great-power wars had never lasted permanently, Kant proposed a federation (league) of the world's states. Through such a federation, Kant proposed, the majority of states could unite to punish any one state that committed aggression. This union would safeguard the collective interests of all the nations together against the narrow self-interest of one nation that might otherwise profit from aggression. The federation would also protect the self-determination of small nations that all too easily became pawns in great-power games.[14]

After the horrors of World War I, a *League of Nations* was actually formed. But it was flawed in two ways. Its membership did not include all the great powers (nor the most powerful one, the United States). And its members proved unwilling to bear the costs of collective action to oppose aggression when it did occur in the 1930s, starting with Japan and Italy). After World War II, the United Nations was created as the League's successor to promote collective security (see Chapter 7).

Several regional IGOs also currently perform collective security functions (deterring aggression) as well as economic and cultural ones. In Latin America and the United States, there is the *Organization of American States (OAS)*. In the Middle East (including North Africa), there is the *Arab League*. In Africa (also including North Africa), there is the *Organization of African Unity (OAU)*.

> **collective security** The formation of a broad alliance of most major actors in an international system for the purpose of jointly opposing aggression by any actor; sometimes seen as presupposing the existence of a universal organization (such as the United Nations) to which both the aggressor and its opponents belong. See also *League of Nations*.

---

[13] Paul Taylor and A. J. R. Groom, eds., *International Institutions at Work* (NY: St. Martin's, 1988). John Gerard Ruggie, ed., *Multiculturalism Matters: The Theory and Praxis of an Institutional Form* (see footnote 5 in this chapter). Robert O. Keohane, "International Institutions: Two Approaches," *International Studies Quarterly* 32.4 (1988): 379–96.

[14] Immanuel Kant, *Perpetual Peace*, ed. Lewis White Beck (1795; Indianapolis: Bobbs-Merrill, 1957).

The success of collective security depends on two points. First, the members must keep their alliance commitments to the group. When a powerful state commits aggression against a weaker one, it often is not in the immediate interest of other powerful states to go to war over the issue. It can be very costly to suppress a determined aggressor.

A second requisite for collective security is that enough members must agree on what constitutes aggression. In international relations, it is often a hotly debated point whether a state has acted aggressively or defensively. The UN Security Council is structured so that aggression is defined by what all 5 permanent members, in addition to at least 4 of the other 10 members, can agree on (see "The Security Council" on pp. 256–258). But this collective security system does not work against aggression by a great power. When the Soviet Union invaded Afghanistan, or the United States mined the harbours of Nicaragua, or France blew up the Greenpeace ship *Rainbow Warrior*, the UN could do nothing—because those states can veto Security Council resolutions.[15]

Both requirements were met in the case of Kuwait in 1990–1991. The aggressor, Iraq, was a member of the UN, as was the victim, Kuwait. It was the first time since the founding of the UN that one member had invaded, occupied, and annexed another member—attempting to erase it as a sovereign state. The invasion was so blatant a violation of Kuwaiti sovereignty and territorial integrity that the Security Council had little trouble labelling it aggression. The aggression was flagrant, the rules of world order were being redefined as the Cold War ended, and of course the West's oil supply was threatened. In a series of resolutions, the Council condemned Iraq, applied mandatory economic sanctions (requiring all UN members to stop trading with Iraq), and ultimately authorized the use of force by a multinational coalition. Collective security worked in the Iraqi case because the conquest of Kuwait brought all the great powers together and because they were willing to bear the costs of confronting Iraq. (China abstained on the resolution authorizing force and did not contribute to the coalition, but it did not veto the resolution.)

In 2002–2003, the United States could not convince the UN that collective security was being threatened by Iraq. The U.S. claimed that Iraq possessed weapons of mass destruction that it planned to use against the U.S. or its allies. The Security Council debated Iraq's failure to abide by its promise to disclose all of its weapons of mass destruction. Iraq claimed they had all been destroyed after the Gulf War, but the U.S. insisted Iraq retained significant stockpiles. In early 2003, a resolution authorizing military force was withdrawn after France promised to veto it; Germany, Russia, and China had also all strongly opposed the resolution and a war against Iraq. When the UN did not act, the U.S. formed a "Coalition of the Willing" that included the United Kingdom and Australia (but not Canada), and invaded Iraq. Saddam Hussein's regime was overthrown, but no weapons of mass destruction were ever found (thus confirming the UN's reluctance to support armed intervention in the name of collective security).

The concept of collective security has been broadened in recent years. Toward the end of the Cold War, the liberal premises of international community and mutual state interests provided the foundations for a new idea called *common security* (or "mutual security"), the notion that because the security of all states, enemies as well as friends, is interdependent, the insecurity of one state makes all states less secure.[16] A local dispute

[15] Joseph Lepgold and Thomas G. Weiss, eds., *Collective Conflict Management and Changing World Politics* (Albany: SUNY P, 1998).

[16] Palme Commission [Independent Commission on Disarmament and Security Issues], *Common Security: A Programme for Disarmament* (London: Pan, 1982). Emma Rothschild, "What Is Security?" *Daedalus* 124.3 (1995): 53–98. Barry Buzan, Ole Waever, and Jaap de Wilde, *Security: A New Framework for Analysis* (Boulder, CO: Rienner, 1997).

in one part of the world can threaten another part; economic and ethnic rivalries can spill over into violent conflicts; the costs of preparing for war can bankrupt great powers even in peacetime. This new reality—if state leaders recognized it—would resolve the security dilemma (see p. 74), because a state's own security interests would be (indirectly) *diminished* if it threatened another state.

The theory and practice of common security were promoted during the late 1980s by Soviet President Gorbachev, who won the Nobel peace prize for his accomplishments (although he was swept from office when the Soviet Union collapsed). Gorbachev argued that as states became more closely connected economically and culturally, it was futile and wasteful to arm against each other, especially with nuclear weapons.

Another elaboration of security was developed by Canadian policy-makers. The idea of **human security** expands the notion of security away from one that is focused on states to a view of security that examines all of the complex ways in which people are made secure, including through human rights protections; access to education, food and shelter; availability of health services; and an environmentally sustainable environment. Human security (see also pp. 193–194) acknowledges that a world in which states are secure is not necessarily one in which people are secure. A considerable amount of violence takes place within states, not just between them, and it is usually states that are the biggest perpetrators of human rights abuses. State policies can also be responsible for poverty, disease, famine, and environmental disasters. By this view, the foreign policy of states such as Canada should aim to promote remedies that enhance human security over and above state security.[17]

Liberals have sought to reform rather than radically reshape the international system as we know it. They have tried to overhaul the realist model but not to reject its terms of reference entirely (this is one reason that realists and liberals can continue to debate and to understand each other's argument even while disagreeing; another reason they can understand each other, as discussed below, is that both would fall into the category of "problem-solving theories"). Liberal scholars and liberal state leaders alike have argued that international cooperation and the avoidance of violence are ultimately better for states themselves, more rational for state leaders to pursue, and more likely to promote peace and prosperity.

human security Expands the notion of security away from a focus on states to one that examines all of the complex ways in which people are made secure, including through human rights protections; access to education, food, and shelter; availability of health services; and an environmentally sustainable environment

PEACE STUDIES

Another approach of growing importance that challenges some fundamental concepts behind realism is *peace studies*. Peace studies falls largely within the paradigm of liberal approaches, but also contains some elements of critical theory. Some peace studies scholars emphasize possibilities for reform of the international system, others seek a more fundamental transformation in both the way we think about world politics and what should be done to promote peace. Many universities have created interdisciplinary peace studies programs through which scholars and students organize discussions and courses about peace.[18] Typically, such programs include not only political scientists but psychologists who have studied conflict, physicists who have studied nuclear weapons, religious scholars who

---

[17] Denis Stairs, "The Changing Office and the Changing Environment of the Minister of Foreign Affairs in the Axworthy Era," *Canada Among Nations 2001: The Axworthy Legacy*, ed. Fen Osler Hampson, Norman Hillmer, and Maureen Appel Molot (Toronto: Oxford UP, 2001).

[18] David P. Barash, *Introduction to Peace Studies* (Belmont, CA: Wadsworth, 1991). Michael T. Klare, ed., *Peace and World Security Studies: A Curriculum Guide*, 6th ed. (Boulder, CO: Rienner, 1994). Paul Smoker, Ruth Davies, and Barbara Munske, eds., *A Reader in Peace Studies* (NY: Pergamon, 1990). George A. Lopez, ed., "Peace Studies: Past and Future," *Annals of the American Academy of Political and Social Science*, 504 (Newbury Park, CA: Sage, 1989).

have studied practical morality, and so forth. With these various disciplinary backgrounds, scholars of peace studies tend to be more eclectic than political scientists and much more broad-ranging in the topics they consider worthy of study in international security affairs.[19]

Broadening the Focus

In particular, peace studies seeks to shift the focus of IR away from the interstate level of analysis and toward a broad conception of social relations at the individual, domestic, and global levels of analysis. Peace studies connects war and peace with individual responsibility, with economic inequality, with gender relations, with cross-cultural under-standing, and with other aspects of social relationships. Peace studies seeks the potentials for peace not in the transactions of state leaders but in the transformation of entire societies (through social revolution) and in transnational communities (bypassing states and ignoring borders to connect people and groups globally).[20]

Another way in which peace studies seeks to broaden the focus of inquiry is to reject the supposed objectivity of traditional (realist and liberal) approaches. Most scholars of peace studies think that a good way to gain knowledge is to participate in action, such as peace movements—not just to observe objectively. This approach seeks to integrate theory with practice.

In addition to gaining better knowledge about their theories, peace studies scholars participate in the practice of seeking peace because they want to use their theories and knowledge to influence the world they live in. They are not interested just in describing the world as it is, but in exploring how it should, or could, be, and helping make it that way. The main reason for studying war and peace, in this view, is to lessen war and promote the chances for peace. This lack of objectivity is called a **normative bias** because scholars impose their personal norms and values on the subject. Some political scientists (especially realists) dismiss peace studies because it lacks scientific objectivity about outcomes.

normative bias The personal norms and values that IR scholars bring to their studies, such as a preference for peace rather than war.

Scholars in peace studies are quick to respond, however, that realism itself has normative biases and makes policy prescriptions. Realists (from Sun Tzu to Henry Kissinger) even take jobs as advisers to state leaders, urging them to follow the principles of realism. Because realism's assumptions—that actors pursue only their own interests, that violence is a normal and acceptable way to achieve ends, that order is more important than justice—are debatable as objective statements of fact; they might better be seen as value statements. Realism, then, becomes more of an ideology than a theory.

Thus scholars in peace studies defend both their broader approach to the subject and their willingness to bring their own values into play when studying that subject. These characteristics of peace studies can be seen in its approach to war—the central topic in international security affairs.

Conflict Resolution

conflict resolution The development and implementation of peaceful strategies for settling conflicts.

The development and implementation of peaceful strategies for settling conflicts—using alternatives to violent forms of leverage—are known by the general term **conflict resolution.**

---

[19] Ursula Franklin, *The Real World of Technology*, rev. ed., (Toronto: Anansi, 1999).

[20] Francesca M. Cancian and James William Gibson, *Making War/Making Peace: The Social Foundations of Violent Conflict* (Belmont, CA: Wadsworth, 1990). Anatol Rapoport, *Peace: An Idea Whose Time Has Come* (Ann Arbor: U Michigan P, 1992). Johan Galtung, *Peace by Peaceful Means: Peace and Conflict, Development and Civilization* (Thousand Oaks, CA: Sage, 1996).

These methods are at work, competing with violent methods, in virtually all international conflicts. Recently the use of conflict resolution has been increasing, becoming more sophisticated, and succeeding more often.[21]

Most conflict resolution uses a third party whose role is **mediation** between two conflicting parties.[22] Most of today's international conflicts have one or more mediating parties working regularly to resolve the conflict short of violence. There is no hard-and-fast rule saying what kinds of third parties mediate what kinds of conflicts. Presently the UN is the most important mediator on the world scene. Some regional conflicts are mediated through regional organizations, single states, or even private individuals. For instance, the former president of Costa Rica, Oscar Arias, won the 1987 Nobel peace prize for mediating a multilateral agreement among Central American presidents to end several brutal wars in the region.[23]

mediation The use of a third party (or parties) in *conflict resolution.*

In the mid-1990s, former U.S. President Jimmy Carter emerged as a virtual one-man band for international mediation. He closed agreements on nuclear proliferation in North Korea, on democratic transition in Haiti, and on ceasefires in Bosnia and the Sudan. Although each agreement was criticized, Carter has clearly developed himself into a specialized instrument of diplomacy that can be brought into play in international bargaining—in some cases as a genuine alternative to military options.

The involvement of the mediator can vary. Some mediation is strictly *technical*—a mediator may take an active but strictly neutral role in channelling communication between two states that lack other channels of communication.[24] For example, Pakistan secretly passed messages between China and the United States before the breakthrough in U.S.-Chinese relations in 1971. Such a role is sometimes referred to as offering the mediator's *good offices* to a negotiating process. In facilitating communication, a mediator listens to each side's ideas and presents them in a way the other side can hear. The mediator works to change each side's view of difficult issues. In these roles, the mediator is like the translator between the two sides, or a therapist helping them work out psychological problems in their relationship.

Mediators may also actively *propose solutions* based on an assessment of each side's demands and interests. Such solutions may be compromises, may recognize the greater validity of one side's position (or power), or may be creative ideas that meet the needs of both parties. A fifty-fifty compromise is not always the best or fairest solution—it may simply reward the side with the more extreme starting position.

---

[21] Lester R. Kurtz, ed., *Encyclopedia of Violence, Peace, and Conflict,* 3 vols. (San Diego: Academic, 1999). Ho-Won Jeong, *Conflict Resolution: Dynamics, Process, and Structure* (Brookfield, VT: Ashgate, 2000). Antonia Handler Chayes and Abram Chayes, *Planning for Intervention: International Cooperation in Conflict Management* (Cambridge, MA: Kluwer Law, 1999). Michael S. Lund, *Preventing Violent Conflicts: A Strategy for Preventive Diplomacy* (Washington, DC: U.S. Institute of Peace, 1996). Dennis J. D. Sandole and Hugo Van der Merwe, eds., *Conflict Resolution: Theory and Practice* (NY: St. Martin's, 1993). Hugh Miall, *The Peacemakers: Peaceful Settlement of Disputes since 1945* (NY: St. Martin's, 1992). Raimo Väyrynen, ed., *New Directions in Conflict Theory: Conflict Resolution and Conflict Transformation* (Newbury Park, CA: Sage, 1991). John W. Burton, *Conflict Resolution and Prevention* (NY: St. Martin's, 1990).

[22] Chester A. Crocker, Fen Osler Hampson, and Pamela Aall, eds., *Herding Cats: The Management of Complex International Mediation* (Washington, DC: U.S. Institute of Peace, 1999). Jacob Bercovitch, ed., *Resolving International Conflicts: The Theory and Practice of Mediation* (Boulder, CO: Rienner, 1996). Thomas Princen, *Intermediaries in International Conflict* (Princeton NJ: Princeton UP, 1992).

[23] Jack Child, *The Central American Peace Process, 1983–1991: Sheathing Swords, Building Confidence* (Boulder, CO: Rienner, 1992).

[24] Janice Gross Stein, ed., Getting to the Table: The Processes of International Prenegotiation (Baltimore: Johns Hopkins UP, 1989).

KEEPING THE PEACE
Proponents of peacekeeping argue that it is a way to use militaries in zones of conflict in decidedly non-militaristic ways.

If both sides agree in advance to abide by a solution devised by a mediator, the process is called *arbitration*. In that case, both sides present their arguments to the arbitrator, who decides on a "fair" solution. For example, the Israelis and Egyptians submitted their border dispute over the hotel at Taba (see p. 162) to arbitration when they could not come to an agreement on their own. Similarly, Chile and Argentina gave their border problems to a panel of Latin American judges in the 1980s and 1990s. When Serbian and Bosnian negotiators could not agree on who should get the city of Brcko, they turned the issue over to arbitration rather than hold up the entire 1995 Dayton Agreement. Arbitration often uses a panel of three people, one chosen by each side unilaterally and a third on whom both sides agree. In 2002, such a panel (with the UN choosing the third member) delineated the Ethiopian-Eritrean border following a costly war.

Why should a state nonviolently settle a conflict that might be settled by military means? It must see that doing so would be in its better interest. To get national leaders to come to this conclusion one must create conditions to bring into play mutual interests that already exist or create new mutual interests.

In many situations, two conflicting parties could benefit from a solution other than war but lack the trust and communication channels to find such a solution. Neutral mediation with various degrees of involvement can bring about awareness of the two parties' common interests. For example, Egypt and Israel had a common interest in making peace in the late 1970s, but they also had a high level of mistrust. U.S. President Jimmy Carter invited the two heads of state to a private and relaxed setting—his Camp David retreat—where they could go through the issues without the restrictions of formal negotiations.

When heads of state do not see their common interests, ordinary citizens might try to raise awareness of such mutual interests on both sides. Travel and discussion by private individuals and groups toward this end has been called *citizen diplomacy,* and it occurs fairly regularly (though not very visibly) when conflicting states are stuck in a cycle of hostility.[25]

Conflicting parties (and mediators) can also work to *restructure* the terms of bargaining—in effect extending the possible solutions for one or both sides so that their interests overlap. Often a mediator can come up with a win-win solution.[26] This may be as simple as providing means for one or both parties to *save face* when giving up some demand. In other cases, creative solutions may satisfy both parties. For instance, at the Camp David negotiations, Egypt insisted on regaining sovereignty over all its territory in the Sinai desert. Israel insisted on security against the threat of attack from the Sinai. The win-win

---

[25] Gale Warner and Michael Shuman, *Citizen Diplomats: Pathfinders in Soviet-American Relations and How You Can Join Them* (NY: Continuum, 1987).

[26] Roger Fisher and William Ury, with Bruce Patton, *Getting to Yes: Negotiating Agreement Without Giving In* (NY: Penguin, 1983).

solution was a return of the territory to Egyptian sovereignty but with most of it demilitarized so that Egypt could not use it to stage an attack. A win-win solution often trades off two disputed items on which the states place different priorities. Each side can then prevail on the issue that it considers important while yielding on an issue it does not care about as much.

Another way to create mutual interests is to break a conflict into pieces (fractionation) and start with those pieces in which a common interest and workable solution can be found. These may be largely symbolic *confidence-building* measures at first but can gather momentum as the process proceeds. A gradual increase in trust reduces the risks of nonviolent settlements relative to their costs and creates an expectation that the issues at stake can be resolved nonviolently.

A mediator who is in a position to apply positive or negative leverage to the two parties can use that leverage to influence each side's calculation of interests (again opening up new mutual interests). For instance, the promise of future U.S. aid to both Israel and Egypt was an important sweetener in bringing them to a substantive agreement at Camp David.

War and Militarism

Most scholars in peace studies reject realism's willingness to treat war as normal, or its willingness to be objective about the merits of war or peace. Peace studies resonates with Benjamin Franklin's observation that "there never was a good war or a bad peace."[27] In particular, peace studies scholars object to realism's willingness to treat nuclear weapons as just another instrument of state military power. In general, peace studies tries to call into question the nature of war and its role in society.

Peace studies scholars argue that war is not just a natural expression of power, but one closely tied to militarism in (some) cultures.[28] **Militarism** is the glorification of war, military force, and violence through TV, films, books, political speeches, toys, games, sports, and other such avenues. Militarism also refers to the structuring of society around war—for example, the dominant role of a military-industrial complex in a national economy, the dominance of national security issues in domestic politics, and so forth. Militarism is thought to underlie the propensity of political leaders to use military force.

militarism The glorification of war, military force, and violence.

Historically, militarism has had a profound influence on the evolution of societies. War has often been glorified as a "manly" enterprise that ennobles the human spirit (especially before World War I, which changed that perspective). Even Mahatma Gandhi (discussed later) conceded that "war is an unmitigated evil. But it certainly does one good thing. It drives away fear and brings bravery to the surface."[29] Not only evil acts but also exemplary acts of humanity are brought forth by war—sacrifice, honour, courage, altruism on behalf of loved ones, and bonding with a community larger than oneself.

The culture of modern states—and of realism—celebrates and rewards these qualities of soldiers, just as hunter-gatherer cultures created rituals and rewards to induce participation in warfare. Many countries have holidays in honour of warriors, provide them (or their survivors) with veterans' benefits, and bury them in special cemeteries where their individual identities are symbolically submerged into a larger collective identity. Because

---

[27] Benjamin Franklin, letter to Josiah Quincy, 11 September 1773.

[28] Lt. Col. Dave Grossman, *On Killing: The Psychological Cost of Learning to Kill in War and Society* (Boston: Little, Brown, 1995). Elise Boulding, ed., *New Agendas for Peace Research: Conflict and Security Reexamined* (Boulder, CO: Rienner, 1992).

[29] Mohandas K. Gandhi, *Non-Violence in Peace and War*, vol. 1 (1942; NY: Garland, 1972) 270.

militarism seems so pervasive and so strongly associated with the state, many scholars in peace studies question whether the very nature of states must change before lasting peace will be possible.

The United States is considered by some scholars to be a particularly militarized society. In the 1950s, children hid under school desks to practise for a nuclear attack. In the 1960s and 1970s, the Vietnam War dominated the experiences of young people. In the 1980s, fear of nuclear war returned, in 1991 came the Gulf War, and in 2003 the Iraq war. The Junior Reserve Officer Training Program, a Pentagon-designed military training program, has been adopted by school boards across the U.S., in part because it comes with extra funding from the Defense Department (especially important for under-funded public schools).[30] Scholars in peace studies have made a connection between U.S. uses of military force and the American gun mania, high murder rate, Wild West myths, television violence, and other aspects of American life indicating that violence is socially acceptable.

Peace studies seeks examples of less-militarized cultures to show that realism's emphasis on military force is not universal or necessary. Some point to countries such as Canada and Ireland that have devoted themselves more to peacekeeping than war-making (though both do use peacekeeping as part of their rationales to maintain military forces). Costa Rica has had no army for 50 years (just lightly armed forces), even during the 1980s when wars occurred in neighbouring Nicaragua and Panama. Japanese culture since World War II has developed strong norms against war and violence. Public opinion, even more than Japan's constitution, prevents political leaders from considering military force a viable instrument of foreign policy.

Anthropologists have tried to connect the domestic characteristics of hunter-gatherer societies with their external propensity to engage in warfare. There is some evidence that war occurs more frequently in societies with internal (especially gender) inequalities, with harsh child-rearing practices, and with fathers who are absent from child-rearing. By contrast, relatively peaceful societies are more likely to have open decision-making processes, relative gender equality, and permissive and affectionate child-rearing.[31] But all these

SHADOW OF WAR
Militarism in a culture, or the lack thereof, can influence foreign policy. In societies at war, children's psychological trauma contributes to the intergroup conflicts decades later. Generations of Palestinians have grown up in a society permeated by violent conflict with Israel. This boy holds a Palestinian gunman's assault rifle during fighting in Bethlehem, 2001.

[30] Cynthia Enloe, *Maneuvers: The International Politics of Militarizing Women's Lives* (Berkeley: U of California P, 2000).

[31] Marc Howard Ross, "A Cross-Cultural Theory of Political Conflict and Violence," *Political Psychology* 7 (1986): 427–69. Carol R. Ember, "A Cross-Cultural Perspective on Sex Differences," *Handbook of Cross-Cultural Human Development*, ed. Ruth H. Munroe et al. (NY: Garland, 1980) 531–80. Beatrice B. Whiting and John W. M. Whiting, *Children of Six Cultures: A Psycho-Cultural Analysis* (Cambridge, MA: Harvard UP, 1975).

societal attributes could as well be *effects* of war as causes. And, as virtually all kinds of society seem to have the potential for warfare under some conditions (see Chapter 5), distinctions such as "warlike" are only relative.

Positive Peace

Just as war is seen in peace studies as a pervasive aspect of society as a whole, so can peace be reconceptualized in a broader way.[32] According to peace studies scholars, peace should be defined as more than just the absence of war. The mere absence of war does not guarantee that war will not recur. As Kant pointed out, each peace treaty ending a European great-power war in the sixteenth through eighteenth centuries merely set the stage for the next war. Nor can the absence of great-power war in the Cold War be considered true peace: proxy wars in the global South killed millions of people while a relentless arms race wasted vast resources. Because realism assumes the normalcy of military conflicts, it recognizes only a negative kind of peace—the temporary absence of war.

By contrast, **positive peace** refers to a peace that resolves the underlying reasons for war—peace that is not just a ceasefire but a transformation of relationships. Under positive peace, not only do state armies stop fighting each other, but they stop arming, stop forming death squads against internal protest, and reverse the economic exploitation and political oppression that scholars in peace studies believe are responsible for social conflicts that lead to war.

Proponents of the positive peace approach see broad social and economic issues—assumed by realists to be relatively unimportant—as inextricably linked with positive peace. Some scholars define poverty, hunger, and oppression as forms of violence—which they call **structural violence** because it is caused by the structure of social relations rather than by direct actions such as shooting people. Structural violence in this definition kills and harms many more people each year than do war and other forms of direct political violence. Positive peace is usually defined to include the elimination of structural violence because it is considered a source of conflict and war.

In this view, negative peace that merely prevents violence may actually lock in place an unjust status quo. That injustice is epitomized in the global North-South disparity (see Chapter 12) with its massive structural violence against the South. Thus, a narrow, negative definition of peace is seen as inadequate because it conflicts with the achievement of justice, which in turn is necessary for positive peace.

Advocates of positive peace also criticize militaristic culture. The "social construction of war"—a complex system of rules and relations that ultimately supports the existence of war—touches our lives in many ways: from children's war toys to patriotic rituals in schools; from teenagers' gender roles to military training for young men; from the taxes we pay to the sports we play. The positive peace approach seeks to change the whole system, not just one piece of it.

Positive peace encompasses a variety of approaches to social change. These include alternative mechanisms for conflict resolution to take the place of war; popular pressure on governments through peace movements and political activism; strengthening of norms against the use of violence (including the philosophy of nonviolence); the development of international or global identity transcending national, ethnic, and religious divisions;

positive peace A peace that resolves the underlying reasons for war; not just a ceasefire but a transformation of relationships, including elimination or reduction of economic exploitation and political oppression.

structural violence A term used by some scholars to refer to poverty, hunger, oppression, and other social and economic sources of conflict.

---

[32] Robert Elias and Jennifer Turpin, eds., *Rethinking Peace* (Boulder, CO: Rienner, 1994). Linda Rennie Forcey, ed., *Peace: Meanings, Politics, Strategies* (NY: Praeger, 1989). Istvan Kende, "The History of Peace: Concept and Organizations from the Late Middle Ages to the 1870s," *Journal of Peace Research* 26.3 (1989): 233–47. Kenneth E. Boulding, *Stable Peace* (Austin: U Texas P, 1978).

and egalitarian relations within societies in the economic, social, and political realms (including changes in gender roles). All these topics—not considered legitimate subjects of study by realists—are put on the table for discussion by peace studies.

Many people think that positive peace would depend on overcoming ethnic conflict, racism, xenophobia, and other sources of tension between groups with different cultures, languages, and religions—tensions that may contribute to war and violence (see "Ethnic Conflict" on pp. 173–178). One approach explores travel, tourism, cultural exchanges (concerts, films), and citizen diplomacy as means of overcoming intergroup conflicts. Some decades ago, a world language called *Esperanto* was created in hopes of encouraging worldwide communication and global identity; the results have been disappointing over-all. But the UN General Assembly with its simultaneous translation does serve as a kind of global town hall.

Another approach to intergroup conflict is reform in the educational system. For example, Western European countries revised textbooks after World War II to remove nationalistic excesses and promote respect for neighbouring countries (see p. 177). Japan's failure to fully include in textbooks its own World War II misdeeds fuels continuing tension with Korea and China.

Positive peace is usually defined to include political equality and human rights as well. When a small ruling group or dictator holds political power, fewer checks on government violence operate than when democratic institutions exist (see pp. 152–154). And when avenues of legitimate political participation are open, citizens are less likely to turn to violence.

More controversial within peace studies is the question of whether positive peace requires that states' authority be subordinated to a **world government**.[33] The creation of a world government has long been debated by scholars and pursued by activists; many plans have been drawn up, though none has yet succeeded. Some scholars believe progress is being made (through the UN) toward the eventual emergence of a world government. Others think the idea is impractical or even undesirable (merely adding another layer of centralized control, when peace demands decentralization and freedom).

world government
A centralized world governing body with strong enforcement powers.

Peace Movements

Scholars in peace studies also study how to achieve the conditions for positive peace. Approaches vary, from building a world government to strengthening democratic governance, from redistributing wealth to strengthening spiritual communities. But most in peace studies share a skepticism that state leaders left to themselves would ever achieve positive peace. Rather, they believe the practice of IR will change only as a result of pressures from individuals and groups.

The most commonly studied method of exerting such pressure is through **peace movements**—people taking to the streets in protest against war and militarism.[34] Such protests occur in many, though not all, states involved in wars. In peace studies it is believed that people all over the world want peace more than governments do.

peace movements
Movements against specific wars or against war and militarism in general, usually involving large numbers of people and forms of direct action such as street protests.

---

[33] Wesley T. Wooley, *Alternatives to Anarchy: American Supranationalism since World War II* (Bloomington: Indiana UP, 1988).

[34] Steve Breyman, *Why Movements Matter: The West German Peace Movement and U.S. Arms Control Policy* (Albany: SUNY P, 2001). Cecelia Lynch, *Beyond Appeasement: Interpreting Interwar Peace Movements in World Politics* (Ithaca, NY: Cornell UP, 1999). April Carter, *Peace Movements: International Protest and World Politics since 1945* (White Plains, NY: Longman, 1992).

GIVE PEACE A CHANCE
Peace demonstrators play a role in many international conflicts. Here, 750 000 demonstrators in London oppose the upcoming Iraq War, as millions took to the streets worldwide in February 2003.

In addition to mass demonstrations, common *tactics* of peace movements include getting antiwar messages into the media, participating in civil disobedience (nonviolently breaking laws and inviting arrest to show one's beliefs), and occasionally organizing consumer boycotts. Favourite *targets* of peace movements include conscription, government buildings, taxes, and nuclear test sites. Like other interest groups, peace movements also participate in elections and lobbying (see pp. 143–144). And peace movements try to educate the public by spreading information about a war or arms race that the government may be suppressing or downplaying.

Peace activists often disagree on goals. Some, more *internationalist* in orientation, see international organizations (today, the UN) as the best hope for peace and have supported wars against aggression. *Pacifists* oppose all wars, and sometimes distrust international organizations whose members are state governments.[35]

In Japan, peace movements are extremely broad-based (enjoying wide popular support) and are pacifist in orientation (as a result of reaction against militarism before and during World War II). In the Soviet Union and Eastern Europe during the Cold War, official state-sponsored peace groups linked international peace to the struggle against Western imperialism while unofficial peace groups linked peace to the struggle for human rights and democracy at home. In Canada, peace groups have protested specific policies, such as cruise missile testing, and militarism more generally.

These divergent tendencies in peace movements come together at peak times in opposition to particular wars or arms races. But beyond this reactive mode of politics, peace movements often have had trouble defining a long-term direction and agenda. Scholars of peace studies are interested in studying the successes and failures of peace movements to understand how popular influence on foreign policy can affect state decisions.

---

[35] Dwight D. Eisenhower, *Ike's Letters to a Friend, 1941–1958*, ed, Robert Griffith (Lawrence: UP Kansas), 1984.

Nonviolence

The philosophies of **nonviolence** and **pacifism** are based on a unilateral commitment to refrain from using any violent forms of leverage in bargaining. No state today follows such a strategy; indeed, it is widely believed that in today's world, a state that adopted a non-violent philosophy would risk exploitation or conquest.[36]

Pacifism nonetheless figures prominently in debates concerning the peaceful solution of conflicts and the achievement of positive peace. Many states contain substantial num-bers of citizens, often organized into popular movements, who believe that only pacifism—an ironclad commitment to renounce violence—can change the nature of IR so as to avoid future wars. As pacifist A. J. Muste put it: "There is no way to peace; peace is the way." Japan has a sizeable pacifist movement, and pacifists have historically formed the hard core of the peace movement in Canada, the United States, and Western Europe as well.

Religious faith has often provided a foundation for philosophies of nonviolence and pacifism. Despite the millions killed in the name of religion throughout history, many pacifists draw inspiration from the teachings of religious figures, including Jesus Christ and Buddha.

The term *pacifism* has fallen into disfavour because it has been taken to imply passiv-ity in the face of aggression. The more popular term, nonviolence, reflects especially the philosophy and practice of *Mahatma Gandhi*, who led India's struggle for independence from the British empire before 1948. Gandhi emphasized that nonviolence must be *active* in seeking to prevent violence, to resolve conflicts without violence, and especially to stand up against injustice enforced violently. Gandhi organized Indians to resist the British colonial occupation without resorting to violence, even when British troops shot down unarmed Indian protesters.

Can a party to a conflict ever gain by renouncing potential means of leverage because they are violent? Proponents of nonviolence think so. They emphasize the *practical* side of nonviolence in addition to its morality. As a tactic in bargaining, it uses moral norms as leverage. That is, by renouncing one kind of leverage (violent force) it gains other kinds of leverage (popular support and the force of a just cause). Furthermore, reassuring the other side that one will not employ violent leverage makes it easier for the other side to put such options aside as well (by eliminating the security dilemma).

As a tool of the *powerless* standing up against injustices by the powerful, nonviolence is often the most cost-effective approach—because the costs of violent resistance would be prohibitive.[37] Thus, nonviolence has traditionally been promulgated by people with the greatest stake in social change but the least access to the instruments of large-scale violence. In the United States, the philosophy of nonviolence spread widely in the 1960s in the civil rights movement, especially through the work of Martin Luther King, Jr. The powerful, unfortunately, have fewer practical incentives to adopt nonviolence because they have greater access to types of leverage that rely on violence.

The dilemma of nonviolence is how to respond to violence.[38] Gandhi believed that there was always a third alternative to passivity or response in kind. Nonviolence does not

---

[36] Richard B. Miller, *Interpretations of Conflict: Ethics, Pacifism, and the Just-War Tradition* (Chicago: U Chicago P, 1991).

[37] Peter Ackerman and Jack DuVall, *A Force More Powerful: A Century of Nonviolent Conflict* (NY: St. Martin's, 2001). Paul Wehr, Heidi Burgess, and Guy Burgess, eds., *Justice without Violence* (Boulder, CO: Rienner, 1994). Ralph Crow, Philip Grant, and Saad E. Ibrahim, eds., *Arab Nonviolent Political Struggle in the Middle East* (Boulder, CO: Rienner, 1990).

[38] Gene Sharp, *Civilian-Based Defense: A Post-Military Weapons System* (Princeton, NJ: Princeton UP, 1990).

always succeed when faced with violence, but then neither does violent response. However, political leaders may believe they have done their duty if they respond violently without success, but not if they respond nonviolently without success. Ironically, in order to be effective as a strategy, nonviolence must not appear too strategic—being used only as a practical means to achieve a bargaining advantage. Rather, successful mobilization of the moral leverage implicit in nonviolence depends on its being perceived as steadfast whatever the cost.

Nonviolence overlaps in many ways with the other subjects of interest to the peace studies community, such as peace movements and positive peace. Yet within peace studies there are also substantial differences among scholars who emphasize different aspects of peace and how to achieve it. These differences are deepened by the multidisciplinary nature of peace studies (sociologists, political scientists, psychologists, anthropologists, etc.). Peace studies tends to be inclusive and tolerant, hoping that different scholars (and activists) can find a core of agreement on the meaning of peace. This tolerance can mask incompatibilities within peace studies, however. Those who think that war can be ended through international mediation may find they have little common ground with those who think that individual meditation is the way to end war.

CRITICAL THEORY

One of the first scholars to write about critical theory in international relations was Canadian political scientist Robert W. Cox. Cox distinguished two types of theory: problem solving and critical theory. **Problem-solving theory** takes the world as it finds it, and attempts to make institutions and relationships work more smoothly within that given framework. Critical theory, by contrast, "stands apart from the prevailing order of the world and asks how that order came about."[39] **Critical theory** questions the very framework (the very world) that problem-solving theory takes for granted, and is concerned with relations of inequality and the issues that go unsaid or are made invisible within more mainstream approaches to IR. Part of that questioning is related to the political commitments of critical theory, following as it does on Marx's observation that the point is not simply to understand the world but to change it.

Cox's elaboration of critical theory was informed by the work of Antonio Gramsci, and his work has been described as falling within the realm of Gramscian political economy. Other influences on critical theory come from the Frankfurt School of critical theory as developed by social theorists such as Jürgen Habermas, Theodor Adorno, and Max Horkheimer. Still other influences have come from postmodernism, feminism, Marxism, post-positivism, dependency theory, anti-racism and post-colonialism, among others. There is enormous debate among critical theorists about which relations of inequality are the most important in any given time or place. There is also debate among some of these scholars about whether all of these influences really should be grouped under the term "critical." Postmodernism, for example, aims at deconstructing the taken-for-granted assumptions of all social phenomena, including IR, and in this way is deeply critical. But postmodernists are also usually very reluctant to define "emancipation" as

problem-solving theory
Theory that takes the world as it finds it, and attempts to make institutions and relationships work more smoothly within that given framework. Problem-solving theory is usually contrasted with critical theory, which stands apart from the prevailing order of the world and asks how that order came about.

critical theory Theory that questions the very framework (the very world) that problem-solving theory takes for granted, and that is concerned with relations of inequality and the issues that are unexplored or made invisible within more mainstream approaches to IR.

---

[39] Robert W. Cox, "Social Forces, States and World Orders: Beyond International Relations Theory," *Approaches to World Order*, Robert W. Cox with Timothy J. Sinclair (Cambridge: Cambridge UP, 1996). See also Robert W. Cox (with Michael G. Schechter), *The Political Economy of a Plural World: Critical Reflections on Power, Morals and Civilization* (London: Routledge, 2002); Stephen Gill, ed., *Gramsci, Historical Materialism and International Relations* (Cambridge: Cambridge UP, 1993); Mark Neufeld, *The Restructuring of International Relations Theory* (Cambridge: Cambridge UP, 1995).

their goal (in part because they believe all such claims should be deconstructed), so they are viewed as falling outside of critical theory by some observers. For our purposes, all theories that follow Cox's original distinction—that is, those theories that do not take the world as "given"—will be grouped into this category, but students of IR should be aware of these kinds of debates. As one author has suggested, critical theory is best described as a "constellation" of theories rather than a single unified theory.[40]

This chapter will examine several examples of theoretical traditions within the constellation of critical theory. Chapter 11 will elaborate upon some of the critical theory interventions in IPE. It is important to note that "critical theory" should not be treated synonymously with critical analysis or criticism. *All* theories make criticisms of one another, and of events that take place or issues that arise in the world of global politics. *All* students and scholars of IR also develop critical analyses—they explain why (or why not) any given argument is persuasive or convincing. Critical theory does not have a monopoly on either criticism or critical analysis (any more than realism has a monopoly on reality).

Feminism

Feminist scholarship has cut a broad swath across academic disciplines, from literature to psychology to history. In recent years, it has made inroads in international relations, once considered one of the fields most resistant to feminist arguments. Feminist scholarship in IR has produced a rapidly growing literature in the past two decades.[41]

Feminist scholarship encompasses a variety of strands of work, but all have in common the insight that gender matters in understanding how IR works, and this is true in issues of war and security, global political economy, North-South issues, and international institutions. Feminist scholarship in various disciplines seeks to uncover hidden assumptions about gender in how we study a subject such as IR. What mainstream scholars traditionally claim to be universal often turns out to be true only of males.

Some feminists examine how *women* interact with, or are affected by, international relations. Others argue that *gender* informs all aspects of IR in one way or another, whether women are present or not. Examining gender (as opposed to sex) means looking at the assumptions about women and men that prevail in any given time or place, and the material condition of both women and men's lives. Gender also acknowledges that women's and men's lives are shaped not only by their sex, but by their class, race, ethnicity, sexuality, and geographic location.

Some feminists have argued that the core assumptions of realism—especially of anarchy and sovereignty—reflect a masculine worldview based on the ways in which *males* tend to interact and to see the world. Or, more accurately, the way males are *expected* to interact and see the world, because not even all men are able to live up to the expectations associated with masculinity. In this view, the realist approach simply assumes the

---

[40] Richard Wyn Jones, "Introduction: Locating Critical International Relations Theory," *Critical Theory and World Politics*, ed. Richard Jones (Boulder, CO: Rienner, 2001). See also Claire Tureene Sjolander and Wayne S. Cox, eds., *Beyond Positivism: Critical Reflections on International Relations* (Boulder, CO: Rienner, 1994). Steve Smith, Ken Booth, and Marysia Zalewski, eds., *International Theory: Positivism and Beyond* (Cambridge: Cambridge UP, 1996). Michael J. Shapiro and Hayward R. Alker, eds., *Challenging Boundaries: Global Flows, Territorial Identities* (Minneapolis: U Minnesota P, 1996).

[41] V. Spike Peterson and Anne Sisson Runyan. *Global Gender Issues*, 2nd ed. (Boulder, CO: Westview, 1999). J. Ann Tickner, *Gendering World Politics: Issues and Approaches in the Post–Cold War Era* (NY: Columbia UP, 2001). Jill Steans, *Gender and International Relations: An Introduction* (Piscataway, NJ: Rutgers UP, 1998). Sandra Whitworth, *Feminism and International Relations* (NY: St. Martin's, 1994). Joshua S. Goldstein, *War and Gender: How Gender Shapes the War System and Vice Versa* (Cambridge UP, 2001).

A GUY THING
Feminists from various traditions argue that the gender makeup of international summits is important. Here, flanked by European Union officials, are the leaders of Japan, Germany, Canada, Russia, France, the United States, Britain, and Italy (2003).

male as norm when discussing foreign policy decision-making, state sovereignty, or the use of military force.

This is a somewhat complex critique. Because in fact the vast majority of heads of state, of diplomats, and of soldiers *are* male, it may be realistic to study them as males. What some feminist critics then ask is that scholars explicitly recognize the gendered nature of their subject (rather than implicitly assuming all actors are gender-neutral). In this view, our understanding of male actors in IR can be increased by considering how their gender identity affects their views and decision processes. And females also influence IR—influences often ignored by realism. Feminist scholars argue that we can better understand IR by including the roles and effects of women.

Beyond revealing the hidden assumptions about gender in a field of scholarship, feminists often *challenge traditional concepts of gender* as well. In IR, these traditional concepts revolve around the assumptions that men fight wars and run states, whereas women are either uninformed or uninterested in the topics and issues of global politics. Such gender roles are based in the broader construction of masculinity as suitable to *public* and political spaces, whereas femininity is associated with the sphere of the *private* and domestic. An example of this gendered construction was provided by White House Chief of Staff Donald Regan's comment at a 1985 Reagan-Gorbachev summit meeting that women do not care about throw weights of ICBMs (see p. 221) and would rather watch Nancy Reagan. Later he said that U.S. women would not support sanctions against white-ruled South Africa because they would not want to lose their diamonds (a South African export). Feminists call into question, at a minimum, the stereotypes of women as caring more about fashion and jewellery than arms control and apartheid.

Beyond a basic agreement that gender is important, there is no single feminist approach to IR but several such approaches. Although they are interwoven (all paying attention to gender or to the status of women), they often run in different directions. On some core issues, the different strands of feminism have conflicting views, creating interesting debates *within* feminism.

One strand, **standpoint feminism,** focuses on valorizing the feminine—that is, valuing the unique contributions of women *as* women. Standpoint feminists argue that most of global politics has been both created and analyzed from the standpoint of men, and we

standpoint feminism
A strand of feminism that believes gender differences are not just socially constructed and that views women as inherently less warlike than men (on average).

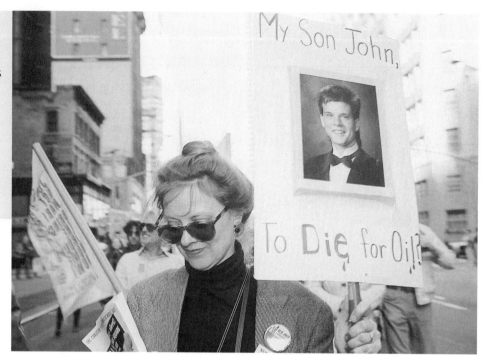

ANOTHER MOTHER FOR PEACE
Standpoint feminists see women as inherently less warlike than men and more adept at making peace, because of their potential and actual experiences as mothers. Here a mother demonstrates against the first Gulf War, 1990.

need to bring the standpoint of women to bear on IR, because women have a unique contribution and point of view. Because of their greater experience with nurturing and human relations, women are seen as potentially more effective than men (on average) in conflict resolution as well as in group decision-making. Standpoint feminists believe there are real differences between the genders that are not just social constructions and cultural indoctrination (although these contribute to gender roles, too). Some standpoint feminists believe there is a core biological essence to being male or female (sometimes called *essentialism*), others think that women's difference is more culturally than biologically determined. In either case, feminine perspectives create a *standpoint* from which to observe, analyze, and criticize the traditional perspectives on IR.[42]

Another strand, **liberal feminism,** rejects these claims as being based on stereotyped gender roles. Liberal feminists see the "essential" differences in men's and women's abilities or perspectives as trivial or nonexistent—men and women are equal. They deplore the exclusion of women from positions of power in IR but do not believe that including women would change the nature of the international system. Liberal feminists seek to include women more often as subjects of study—such as women state leaders, women soldiers, and other women operating outside the traditional gender roles in IR.

A third approach adds to feminism some of the insights from postmodernism, discussed later in this chapter. **Post-positivist feminism** tends to reject the assumptions about gender made by both standpoint and liberal feminists. While standpoint feminists consider gender differences to be important and fixed, and liberal feminists consider those differences to be trivial, post-positivist feminists are more interested in the ways in which representations of difference may impact upon, or be used to legitimize, certain events in IR.

liberal feminism A strand of feminism that emphasizes gender equality and views the "essential" differences in men's and women's abilities or perspectives as trivial or nonexistent.

post-positivist feminism An effort to combine feminist and postmodernist perspectives with the aim of uncovering the hidden influences of gender in IR and showing how arbitrary the construction of gender roles is.

---

[42] Robert O. Keohane, "International Relations Theory: Contributions of a Feminist Standpoint," *Millennium* 18.2 (1989): 245–53.

HER ROLE AND HIS Feminist scholars emphasize the importance of gender roles in IR, especially the traditional distinction between males in the political-military roles and females in the domestic-family roles. Here in Sarajevo, a UN soldier provides cover as a Bosnian citizen runs along "sniper's alley" (1994).

The Masculinity of Realism

Standpoint feminism provides a perspective from which to re-examine the core assumptions of realism—especially the assumption of autonomy—from which flow the key realist concepts of sovereignty and anarchy. To realists, the international system consists of autonomous actors (states) that control their own territory and have no right to infringe on another's territory. Do these concepts rest on a "masculine" view of the world? If so, what would a "feminine" approach to international security be like? Some standpoint feminists have argued that realism emphasizes autonomy and separation because men find separation easier to deal with than interconnection.

This view rests on a psychological theory that boys and girls grow up from a young age with different views of separateness and connection.[43] In this theory, because a child's primary caretaker is almost always female in the early years, girls form their gender identity around the perception of *similarity* with their caretaker (and by extension the environment in which they live), but boys perceive their *difference* from the caretaker. From this experience, boys develop social relations based on individual *autonomy*, but girls' relations are based on *connection*. As a result, women are held to be more likely than men to fear abandonment, whereas men are more likely to fear intimacy.

In *moral* reasoning, according to this research, boys tend to apply abstract rules and stress individual rights (reflecting their sense of separation from the situation), but girls pay more attention to the concrete contexts of different situations and to the responsibility of group members for each other. In playing *games*, boys resolve disputes through arguments about the rules and then keep playing, but girls are more likely to abandon a game rather

---

[43] Carol Gilligan, *In a Different Voice: Psychological Theory and Women's Development* (Cambridge, MA: Harvard UP, 1982). Nancy Chodorow, *The Reproduction of Mothering* (Berkeley: U California P, 1978).

Thinking Theoretically

Feminist theories provide explanations that differ from both realist and liberal theories. In the case of response to aggression, such as in Kuwait and Bosnia, feminists might call attention to the importance of gender roles such as the desire on the part of state leaders to prove their manhood by standing up to the bad guys.

In the case of Kuwait, President George H. W. Bush had long been criticized as being a "wimp" (an insult to his manhood), and his determination to respond to Iraq's aggression became a personal battle with Saddam Hussein. A key moment in Bush's decision process was said to be when Britain's prime minister, Margaret Thatcher—a woman—urged him to act firmly, saying, "Don't go all wobbly on us, George."

Some of the initial reaction to the attacks against the United States on September 11 also indicated that a swift, tough, and manly reaction was demanded. Former Defense Intelligence Agency officer Thomas Woodrow wrote that "To do less [than use tactical nuclear capabilities against the bin Laden camps in the desert of Afghanistan] would be rightly seen ... as cowardice on the part of the United States." Journalist Steve Dunleavy commented that "This should be as simple as it is swift—kill the bastards. A gunshot between the eyes, blow them to smithereens, poison them if you have to. As for cities or

countries that host these worms, bomb them into basketball courts." Not to be outdone, George W. Bush sought to establish his credentials when he said of Osama bin Laden: "Wanted Dead or Alive."

For feminists, this kind of masculinist frame can lead decision-makers down paths that could, and should, be avoided. In turn, it likely forecloses other policy options precisely because they are not "manly" enough. Some observers suggested that the U.S. government could make an enormously profound statement after September 11 by "bombarding Afghanistan with massive supplies of food instead of warheads. Such an approach would surely earn America's commander-in-chief the media label of wimp—and much worse. Obviously, it's the sort of risk that the president wouldn't dare to take."*

* Thomas Woodrow, "Time to Use the Nuclear Option," *Washington Times* 14 Sept. 2001. Steve Dunleavy, *New York Post* 12 Sept. 2001. Norman Solomon, "The 'Wimp' Factor: Goading to Shed Blood," *Media Beat* 28 Sept. 2001 <http://www.fair.org/media-beat/010928.html>. See also Sandra Whitworth, "11 September and the Aftermath," *Studies in Political Economy* 67 (Spring 2002): 33–38. Krista Hunt, "The Strategic Co-optation of Women's Rights: Discourse in the 'War on Terrorism,' " *International Feminist Journal of Politics* 4.1 (2002): 116–21. "Forum: The Events of 11 September 2001 and Beyond," *International Feminist Journal of Politics* 4.1 (2002): 95–115.

than argue over the rules and risk the social cohesion of their group. In *social relations*, boys form and dissolve friendships more readily than girls, who are more likely to stick loyally with friends. All these gender differences in children reflect the basic concept that for girls connection matters more than independence, but for boys the reverse is true.

Realism, of course, rests on the concept of states as separate, autonomous actors that make and break alliances freely while pursuing their own interests (but not interfering in each other's internal affairs). Such a conception of autonomy parallels the masculine psyche just described. Thus, some feminists find in realism a hidden assumption of masculinity. Furthermore, the sharp distinction that realists draw between international politics (anarchic) and domestic politics (ordered) parallels the distinction in gender roles between the public (masculine) and private (feminine) spheres. Thus, realism constructs IR as a man's world.

By contrast, an international system based on *feminine* principles might give greater importance to the *interdependence* of states than to their autonomy, stressing the responsibility of people to care for each other with less regard for states and borders. In the struggle between the principles of human rights and of sovereignty (noninterference in internal affairs), human rights would receive priority. In the choice of forms of leverage when conflicts arise between states, violence might be less prevalent. The concept of national security might be based on human security (see pp. 95–97) rather than narrow self-interest.

The realist preoccupation with the interstate level of analysis presumes that the logic of war itself is autonomous and can be separated from other social relationships such as economics, domestic politics, sexism, and racism. Standpoint feminism, however, reveals the *connections* of these phenomena with war. It suggests new avenues for understanding war at the domestic and individual levels of analysis—underlying causes that realists largely ignore.

From this feminist perspective, neoliberalism has gone backward from traditional liberalism by accepting the realist assumption of separate unitary states as the important actors, and downplaying substate and transnational actors including women. Neoliberalism's conception of cooperation as rule-based interactions among autonomous actors also reflects masculinist assumptions.

Gender in War and Peace

In addition to its emphasis on autonomy and anarchy, realism stresses military force as the key form of leverage in IR. Here, too, many standpoint feminists see in realism a hidden assumption of masculinity. They see war as not only a male occupation, but the quintessentially male occupation. In this view, men are inherently the more warlike sex, and women the more peaceful. Thus, although realism may accurately portray the importance of war and military force in IR as we now know it, this merely reflects the male domination of the international sphere to date—not a necessary, eternal, or inescapable logic of relations among states.[44]

Standpoint feminists find plenty of evidence to support the idea of war as a masculine pursuit. Anthropologists have found that in all known cultures, males are the primary (and usually the only) combatants in warfare, despite the enormous diversity of those cultures in so many other ways. (Of course, voting and political leadership were also male domains for most of history, yet feminists would hardly call those activities essentially masculine.)

One supposed link between war and masculinity is the male sex hormone testosterone (along with related hormones), which some biologists have connected with aggressive behaviour in animals. However, testosterone does not *cause* aggression. Rather, social interactions "feed back" to affect testosterone levels (winners' testosterone rises while losers' levels fall). Thus testosterone is a link in a complex system of relationships between the organism and the social environment. Complex behaviours such as aggression and war cannot be said to be biologically *driven* or predetermined, because humanity's most striking biological capability is flexibility.

Even some feminists who see gender differences as strictly cultural, and not biological at all, view war as a masculine construction. In one theory, for example, war may fill a void left for men by their inability to give birth; war provides a meaning to life and gives men an opportunity through heroism to transcend their individual isolation and overcome their fear of death—opportunities that women potentially get through childbirth. In addition, heroism on the battlefield, especially before modern mechanized war, promised men a form of immortality, as their deeds would live on in collective memory.[45]

By contrast, women are usually portrayed by standpoint feminists as more peaceful creatures than men—whether because of biology, culture, or (most likely) both. These feminists emphasize women's unique abilities and contributions as *peacemakers*. They

---

[44] Lois Ann Lorentzen and Jennifer Turpin, eds., *The Women and War Reader* (NY: New York UP, 1998). Jean Bethke Elshtain and Sheila Tobias, eds., *Women, Militarism, and War: Essays in History, Politics, and Social Theory* (Lanham, MD: UP of America, 1989).

[45] Nancy C. M. Hartsock, "Masculinity, Heroism, and the Making of War," *Rocking the Ship of State: Toward a Feminist Peace Politics*, ed. Adrienne Harris and Ynestra King (Boulder, CO: Westview, 1989) 133–52.

stress women's roles as *mothers* and potential mothers. Because of such caregiving roles, women are presumed to be more likely than men to oppose war and more likely to find alternatives to violence in resolving conflicts.[46]

Both biologically and anthropologically, there is no firm evidence connecting women's caregiving functions (pregnancy and nursing) with any particular kinds of behaviour such as reconciliation or nonviolence—although females have been studied less than males. The role of women varies considerably from one society to another. Although they rarely take part in combat, women sometimes provide logistical support to male warriors and sometimes help to drive the men into a war frenzy by dancing, shaming nonparticipating males, and other activities supportive of war. Yet in other cultures, women restrain the men from war or play special roles as mediators in bringing wars to an end.

The idea of women as peacemakers has a long history. In ancient Athens, the (male) playwright Aristophanes speculated in his play *Lysistrata* about how women might end the unpopular Peloponnesian War with Sparta, then in progress. In the play, a young woman named Lysistrata organizes the Athenian and Spartan women to withhold sex from the men until the latter stop the war (the women also make off with the war treasury). In short order, the men come to their senses and make peace.[47]

Women have formed their own organizations to work for peace on many occasions. In 1852, *Sisterly Voices* was published as a newsletter for women's peace societies. Bertha von Suttner in 1892 persuaded Alfred Nobel to create the Nobel peace prize (which Suttner won in 1905). During World War I, in 1915, Jane Addams and other feminists convened an international women's peace conference at the Hague. They founded the Women's Peace Party (now called the Women's International League for Peace and Freedom).[48]

After World War I, the *suffrage* movement won the right for women to vote. Standpoint feminists thought that women would vote for peace and against war, changing the nature of foreign policy, but women generally voted as their husbands did. Similarly, decades later when women participated in liberation struggles against colonialism in the global South, some feminists thought such participation would lead to different kinds of foreign policies in the newly independent countries, but in general such changes did not materialize (partly because women were often pushed aside from political power after the revolution).

Public opinion polling on foreign policy issues partially vindicates standpoint feminists. In most Western countries in which people are polled on such issues, a **gender gap** shows women to be less supportive than men when asked about military action. Meanwhile, feminists in recent decades have continued to organize women's peace organizations.[49] In the 1980s, Women's Action for Nuclear Disarmament (WAND) opposed

gender gap Refers to polls showing women lower than men on average in their support for military actions (as well as for various other issues and candidates).

---

[46] Virginia Woolf, *Three Guineas* (1938; London: Hogarth, 1977). Ruth Roach Pierson, *Women and Peace: Theoretical, Historical and Practical Perspectives* (London: Croom Helm, 1987). M. K. Burguieres, "Feminist Approaches to Peace: Another Step for Peace Studies," *Millennium* 19.1 (1990): 1–18. Birgit Brock-Utne, *Educating for Peace: A Feminist Perspective* (NY: Pergamon, 1985). Betty Reardon, *Sexism and the War System.* (NY: Teachers College, 1985). Micaela De Leonardo, rev. of *Morals, Mothers, and Militarism: Antimilitarism and Feminist Theory, Feminist Studies* 11 (1985): 599–617.

[47] Aristophanes, *Lysistrata,* ed. Jeffrey Henderson (NY: Oxford UP, 1987).

[48] Marie Louise Degen, *The History of the Woman's Peace Party* (1939, Johns Hopkins UP; NY: Burt Franklin Reprints, 1974).

[49] Amy Swerdlow, "Pure Milk, Not Poison: Women Strike for Peace and the Test Ban Treaty of 1963," *Rocking the Ship of State,* ed. Harris and King (see footnote 20 in this chapter) 225–37. Carolyn M. Stephenson, "Feminism, Pacifism, Nationalism, and the United Nations Decade for Women," *Women and Men's Wars,* ed. Judith Stiehm (Oxford: Pergamon, 1983) 341–48. Gwyn Kirk, "Our Greenham Common: Feminism and Nonviolence," *Rocking the Ship of State,* ed. Harris and King (see footnote 20 in this chapter) 115–30.

the nuclear arms buildup, and women encamped for years at Britain's Greenham Common air base. In Israel, the "women in black" held vigils to protest their government's military actions against Palestinians. In 1995, the UN-sponsored Beijing conference on women brought together women activists from around the world, and helped deepen feminists' engagement with global issues such as North-South inequality.

Through these various actions, standpoint feminists began developing a feminist practice of international relations that could provide an alternative to the masculine practice of realism. The motto of the UN Educational, Scientific, and Cultural Organization (UNESCO) is, "Since war begins in the minds of men, it is in the minds of men that the foundations for peace should be sought." For standpoint feminists, war does indeed begin in the minds of men, but the foundations for peace would better be sought in the minds of women.

Women in IR

Liberal feminists are skeptical of standpoint feminist critiques of realism. They believe that when women are allowed to participate in IR, they play the game basically the same way men do, with similar results. They think that women can practise realism—based on autonomy, sovereignty, anarchy, territory, military force, and all the rest—just as well as men can. Liberal feminists therefore tend to reject the critique of realism as masculine. They, along with other feminists, argue that standpoint arguments about the fundamental differences between women and men may appeal to prevailing stereotypes, but they do not tell us much about women's experiences in world politics or how gender impacts IR.

Liberal feminism focuses on the integration of women into the overwhelmingly male preserves of foreign policy-making and the military. In most states, these occupations are typically at least 90 percent male. For instance, in 1995 the world's diplomatic delegations to the UN General Assembly were 80 percent male overall, and the heads of those delegations were 97 percent male. The Canadian military, with one of the highest proportions of women anywhere in the world or in history, is still 85 percent male.[50]

For liberal feminists, the main effect of this gender imbalance on the nature of IR—that is, apart from effects on the status of women—is to waste talent. Since liberal feminists think that women have the same capabilities as men, the inclusion of women in traditionally male occupations (from state leader to foot soldier) would bring additional capable individuals into those areas. Gender equality would thus increase national capabilities by giving the state a better overall pool of diplomats, generals, soldiers, and politicians.

In support of their argument that, on average, women handle power just as men do, liberal feminists point to the many examples of women who have served in such positions. No distinctly feminine feature of their behaviour in office distinguishes these leaders from their male counterparts. Rather, they have been diverse in character and policy. Of course, women in traditionally male roles may have been selected (or self-selected) on the basis of their suitability to such roles: they may not act the way "average" women would act. Still, they do show that individuals cannot be judged accurately using group characteristics alone.

Female state leaders do not appear to be any more peaceful, or any less committed to state sovereignty and territorial integrity, than are male leaders. It has even been suggested that women in power tend to be more warlike to compensate for being females in traditionally male roles.

---

[50] Joni Seager, *The Penguin Atlas of Women in the World*, 2nd ed. (London: Penguin, 2003).

FLOWER GIRLS

Consistent with liberal feminism's premises, the first female U.S. secretary of state, Madeleine Albright, was at least as hard-line as her male colleagues. She advocated the use of force in Bosnia and the expansion of NATO in Eastern Europe. Here, however, she told refugee girls from Afghanistan (where the Taliban faction harshly restricted women) that women worldwide "are all the same, and we have the same feelings"—a line more consistent with difference feminism (1997).

Only one female has led a great power in the past century—Britain's Margaret Thatcher in the 1980s. She went to war in 1982 to recover the Falkland/Malvinas Islands from Argentina (at issue were sovereignty and territorial integrity). Among middle powers, Indira Gandhi likewise led India in war against Pakistan in 1971, as did Israel's Golda Meir against Egypt and Syria in 1973. But Benazir Bhutto of Pakistan and Corazón Aquino of the Philippines struggled to control their own military forces in the late 1980s. Turkey's Tansu Çiller led a harsh war to suppress Kurdish rebels in the mid-1990s. But Violetta Chamorro of Nicaragua kept the peace between factions that had fought a brutal civil war in the 1980s. The president of Sri Lanka, Chandrika Bandaranaike Kumaratunga, and her mother, the prime minister, tried to make peace with separatist rebels, but returned to war when that initiative failed. Indonesia's president Megawati Sukarnoputri has tried to hold together a fractious Indonesia in recent years. Other states, such as Finland, Norway, Iceland, and (briefly) Canada, have had female leaders when war and peace were not major political issues in those countries. Overall, women state leaders, like men, seem capable of leading in war or in peace as circumstances demand.[51]

Liberal feminists believe that women soldiers, like women politicians, have a range of skills and abilities comparable to men's. Again the main effect of including more women would be to improve the overall quality of military forces.[52]

Although women have served with distinction in military forces, they have been excluded from combat roles in almost all those forces. (It is a myth that women in the Israeli army serve in combat infantry roles.) In some countries, military women are limited to traditional female roles such as nurses and typists. Even where women may hold nontraditional positions such as mechanics and pilots, most women remain in the trad-

---

[51] Claire T. Sjolander, Deborah Stienstra, and Heather A. Smith, eds., *Feminist Approaches to Canadian Foreign Policy* (Toronto: Oxford UP, 2003). Francine D'Amico and Peter R. Beckman, eds., *Women in World Politics: An Introduction* (Westport, CT: Bergin & Garvey, 1995). Barbara J. Nelson, and Najma Chowdhury, eds., *Women and Politics Worldwide* (New Haven, CT: Yale UP, 1994). Michael A. Genovese, ed., *Women as National Leaders: The Political Performance of Women as Heads of Government* (Thousand Oaks, CA: Sage, 1993). Nancy E. McGlen and Meredith Reid Sarkees, *Women in Foreign Policy: The Insiders* (NY: Routledge, 1993).

[52] Linda Grant De Pauw, *Battle Cries and Lullabies: Women in War from Prehistory to the Present* (Norman, OK: U Oklahoma P, 1998). Linda Bird Francke, *Ground Zero: The Gender Wars in the Military* (NY: Simon & Schuster, 1997). Judith Hicks Stiehm, ed., *It's Our Military, Too!* (Philadelphia: Temple UP, 1996). Antonia Fraser, *The Warrior Queens* (NY: Knopf, 1989). Elisabetta Addis, Valerie E. Russo, and Lorenza Ebesta, eds., *Women Soldiers: Images and Realities* (NY: St. Martin's, 1994). Eva Isaksson, ed., *Women and the Military System* (NY: St. Martin's, 1988).

itional roles. And certain jobs still remain off-limits; for instance, on submarines or in combat infantry. Thus there are relatively few cases to judge women's abilities in combat.

Those cases include historical examples of individual women who served in combat (sometimes disguised as men, sometimes not). In the fifteenth century, Joan of Arc rallied French soldiers to defeat England, turning the tide of the Hundred Years' War. (The English burned her at the stake as a witch after capturing her.) In recent years, U.S. women soldiers have found themselves in combat in both the Gulf and Iraq Wars (present-day mobile tactics and fluid front lines make it hard to separate combat from support roles). Women pilot helicopters and planes, have been killed, and have been taken prisoner. Images from Iraq of rescued POW Jessica Lynch were used extensively by the U.S. as evidence of the stoic courage exhibited by female soldiers. By contrast, the release of images depicting a female U.S. soldier involved in the physical and sexual torture of Iraqi prisoners showed that women can also be equal partners in the ruthless side of soldiering.

Women have repeatedly participated in combat in rebel forces fighting guerrilla wars in Vietnam, Nicaragua, and elsewhere, as well as in terrorist or paramilitary units in countries such as Peru, Germany, Italy, and Palestine. Women in Eritrea's guerrilla forces became part of that country's regular army after independence and then served in front-line combat units during the Eritrea-Ethiopia war in the late 1990s. All these cases suggest that (at least some) women are able to hold their own in combat. Women have also served on peacekeeping missions, and governments such as Canada that are actively involved in peacekeeping missions make no distinction between male and female soldiers.

Some argue that women are more vulnerable (that is, to rape) if taken as POWs. Again liberal feminists disagree. All POWs are vulnerable, and both men and women POWs can be sexually abused. One of the female soldiers who had been captured during the Gulf War commented that the only difference between male and female POWs is no one thinks to ask the male soldiers if they were raped, whereas it is the first question asked of female POWs.

The main reason that military forces give for their exclusion of women from combat is fear about what effect their presence might have on the male soldiers, whose discipline and loyalty have traditionally been thought to depend on male bonding and single-minded focus (in other words, because of prevailing assumptions about women and men). Opponents of women in the military claimed vindication, ironically, from a series of high-

FIGHTING FEMALES
Women soldiers have performed as well as men in military tasks, as predicted by liberal feminists. But in state armies, women are barred from virtually all infantry combat units worldwide. Guerrilla forces more often include women, such as these soldiers of the Tamil Tigers rebels in Sri Lanka, 2002.

profile cases of sex discrimination, harassment, adultery, and rape in the U.S. military in the mid-1990s and early 2000s. By February 2004 reports emerged from Iraq, for example, that more than 100 female U.S. soldiers had reported being sexually assaulted by fellow soldiers. The presence of females in the ranks, critics argue, was breaking down discipline and morale. Liberal feminists reject such arguments and argue that group bonding in military units does not depend on gender segregation. (After all, similar rationales were once given for racial segregation in U.S. military forces.)[53] Thus, a heated public debate continues on the question of women in the military.

The effects of war on noncombatant women has also received growing attention.[54] Attacks on women in Algeria, Rwanda, Bosnia, and Afghanistan pointed to a possible new trend toward women as military targets. Systematic rape was used as a terror tactic in Bosnia and Rwanda, and the Japanese army in World War II operated an international network of sex slaves known as "comfort women." Rape has long been treated as a normal if regrettable by-product of war, but recently certain instances of rape were declared war crimes (see p. 283) by the international war crimes tribunal for the former Yugoslavia.

In sum, liberal feminists reject the argument that women bring uniquely feminine assets or liabilities to foreign and military affairs. They do not critique realism as essentially masculine in nature but do criticize state practices that exclude women from participation in international politics and war.

In addition to the liberal and standpoint strands of feminism, the third strand, postmodern feminism, is connected with the rise of postmodernism in the social sciences.

POSTMODERNISM

postmodernism
An approach that denies the existence of a single fixed reality, and pays special attention to texts and to discourses—that is, to how people write and talk about a subject.

Postmodernism, like feminism, is a broad approach to scholarship that has left its mark on various academic disciplines, especially the study of literature. Because of their literary roots, postmodernists pay special attention to *texts* and to *discourses*—how people write and talk about their subject (IR).[55] Postmodern critiques of realism thus concentrate on analyzing realists' words and arguments.[56]

Deconstructing Realism

A central idea of postmodernism is that there is no single, objective reality but a multiplicity of experiences and perspectives that defy easy categorization. Postmodernists also reject the way in which international relations has been studied; they reject what is called positivism, the assumption, among other things, that the methodologies of the natural sci-

---

[53] Julian Borger, "U.S. Soldiers Accused of Raping 100 Colleagues," *The Guardian* 26 Feb. 2004. Mary Fainsod Katzenstein and Judith Reppy, eds., *Beyond Zero Tolerance: Discrimination in Military Culture* (Lanham, MD: Rowman & Littlefield, 1999).

[54] United Nations Secretary-General Study, *Women, Peace and Security* (New York: United Nations, 2002). Wenona Giles and Jennifer Hyndman, *Sites of Violence: Gender and Conflict Zones* (Berkeley: U of California P, 2004).

[55] Pauline Marie Rosenau, *Post-Modernism and the Social Sciences: Insights, Inroads, and Intrusions* (Princeton, NJ: Princeton UP, 1992).

[56] Richard K. Ashley and R. B. J. Walker, "Speaking the Language of Exile: Dissident Thought in International Studies" [Introduction to special issue], *International Studies Quarterly* 34.3 (1990): 259–68. Yosef Lapid, "The Third Debate: On the Prospects of International Theory in a Post–Positivist Era," *International Studies Quarterly* 33.3 (1989): 235–54. James Der Derian, *On Diplomacy: A Genealogy of Western Estrangement* (NY: Basil Blackwell, 1987).

ences help us to understand the social world. They reject also that theories can be validated (or falsified) only through empirical reference to the "real world."[57] For this reason, postmodernism itself is difficult to present in a simple or categorical way. Indeed, some theorists share with postmodernism their rejection of positivism, but do not agree with all the elements of postmodernism (and so use instead the term post-positivism). This section will merely convey some important postmodern themes, necessarily oversimplified, and show how postmodernism can help illuminate some problems of realism.

From a postmodern perspective, realism cannot justify its claim that states are the central actors in IR and that states operate as unitary actors with coherent sets of objective interests (which they pursue through international power politics). Postmodern critics of realism see nothing objective about state interests, and certainly nothing universal (in that one set of values or interests applies to all states).

More fundamentally, postmodernism calls into question the whole notion of states as actors. States have no tangible reality; they are "fictions" that we (as scholars and citizens) construct to make sense of the actions of large numbers of individuals. For postmodernists, the stories told about the actions and policies of states are just that—stories. From this perspective, it is an arbitrary distinction that leads bookstores to put spy novels on the fiction shelf whereas biographies and histories go on the nonfiction shelf. None of these is an objective reality, and all are filtered through an interpretive process that distorts the actual experiences of those involved.[58]

Contrary to realism's claim that states are unitary actors, postmodernists see multiple realities and experiences below the surface of the fictional entities that realists construct (states). The Soviet Union, for example, was treated by realists as a single actor with a single set of objective interests. Indeed, it was considered the second most important actor in the world. Realists were amazed when the Soviet Union split into 15 pieces, each containing its own fractious groups and elements. It became clear that the "unitary state" called the Soviet Union had masked (and let realists ignore) the divergent experiences of constituent republics, ethnic groups, and individuals.

Postmodernists seek to "deconstruct" such constructions as states, the international system, and the associated stories and arguments (texts and discourses) with which realists portray the nature of international relations. To *deconstruct* a text—a term borrowed from literary criticism—means to tease apart the words in order to reveal hidden meanings, looking for what might be omitted or included only implicitly. The hidden meanings not explicitly addressed in the text are often called the **subtext**.[59]

What is subtext in the stories realists tell about IR? What does realism omit from its accounts of IR? We have just discussed one major omission—women and gender. Furthermore, in its emphasis on states, realism omits the roles of individuals, domestic politics, economic classes, MNCs, and other nonstate actors. In its focus on the great powers, realism omits the experiences of countries of the global South. In its attention to military forms of leverage, it omits the roles of various nonmilitary forms of leverage.

subtext Meanings that are implicit or hidden in a text rather than explicitly addressed. See also *postmodernism*.

---

[57] Steve Smith, "Positivism and Beyond," *International Theory: Positivism and Beyond*, ed. Steve Smith, Ken Booth, and Marysia Zalewski (Cambridge: Cambridge UP,1996) 11–46.

[58] Michael J. Shapiro, "Textualizing Global Politics," *International/Intertextual Relations: Postmodern Readings of World Politics*, ed. James Der Derian and Michael J. Shapiro (NY: Lexington, 1989) 11–22. Michael J. Shapiro and Hayward R. Alker, eds., *Challenging Boundaries: Global Flows, Territorial Identities* (Minneapolis: U Minnesota P, 1996).

[59] David Campbell, *Politics without Principle: Sovereignty, Ethics, and the Narratives of the Gulf War*(Boulder, CO: Rienner, 1993). Anders Stephanson, *Kennan and the Art of Foreign Policy* (Cambridge, MA: Harvard UP, 1989). William Chaloupka, *Knowing Nukes: The Politics and Culture of the Atom* (Minneapolis: U Minnesota P, 1992).

Realism focuses so narrowly because its aim is to reduce IR down to a simple, coherent model. The model is claimed to be objective, universal, and accurate. To postmodernists, the realist model is none of these things: it is a biased model that creates a narrow and one-sided story for the purpose of promoting the interests of powerful actors. Postmodernists seek to destroy this model along with any other model (including neoliberalism) that tries to represent IR in simple, objective categories. Postmodernists instead want to celebrate the diversity of experiences that make up IR without needing to make sense of them by simplifying and categorizing.[60]

Post-positivist Feminism

One line of criticism directed at realism combines feminism with insights from postmodernism.[61] *Post-positivist feminism* seeks to deconstruct realism (and liberalism) with the specific aim of uncovering the pervasive hidden influences of gender in IR while showing how arbitrary the construction of gender roles is. This category is called post-positivist feminism (as opposed to postmodern feminism) because not all of the feminist scholars described here would adopt the term "postmodernism," but most would acknowledge the influence of postmodern thought on their own work.

Post-positivist feminists agree with standpoint feminists that realism carries hidden meanings about gender roles but deny that there is any fixed inherent meaning in either male or female genders. Rather, feminist post-positivists look at the interplay of gender and power in a more open-ended way. Post-positivist feminists criticize liberal feminists for trying merely to integrate women into traditional structures of war and foreign policy. They criticize standpoint feminists as well, for glorifying traditional feminine virtues.

In studying war, post-positivist feminists have challenged the archetypes of the (male) "just warrior" and the (female) "beautiful soul." They argue that women are not just passive bystanders or victims in war, but active participants in a system of warfare tied to both genders. Women act not only as nurses and journalists at the "front" but as mothers, wives, and girlfriends on the "home front."[62] These scholars believe that stories of military forces should not omit the roles of prostitutes at military bases, that stories of armed conflict should not omit the details of women's activism in zones of conflict, nor should stories of diplomacy omit the roles of diplomats' wives.[63]

---

[60] R. B. J. Walker and Saul H. Mendlovitz, eds., *Contending Sovereignties: Redefining Political Community* (Boulder, CO: Rienner, 1990). R. B. J. Walker, *Inside/Outside: International Relations as Political Theory* (NY: Cambridge UP, 1993). Cynthia Weber, *Simulating Sovereignty: Intervention, the State and Symbolic Exchange* (NY: Cambridge UP, 1995). Jim George, *Discourses of Global Politics: A Critical (Re)Introduction to International Relations* (Boulder, CO: Rienner, 1994).

[61] V. Spike Peterson, ed., *Gendered States: Feminist (Re)Visions of International Relations Theory* (Boulder, CO: Rienner, 1992). Christine Sylvester, *Feminist Theory and International Relations in a Postmodern Era* (NY: Cambridge UP, 1994).

[62] Jean Bethke Elshtain, *Women and War*, 2nd ed. (Chicago: U Chicago P, 1995). Gail Braybon and Penny Summerfield, *Out of the Cage: Women's Experiences in Two World Wars* (NY: Pandora, 1987).

[63] Cynthia Enloe, *Bananas, Beaches, and Bases: Making Feminist Sense of International Politics* (Berkeley: U California P, 1989). Wenona Giles, Malathi de Alwis, Edith Klein, and Neluka Silva, eds., *Feminists under Fire: Exchanges across War Zones* (Toronto: Between the Lines, 2003). Simona Sharoni, *Gender and the Israeli-Palestinian Conflict: The Politics of Women's Resistance* (Syracuse, Syracuse UP, 1995). Tami Jacoby, *Women in Zones of Conflict* (Montreal: McGill-Queen's UP, forthcoming). Jan Jindy Pettman, *Worlding Women: A Feminist International Politics* (NY: Routledge, 1996). Katherine H. S. Moon, *Sex among Allies: Military Prostitution in U.S.–Korea Relations* (NY: Columbia UP, 1997).

Post-positivist feminists reject not only realism but also some of the alternative approaches that emphasize the protection of women and other noncombatants. Just war doctrine (see pp. 287–288) is considered too abstract—a set of concepts and rules that does not do justice to the richness of each historical context and the varied roles of individual men and women within it.[64] Liberal pluralism is considered too problem-solving in orientation, and unsophisticated in its analysis of the relations of power between women and men, relations of power which will not be transformed simply by "getting more women in" to governments and militaries.

Many post-positivist feminists also engage with questions of masculinity, but they take a very different view of masculinity than that offered by standpoint feminists. By this view there is no single masculinity or femininity, but rather multiple masculinities and femininities. There are forms of masculinity, for example, that privilege physical strength and machismo attitudes as well as those that privilege rational thought or entrepreneurial spirit. In different times or places, communities or institutions, any one vision of masculinity may predominate over others, or, for some theorists of masculinity, become hegemonic.[65]

Post-positivist feminists have tried to deconstruct the language of realism, especially where it reflects influences of gender and sex. For instance, the first atomic bombs had male gender (they were named "Fat Man" and "Little Boy"); the coded telegram informing Washington, D.C., that the first hydrogen bomb had worked said simply, "It's a boy" (presumably being born a girl would have indicated a failure). The plane that dropped the atomic bomb on Hiroshima (the *Enola Gay*) had female gender; it was named after the pilot's mother. Likewise the French atom-bomb test sites in the South Pacific were all given women's names.[66] Similarly, pilots have pasted pinup photos of nude women onto conventional bombs before dropping them. In all these cases, post-positivist feminists would note that the feminine gender of vehicles, targets, or decorations amplifies the masculinity of the weapon itself.

These efforts find sex and gender throughout the subtext of realism. For example, the terms *power* and *potency* refer to both state capability and male virility. Military force depends on phallic objects—weapons designed to shoot projectiles, penetrate targets, and explode. In basic training, men chant: "This is my rifle [holding up rifle], this is my gun [pointing to crotch]; one's for killing, the other's for fun."[67] Nuclear weapons are also repeatedly spoken of in sexual terms, perhaps due to their great "potency." Female models are hired to market tanks, helicopter missiles, and other "potent" weapons to male procurement officers at international military trade shows.[68] The phallic character of weapons has seemingly persisted even as technology has evolved from spears to guns to missiles.

---

[64] Elshtain, *Women and War* (see footnote 62 in this chapter). Sara Ruddick, *Maternal Thinking: Towards a Politics of Peace*. (London: Women's Press, 1989).

[65] Marysia Zalewski and Jane Parpart, eds., *The "Man" Question in International Relations* (Boulder: Westview Press, 1998). R.W. Connell, *Masculinities* (Berkeley: U California P, 1995). Marieke de Goede, "Mastering 'Lady Credit': Discourses of Financial Crisis in Historical Perspective," *International Feminist Journal of Politics* 2.1 (2000): 73. Charlotte Hooper, *Manly States: Masculinities, International Relations and Gender Politics* (NY: Columbia UP, 2001). Lily Ling, "Hypermasculinity on the Rise, Again: A Response to Fukuyama on Women and World Politics," *International Feminist Journal of Politics* 2.2 (2000): 278–86. Abouali Farmanfarmaian, "Did You Measure Up? The Role of Race and Sexuality in The Gulf War," *Collateral Damage: The New World Order at Home and Abroad*, ed. C. Peters (Boston: South End, 1992) 111–38.

[66] Carol Cohn, "Sex and Death in the Rational World of Defense Intellectuals," *Signs* 12 (1987): 687–718.

[67] Gwynne Dyer, *War* (NY: Crown, 1985).

[68] Center for Defense Information [Washington, DC], "Weapons Bazaar," slide show (1985).

SEX IN THE SUBTEXT
Feminist post-positivists try to reveal hidden subtexts connecting gender with IR, such as the roles of sex and death in the constructions of masculinity by U.S. airmen in England, 1944.

Realism and liberalism ignore all the sexual aspects of weaponry, limiting themselves to such issues as a weapon's explosive power, its range, and other technical information about its use as state leverage. But if sexual assumptions enter into decisions about whether and when to use bombs or other military forces, or where and how to establish colonies, then realism and liberalism cannot adequately explain those decisions.[69] Post-positivist feminism thus reveals another reality—the desire of male politicians and soldiers to exhibit, or be perceived to exhibit, sexual competency—which competes with the realities of realism and neoliberalism, with their focus on maximizing national interests (narrowly or broadly construed).

Some post-positivist feminists point out that the more likely reason militaries prefer gender segregation is because the creation of soldiers depends on a series of myths, including the superiority of one's nation (and usually race), the celebration of violence and the promise that women maintain the homefront while soldiers "man" the battlefront. As feminist author Cynthia Enloe writes: "If male aircraft pilots can't have a few drinks and send women down a hotel corridor gauntlet, how are they supposed to militarily bond with one another? And if a woman who isn't sexually attracted to even benign versions of male heterosexuality is permitted to openly express her sexual indifference to masculinized pilots, then what's the prize waiting at the end of the war?[70]

By radically shifting the focus and approach of IR scholarship, post-positivist feminists hope to challenge traditional understandings of IR, rationality, and the kinds of questions that can be asked about global level politics.

---

[69] Anne McClintock, *Imperial Leather: Race, Gender and Sexuality in the Colonial Conquest* (NY: Routledge, 1995).

[70] Cynthia Enloe, "The Right to Fight: A Feminist Catch-22," *Ms.* July–Aug 1993: 84–87. See also Deborah Harrison and Lucie Laliberté, *No Life Like It: Military Wives in Canada* (Toronto: Lorimer, 1994). Deborah Harrison, *The First Casualty: Violence against Women in Canadian Military Communities* (Toronto: Lorimer, 2002).

Constructivism

A related stream of IR theory, called **constructivism,** maintains postmodernists' skepticism of the assumptions of realism and liberalism but focuses on where state interests and identities come from. Some would argue that constructivists are not particularly critical in orientation, because of their focus on an otherwise realist issue (state interests). Constructivists do depart from realism, however, at least insofar as they do not simply take state interests as given, but rather insist that the construction of state interests needs to be explored.[71]

One constructivist approach focuses on how people use language to make or "construct" the social world and how the social world in turn shapes individuals.[72] Rules (including legal rules and nonlegal norms) are seen as crucial because they stand in between people and society, enabling the two-way process of construction to be an ongoing one. Rules are statements telling people how they should behave under certain conditions, and this version of constructivism analyzes rules in terms of the kinds of "speech acts" that compose them. Anarchy, sovereignty, regimes, and other basic IR concepts are then seen in terms of how they relate to rules, in this broad sense.

A different constructivist approach considers how states' interests and identities are shaped by rule-governed (or norm-governed) interactions.[73] Liberalism tends to see rules and norms mainly as mediators and coordinators of states' self-interested behaviour. For constructivists, however, norms do more than help states to pursue their selfish interests in mutually beneficial ways and to overcome collective goods problems. Rather, norms affect how states conceive of their interests and, indeed, identities, in the first place. Thus, the state's conception of its interests, its presentation of itself on the international stage, and its behaviour all might change as a result of interstate interactions. States, like people, come to see themselves as others see them.

Constructivists reject the assumption that states always want more rather than less power and wealth, or the assumption that state interests exist independently of a context of interactions among states.[74] Rather, constructivists assume that complex cultures shape state behaviour regarding international security and military force.[75] For example, a small state asked to mediate a conflict between two larger states might acquire a new identity as peacemaker or mediator, and with that new identity would come an interest in *acting* as a peacemaker would.

constructivism A movement in IR theory that examines how changing international norms help shape the content of state interests and the character of international institutions.

---

[71] Jeffrey T. Checkel, rev. of *The Constructivist Turn in International Relations Theory*, *World Politics* 50.2 (1998): 324–48.

[72] Nicholas Onuf, "Constructivism: A User's Manual," *International Relations in a Constructed World*, ed. Vendulka Kubálková, Nicholas Onuf, and Paul Kowert (Armonk, NY: Sharpe, 1998) 58–78. Vendulka Kubálková, ed., *Foreign Policy in a Constructed World* (Armonk, NY: Sharpe, 2001). Karin Fierke and Knud Erik Jorgensen, eds., *Constructing International Relations* (Armonk, NY: Sharpe 2001). Friedrich V. Kratochwil, *Rules, Norms, and Decisions: On the Conditions of Practical and Legal Reasoning in International Relations and Domestic Affairs* (NY: Cambridge UP, 1989).

[73] Rodney Bruce Hall, *National Collective Identity: Social Constructs and International Systems* (NY: Columbia UP, 1999). Christian Reus-Smit, *The Moral Purpose of the State: Culture, Social Identity, and Institutional Rationality in International Relations* (Princeton, NJ: Princeton, 1999). Martha Finnemore, *National Interests in International Society* (Ithaca, NY: Cornell UP, 1996).

[74] Alexander Wendt, *Social Theory of International Politics* (NY: Cambridge UP, 1999). Alexander Wendt, "Anarchy Is What States Make of It: The Social Construction of Power Politics," *International Organization* 46.2 (1992): 391–426.

[75] Jutta Weldes, Mark Laffey, Hugh Gusterson, and Raymond Duval, eds., *Cultures of Insecurity: States, Communities and the Production of Danger* (Minneapolis: U Minnesota P, 1999). Peter J. Katzenstein, ed., *The Culture of National Security: Norms and Identity in World Politics* (NY: Columbia UP, 1996). Thomas U. Berger, *Cultures of Antimilitarism: National Security in Germany and Japan* (Baltimore: Johns Hopkins UP, 1998)

Postcolonialism

Postmodern and post-positivist theorists engage in the ways in which discursive constructions of men and women, states and militaries, laws and institutions, all impact how we understand and engage with politics at the global level. Postcolonial theorists draw on these insights and argue further that imperialism constitutes one of the crucial moments, or processes, through which modern identities in all of their guises became established. For postcolonial theorists, the project of theorizing in IR should be to explore the intersectionality of race, class, gender, and imperialism. It is through the colonial encounter, by this view, that widespread and naturalized identities emerged that shape how we think about the world and each other. These include the following kinds of binaries: developed/undeveloped, core/periphery, rational/irrational, male/female, First World/ Third World, modern/traditional, civilized/backward, white/black, advanced/barbaric. Importantly, for postcolonial theorists, representations of the "south" or the "colonial other" have less to do with the south than they do with "our" world. Depictions of the "other," in other words, tell us what we think about "ourselves" (usually all of the words found on the "superior" side of the binaries).[76]

Postcolonial theorists also argue that IR itself is part of the colonial project. The failure of mainstream approaches like realism and liberalism to explore imperialism, inequality, and difference is not, by this view, an innocent omission. Emphasizing differences between states rather than the many profound differences and inequalities that mark the world (both within and between states) is a way to make some sets of questions accepted and legitimate (war and peace, trade, finance) while others are cast to the margins (racism and colonialism). It is, moreover, a parochial and impoverished way to understand the enormous diversity and complexity of the contemporary world.[77]

The contemporary colonial project, by this view, is not carried only by warriors but by a variety of practices and actors, including those that liberals would argue are the "benign" or more overtly positive side of global politics, such as the UN and the functioning of international law. Peacekeeping and humanitarian interventions are also subject to interrogation by postcolonial theorists as part of the "civilizing mission" of Western institutions, often informed by overtly racist assumptions about the peoples of countries to which such missions are deployed.[78] Postcolonialism offers some of the most profound critiques of IR found within the "constellation" of critical theories.

In sum, through a variety of methods and concepts, critical theorists challenge mainstream accounts of international relations. They seek to replace oversimplified models with one in which multiple realities coexist—realities of gender and sexuality, of race and class, and of imperialism and colonialism. They seek to better understand IR by listening

---

[76] Geeta Chowdhry, and Sheila Nair, eds., *Power, Postcolonialism and International Relations.* (London: Routledge, 2002). Roxanne Lynn Doty, *Imperial Encounters: The Politics of Representation in North-South Relations* (Minneapolis: U Minnesota P, 1996). Edward Said, *Orientalism* (NY: Vintage, 1979). Edward Said, *Culture and Imperialism* (NY: Knopf, 1993).

[77] Naeem Inayatullah and David L. Blaney, *International Relations and the Problem of Difference* (NY: Routledge, 2004). J. Marshall Beier, *International Relations in Uncommon Places: Indigeneity, Cosmology, and the Limits of International Theory* (NY: Palgrave MacMillan, forthcoming 2005).

[78] Sherene Razack, *Dark Threats and White Knights: The Somalia Affair, Peacekeeping and the New Imperialism* (Toronto: U Toronto P, 2004). Jayan Nayar, "Orders of Inhumanity," *Reframing the International: Law, Culture and Politics*, ed. Richard Falk, Edwin J. Lester Ruiz, and R.B.J. Walker (NY: Routledge, 2002). Anne Orford, "Feminism, Imperialism and the Mission of International Law," *Nordic Journal of International Law* 71.2 (2002): 275–96. Anne Orford, "Muscular Humanitarianism: Reading the Narratives of the New Interventionism," *European Journal of International Law* 10.4 (1999): 679–711.

to voices silenced by power—the voices of women, of oppressed ethnic minorities, and of "others" whose interests and actions are not done justice to by states or by theories of IR that focus exclusively on states or other more traditional actors, such as international organizations or MNCs.

With this chapter and the previous one as theoretical background, the next four chapters will cover the major topics in international security studies, broadly defined. The questions in the domain of foreign policy studies are the subject of Chapter 4.

Thinking Critically

1. U.S.-Canadian relations seem better explained by liberalism than realism. Yet realist scholars of Canadian foreign policy would debate this. Discuss the contrasting tenets of realism and liberalism, showing how each applies to the relationship.

2. Peace studies claims that internal characteristics of states (at the domestic level of analysis) strongly affect the propensity for war or potential for lasting peace. For one society, show how internal characteristics—social, economic, and/or cultural—influence that society's external behaviour.

3. Would IR operate differently if most leaders of states were women? What would the differences be? What evidence (beyond gender stereotypes) supports your answer?

4. How would a feminist or postcolonial understanding of militarism impact on how you see international relations? Could these approaches also change the way policies are made in IR? Would they want to?

5. Deconstruct this book by identifying implicit themes, subjects not covered, and hidden biases.

6. Write your own critical-thinking question concerning the topics discussed in this chapter. What are the merits of your question? How would you go about answering it?

Chapter Summary

- The central claims of realism—regarding anarchy, state actors, rationality, and the utility of military force—have been challenged on a variety of grounds.

- Liberals dispute the realist notion that narrow self-interest is more rational than mutually beneficial cooperation.

- Neoliberalism argues that even in an anarchic system of autonomous rational states, cooperation can emerge through the building of norms, regimes, and institutions.

- Collective goods are benefits received by all members of a group regardless of their individual contribution. Shared norms and rules are important in getting members to pay for collective goods.

- International regimes—convergent expectations of state leaders about the rules for issue areas in IR—help provide stability in the absence of a world government.

- Hegemonic stability theory suggests that the holding of predominant power by one state lends stability to international relations and helps create regimes.

- In a collective security arrangement, a group of states agrees to respond together to aggression by any participating state; the UN and other IGOs perform this function.

- Peace studies programs are interdisciplinary and seek to broaden the study of international security to include social and economic factors ignored by realism.

- Peace studies acknowledges a normative bias—that peace is good and war is bad—and a willingness to put theory into practice by participating in politics.

- Mediation and other forms of conflict resolution are alternative means of exerting leverage on participants in bargaining. Increasingly these means are succeeding in settling conflicts without (or with no further) use of violence.

- For scholars in peace studies, militarism in many cultures contributes to states' propensity to resort to force in international bargaining.

- Positive peace implies not just the absence of war but addressing conditions that scholars in peace studies connect with violence—especially injustice and poverty.

- Peace movements try to influence state foreign policies regarding military force; such movements are of great interest in peace studies.

- Nonviolence—the renunciation of force—can be an effective means of leverage, especially for poor or oppressed people with few other means available.

- Feminist scholars of IR agree that gender is important in understanding IR but diverge into several strands regarding their conception of the role of gender.

- Standpoint feminists argue that real (not arbitrary) differences between men and women exist. Men think about social relations more often in terms of autonomy (as do realists), but women think in terms of connection.

- Standpoint feminists argue that men are more warlike on average than women. Although individual women participants (such as state leaders) may not reflect this difference, the participation of large numbers of women would change the character of the international system, making it more peaceful.

- Liberal feminists disagree that women have substantially different capabilities or tendencies as participants in IR. They argue that women are equivalent to men in virtually all IR roles. As evidence, liberal feminists point to historical and present-day women leaders and women soldiers.

- Postmodern critics reject the entire framework and language of realism, with its unitary state actors. Postmodernists argue that no simple categories can capture the multiple realities experienced by participants in IR.

- Post-positivist feminists seek to uncover gender-related subtexts implicit in realist discourse, including sexual themes connected with the concept of power.

- Constructivists reject realist assumptions about state interests, tracing those interests in part to international rules and norms.

- Postcolonial theorists explore the intersectionality of race, class, gender, and imperialism.

Key Terms

neoliberalism   90

tit for tat   90

collective goods problem   91

free riders   91

international regime   92

hegemonic stability theory   93

collective security   95

human security   97

normative bias   98

conflict resolution   98

mediation   99

militarism   101

positive peace   103

structural violence   103

world government   104

peace movements   104

nonviolence/pacifism   106

problem-solving theory   107

critical theory   107

standpoint feminism   109

liberal feminism   110

post-positivist feminism   110

gender gap   114

postmodernism   118

subtext   119

constructivism   123

Weblinks

Here are additional scholarly journals that focus on issues of interest to liberal pluralism and critical theory:

Alternatives: Global, Local, Political:
http://www.rienner.com/viewbook.cfm?BOOKID=1312

Global Governance:
http://www.arts.ualberta.ca/globalgovernance

Human Rights Quarterly:
http://muse.jhu.edu/journals/human_rights_quarterly

International Feminist Journal of Politics:
http://www.tandf.co.uk/journals/titles/14616742.asp

Millennium: Journal of International Studies:
http://www.lse.ac.uk/Depts/intrel/millenn/

Review of International Political Economy:
http://www.sussex.ac.uk/Units/IRPol/RIPE

Review of International Studies:
http://titles.cambridge.org/journals/journal_catalogue.asp?mnemonic=ris

Foreign Policy

4

MAKING FOREIGN POLICY

MODELS OF DECISION-MAKING: THE RATIONAL ACTOR MODEL
Individual Decision-Makers

MODELS OF DECISION-MAKING: THE ORGANIZATIONAL PROCESS AND BUREAUCRATIC POLITICS MODELS
Organizational Process Model
Bureaucratic Politics or
   Government Bargaining Model
Group Dynamics
Crisis Management
Substate Actors
Public Opinion

MODELS OF DECISION-MAKING: ELITE ANALYSIS AND INSTRUMENTAL MARXISM
The Military-Industrial Complex
Making and Writing Foreign
   Policy
Democracy and Foreign Policy
The Democratic Peace

Condoleezza Rice before 9/11 Commission, April 2004.

MAKING FOREIGN POLICY

Looking at states as though they were unitary actors is useful up to a point, but not very accurate. A state is not a single conscious being; its actions are a composite of individual human choices—by its citizenry, its political leaders, its diplomats and bureaucrats—aggregated through the state's internal structures. This chapter looks at the state from inside out, trying to understand the processes and structures *within* states that make them take the actions they do toward other states.

Foreign policies are the strategies used by governments to guide their actions in the international arena (various alternative definitions have been proposed). Foreign policies spell out the objectives state leaders have decided to pursue in a given relationship or situation as well as the general means by which they intend to pursue those objectives. Day-to-day decisions made by various arms of government are guided by the goal of implementing foreign policies.

Every day, states take actions in international affairs. Diplomats are appointed to posts, given instructions for their negotiations, or recalled home. Trade negotiators agree to reduce their demands by a few percent. Military forces are moved around and occasionally sent into battle. Behind each of these actions are decisions by foreign policy bureaucrats in national capitals (including but not limited to the top state leaders). These decisions in turn generally reflect the overall policies states have developed to govern their relationships with other states.

The study of foreign policies includes understanding the various states' substantive policies, for example, understanding why Canada supported the United States during the first Persian Gulf War in 1991 and did not support the United States in the Iraq War of

2003. But, in general, IR scholars are less interested in specific policies than in the **foreign policy process**—how policies are arrived at, and implemented, in various states.[1]

States establish various organizational structures and functional relationships to create and carry out foreign policies. Officials and agencies collect information about a situation through various channels; they write memoranda outlining possible options for action; they hold meetings to discuss the matter; some of them meet privately outside these meetings to decide how to steer the meetings. Such activities, broadly defined, are what is meant by "the foreign policy process." IR scholars are especially interested in exploring whether certain kinds of policy processes lead to certain kinds of decisions—whether certain processes produce better outcomes (for the state's self-defined interests) than do others.

Foreign policy outcomes result from multiple forces working at once on the various levels of analysis. The outcomes depend on individual decision-makers, on the type of society and government they are working within, and on the international and global context of their actions. Since the study of foreign policy concentrates on forces within the state, its main emphasis is on the individual and domestic levels of analysis.

Comparative foreign policy is the study of foreign policy in various states in order to discover whether similar types of societies or governments consistently have similar types of foreign policies (comparing across states or across different time periods for a single state). Such studies have focused on three characteristics in particular: size, wealth, and extent of democratic participation in government.[2] An alternative approach categorizes societies according to their relative populations, natural resources, and levels of technology.[3]

A major focus of such studies is whether certain characteristics of a state or society predispose it to be more warlike or aggressive. In particular, during the Cold War scholars debated whether communism or capitalism was inherently more warlike in nature. However, no simple rule has been found to predict a state's warlike tendencies based on attributes such as size, wealth, and type of government. There is great variation among states, and even within a single state over time. Both capitalist and communist states have proven capable of naked aggression or peaceful behaviour, depending on circumstances.

Some political scientists have tried to interpret particular states' foreign policies in terms of each one's *political culture and history*. For example, both superpowers in the Cold War had been shaped by long periods of geographical expansion, which reached limits only in the twentieth century. This may help explain the global, expansionist foreign policies of both superpowers during the Cold War. But the Soviet Union (Russia) had experienced repeated devastating land invasions over the centuries (culminating in World War II) while the United States had experienced two centuries of safety behind great oceans. Thus the military might of the Soviet Union, and its control of buffer states in Eastern Europe, seemed defensive in nature to Soviet leaders but appeared aggressive to U.S. leaders.

Most studies of foreign policy have not focused on the comparison of policies of different states, however; they have instead concentrated on understanding in a more general way the kinds of processes used in various states to reach (and implement) foreign policies. Scholars have tried to probe the effects of these processes on the resulting outcomes.

foreign policy process
The process by which foreign policies are arrived at and implemented.

---

[1] Kim Richard Nossal, *The Politics of Canadian Foreign Policy* (Scarborough: Prentice Hall Canada, 1997). Laura Neack, *The New Foreign Policy: U.S. and Comparative Foreign Policy in the 21st Century* (Lanham, MD: Rowman & Littlefield, 2003). Deborah J. Gerner, "Foreign Policy Analysis: Exhilarating Eclecticism, Intriguing Enigmas," *International Studies Notes* 16.3 (1991): 4–19.

[2] Steven W. Hook, *Comparative Foreign Policy* (Upper Saddle River, NJ: Prentice Hall, 2002). James N. Rosenau, *The Scientific Study of Foreign Policy*, 2nd ed. (London: Frances Pinter, 1980).

[3] Robert C. North, *The World That Could Be* (Palo Alto, CA: Stanford Alumni Association, 1976).

UNEASY CROWN
Foreign policy outcomes result from processes at several levels of analysis. Heads of state act on the interstate and domestic levels—for example, managing Nepal's conflict with India and its response to a Maoist insurgency. But they are also individuals, subject to forces at the individual level of analysis that defy rationality—such as mistakes, misperceptions, accidents, and assassinations. Here the new king of Nepal (a constitutional monarchy) is crowned after a palace massacre killed much of the royal family, 2001.

The foreign policy process is a process of *decision-making*. States take actions because people in governments choose those actions. People whose job it is to make decisions about international relations—*decision-makers*—have to go through the same kinds of processes, in one way or another, that anyone would go through even in deciding what to eat for dinner.

Decision-making is a *steering* process in which adjustments are made as a result of feedback from the outside world. Decisions are carried out by actions taken to change the world, and then information from the world is monitored to evaluate the effects of actions. These evaluations—along with information about other, independent changes in the environment—go into the next round of decisions (see Figure 4.1). The steering process, with its external feedback, is based on the *goals* of the decision-maker. Along the way to these goals, decision-makers set *objectives* as discrete steps to be reached. Objectives fall along a spectrum from core, long-term objectives to very short-term, practical objectives.

MODELS OF DECISION-MAKING: THE RATIONAL ACTOR MODEL

rational actor model (of decision-making) A model in which decision-makers calculate the costs and benefits of each possible course of action, then choose the one with the highest benefits and lowest costs.

A common starting point for studying the decision-making process is the **rational actor model.**[4] In this model, decision-makers calculate the costs and benefits of each possible course of action, then choose the one with the highest benefits and lowest costs. This model is favoured by realists. For some scholars, the state is seen as generating decisions in a manner analogous to the decision-making process undertaken by an individual. Whether it is understood as actual individuals involved in decision-making, or by analogy to individual decision-making, the rational actor model envisions a number of steps in the decision-making process:

1. *Clarify goals* in the situation.

2. *Order them* by importance (in case different goals conflict).

---

[4] It, along with the organizational process and bureaucratic politics models discussed later, derives from Graham Allison; see Graham T. Allison and Philip Zelikow, *Essence of Decision: Explaining the Cuban Missile Crisis*, 2nd ed. (NY: Longman, 1999). Jonathan Bendor and Thomas H. Hammond, "Rethinking Allison's Models," *American Political Science Review* 86.2 (1992): 301–22.

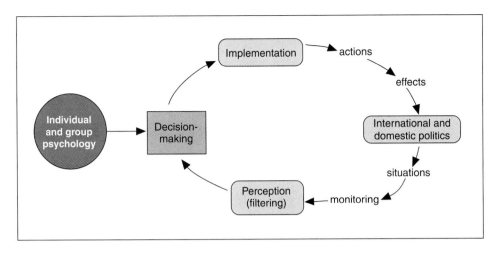

Figure 4.1 Decision-Making as Steering

3. *List the alternatives* available to achieve the goals.

4. *Investigate the consequences* (probable and possible outcomes) of those alternatives.

5. *Choose* the course of action that will produce the best outcome (in terms of reaching one's goals).

The choice may be complicated by *uncertainty* about the costs and benefits of various actions. In such cases, decision-makers must attach probabilities to each possible outcome of an action. Some decision-makers are relatively *accepting of risk*, whereas others are *averse to risk*. These factors affect the importance that decision-makers place on various alternative outcomes that could result from an action. For example, U.S. President George W. Bush's decision to invade Iraq showed high acceptance of risk. The potential benefits were great (including seizing possible weapons of mass destruction), and Bush was willing to risk the lives of American and Coalition military personnel on the chance that such a gamble might pay off.

The rational actor model may imply that decision-making is simpler than is actually the case. A decision-maker may hold different conflicting goals simultaneously. The goals of different individuals involved in making a decision may diverge, as may the goals of different state agencies. The rational model of decision-making thus is somewhat complicated by uncertainty and the multiple goals of decision-makers.

Although the rational model is the usual starting point for thinking about foreign policy decision-making, there are many reasons to question whether decisions can be considered rational. These nonrational elements in decision-making are best understood from a *psychological* analysis of individual and group decision-making processes.[5]

Individual Decision-Makers

Individuals are the only true actors in IR. Every international event is the result, intended or unintended, of decisions made by individuals. IR does not just happen. President Harry Truman, who made the decision to drop U.S. nuclear bombs on two Japanese cities in

---

[5] Philip E. Tetlock, "Psychological Advice on Foreign Policy: What Do We Have to Contribute?" *American Psychologist* 41 (1986): 557–67. Zeev Maoz, *Domestic Sources of Global Change* (Ann Arbor: U Michigan P, 1996).

Thinking Theoretically

In 1988 during the Canadian federal election campaign, the Liberal Party promised to tear up the Free Trade Agreement between the U.S. and Canada if it was elected. Although the Liberals and the New Democratic Party (also opposed to free trade) together received a combined majority of the popular vote in that election, the Progressive Conservative Party, which supported free trade, won more seats in Parliament. The Free Trade Agreement subsequently went into effect on 1 January 1989. However, five years later, when the Liberals, under Prime Minister Jean Chrétien, formed the Canadian government, their position on free trade had changed. Once elected, the Liberal Party not only retained the agreement but signed on to the North American Free Trade Agreement (NAFTA) and sought to expand it to the entire Western Hemisphere (with the exception of Cuba) under the Free Trade Agreement of the Americas (FTAA). What theories might help explain this switch? A variety of explanations might be drawn from the three theoretical perspectives.

One theory, the organizational process model, holds that government bureaucracies churn out policy in a routine manner, with only incremental change as political leaders come and go. The liberal pluralist (not to be confused with Liberal Party) elements of this model include its understanding of the state as a complex organization cross-cut by numerous departments and agencies, its emphasis on substate actors, and its view of change as incremental. This reasoning could explain the continuity in Canadian policy on free trade, even when a new leader and party came in with new ideas. The relevant departments "educated" the Liberal Party and Prime Minister Chrétien, and policy remained relatively unchanged.

A different theoretical approach, drawing on realist themes, explains decisions such as free trade agreements as actions taken rationally (benefits exceed costs) in pursuit of national interests. These interests for realists tend to be defined, rather narrowly, as access to tangible power resources such as territory, energy supplies, wealth, strategic military bases, and the like. By this line of reasoning, the Liberals did not change the Canadian position on free trade because Canadian interests had not changed. For realists, neither political rhetoric nor changes in government matter as much as basic national interests and capabilities. The Liberal Prime Minister Jean Chrétien made roughly the same cost-benefit calculation as had the Progressive Conservative Prime Minister Brian Mulroney.

A critical theory perspective might suggest that mainstream political parties like the Liberal Party usually have close ties with, and depend upon the support of, Canadian business and other elites within Canadian society. Those interests support either what is good for business or, more broadly, what facilitates the continued and smooth functioning of capitalism. For critical theorists, no matter what political parties may say as part of their election platforms, when they are in power, they will make decisions that support those business and elite interests.

The difficulty within the study of international relations is that there are no "experiments" in which theories can be tested against each other. Often scholars and students of IR can only make judgments based on how persuasive a case each perspective presents. This means assessing the coherence of the argument and the quality of the evidence mounted in support of contending positions. Which position do you find most convincing?

1945, understood this. He had a sign on his desk: "The buck stops here." If he chose to use the bomb (as he did), more than 100 000 civilians would die. If he chose not to, the war might drag on for months with tens of thousands of U.S. casualties. Truman had to choose. Some people applaud his decision; others condemn it. But for better or worse, Truman as an individual had to decide, and to take responsibility for the consequences. Similarly, the decisions of individual citizens, although they may not seem important when taken one by one, are what create the great forces of world history.

The study of individual decision-making revolves around the question of rationality. To what extent are national leaders (or citizens) able to make rational decisions in the national interest—if indeed such an interest can be defined—and thus to conform to a realist view of IR? Individual rationality is not equivalent to state rationality: states might filter individuals' irrational decisions so as to arrive at rational choices, or states might distort individually rational decisions and end up with irrational state choices. But realists tend to assume that both states and individuals are rational and that the goals or interests of states correlate with those of leaders. Partly this assumption reflects the role of strong individuals such as monarchs and dictators in many states, where the rationality and interests of the leader determine those of the state.

The most simplified rational-actor models go so far as to assume that interests are the same from one actor to another. If this were so, individuals could be substituted for each other in various roles without changing history very much. And states would all behave similarly to each other (or rather, the differences between them would reflect different resources, geography, and similar features, not differences in the nature of national inter- ests). Many realists make this type of assumption, but it is at best a great oversimplifica- tion.[6] In truth, individual decisions reflect the *values* and *beliefs* of the decision-maker.

How can IR scholars characterize an individual's values and beliefs? Sometimes beliefs and values are spelled out in ideological autobiographies such as Hitler's *Mein Kampf*. Other times IR researchers try to infer beliefs through a method called *content analysis*—analyzing speeches or other documents to count the number of times key words or phrases are repeated, and in what contexts. Scholars of IR have also described *opera- tional codes*—routines and methods that mediate between beliefs and practical actions. They have traced out such operational codes, for example, for Soviet communist leaders.[7] Other scholars have created computer-based models of beliefs.[8]

The goals of individuals differ, as do the ways in which they pursue those goals. Individual decision-makers not only have differing values and beliefs, but also have unique personalities—their personal experiences, intellectual capabilities, and personal styles of making decisions. Some IR scholars study individual psychology to understand how personality affects decision-making. *Psychoanalytic approaches* hold that personal- ities reflect the subconscious influences of childhood experiences. For instance, some scholars believe Canadian Prime Minister Pierre Elliott Trudeau's adolescent fears of being left behind, his own sense that he was neither physically strong nor intellectually bright (despite all evidence to the contrary), contributed to a later refusal to back down in a fight. During the 1970 October Crisis, Trudeau earned the admiration of many foreign leaders for his refusal to yield to terrorist demands of the Front de Libération de Québec (FLQ), but his suspension of civil liberties earned him much criticism at home.[9]

U.S. President Clinton's early years in office drew much criticism for a foreign policy that seemed to zigzag. A notable Clinton personality trait was his readiness to compromise. Clinton himself has noted that his experience of growing up with a violent, alcoholic step- father shaped him into a "peacemaker, always trying to minimize the disruption."[10]

---

[6] James M. Goldgeier, *Leadership Style and Soviet Foreign Policy: Stalin, Khrushchev, Brezhnev, Gorbachev* (Baltimore: Johns Hopkins UP, 1994). Barbara Farnham, *Roosevelt and the Munich Crisis: A Study of Political Decision-Making* (Princeton, NJ: Princeton UP, 1997).

[7] Alexander L. George, "The 'Operational Code': A Neglected Approach to the Study of Political Leaders and Decision Making," *International Studies Quarterly* 13.2 (1969): 199–222.

[8] Charles S. Taber, "POLI: An Expert System Model of U.S. Foreign Policy Belief Systems," *American Political Science Review* 86.4 (1992). Valerie M. Hudson, ed., *Artificial Intelligence and International Politics* (Boulder, CO: Westview, 1991).

[9] Richard Gwyn, *The Northern Magus: Pierre Trudeau and Canadians* (Toronto: McClelland & Stewart, 1980).

[10] Nancy Collins, "A Legacy of Strength and Love," interview with President Clinton, *Good Housekeeping* 221.5 (Nov. 1995): 113–115.

Beyond individual *idiosyncrasies* in goals or decision-making processes, there are at least three *systematic* ways in which individual decision-making diverges from the rational actor model. First, decision-makers suffer from **misperceptions and selective perceptions** (taking in only some kinds of information) when they compile information on the likely consequences of their choices.[11] Decision-making processes must by necessity reduce and filter the incoming information on which a decision is based; the problem is that such filtration often is biased. **Information screens** are subconscious filters through which people put the information coming in about the world around them. Often they simply ignore any information that does not fit their expectations. Information is also screened out as it passes from one person to another in the decision-making process. For example, prior to the September 2001 terrorist attacks, U.S. intelligence agencies failed to adequately interpret available evidence, in part because too few analysts were fluent in Arabic. Similarly, Soviet leaders in 1941 and Israeli leaders in 1973 ignored evidence of pending invasions of their countries.

Second, the rationality of individual cost-benefit calculations is undermined by emotions that decision-makers feel while thinking about the consequences of their actions—an effect referred to as *affective bias*. (Positive and negative affect refer to feelings of liking or disliking someone.) As hard as a decision-maker tries to be rational in making a decision, the decision-making process is bound to be influenced by strong feelings held about the person or state toward which a decision is directed. (Affective biases also contribute to information screening, as positive information about disliked people or negative information about liked people is screened out.)

Third, *cognitive biases* are systematic distortions of rational calculations based not on emotional feelings but simply on the limitations of the human brain in making choices. The most important seems to be the attempt to produce *cognitive balance*—or to reduce *cognitive dissonance*. These terms refer to the tendency people have to try to maintain mental models of the world that are logically consistent (this seldom succeeds entirely). For instance, after deciding whether to intervene militarily in a conflict, a state leader will very likely adjust his or her mental model to downplay the risks and exaggerate the gains of the chosen course of action.[12]

One implication of cognitive balance is that decision-makers place greater value on goals that they have put much effort into achieving—the *justification of effort*. This is especially true in a democracy where politicians must face their citizens' judgment at the polls and so do not want to admit failures. Although it is still too early to judge with any certainty, British and American involvement in Iraq may have trapped decision-makers in this way. After sending hundreds of thousands of troops halfway around the world it will be difficult for U.S. or British leaders to admit to themselves that the costs of the war may be greater than the benefits.

Decision-makers also achieve cognitive balance through *wishful thinking*—an overestimate of the probability of a desired outcome. A variation of wishful thinking is to assume that an event with a *low probability* of occurring will *not* occur. This could be a dangerous way to think about catastrophic events such as accidental nuclear war.

misperceptions and selective perceptions The selective or mistaken processing of the available information about a decision; one of several ways—along with affective and cognitive bias—in which individual decision-making diverges from the *rational model*.

information screens The subconscious or unconscious filters through which people put the information coming in about the world around them.

---

[11] Robert Jervis, *Perception and Misperception in International Politics* (Princeton, NJ: Princeton UP, 1976). Robert Jervis, *The Logic of Images in International Relations* (NY: Columbia UP, 1989).

[12] Yaacov Y. I. Vertzberger, *The World in Their Minds: Information Processing, Cognition, and Perception in Foreign Policy Decisionmaking* (Palo Alto, CA: Stanford UP, 1990). Richard Hermann, "The Empirical Challenge of the Cognitive Revolution: A Strategy for Drawing Inferences about Perceptions," *International Studies Quarterly* 32.2 (1988): 175–204. Martha L. Cottam, *Foreign Policy Decision Making: The Influence of Cognition* (Boulder, CO: Westview, 1986).

Cognitive balance often leads decision-makers to maintain a hardened image of an *enemy* and to interpret all the enemy's actions in a negative light (since the idea of bad people doing good things would create cognitive dissonance).[13] Obviously, this cognitive bias overlaps with the affective bias felt toward such enemies.

A *mirror image* refers to two sides in a conflict maintaining very similar enemy images of each other ("we are defensive, they are aggressive," etc.). This happens frequently in ethnic conflicts. A decision-maker may experience psychological *projection* of his or her own feelings onto another actor. For instance, if (hypothetically) Indian leaders wanted to gain nuclear superiority over Pakistan but found that goal inconsistent with their image of themselves as peaceful and defensive, the resulting cognitive dissonance might be resolved by believing that Pakistan was trying to gain nuclear superiority (the example works as well with the states reversed).

Another form of cognitive bias, related to cognitive balance, is the use of *historical analogies* to structure one's thinking about a decision. This can be quite useful or quite misleading, depending on whether the analogy is appropriate.[14] As each historical situation is unique in some way, when a decision-maker latches onto an analogy and uses it as a shortcut to a decision, the rational calculation of costs and benefits may be cut short as well. For example, U.S. leaders used the analogy of Munich in 1938 to convince themselves that appeasement of communism in the Vietnam War would lead to increased communist aggression in Asia. In retrospect, the differences between North Vietnam and Nazi Germany made this a poor analogy. Vietnam then became a potent analogy that helped convince U.S. leaders to avoid involvement in certain overseas conflicts, including Bosnia; this was called the "Vietnam syndrome" in U.S. foreign policy.

All these psychological processes—misperception, affective biases, and cognitive biases—interfere with the rational assessment of costs and benefits in making a decision.[15] Two specific modifications to the rational model of decision-making have been proposed to accommodate psychological realities.

First, the model of *bounded rationality* takes into account the costs of seeking and processing information. Nobody thinks about every single possible course of action when making a decision. Instead of **optimizing,** or picking the very best option, people usually work on the problem until they come up with a "good enough" option that meets some minimal criteria; this is called **satisficing,** or finding a satisfactory solution.[16] The time constraints faced by top decision-makers in IR—who are constantly besieged with crises requiring their attention—generally preclude their finding the very best response to a situation. These time constraints were described by U.S. Defense Secretary William Cohen in 1997: "The unrelenting flow of information, the need to digest it on a minute-by-minute basis, is quite different from anything I've experienced before.... There's little time for contemplation; most of it is action."[17]

optimizing Picking the very best option; contrasts with *satisficing,* or finding a satisfactory but less than best solution to a problem. The model of "bounded rationality" postulates that decision-makers generally satisfice rather than optimize.

satisficing The act of finding a satisfactory or "good enough" solution to a problem.

---

[13] Sam Keen, *Faces of the Enemy: Reflections of the Hostile Imagination* (San Francisco: Harper & Row, 1986).

[14] George W. Breslauer and Philip E. Tetlock, eds., *Learning in U.S. and Soviet Foreign Policy* (Boulder, CO: Westview, 1991). Yuen Foong Khong, *Analogies at War: Korea, Munich, Dien Bien Phu, and the Vietnam Decisions of 1965* (Princeton, NJ: Princeton UP, 1992).

[15] Barbara W. Tuchman, *The March of Folly: From Troy to Vietnam* (NY: Knopf/Random House, 1984). Richard B. Parker, *The Politics of Miscalculation in the Middle East* (Bloomington: Indiana UP, 1993). Andrew Bennett, *Condemned to Repetition? The Rise, Fall, and Reprise of Soviet-Russian Military Interventionism, 1973–1996* (Cambridge, MA: MIT, 1999).

[16] Herbert A. Simon, *Models of Bounded Rationality* (Cambridge, MA: MIT, 1982).

[17] *Washington Post,* 5 March 1997: A22.

Second, *prospect theory* provides an alternative explanation (rather than simple rational optimization) of decisions made under risk or uncertainty.[18] According to this theory, decision-makers go through two phases. In the editing phase they frame the options available and the probabilities of various outcomes associated with each option. Then in the evaluation phase they assess the options and choose one. Prospect theory holds that evaluations take place by comparison with a *reference point*, which is often the status quo but might be some past or expected situation. The decision-maker asks if she or he can do better than that reference point, but the value placed on outcomes depends on how far from the reference point they are. The theory also holds that individuals *fear losses* more than they relish gains. Decision-makers are therefore often willing to forgo opportunities rather than risk a setback.

Individual decision-making thus follows an imperfect and partial kind of rationality at best. Not only do the goals of different individuals vary, but decision-makers face a series of obstacles in receiving accurate information, constructing accurate models of the world, and reaching decisions that further their own goals. The rational model is only a simplification at best and must be supplemented by an understanding of individual psychological processes that affect decision-making.

Not even an absolute dictator, however, makes decisions all alone. State decisions result from the interactions of groups of people. Leaders surround themselves with advisers to help them think about decisions. Decision-making bodies—from committees and agency task forces to legislatures and political parties—all rely on the interactions of relatively small groups of people reasoning or arguing together. The psychology of group dynamics, as will be discussed below, thus has great influence on the way foreign policy is formulated.

MODELS OF DECISION-MAKING: THE ORGANIZATIONAL PROCESS AND BUREAUCRATIC POLITICS MODELS

Liberal pluralist analysts (and some realists) argue that the state is more complex than is suggested by the rational actor model. From this perspective, governments are complex organizations, with many departments and agencies each charged with particular areas of responsibility. In Canada, for example, the Departments of National Defence, International Trade, and Foreign Affairs are all involved in Canada's relationship to the rest of the world, but they are involved in different aspects of that relationship: one is charged with the defence of the nation, one focuses on trade, while the third concentrates on peace and diplomacy.

Organizational Process Model

Once the state is understood as a complex organization, the manner in which that organization generates decisions is also understood quite differently. One alternative to the rational actor model is called the **organizational process model.** In this model, foreign policy decision-makers generally skip the labour-intensive process of identifying goals and

organizational process model A decision-making model in which policy-makers or lower-level officials rely largely on standardized responses or standard operating procedures.

---

[18] James W. Davis, *Threats and Promises: The Pursuit of International Influence* (Baltimore: Johns Hopkins UP, 2000). Rose McDermott, *Risk-Taking in International Politics: Prospect Theory in American Foreign Policy* (Ann Arbor: U Michigan P, 1998). Barbara Farnham, ed. *Avoiding Losses/Taking Risks: Prospect Theory and International Conflict* (Ann Arbor: U Michigan P, 1994). Jack S. Levy, "Prospect Theory, Rational Choice, and International Relations," *International Studies Quarterly* 41.1 (1997): 87–112.

alternative actions in response to every situation as it arises, relying instead for most decisions on standardized responses or *standard operating procedures*. For example, the Department of Foreign Affairs every day receives upwards of a thousand reports or inquiries from its embassies around the world and sends out as many responses or instructions in return. The vast majority of those cables, phone calls, and emails are never seen by the top decision-makers (the minister of Foreign Affairs or the prime minister); instead, they are handled by low-level decision-makers who apply general principles—or who simply try to make the least controversial, most standardized decision. These low-level decisions may not even reflect the high-level policies adopted by top leaders, but rather have a life of their own. The organizational process model implies that much of foreign policy results from "management by muddling through."[19]

What is distinctive about decisions that are understood to be generated through the organizational processes model is their preprogrammed character. Departments or agencies within a government do not wait to respond to events as they happen; rather, they prepare "standard" responses that can be implemented when the need arises. These standard operating procedures allow the coordination of hundreds of individuals within an organization, but they do not address new situations very well.

Bureaucratic Politics or Government Bargaining Model

Another alternative to the rational model is the **bureaucratic politics model** (also called the *government bargaining model*). This model also envisions the state as a complex organization, but suggests that what is distinctive about foreign policy decision-making is the bargaining process among various government agencies with somewhat divergent interests in the outcome.[20] In 1996, the Canadian government became actively involved in supporting a ban on anti-personnel landmines, a particularly insidious weapon that annually claimed some 26 000 casualties, many of whom were civilians. In Canada, the push to achieve a ban came from the Department of Foreign Affairs (at that time called the Department of Foreign Affairs and International Trade, or DFAIT). The Department of National Defence, by contrast, resisted the ban, arguing in part that landmines were legitimate weapons and could not be eliminated until "effective and humane alternatives" could be found. In the end, DFAIT's position was the most successful, and a Convention to Ban Anti-Personnel Landmines was signed by 122 countries in Ottawa in December of 1997.[21]

The bureaucratic politics model emphasizes the way in which certain agencies or departments within government traditionally clash, and an endless tug-of-war shapes the foreign policies that emerge. In an extreme example of interagency rivalry, the U.S. State Department and the CIA backed opposite sides in a civil war in Laos in 1960.

In general, bureaucracies promote policies in which their own capabilities would be effective and their power would increase. There is a saying within this model that "where

bureaucratic politics model A decision-making model that sees foreign policy decisions as flowing from a bargaining process among various government agencies that have somewhat divergent interests in the outcome ("where you stand depends on where you sit"). Also called the *government bargaining model*.

---

[19] Deborah D. Avant, *Political Institutions and Military Change: Lessons from Peripheral Wars* (Ithaca, NY: Cornell UP, 1995). Jack S. Levy, "Organizational Routines and the Causes of War," *International Studies Quarterly* 30.2 (1986): 193–222.

[20] David A. Welch, "The Organizational Process and Bureaucratic Politics Paradigms: Retrospect and Prospect," *International Security* 17.2 (1992): 112–46.

[21] Maxwell A. Cameron, Robert J. Lawson, and Brian W. Tomlin, *To Walk Without Fear: The Global Movement to Ban Landmines* (Toronto: Oxford UP, 1998).

you stand" on an issue "depends on where you sit" (in the bureaucratic structure). In the example of the landmines debate above, the Department of National Defence claimed that any issue concerning a weapon fell exclusively within its area of responsibility, and so DND ought to determine the policy stance of the Canadian government on that issue. DND failed in persuading the prime minister, or the government in general, to adopt this position. One can often predict just from the job titles of participants how they will argue on a policy issue. The government bargaining model pays special attention to the inter-agency negotiations that result from conflicts of interest between agencies of the same government. The conflicting and overlapping interests of agencies can be complex, especially in large governments such as those of the great or middle powers, with dozens of agencies that deal with international relations. And although representatives of bureaucratic agencies usually promote the interests of their own bureaucracies, sometimes heads of agencies try to appear loyal to the state leader by forgoing the interests of their own agencies.

Units within agencies have similar tensions. In many countries, the different military services (army, navy, air force) pull in somewhat different directions, even if they ultimately unite to battle the foreign ministry. Bureaucrats working in particular units or projects become attached to them. Officials responsible for a new weapon system will lose bureaucratic turf, and perhaps their jobs, if the weapon's development is cancelled.

Of special concern in many poor states is the institutional interest that military officers have in maintaining a strong military. If civilian state leaders allow officers' salaries to fall or the size of the military forces to be cut, they may well face institutional resistance from the military—in the extreme case a military takeover of the government (see pp. 208–211). These issues were factors in attempted military coups in the Philippines, Venezuela, and other states in the 1990s.

Different states develop different institutional capabilities, in terms of both size (of budget and personnel) and specialization. These differences in institutions help explain differences in states' foreign policies.

In general, bureaucratic rivalry as an influence on foreign policy challenges the notion of states as unitary actors in the international system. Such rivalries suggest that a state does not have any single set of goals—a national interest—but that its actions may result from the bargaining of subunits, each with its own set of goals.[22] Furthermore, such a perspective extends far beyond bureaucratic agencies because other substate actors have their own goals, which they seek to advance by influencing foreign policy.

Group Dynamics

Both the organizational process and bureaucratic politics models signal that it is the larger organization, or group, that is an important consideration in understanding foreign policy decision-making. This view necessarily raises questions about the implications of group psychology for foreign policy decision-making. In one respect, groups promote rationality by balancing out the blind spots and biases of any individual. Advisers or legislative committees may force a state leader to reconsider a rash decision. And the interactions of different individuals in a group may result in the formulation of goals that more closely reflect state interests rather than individual idiosyncrasies. However, group dynamics also introduce new sources of irrationality into the decision-making process. These fall into two gen-

---

[22] Richard D. Anderson, Jr., Margaret G. Hermann, and Charles F. Hermann, "Explaining Self-Defeating Foreign Policy Decisions: Interpreting Soviet Arms for Egypt in 1973 through Process or Domestic Bargaining Models?" (Comment and Response), *American Political Science Review* 86.3 (1992): 759–67.

eral categories: the psychological dynamics that occur within groups, and the ways that the structure of group decision-making processes can bias the outcomes.

Group Psychology The most important psychological problem is the tendency for groups to reach decisions without accurately assessing their consequences, since individual members tend to go along with ideas they think the others support. This is called **groupthink**.[23] The basic phenomenon is illustrated by a simple psychology experiment. A group of six people is asked to compare the lengths of two lines projected onto a screen. When five of the people are secretly instructed to say that line A is longer—even though anyone can see that line B is actually longer—the sixth person is likely to agree with the group rather than believe her or his own eyes.

Unlike individuals, groups tend to be overly optimistic about the chances of success and are thus more willing to take risks. Doubts about dubious undertakings are suppressed by participants because everyone else seems to think an idea will work. Also, because the group diffuses responsibility from individuals, nobody feels accountable for actions.

In a spectacular case of groupthink, President Ronald Reagan's close friend and director of the U.S. Central Intelligence Agency (CIA), William Casey, bypassed his own agency and ran covert operations spanning three continents using the National Security Council (NSC) staff in the White House basement. The NSC sold weapons to Iran in exchange for the freedom of U.S. hostages held in Lebanon, and then used the Iranian payments to illegally fund Nicaraguan Contra rebels. The *Iran-Contra scandal* resulted when these operations, managed by an obscure NSC aide named Oliver North, became public. Because the operation was secret, the small group involved was cut off from skeptical views, and its few participants seem to have talked themselves into thinking that the operation was a smart idea. They discounted risks such as being discovered and exaggerated the benefits of opening channels to Iranian moderates (who proved elusive). The involvement of a top authority figure surely reassured other participants.

groupthink The tendency of individual members of a group to go along with ideas they think other group members support, leading to the adoption of decisions that conform to group sentiment but not necessarily to the available evidence (and in extreme cases, that contravene legal or ethical norms).

---

[23] Irving L. Janis, *Victims of Groupthink: A Psychological Study of Foreign-Policy Decisions and Fiascoes* (Boston: Houghton Mifflin, 1972). Paul Hart, Eric K. Stern, and Bengt Sundelius, eds., *Beyond Groupthink: Political Group Dynamics and Foreign Policy-Making* (Ann Arbor: U Michigan P, 1997).

A U.S. Senate intelligence committee concluded in 2004 that the CIA succumbed again to groupthink when it collected and presented its evidence in support of the U.S. invasion of Iraq. The report claimed that the agency used overstated, misleading, and incorrect information to convince the president, the Senate, and U.S. allies that Saddam Hussein was amassing weapons of mass destruction. Analysts within the CIA ignored information that contradicted their presumptions about Iraqi weapons, and focused only on evidence that supported their conclusions. Calling it "the most devastating intelligence failure in the history of the nation," the senators who authored the report said that this case of groupthink resulted in an avoidable war, with significant loss of life on all sides. It also inflamed anti-American sentiment around the world, making the U.S. and its citizens more, rather than less, vulnerable.[24]

Decision Structure   The *structure of a decision-making process*—the rules for who is involved in making the decision, how voting is conducted, and so forth—can affect the outcome, especially true when a group has *indeterminate preferences* because no single alternative appeals to a majority of participants. Experienced participants in foreign policy formation are familiar with the techniques for manipulating decision-making processes to favour outcomes they prefer. A common technique is to control a group's formal *decision rules*. These rules include the items of business the group discusses and the order in which proposals are considered (especially important when participants are satisficing). Probably most important is the ability to *control the agenda* and thereby structure the terms of debate. A group's voting procedures also affect the choices it makes. Procedures requiring more votes for adoption tend to favour conservative approaches to policy, whereas those allowing adoption with a mere plurality of votes tend to allow more frequent changes in policy.

The structure of decision-making also reflects the composition of a decision group. Who is represented? Often the group is composed of individuals cast in particular *roles* in the group. (Some IR scholars treat role as a distinct level of analysis between the individual and domestic levels.) Roles can be institutional—a participant representing a viewpoint shared by her or his particular group, for example, an intelligence agency. Different sorts of roles within particular groups can be based on factions, mediators, swing voters, and so forth. One adviser might often play the role of introducing new ideas, another the role of defending the status quo, and a third the role of staying neutral so as to gain the leader's ear last.

State leaders often rely on an inner circle of advisers in making foreign policy decisions. In Canada, the Cabinet is formally the inner circle, a group of ministers which, in principle, collectively makes foreign policy decisions. Some groups depend heavily on *informal* consultations in addition to formal meetings. Some leaders create a "kitchen cabinet"—a trusted group of friends who discuss policy issues with the leader even though they have no formal positions in government. For instance, Israel's Golda Meir held many such discussions at her home, sometimes literally in the kitchen. Russian President Boris Yeltsin relied on the advice of his bodyguard, who was a trusted friend. Canadian Prime Minister Lester B. Pearson often made foreign policy decisions together with his Minister of External Affairs, Paul Martin (father of Prime Minister Paul Martin), and together they informed Cabinet colleagues after the fact.[25]

---

[24] Janice Tibbetts, "CIA's 'group-think' blamed for U.S. decision to go to war," *Ottawa Citizen* 10 July 2004: A9.

[25] Kim Richard Nossal, *The Politics of Canadian Foreign Policy* (see footnote 1 in this chapter). During Pearson's time, the ministry of Foreign Affairs was called the Department of External Affairs.

Informal settings may be used in another way—to shake up formal decision groups and draw participants away from their usual bureaucratic roles. Soviet Premier Leonid Brezhnev in 1972 took President Richard Nixon on a speedboat ride before settling down for discussions at Brezhnev's dacha (villa) in the countryside.

Crisis Management

The difficulties in reaching rational decisions, both for individuals and for groups, are heightened during a crisis.[26] *Crises* are foreign policy situations in which outcomes are very important and time frames are compressed. There is no firm boundary between crises and routine policy-making. But if a situation drags on for months or loses the dedicated attention of the top political leaders, it is not considered a crisis anymore. Crisis decision-making is harder to understand and predict than is normal foreign policy-making.

In a crisis, decision-makers operate under tremendous time constraints. The normal checks on unwise decisions may not operate. Communications become shorter and more stereotyped, and information that does not fit a decision-maker's expectations is more likely to be discarded simply because there is no time to consider it. In framing options there is a tendency to restrict the choices, again to save time, and a tendency to overlook creative options while focusing on the most obvious ones.

Groupthink occurs easily during crises. During the 1962 Cuban Missile Crisis, U.S. President John Kennedy created a small, closed group of advisers who worked together intensively for days on end, cut off from outside contact and discussion. Even the president's communication with Soviet leader Nikita Khrushchev was rerouted through Kennedy's brother Robert and the Soviet ambassador, cutting out the State Department. Recognizing the danger of groupthink, Kennedy would leave the room from time to time—removing the authority figure from the group—to encourage free discussion. Through this and other means, the group managed to identify a third option (a naval blockade) beyond their first two choices (bombing the missile sites or doing nothing).

Participants in crisis decision-making are not only rushed, they experience severe psychological *stress*. As most of us have experienced personally, people usually do not make decisions wisely when under stress. Stress amplifies the biases just discussed. Decision-makers tend to overestimate the hostility of adversaries and to underestimate their own hostility toward those adversaries. Dislike easily turns to hatred, and anxiety to fear. More and more information is screened out in order to come to terms with decisions being made and to restore cognitive balance. Crisis decision-making also leads to physical exhaustion. *Sleep deprivation* sets in within days as decision-makers use every hour to stay on top of the crisis. University students who have "pulled an all-nighter"—or several in a row—know that within days people deprived of sleep lose touch with reality, experience everything as exaggerated, and suffer from depression and even hallucinations. Unless decision-makers are careful about getting enough sleep, these are the conditions under which vital foreign policy decisions may be made. In addition to sleep deprivation, physiological stress comes from drugs used by top policy-makers—often nicotine and caffeine in high doses, and sometimes alcohol.

Because of the importance of sound decision-making during crises, voters pay great attention to the psychological stability of their leaders. Before Israeli Prime Minister

---

[26] Michael Brecher and Jonathan Wilkenfeld, *A Study of Crisis* (Ann Arbor: U Michigan P, 2000). David Houghton, *U.S. Foreign Policy and the Iran Hostage Crisis* (NY: Cambridge UP, 2001). James L. Richardson, *Crisis Diplomacy: The Great Powers since the Mid-Nineteenth Century* (NY: Cambridge UP, 1994). Richard Ned Lebow, *Between Peace and War: The Nature of International Crisis* (Baltimore: Johns Hopkins UP, 1981).

Yitzhak Rabin won election in 1992, he faced charges that he had suffered a one-day nervous breakdown when he headed the armed forces just before the 1967 war. Not so, he responded; he was just smart enough to realize that the crisis had caused both exhaustion and acute nicotine poisoning; he needed to rest up for a day in order to go on and make good decisions.

Whether in crisis mode or normal routines, individual decision-makers do not operate alone. Their decisions are shaped by the government and society in which they work. Foreign policy is constrained and shaped by substate actors ranging from government agencies to political interest groups and industries.

Substate Actors

Foreign policy is shaped not only by the internal dynamics of individual and group decision-making but also by the states and societies within which decision-makers operate.

Bureaucracies   The substate actors closest to the foreign policy process are the state's bureaucratic agencies maintained for developing and carrying out foreign policy. Different states maintain different foreign policy bureaucracies but share some common elements.

Virtually all states maintain a *diplomatic corps*, or *foreign service*, of diplomats working in *embassies* in foreign capitals (and in *consulates* located in noncapital foreign cities), as well as diplomats who remain at home to help coordinate foreign policy. States appoint *ambassadors* as their official representatives to other states and to international organizations. Diplomatic activities are organized through a *foreign ministry* or the equivalent (for example, Foreign Affairs Canada, or the U.S. State Department).

In many democracies, some diplomats are *political appointees* who come and go with changes in government leaders (often as patronage for past political support). Others are *career diplomats*, who come up through the ranks of the foreign service and tend to outlast changes in administration. Skilled diplomats are assets that increase a state's power.

Diplomats provide much of the information that goes into making foreign policies, but their main role is to carry out rather than create policies. Nonetheless, foreign ministry bureaucrats can often make foreign relations so routine that top leaders and political appointees can come and go without greatly altering the country's relations. The national interest is served, the bureaucrats believe, by the stability of overall national goals and positions in international affairs.

Tension is common between state leaders and foreign policy bureaucrats. Career diplomats try to orient new leaders and their

WORKING UNDER STRESS
Crisis management takes a high toll psychologically and physiologically. President Eduard Shevardnadze of Georgia seems to show this strain in 1992—just the beginning of years of civil war and perpetual crisis in that country. Shevardnadze, formerly Gorbachev's foreign minister, returned to lead his native Georgia when the Soviet Union dissolved. He eventually resigned from office in November of 2003 following a wave of popular protest.

appointees, and to control the flow of information they receive (creating information screens). Politicians for their part struggle to exercise power over the formal bureaucratic agencies because the latter can be too "bureaucratic" (cumbersome, routinized, conservative) to control easily. Also, these agencies are often staffed (at lower levels) mostly by career officials who may not owe loyalty to political leaders.

Sometimes, state leaders appoint a close friend or key adviser to manage the foreign policy bureaucracy. President George Bush (senior) did this with his closest friend, James Baker. Chinese leader Mao Zedong put his loyal ally, Zhou Enlai, in charge of foreign policy.

At times, frustration with the bureaucracy leads politicians to bypass normal channels of diplomacy. For example, during the 1962 Cuban Missile Crisis, President Kennedy used an ad hoc circle of 13 advisers, and negotiated through his brother Robert (the attorney general) instead of the State Department.

Interest Groups   Foreign policy-makers operate not in a political vacuum but in the context of the political debates in their society. In all states societal pressures influence foreign policy, although these are aggregated and made effective through different channels in different societies. In pluralistic democracies, interested parties influence foreign policy through interest groups and political parties. In dictatorships, similar influences occur but less visibly. Thus foreign policies adopted by states generally reflect some kind of process of domestic coalition formation.[27] Of course, international factors also have strong effects on domestic politics.[28]

Interest groups are coalitions of people who share a common interest in the outcome of some political issue and who organize themselves to try to influence the outcome. For instance, French farmers have a big stake in international negotiations in the European Union (which subsidizes agriculture) and in world trade talks (which set agricultural tariffs). The farmers exert political pressure on the French government through long-established and politically sophisticated associations and organizations. They lobby for desired legislation and contribute to politicians' campaigns. More dramatically, when their interests are threatened, French farmers have turned out in large numbers across the country to block roads, stage violent street demonstrations, and threaten to grind the national economy to a halt unless the government adopts their position. Similarly (but often less dramatically), interest groups form around businesses, labour unions, churches, veterans, senior citizens, members of an occupation, or citizens concerned about an issue such as the environment.

Lobbying is the process of talking with legislators or officials to influence their decisions on some set of issues. Three important elements that go into successful lobbying are the ability to gain a hearing with busy officials, the ability to present cogent arguments for one's case, and the ability to trade favours in return for positive action on an issue. These favours—legal and illegal—range from campaign contributions through dinners at nice restaurants and trips to golf resorts, to securing illicit sexual liaisons and paying bribes. In many states, corruption is a major problem in governmental decision-making (see

interest groups Coalitions of people who share a common interest in the outcome of some political issue and who organize themselves to try to influence the outcome.

---

[27] Tony Smith, *Foreign Attachments: The Power of Ethnic Groups in the Making of American Foreign Policy* (Cambridge, MA: Harvard UP, 2000). Helen Milner, *Interests, Institutions, and Information: Domestic Politics and International Relations* (Princeton, NJ: Princeton UP, 1997). Peter B. Evans, Harold K. Jacobson, and Robert D. Putnam, eds., *Double-Edged Diplomacy: International Bargaining and Domestic Politics* (Berkeley: U California P, 1993). Bruce Bueno de Mesquita and David Lalman, *War and Reason: Domestic and International Imperatives* (New Haven, CT: Yale UP, 1992). Jack L. Snyder, *Myths of Empire: Domestic Politics and International Ambition* (Ithaca, NY: Cornell UP, 1991).

[28] Peter Gourevitch, "The Second Image Reversed: International Sources of Domestic Politics," *International Organization* 32.4 (1978): 881–911.

MAKING THEMSELVES HEARD
Foreign policies are affected by the pulling and tugging of various domestic interest groups. European farmers and truckers have tried to influence policies by repeatedly blocking rail and road traffic. Here Belgian truckers block a border crossing to Germany, 2000.

pp. 462–464), and interest groups may induce government officials by illegal means to take certain actions.

Ethnic groups within one state often become interest groups concerned about their ancestral nation outside that state. Many members of ethnic groups feel strong emotional ties to their relatives in other countries; because the rest of the population generally does not care about such issues one way or the other, even a small ethnic group can have considerable influence on policy toward a particular country. Such ethnic ties are emerging as a powerful foreign policy influence in various ethnic conflicts in poor regions. The effect is especially strong in the United States, which is ethnically mixed and has a pluralistic, interest-group form of democracy. For example, Cuban Americans organize to influence U.S. policy toward Cuba, as do Greek Americans on Greece, Jewish Americans on Israel, and African Americans on Africa. Although ethnic groups do not exert the same organized pressure in countries such as Canada, they do sometimes try to influence foreign policy or are called upon by government for advice and input. For example, after the massacre of pro-democracy protesters in Beijing's Tiananmen Square in June of 1989, the Department of External Affairs assembled members of the Canadian Chinese community along with China scholars, business people, and non-governmental organization (NGO) representatives to help the Canadian government determine a policy response to the massacre.[29]

Clearly, interest groups have goals and interests that may or may not coincide with the national interest as a whole (if indeed such an interest can be identified). As with bureaucratic agencies, the view of the state as a unitary actor can be questioned. The head of General Motors once said that "what's good for General Motors is good for the country, and vice versa." This is not self-evident. Nonetheless, defenders of interest group politics argue that various interest groups tend to push and pull in different directions, with the ultimate decisions generally reflecting the interests of society as a whole.

Public Opinion

public opinion In IR, the range of views on foreign policy issues held by the citizens of a state.

Interest groups and other substate actors often seek to influence **public opinion**—the range of views on foreign policy issues held by the citizens of a state. Public opinion has greater influence on foreign policy in democracies than in authoritarian governments. But

---

[29] Bernard M. Frolic, *Canada and the People's Republic of China: Twenty Years of a Bilateral Relationship 1970–1990* (Ottawa: Lowe-Martin, 1992).

even dictators must pay attention to what citizens think. No government can rule by force alone: it needs legitimacy to survive. It must convince people to accept (if not to like) its policies, because in the end policies are carried out by ordinary people—soldiers, workers, petty bureaucrats.

Because of the need for public support, even authoritarian governments spend great effort on *propaganda*—the public promotion of their official line—to win support for foreign policies. States use television, newspapers, and other information media in this effort. For instance, when China invited U.S. President Richard Nixon to visit in 1972, the Chinese government mounted a major propaganda campaign to explain to its people that the United States was not so bad after all. In many countries the state owns or controls major mass media such as television and newspapers, mediating the flow of information to its citizens; however, new information technologies with multiple channels make this harder to do.

In democracies, where governments must stand for election, public opinion is even more important. An unpopular war can force a leader or party from office, as happened to U.S. President Lyndon Johnson in 1968 during the Vietnam War. Or a popular war can help secure a government's mandate to continue in power, as happened to Margaret Thatcher in Britain after the 1982 Falkland Islands War. A key influence on public opinion is the content of scenes appearing on television: U.S. soldiers were sent to Somalia to assist in relief efforts in 1992 after TV news showed the heartrending results of civil war and famine there. But after TV news showed an American soldier's body being dragged through the streets by members of a Somali faction after a deadly firefight that killed 18 U.S. soldiers, public opinion shifted quickly against the Somalia operation.

Journalists serve as the gatekeepers of information passing from foreign policy elites to the public. The media and government often conflict, because of the traditional role of the press as a watchdog and critic of government actions and powers. The media try to uncover and publicize that which the government wants to hide, especially in situations involving scandal. Foreign policy decision-makers also rely on the media for information about foreign affairs; many world leaders turn into media outlets such as CNN to find out about events going on around the world.

Yet the media also depend on government for information; the size and resources of the foreign policy bureaucracies dwarf those of the press. These advantages give the government great power to *manipulate* journalists by feeding them information in order to shape the news and influence public opinion. Government decision-makers can create dramatic stories in foreign relations—through summit meetings, crises, actions, and so forth. Bureaucrats can also *leak* secret information to the press in order to support their own point of view and win bureaucratic battles. Finally, the military and the press have a running battle about journalists' access to military operations; for instance, in the invasion of Grenada and the Gulf War, U.S. military censors limited media coverage. During the 2003 Iraq War, by contrast, some journalists became "embedded" with particular military units. This provided them with access to information but also raised questions about whether their objectivity had been compromised.

In democracies, where the flow of information and opinions is not tightly restricted by the state, public opinion can be accurately measured through *polling*—analyzing the responses of a sample group to questionnaires, to infer the opinions of a larger population. This is impossible to do in societies where secret police monitor any expressions of opposition to state policies. But in societies where individuals feel free to speak out, polling has developed into an important part of the foreign policy-making process.

Occasionally a foreign policy issue is decided directly by a referendum of the entire citizenry, a tradition that is strong in countries such Switzerland and Denmark, for example.[30] In 1992, the Maastricht Treaty on closer European political union (see pp. 377–379) was narrowly defeated in a popular referendum in Denmark, despite the support of the government, all major political parties, labour unions, and other political groups. (A later referendum narrowly approved the treaty.) In France the treaty barely squeaked through. Because of these signs of public opposition to the Maastricht Treaty, European leaders were forced to reconsider the pace of European integration.

Even in the most open democracies, states do not merely *respond* to public opinion. Decision-makers enjoy some autonomy to make their own choices, and they are pulled in various directions by bureaucracies and interest groups, whose views often conflict with the direction favoured by public opinion at large. Furthermore, public opinion is seldom unified on any policy, and sophisticated polling can show that particular segments of the population (regions of the country, genders, income groups, races, etc.) often differ in their perceptions of foreign policy issues. So a politician may respond to the opinion of one constituency rather than the whole population. Public opinion varies considerably over time on many foreign policy issues. States use propaganda or try to manipulate the media to keep public opinion from diverging too much from state policies.

In democracies, public opinion generally has *less effect on foreign policy than on domestic policy*. National leaders traditionally have additional latitude to make decisions in the international realm. This derives from the special need of states to act in a unified way to function effectively in the international system, as well as from the traditions of secrecy and diplomacy that remove IR from the realm of ordinary domestic politics. In Canada in 1982, for example, a public outcry erupted over news that the Canadian government planned to allow the United States Air Force to test cruise missiles over Canadian territory. Public protests, rallies, and opinion polls that showed the majority of Canadians were opposed could not alter the Trudeau government's plans to go ahead with the testing.[31] In the nuclear age, IR was further distanced from everyday political life in the nuclear states by the public's willingness to trust experts and officials to deal with the technical and frightening issues of nuclear strategy. Over time, however, peace movements have sometimes pushed governments toward disarmament (see "Peace Movements" on pp. 104–105).

In the case of Japan, public opinion is a major political force restraining the military spending of the government, its commitment of military forces beyond Japan's borders, and especially the development of nuclear weapons (which is within Japan's technical abilities). The ruling party has slowly but steadily pushed to increase Japan's military spending and allow Japanese military forces to expand their role modestly (in the 1980s, to patrol Asian sea lanes vital to Japanese trade; in the 1990s, to participate in UN peacekeeping operations; and more recently to send military personnel to Iraq in 2003 as part of the U.S.-led coalition). Repeatedly, these efforts have been slowed or rebuffed by strong public opinion against the military. In Japan, people remember the horrible consequences of militarism in the 1930s and World War II, culminating in the nuclear bombings of 1945. They are suspicious of any increase in the size or role of military forces, and dead set against Japan's having nuclear weapons. In this case public opinion constrains the state's conduct of foreign policy, and has slowed the pace of change.

The *attentive public* in a democracy is that minority of the population that stays informed about international issues. This segment varies somewhat from one issue to another, but there is also a core of people who care in general about foreign affairs and fol-

---

[30] John T. Rourke, Richard P. Hiskes, and Cyrus Ernesto Zirakzadeh, *Direct Democracy and International Politics: Deciding International Issues through Referendums* (Boulder, CO: Rienner, 1992).

[31] Kim Richard Nossal, *The Politics of Canadian Foreign Policy* (see footnote 1 in this chapter).

low them closely. This is the element of the public that, in many ways, governments most seek to influence and secure their consent for foreign policy decisions.[32] The most active members of the attentive public on foreign affairs constitute a foreign policy *elite*—people with power and influence who affect foreign policy. This elite includes people within governments as well as outsiders such as businesspeople, journalists, lobbyists, and professors of political science. Public opinion polls show that elite opinions sometimes (but not always) differ considerably from those of the general population, and sometimes from those of the government as well.[33]

Governments sometimes adopt foreign policies for the specific purpose of generating public approval and hence gaining domestic legitimacy.[34] This is the case when a government undertakes a war or foreign military intervention at a time of domestic difficulty, to distract attention and gain public support—taking advantage of the **rally 'round the flag syndrome** (the public's increased support for government leaders during wartime, at least in the short term). Citizens who would readily criticize their government's policies on education or health care will often refrain from criticism when the government is at war and the lives of the nation's soldiers are on the line. In the U.S., President Bush (senior) enjoyed extremely high popularity ratings in both the 1989 Panama and the 1991 Gulf wars, as did President Bush (junior) during the war in Afghanistan in late 2001.

> **rally 'round the flag syndrome** The public's increased support for government leaders during wartime, at least in the short term.

However, wars that go on too long, or are not successful, can turn public opinion against the government and even lead to a popular uprising to overthrow the government. In Argentina, the military government in 1982 led the country into war with Britain over the Falkland/Malvinas Islands. At first Argentineans rallied around the flag, but after losing the war they rallied around the cause of getting rid of the military government, and they replaced it with a new civilian government that prosecuted the former leaders. As the U.S. war in Iraq dragged on, so too did support for President George W. Bush begin to wane.

MODELS OF DECISION-MAKING: ELITE ANALYSIS AND INSTRUMENTAL MARXISM

Another alternative model of decision-making focuses on the class or elite background of decision-makers (called either the **elite model** or **instrumental Marxism,** a more critical variant). Elite theorists and instrumental Marxists argue that decision-makers within governments or state agencies share a common business or class background, and that their decisions will reflect their business or class interests. For instance, European imperialism benefited banks and big business, which made huge profits from exploiting cheap labour and resources in overseas colonies.

> **elite model** (with a more critical variant called **instrumental Marxism**). Elite theorists and instrumental Marxists argue that decision-makers within governments or state agencies share a common business or class background, and that their decisions will reflect their business or class interests.

Proponents of this perspective argue that it not only explains large processes, such as imperialism, but also particular foreign policy decisions. In 1951 in Guatemala, the election of a socialist president, Jacobo Arbenz, caused some alarm in the United Fruit Company (UFC), a U.S.-based company with extensive land holdings in Guatemala.

---

[32] Noam Chomsky, "The Manufacture of Consent," *The Chomsky Reader* (NY: Pantheon Books, 1987).

[33] Richard Sobel, *The Impact of Public Opinion on U.S. Foreign Policy since Vietnam* (NY: Oxford UP, 2001). Ole R. Holsti, *Public Opinion and American Foreign Policy* (Ann Arbor: U Michigan P, 1996). Shoon Murray, *Anchors against Change: American Opinion Leaders' Beliefs after the Cold War* (Ann Arbor: U Michigan P, 1996). Miroslav Nincic, "A Sensible Public: New Perspectives on Popular Opinion and Foreign Policy," *Journal of Conflict Resolution* 36.4 (1992): 772–89.

[34] T. Clifton Morgan and Kenneth N. Bickers, "Domestic Discontent and the External Use of Force," *Journal of Conflict Resolution* 36.1 (1992): 25–52. Bruce Bueno de Mesquita, Randolph M. Siverson, and Gary Woller, "War and the Fate of Regimes: A Comparative Analysis," *American Political Science Review* 86.3 (1992): 638–46.

Arbenz had pledged his government to buy back Guatemalan land from UFC. At that time, John Foster Dulles was the U.S. Secretary of State and his brother Allen Dulles was the head of the Central Intelligence Agency (CIA). Before becoming Secretary of State, John Foster Dulles had represented the United Fruit Company through his former law firm, and Allen Dulles had served on the company's Board of Trustees. For elite theorists and instrumental Marxists, it was the particular interest that the Dulles brothers had in UFC that explains the June 1954 U.S.-sponsored coup in Guatemala, a coup that used American planes to bomb the capital, and CIA-trained Guatemalans as personnel. The Arbenz government was overthrown, and the military dictatorship that replaced it quickly abandoned any plans for land reform.[35]

The Military-Industrial Complex

military-industrial complex
A huge, interlocking network of governmental agencies, industrial corporations, and research institutes, all working together to promote and benefit from military spending.

During the Cold War, Marxists and elite theorists frequently argued that U.S. foreign policy and that of its Western allies were driven by the profit motive of arms manufacturers.[36] Even a U.S. president expressed concern about the **military-industrial complex,** a huge, interlocking network of governmental agencies, industrial corporations, and research institutes, working together to supply a nation's military forces. Because of the domestic political clout of these actors, the complex was a very powerful influence on foreign policy in *both* the United States and the Soviet Union during the Cold War. Some of that influence remains, though it has diminished. The military-industrial complex was a response to the growing importance of technology (nuclear weapons, electronics, and others) and of logistics in Cold War military planning.

States at war have long harnessed their economic and technological might for the war effort. But during the Cold War military procurement occurred on a massive scale in "peacetime," as the superpowers raced to develop new high-technology weapons. This race created a special role for scientists and engineers in addition to the more traditional role of industries that produce war materials. In response to the Soviet satellite *Sputnik* in 1957, the United States increased spending on research and development and created new science education programs. By 1961, President Dwight Eisenhower warned in his farewell speech that the military-industrial complex was gaining "unwarranted influence" in U.S. society and that militarization could erode democracy in the United States. The threat to democracy was that the interest of the military-industrial complex in the arms race conflicted with the interest of ordinary citizens in peace, while the size of the complex gave it more political clout than ordinary citizens could muster.

The complex encompasses a variety of constituencies, each of which has an interest in military spending. *Corporations* that produce goods for the military profit from government contracts. So do military *officers* whose careers advance by building bureaucratic empires around new weapons systems. And so do universities and scientific institutes that receive military research contracts—a major source of funding for scientists in Russia and the United States.

Subcontractors and parts suppliers for big U.S. weapons projects are usually spread around the country, so that local citizens and politicians join the list of constituents ben-

---

[35] Nick Cullather, *Secret History: The CIA's Classified Account of Its Operations in Guatemala, 1952–1954* (Palo Alto, CA: Stanford UP, 1999). Walter LaFeber, *Inevitable Revolutions: the United States in Central America,* 2nd ed. (NY: Norton, 1993). Stephen Schlesinger and Stephen Kinzer, *Bitter Fruit: The Untold Story of the American Coup in Guatemala* (NY: Doubleday, 1982).

[36] V. Konobeyev, "The Capitalist Economy and the Arms Race," *International Affairs* [Moscow] 8 (1982): 28–48.

efiting from military spending. Recently, a similar phenomenon has emerged in the European Union, where weapons development programs have been parcelled out to several European states. A new fighter jet is less likely to be cancelled if one country gets the contract for the wings, another for the engines, and so forth.

Executives in military industries, as the people who best understand their industries, are often appointed as government officials responsible for military procurement decisions and then return to their companies again—a practice called the *revolving door*. In democracies, military industries also try to influence public opinion through *advertising* that ties their products to patriotic themes. Finally, U.S. military industries give generous *campaign contributions* to national politicians who vote on military budgets, and sometimes bribes to Pentagon officials as well. Military industry became an important source of *political action committee (PAC)* money raised by members of Congress. In the 1996 U.S. elections, for example, one company alone, Lockheed Martin, contributed more than $2 million to congressional campaigns.[37]

When the Cold War ended, the military-industrial complex in both superpowers endured cutbacks in military budgets. In Russia, military industries formed the backbone of a political faction seeking to slow down economic reforms and continue government subsidies to state-owned industries. They succeeded in replacing Russia's reformist prime minister with an industrial manager in late 1992. In the United States, meanwhile, the lingering influence of the military-industrial complex may help to explain why Congress kept funding certain Cold War weapons (such as the Seawolf submarine and B-2 bomber) after their purpose seemingly disappeared.

Although the Canadian arms industry is not as large as that found in either the United States or Russia, Canada's role as a producer of weapons may impact on some foreign policy decisions, and has also attracted criticism. The Canadian Defence Industry Association estimates that defence industries in Canada generate over $4 billion in revenues, approximately 30 percent of which is from exports to the United States and some 37 percent from exports to the rest of the world. Critics charge that the Liberal government's enthusiasm for projects like the U.S. National Missile Defense plan stems more from the benefits derived to the defence industry than any real impact on national security (estimated at between one-quarter to over 1 billion dollars annually).[38] Although no scholarly studies have yet been conducted to test this relationship, such benefits suggest that the military-industrial complex in Canada may exert some leverage on foreign policy decisions.

Canada's involvement in the arms industry also draws criticisms from other sources. The human rights organization Amnesty International, for example, criticized the Canadian government in 2003 for exporting arms to a number of authoritarian and military regimes. In one case, helicopters made in Canada were exported first to the United States, which then sent them on to Colombia. Under federal guidelines, the government would not have allowed the helicopters to be sold directly to Colombia because of human rights abuses there, but the sale was permitted because the final destination appeared to be the United States.[39]

---

[37] James Der Derian, *Virtuous War: Mapping the Military-Industrial-Media-Entertainment Network* (Boulder, CO: Westview, 2001). Jennifer Washburn, "When Money Talks, Congress Listens," *Bulletin of the Atomic Scientists* 53.4 (July-Aug. 1997): 40.

[38] Stephen James-Kerr, "Meet Canada The Global Arms Dealer," *Znet*, 23 May 2003 <http://www.zmag.org/content/showarticle.cfm?SectionID=15&ItemID=3668)>.

[39] Amnesty International, *A Catalogue of Failures: G8 Arms Exports and Human Right Violations*, IOR 30/003/2003 /<http://amnesty.org/pages/ENG-IOR300032003>

Making and Writing Foreign Policy

Some critical theory approaches to international relations examine foreign policies not to determine how particular foreign policies are made, but rather to explore what foreign policy "makes possible" for states. From this perspective, for example, it is not simply that the military-industrial complex exerts influence on state decision-makers to make particular choices. Rather, the depiction of some states or actors as dangerous, or backwards, or barbarous, makes possible certain foreign policy choices (such as deterrence, intervention, imperialism) and even how we understand particular states, like the United States.

This approach suggests, for example, that there was nothing natural or inevitable about treating the Soviet Union as the declared enemy of the U.S. in the post–World War II period. In fact, there was a lot of evidence to suggest that the Soviet Union had largely defensive rather than offensive foreign policy goals. But understanding, or depicting the Soviet Union as a particularly deadly enemy permitted not only a massive military buildup and the suppression of dissent (during the McCarthy era of the 1950s) but also provided the legitimation for the U.S. to become hegemonic over the Western international system. By this view, then, when the Cold War collapsed, the United States went in search of new enemies: drugs, rogue states, and "madmen" like Saddam Hussein.[40]

This approach to foreign policy analysis is dramatically different from the rational actor model, the operational processes model, or the bureaucratic politics model. It argues that we question, or deconstruct, our taken-for-granted assumptions about foreign policies, enemies, and who "we" are in world politics. Even analyses of democracy and foreign policy, as discussed in the section that follows, would for critical theorists require an "unpacking" of basic assumptions.

Democracy and Foreign Policy

For many observers of global politics, the differences in the foreign policy process from one state to another are more influenced by a state's type of government than by the particular constellation of bureaucracies, interest groups, or individuals within it. Government types include military dictatorship, communist party rule, one-party (noncommunist) rule, and various forms of multiparty democracy. Relatively democratic states tend to share values and interests, and hence to get along better with each other than with nondemocracies.

authoritarian (government) A government that rules without the need to stand for free elections, respect civil and political rights, allow freedom of the press, and so forth.

democracy A government of "the people," usually through elected representatives, and usually with a respect for individual rights in society (especially rights to hold political ideas differing from those of the government).

Nondemocratic governments are often called **authoritarian.** These governments rule without needing to stand for free elections, to respect civil and political rights, to allow freedom of the press, and so forth. By contrast, a **democracy** is a government of the people, usually through elected representatives, and usually with a respect for individual rights in society (especially rights to hold political ideas differing from those of the government).

In practice, most states lie along a spectrum, with some mix of democratic and authoritarian elements. For example, because of campaign contributions, democracies in North America and Japan give greater influence to rich people than to poor people. In many states, governments control TV and radio stations, putting opposition politicians at a disadvantage in elections. In Angola, relatively fair elections were held in 1992, but the losing side rejected the results and resorted to military attacks. In Burma, a military gov-

---

[40] David Campbell, *Writing Security: United States Foreign Policy and the Politics of Identity* (Minneapolis: U Minnesota P, 1992). Roxanne Lynn Doty, *Imperial Encounters: The Politics of Representation in North-South Relations* (Minneapolis: U Minnesota P, 1996). David Mutimer, *The Weapons State: Proliferation and the Framing of Security* (Boulder, CO: Rienner, 2000). Charles E. Nathanson, "The Social Construction of the Soviet Threat: A Study in the Politics of Representation," *Alternatives* XIII (1988): 443–83.

The Changing World Order
Authoritarian Governments: Hindrance or Help?

World order and domestic politics affect each other. For example, the war on terrorism has reshaped U.S. domestic politics, notably in the dramatic, "rally 'round the flag" boost in President Bush's popularity immediately after the September 11 attacks. The bipartisan cohesiveness that emerged in the months after September 11 in turn affected world order by increasing U.S. willingness and ability to take military action abroad. That cohesiveness, both within the United States and internationally, is beginning to fade as serious questions have been raised about the U.S.-led attack on and occupation of Iraq.

Similarly, the changing world order closely connects with the issue of democracy in the Arab and Muslim worlds. Bahrain in 2002 changed from an emirate to a constitutional monarchy with an elected parliament—a modest step towards democracy. Saudi Arabia's lack of democracy has received new attention. The pace of democratization in the Middle East and South Asia may shape the potential of Islamic revolutionaries to undermine the present interstate system. Authoritarian governments in many countries in these regions stifle political expression, often leaving the mosque as the prime gathering point for opposition and revolution as a main alternative given a lack of other political reform outlets. In Iran in recent years, modest democratization had strengthened moderates, resulting in less radical policies, although recently moderates in Iran encountered setbacks after being barred from running for election in 2004 (resulting in the lowest voter turnout in a quarter century).

Yet, in other countries, the U.S. relies on authoritarian governments to suppress religious extremists who support terrorism. (Similarly, in the Cold War, the U.S. supported authoritarian governments that suppressed communists.) Can these governments loosen their grip without potentially bringing extremists to power in states like Saudi Arabia or Pakistan? When Algeria democratized a decade ago, Islamic parties were poised to win until the military seized control again. Could the people of some country vote an Osama bin Laden into power and give him the keys to the interstate club, or even the nuclear club, the way Germans voted Hitler in during the 1930s? Is it hypocritical for countries like the U.S. both to champion democracy and at the same time support authoritarian governments in situations where a democratic outcome may not be in its national interest?

So is democracy a good thing or a bad thing in global politics? On what does it depend?

ernment held elections, lost them, and then simply refused to step aside or allow the newly elected parliament to meet. In Algeria, the military cancelled elections midway as Islamic parties were winning.

The Democratic Peace

How do the foreign policies of democracies differ from those of authoritarian governments? We have already referred to a number of differences in the nature of internal decision-making, the effects of interest groups, and the importance of public opinion. Although public opinion and interest group activism operate in some form in virtually all states, they are more influential in democracies.

Some 200 years ago, philosopher Immanuel Kant argued that lasting peace would depend on states' becoming republics, with legislatures to check the power of monarchs (or prime ministers) to make war. He thought that checks and balances in government would act as a brake on the use of military force—as compared to autocratic governments where a single individual (or small ruling group) could make war without regard for the effect on the population.

IR scholars have examined whether empirical data support the idea that democracy is linked with a kind of foreign policy fundamentally different from that of authoritarianism.[41] One theory they considered was that democracies are generally *more peaceful* than authoritarian governments (fighting fewer, or smaller, wars). This turned out to be *not true*. Democracies fight as many wars as do authoritarian states. Indeed, the three most war-prone states of the past two centuries (according to political scientists who count wars) were France, Russia, and Britain. Britain was a democracy throughout, France for part of the period, and Russia not at all.

What *is* true about democracies is that although they fight wars against authoritarian states, *democracies almost never fight each other*. No major historical cases contradict this generalization, which is known as the **democratic peace.** Why this is so is not entirely clear. As there have not been many democracies for very long, the generalization could be just a coincidence, though this seems unlikely. It may be that democracies do not tend to have severe conflicts with each other, as they tend to be capitalist states whose trade relations create strong interdependence

WE WANT TO VOTE

Upsurges of democratic movements throughout the world in recent years testify to the power of the idea of democracy. Since democracies rarely fight each other, worldwide democratization might lead to lasting peace. Here, South Africans line up to vote in that country's first all-race elections, which ended apartheid and elected Nelson Mandela as president, 1994.

democratic peace The proposition, strongly supported by empirical evidence, that democracies almost never fight wars against each other (although they do fight against authoritarian states).

(war would be costly since it would disrupt trade). Or, citizens of democratic societies (whose support is necessary for wars to be waged) may simply not see the citizens of other democracies as enemies. By contrast, authoritarian governments of other states can be seen as enemies. Note that the peace among democracies gives empirical support to a long-standing liberal claim that, because it is rooted in the domestic level of analysis, contradicts a fundamental premise of realism—that the most important explanations are to be found at the interstate level.

Over the past two centuries, democracy has become more and more widespread as a form of government, and this trend is changing the nature of the foreign policy process worldwide. Many states do not yet have democratic governments (the most important of these is China). And existing democracies are imperfect in various ways—from political apathy in countries like Canada and the United States, and corruption in Japan to autocratic traditions in Russia. Nonetheless, the trend is toward democratization in most of the world's regions.

[41] Bruce Russett and John Oneal, *Triangulating Peace: Democracy, Interdependence, and International Organizations* (NY: Norton, 2000). Joanne Gowa, *Ballots and Bullets: The Elusive Democratic Peace* (Princeton, NJ: Princeton UP, 1999). Spencer R. Weart, *Never at War: Why Democracies Will Not Fight One Another* (New Haven, CT: Yale UP, 1998). Miriam Fendius Elman, ed., *Paths to Peace: Is Democracy the Answer?* (Cambaridge, MA: MIT P, 1997). Bruce Russett, *Grasping the Democratic Peace: Principles for a Post–Cold War World* (Princeton, NJ: Princeton UP, 1993).James Lee Ray, *Democracy and International Conflict: An Evaluation of the Democratic Peace Proposition* (Columbia: U South Carolina P, 1995). Michael W. Doyle, "Liberalism and World Politics," *American Political Science Review* 80 (1986): 1151–70. Zeev Maoz, "The Controversy over the Democratic Peace: Rearguard Action or Cracks in the Wall?" *International Security* 22.1 (1997): 162–98. John M. Owen, *Liberal Peace, Liberal War: American Politics and International Security* (Ithaca, NY: Cornell UP, 1997).

In the past two decades the trend has accelerated in several ways. New democracies emerged in several (though not all) states of the old Soviet bloc. Military governments were replaced with democratically elected civilian ones throughout most of Latin America as well as in several African and Asian countries. South Africa, the last white-ruled African country, adopted majority rule in 1994. In several of these cases (for instance, in the Philippines in 1986), long-standing dictatorships were ended by nonviolent popular movements. Elsewhere (for instance, in Nicaragua) civil wars ended with internationally supervised democratic elections. In several other authoritarian states, such as China, public pressures for greater democratic participation in government became evident. Most recently, long-standing dictator-

> ### The Information Revolution
> ## Informed or Brainwashed?
>
> Democratization accelerated in the 1990s worldwide, potentially enlarging the zone of "democratic peace" since democracies rarely fight each other. New information technologies may allow citizens greater access to political processes, including those that cross borders. However, these technologies may also give those with wealth and power new means of influence, as when state-controlled media whip up nationalism or when advertising promotes Western products and values in the global South. Will the information revolution usher in global democracy and peace, or sharpen divisions?
>
> **To explore this question, go to www.pearsoned.ca/goldstein.**

ships or military governments were replaced peacefully by democratic governments in Indonesia and Nigeria, both regional giants. However, movement in the other direction still occurs—military governments took over in Pakistan and in Ivory Coast in 1999, for example—but less often.

We do not know where these trends toward democracy will lead, but because it is now conceivable that someday all or most of the world's states will be democratically governed, wars may become less frequent. As Kant envisaged, an international community based on peaceful relations may emerge. However, although mature democracies almost never fight each other, a period of *transition* to democracy may be more prone to war than either a stable democracy or a stable authoritarian government.[42] Therefore the process of democratization does not necessarily bode well for peace in the short term.

A further caution is in order. The generalization about democracies almost never fighting each other is historically valid but not necessarily applicable in the future. By way of analogy, there was a generalization during the Cold War that communist governments never yield power peacefully. That generalization held up until suddenly a series of communist governments did just that around 1990. As the world has more democracies for a longer time, the generalization about their almost never fighting each other might not hold up.

The attempt to explain foreign policy in a general and *theoretical* way has met only limited success. This is one reason realists continued to find simple unitary actor models of the state useful; the domestic and individual elements of the foreign policy process add much complexity and unpredictability. One area of foreign policy where knowledge stands on a somewhat firmer basis is the *descriptive* effort to understand how particular mechanisms of foreign policy formation operate in various states. This chapter has largely bypassed such approaches because they belong properly to the field of comparative politics.

To summarize, foreign policy is a complex outcome of a complex process. It results from the struggle of competing themes, competing domestic interests, and competing government agencies. No single individual, agency, or guiding principle determines the outcome. Yet, foreign policy does achieve a certain overall coherence. States do form foreign policy on an issue or toward a region; it is not just an incoherent collection of decisions

---

[42] Jack Snyder, *From Voting to Violence: Democratization and Nationalist Conflict* (NY: Norton, 2000) Michael D. Ward and Kristian S. Gleditsch, "Democratizing for Peace," *American Political Science Review* 92.1 (1998): 51–61.

and actions taken from time to time. Out of the turbulent internal processes of foreign policy formation come relatively coherent interests and policies that states pursue.

Of course, those aggregate state interests and policies frequently come into conflict with the interests and policies of other states. Such conflicts are the subject of the next chapter.

Thinking Critically

1. India and Pakistan are neighbours and enemies. Given the problems of misperception and bias in foreign policy decision-making, what steps could you propose that each government adopt to keep these problems from interfering in the rational pursuit of national interests?

2. Sometimes aggressive international actions are attributed to a "madman" such as Iraq's Saddam Hussein or Nazi Germany's Adolf Hitler. Do you agree that such leaders (each of whose actions severely damaged his state's well-being) must be "mad"? What other factors could account for their actions? How else might the charge of "madness" be understood?

3. Imagine a sudden, unexpected crisis caused by an event such as the explosion of a nuclear weapon (of unknown origin) in Moscow. Given the dangers inherent in crisis decision-making, what steps could the leaders of affected states take to prevent the situation from spinning out of control? Which of these steps might be taken *before* any crisis occurred, to prepare for a future crisis?

4. Inasmuch as democracies almost never fight wars with each other, do existing democracies have a national security interest in seeing democratization spread to China and other authoritarian states? If so, how can that interest be reconciled with the long-standing norm of noninterference in the internal affairs of other sovereign states?

5. Traditionally, foreign policy elites have faced only sporadic pressure from mass public opinion. Is the role of television or the internet changing this relationship?

Chapter Summary

-   Foreign policies are strategies governments use to guide their actions toward other states. The foreign policy process is the set of procedures and structures that states use to arrive at foreign policy decisions and to implement them.

-   In the rational actor model of decision-making, officials choose the action whose consequences best help to meet the state's established goals.

-   The actions of individual decision-makers are influenced by their personalities, values, and beliefs as well as by common psychological factors that diverge from rationality. These factors include misperception, selective perception, emotional biases, and cognitive biases (including the effort to reduce cognitive dissonance).

-   Another view of decision-making focuses not on the actions of individuals, but rather sees governments as complex organizations with multiple departments and agencies charged with different features of a country's foreign policy. In the organizational process model, decisions result from routine administrative procedures, and in the government bargaining (or bureaucratic politics) model, decisions result from negotiations among governmental agencies with different interests in the outcome.

-   These models signal that foreign policy decisions are also influenced by the psychology of groups (including "groupthink"), the procedures used to reach decisions, and the roles of participants.

- During crises, the potentials for misperception and error are amplified.
- Struggles over the direction of foreign policy are common between professional bureaucrats and politicians, as well as between different government agencies.
- Domestic constituencies (interest groups) have distinct interests in foreign policies and often organize politically to promote those interests.
- Public opinion influences governments' foreign policy decisions (more so in democracies than in authoritarian states), but governments also manipulate public opinion.
- An elite or instrumental Marxist model of decision-making focuses on the ways in which foreign policies tend to reflect the interests of particular business or capitalist class interests.
- Another critical approach focuses on the interests of military-industrial complexes consisting of military industries and others with an interest in high military spending.
- Some critical approaches to foreign policy do not explore how policy is made, but rather what particular policies "make possible" for states; this approach tends to deconstruct foreign policies and the many taken-for-granted assumptions associated with them.
- Even terms like *democracy* are subject to interrogation, although most liberals and realists would argue that while democracies have historically fought as many wars as authoritarian states, democracies have almost never fought wars against other democracies. This is called the democratic peace.

Key Terms

foreign policy process   129
rational actor model   130
misperceptions and selective perceptions
    134
information screens   134
optimizing   135
satisficing   135
organizational process model   136
bureaucratic politics model   137
groupthink   139

interest groups   143
public opinion   144
rally 'round the flag syndrome   147
elite model (instrumental Marxism)
    147
military-industrial complex   148
authoritarian (government)   150
democracy   150
democratic peace   152

Weblinks

The following are a sampling of government departments, journals, and research centres that are concerned with questions of foreign policy:

Canadian Foreign Policy:
http://www.carleton.ca/npsia/cfpj

Canadian Institute of International Affairs:
http://www.ciia.org

Foreign Affairs Canada:
http://www.fac-aec.gc.ca/menu-en.asp

Foreign Policy in Focus:
http://www.fpif.org/index.html

U.S. State Department:
http://www.state.gov

International Conflict

5

THE CAUSES OF WAR
Theories about War

CONFLICTS OF INTEREST
Territorial Disputes
Control of Governments
Economic Conflict

CONFLICTS OF IDEAS
Ethnic Conflict
Religious Conflict
Ideological Conflict

MEANS OF LEVERAGE
Types of War
Terrorism

HUMAN SECURITY

Israeli security wall under construction, 2002.

THE CAUSES OF WAR

The Roman writer Seneca said nearly 2000 years ago, "Of war men ask the outcome, not the cause."[1] This is not true of political scientists. They ask two fundamental questions: Why do international actors (states and nonstate actors alike) come into conflict with each other? And why do those conflicts sometimes lead to violence and war? This chapter addresses both questions.

Conflict among states, for realists in particular, is not an unusual condition but an ordinary one. **Conflict** may be defined as a difference in preferred outcomes in a bargaining situation. International conflicts will always exist. In such conflict bargaining, states develop capabilities that give them leverage to obtain more favourable outcomes than they could obtain without such leverage. Whether fair or unfair, the ultimate outcome of the bargaining process is a **settlement** of the particular conflict.

Violence is an effective form of leverage in some bargaining situations (see p. 62). So states develop capabilities for using violence in international conflicts (these military capabilities are discussed in Chapter 6). But these capabilities only sometimes come into play in international conflicts. In fact, the great majority of international conflicts do not lead to war, but are resolved in other ways. The study of the causes of war, then, is really an effort to understand the *outbreak of war*—resorting to violence as a means of leverage in international conflicts. But understanding the outbreak of war requires studying the underlying conflicts as well.

conflict A difference in preferred outcomes in a bargaining situation.

settlement The outcome of a bargaining process.

---

[1] Hercules Furens Seneca, *Seneca's Tragedies*, vol. 1, trans. Frank Justus Miller (London: Heinemann, 1917).

The question of why war breaks out can be approached in different ways. More descriptive approaches, favoured by historians, tend to focus narrowly on specific direct causes of the outbreak of war, which vary from one war to another.[2] For example, one could say that the assassination of Archduke Ferdinand in 1914 "caused" World War I. More general, theoretical approaches, favoured by many political scientists, tend to focus on the search for general explanations, applicable to a variety of contexts, about why wars break out.[3] For example, one can see World War I as caused by shifts in the balance of power among European states, with the assassination being only a catalyst.

Theories about War

Broad generalizations about the causes of war have been elusive. Wars do not have a single or simple cause. Some scholars distinguish *necessary* causes (conditions that must exist for a war to occur, but might not trigger one) from *sufficient* causes (conditions that will trigger war but are responsible for only some wars).[4] Many theories about war have been put forward, but few have universal validity. Levels of analysis can help us organize these theories (types of explanations of war).[5] Wars have been viewed as resulting from forces and processes operating on all the levels.

The Individual Level On the *individual* level of analysis, the question of why conflicts turn violent revolves around the familiar issue of rationality. One theory, consistent with realism, holds that the use of war and other violent means of leverage in international conflicts is normal and reflects *rational* decisions of national leaders: that "wars begin with conscious and reasoned decisions based on the calculation, made by *both* parties, that they can achieve more by going to war than by remaining at peace."[6]

An opposite theory holds that conflicts often escalate to war because of *deviations* from rationality in the individual decision-making processes of national leaders. These potentials were discussed in Chapter 4—information screens, cognitive biases, groupthink, and so forth. A related theory holds that the education and mentality of whole populations of individuals determine whether conflicts become violent. In this view, public nationalism or ethnic hatred—or even an innate tendency toward violence in human nature—may pressure leaders to solve conflicts violently. Some IR researchers and activists alike believe that the re-education of populations can result in fewer conflicts turning violent.

---

[2] Michael Howard, *The Invention of Peace: Reflections on War and the International Order* (New Haven, CT: Yale, 2001). Robert I. Rotberg and Theodore K. Rabb, eds., *The Origin and Prevention of Major Wars* (NY: Cambridge UP, 1989).

[3] John A. Vasquez, ed., *What Do We Know About War?* (Lanham, MD: Rowman Littlefield, 2000). Zeev Maoz and Azar Gat, eds., *War in a Changing World* (Ann Arbor: U Michigan P, 2001). Dale C. Copeland, *The Origins of Major War* (Ithaca, NY: Cornell UP, 2001). Stephen Van Evera, *Causes of War: Power and the Roots of Conflict* (Ithaca, NY: Cornell, 1999). Michael E. Brown, Owen R. Coté, Jr., Sean M. Lynn-Jones, and Steven E. Miller, eds., *Theories of War and Peace* (Cambridge, MA: MIT P, 1998). Hidemi Suganami, *On the Causes of War* (NY: Oxford UP, 1996). John A. Vasquez, *The War Puzzle* (NY: Cambridge UP, 1993). Seyom Brown, *The Causes and Prevention of War* (NY: St. Martin's, 1987). Kalevi J. Holsti, *Peace and War: Armed Conflicts and International Order* (NY: Cambridge UP, 1991). Geoffrey Blainey, *The Causes of War* (London: Macmillan, 1973).

[4] Benjamin A. Most and Harvey Starr, *Inquiry, Logic and International Politics* (Columbia: U South Carolina P, 1989).

[5] Jack S. Levy, "The Causes of War: A Review of Theories and Evidence," *Behavior, Society, and Nuclear War*, ed. P. E. Tetlock et al., vol. 1 (NY: Oxford UP, 1989).

[6] Michael Howard, *The Causes of Wars and Other Essays* (Cambridge: Harvard UP, 1984) 22. Emphasis in original.

Neither of these theories holds up very well. Some wars clearly reflect rational calculations of national leaders, whereas others clearly were mistakes and cannot be considered rational. Certainly some individual leaders seem prone to turn to military force to try to settle conflicts on favourable terms. But no reliable guide has been discovered that yet predicts who will be a more warlike or more peaceful leader. A warlike leader can become peaceful, as did Egypt's Anwar Sadat, for example. Individuals of many cultural backgrounds and religions lead their states into war, as do both male and female leaders.

The Domestic Level   The *domestic* level of analysis draws attention to the characteristics of states or societies that may make them more or less prone to use violence in resolving conflicts. During the Cold War, the Soviet Union and its allies frequently said that the aggressive and greedy *capitalist* states were prone to using violence in international conflicts, whereas Western leaders claimed that the expansionist, ideological, and totalitarian nature of *communist* states made them especially prone to using violence. In truth, both types of society have used violence regularly in international conflicts.

Likewise, we have seen (in Chapter 4) that both democracies and authoritarian states fight wars (though democracies almost never fight other democracies). Rich industrialized states and poor agrarian ones both use war at times. In fact, anthropologists have found that a wide range of *preagricultural* hunter-gatherer societies are also prone to warfare under certain circumstances.[7] Thus the potential for warfare seems to hold across cultures, types of society, and time periods—although the importance and frequency of war vary greatly from case to case.

Few useful generalizations can be made about what kinds of domestic society are more prone or less prone to war (given that all are war-prone to some extent). The same society may change greatly over time. For example, Japan was prone to using violence in international conflicts before World War II, but averse to such violence since then. The !Kung bush people in Angola and Namibia—a hunter-gatherer society—were observed by anthropologists in the 1960s to be extremely peaceful. Yet anthropologists in the 1920s had observed them engaging in murderous inter-group violence.[8] If there are general principles to explain why some societies at some times are more peaceful than others and why they change, political scientists have not yet identified them.

The Interstate Level   The theories at the *interstate* level explain wars in terms of power relations among major actors in the international system and are favoured by realists. For example, power transition theory holds that conflicts generate large wars at times when power is relatively equally distributed and a rising power is threatening to overtake a declining hegemon in overall position. At this level, too, there are competing theories that seem incompatible. Deterrence, as we have seen, is supposed to stop wars by building up power and threatening its use. But the theory of arms races holds that wars are caused, not prevented, by such actions. As is noted in Chapter 2, no general formula has been discovered to tell us in what circumstances each of these principles holds true.

Lacking a reliable method for predicting what power configurations among states will lead to war, some political scientists have tried to estimate statistically the *probabilities* that

---

[7] Lawrence H. Keeley, *War before Civilization: The Myth of the Peaceful Savage* (NY: Oxford UP, 1996). Robert L. O'Connell, *Ride of the Second Horseman: The Birth and Death of War* (NY: Oxford UP, 1995). Barbara Ehrenreich, *Blood Rites: Origins and History of the Passions of War* (NY: Metropolitan/Holt, 1997). Carol R. Ember and Melvin Ember, "Resource Unpredictability, Mistrust, and War: A Cross-Cultural Study," *Journal of Conflict Resolution* 36.2 (1992): 242–62. Robert A. Rubinstein and Mary LeCron Foster, eds., *The Social Dynamics of Peace and Conflict: Culture in International Security* (Boulder, CO: Westview, 1988).

[8] Irenaus Eibl-Eibesfeldt, *The Biology of Peace and War: Men, Animals, and Aggression* (NY: Viking, 1979).

WHY WAR?
Political scientists do not agree on a theory of why great wars like World War II occur and cannot predict whether they could happen again. The city of Stalingrad (Volgograd) was decimated during Germany's invasion of the Soviet Union, 1943.

one or another type of interstate relationship might lead to war.[9] Current research focuses on the effects of democracy, government structure, trade, and related factors in explaining the escalation or settlement of "militarized interstate disputes."[10]

Scholars use quantitative and statistical methods to test various ideas about international conflict, such as analyzing data about wars, weapons, and arms races.[11] For example, researchers are analyzing conflicts between democracies to see why they almost never escalate to war (see "Democracy and Foreign Policy" on pp. 150–151). The quality of data, however, is a major problem for statistical studies of infrequent occurrences such as wars.

The Global Level   At the *global* level of analysis, a number of theories of war have been proposed. Of the several variations on the idea that major warfare in the international system is *cyclical*, one approach links large wars with *long economic waves* (also called *Kondratieff cycles*) in the world economy, of about 50 years' duration. Another approach links the largest wars with a 100-year cycle based on the creation and decay of

---

[9] Quincy Wright, *A Study of War* (1942; Chicago: U Chicago P, 1965). Lewis F. Richardson, *Arms and Insecurity* (Pittsburgh: Boxwood, 1960). Daniel S. Geller and J. David Singer, *Nations at War: A Scientific Study of International Conflict* (NY: Cambridge UP, 1998). John A. Vasquez and Marie T. Henehan, eds., *The Scientific Study of Peace and War: A Text Reader* (Lanham, MD: UP America/Lexington, 1999). Manus I. Midlarsky, ed., *Handbook of War Studies II* (Ann Arbor: U Michigan P, 2000). Claudio Cioffi-Revilla, *The Scientific Measurement of International Conflict: Handbook of Datasets on Crises and War, 1495–1988 A.D.* (Boulder, CO: Rienner, 1990).

[10] Stuart A. Bremer and Thomas R. Cusack, *The Process of War: Advancing the Scientific Study of War* (Newark, NJ: Gordon & Breach, 1995). J. David Singer and Paul F. Diehl, eds., *Measuring the Correlates of War* (Ann Arbor: U Michigan P, 1990). Melvin Small and J. David Singer, *Resort to Arms: International and Civil Wars, 1816–1980* (Beverly Hills: Sage, 1982).

[11] Peter Wallensteen, ed., *Peace Research: Achievements and Challenges* (Boulder, CO: Westview, 1988). Peter Van Den Dungen, "Jean De Bloch: A 19th Century Peace Researcher," *Peace Researcher* 15.3 (1983): 21–27.

world orders (see "Hegemony" on pp. 80–83). These cycle theories at best can explain only general tendencies toward war in the international system over time.[12]

An opposite approach in some ways is the theory of linear long-term change—that war as an outcome of conflict is becoming less likely over time due to the worldwide development of both technology and international norms. Some IR scholars argue that war and military force are becoming *obsolete* as a leverage in international conflicts because these means of influence are not very effective in today's highly complex, interdependent world. A parallel line of argument holds that today's military technology is too powerful to use in most conflicts; this is especially applicable to nuclear weapons.

A possibly complementary theory traces the obsolescence of war to the evolution of international norms against the use of force. War once was seen as a normal way to resolve disputes but now is considered distasteful. An analogy has been drawn to the practices of slavery and duelling—once considered normal but now obsolete.[13] However, all these arguments about the linear evolution of warfare in the international system rest on mixed empirical evidence. In truth, although major wars have become shorter and less frequent, they are more destructive than ever when they occur. And even in the absence of major wars, smaller wars around the world have not yet evolved out of existence. War may be obsolete, but it still occurs with great frequency.[14]

Thus, although the levels of analysis suggest many explanations for why conflicts lead to war, few such generalizations hold up. On all the levels of analysis, competing theories offer very different explanations for why some conflicts become violent and others do not. For these reasons, political scientists cannot yet predict with any confidence which of the world's many international conflicts will lead to war. We can gain insight, however, by studying various types of conflicts to understand better what it is that states are fighting about. We can also examine some of the alternative forms of leverage, violent and nonviolent, that states use in conflicts.

CONFLICTS OF INTEREST

One way of looking at international conflicts, deriving from realist assumptions, is to assume that all states want maximum power relative to other states. Conflict then becomes a universal condition among states, and they fight about power, status, and alliances in the international system. This realist approach offers insights into power rivalries that sometimes become detached from underlying conflicts over territory, religion, or other specific causes. China attacked Vietnam in 1979 to "teach Vietnam a lesson" after Vietnam invaded Cambodia and overthrew the Chinese-aligned Khmer Rouge government there. China did not want Vietnamese territory; it just wanted to administer punishment for an act it disapproved of. In such cases the struggle for power in an abstract sense takes on its own logic.

But why do states want power? Power gives states specific benefits—the ability to gain better outcomes in bargaining over particular issues that matter to their well-being. Most international conflicts—including those behind the dozens of wars going on at present—are disputes about concrete grievances and demands. They are about territorial borders, ethnic hatreds, revolutions, and so forth. To understand the nature of international con-

---

[12] Joshua S. Goldstein, *Long Cycles: Prosperity and War in the Modern Age* (New Haven, CT: Yale UP, 1988). George Modelski, *Long Cycles in World Politics* (Seattle: U Washington P, 1987).

[13] John Mueller, *Retreat from Doomsday: The Obsolescence of Major War* (NY: Basic, 1989).

[14] Patrick Brogan, *The Fighting Never Stopped: A Comprehensive Guide to World Conflict since 1945* (NY: Random/Vintage, 1991). Phillipe Delmas, *The Rosy Future of War*, trans. C. Atamian and C. Hewitt (NY: Free Press, 1997).

flicts, including their potential for becoming violent, one must study the underlying interests and goals of the actors involved.

The following sections discuss six types of international conflict. Three are conflicts over tangible material interests:

1. Territorial border disputes, including secession attempts
2. Conflicts over who controls national governments
3. Economic conflicts over trade, money, natural resources, drug trafficking, and other such economic transactions

The other three types of conflict concern less-tangible clashes of ideas:

4. Ethnic conflicts
5. Religious conflicts
6. Ideological conflicts

These six types of conflict are not mutually exclusive, and they overlap considerably in practice. For example, the conflicts between Russia and Ukraine after the 1991 Soviet breakup were complex. The two new states had a *territorial* dispute over the Crimean peninsula, which Soviet leader Nikita Khrushchev had transferred to Ukraine in the 1950s. There and elsewhere, *ethnic* Russians living in Ukraine, and Ukrainians in Russia, experienced ethnic conflict. There are *religious* differences between Ukrainian and Russian forms of Christianity. The two states also had *economic* conflicts over trade and money after the Soviet breakup, which created new borders and currencies. These multiple conflicts did not lead to the use of military force, however. Again, conflict is not the same as war—most conflicts do not entail the use of violence. Conflicts of interest lie at the heart of all international bargaining, from trade negotiations to arms control. Only sometimes do they turn violent.

Territorial Disputes

Among the international conflicts that concern tangible "goods," those about territory have special importance because of the territorial nature of the state (see "Anarchy and Sovereignty" on pp. 71–74). Conflicts over control of territory are really of two varieties: territorial disputes (about where borders are drawn) and conflicts over control of entire states within existing borders (discussed next under "Control of Governments"). Consider first differences over where borders between two states should be drawn—that is, about which state should control disputed territory.

Because states value home territory with an almost fanatical devotion, border disputes tend to be among the most intractable in IR. States will seldom yield territory in exchange for money or any other positive reward. Nor do states quickly forget territory that they lose involuntarily. For example, after defeating France in 1871, Germany took the French provinces of Alsace and Lorraine. French indignation over the loss and French nationalism among the inhabitants of the province made Germany's possession of the territory difficult; ultimately it was returned after Germany lost World War I. The goal of regaining territory lost to another state is called **irredentism.** This form of nationalism leads directly to serious interstate conflicts.[15]

irredentism A form of nationalism whose goal is the regaining of territory lost to another state; it can lead directly to violent interstate conflicts.

---

[15] Paul F. Diehl, ed., *A Road Map to War: Territorial Dimensions of International Conflic.* (Nashville, TN: Vanderbilt, 1999). Paul F. Diehl and Gary Goertz, *Territorial Changes and International Conflict* (NY: Routledge, 1992). Arie Marcelo Kacowicz, *Peaceful Territorial Change* (Columbia: U South Carolina P, 1994). Naomi Chazan, ed., *Irredentism and International Politics* (Boulder, CO: Rienner, 1991).

Because of their association with the integrity of states, territories are valued far beyond any inherent economic or strategic value they hold. For example, after Israel and Egypt made peace in 1978, it took them a decade to settle a border dispute at Taba, a tiny plot of beachfront on which Israeli developers had built a hotel just slightly across the old border. The two states finally submitted the issue for binding arbitration, and Egypt ended up in possession. For Egypt, regaining every centimetre of territory was a matter of national honour and a symbol of the sovereignty and territorial integrity that defined Egyptian statehood. In 2002, Bolivian public opinion opposed a gas export pipeline through Chile to the sea, because Chile had seized the coastline from Bolivia more than a century earlier, in 1879.

An exception to this attitude toward territories used to exist in regard to colonies and other territorial possessions. Because these were not part of the home territory or associated with the idea of the nation, they were valued only as property to be won, lost, sold, or traded in political deals and wars. France and Russia sold their territories in Louisiana and Alaska, respectively, to the United States. Such territories are valued for their natural resources or their geopolitical location. Britain since 1704 has possessed the tiny Rock of Gibraltar commanding the entrance to the Mediterranean; the United States since 1898 has owned the Pacific island of Guam, used for military bases. But today, with few colonies remaining, most of the world's territory is home territory to some state.

The value states place on home territory seems undiminished despite the apparent reduction in the inherent value of territory over time as technology has developed. Historically, territory was the basis of economic production—agriculture and the extraction of raw materials. Even in Sun Tzu's time, it was said that "land is the foundation of the state." It was in these agrarian societies that the international system developed. Winning and losing wars meant gaining or losing territory, with which came wealth and hence long-term power. Today, however, much more wealth derives from trade and technology than from agriculture. The costs of most territorial disputes appear to outweigh any economic benefits that the territory in question could provide. There are exceptions, however, such as the capture of diamond-mining areas in several African countries by rebels who use the diamond revenues to finance war. In 2002, 40 states created a program of UN certification for legitimate diamonds, trying to keep "conflict diamonds" off the international market. (See also "Trafficking," pp. 171–173.)

Means of Controlling Territory Historically, military means have been the most effective leverage for controlling territory, and wars have often redrawn the borders of states. Military forces can seize control on the ground in a way that is hard to contest by any means except other military forces. For example, when Saddam Hussein redrew the borders of Iraq to include Kuwait, his opponents found no better means to dislodge him (economic sanctions, diplomatic isolation, negotiations, and so on) than to use military force themselves. The 2003 invasion of Iraq by the United States and Britain was ostensibly not aimed at controlling Iraqi territory, but did topple Saddam Hussein's regime.

Since World War II, however, there has been a strong norm in the international system *against* trying to alter borders by force. Such attempts are considered grave matters by the international community. Thus, when Iraq annexed Kuwait and erased its borders, most states treated the act as not merely distasteful but intolerable. By contrast, it is considered a lesser offence for one state merely to topple another's government and install a puppet regime, even if done violently. The principle is: governments come and go; borders remain.

The norm of territorial integrity was illustrated in 1992 when a group of Pakistani nationalists tried to march across the border into a part of India populated by fellow Muslims. Pakistani police fired on their own nationalists to keep them from reaching the border (and possibly triggering a war with India). Because the Pakistani action upheld

TERRITORIAL INTEGRITY

Efforts by a region to secede from a state are a frequent source of international conflict, but international norms generally treat such conflicts as internal matters unless they spill over borders. Russia's 1995 assault on its mainly Muslim republic of Chechnya, which had declared independence from the Russian Federation, was repelled, but in 1999–2000 Russia regained control over most of the territory in an even fiercer offensive. Despite human rights violations, the international community tacitly accepted Russia's actions. Here the Russian Army takes control of the capital, Grozny, which was totally destroyed in the attack (2000).

the integrity of the border, and because they fired on their own citizens, not those of another country, Western democracies did not disapprove of Pakistan's use of force against the demonstrators.

Secession Efforts by a province or region to secede from an existing state are a special type of conflict over borders—not the borders of two existing states but the efforts by a substate area to draw international borders around itself as a new state. Dozens of secession movements exist around the world, of varying sizes and political effectiveness, but they succeed in seceding only rarely. The existing state almost always tries to hold onto the area in question. For instance, the mainly Muslim republic of Chechnya, one of the republics of Russia (the Russian Federation), tried to split away from Russia in the early 1990s after the Soviet Union collapsed. In 1994–1995, Russia sent in a huge military force that destroyed the Chechen capital, but faced fierce resistance from Chechen nationalist guerrillas, and withdrew in defeat. In 1999–2000, another destructive Russian campaign won a tentative grip on power in the province but has been resisted by Chechen fighters, who have attacked civilian targets within Russia. The pro-Russian Chechen president was assassinated in 2004.

As this example suggests, wars of secession can be large and deadly, and they can easily spill over international borders or draw in other countries. This spillover is particularly likely if members of an ethnic or a religious group span two sides of a border, constituting the majority group in one state and a majority in a nearby region of another state, but a minority in the other state as a whole. This pattern occurs in Bosnia-Serbia, Moldova-Russia, Iraq-Iran, and India-Pakistan. In some cases, secessionists want to merge their territories with the neighbouring state (as in the effort to carve out a "greater Serbia"), which amounts to redrawing the international border. International norms frown on such an outcome. (Ethnic and religious conflict are discussed later in this chapter.)

The strong international norms of sovereignty and territorial integrity treat secession movements as domestic problems that are of little concern to other states. In the case of Chechnya, the Western governments objected not to Russia's goal of maintaining control of the republic, but only to Russia's methods of waging the war—which included indiscriminate bombing and shelling of civilian areas. These actions violated standards of human rights, which are however a weaker set of norms than those promoting state sovereignty.

Thus, the international community expressed concern over Russia's treatment of Chechen civilians, but U.S. President Clinton went to Moscow for a summit meeting while the Russian military was still fighting in Chechnya. Even when secession conflicts occasionally spill over international borders, as with Turkey's incursions into Iraq since 1995, the international community tends to treat the matter lightly as long as the cross-border incursion is temporary. The general principle seems to be: "We existing states all have our own domestic problems and disaffected groups or regions, so we must stick together behind sovereignty and territorial integrity." This solidarity only increased after the 2001 terrorist attacks on the U.S., after which Russia's position on Chechnya found a more receptive hearing within the U.S. administration.

Messy border problems have been created in some recent cases in which multinational states broke up into pieces. In such cases, borders that had been internal become international; since these borders are new they may be more vulnerable to challenge.

Certainly this is the case in the former Yugoslavia, where ethnic groups had intermingled and intermarried, leaving mixed populations in most of the Yugoslav republics. When Yugoslavia broke up in 1991–1992, several republics declared their independence as separate states. Two of these, Croatia and Bosnia, contained minority populations of ethnic Serbs. Serbia seized effective control of significant areas of Croatia and Bosnia that contained Serbian communities or linked such populations geographically. Non-Serbian populations in these areas were driven out or massacred—**ethnic cleansing.** Then, when Croatia reconquered most of its territory in 1995, Serbian populations in turn fled from Croatia. Ethnic nationalism proved stronger than multi-ethnic tolerance in both Serbia and Croatia, making borders problematic.

The breakup of a state need not lead to violence, however. Czechoslovakia split into the Czech Republic and Slovakia in a cooperative and civil manner. And the breakup of the Soviet Union did not lead to violent territorial disputes between republics in *most* cases, even where ethnic groups were split across new international borders (such as Ukraine-Russia).

The norm against forceful redrawing of borders does not apply to cases of decolonization. For example, when Portugal's empire crumbled in 1975, its colony of East Timor was brutally invaded and annexed by neighbouring Indonesia. Because East Timor was not a UN member state (most states did not recognize its independence), Indonesia got away with this move (although the move was not officially recognized by most states). As with Chechnya, the problem was treated mainly as one of human rights. However, the international community never formally recognized Indonesia's control over East Timor, and decades later East Timor achieved independence, joining the UN in 2003. Similarly, since Spain pulled out of Western Sahara, Morocco has retained control (after fighting independence guerrillas, and still under dispute pending a long-stalled referendum).

ethnic cleansing Forced displacement of an ethnic group or groups from a particular territory, accompanied by massacres and other human rights violations; it has occurred after the breakup of multinational states, notably in the former Yugoslavia.

The transfer of Hong Kong from British to Chinese control in 1997 also illustrates how colonial territory is dispensable (Britain's perspective) while home territory is nearly sacred (China's perspective). From neither perspective do the views of the inhabitants of a territory carry much weight. The peaceful transfer of Hong Kong is one of the few recent cases in which territory has changed hands in the international system.

Interstate Borders Border disputes between existing states are taken more seriously by the international community, but are less common than secessionist conflicts. Because of the norm of territorial integrity, few important border conflicts remain among long-established states. At one time, huge chunks of territory were passed between states at the stroke of a pen (on a peace treaty or marriage contract). However, this kind of wholesale redrawing of borders has not occurred among established states for 50 years. Since the end of World War II, only a minuscule amount of territory has changed hands between established states through force. Such efforts have been made, but have failed. For instance, when Iraq attacked Iran in 1980, one objective was to control the Shatt-al-Arab waterway (with access to the Persian Gulf) because of its commercial and strategic value. But 10 years and a million deaths later, the Iran-Iraq border was back where it started. Bits of land have changed hands in recent decades through war, but it is remarkable how small those bits have been. (Again, this does not apply to the formation of new states and the fragmenting of old ones.)

Furthermore, when territorial disputes do occur between established states, they *can* sometimes be settled peacefully, especially when the involved territory is small compared with the states disputing it. The Soviet Union simply agreed to China's boundary preferences in 1986 after the two states had disputed ownership of some minor river islands for years (including military skirmishes in 1969). El Salvador and Honduras got the World Court to adjudicate their border disputes in 1992. And in 1994 a panel of Latin American judges settled a century-long border dispute between Argentina and Chile over some mountainous terrain that both claimed. The 3–2 ruling, after the countries submitted the dispute for judicial arbitration, awarded the territory to Argentina and provoked howls of protest from Chile. But despite the strong feelings evoked by the loss of territory, Argentina and Chile had settled 22 of 24 remaining border disputes peacefully over the previous 10 years (after nearly going to war in 1978 over disputed islands).

At the end of 2003, Nigeria transferred sovereignty over 33 villages to Cameroon under terms of a World Court ruling. A joint delegation of officials, with UN experts and observers, travelled by dirt road and canoe to oversee the flag lowering and raising in each village. Why would Nigeria—a country with nine times Cameroon's population, more than triple its GDP, and a much stronger military—voluntarily cede territory? Doing so would seem to run counter to the predictions of realism. Rather, as liberals might emphasize, Nigeria acted out of a different calculation of power than merely controlling territory. Turning the dispute over to the World Court and bringing in the UN to assist with implementation brought the kind of stability needed for foreign investment to develop the area's resources, primarily oil. Nigeria cares more about economic development than about a few remote villages in contested territory. A harder test came in 2004 when, under the same ruling, Nigeria was to hand over the Bakassi peninsula on the coast, thought to be rich in oil. The outcome is not known at the time of this writing, but by mid-2004 Nigeria had achieved agreement from Cameroon and the UN to delay the handover until later in the year. Again, the overall benefits of political stability and international cooperation might make it worthwhile for Nigeria to comply with the ruling, even at the cost of some missed oil revenues, rather than defy the World Court.

Lingering Disputes Today, only a few of the world's interstate borders are disputed. Nonetheless, those that persist are important sources of international conflict. Among the most difficult are the borders of *Israel*, which have never been firmly defined and recognized by its neighbours. The 1948 ceasefire lines resulting from Israel's war of independence expanded in the 1967 war, then contracted again on the Egyptian border with the Camp David peace treaty of 1978. The remaining territories occupied in 1967—the *West Bank* near Jordan, the *Gaza Strip* near Egypt, and the *Golan Heights* of Syria—are central to the Arab-Israeli conflict. Israeli-Palestinian agreements since 1993 tried to move toward Palestinian autonomy in parts of the West Bank and Gaza Strip, and negotiations seemed headed toward creation of a state of Palestine in all or most of the occupied territories, at peace with Israel. However, the 2000 "Camp David II" summit failed—over how to divide Jerusalem, and other emotional issues—and a new phase of violence and hate began.

Another major border dispute is in the *Kashmir* area where India, Pakistan, and China intersect. The India-held part of Kashmir is predominantly inhabited by Muslims, a group that is the majority in Pakistan but a minority in India. A *Line of Control* divides the disputed province. Pakistan accuses India of oppressing Kashmiris and thwarting an international agreement to decide Kashmir's future by a popular referendum. India accuses Pakistan of aiding and infiltrating Islamic radicals who carry out attacks in Indian-occupied Kashmir. The two countries went to war twice before over the issue, and nearly did so again in 2002—but that time with both sides holding dozens of nuclear-armed missiles that some experts estimated would kill more than 10 million people in an India-Pakistan war. Perhaps chastened by this experience, the two countries improved relations in 2003 and began a ceasefire that stopped the incessant low-level fighting along the Line of Control, although not the fighting between Indian authorities and insurgents.

Among the former Soviet republics, the most serious border dispute is over *Nagorno-Karabakh*, an Armenian-populated territory within neighbouring Azerbaijan. After a costly war, Armenia gained military control of the region. Russia and Ukraine had a conflict over the Crimean peninsula, formerly Russian but part of Ukraine since the 1950s.

Peru and Ecuador fought border skirmishes in 1995 over a nearly inaccessible stretch of mountainous terrain, part of a sizable area signed over to Peru following its victory in a brief war with Ecuador in 1941. The conflict, which involved no tangible assets worth fighting over, illustrated once again the almost mystical power of territory as a symbol of national honour, and the continuing usefulness of nationalism in generating political support for state leaders (the popularity of both presidents increased as the conflict heated up). International mediation cooled off the dispute after a month of fighting.

Many of the world's other remaining interstate territorial disputes—and often the most serious ones—concern the control of small islands, which often provide strategic advantages, natural resources (such as offshore oil), or fishing rights. China asserts a right to the tiny disputed *Spratly Islands* in the South China Sea. The islands and the surrounding waters, which may hold substantial oil reserves, are closer to Vietnam, the Philippines, Malaysia, and Brunei than to China, and are claimed in part or in full by all of those countries and by Taiwan (see Figure 5.1). All of those states except Brunei have resorted to military occupation at times to stake their claims, but in 2002 the countries agreed to avoid conflicts over the islands. After a small Chinese-Vietnamese naval battle in 1988, the countries agreed to refrain from destabilizing activities and to work for a peaceful resolution. But incidents and tensions have continued since then. The Spratly Islands conflict has importance beyond the immediate dispute since it may signal China's intentions as a rising great power. Japan and China also dispute tiny islands elsewhere, as do Japan and South Korea. These disputes involve low economic stakes, but have become a focus of nationalist sentiments on both sides, fuelled partly by memories of World War II, when Japan occupied China and Korea. In 2004, South Korea issued four postage stamps depicting a tiny island also claimed by Japan. They sold out within hours.

In the Middle East, Iran and the United Arab Emirates dispute ownership of small islands near the mouth of the Persian Gulf. In 2002, Spain sent soldiers to oust a handful of Moroccan troops from islands off Morocco's coast. In South America, Argentina and Britain still dispute control of the *Falkland Islands* (*Islas Malvinas*), over which they fought a war in 1982. And the major bone of contention in Russian-Japanese relations is the ownership of the small but strategically located *Kuril Islands* occupied by the Soviet Union in 1945. In 2001, Japan objected when Russia granted South Korea fishing rights near the islands (a provisional settlement was reached). With islands now bringing control of surrounding economic zones, international conflicts over islands will undoubtedly continue in the coming years.

Territorial Waters States treat **territorial waters** near their shores as part of their national territory. Definitions of such waters are not universally agreed upon, but norms have developed in recent years, especially after the *UN Convention on the Law of the Sea (UNCLOS)* (see pp. 502–505). Waters within three nautical miles (5.6 kilometres) of shore have traditionally been recognized as territorial, but beyond that there are disputes about how far out national sovereignty extends and for what purposes. UNCLOS generally allows a 12-nautical mile (22.2-kilometre) limit for shipping, and a 200-nautical mile (370.4-kilometre) *exclusive economic zone (EEZ)* covering fishing and mineral rights (but allowing for free navigation by all). The EEZs together cover a third of the world's oceans.

Figure 5.1 Disputed Islands

The Spratly Islands exemplify contemporary conflicts over territory and natural resources around islands. All or part of the Spratlys are claimed by China, Vietnam, Malaysia, Brunei, the Philippines, and Taiwan.

It is because of the EEZs that sovereignty over a single tiny island can now bring with it rights to as much as 259 000 square kilometres of surrounding ocean. But these zones overlap greatly, and shorelines do not run in straight lines; thus numerous questions of interpretation arise about how to delineate territorial and economic waters. For example, Libya claims ownership of the entire Gulf of Sidra, treating it as a bay; the United States treats it as a curvature in the shoreline and insists that most of it is international waters. In 1986, the United States sent warships into the Gulf of Sidra to make its point. U.S. planes shot down two Libyan jets that challenged the U.S. manoeuvres.

In 1994–1995, Canada sent its navy to harass Spanish fishing boats just beyond the 200-nautical mile zone (but affecting fish stocks within the zone). In the Sea of Okhotsk, Russia's EEZ includes all but a small "doughnut hole" of international waters in the middle (see p. 504). Non-Russian boats have fished intensively in the "hole," which of course depletes fish stocks in Russia's EEZ.

The Arctic waters have been a consistent security issue for Canada. During the Cold War the concern focused on Soviet proximity to Canada via the Arctic Circle. Canada has also faced challenges to its sovereignty in parts of the Arctic; in 1985, for example, a U.S. Coast Guard icebreaker traversed the Northwest Passage without seeking Canadian permission, precipitating greater Canadian Forces presence in Canadian Arctic waters.[16]

territorial waters The waters near states' shores generally treated as part of national territory. The UN Convention on the Law of the Sea provides for a 12-nautical mile territorial sea (exclusive national jurisdiction over shipping and navigation) and a 200-nautical mile exclusive economic zone (EEZ) covering exclusive fishing and mineral rights (but allowing for free navigation by all). See also *high seas* and *UN Convention on the Law of the Sea (UNCLOS)*.

---

[16] Ron Purver, "The Arctic in Canadian Security Policy, 1945 to the Present," *Canada's International Security Policy,* ed. David B. Dewitt and David Leyton-Brown (Scarborough, ON: Prentice Hall, 1995).

airspace The space above a state that is considered its territory, in contrast to outer space, which is considered international territory.

Airspace **Airspace** above a state is considered the territory of the state. Any airplane that wants to fly over a state's territory must have the state's permission. For example, in a 1986 raid on Libya, U.S. bombers based in Britain had to fly a long detour over the Atlantic Ocean because France (between Britain and Libya) would not grant permission for U.S. planes to use its airspace during the mission.

Outer space, by contrast, is considered international territory, like the oceans. International law does not define exactly where airspace ends and outer space begins. However, orbiting satellites fly higher than airplanes, move very fast, and cannot easily change direction to avoid overflying a country. Also, very few states can shoot down satellites, though many can shoot airplanes. Since satellites have become useful to all the great powers as intelligence-gathering tools, and since all satellites are extremely vulnerable to attack, a norm of demilitarization of outer space has developed. No state has ever attacked the satellite of another, and doing so would be a severe provocation.

Control of Governments

Despite the many minor border disputes that continue to plague the world, most of the struggles to control territory do not involve changing borders. Rather, they are conflicts over which governments will control entire states.

In theory, states do not interfere in each other's governance. In practice, states often have strong interests in the governments of other states and use a variety of means of leverage to influence who holds power in those states. When one state wants to alter or replace the government of a second state, a conflict always exists between the two governments. In addition, the first state may come into conflict with other parties that oppose changing the second state's government. These conflicts over governments take many forms, some mild and some severe, some deeply entwined with third parties and some more or less bilateral. Sometimes a state merely exerts subtle influences on another state's elections; at other times, a state supports rebel elements seeking to overthrow the second state's constitutional order altogether.

STRUGGLE FOR CONTROL
Conflicts over who controls a national government, especially armed rebellions, can easily become internationalized. In 2003, U.S. and British forces overthrew Saddam Hussein's government in Iraq by force. Here, a statue of Saddam is toppled in central Baghdad (with a live worldwide TV audience) after U.S. forces took the city, April 2003.

During the Cold War, both superpowers actively promoted changes of government in countries of the global South through covert operations and support of rebel armies. The civil wars in Angola, Afghanistan, and Nicaragua are good examples. Both superpowers poured in weapons, money, military advisers, and so forth—all in hopes of influencing the composition of the country's government.

Occasionally, one state invades another in order to change its government. The Soviet Union did this in Czechoslovakia in 1968; the United States did it in Grenada in 1983 and in Iraq in 2003. It is sometimes hard for new governments created in this way to gain legitimacy both domestically and internationally. People generally resent having foreigners choose their government for them—even if they didn't like the old government—and the international community frowns on such overt violations of national sovereignty. For instance, the government installed in Afghanistan after the Soviet invasion of 1979 was seen as a Soviet puppet and was finally toppled after a dozen years of rule marked by constant war.

Even in Cambodia—where the Khmer Rouge government's atrocities led many people inside and outside the country to welcome the Vietnamese invasion that installed a new Cambodian government in 1979—the new government could not consolidate its international position for more than a decade. It did not gain Cambodia's seat in the UN, and the United States and China sent assistance to rebel groups that fought a long and bloody civil war against the Vietnamese-backed Cambodian government. (In the 1990s, the UN mediated a ceasefire and implemented a peace plan under which the UN basically ran the government while organizing elections.)

International conflicts over the control of governments—along with territorial disputes—are likely to lead to the use of violence. They involve core issues of the status and integrity of states, the stakes tend to be high, and the interests of involved actors are often diametrically opposed. Other types of conflict are both more widespread and sometimes less likely to lead to violence. Chief among these is economic conflict among states.

Economic Conflict

Economic competition is the most pervasive form of conflict in international relations because economic transactions are pervasive. Every sale made and every deal reached across international borders entails a resolution of conflicting interests. Costa Rica wants the price of coffee, which it exports, to go up; Canada, which imports coffee, wants the price to go down. Angola wants foreign producers of Angolan oil to receive fewer profits from oil sales; those companies' home states want them to take home more profits. In a global capitalist market, all economic exchanges involve some conflict of interest.

However, such economic transactions also contain a strong element of mutual economic gain in addition to the element of conflicting interests (see Chapters 3 and 8). This is a view most favoured by liberals, particularly economic liberals. These mutual gains provide the most useful leverage in bargaining over economic exchanges: states and companies enter into economic transactions because they profit from doing so. The use of violence would for the most part interrupt and diminish such profit by more than could be gained as a result of the use of violence.

For liberals, then, economic conflict seldom leads to violence today because military forms of leverage are no longer very effective in economic conflicts. With the tight integration of the world economy and the high cost of military actions, the use of force is seldom justified to solve an economic issue. Thus, most economic conflicts are not issues in international security; they are discussed in Chapters 8 through 13 (international political economy).

But such restraint has not always been the case. In the sixteenth century, England's Sir Francis Drake intercepted Spanish ships bringing gold and silver from Central America and took the loot in the name of queen and country—a practice known as *privateering*. In the seventeenth century, England fought several naval wars against the Netherlands. An English general, when asked the reason for England's declaration of war in 1652, replied, "What matters this or that reason? What we want is more of the trade the Dutch now have."[17] In 1861, France, Britain, and Spain invaded Mexico when it failed to pay its international debts.

For critical theorists, economic relations bear on international security in a variety of ways. For some critical theorists, war has been an intrinsic part of capitalism and imperialism. This includes both wars fought between colonial powers over imperial possessions and the brutally one-sided wars of imperial conquest in which lands were occupied, peoples enslaved, and resources looted.[18] Realists too sometimes make links between economics and security. The theory of **lateral pressure** also connects economic competition with security concerns. This theory holds that the economic growth of states leads to geographic expansion as they seek natural resources beyond their borders (by various means, peaceful and violent). As great powers expand their economic activities outward, their competition leads to conflicts and sometimes to war. The theory has been used to help explain both World War I and the expansion of Japan prior to World War II.[19]

Another kind of economic conflict that affects international security concerns the *military-industrial complex* and the interests associated with the production of military equipment, especially high-technology weapons such as fighter aircraft or missiles. By this view, the arms trade is related to the outbreak of international violence in ways more complicated than simply making weapons available to belligerents. Countries that export weapons are rarely the countries in which armed conflict takes place. If a country is an exporter of arms, and if its industrial base depends on the manufacture of weapons, then, as some critical theorists note, those countries have an interest in ensuring there is always a market for their goods. It is, in other words, in the interests of weapons exporters—most of which are Northern, industrialized states—to make sure there is always a war going on somewhere.[20]

A different kind of economic conflict revolves around the distribution of wealth within and among states. As discussed in Chapter 12, there are tremendous disparities in wealth in our world, disparities that create a variety of international security problems with the potential for violence.

Revolutions in poor countries are often fuelled by disparities of wealth within the country as well as its poverty relative to other countries. These revolutions in turn frequently draw in other states as supporters of one side or the other in a civil war. If successful, revolutions can abruptly change a state's foreign policy, leading to new alliances and power alignments.

lateral pressure (theory of) Theory that the economic and population growth of states fuels geographic expansion as they seek natural resources beyond their borders, which in turn leads to conflicts and sometimes to war.

---

[17] Michael Howard, *War in European History* (NY: Oxford UP, 1976) 47.

[18] Eric J. Hobsbawm, *Age of Extremes* (London: Little, Brown, 1994). Robbie Robertson, *Three Waves of Globalization: A History of a Developing Global Consciousness* (London: Zed Books, 2003).

[19] Nazli Choucri and Robert C. North, *Nations in Conflict: National Growth and International Violence* (San Francisco: Freeman, 1975). Richard K. Ashley, *The Political Economy of War and Peace: The Sino-Soviet-American Triangle and the Modern Security Problematique* (London: Pinter, 1980). Nazli Choucri, Robert C. North, and Susumu Yamakage, *The Challenge of Japan: Before World War II and After* (NY: Routledge, 1993).

[20] Marilyn Waring, *Counting for Nothing: What Men Value and What Women are Worth*, 2nd ed. (Toronto: U Toronto P, 1999). Dr. Helen Caldicott, *The New Nuclear Danger: George W. Bush's Military-Industrial Complex* (NY: New Press, 2002).

Critical approaches to international relations drawn from Marxist thought treat class struggle between rich and poor people as the basis of interstate relations. According to these approaches, capitalist states adopt foreign policies that serve the interests of the rich owners of companies. Conflicts and wars between the global North and South—rich states versus poor states—are seen as reflections of the domination and exploitation of the poor by the rich—imperialism in direct or indirect form. For example, most Marxists saw the Vietnam War as a U.S. effort to suppress revolution in order to secure continued U.S. access to cheap labour and raw materials in Southeast Asia. The 1991 Gulf War and the 2003 War in Iraq were seen in similar terms, though focused there on access to oil. Many Marxists portray conflicts among capitalist states as competition over the right to exploit poor areas. Soviet founder V. I. Lenin portrayed World War I as a fight over the imperialists' division of the world.

Trafficking Trafficking today takes many forms, and includes trafficking in resources such as gems and timber; trafficking in drugs; and trafficking in persons.

Gems, timber, and other resources may be trafficked by belligerents in a conflict as a means to finance their efforts. Sometimes these conflicts are civil (internal) in scope, but because they are related to the global political economy through shadow or war economies, they are also international. In some cases, continued fighting, rather than "defeating an enemy" is the goal, because ongoing institutionalized violence serves as an effective cover and vehicle for the extraction and trafficking of the resources.[21] Many contemporary conflicts are fought over access to resources, such as in the Democratic Republic of the Congo and Sierra Leone. For some observers of global politics, resource wars over timber, gems, strategic minerals, and oil will become the most common sources of international conflict in the coming decades.[22]

Trafficking in persons is more often an effect of contemporary conflict than it is a cause, but it can certainly exacerbate conflicts. In some cases, children are trafficked during conflicts, often to serve as combatants. Women and children have been trafficked also, usually for purposes of prostitution, sexual exploitation, forced labour, and slavery. Trafficked women and children can become part of the barter of war, traded between camps of rebels and soldiers. When resource extraction is a defining part of local conflict, trafficked children and women can also be used as workers in the mines or other elements of the extraction process.[23]

Drug trafficking supplies illegal products that are treated as a security threat because of their effect on national (and military) morale and efficiency. Drug trafficking also has become linked with security concerns because military forces participate regularly in operations against the heavily armed drug traffickers.[24] Conflicts over drugs generally concern states on one side and nonstate actors on the other. But other states can be drawn in because the activities in question cross national borders and may involve corrupt state officials.

---

[21] Mats Berdal and David M. Malone, eds., *Greed and Grievance: Economic Agendas in Civil Wars* (Boulder, CO: Rienner, 2000). Mark Duffield, *Global Governance and the New Wars* (London: Zed Books, 2001).

[22] Michael T. Klare, *Resource Wars: The New Landscape of Global Conflict* (NY: Holt, 2001).

[23] *Integration of the human rights of women and the gender perspective: Violence against women: Report of the Special Rapporteur on violence against women, Ms. Radhika Coomaraswamy, on trafficking in women, women's migration and violence against women, submitted in accordance with Commission on Human Rights resolution 1977/44*, UN Economic and Social Council (29 Feb. 2000), E/CN.4/2000/68.

[24] LaMond Tullis, *Unintended Consequences: Illegal Drugs and Drug Policies in Nine Countries* (Boulder, CO: Rienner, 1995). Francisco E. Thoumi, *Political Economy and Illegal Drugs in Colombia* (Boulder, CO: Rienner, 1994). Celia Toro, *Mexico's "War" on Drugs: Causes and Consequences* (Boulder, CO: Rienner, 1995).

These international ramifications are evident in the efforts of the U.S. government to prevent *cocaine cartels* based in Colombia from supplying cocaine to U.S. cities. Such cocaine derives from coca plants mostly grown by peasant farmers in mountainous areas of Peru, Bolivia, and Colombia itself. Processed in simple laboratories in the jungle, the cocaine moves from Colombia through other countries, such as Panama, before arriving in the United States. In each of these states (including the United States), the drug smugglers have bribed some corrupt officials, including military or police officers, to stay clear. But other state officials in each country are working with U.S. law enforcement agencies and the U.S. military to crack down on the cocaine trade. The crackdown inevitably brings some negative side effects. In 2001, Peruvian jets working with U.S. radar trackers shot down a small plane over the Andes that turned out to be carrying U.S. missionaries, not cocaine traffickers.

The truth is that the populations in several of these countries, especially in cocaine-producing regions, benefit substantially from the drug trade. For peasant farmers in Bolivia or for residents of the Colombian cocaine cartels' home provinces, the cocaine trade may be their only access to a decent income. This dilemma worsened in 2001 as coffee prices dropped to their lowest level in decades. Similarly, in 2003 many Ethiopian coffee farmers switched to growing the drug *khat* for export when low coffee prices left them unable to feed themselves. Benefits to corrupt state officials or rebel armies are also substantial. In rural Peru and Colombia, leftist guerrillas have funded their operations by controlling peasants' production of coca.

The cocaine trade thus creates several conflicts between the United States and the states of the region. Most such interstate conflicts are resolved through positive forms of leverage, such as financial or military aid. State officials are also often willing to make common cause with the United States because they are threatened by the drug traffickers, who control great wealth and power, and who, being outlaws, have few incentives against using violence.

Because of the long history of U.S. military intervention in Latin America, state cooperation with U.S. military forces is a sensitive political issue. Governments in the region must respect a delicate balance between the need for U.S. help and the need to uphold national sovereignty. In some countries, governments have faced popular criticism for allowing the "Yankees" to "invade" in the drug war. In one case, the U.S. military literally did invade. In 1989, U.S. forces invaded Panama, arrested its leader, dictator Manuel Noriega, and convicted him in U.S. courts of complicity in drug trafficking through Panama.

DRUG WARS
Because drug trafficking crosses national borders and involves lots of guns and money, it is a source of interstate conflict. The United States invaded Panama to stop dictator Manuel Noriega's collusion with traffickers shipping illegal drugs to the United States. Here, U.S. forces train in Panama near a billboard advertising the United States's own drug export to Panama (tobacco), 1989.

The growing world trade in *heroin* created some similar conflicts in the late 1990s. Most of the raw material (opium poppies) came from two poor and conflict-ridden countries with authoritarian governments, Afghanistan and Burma. Afghan production of opium poppies doubled after 1998, making it the supplier of three-quarters of the world total. The Taliban government that controlled most of Afghanistan (see pp. 180–181) then abruptly halted production by early 2001, perhaps in hopes of gaining international aid or perhaps to drive up the price of the Taliban's own large stockpiles. Since the opium trade enriches local officials and farmers, it may return if post-Taliban Afghanistan remains poor and politically unstable.

Like the other sources of international conflict discussed so far, conflicts over trafficking in drugs, gems, and resources arise from conflicting interests regarding tangible items such as money, territory, or control of governments. More difficult to understand, in some ways, are international conflicts rooted in clashes of ideas. Of course, the two overlap—especially around the material and intangible aspects of nationalism—but conflicts of ideas also require special attention in their own right.

CONFLICTS OF IDEAS

Conflicts over tangible issues (whether territory, government, or resources) often are associated with conflicts over ideas. In many cases, it is difficult to identify which element is the most important contributing factor in any given conflict. Although conflicts over ideas are inseparable from their more tangible elements, such as ethnic, religious, or ideological difference, each is described separately here.

Ethnic Conflict

Ethnic conflict is described by some observers as quite possibly the most important source of conflict in the numerous wars now occurring throughout the world.[25] **Ethnic groups** are large groups of people who share ancestral, language, cultural, or religious ties and a common *identity* (individuals identify with the group). Ethnic groups often form the basis for *nationalist* sentiments. Not all ethnic groups identify as nations; for instance, within Canada various ethnic groups coexist (though sometimes uneasily) with a common *national* identity as Canadians. But in locations where millions of members of a single ethnic group live as the majority population in their ancestors' land, they usually think of themselves as a nation. In most such cases they aspire to have their own state with its formal international status and territorial boundaries.[26]

Territorial control is closely tied to the aspirations of ethnic groups for statehood. Any state's borders will deviate to some extent (sometimes substantially) from the actual location of ethnic communities. Members of the ethnic group will be left outside its state's borders, and members of other ethnic groups will be located within the state's borders. The resulting situation can be dangerous, with part of an ethnic group controlling a state and another part living as a minority within another state controlled by a rival ethnic

ethnic groups Large groups of people who share ancestral, language, cultural, or religious ties and a common identity.

---

[25] Ted Robert Gurr, *Peoples versus States: Minorities at Risk in the New Century* (Washington, DC: U.S. Institute of Peace, 2000). Stephen M. Saideman, *The Ties That Divide* (NY: Columbia UP, 2001). Milton J. Esman, *Ethnic Politics* (Ithaca, NY: Cornell UP, 1995). Stephen Iwan Griffiths, *Nationalism and Ethnic Conflict* (NY: Oxford UP, 1993). Donald L. Horowitz, *Ethnic Groups in Conflict* (Berkeley: U California P, 1985). Donald Rothchild, *Managing Ethnic Conflict in Africa: Pressures and Incentives for Cooperation* (Washington, DC: Brookings, 1997).

[26] Lars-Erik Cederman, *Emergent Actors in World Politics: How States and Nations Develop and Dissolve* (Princeton, NJ: Princeton UP, 1997).

Figure 5.2 Kurdish Area

Ethnic populations often span international borders. Shaded region shows the approximate area of Kurdish settlements.

group. Frequently the minority group suffers discrimination in the other state and the "home" state tries to rescue or avenge them.

Other ethnic groups lack any home state. Kurds share a culture, and many of them aspire to create a state of Kurdistan. But Kurds reside in four states—Turkey, Iraq, Iran, and Syria—all of which strongly oppose giving up control of part of their own territory to create a Kurdish state (see Figure 5.2). In recent years, rival Kurdish guerrilla armies have fought both Iraqi and Turkish military forces, and each other. Repeatedly in the late 1990s, Turkey sent large military forces into northern Iraq to attack Kurdish guerrilla bases.[27] Kurds enjoyed autonomy in part of northern Iraq under U.S. protection in the 1990s and may receive quasi-autonomous status in post-war Iraq.

In ethnic conflicts there are often pressures to redraw borders by force. For example, the former Soviet republic of Moldova is inhabited mostly by ethnic Romanians but also by quite a few ethnic Russians, who are concentrated at the eastern end of Moldova (farthest from Romania). A river separates a strip of land at the east end from the rest of Moldova, and ethnic Russians make up the majority in that strip of territory. When Moldova became independent in 1991 and began asserting its Romanian identity—even considering merging into Romania—the Russians living in the eastern strip of land sought to break away and make the river a new international border. Armed conflict ensued, and both Russia and Romania threatened to intervene. Eventually a ceasefire and a peacekeeping arrangement were implemented, with no formal change in borders.

When ethnic populations are minorities in territories controlled by rival ethnic groups, they may even be driven from their land or (in rare cases) systematically exterminated. By driving out the minority ethnic group, a majority group can assemble a more unified, more contiguous, and larger territory for its nation-state, as ethnic Serbs did through "ethnic cleansing" after the breakup of Yugoslavia.

Outside states often worry about the fate of "their people" living as minorities in neighbouring states. For instance, Albania is concerned about ethnic Albanians who are the majority population in the Serbian province of Kosovo. But if Kosovo became independent of Serbia (or merged with Albania), then Serbia would worry about the minority of ethnic Serbs living in Kosovo. Similar problems have fuelled wars between Armenia and Azerbaijan (in the former Soviet Union) and between India and Pakistan. Before World War II, Adolf Hitler used the fate of ethnic German communities in Poland and Czechoslovakia to justify German territorial expansion into those neighbouring states. It appears likely that the dangerous combination of ethnic conflict and territorial disputes will lead to more wars in the future.

In extreme cases, such as Hitler's Germany, governments use genocide—systematic extermination of ethnic or religious groups in whole or in part—to try to destroy scapegoated groups or political rivals. In Rwanda, where the Hutu group is the majority and the Tutsi group the minority, a Hutu-nationalist government in 1994 slaughtered more than half a million Tutsis (and Hutus opposed to the government) in a matter of weeks. The weak international response to this atrocity reveals how frail are international norms of human rights compared to norms of noninterference in other states' internal affairs—at least when no strategic interests are at stake. Former United Nations Commander in Rwanda, retired Canadian Lieutenant-General Roméo Dallaire, has also suggested that the world community's indifference to the genocide was in no small measure a result of the racism of Northern decision-makers toward a country populated by black Africans.[28]

---

[27] Henri J. Barkey and Graham E. Fuller, *Turkey's Kurdish Question* (Lanham, MD: Rowman & Littlefield, 1998).

[28] Roméo Dallaire, *Shake Hands with the Devil: The Failure of Humanity in Rwanda* (Toronto: Random House Canada, 2003).

The Hutu ultranationalists quickly lost power when Tutsi rebels defeated the government militarily, but they regrouped across the border in Zaire, with hundreds of thousands of Hutu refugees. In 1997, a Tutsi-led army with support from Rwanda and other neighbouring states swept through Zaire, toppled its government, and dispersed or killed many of the refugees. The Hutu-Tutsi conflict thus sparked an intense series of wars that directly affected a half-dozen states, brought down several governments, and destroyed or damaged millions of lives.

Often, in former colonies whose borders were drawn arbitrarily, some ethnic groups span two or more states while others find themselves sharing a state with groups that are traditionally rivals or enemies. For example, Nigeria includes 250 ethnic groups, the largest being two Muslim groups in the north and two Christian groups in the south. Although Nigeria's ethnic populations are slowly developing an overarching national identity as Nigerians, old tensions continue to disrupt politics. For example, after a northern-dominated military government was replaced by an elected president from the south in 1999, as Nigeria democratized, ethnic violence killed hundreds of people.

The Cold War, with its tight system of alliances and authoritarian communist governments, seems to have helped to keep ethnic conflicts in check. In the Soviet Union and Yugoslavia—multinational states—the existence of a single strong state (willing to oppress local communities) kept the lid on ethnic tensions and enforced peace between neighbouring communities. The breakup of these states allowed ethnic and regional

TELLING THE WORLD
Canadian Lieutenant-General Roméo Dallaire served as the United Nations Commander in Rwanda in 1994, and was unable to convince the United Natoins to prevent the slaughter of over half a million Tutsis and moderate Hutus.

DRIVING OUT THE OUT-GROUP
Ethnocentrism based on an in-group bias can promote intolerance and ultimately dehumanization of an out-group, as in Bosnian and Rwandan genocide, South African apartheid, the persecution of Jews and other minorities in Nazi Germany, and slavery in the United States. Ethnic conflicts play a role in many international conflicts. Canadians, as part of a multi-ethnic society, view such conflicts somewhat differently than citizens of more homogeneous great powers. Here, members of the ethnic majority group in one Indonesian province burn a refugee camp where a minority group had taken shelter after being driven from their homes, 2001.

conflicts to take centre stage, sometimes bringing violence and war. Many realist and neo-realist commentators noted that the end of the Cold War might result in rising ethnic conflict. Critical theorists would argue that ethnic conflict is often used to camouflage the underlying causes of conflict, and is used in a way that depicts those who face ethnic conflict as "barbarians" and thus, as Dallaire suggested about Rwanda, not worthy of the international community's attention. Of course, not all ethnic groups get along so poorly together. After the fall of communism, most of the numerous ethnic rivalries in the former Soviet Union did not lead to warfare, and in Czechoslovakia and elsewhere ethnic relations were relatively peaceful after the fall of communism.

Causes of Ethnic Hostility Why do ethnic groups frequently dislike each other? Often there are long-standing historical conflicts over specific territories or natural resources, or over one ethnic group's economic exploitation or political domination of another. Over time, ethnic conflicts may transcend these concrete historical causes and take on a life of their own. They become driven not by tangible grievances (though these may well persist) but by the kinds of processes described by social psychology that are set in motion when one group of people has a prolonged conflict with another and experiences violence at the hands of the other group.[29]

The ethnic group is a kind of extended *kinship* group—a group of related individuals sharing some ancestors. Even when kinship relations are not very close, a *group identity* makes a person act as though the other members of the ethnic group were family. For instance, African Canadian men who call each other "brother" express group identity as kinship. Likewise Jews around the world treat each other as family even though each community has intermarried over time and may have more ancestors in common with local non-Jews than with distant Jews. Perhaps, as technology allows far-flung groups to congregate in cyberspace, there will be less psychological pressure to collect ethnic groups physically in a territorial nation-state.

Ethnocentrism, or *in-group bias*, is the tendency to see one's own group in favourable terms and an *out-group* in unfavourable terms. Some scholars believe that ethnocentrism has roots in a biological propensity to protect closely related individuals, but this idea is quite controversial.[30] More often in-group bias is understood in terms of social psychology.

No *minimum criterion* of similarity or kin relationship is needed to evoke the group identity process, including in-group bias. In psychological experiments, even trivial differentiations can evoke these processes. If people are assigned to groups based on a known but unimportant characteristic (such as preferring, say, circles to triangles), before long the people in each group show in-group bias and find they don't much care for the other group's members.[31]

In-group biases are far stronger when the other group looks different, speaks a different language, or worships in a different way (or all three). All too easily, an out-group can be dehumanized and stripped of all human rights. This **dehumanization** includes the common use of animal names—"pigs," "dogs," and so forth—for members of the out-group. U.S. propaganda in World War II depicted Japanese people as apes. Especially in

ethnocentrism (in-group bias) The tendency to see one's own group (in-group) in favourable terms and an out-group in unfavourable terms.

dehumanization Stigmatization of enemies as subhuman or nonhuman, leading frequently to widespread massacres or, in the worst cases, destruction of entire populations. See also *crimes against humanity* and *genocide*.

---

[29] Betty Glad, ed., *Psychological Dimensions of War* (Newbury Park, CA: Sage, 1990).

[30] Paul Shaw and Yuwa Wong, *Genetic Seeds of Warfare: Evolution, Nationalism, and Patriotism* (Boston: Unwin Hyman, 1989). J. Groebel and R. A. Hinde, eds., *Aggression and War: Their Biological and Social Bases* (NY: Cambridge UP, 1989). Albert Somit, *Humans, Chimps, and Bonobos: The Biological Bases of Aggression, War, and Peacemaking* [review essay]. *Journal of Conflict Resolution* 34.3 (1990): 553–82. Diane McGuinness, ed., *Dominance, Aggression, and War* (NY: Paragon, 1987).

[31] H. Tajfel and J. C. Turner, "The Social Identity Theory of Intergroup Behavior," *Psychology of Intergroup Relations*, 2nd ed., ed. S. Worchel and W. Austin (Chicago: Nelson-Hall, 1986) 7–24.

wartime, when people see members of an out-group killing members of their in-group, dehumanization can be extreme. The restraints on war that have evolved in regular interstate warfare, such as not massacring civilians (see "War Crimes" on pp. 283–286), are easily discarded in inter-ethnic warfare.

In several countries where long internal wars in the 1990s had led to dehumanization and atrocities—notably in South Africa—new governments used *truth commissions* to help the society heal and move forward. The commission's role was to hear honest testimony from the period, to bring to light what really happened during these wars, and in exchange to offer most of the participants asylum from punishment. Sometimes international NGOs helped facilitate the process. However, human rights groups objected to a settlement in Sierra Leone in 1999 that brought into the government a faction that had routinely cut off civilians' fingers as a terror tactic. (The war did end, however, and combatants were disarmed in 2001.) Thus, after brutal ethnic conflicts give way to complex political settlements, most governments try to balance the need for justice and truth with the need to keep all groups on board.

Experience in Western Europe shows that education over time can overcome ethnic animosities between traditionally hostile nations, such as France and Germany. After World War II, governments rewrote the textbooks with which a new generation would learn its peoples' histories. Previously each state's textbooks had glorified its own past deeds, played down its misdeeds, and portrayed its traditional enemies in unflattering terms. In a continent-wide project, new textbooks that gave a more objective and fair rendition were created. This project helped pave the way for European integration in subsequent decades. By contrast, many educators in both Israel and Palestine report that textbooks and other teaching tools continue to depict the other side as a barbaric, irrational enemy while their own side (and this is true of each "side") is portrayed as rational, just, and innocent parties in the conflict.

The existence of a threat from an out-group promotes the cohesion of an in-group, thereby creating a somewhat self-reinforcing process of ethnic division. However, ethnocentrism also often causes members of a group to view themselves as disunited (because they see their own divisions up close) and the out-group as monolithic (because they see it only from outside). This usually reflects a group's sense of vulnerability. Furthermore, overstating the threat posed by an enemy is a common way for political leaders to bolster their own position within an in-group. In the Arab-Israeli conflict, Israelis tend to see themselves as fragmented into dozens of political parties and diverse immigrant communities pulling in different directions, while they see Arabs as a monolithic bloc united against them. Meanwhile, Arab Palestinians see themselves as fragmented into factions and weakened by divisions among the Arab states, while Israelis appear monolithic to them.

Over time, rival ethnic groups may develop a pattern of *feuding*. Each side retaliates for actions of the other in a continuing circle of violence. Reflecting in-group bias, each side often believes it is acting defensively and that the other side "started it."

Ethnic conflicts are hard to resolve because they are not about "who gets what" but about "I don't like you." To cast the conflict in terms of a bargaining situation, each side places value on the other's loss of value (making a zero-sum game; see p. 69). A person

The Information Revolution
Nations and States

Many current international conflicts result from the mismatch of states' territorial borders with the actual distributions of ethnic or national populations. As technology allows communities to transcend geography, can national identity connect dispersed populations without generating territorial conflicts?

To explore this question, go to www.pearsoned.ca/goldstein.

Thinking Theoretically

Ethnic Hutu extremists in the government of Rwanda in 1994 carried out an organized genocide, giving orders throughout the country to kill ethnic Tutsis and those Hutus who had opposed the government. In short order, about 500 000 men, women, and children were massacred, mostly by machete, and their bodies dumped into rivers; thousands at a time washed up on lakeshores in neighbouring Uganda. What theories could help explain this event?

Hutu hatred toward Tutsis could reflect concrete interests and experiences of the two groups, especially since the minority Tutsis had earlier held power over the Hutu, and Belgian colonialism had exploited local rivalries. Realists might try to explain how the interests of Hutu extremists were served by their actions in exterminating rivals for power. This explanation is undermined, however, by the outcome in this case: the Hutu extremists lost power as a result of the episode.

We might instead view Hutu-Tutsi hatred as part of a pattern of age-old ethnic hatreds that are cropping up in the post–Cold War era, especially in so-called backward areas such as Africa. (This age-old-hatreds theory was often articulated by Western politicians in the Bosnia case, portraying the Balkans, like Africa, as "backward" and conflict-prone.) However, this theory holds up even worse than the realist explanation, since one of the world's most civilized, "advanced" states, Germany, exterminated its Jews even more efficiently than Rwanda did its Tutsis—the difference being simply that the "advanced" society could kill with industrial chemicals instead of at knifepoint.

Social psychology theories would tend to view the Rwandan genocide as pathological—a deviation from both rationality and social norms. In-group biases based on fairly arbitrary group characteristics become amplified by a perceived threat from an out-group, exaggerated by history, myth, and propaganda (including schooling). Such feelings can be whipped up by politicians pursuing their own power. A key threshold is crossed when the out-group is dehumanized; norms of social interaction, such as not slitting children's throats, can then be disregarded.

inflamed with hatred of an enemy is willing to *lose* value in absolute terms—to lose money, the support of allies, or even life—to deprive the enemy of value as well. Suicide bombers exemplify this fanatical hatred. Almost all the means of leverage used in such conflicts are negative, and bargains are very hard to reach. So ethnic conflicts tend to drag on without resolution for generations.

Ethnic groups are only one point along a spectrum of kinship relations—from nuclear families through extended families, villages, provinces, and nations, up to the entire human race. Loyalties fall at different points along the spectrum. Again there is no minimum criterion for in-group identity. For instance, experts said that of all the African countries, Somalia was surely immune from ethnic conflicts because Somalis were all from the same ethnic group and spoke the same language. Then in 1991–1992 a ruinous civil war erupted between members of different clans (based on extended families), leading to mass starvation and the intervention of foreign military forces (which by 1995 had to withdraw after a humiliating failure to tame the violence).

It is unclear why people identify most strongly at one level of group identity.[32] In Somalia, loyalties are to clans; in Serbia, they are to the ethnic group; in Canada and elsewhere, multi-ethnic states have managed to gain people's primary loyalty. States reinforce their citizens' identification with the state through flags, anthems, pledges of allegiance, patriotic speeches, and so forth. Perhaps someday people will shift loyalties even further, developing a *global identity* as humans first and members of states and ethnic groups second.

---

[32] Jill Krause and Neil Renwick, eds., *Identities in International Relations* (NY: St. Martin's, 1996).

Religious Conflict

One reason ethnic conflicts often transcend material grievances is that they find expression as *religious* conflicts. Since religion can be the core of a community's value system, people whose religious practices differ are easily disdained and treated as unworthy or even inhuman. When overlaid on ethnic and territorial conflicts, religion often surfaces as the central and most visible division between groups. For instance, most Indians are Hindus and most Pakistanis are Muslims. Most people in Azerbaijan are Muslims; Armenians are Christians. Most Croats are Roman Catholic Christians, whereas most Serbs are Orthodox Christians and most Bosnians and Albanians are Muslims.

Nothing inherent in religion mandates conflicts—in many places members of different religious groups coexist peacefully. But religious differences hold the potential for conflict, and for making existing conflicts more intractable, because religions involve core values, which are held as absolute truth.[33] This is increasingly true as *fundamentalist* movements have gained strength in recent decades. (The reasons for the spread of fundamentalism are disputed, but it is clearly a global-level phenomenon.) Members of these movements organize their lives and communities around their religious beliefs; many are willing to sacrifice and even die for those beliefs. Fundamentalist movements have become larger and more powerful in recent decades in Christianity, Islam, Judaism, Hinduism, and other religions. Such movements challenge the values and practices of **secular** political organizations—those created apart from religious establishments (the separation of religion and state). For example, an Islamic movement in Turkey and a Christian movement in the United States both seek to change long-standing secular traditions by incorporating religious values into the government.

Among the secular practices threatened by fundamentalist movements are the rules of the international system, whereby states are treated as formally equal and sovereign whether they are "believers" or "infidels." As transnational belief systems, religions often are taken as a higher law than state laws and international treaties. Iranian "revolutionary guards" train and support Islamic fundamentalists in other states, such as Algeria, Egypt, Jordan, and Lebanon. Jewish fundamentalists build settlements in Israeli-occupied territories and vow to cling to the land even if their government evacuates it. Christian fundamentalists in the United States are trying to convince their government to withdraw from the UN Population Fund. All these actions in one way or another run counter to the norms of the international system.[34]

Currently, violent conflicts are being prosecuted in the name of all the world's major religions. **Islam,** the religion practised by **Muslims** (or *Moslems*), has been frequently stereotyped in European and North American political discourse, especially at times of conflict such as the 1973 oil embargo, the 1979 Iranian revolution, the 1991 Gulf War, the 2003 War in Iraq and the ongoing so-called war on terrorism. Islam is no more conflict-prone than other religions. Islam is in fact broad and diverse. Its divergent populations include Sunni Muslims, Shiite Muslims, and many smaller branches and sects. The areas of the world that are predominantly Islamic stretch from Nigeria to Indonesia, centred in the Middle East. Most countries with mainly Muslim populations belong to the Islamic Conference, an IGO (see Figure 5.3).

secular (state) A state created apart from religious establishments and in which there is a high degree of separation between religious and political organizations.

Islam/Muslims A broad and diverse world religion whose divergent populations include Sunni Muslims, Shiite Muslims, and many smaller branches and sects, practised by Muslims from Nigeria to Indonesia, centred in the Middle East.

---

[33] R. Scott Appleby, *The Ambivalence of the Sacred: Religion, Violence, and Reconciliation* (Lanham, MD: Rowman & Littlefield, 1999).

[34] Mark Juergensmeyer, *The New Cold War? Religious Nationalism Confronts the Secular State* (Berkeley: U California P, 1993).

Figure 5.3
Members of the
Islamic Conference

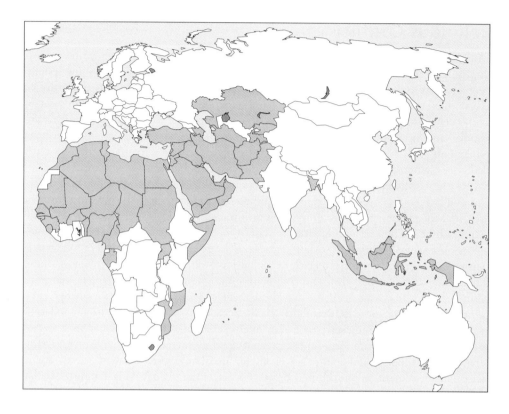

In several countries, Islamic fundamentalists reject Western-oriented secular states in favour of governments more explicitly oriented to Islamic values.[35] These movements reflect long-standing *anti-Western* sentiment in these countries—against the old European colonizers who were Christian—and are in some ways *nationalist* movements expressed through religious channels. In some Middle Eastern countries with authoritarian governments, religious institutions (mosques) have been the only available avenue for political opposition. Religion has therefore become a means for expressing opposition to the status quo in both politics and culture. (Similarly political roles have developed for other religions elsewhere, notably the Falun Gong movement in China in the late 1990s.)

Islamic movements have gained strength in recent years. In 1979, an Islamic republic was created in Iran. Pakistan and Sudan adopted Islamic laws without a revolution, as did the mostly Muslim northern provinces of Nigeria.

An Islamic government was established in Afghanistan in 1992 after a civil war (and following a decade of ill-fated Soviet occupation). Rival Islamic factions then continued the war with even greater intensity for several years. By 1997 a faction called Taliban had taken control of most of Afghanistan and imposed an extreme interpretation of Islamic law. With beatings and executions, the regime forced women to wear head-to-toe coverings, girls to stay out of school, and men to grow beards, among other repressive policies. The Afghanistan war became by the late 1990s the world's most destructive war and threatened to fuel conflicts in Russia, China, and other nearby countries where various

---

[35] James Turner Johnson and John Kelsay, *Cross, Crescent, and Sword: The Justification and Limitation of War in Western and Islamic Tradition* (NY: Greenwood, 1990). James Piscatori, *Islam in a World of Nation-States* (NY: Cambridge UP, 1984). Scott W. Hibbard and David Little, *Islamic Activism and U.S. Foreign Policy* (Washington, DC: U.S. Institute of Peace, 1997). Leonard Binder, *Islamic Liberalism: A Critique of Development Ideologies* (Chicago: U Chicago P, 1988).

forms of Muslim nationalism are at odds with state governments. As noted earlier, Afghanistan is also the world's primary source of opium for narcotics.

The incendiary mixture in Afghanistan in the 1990s—unending war, grinding poverty, religious fundamentalism, and an ideologically driven repressive government—did not spread like wildfire to neighbouring countries. It did, however, jump the oceans to hit the United States in September 2001. The Taliban's allies and counterparts from other countries used Afghanistan as a base for terrorist operations, culminating in the 2001 attacks. In response, the U.S. exerted its power to remove the Taliban from power in Afghanistan and disrupt the Al Qaeda terrorist network headquartered there.

The Changing World Order

Religious and Ethnic Difference in World Order

When the Cold War between the United States and the Soviet Union unravelled in the late 1980s, there was much speculation about the shape of future conflict. Some realist commentators suggested that we would all soon miss the Cold War because tensions between the two superpowers had kept a lid on other sources of conflict, those for example deriving from ethnic or religious differences. Some suggested that we would soon see a clash of civilizations between "the West" and "the rest" and others predicted a "coming anarchy."

From this perspective, the Cold War provided something of a bipolar balance between the U.S. and the Soviet Union. This did not mean conflict would never occur during the Cold War, but rather that there were some things that could be anticipated, given the balance of power: such as, *who* to be concerned about (if you lived in the West, then the Soviet Union; if you lived in the communist bloc, then the United States); *what* to be concerned about (nuclear weapons), and *how* to address the threat (nuclear deterrence). That a war between the Soviet Union and United States had never taken place, and that nuclear weapons had never been used in such a conflict, was seen as evidence in support of the idea of this balance. With the collapse of the Cold War, all of the old certainties of the Cold War rivalry were gone, and the world had become a more dangerous and unpredictable place.

Other commentators, informed by a liberal-pluralist approach, anticipated instead the possibility of a peace dividend at the end of the Cold War. By this view, the vast expenditures on military armaments that had taken place during the Cold War to maintain nuclear weapons and the infrastructure that sustained them could be redirected into social spending: housing, education, and health care. By this view, too, there would be more room for international institutions: while Cold War rivalries had made organizations like the United Nations largely ineffective, this institution would now be able to fulfill its most important goal, to protect future generations from the scourge of war.

Critical theorists challenged both the realist and liberal predictions. Critical theorists noted that the Cold War had not been a period of peace and stability for most people in the world. Living under the threat of nuclear annihilation was not actually a situation of peace. More importantly, while it was true that a Third World War had not broken about between the Soviet Union and the United States, Cold War rivalry nonetheless had played out in violent conflicts throughout the world, usually in the global South, resulting in millions of casualties. Critical theorists were also sceptical about the prospects for either a peace dividend or a larger role for institutions like the UN. By this view, a hegemonic power like the United States would soon go in search of new legitimations for its hegemony and continued military spending—hence, for critical theorists, the current interest in terrorists, religious fundamentalism, and ethnic conflict.

Events of the last decade have neither confirmed nor refuted any of these perspectives. Rising conflicts in the global South attributed to ethnic or religious difference appear to confirm the realist view, as do the terrorist attacks against the United States in September 2001. The exponential increase of UN missions around the world appears to confirm what the liberal pluralists had anticipated: a much larger role for international institutions. The new so-called war on terror, which targets Muslims and Arab peoples, seems to confirm the critical view.

Which of these views do you find most persuasive? Are any of them reflective of a new world order?

In Algeria, an especially brutal war evolved in the mid-1990s between the secular military government and an Islamic revolutionary movement. Islamic parties were winning democratic elections for a new parliament in 1991, when the military intervened to take power and stop the elections. The Islamic movement went underground, and the ensuing war between the military and the rebels killed as many as 100 000 people. In a murky and brutal struggle, both sides eventually turned to seemingly purposeless massacres. In 1999, a reformist politician returned from exile was elected president, and a peace deal was struck with the main rebel faction—raising hopes for a more durable peace—but intermittent violence continues.

In Jordan, Islamic parties won the largest bloc of seats in Parliament but violence did not ensue. Meanwhile, in the 1990s Islamic parties gained ground in Turkey—a fiercely secular state in which the military has intervened to prevent religious expression in politics. The main Islamic party has been repeatedly banned but has returned under new names, and a former Islamist became prime minister in 2003.

The more radical Islamic movements not only threaten some existing governments—especially those tied to the West—they also often undermine norms of state sovereignty (for better or worse). They are creating new transnational ties. They reject Western political conceptions of the state (based on individual autonomy) in favour of a more traditional Islamic orientation based on community. Some aspire to create a single political state encompassing most of the Middle East, as existed in A.D. 600–1200.

For better or worse, such a development would create a profound challenge to the present international system—particularly to its current status quo powers—and would therefore be opposed at every turn by the world's most powerful states. From the perspective of some outsiders, the religious conflicts boiling and simmering at the edges of the Islamic world look like an expansionist threat to be contained. The view from within looks more like being surrounded and repressed from several directions—a view reinforced by massacres of Muslims in Bosnia, Chechnya, and India in the 1990s and by the invasion of Iraq in 2003.

Overall, Islamic activism (and the opposition to it) is more complex

FROM FAITH TO FRENZY
Religious intolerance can exacerbate tensions between groups, sometimes crossing the line to violence, with international implications. For example, Hindu-Muslim conflict affects India's relations with its Muslim neighbours, including Pakistan, Bangladesh, and Indonesia. Here, a Hindu mob destroys a Muslim mosque at Ayodhya, India (1992). The incident provoked days of civil violence in India, mostly directed against Muslims, in which thousands died.

than simply a religious conflict; it concerns power, economic relations, ethnic chauvinism, and historical empires as well.

The same forces contribute to religious activism in non-Muslim countries. In India, Hindu fundamentalists have provoked violent clashes and massacres that have reverberated internationally. In 1992 a Hindu mob destroyed a Muslim mosque at Ayodhya. The incident provoked days of civil violence, mostly directed against Muslims, in which thousands died. In 2002, a similar frenzy of burning, torturing, and raping by Hindu nationalist extremists killed more than 2000 Muslims in India's Gujarat state, where the Hindu nationalist party controls the state government. In Israel, Jewish fundamentalists have used violence, including the assassination of Israel's own prime minister in 1995, to try to derail Arab-Jewish peace negotiations.

Recently it has been suggested that international conflicts in the coming years may be generated by a clash of civilizations—based on the differences between the world's major cultural groupings, which overlap quite a bit with religious communities.[36] The idea has been criticized for being overly general, and for assuming that cultural differences naturally create conflict.

Ideological Conflict

To a large extent, ideology is like religion: it symbolizes and intensifies conflicts between groups and states more than it causes them. Ideologies have a somewhat weaker hold on core values and absolute truth than religions do, so they pose somewhat fewer problems for the international system.

For realists, ideological differences among states do not matter much, because all members of the international system pursue their national interests in the context of relatively fluid alliances. For example, during the Cold War there was a global ideological struggle between capitalist democracy and communism. But the alliances and military competitions in that struggle were fairly detached from ideological factors. The two communist giants—the Soviet Union and China—did not stay together very long. And even the two great rival superpowers managed to live within the rules of the international system for the most part (such as both remaining UN members).

Over the long run, even countries that experience revolutions based on strong ideologies tend to lose their ideological fervour—be it Iran's Islamic fundamentalism in 1979, China's Maoist communism in 1949, Russia's Leninist communism in 1917, or U.S. democracy in 1776. In each case, the revolutionaries expected that their assumption of power would dra-

LET A HUNDRED FLOWERS BLOOM
Ideology plays only a limited role in most international conflicts. After revolutions, such as China's in 1949, ideologies such as Maoism may affect foreign policy. But over the next 10 or 20 years such countries typically revert to a foreign policy based more on national interests (for China, territorial integrity and trade-based prosperity) than ideology (communism). Nonetheless, the clashing cultures of Western-style democracy and Chinese-style communism still are a source of conflict. Here, students demonstrate for democracy in Tiananmen Square, Beijing, 1989. The violent repression of those demonstrations cast a shadow over Chinese relations with numerous countries of the West, including Canada.

---

[36] Samuel P. Huntington, *The Clash of Civilizations and the Remaking of World Order* (NY: Simon & Schuster, 1996). Samuel P. Huntington, "The Clash of Civilizations?" *Foreign Affairs* 72.3 (1993): 22–49.

matically alter their state's foreign policy, because in each case their ideology had profound international implications.

Yet, within a few decades, each of these revolutionary governments turned to the pursuit of national interests above ideological ones. The Soviet Union soon became in many ways just another great power on the European scene—building up its own armed forces, expanding its territory at the expense of Poland, and making alliances with former enemies. Likewise, China's Chairman Mao wanted to spread a "prairie fire" of revolution through the global South to liberate it from U.S. imperialism, but within a few decades Mao was welcoming the very embodiment of U.S. imperialism, President Nixon, to pursue mutual national interests. Iran's Ayatollah Khomeini took power in 1979 determined to revamp foreign policy and struggle against Western, non-Islamic influences—especially the "Great Satan" United States. Twenty years later, however, a liberal reformer had been elected president (albeit with limited powers) and Iranians were expanding contacts with the West.

Sometimes even self-proclaimed ideological struggles are not really ideological. In Angola in the 1980s, the United States backed a rebel army called UNITA against a Soviet-aligned government—supposedly a struggle of democracy against Marxism. In truth, the ideological differences were quite arbitrary. The government mouthed Marxist rhetoric to get the Soviet Union to give it aid (a policy that was reversed as soon as Soviet aid dried up). The "democratic" rebels meanwhile adopted democratic rhetoric to get U.S. support but practised nothing of the sort. In fact, they had earlier received Chinese support and had mouthed Maoist rhetoric. When UN-sponsored elections were won by the government, the "democratic" UNITA refused to accept the results and resumed fighting. This conflict, which finally ended in 2002, really had nothing to do with ideology.

In the short term, revolutions *do* change international relations—they make wars more likely—but not because of ideology. Rather, the sudden change of governments can alter alliances and change the balance of power. With calculations of power being revised by all parties, it is easy to miscalculate or to exaggerate threats on both sides. But ideology itself plays little role in this post-revolutionary propensity for wars: revolutions are seldom exported to other states.[37]

We should not assume, however, that ideology and political philosophies play no role at all in international politics. Ideologies can help to *mobilize* national populations to support a state in its international dealings, such as war. Fascism (the Nazi ideology) inflamed German nationalism before World War II, legitimizing German aggression by placing it in an ideological framework. And ideology can sharpen and intensify the conflict between two rivals, as happened to the superpowers during the Cold War. In some proxy wars of that era—for instance, in Vietnam in the 1960s and Nicaragua in the 1980s—the rebels and governments had real ideological differences that resonated with the Cold War rivalry.

Political democracy is an ideology also, and it may be the exception to the rule that ideology does not affect IR much. Democracy has become a global-level force in world politics, transcending the interests of particular states. A commitment to democracy does not yet outweigh a commitment to national interest in states' foreign policies, and perhaps never will, but global democracy is slowly emerging as a norm that states increasingly are pursuing in their dealings with other states (see "Democracy and Foreign Policy" on pp. 150–151). Democracies and nondemocracies may increasingly find themselves in conflict with each other if this trend continues. Because democracies almost never fight wars with each other (although they still have conflicts), the spread of democratic ideology

---

[37] Stephen M. Walt, *Revolution and War* (Ithaca, NY: Cornell UP, 1996).

may have great implications for future prospects for peace. At the same time, some international interventions (most recently the 2003 Iraq war) have been done in the name of promoting democracy—a rationale that critical theorists, and other observers of global politics, find deeply suspect.

All six types of conflict just discussed can be pursued through peaceful or violent means. We can better understand conflict by examining the types of leverage, violent and otherwise, that come into play in international conflicts.

MEANS OF LEVERAGE

Conflicts are settled when some explicit or implicit bargaining process arrives at an outcome acceptable to both parties (see "Bargaining and Leverage" on pp. 61–62). Acceptable does not mean that both parties are happy or that the outcome is fair—only that neither party thinks it worth the effort to try to change the outcome. Perhaps both parties are satisfied that they have struck a beneficial or fair deal, or one party has been stripped of its leverage (in the extreme case, destroyed altogether) and has no prospect of improving a bad outcome through further bargaining.

War and other violent actions taken in international conflicts are aimed at settling conflicts on favourable terms by inflicting violence as a negative form of leverage. States can also have alternative means of leverage and strategies that often work better than war in resolving conflicts (ending them on mutually acceptable terms).

Types of War

War has been defined in various ways. For present purposes, we may define *war* as sustained inter-group violence (deliberately inflicting death and injury) in which state military forces participate on at least one side—on both sides in the case of *interstate war* and generally on only one side in the case of civil war. Around this definition are grey areas. In a world of standing military forces it is hard to say exactly where peace ends and war begins. A military battle that is not sustained over time may or may not be considered a war. The brief Chinese-Soviet border clashes in March and July 1969, for example, entailed several small battles at a few points along the border, in which some hundreds of people were killed. Similarly ambiguous is a long-term violent struggle involving irregular (substate) forces, such as in Northern Ireland. There, uniformed British military forces waged a sustained violent struggle with a nonstate army, the Irish Republican Army (IRA), until a ceasefire that has held on and off since 1995.

Thus, many different activities are covered by the general term *war*. Consequently, it is not easy to say how many wars are going on in the world at the moment. Political scientists can count the number of militarized disputes or the number of international conflicts that regularly entail violence. But most lists of wars set some minimum criteria—for instance, a minimum of a thousand battle deaths—to distinguish the large-scale violence implied by war from the more common lower-level violence that occurs in many international conflicts. Criteria that are not often used include formal declarations of war (now largely obsolete) or other legal standards. For example, Japan and the Soviet Union never signed a treaty ending World War II but are not considered to be at war.

Figure 5.4 shows the locations of the 15 wars in progress in 2004. Table 5.1 (p. 187) summarizes these wars. Of the 15 wars, none is in North America, Western Europe, Japan/Pacific, or China. All but Chechnya are in the global South—mainly in Africa, South Asia, and the Middle East.

Figure 5.4 Wars in Progress, January 2004

* Estimated deaths to date over 100 000
* Estimated deaths to date under 100 000

Table 5.1 Wars by Region

Region	Most Important Wars, January 2004
Africa	**Rwanda, Burundi, Uganda, Sudan, Somalia**
South Asia	**Afghanistan,** India, Nepal, Burma, Indonesia, Philippines
Middle East	**Iraq,** Israel-Palestine
Russia/E. Europe	Russia (Chechnya)
Latin America	Colombia, Peru
N. America, W. Europe, Japan/Pacific, China	None

Note: Bold face indicates reported casualties of over 100 000.

The largest and most active wars in spring 2004 were in Iraq, Sudan, and Colombia. (In early 2002, governments killed the top rebel leaders in both Angola and Algeria, hastening peace.) The first serious interstate war in years was the attack on Iraq in 2003. Wars are sputtering on and off in Israel-Palestine, the Rwanda-Burundi area (including Uganda), Somalia, Tajikistan/Kyrgyzstan, Nepal, Burma, Indonesia, and the Philippines.

More importantly, a number of intense wars have ended, at least tentatively, in formal peace settlements in recent years. These wars, each of which inflicted grave damage, include those in Sierra Leone, Angola, East Timor, the former Yugoslavia, Lebanon, Guatemala, and possibly Northern Ireland (along with South Africa and Mozambique earlier in the 1990s). In 2003, notwithstanding the war in Iraq, a new wave of settlements ended several more of the world's remaining wars of greatest duration and lethality. Liberia, Ivory Coast, and (more tentatively) Democratic Congo all established power-sharing governments and brought in international peacekeepers—following the path of Sierra Leone (which in 2003 held democratic elections). India and Pakistan began their first ceasefire in a decade, as did Burma's government and its largest rebel militia. In Sri Lanka, a ceasefire continued and negotiations inched forward. In Sudan, the warring sides signed a peace agreement that may end one of the world's last active wars that has killed more than a million people. It calls for withdrawing government forces from the south of the country, establishing a power-sharing transitional government and army, and holding a referendum in the rebel areas in six years. The diminishing number and size of wars reflects the peaceful trends of the post–Cold War era.

Wars are very diverse. Several types of war tend to arise from different situations and play different sorts of roles in bargaining over conflicts. Starting from the largest wars (which obviously meet the criteria), we may distinguish the following main categories.

Hegemonic war is a war over control of the entire *world order*—the rules of the international system as a whole, including the role of world hegemony (see "Hegemony" on p. 80). This class of wars (with variations in definition and conception) is also known as *world war, global war, general war,* or *systemic war.*[38] The last hegemonic war was World War II. This kind of war probably cannot occur any longer without destroying civilization.

Total war is warfare by one state waged to conquer and occupy another. The goal is to reach the capital city and force the surrender of the government, which can then be replaced with one of the victor's choosing (see pp. 168–169). In rare cases, the victor

hegemonic war War for control of the entire world order—the rules of the international system as a whole. Also known as world war, global war, general war, or systemic war.

total war Warfare by one state waged to conquer and occupy another; modern total war originated in the Napoleonic Wars, which relied upon conscription on a mass scale.

---

[38] Jack S. Levy, "Theories of General War," *World Politics* 37.3 (1985): 344–74. William R. Thompson, *On Global War: Historical-Structural Approaches to World Politics* (Columbia: U South Carolina P, 1988).

annexes the loser into its own state, as Iraq tried to do with Kuwait. Total war as we know it began with the massively destructive Napoleonic Wars, which introduced large-scale conscription and geared the entire French national economy toward the war effort. The practice of total war evolved with industrialization, which further integrated all of society and economy into the practice of war. The last total war among great powers was World War II, which ended with Germany and Japan in ruins, occupied by the Western alliance.

In total war, with the entire society mobilized for the struggle, the entire society of the enemy is considered a legitimate target. For instance, in World War II Germany attacked British civilians with V-2 rockets, while British and U.S. strategic bombing killed 600 000 German civilians (and hundreds of thousands more Japanese) in an effort to weaken morale.

Limited war includes military actions carried out to gain some objective short of the surrender and occupation of the enemy. For instance, the U.S.-led war against Iraq in 1991 retook the territory of Kuwait but did not go on to Baghdad to topple Saddam Hussein's government. Many border wars have this character: after occupying the land it wants, a state may stop short and defend its gains.

Raids are limited wars that consist of a single action—a bombing run or a quick incursion by land. In 1981 Israeli warplanes bombed an Iraqi nuclear research facility to stop Iraq from making progress toward the development of nuclear weapons. (Without this raid, Iraq might have had nuclear weapons when it invaded Kuwait in 1990.) The action had a narrow objective—destruction of the facility—and was over within hours. Raids fall into the grey area between wars and nonwars because their destruction is limited and they are over quickly. Raiding that is repeated or fuels a cycle of retaliation usually becomes a limited war or what is sometimes called "low-intensity conflict."

Not all wars fit neatly into one of these categories. The Iraq War of 2003, for example, seems to be a total war at least insofar as its aim was to overthrow the Iraqi government and civilians were inevitably targeted during the campaign. But the United States and its coalition partners did not mobilize their entire societies in pursuit of this aim, and also insisted that their goal was to see a democratically elected government. For these reasons it seems more like a limited war. Yet as resistance against the U.S.- and British-led occupation grew in 2004, from the perspective of many people inside Iraq, this may be a total war, no matter what the perspective of the coalition partners.

Civil war refers to war between factions within a state trying to create, or prevent, a new government for the entire state or some territorial part of it. (The aim may be to change the entire system of government, to merely replace the people in it, or to split a region off as a new state.) The U.S. Civil War of the 1860s is a good example of a secessionist civil war, as is the war of Eritrea province in Ethiopia (now the internationally recognized state of Eritrea) in the 1980s. The war in El Salvador in the 1980s is an example of a civil war for control of the entire state (not secessionist). Civil wars seem to be often among the most brutal wars—sometimes brother fighting brother, often with no clearly defined front lines. People fighting their fellow citizens act no less cruelly than those fighting people from another state. The 50 000 or more deaths in the civil war in El Salvador, including many from massacres and death squads, were not based on ethnic differences. (Of course, many of today's civil wars do contain ethnic conflicts as well.)

Guerrilla war, which includes certain kinds of civil wars, is warfare without front lines. Irregular forces operate in the midst of, and often hidden or protected by, civilian populations. The purpose is not to directly confront an enemy army but rather to harass and punish it so as to gradually limit its operation and effectively liberate territory from its control. U.S. military forces in South Vietnam fought against Viet Cong guerrillas in the 1960s and 1970s, with rising frustration. The United States could occupy a location

limited war Military actions that seek objectives short of the surrender and occupation of the enemy.

civil war A war between factions within a state trying to create, or prevent, a new government for the entire state or some territorial part of it.

guerrilla war Warfare without front lines and with irregular forces operating in the midst of, and often hidden or protected by, civilian populations.

by daylight, but by night the guerrillas would slip back and reclaim control. Efforts to combat such a guerrilla army—**counterinsurgency**—often include programs to "win the hearts and minds" of rural populations so that they stop sheltering the guerrillas.

In guerrilla war, without a fixed front line, there is much territory that neither side controls; both sides exert military leverage over the same places at the same time. Thus, guerrilla wars are extremely painful for civilians. The situation is doubly painful because conventional armies fighting against guerrillas and paramilitaries often cannot distinguish them from civilians and punish both together. As a result, civilians now constitute between 75 and 90 percent of the casualties in armed conflict. Civilians also are usually targeted differently, depending on whether they are men or women: men are more likely to be killed or abducted to serve as soldiers in guerrilla forces while women often face sexual assault, the risk of being trafficked, and loss of livelihoods.[39]

Warfare increasingly is irregular and guerrilla-style; it is less and less often an open conventional clash of large state armies.[40] On the whole, state and nonstate actors have a range of political goals that lead them to employ violent forms of leverage, and a range of options for employing force.

counterinsurgency An effort to combat guerrilla armies, often including programs to "win the hearts and minds" of rural populations so that they stop sheltering guerrillas.

Terrorism

Since September 2001, governments and ordinary people in the West have paid much more attention to terrorism than previously. But terrorism itself is not new. Terrorism is basically just another step along the spectrum of violent leverage, from total war to guerrilla war. Indeed terrorism and guerrilla war often occur together. Yet terrorism differs from other kinds of wars.

Terrorism refers to political violence that targets civilians deliberately and indiscriminately. Beyond this basic definition other criteria can be applied, but the definitions become politically motivated: one person's freedom fighter is another's terrorist. More than guerrilla warfare, terrorism is a shadowy world of faceless enemies and irregular tactics marked by extreme brutality.[41]

In Canada, the 1970 kidnapping of British Trade Commissioner James Cross and the kidnapping and murder of Québec Minister of Labour Pierre Laporte by the Front de Libération du Québec (FLQ) constituted one of the only terrorist acts committed on Canadian soil. The Liberal government of Pierre Elliott Trudeau invoked the War Measures Act, declared martial law, suspended civil liberties throughout the country, and deployed Canadian Forces to Québec. This was the first time that Canada had invoked the War Measures Act during peacetime. Some observers felt the federal government's reaction was an appropriate response to a perceived insurrection, while many others argued it was

---

[39] Simon Chesterman, ed., *Civilians in War* (Boulder: Rienner, 2001). United Nations Secretary General Study, *Women, Peace and Security* (NY: United Nations, 2002).

[40] Ariel E. Levite, Bruce W. Jentleson, and Larry Berman, eds., *Foreign Military Intervention: The Dynamics of Protracted Conflict* (NY: Columbia UP, 1992). Michael Klare and Peter Kornbluh, eds., *Low-Intensity Warfare: Counterinsurgency, Proinsurgency, and Antiterrorism in the Eighties* (NY: Random/Pantheon, 1991). Edward E. Azar and Chung-in Moon, eds., *National Security in the Third World: The Management of Internal and External Threats* (Aldershot, UK: Elgar, 1988).

[41] Annamarie Oliverio, *The State of Terror* (Albany: SUNY P, 1998). Adrian Guelke, *The Age of Terrorism and the International Political System* (NY: Tauris/St. Martin's, 1995). Edward S. Herman and Gerry O'Sullivan, *The "Terrorism" Industry: The Experts and Institutions That Shape Our View of Terror* (NY: Random/Pantheon, 1991). Walter Reich, ed., *Origins of Terrorism: Psychologies, Ideologies, Theologies, States of Mind* (NY: Cambridge UP, 1990). David C. Rapoport, ed., *Inside Terrorist Organizations* (NY: Columbia UP, 1988).

an overreaction in its overestimation of the nature of the threat posed by the FLQ, its suspension of the civil liberties of all Canadians, and the arbitrary arrest of any Canadian thought to have communist or FLQ sympathies. The suspension of civil liberties, and arbitrary arrest, is a common tactic employed by states in the face of terrorism, as seen most recently since the attacks on the World Trade Center in the United States.

Another terrorist incident in which Canada was involved occurred in 1985 with the bombing of an Air India Boeing 747 jetliner, killing 329 people, some 280 of them Canadian. Two British Columbia men face murder charges for the explosion, and are alleged to have planted the bomb in luggage checked at the Vancouver airport and then transferred to the Air India flight in Toronto. Two luggage handlers were killed in a bomb explosion at Japan's Narita Airport on the same day. The Canadians have also been charged in their deaths.[42]

Despite these events, most terrorist incidents in the past have occurred in the Middle East, Europe, and South Asia. In an interdependent world, Canada can no longer keep global problems such as terrorism at a distance. For years before the 2001 attacks, the Al Qaeda terrorist organization had thousands of members operating in dozens of countries, including Canada. Canada's border with the United States has also been raised as a source of concern for authorities in both the U.S. and Canada, particularly so after the arrest of a suspected terrorist at the British Columbia border planning to attack the Seattle Space Needle during millennium celebrations.[43]

Generally, the purpose of terrorism is to demoralize a civilian population in order to use its discontent as leverage on national governments or other parties to a conflict. Related to this is the aim of creating drama in order to gain media attention for a cause. When the IRA planted bombs in London, it hoped to make life miserable enough for Londoners that they would insist their government settle the Northern Ireland issue; the bombing also sought to keep the issue of Northern Ireland in the news. The British government would then be pressured to concede terms more favourable to the IRA than would otherwise be the case. Terrorism is seldom mindless; it is usually a calculated use of violence as leverage. However, motives and means of terrorism vary widely, having in common only that some actor is using violence to send a message to other actors.

The primary effect of terrorism is psychological. In part the effectiveness of terrorism in capturing attention is due to the dramatic nature of the incidents, especially as shown on television news. Terrorism also gains attention because of the randomness of victims. Although only a few dozen people may be injured by a bomb left in a market, millions of people realize "it could have been me," because they, too, shop in markets. Attacks on airplanes augment this fear because many people already fear flying. Terrorism thus amplifies a small amount of power by its psychological effect on large populations; this is why it is usually a tool of the powerless.

In the shockingly destructive attack on the World Trade Center in the United States, tangible damage was far greater than in previous terrorist attacks—reaching into thousands of lives and tens of billions of dollars. The psychological impact was even stronger than the physical damage—changing the U.S. political and cultural landscape instantly. But in contrast to historical instances of terrorism, real costs began to loom large. The same terrorist network was reportedly trying to obtain nuclear weapons (see pp. 217–220) with which to

[42] Zuhair Kashmeri, "Sabotage Feared as 329 Die in Jet," *The Globe and Mail* 4 Aug. 1986. Robert Matas, "Air-India Trial Puts Focus on Lax Security," *The Globe and Mail* 13 May 2003: A1.

[43] James Fergusson, "National Missile Defense, Homeland Defense, and Outer Space: Policy Dilemmas in the Canada-US Relationship," *Canada among Nations 2001: The Axworthy Legacy*, ed. Fen Osler Hampson, Norman Hillmer, and Maureen Appel Molot (NY: Oxford UP, 2001).

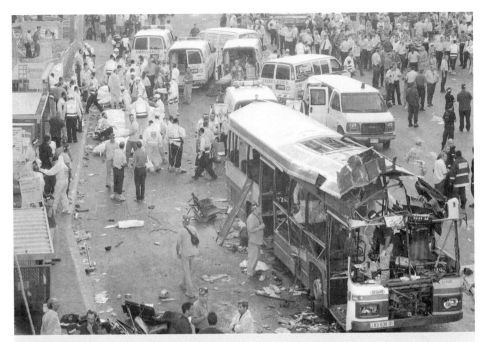

CRUDE BUT SOMETIMES EFFECTIVE

Terrorist attacks often reflect the weakness of the perpetrators and their lack of access to other means of leverage. Terror can sometimes amplify a small group's power and affect outcomes. In the "Intifada II" that started after the failed Israeli-Palestinian negotiations of 2000, several Palestinian factions escalated terrorist attacks against Israeli civilians—ensuring that the peace negotiations, which they opposed, could not resume. Here, a bomb in Jerusalem killed 16 and wounded 70 in June 2003.

kill not thousands but tens of thousands of Americans. Similarly, although the mailed anthrax attacks in fall 2001 killed only a few people, and had far more psychological than physical effect, nonetheless the door had been opened to a new bioterrorism that also could kill tens of thousands.

Generally, terrorism has failed to accomplish its perpetrators' goals. The September 2001 attacks presumably aimed to weaken the United States, to change U.S. policy on two issues—support for Israel and stationing of troops in Saudi Arabia—and to mobilize Muslims against the West, strengthening Islamic radicals including Al Qaeda. Instead, in the immediate aftermath of the attack, the U.S. became more united domestically (e.g., national will, solidarity) and found widespread support internationally (e.g., alliances, moral support, use of military bases). The attacks had a large economic cost, especially given a pre-existing recession, but not enough to permanently weaken the country. U.S. determination to support Israel and keep troops in Saudi Arabia remained unchanged. But the attacks did show that even democratic countries like the United States will not hesitate to suspend civil liberties, or employ tactics like racial profiling, when confronted by a terrorist threat.

Terrorist attacks on Spain in 2004, allegedly in reaction to Spain's involvement in the war against Iraq, had an almost immediate impact on Spanish foreign policy. The Spanish public had been overwhelmingly opposed to Spain sending troops to Iraq, and three days after the bombing of commuter trains in Madrid, a general election resulted in a change of government, one committed to withdrawing from Iraq. The classic cases of terrorism—from the 1970s to the present—are those in which a *nonstate* actor uses attacks against *civilians* by secret *nonuniformed* forces, operating *across international borders*, as a leverage against *state* actors. Radical political factions or separatist groups hijack or blow up airplanes, or plant bombs in cafés, clubs, or other crowded places. For example, a Palestinian faction held hostage and then killed Israeli athletes at the 1972 Olympic Games in Munich. Such tactics create spectacular incidents that draw attention to the terrorists' cause. Typically, the message is, "We won't go away; we will make you unhappy until you deal with us."

Often terrorism is used by radical factions of movements that have not been able to get attention or develop other effective means of leverage. It is often a tactic of desperation, and it almost always reflects weakness in the power position of the attacker. For instance, the Palestinian radicals in 1972 had seen Arab states defeated by Israel in war and could not see a way to gain even a hearing for their cause. By capturing media attention worldwide with dramatic incidents of violence—even at the cost of rallying world public opinion against their cause—the radicals hoped to make Palestinian aspirations an issue that Western governments could not ignore when deciding on policies toward the Middle East.

States themselves carry out acts designed to terrorize their own populations or those of other states, and use many of the same techniques, including assassinations and bombings. Scholars do not agree on whether to use the label "terrorism" for such acts. Realists and liberals reject the label when states resort to these kinds of tactics, preferring to call it repression or war. Russia's indiscriminate attacks in Chechnya province in 1995 are an example. (By contrast, they would describe the later bombings of Moscow apartment buildings by Chechen radicals, the seizing of a Moscow theatre in 2002 or the assassination of the Chechen president in 2004 as clearly terrorism.) Critical theorists insist that that it is the acts of violence, not who commits them, that should be the defining characteristic of terrorism. From this perspective, states are the biggest, and most frequent, terrorists.[44] Of course, because war itself is hard to define, so is terrorism; warring parties often call each other terrorists. In the Central American civil wars of the 1980s, both the states and the guerrillas employed tactics that, if taken in peacetime, would easily qualify as terrorism.

The narrowest definition of terrorism would exclude acts either by or against *uniformed military forces* rather than civilians. This definition would exclude the killing of 243 U.S. Marines by a car bomb in Lebanon in 1983, and the 2001 attack on the Pentagon, because they were directed at military targets. It would also exclude the bombing of German cities in World War II although the purpose was to terrorize civilians. But in today's world of undeclared war, guerrilla war, civil war, and ethnic violence, there is a large grey zone around clear cases of terrorism. Disagreements about whether terrorism included Palestinian attacks on Israel, and Pakistani attacks in Kashmir, scuttled efforts to pass a UN treaty on terrorism in late 2001.

state-sponsored terrorism
The use of terrorist groups by states, usually under control of a state's intelligence agency, to achieve political aims.

State-sponsored terrorism refers to the use of terrorist groups by states—usually under control of the state's intelligence agency—to achieve political aims.[45] In 1988 a bomb scattered pieces of Pan Am Flight 103 over the Scottish countryside. Combing the fields for debris, investigators found fragments of a tape recorder that had contained a sophisticated plastic-explosive bomb. A tiny strand of wire from the triggering device turned out to be a

---

[44] Noam Chomsky, "Who Are the Global Terrorists?" *Worlds in Collision: Terror and the Future of Global Order,* ed. Ken Booth and Tim Dunne (London: Palgrave Macmillan, 2002). James Der Derian, "The Terrorist Discourse: Signs, States and Systems of Global Political Violence," *Antidiplomacy: Spies, Terror, Speed, and War* (Cambridge: Blackwell, 1992).

rare variety, through which the investigators traced the origins of the bomb. The U.S. and British governments identified two Libyan intelligence agents who had smuggled the tape recorder onto Flight 103 in Frankfurt. In 1992, backed by the UN Security Council, they demanded that Libya turn over the two agents for trial. When Libya refused, the UN imposed sanctions, including a ban on international flights to or from Libya. In 1999, Libya turned over the suspects for trial—two received life in prison while a third was acquitted—and the sanctions were lifted. In 2003, Libya formally took responsibility for the bombing and struck a multibillion-dollar compensation deal with the victims' families, in an effort to secure a place of some legitimacy in the international community.

The United States in recent years has accused seven states of supporting international terrorism: North Korea, Iran, Iraq, Syria, Libya, Sudan, and Cuba. In 1996, the United States barred U.S. companies from doing business in those states. However, these kinds of sanctions are of limited effect since most industrialized states do not share U.S. views of one or more of these target states. Cuba can do business with Canada, Iran with France, and Libya with Italy. The U.S. position was also undermined when it carved an exception in its rule to allow a U.S. oil company to bid on a lucrative pipeline project in Sudan.

More often, state involvement in terrorism is very difficult to trace. Indeed, had the bomb on Flight 103 exploded as scheduled over the Atlantic Ocean, instead of prematurely, the clues would not have been found. When a political faction issues a communiqué claiming credit for a terrorist action, it never includes a statement such as, "The participants wish to thank the government of 'X' for its generous support, which made today's action possible."

Counterterrorism has become a sophisticated operation as well as a big business—a trend that accelerated after September 2001. International agencies, notably the *Interpol* police agency (and in Europe, *Europol*), coordinate the actions of states in tracking and apprehending suspected terrorists (as well as drug traffickers and other criminals). National governments have investigative agencies, such as the RCMP and CSIS in Canada or the FBI and CIA in the United States, to try to break through the wall of secrecy around terrorist operations. Lately, many private companies have expanded the business of providing security services, including antiterrorist equipment and forces, to companies and individuals doing business internationally. These companies have been very busy since September 2001, as governments, companies, and individuals worldwide adapt to the new security environment that comes from a global terrorist threat.

HUMAN SECURITY

Human security became a foreign policy priority of the Canadian government under former Canadian Minister of Foreign Affairs Lloyd Axworthy. Human security has not been clearly defined, but it signals a departure from the strictly state-based understanding of conflict and security that tends to dominate IR. During the Cold War, there was at least some consensus that security meant national security. Scholars of international relations focused on causes of war, sources of threat, and means of addressing those threats (much as this chapter has done). Advocates of the notion of human security argue that security should include a broader conception of what makes people secure. So in addition to

[45] Walter Laqueur, *A History of Terrorism* (Piscataway, NJ: Transaction, 2001). Paul R. Pilar, *Terrorism and U.S. Foreign Policy* (Washington, DC: Brookings, 2001). Jessica Stern, *The Ultimate Terrorist* (Cambridge, MA: Harvard UP, 2000). Rosemary H. T. O'Kane, *Terror, Force, and States: The Path from Modernity* (Aldershot, UK: Elgar, 1996). Michael Stohl and George A. Lopez, eds., *Terrible Beyond Endurance? The Foreign Policy of State Terrorism* (Westport, CT: Greenwood, 1988).

thinking about violence and conflict, scholars and policy-makers who talk about human security also focus on freedom from want (economic and social justice issues) and political freedoms such as human rights.[46]

Some of the discussions of human security originated from a 1994 report by the United Nations Development Program (UNDP) that was then picked up by policy-makers like Axworthy. In that report, the UNDP identified seven elements of security: economic security, food security, health security, environmental security, community security, personal security, and political security. Some of these elements can be addressed through more traditional military means, but other elements require attention to questions of human rights and sustainable economic development. Human security also demands that decision-makers consider the specific impact of more traditional forms of conflict on particularly vulnerable groups, such as the elderly, children, and women.[47]

As part of its pursuit of a human security agenda, the Canadian government established the Canadian Consortium on Human Security at the University of British Columbia to provide research and policy advice on human security questions (see weblinks at the end of the chapter). Canada was also actively involved in the convention to ban landmines (see Chapters 4 and 7) as part of its commitment to promoting human security, as well as small arms control and efforts to protect refugees, address issues of women and children in armed conflict and the establishment of the International Criminal Court (see p. 283). It remains to be seen what kind of impact notions of human security will have on foreign policy decisions of other states, particularly larger states such as the United States, Britain and Russia.

Just as there are many possible outcomes of conflict, many types of war, and varied propensities for violence among different states, so too is there great diversity in how force is used if conflict leads to violence. States develop a wide array of military forces, which vary tremendously in their purposes and capabilities—having in common only that they are instruments used to apply violence in some form. It is to these military forces that we now turn.

Thinking Critically

1. Suppose that you were the mediator in negotiations between two states, each claiming the same piece of land. What principles could you follow in developing a mutually acceptable plan for ownership of the territory? What means could you use to convince the two states to accept your plan?

2. How many of the six types of international conflict discussed in this chapter can you connect with the phenomenon of nationalism discussed on pp. 30–31? What are the connections in each case?

3. European textbooks were revised after World War II to reduce ethnic and national stereotypes and to give a fairer portrayal of Europe's various nations. What about the textbooks you used to learn your country's history? Did they give an accurate picture, or did they overstate the virtues of your own ethnic group or nation at the expense of others? How?

---

[46] Fen Osler Hampson, *Madness in the Multitude: Human Security and World Disorder* (Toronto: Oxford UP, 2002).

[47] Fen Osler Hampson, *Madness in the Multitude* (see note 46 above). Fen Osler Hampson, Norman Hillimer, and Maureen Appel Molot, *Canada among Nations: The Axworthy Legacy* (Toronto: Oxford UP, 2001).

4. The rise of fundamentalism among the world's major religions challenges traditional notions of state sovereignty. How might this trend strengthen, or weaken, the United Nations and other attempts to create supranational authority (which also challenge state sovereignty)?

5. Given the definition of war provided on p. 185, name three current international situations that clearly fit the definition of war and three that are ambiguous "quasi-wars" (almost but not quite fitting the definition). Which do you think are more serious, the wars or the quasi-wars? Do they involve different types of actors? Different kinds of conflicts? Different capabilities?

Chapter Summary

- War and other forms of international violence are used as leverage to try to improve the terms of settlement of conflicts.

- Many theories have been offered as general explanations about when such forms of leverage come into play—the causes of war. Contradictory theories have been proposed at each level of analysis and, with two exceptions, none has strong empirical support. Thus, political scientists cannot reliably predict the outbreak of war.

- The two exceptions are (1) that there are virtually no societies in which war and inter-group violence as means of leverage are unknown, and (2) that democratic states almost never fight wars against other democracies.

- States come into conflict with each other and with nonstate actors for a variety of reasons. For realists, conflicts will always exist among international actors.

- Territorial disputes are among the most serious international conflicts because states place great value on territorial integrity. With a few exceptions, however, almost all the world's borders are now firmly fixed and internationally recognized.

- Conflicts over the control of entire states (through control of governments) are also serious and are relatively likely to lead to the use of force.

- From the perspective of economic liberals, economic conflicts lead to violence much less often, because positive gains from economic activities are more important inducements than negative threats of violence. Critical theorists, by contrast, would argue that economic relations of inequality are at the root of most conflicts.

- Trafficking in gems, minerals, timber, and drugs creates several kinds of conflict that draw in state and nonstate actors alike. Conflicts over resources such as minerals, timber, oil, and water are viewed by some as the most likely source of future international conflicts. Trafficking in persons, to serve as combatants, prostitutes, or forced labourers, can exacerbate conflicts

- Ethnic conflicts, especially when linked with territorial disputes, are very difficult to resolve because of psychological biases. It is hard to explain why people's loyalties are sometimes to their ethnic group, sometimes to a multi-ethnic nation.

- Fundamentalist religious movements of all kinds pose a broad challenge to the rules of the international system in general and state sovereignty in particular.

- Ideologies do not matter very much in international relations. State leaders tend to use ideologies to justify whatever actions are in their interests.

- When violent means are used as leverage in international conflicts, a variety of types of war result. These vary greatly in size and character, from guerrilla wars and raids to hegemonic war for leadership of the international system. Along this spectrum of uses of violence, the exact definition of war is uncertain.

- Like other violent means of leverage, terrorism is used to gain advantage in international bargaining situations. Terrorism is effective if it damages morale in a population and gains media exposure for the cause.

- The 2001 attacks against the United States differed from earlier terrorism both in their scale of destruction and in the long reach of the global Al Qaeda terrorist network. The attacks forced dramatic changes in U.S. and worldwide security arrangements.

- *Human security* is a term that has been promoted by the Canadian government as a means to rethink conflict as a strictly state-based issue. Human security refers to the various ways people are made to be secure, not simply to military means of security.

Key Terms

conflict   156
settlement   156
irredentism   161
ethnic cleansing   164
territorial waters   167
airspace   168
lateral pressure   170
ethnic groups   173
ethnocentrism   176
dehumanization   176

secular (state)   179
Islam/Muslims   179
hegemonic war   187
total war   187
limited war   188
civil war   188
guerrilla war   188
counterinsurgency   189
state-sponsored terrorism   192

Weblinks

The following are a sampling of research centres or NGOs that focus on different aspects of international conflict and security:

Canadian Consortium on Asia Pacific Security:
http://www.iir.ubc.ca/cancaps

Canadian Consortium on Human Security:
http://www.humansecurity.info/CCHS_web/Home/en

Canadian Peacebuilding Coordinating Committee:
http://www.peacebuild.ca

Canadian Security Intelligence Service:
http://www.csis-scrs.gc.ca/eng/menu/welcome_e.html

International Peace Academy:
http://www.ipacademy.org

York Centre for International and Security Studies:
http://www.yorku.ca/yciss

Militaries and Military Force 6

Fighters in Sierra Leone, 2000.

THE USE OF FORCE

A state leader in a conflict bargaining situation can apply various kinds of leverage to reach a more favourable outcome (see Figure 6.1). One set of levers represents nonviolent means of influencing other states, such as foreign aid, economic sanctions, personal diplomacy, and so forth (less tangible means include use of norms, morality, and other ideas). A second set of levers—the subject of this chapter—represents violent actions. These levers threaten to set armies marching or missiles flying.

When state leaders resort to force in an international conflict, they do not push all the violence levers at once. Rather, they choose applications of force that suit their objectives, and their strategies for achieving those objectives. Furthermore, different levers are available to leaders of different states—different military capabilities that they earlier decided to create and maintain (see pp. 200–201). In order to understand the decisions that leaders make about using military force, realists argue that it is important to know how various military capabilities work, how much they cost, and what effects they have.

Violence as a means of leverage tends to be costly to both the attacker and the attacked. It is therefore not the most effective instrument in most situations: states can generally achieve their objectives in a more cost-effective way by using means of leverage such as economic actions (Chapters 8 and 9), foreign aid (Chapter 12), communication (Chapter 10), or international organizations (Chapter 7). Military force tends to be a last resort. There is also evidence that the utility of military force relative to non-military means is slowly declining over time.

Yet most states still devote vast resources to military capabilities compared to other means of influence. For example, a country like the United States has about

Figure 6.1 Military and Nonmilitary Means of Leverage

Conventional armed force is the most commonly used military form of leverage.

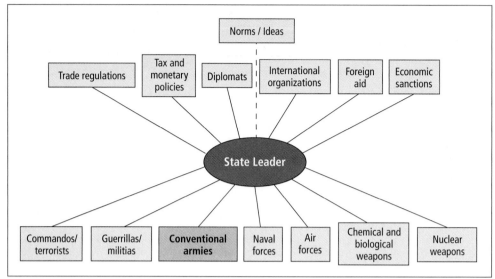

20 000 diplomatic personnel but 2 million soldiers; it spends about US$10 billion a year on foreign aid but about US$400 billion on military forces. Though the numbers are smaller in a country like Canada, the ratios are similar: about 7000 diplomatic personnel work for the Foreign Affairs Canada, but 60 000 regular forces personnel, 20 000 reserves, and a further 20 000 public servants are employed by the Department of National Defence. The Canadian government spends approximately $13 billion annually on defence and $3 billion annually in international assistance.

For many states, the reason for this dedication of resources is largely defensive. Military capabilities are maintained in an effort to ensure *state security*—the ability to feel safe against the threat of military attack (or other uses of force as leverage by other states). The overall utility of military force in IR may be declining, but for the narrow purpose of repelling a military attack there is often no substitute for military means. Because of the security dilemma, states believe they must devote large resources to military capabilities if even only a few other states are doing so. The shocking attacks on the U.S. in 2001 underscored many states' sense of insecurity and their need to maintain capable military forces. Military expenditure, however, does little to enhance human security (see pp. 193–194), and may even detract from it.

Beyond defending their territories, states develop military capabilities for several other purposes. They often hope to *deter* attack by having the means to retaliate. They may also hope to *compel* other states to behave in certain ways, by threatening an attack if the state does not comply. The sizes and types of military forces make particular threats credible.

States are increasingly using military forces for purposes other than fighting (or threatening) wars. These purposes include humanitarian assistance after disasters, surveillance of drug trafficking, and repression of domestic political dissent, among others. Peacekeeping operations (see pp. 258–264) are a specialization of certain military forces, especially that of Canada, and a focus of NATO's Partnership for Peace program (see p. 245).

Military capabilities are generally divided into two types—conventional forces and weapons of mass destruction (nuclear, chemical, and biological weapons). Almost all of the actual uses of military force to date have involved conventional forces. Weapons of mass destruction nonetheless come into play in international bargaining because even the implicit threat of their use is leverage. Although the superpower nuclear arms race has ended, the spread of weapons of mass destruction to new states and to nonstate actors is an increasing concern.

This chapter discusses the various kinds of military forces used by state leaders. It first considers the major strategic concerns of state leaders in acquiring and maintaining military forces, especially in deciding how much to spend on military budgets. The chapter then considers the civil-military link that allows political leaders to control military forces to be used as leverage in international bargaining. Finally, the chapter sketches the variety of types of military forces that states maintain, including efforts to obtain weapons of mass destruction.

CONFIGURING FORCES

Given the range of military capabilities available to states (at various costs), how should state leaders choose which to acquire?

Military Economics

Choices about military forces depend on the connection between a state's military spending and its economic health. Not long ago, it was widely believed in some countries that "war is good for the economy" (seemingly, military spending had helped end the Great Depression in the late 1930s). If this were true, state leaders would not face difficult choices in setting military budgets. High military spending would give them both more military capabilities for use in international conflicts *and* more economic growth for domestic needs (buying popular and political support in various ways).

Unfortunately for state leaders, the economics of military spending is not so favourable. Over the long run, military spending tends to compete with other economic needs, such as investment in civilian industry or government projects. Over time, allocating economic resources for military purposes deprives the rest of the economy and reduces its growth. High-technology military development (using engineers, scientists, and technicians) tends to starve civilian sectors of talent and technology. Fewer jobs are created in the military than in education, housing, construction, and similar areas (military spending is more capital-intensive and less labour-intensive). Conversely, reductions in military spending tend to free up economic resources for more productive purposes and strengthen the growth of the economy in the long term.

Thus, over the long term, state leaders face a trade-off between increasing their available military leverage and increasing their overall economic health. This trade-off explains in part why, during the Cold War, the great power with the highest military spending—the Soviet Union, at perhaps 20 percent of GDP—had the worst economic performance, whereas the great power with the lowest military spending (Japan, with around 1 percent of GDP) had the best economic performance.[1]

When the Cold War ended, U.S. leaders promised to cut military spending to reap a peace dividend: more money for cities, education, the environment, and so forth.[2] The savings in the next decade, estimated at more than US$100 billion, may not have changed those problems much but did help reduce the U.S. budget deficit. And, while

---

[1] Alex Mintz and Steve Chan, *Defense, Welfare and Growth: Perspectives and Evidence* (NY: Routledge, 1992). Richard J. Samuels, *Rich Nation, Strong Army: National Security and the Technological Transformation of Japan* (Ithaca, NY: Cornell UP, 1994).

nuclear arsenals were reduced, high-tech investment in areas like the National Missile Defense program tend to offset any savings. The U.S. also began to demand that prosperous allies in Europe and Japan pay more for maintaining U.S. military forces there—a concept known as *burden sharing*. The U.S. has also pressured countries like Canada to devote more resources to maintaining their militaries. At the same time, Russia and the other former Soviet republics drastically curtailed military spending, which their tattered economies could not support.

Unfortunately, the short-term effects of military spending (or reductions in spending) tend to run counter to the long-term effects. The immediate effect of a sharp reduction in military spending (as at the end of a war) is often to throw people out of work and disrupt economic growth. Conversely, the effect of increased military spending in the short term can be to pick up the slack in a national economy operating below capacity (as the United States and Canada were in the 1930s, for example). Because of these short-term effects, U.S. military spending cuts after the Cold War deepened a recession there in the early 1990s. Only later in the decade did the United States enjoy unprecedented prosperity.

Russia's cuts in military spending did little to stop its economic free fall. There and throughout the former Soviet Union—and somewhat less desperately in the West—political leaders scrambled to develop plans for **economic conversion**—use of former military facilities and industries for new civilian production.[3]

Canada was quick to take advantage of its comparative advantage in peacekeeping at the end of the Cold War. Not only were Canadian forces deployed on more missions during the 1990s, but Canada also became actively involved in training peacekeepers, both its own and those from other countries. Training was delivered either on Canadian military bases or at the Pearson Peacekeeping Centre in Cornwallis, Nova Scotia.[4]

Both the long- and short-term effects of military spending are magnified by actual warfare. War not only stimulates high military spending, it destroys capital (people, cities, farms, and factories in battle areas) and causes inflation (reducing the supply of various goods while increasing demand for them). Governments must pay for war goods by borrowing money (increasing government debt), by printing more currency (fuelling inflation), or by raising taxes (reducing spending and investment). U.S. revolutionary Thomas Paine warned in 1787 that "war … has but one thing certain, and that is to increase taxes."[5]

Nonetheless, war and high military spending can have certain economic benefits. The short-term stimulation resulting from a boost in military spending has been mentioned. Another potential benefit, particularly important from the perspective of realism, is the acquisition of territory (containing resources and capital). Another potential economic

economic conversion The use of former military facilities and industries for new civilian production.

---

[2] Michael D. Ward and David R. Davis, "Sizing Up the Peace Dividend: Economic Growth and Military Spending in the United States, 1948–1996," *American Political Science Review* 86.3 (1992): 748–58. Alex Mintz, ed., *The Political Economy of Military Spending in the United States* (NY: Routledge, 1992). William W. Kaufmann, *Glasnost, Perestroika, and U.S. Defense Spending* (Washington, DC: Brookings, 1990).

[3] Ian Anthony, *The Future of the Defense Industries in Central and Eastern Europe* (NY: Oxford UP, 1994). Lawrence R. Klein, Fu-chen Lo, and Warwick J. McKibbin, eds., *Arms Reduction: Economic Implications in the Post–Cold War Era* (NY: UN UP, 1995). Bonn International Center for Conversion, *Conversion Survey 1997: Global Disarmament and the Disposal of Surplus Weapons* (NY: Oxford UP, 1997). Lloyd J. Dumas and Marek Thee, eds., *Making Peace Possible: The Promise of Economic Conversion* (NY: Pergamon, 1989).

[4] Jocelyn Coulon, *Soldiers of Diplomacy: The United Nations, Peacekeeping, and the New World Order* (Toronto: U Toronto P, 1998). Joseph T. Jockel, *Canada and International Peacekeeping* (Washington: Center for Strategic and International Studies, 1994).

[5] Thomas Paine, *The Writings of Thomas Paine*, vol. 2 (NY: Knickerbocker, 1894).

benefit of war is to stir up a population's patriotism so that it will work harder for less pay. But overall, the benefits rarely equal the economic costs of war.

State leaders, then, face complex choices in setting overall levels of military spending. Over the long term, lower military spending is economically preferable, but in the short term higher military spending can stimulate the economy. Sudden changes in military spending, up or down, are usually disruptive to economic health and stability. But such sudden changes usually reflect the beginnings or ends of wars, which entail even more complex trade-offs of costs and benefits (economic *and* political) for state leaders.

The Choice of Capabilities

Despite the complexity of these trade-offs, state leaders must adopt military budgets, choose particular military capabilities to obtain, and often structure other economic activities to support those choices (for instance, nurturing the military-industrial complex). Leaders try to assess the threats to their state from other states' military capabilities and then develop affordable strategies to reduce those threats.

THE WAR IS OVER
U.S. and Russian nuclear forces were greatly reduced in the 1990s. Here, U.S. B-52 bombers are being chopped up, under the eye of Russian satellites, to bring force levels down.

The most basic choice facing state leaders is how much to spend on military capabilities. This varies widely, from Costa Rica, with virtually no military spending at all, to states such as North Korea, which devotes 20 percent or more of all economic activity to military purposes. If military budgets are too low, states may be unprepared to meet a security threat; in the worst case, they may even be overrun and conquered militarily. But if leaders set military budgets too high, they will overburden the national economy in the long run. (So far, Costa Rica has not been attacked despite recent wars in neighbouring Nicaragua and Panama, whereas North Korea is virtually bankrupt.)

In recent years, U.S. leaders have been rethinking military capabilities. Given the tremendous U.S. lead over other great powers, how much U.S. superiority is enough? In Canada, by contrast, the concern has been that reductions in military spending during the 1980s and 1990s have so reduced the quality of infrastructure and equipment that members of the Canadian Forces are at risk. Whether Canada could actually defend itself against an attack, given the size of the Canadian military, is also a question that is raised regularly.

Rationales for various policies in the United States have been proposed by the Pentagon, members of Congress, and private think-tanks—matching up certain configurations of forces with certain scenarios in which the United States might want military options. The primary mission of U.S. armed forces during the Cold War was containing the Soviet Union, especially from attacking Western Europe. The Gulf War suggested a new type of mission based on the ability to deploy a large armed force to a regional conflict area. In the 1990s, U.S. strategy called for the ability to fight two regional wars at once. In 2001, this goal was reduced to fighting one war at a time, to make resources available for high-technology weaponry and homeland defence, including ballistic missile defence (see p. 221).[6]

---

[6] Michael E. O'Hanlon, *Defense Policy Choices for the Bush Administration 2001–05* (Washington, DC: Brookings, 2001). George C. Wilson, *This War Really Matters: Inside the Fight for Defense Dollars* (Washington, DC: CQ, 2000).

Thinking Theoretically

During the Cold War, the superpowers poured money into military budgets, at rates ranging from 5 to 10 percent of GDP for the United States and perhaps 20 percent for the Soviet Union. What theories can explain the superpowers' military spending levels, as well as the sharp decreases in military spending in the 1990s?

One approach is based on reciprocity (see pp. 65–66). Each superpower responds to the other's military spending by raising or lowering its own military budget in the next time period. From this perspective, the superpower arms race may fit the model of a repeated Prisoner's Dilemma, as in laboratory experiments in which university students play PD repeatedly, both sides eventually learn to get out of the cycle of mutual defection (the spiralling arms race), and lock into stable cooperation. This pattern could explain the recent sharp decrease in military spending.

An alternative model has each superpower's military spending domestically driven. This would follow from ideas such as the organizational process model of foreign policy (see pp. 136–137) or, from a critical theory perspective, the power of the military-industrial complex (see pp. 148–150). Hundreds of research studies have tried to test these models against the empirical evidence provided by 40 years of military budgets. Typically they use a math-ematical model of the arms race, and then use quantitative data on arms spending to test statistically whether the model explains the data well. The statistical test shows how well, on average, a country's military spending correlates with the other country's previous spending.

So which theory is supported by these tests? The answer is that none can be evaluated with much confidence because the quantitative data on military spending are unreliable. Not only did both superpowers conceal military spending (and even military activity from which spending levels might be inferred), but comparing the two was problematic. Costs of weapons and salaries were very different in the two countries; the soldiers and equipment were not of comparable quality; rubles were not convertible into dollars; and macroeconomic indicators such as GDP were not compatible across communist and capitalist economies. As a result, no one could say for sure if Soviet military spending was going up or down in a given year, or whether Soviet spending was more or less than U.S. spending. Thus, military spending can be explained by at least three good theories—good in the sense that they can explain the outcome in terms of a general model with implications for other cases—and neither model can be ruled out by empirical evidence.

Outside the United States, other states were making similar assessments—most dramatically in Russia and the other republics of the former Soviet Union. Although they tried to reduce military spending as quickly as possible, there were no jobs for laid-off soldiers and military-industrial workers and no housing for troops brought home from Eastern Europe. For the next few years at least, military forces in Russia and most of the other former Soviet republics appear destined to limp along in a much reduced and weakened condition.

The cutbacks are less dramatic in Western Europe, where NATO members spend several percent of GDP on military forces. In Japan, where military spending was already only 1 percent of GDP, dramatic cutbacks are not in the works. In China, military spending does not affect economic growth greatly because the army is largely self-supporting (running its own farms, factories, etc.)—which also makes Chinese military spending hard to calculate. Chinese military forces underwent substantial reduction, along with modernization, in the 1980s and 1990s. Because it lags in technology, however, China's army remains the weakest of the great-power militaries (except perhaps Russia's).

Great powers continue to dominate the makeup of world military forces. Table 6.1 summarizes the most important forces of the great powers. Together, they account for two-thirds of world military spending, a third of the world's soldiers, about 50 percent of the weapons, 99 percent of nuclear weapons, and 90 percent of arms exports. The table also indicates the sizeable military forces maintained by Germany and Japan despite their non-traditional roles in international security affairs since World War II.

Table 6.1 Estimated Great-Power Military Capabilities, 2001–2002

	Military Expenditures[b] (Billions of US$), 2002	Soldiers[c] (Millions)	Weapons[a]				Arms Exported[e] (Billions of US$), 2002
			Tanks	Carriers/ Warships/ Submarines	Combat Airplanes	Nuclear Weapons[d]	
United States	350	1.4	10 000	11/ 112/ 74	3 600	10 000*	7
Russia	10–50*	1.5	20 000*	1/ 40/ 69	1 800	20 000*	3
China	30	2.8	10 000	0/ 29/ 6	2 100*	410	1
France	35	0.3	1 000	0/ 19/ 12	300	350	1
Britain	35	0.2	1 000	0/ 35/ 16	300	185	3
Germany	30	0.2	3 000	0/ 14/ 0	400	0	0
Japan	50	0.2	1 000	0/ 39/ 20	300	0	0
Approximate % of world total	67%	30%	25%	100/60/50%	40%	99%	83%

Notes: In the 1990s, the military forces of many of these states—Russia above all—were profoundly restructured. Numbers of weapons or soldiers do not indicate quality (levels of technology) or predict how armed forces would actually perform in combat. Russian forces are disorganized and in disrepair, with rampant desertion, nonoperational equipment, and low morale. Chinese forces are lower-tech than the others. Expenditure data are notoriously unreliable for Russia and China.

Data on soldiers exclude reserves. Tanks include only main battle tanks. Warships are major surface combat ships over 2700 tonnes. Nuclear warheads include both strategic and tactical weapons. Arms exports are deliveries, not orders, for 2002.

*Problematic data: Russian military expenditure estimates vary. Many Chinese aircraft and Russian tanks are old and of limited military use. U.S. and Russian nuclear warheads include deployed strategic weapons (6000 U.S., 6000 Russian) with the remainder held in reserve or retired (awaiting destruction).

Sources: Author's estimates based on data provided by the Institute for Defense and Disarmament Studies (IDDS), Cambridge, MA. Main sources are: [a] IDDS World Arms Database 2001 (www.idds.org); [b] SIPRI Yearbook 2003. Not adjusted for purchasing power parity. [c] Institute for International and Strategic Studies, *The Military Balance 2001–2002:* 299–304; [d] Carnegie Endowment for International Peace (www.ceip.org); [e] Richard F. Grimmett, *Conventional Arms Transfers to Developing Nations, 1993–2000* (Washington, DC: Congressional Research Service, 2001).

Middle powers like Canada, the Netherlands, and Australia remained heavily committed to peacekeeping missions. These missions do not require the same kind of capital expenditure, or acquisition of arms, as other configurations of forces. But they are significant in part because they provide those militaries with opportunities for training and to prepare and approximate "combat readiness" in a context in which the likelihood of facing actual combat is practically nonexistent.

In the global South, military spending varies greatly from one country to another, depending in part on the government in power (military or civilian).[7] Spending also depends heavily on available hard currency, from exports of oil or other products, to pay for arms purchases.

Weapons imports by states of the global South make up two-thirds of all arms sales. About half of the South's arms imports are in the Middle East, where oil exports create a ready source of funding. The remaining arms purchases are spread across Latin America, South Asia, East Asia, and Africa. Of all international arms exports, about half come from the United States, with Russia and France making up two-thirds of the rest. Globally, arms sales declined in the mid-1990s but grew again after 1997.[8]

In recent years, activists have called attention to the sales of small arms, especially assault rifles, to unstable conflict zones where regular and irregular armies commit brutalities. The largest exporters of small arms, by value, are the United States, Italy, Belgium, Germany, Russia, Brazil, and China. The largest importers of small arms are the U.S., Saudi Arabia, Cyprus, Japan, South Korea, Germany, and Canada. Of the US$4 billion in small arms and ammunition exported in 2001, U.S. exports accounted for $741 million (followed by Italy with $300 million, Belgium with $244 million, and Germany with at least $157 million, all in U.S. dollars). Canada is a significant exporter of small arms also, at $53 million.[9] In 2001, 140 states agreed to a voluntary pact to curb small-arms sales to conflict zones. Canada is a strong supporter of limiting small-arms sales, but countries like the United States have blocked proposals to restrict sales of military weapons to rebel movements and to civilians. The U.S. favours export licensing by individual exporters over multilateral efforts to address small arms, and has indicated that it will not sign on to any binding agreements to limit small-arms sales. A follow-up UN conference is planned for 2006.[10]

From a global perspective, the amount of world military spending decreased substantially in the post–Cold War era, by about one-third overall in the 1990s, although it began to increase again after 1998. World military spending is about 2 percent of the total goods and services in the world economy—about US$800 billion every year, or roughly $1 million every 40 seconds. Most is spent by a few big states, over a third by the United States alone. World military spending is a vast flow of money that could, if redirected to other

[7] Norman A. Graham, ed., *Seeking Security and Development: The Impact of Military Spending and Arms Transfers* (Boulder, CO: Rienner, 1994). Ravinder Pal Singh, ed., *Arms Procurement Decision-Making Processes: China, India, Israel, Japan, and South Korea* (NY: Oxford UP/SIPRI, 1997). Bates Gill and J. N. Mak, eds., *Arms Trade, Transparency, and Security in South-East Asia* (NY: Oxford UP/SIPRI, 1997).

[8] Richard F. Grimmett, *Conventional Arms Transfers to Developing Nations, 1993–2000* (Washington, DC: Congressional Research Service, 2001).Randall Forsberg, ed., *The Arms Production Dilemma: Contraction and Restraint in the World Combat Aircraft Industry* (Cambridge, MA: MIT P, 1994). Edward A. Kolodziej, *Making and Marketing Arms: The French Experience and Its Implications for the International System* (Princeton, NJ: Princeton, 1987).

[9] Small Arms Survey, *Small Arms Survey 2004: Rights at Risk* (Oxford: Oxford UP, 2004).

[10] Jeffrey Boutwell and Michael T. Klare, *Light Weapons and Civil Conflict: Controlling the Tools of Violence* (Lanham, MD: Rowman & Littlefield, 1999). "Small Arms, Big Business," *Washington Post* 8 July 2001: A19.

purposes, change the world profoundly and improve major world problems.[11] Of course, "the world" does not spend this money or choose how to direct it; states do.

Beyond these considerations about the size of military forces, the configuration of a state's military forces also presents difficult choices. Should Canada, for example, emphasize its navy or its air force? Should the army have more soldiers or more tanks? Which bases should be closed in periods of military cutbacks? Should Japan build nuclear weapons? Should Syria buy medium-range missiles?

Different missions require different forces. During the Cold War, about half of all military spending in the U.S. budget—and of world military spending—was directed toward the capitalist-communist conflict in Europe. Now other missions, such as intervention in regional conflicts, are more important. Some scholars think that North-South threats are replacing capitalist-communist ones.[12] And other new missions for military forces include humanitarian assistance, drug interdiction, disaster assistance at home (such as the 1997 Manitoba flood and the 1998 ice storm in eastern Ontario and Québec) and aid to other nations in building roads and schools.

Decisions about a state's military role give direction to its entire economy. During the Cold War, U.S. scientific research and industrial innovation were concentrated in the military sector. By contrast, Japan's research and development in those years focused on commercial products, contributing to Japan's prosperity.

Whatever configuration of military forces a state maintains, the leaders of the state face ongoing decisions about when and how to use those forces.

CONTROL OF MILITARY FORCES

The first issue of concern to a state leader in pulling a lever to exert influence is whether the lever is attached to anything. That is, how are the decisions of leaders translated into actual actions in distant locations that carry out the leaders' plans?

Command

The use of military force generally requires the coordination of the efforts of thousands, sometimes millions, of individuals performing many different functions in many locations. Such coordination is what is meant by *command*. One cannot take for granted the ability of a state leader to make military forces take desired actions. At best, military forces are large and complex institutions, operating in especially difficult conditions during wartime. At worst, military forces have a mind of their own (see pp. 208–211). Sometimes, as in the Russian Army's attacks in Chechnya province, or the abuse of Iraqi prisoners by U.S. forces in 2004, the state leader appears to exert only incomplete control over the military.

States control military forces through a *chain of command* running from the highest authority through a hierarchy spreading out to the lowest-level soldiers. The highest authority, or commander in chief, is usually the top political leader—the Canadian

[11] Randall Forsberg, Robert Elias, and Matthew Goodman, "Peace Issues and Strategies," *Institute for Defense and Disarmament Studies. Peace Resource Book 1986* (Cambridge, MA: Ballinger, 1985) 5–13.

[12] John D. Steinbruner, *Principles of Global Security* (Washington, DC: Brookings, 2000). Richard N. Haass, *Intervention: The Use of American Military Force in the Post-Cold War World*, rev. ed. (Washington, DC: Brookings Institution, 1999). Murray J. Douglas and Paul R. Viotti, eds., *The Defense Policies of Nations: A Comparative Study*, 3rd ed. (Baltimore: Johns Hopkins UP, 1994). Ken Booth, ed., *New Thinking about Strategy and International Security* (Boston: Unwin Hyman, 1991). Bjørn Møller, *The Dictionary of Alternative Defence* (Boulder, CO: Rienner, 1992).

UNDER CONTROL

Through a hierarchical chain of command, states control the actions of millions of individual soldiers, creating effective leverage in the hands of state leaders. Here, Chinese women soldiers march in a military parade, Guangzhou, 1991.

prime minister, U.S. president, Russian president, and so forth. The military hierarchy consists of levels of officers and soldiers.

In actual conditions of battle, controlling armed forces is especially difficult because of complex operations, rapid change, and the fog of war created by the gap between battlefield activity and command-level information. Participants are pumped up with adrenaline, deafened by noise, and confused by a mass of activity that—from the middle of it—may seem to make no sense. They are called on to perform actions that run against basic instincts as well as moral norms—killing people and risking death. It is difficult to coordinate forces effectively in order to carry out overall plans of action.

These factors reduce the effectiveness of military forces as instruments of state power. But military forces have developed several means for counteracting these problems. First is the principle of military discipline. Orders given from higher levels of the hierarchy must be obeyed by the lower levels—whether or not those at the lower level agree. Failure to do so is insubordination, or a mutiny if a whole group is involved. Leaving one's unit is called deserting. These are serious offences punishable by prison or death.

Members of most contemporary armed forces are trained into the highly structured lines of authority that make up the chain of command from the moment that they arrive as new recruits. Basic training and other initiation exercises aim to enforce obedience and promote an intense bonding among soldiers. No one, at any level, is allowed to deviate from the chain of command, and soldiers learn that their chances of survival in battle are enhanced if they respond to orders instantly and without question.[13]

Discipline depends not only on punishment but also on patriotism and professionalism on the part of soldiers. Officers play to nationalist sentiments, reminding soldiers that they fight for their nation and family. Whatever the motivation of soldiers, they require training in order to function as instruments of state power. Military training includes both technical training and training in the habit of obeying commands—a central purpose of basic training in every military force. Soldiers are deliberately stripped of their individuality—hair styles, clothes, habits, and mannerisms—to become part of a group. This action has both good and bad effects for the individuals, but it works for the purposes of the military. Then in exercises, soldiers practise over and over until certain operations become second nature.

---

[13] Deborah Harrison and Lucie Laliberté, *No Life Like It: Military Wives in Canada* (Toronto: Lorimer, 1994).

To maintain control of forces in battle, military units also rely on soldiers' sense of group solidarity. Soldiers risk their lives because their "buddies" depend on them.[14] Abstractions such as nationalism, patriotism, or religious fervour are important, but loyalty to the immediate group (along with a survival instinct) is a stronger motivator.

Unfortunately, some of the means by which soldiers learn to bond with one another, and to submit to military authority, are accomplished through denigrating anyone who is seen as "the enemy"—and that can include ethnic minorities, women, homosexuals, and people of colour. Some analysts have suggested that indoctrinating soldiers in this way can influence how they treat the people in countries to which they are deployed, in some of the most extreme cases resulting in soldiers who dehumanize, torture, and kill local peoples. Canada was witness to this when members of the Canadian Airborne Regiment tortured and murdered Somali teenager Shidane Arone in the early 1990s.[15] In 2004 in Iraq, U.S. soldiers were photographed humiliating and torturing Iraqi prisoners.

Troops operating in the field also rely on logistical support in order to function effectively. For states to use military leverage, they cannot just push armies around on a map like chess pieces. Rather, they must support those armies with large quantities of supplies. Leaders in Prussia (Germany) more than a century ago used well-oiled logistics based on railroads to defeat both Austria and France, which were using rapid offensives.

A further difficulty that states must overcome to use military forces effectively is that top officers and political leaders need accurate information about what is going on in the field—intelligence—to make good decisions.[16] They also need extensive communications networks, including the ability to use codes to ensure secrecy. Such functions are known as "command and control," or sometimes C^3I—for command, control, communications, and intelligence. During the Cold War, it was assumed that C^3I capabilities would be the first targets in a nuclear war. This information side of controlling military forces has become ever more important. In the Gulf War, a top U.S. priority was to target Iraqi communications facilities so as to disable Iraq's command and control.

The number of so-called friendly fire deaths in the Gulf War and in Afghanistan suggest that command and communications lines are not always effective. In Afghanistan, four Canadian soldiers were killed and eight were wounded in 2002 when American pilots dropped a 227 kilogram bomb on them. The pilots mistook flashes from the Canadian soldiers' live ammunition exercise on the ground as anti-aircraft fire and assumed they were under attack. This happened despite the fact that the Canadians had informed U.S. command of their planned exercises. But the information did not reach the pilots in time to avert the tragedy.

Finally, states rely on their military officers to develop and implement effective strategies and tactics. Strategies bring the state's military (and nonmilitary) capabilities to bear

---

[14] Joanna Bourke, *An Intimate History of Killing: Face-to-Face Killing in Twentieth-Century Warfare* (NY: Basic, 1999). Dave Grossman, *On Killing: The Psychological Cost of Learning to Kill in War and Society* (Boston: Little, Brown, 1995). Richard Holmes, *Acts of War: The Behavior of Men in Battle* (NY: Free Press, 1985). Anthony Kellett, "The Soldier in Battle: Motivational and Behavioral Aspects of the Combat Experience," *Psychological Dimensions of War*, ed. Betty Glad (Newbury Park, CA: Sage, 1990) 215–35. Paul Fussell, *Wartime: Understanding and Behavior in the Second World War* (NY: Oxford UP, 1989). J. Glenn Gray, *The Warriors: Reflections on Men in Battle* (1959; NY: Harper & Row, 1967).

[15] Sandra Whitworth, *Men, Militarism and UN Peacekeeping: A Gendered Analysis* (Boulder, CO: Rienner, 2004). Alfred W. McCoy, " 'Same Banana': Hazing and Honor at the Philippine Military Academy," *The Journal of Asian Studies* 54.3 (August 1995): 689–726.

[16] Mark M. Lowenthal, *Intelligence: From Secrets to Policy* (Washington, DC: CQ, 2000). Jeffery T. Richelson, *A Century of Spies: Intelligence in the Twentieth Century* (NY: Oxford UP, 1995).

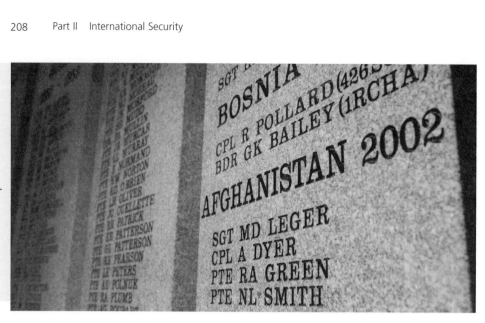

MILITARY MEMORIAL The name of the four Princess Patricia's Canadian Light Infantry soldiers killed by friendly fire in Afghanistan are seen engraved along with other Canadian military dead at a memorial in Calgary, June 19, 2003. The pilots who dropped the bombs that killed the soldiers now face court-martial.

in an overall coordinated manner to achieve an end. Tactics do the same but in a more localized setting (a single battle) and in a more standardized way. Often when state leaders want to achieve certain political aims in international conflicts, they ask military officers to suggest strategies for employing force toward those ends. Strategy and tactics become especially important when a state employs military force in a conflict with another state whose military capabilities are larger or technically superior. For example, Israel defeated the larger Egyptian military forces in 1967 and 1973 partly by employing clever tactics.

States and Militaries

Overcoming chaos and complexity is only part of the task for state leaders seeking to control military forces. Sometimes they must overcome their own military officers as well. Although militaries are considered instruments of state power, in many states the military forces themselves control the government. These **military governments** are most common in countries of the global South, where the military may be the only large modern institution in the country.

Military leaders are able to exercise political control because the same violent forms of leverage that work internationally also work domestically. In fact, domestically there may be little or no counter-leverage to the use of military force. Military officers thus have an inherent power advantage over civilian political leaders. Ironically, the disciplined central command of military forces, which makes them effective as tools of state influence, also lets the state lose control of them to military officers. Soldiers are trained to follow the orders of their commanding officers, not to think about politics.

A **coup d'état** (French for "blow against the state") is the seizure of political power by domestic military forces—a change of political power outside the state's constitutional order.[17] Coups are often mounted by ambitious junior officers against the top generals.

military governments
States in which military forces control the government; more common in countries of the global South, where the military may be the only large modern institution.

coup d'état French for "blow against the state," it refers to the seizure of political power by domestic military forces—that is, a change of political power outside the state's constitutional order.

---

[17] Peter D. Feaver and Richard D. Kohn, eds., *Soldiers and Civilians* (Cambridge, MA: MIT P, 2001). Steven R. David, *Third World Coups d'État and International Security* (Baltimore: Johns Hopkins UP, 1987). Talukder Maniruzzaman, "Arms Transfers, Military Coups, and Military Rule in Developing States," *Journal of Conflict Resolution* 36.4 (1992): 733–55. William J. Foltz and Henry S. Bienen, eds., *Arms and the African: Military Influences on Africa's International Relations* (New Haven, CT: Yale UP, 1985). Robert S. Jackman, Rosemary H. T. O'Kane, Thomas H. Johnson, Pat McGowan, and Robert O. Slater, "Explaining African Coups d'État," *American Political Science Review* 80.1 (1986): 225–50.

Officers who thus break the chain of command can take along with them the sections of the military hierarchy below them. Coup leaders move quickly to seize centres of power—official state buildings as well as television stations and transmitters—before other units of the military can put down the coup attempt or unleash a civil war. Civilian politicians in power and uncooperative military officers are arrested or killed. The coup leaders try to create a sense of inevitability around the change in government and hope that fellow officers throughout the military defect to their side. In some cases, as in Haiti in 2004, it is former members of the military who launch a coup.

The outcome of a coup is hard to predict. If most or all of the military go along with the coup, civilian leaders are generally helpless to stop it. But if most of the military officers follow the existing chain of command, the coup is doomed. In the Philippines in the late 1980s, the top general, Fidel Ramos, remained loyal to the civilian president, Corazón Aquino, in seven coup attempts by subordinate officers. In each case, the bulk of the Philippine military forces stayed loyal to Ramos, and the coups failed. In 1992, Ramos himself was elected president with the backing of a grateful Aquino.

Coups may also be put down by an outside military force. A government threatened with a coup may call on foreign friends for military assistance. But because coups are considered largely an internal affair—and because they are over so quickly—direct foreign intervention in them is relatively rare.

Military governments often have difficulty gaining popular legitimacy for their rule because their power is clearly based on force rather than popular mandate, although the public may support the new regime if the old one was really bad. To stay in power, both military and civilian governments require at least passive acceptance by their people.

Even in nonmilitary governments, the interaction of civilian with military leaders—called civil-military relations—is an important factor in how states use force. Military leaders may undermine the authority of civilian leaders in carrying out foreign policies, or they may even threaten a coup if certain actions are taken in international conflicts.

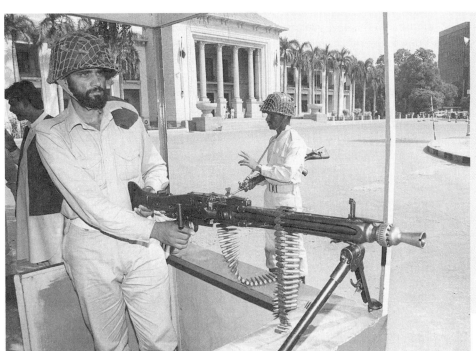

HIGHLY IRREGULAR A coup is a change of government carried out by domestic military forces operating outside the state's constitution. The number of military governments is declining, but dozens remain. Pakistan's military government took power in a 1999 coup and became a key ally in fighting Taliban-ruled Afghanistan in 2001. Here soldiers deploy to the provincial legislature in Lahore after the coup.

NATO forces operate under strong civilian control. However, military desires continue to run counter to civilian decisions at times. After the Vietnam War, top U.S. military officers became more reluctant to send U.S. forces into combat. The U.S. Pentagon now generally supports using military force only when there is a clear goal that can be achieved militarily, when the public supports the action, and when military forces can be used massively for a quick victory. Panama in 1989, Kuwait in 1991, and Afghanistan in 2001 fit these new conditions. Members of the U.S. military were more divided on the invasion of Iraq, with some suggesting that none of these conditions held.

Military officers also want autonomy of decision once force is committed, in order to avoid the problems created in the Vietnam War when President Johnson sat in the White House situation room daily picking targets for bombing raids. In NATO's 1999 bombing of Serbia, specific targets had to be approved by politicians in multiple countries.

Covert operations are the dagger part of the "cloak and dagger" spy business. Several thousand such operations were mounted during the Cold War, when the CIA in the U.S. and the Soviet Union's KGB, waged an ongoing worldwide secret war. CIA covert operations in the 1950s overthrew unfriendly foreign governments—in Iran and Guatemala—by organizing coups against them. The CIA-organized Bay of Pigs invasion in Cuba, in 1961, was its first big failure, followed by other failed efforts against the Castro government (including eight assassination attempts). CIA covert activities were sharply scaled back after congressional hearings in the 1970s revealed scandals. Such covert operations now must be reported to special congressional *oversight* committees through an elaborate set of procedures. After September 2001, the executive branch enjoyed greater authority in conducting covert operations without congressional scrutiny.

The Canadian Security Intelligence Service (CSIS) was established in 1984 and is mandated to provide advance warning to government departments about any activities that may constitute a threat to Canadian security. Prior to 1984, the Royal Canadian Mounted Police (RCMP) provided security intelligence within Canada, but a number of scandals led the Canadian government to decide that a civilian body would be better suited to this role. During the dying years of the Cold War, CSIS was involved primarily in countering the espionage activities of foreign governments. Like the CIA in the United States, it now focuses on counterterrorism but also investigates economic espionage. CSIS does not have quite the "cloak and dagger" reputation of the CIA, but in its early years it was subject to considerable domestic criticism for spying on its own citizens. CSIS is not permitted to take direct action against any perceived threats; instead, responses to security threats are left to the police and military.

The traditions of civil-military relations in a state do not necessarily reflect the extent of democracy there. States in which civilians traditionally have trouble controlling the military include some with long histories of democracy, notably in Latin America. And states with strong traditions of civilian control over military forces include some authoritarian states, such as the former Soviet Union (where the Communist Party controlled the military). This tradition helps to explain the failure of the attempted coup in August 1991 against the head of the Communist Party (Gorbachev). Even with most of the second echelon of party leaders behind them, the coup leaders could not gain the legitimacy needed to take power and to get soldiers to follow their orders.[18]

The tradition of civilian (Communist Party) control of the military in China is more ambiguous. Regional military leaders coordinate their activities through the Central

---

[18] John W. R. Lepingwell, "Soviet Civil-Military Relations and the August Coup," *World Politics* 44.4 (1992): 539–72.

Military Commission, under direction of the Communist Party. But during the Cultural Revolution in the 1960s, and again in the Tiananmen protests in 1989, military forces essentially held power at times of internal splits in the party. Both Mao Zedong and Deng Xiaoping made it a point to control the Military Commission personally.

In a few states, certain military forces operate beyond the reach of the government's chain of command—certainly when rebel guerrilla armies control territories nominally under the jurisdiction of the central government. It is also true in the infrequent but dramatic cases when governmental authority breaks down, such as in Somalia and Afghanistan in the 1990s. Private armies or militias then answer to local warlords rather than to any national government. In such situations one cannot speak of military force as an instrument of state leverage.

No matter how firmly state leaders control the military forces at their disposition, those forces are effective only if they are equipped and trained for the purposes the state leaders have in mind. To understand decisions to use military force, one must understand the various types of forces and weapons and the missions they are to perform.

CONVENTIONAL FORCES

The bargaining power of states depends not only on the overall size of their military forces but on the particular capabilities of those forces in various scenarios. State leaders almost always turn to conventional military forces for actual missions, reserving weapons of mass destruction for making or deterring threats.

If a leader decides that an international conflict could be more favourably settled by applying military force, it matters a great deal whether the application involves bombing another state's capital city, imposing a naval blockade, or seizing disputed territory. Armed forces can apply negative leverage at a distance, but various types of forces have evolved over time for different situations and contexts—on water, on land, or in the air.[19] They match up against each other in particular ways. A tank cannot destroy a submarine, and vice versa. A tank can generally prevail against foot soldiers with rifles, though foot soldiers with antitank missiles might prevail.

Types of Forces

Whatever their ultimate causes and objectives, most wars involve a struggle to *control territory*. Territory holds a central place in warfare because of its importance in the international system, and vice versa. Borders define where a state's own military forces and rival states' military forces are free to move. Military logistics make territoriality all the more important because of the need to control territories connecting military forces with each other. An army's supplies must flow from home territory along *supply lines* to the field. Thus the most fundamental purpose of conventional forces is to take, hold, or defend territory.

Armies

Armies are adapted to this purpose. Infantry soldiers armed with automatic rifles can generally control a local piece of territory. Military forces with such a presence *occupy* a ter-

---

[19] John A. Keegan, *History of Warfare* (NY: Random House, 1993). Martin Van Creveld, *Technology and War: From 2000 B.C. to the Present* (NY: Free Press, 1989). Robert L. O'Connell, *Of Arms and Men: A History of War, Weapons and Aggression* (NY: Oxford UP, 1989). Edward Luttwak and Stuart L. Koehl, *The Dictionary of Modern War* (NY: HarperCollins, 1991)

ritory militarily. Although inhabitants may make the soldiers' lives unhappy through violent or nonviolent resistance, generally only another organized, armed military force can displace occupiers.

Foot soldiers are called the **infantry.** They use assault rifles and other light weapons (such as mines and machine guns) as well as heavy artillery of various types. Artillery is extremely destructive and not very discriminating: it usually causes the most damage and casualties in wars. Armour refers to tanks and armoured vehicles. In open terrain, such as desert, mechanized ground forces typically combine armour, artillery, and infantry. In close terrain, such as jungles and cities, however, foot soldiers are more important.

For this reason, the armies of industrialized states have a greater advantage over poor armies in open conventional warfare, such as in the Kuwaiti desert. In jungle, mountain, or urban warfare, however—as in Vietnam, Somalia, Bosnia, or Iraq—such advantages are eroded, and a cheaper and more lightly armed force of motivated foot soldiers or guerrillas may ultimately prevail over an expensive conventional army.

Land mines are used by armies to defend territory by creating zones (mine fields) in which anyone passing through is subject to injury by stepping on (or driving over) a mine. The mine itself is a simple, small, and cheap container of explosives with a trigger activated by contact or sensor. These mines were a particular focus of public attention in the 1990s because in places such as Angola, Afghanistan, Cambodia, and Bosnia, they were used extensively. Long after such a war ends, land mines continue to maim and kill civilians who try to re-establish their lives in former war zones. As many as 100 million land mines remain from recent wars; they injure about 25 000 people a year (a third of whom are children); although they are cheap to deploy, it costs about $1000 per mine to find and disarm them.

Public opinion and NGOs have pressured governments to restrict the future use of land mines (Chapter 7). After the death in 1997 of Britain's Princess Diana, who had actively supported the campaign, a treaty to ban land mines was signed by more than 100 countries at a 1997 conference organized by Canada's then Minister of Foreign Affairs, Lloyd Axworthy. Russia and Japan signed on shortly afterward, but the United States and China refused to sign. The U.S. government argued that land mines were essential for defending South Korea if the massed troops of North Korea tried to invade across the demilitarized zone. The United States is also a large producer of land mines.

infantry Foot soldiers who use assault rifles and other light weapons (mines, machine guns, and the like).

land mines Concealed explosive devices, often left behind by irregular armies, which kill or maim civilians after wars end. Such mines number more than 100 million, primarily in Angola, Bosnia, Afghanistan, and Cambodia. A movement to ban land mines is underway; nearly 100 states have agreed to do so.

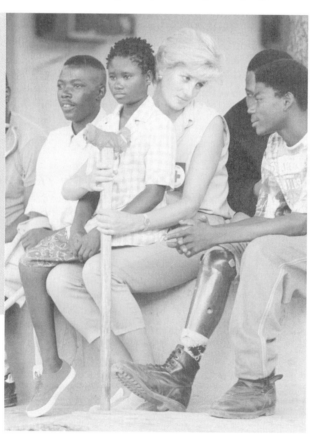

INVISIBLE KILLERS
Land mines continue to kill and maim civilians long after wars end. A movement to ban land mines culminated in a 1997 treaty signed in Ottawa by over 100 countries (not including the United States or China). Britain's Princess Diana, shown here with Angolan mine victims in 1997, was a major supporter of the movement, and her death in 1997 helped galvanize support for the treaty.

Navies *Navies* are adapted primarily to control passage through the seas and to attack land near coastlines.[20] Unlike armies, navies are not tied to territory because the oceans beyond coastal waters are not owned by any state. Controlling the seas in wartime allows states to move their own goods and military forces by sea while preventing enemies from doing so.

Aircraft carriers—mobile platforms for attack aircraft—are instruments of **power projection** that can exert negative leverage against virtually any state in the world. Merely sending an aircraft carrier sailing to the vicinity of an international conflict implies a threat to use force—a modern version of what was known in the nineteenth century as "gunboat diplomacy."

power projection The ability to use military force in areas far from a country's region or sphere of influence.

Aircraft carriers are extremely expensive, and typically require 20 to 25 supporting ships for protection and supply. Few states can afford even one. The United States has 12, France 2, Russia 1, and several other states have a few smaller and less capable carriers. Canada had a number of aircraft carriers during World War II, but has since focused on smaller surface vessels and several submarines.

Surface ships, which account for the majority of warships, rely increasingly on guided missiles and are in turn vulnerable to attack by missiles (fired from ships, planes, submarines, or land). Since the ranges of small missiles now reach from dozens to hundreds of kilometres, naval warfare emphasizes detection at great distances without being detected oneself—a cat-and-mouse game of radar surveillance and electronic countermeasures.

Missile-firing ships are much cheaper and faster than aircraft carriers. They are becoming potent instruments of power projection themselves. (Cruise missiles are discussed later.) Submarines are specialized to attack ships but can also fire missiles at land targets. (Those that fire nuclear missiles are discussed later.) Submarine and antisubmarine warfare place a great premium on detection and evading detection.

Marines (part of the navy in the United States, Britain, and Russia) move to battle in ships but fight on land—amphibious warfare. Marines are also useful for great-power intervention in distant conflicts where they can insert themselves quickly and establish local control. In the 1992–1993 intervention in Somalia, U.S. Marines were already waiting offshore while the UN Security Council was debating whether to authorize the use of force.

Air Forces *Air forces* serve several distinct purposes—strategic bombing of land or sea targets; "close air support" (battlefield bombing); interception of other aircraft; reconnaissance; and airlift of supplies, weapons, and troops.

Traditionally, and still to a large extent, aerial bombing resembles artillery shelling in that it causes great destruction with little discrimination. This has begun to change in a few cases as "smart bombs" improve accuracy. For instance, laser-guided bombs follow a sensor pointed at the target from the air. Television viewers during the 1991 Gulf War watched video images of bombs scoring direct hits (not all were as accurate). For many critics, these images desensitize viewers to the death and destruction that is being created by directing attention instead to "fascinating" new technologies. Most of the bombing in that war was high-altitude saturation bombing using large numbers of "dumb bombs," and here too pilots can fulfill their missions without seeing or experiencing the effects of their actions on the ground

In other more typical wars, such as Russia's repression of Chechnya in 1995, and the invasion of Iraq in 2003, bombing of cities causes high civilian casualties, no matter how "smart" the technology. In cases of low-intensity conflicts and guerrilla wars, especially where forces intermingle with civilians in closed terrain such as Vietnamese jungles or

---

[20] John Keegan, *The Price of Admiralty: The Evolution of Naval Warfare* (NY: Viking, 1988).

PROJECTING POWER
Different types of military forces are adapted to different purposes. Naval forces are used to project power in distant regions. Special forces soldiers, like this member of Canada's Joint Task Force 2 (JTF2), work in covert and commando operations.

Somali cities, bombing is of limited utility. Air forces are also vulnerable to missile fire. In the 2003 Iraq war, the threat of shoulder-fired missiles kept the Baghdad airport closed to all commercial traffic, and most military traffic, for months after the invasion began.

Even more than ships, aircraft rely heavily on electronics, especially radar. The best-equipped air forces have specialized AWACS (Airborne Warning and Control System) airplanes to survey a large area with radar and coordinate the movements of dozens of aircraft. The increasing sophistication of electronic equipment and high performance requirements of attack aircraft make air forces expensive—totally out of reach for some states.

Logistics and Intelligence All military operations rely heavily on logistical support such as food, fuel, and ordnance (weapons and ammunition). Military logistics are a huge operation, and in most armed forces the majority of soldiers are not combat troops. Before the Gulf War, the United States moved an army of half a million people and a vast quantity of supplies to Saudi Arabia in a six-month effort that was the largest military logistical operation in such a time frame in history.

Global reach capabilities combine long-distance logistical support with various power projection forces.[21] These capabilities allow a great power to project military power to distant corners of the world and to maintain a military presence in most of the world's regions simultaneously. Only the United States today fully possesses such a capability—with worldwide military alliances, air and naval bases, troops stationed overseas, and aircraft carriers plying the world's oceans (refer to Table 6.1 on page 203). Britain and France are in a distant second place, able to mount occasional distant operations of modest size, such as the Falkland/Malvinas Islands War. Russia is preoccupied with internal conflicts and its CIS neighbours, and China's military forces are oriented toward regional conflicts and are not global in scope.

Space forces are military forces designed to attack in or from outer space.[22] Ballistic missiles, which travel through space briefly, are not generally included in this category. Only the United States and Russia have substan-

---

[21] Robert E. Harkavy, *Bases Abroad: The Global Foreign Military Presence* (NY: Oxford, 1989).

[22] Bob Preston, ed., *Space Weapons: Earth Wars* (Santa Monica, CA: Rand, 2002). Bhupendra Jasani, ed., *Space Weapons and International Security* (Oxford: Oxford UP, 1987). Stephen Kirby and Gordon Robson, eds., *The Militarisation of Space* (Boulder, CO: Rienner, 1987).

tial military capabilities in space. China joined the manned-space club in 2003, though with far fewer capabilities overall. The development of space weapons has been constrained by the technical challenges and expenses of space operations, and by norms against militarizing space. U.S. policy-makers in 2001 announced a plan to begin testing space-based lasers (for intercepting ballistic missiles) in several years.

Satellites are used extensively for military purposes, but these purposes thus far do not include attack. Satellites perform military surveillance and mapping, communications, weather assessment, and early warning of ballistic missile launches. Satellites also provide navigational information to military forces—army units, ships, planes, and even guided missiles in flight. Analysts pore over masses of satellite reconnaissance data every day. Poorer states can buy satellite photos on the commercial market—including high-resolution pictures that Russia sells for hard currency.

Locations are calculated to within about 15 metres by small receivers, which pick up beacons transmitted from a network of 18 U.S. satellites known as a *Global Positioning System (GPS)*. Handheld receivers are available commercially, so the military forces of nonsuperpowers can ride free on these satellite navigation beacons. But, in general, outer space is an area in which great powers have great advantages over smaller or poorer states.

Intelligence gathering also relies on various other means, such as electronic monitoring of telephone lines and other communications, reports from embassies, and information in the open press. Some kinds of information are obtained by sending agents into foreign countries as spies. They use ingenuity (plus money and technology) to penetrate walls of secrecy that foreign governments have constructed around their plans and capabilities.

Evolving Technologies

Through the centuries, the lethal power of weapons has increased continuously—from swords to muskets, machine guns to missiles. Technological developments have changed the nature of military force in several ways. First, the resort to force in international conflicts now has more profound costs and consequences than it did at the outset of the international system several centuries ago. Great powers in particular can no longer use force to settle disputes among themselves without risking massive destruction and economic ruin.

A second long-term effect of technological change is that military engagements now occur across greater standoff distances between opposing forces. Missiles of all types are accelerating this trend. Its effect is to undermine the territorial basis of war and of the state itself. The state once had a hard shell of militarily protected borders, but today the protection offered by borders is diminishing.[23] For example, Israel's successful defence of its borders could not stop Iraqi scud missiles from hitting Israeli cities during the Gulf War.

The pace of technological change has also made national security more intertwined with economics. Critical technologies with potential military applications are developed by industrialized states and guarded from export. In the 1980s, a major scandal erupted when it was discovered that the Japanese company Toshiba had sold the Soviet Union advanced machinery that would allow the Soviets to produce quieter submarine propellers (an important feature for evading detection).

In recent decades, the technological revolution in electronics has profoundly affected military forces, especially their command and control. **Electronic warfare** (now broadened to *information warfare*) refers to the uses of the electromagnetic spectrum (radio waves, radar, infrared, etc.) in war—employing electromagnetic signals for one's own

electronic warfare The use of the electromagnetic spectrum (radio waves, radar, infrared, etc.) in war, such as employing electromagnetic signals for one's own benefit while denying their use to an enemy.

---

[23] John H. Herz, *International Politics in the Atomic Age* (NY: Columbia UP, 1959).

SMALL BUT DEADLY
The information revolution is making smaller weapons more potent. The U.S.-made Stinger anti-aircraft missile—portable and shoulder-launched—helped turn the tide against the Soviet Union in the war in Afghanistan in the 1980s, with far-reaching consequences. Here, an Afghan fighter holds a Stinger in 1987.

benefit while denying their use to an enemy. Electromagnetic signals are used for sensing beyond the normal visual range, through radar, infrared, and imaging equipment, to see in darkness, through fog, or at great distances. These and other technologies have illuminated the battlefield so that forces cannot be easily hidden.

Electronic countermeasures are technologies designed to counteract enemy electronic systems such as radar and radio communications. **Stealth technology** uses special radar-absorbent materials and unusual shapes in the design of aircraft, missiles, and ships to scatter enemy radar. However, stealth is extremely expensive (the B-2 stealth bomber costs about US$2 billion per plane, or about three times its weight in gold) and is prone to technical problems. Electronics are changing the costs and relative capabilities of weapons across the board. Computer chips in guided missiles have made them a formidable weapon on land, sea, and air. The miniaturization of such weaponry is making smaller and cheaper military forces more powerful than ever. An infantry soldier now can use a shoulder-fired missile costing $10 000 to destroy a main battle tank costing $1 million. Similarly, a small boat firing an anti-ship missile costing $250 000 can potentially destroy a major warship costing hundreds of millions of dollars.

Technological developments are in some ways increasing the advantages of great powers over less-powerful states, while in other ways undermining those advantages. For example, China's military has been developing lower-cost technological strategies to counter U.S. military power in any future war. Land-based missiles could destroy expensive U.S. aircraft carriers. New Chinese anti-aircraft systems reportedly can detect even "stealth" U.S. aircraft while remaining passive and thus not presenting a target. (Conventional radar sends signals to bounce off aircraft; the passive design instead detects tiny variations in existing signals like television broadcasts.)

stealth technology The use of special radar-absorbent materials and unusual shapes in the design of aircraft, missiles, and ships to scatter enemy radar.

U.S. forces in turn are developing new battlefield tactics calling for smaller, more mobile weapons and troop units, along with more unmanned systems, linked by intensive communications networks. Unmanned drones in Afghanistan in 2001 monitored Taliban movements from the air, and were retrofitted with two remote-controlled missiles. Within the decade, the U.S. military may begin deploying a new generation of laser weapons fired from planes at targets on the ground.

Strategies for *cyberwar*—disrupting enemy computer networks to degrade command-and-control, or even hacking into bank accounts electronically—were developed by NATO forces during the 1999 Kosovo war, though mostly not implemented, and will probably figure in future wars. Some experts fear that terrorist attacks too could target computer networks.[24]

WEAPONS OF MASS DESTRUCTION

Weapons of mass destruction include three general types: nuclear, chemical, and biological weapons. They are distinguished from conventional weapons by their enormous potential lethality, given their small size and modest costs, and by their relative lack of discrimination in whom they kill. Because of these differences, weapons of mass destruction offer state leaders types of leverage that differ from conventional military forces. When deployed on ballistic missiles, they can potentially be fired from the home territory of one state and wreak great destruction on the home territory of another state.

To date this has never happened. But the mere threat of such an action undermines the territorial integrity and security of states in the international system. Thus scholars pay special attention to such weapons and the missiles that can deliver them. Of central concern today are the potentials for proliferation—the possession of weapons of mass destruction by more and more states.

Weapons of mass destruction serve different purposes from conventional weapons. With a few exceptions, their purpose is to deter attack (especially by other weapons of mass destruction) by giving state leaders the means to inflict great pain against a would-be conqueror or destroyer. For middle powers, these weapons also provide destructive power more in line with the great powers, serving as symbolic equalizers.

> **weapons of mass destruction** Nuclear, chemical, and biological weapons, all distinguished from conventional weapons by their enormous potential lethality, and by their relative lack of discrimination in whom they kill.

Nuclear Weapons

Nuclear weapons are, in sheer explosive power, the most destructive weapons available to states. A single weapon the size of a refrigerator can destroy a city. Defending against nuclear weapons is extremely difficult at best.

To understand the potentials for nuclear proliferation, one has to know something about how nuclear weapons work. There are two types. *Fission* weapons (atomic bombs or A-bombs) are simpler and less expensive than **fusion weapons** (also called thermonuclear bombs, hydrogen bombs, or H-bombs). The term *bomb* refers to a warhead that can be delivered by missile, bomb, artillery shell, or other means.

When a fission weapon explodes, one type of atom (element) is split, or "fissioned," into new types with less total mass. The lost mass is transformed into energy according to Albert Einstein's famous formula, $E = mc^2$, which shows that a little bit of mass is equivalent to a great deal of energy. In fact, the fission bomb that U.S. forces used to destroy Nagasaki, Japan, in 1945 converted to energy roughly the amount of mass in a single

> **fusion weapons** Extremely destructive, expensive, and technologically sophisticated weapons in which two small atoms fuse together into a larger atom, releasing energy. Also referred to as "thermonuclear weapons" or "hydrogen bombs." See also *fissionable material*.

[24] Gregory J. Rattray, *Strategic Warfare in Cyberspace* (Cambridge, MA: MIT P, 2001). Neil Munro, *The Quick and the Dead: Electronic Combat and Modern Warfare* (NY: St. Martin's, 1991).

The Changing World Order
The Revolution in Military Affairs

Military historians refer to a period of rapid change in the conduct of war as a "revolution in military affairs." These periods usually combine innovative applications of new technology with changes in military doctrine, organization, or operations. Such revolutions may arise from innovations in organization, as when revolutionary France first mobilized an entire nation into a war machine two centuries ago. Or they may arise from new military doctrine, as when Germany used the "blitzkrieg" to overwhelm Poland and France at the outset of World War II, or from technology alone, as with the invention of nuclear weapons.

Many military analysts consider the present period, starting with the 1991 Gulf War, to be a revolution in military affairs. Current technologies allow armed forces to cut through Clausewitz's famous "fog of war" (see p. 206), the confusion and uncertainty that greatly reduces the effectiveness of armies in battle. Stealth airplanes, laser-guided weapons, so-called smart bombs dropped by high-flying aircraft, all are elements of the revolution in military affairs.

From a realist perspective, critics worry that the revolution has brought an unrealistic expectation of low casualties in war, which may make political leaders unduly cautious in applying military force. For example, at the end of the Afghanistan campaign, terrorist leaders including Osama bin Laden slipped away as the United States relied on local warlords to hunt them, when larger numbers of U.S. troops might have captured them (but with U.S. casualties).

Others are concerned that the revolution in military affairs "sanitizes" the conduct of war. Images of bomber

Anti-Taliban Afghans watch U.S. air strikes, 2001.

pilots who take off from an airbase, drop their "payload" on targets halfway around the world, and are home in time to have breakfast with their kids, normalizes militarism and makes bombing raids (which wreak violent death and destruction) appear no different from any other "day at the office."

Others still have pointed out that state militaries do not hold a monopoly on the revolution in military affairs. The people involved in the September 2001 attack against the U.S. used information technology, such as encrypted internet communications, to coordinate forces while keeping authorities in the dark. They carried out precision strikes over long distances with very small, dispersed units. As a result, 19 attackers killed more than 3000 people, and an expenditure of under $1 million caused tens of *billions* of dollars in damage.

---

fissionable material The elements uranium-235 and plutonium, whose atoms split apart and release energy via a chain reaction when an atomic bomb explodes. See also *fusion weapons.*

penny. Two elements can be split in this way, and each has been used to make fission weapons. These elements—known as **fissionable material**—are uranium-235 (or U-235) and plutonium.

Fission weapons work by taking subcritical masses of the fissionable material—amounts not dense enough to start a chain reaction—and compressing them into a critical mass, which explodes. In the simplest design, one piece of uranium is propelled down a tube (by conventional explosives) into another piece of uranium. A more efficient but technically demanding design arranges high explosives precisely around a hollow sphere of plutonium so as to implode the sphere and create a critical mass. Enhanced designs add an outer sphere of neutron-reflecting material to increase the number of speeding neutrons during the explosion.

Although these designs require sophisticated engineering, they are well within the capabilities of many states and some private groups. The obstacle is obtaining fissionable material. Only 4.5 to 45 kilograms are required for each bomb, but even these amounts are not easily obtained. U-235, which can be used in the simplest bomb designs, is especially difficult to obtain. Natural uranium (mined in various countries) has less than 1 percent U-235, mixed with nonfissionable uranium. Extracting the fissionable U-235, referred to as enriching the uranium up to weapons grade (or high grade), is slow, expensive, and technically complex—a major obstacle to proliferation.

Plutonium is more easily produced, from low-grade uranium in nuclear power reactors—although extracting the plutonium requires a separation plant. But a plutonium bomb is more difficult to build than a uranium one—another obstacle to proliferation. Plutonium is also used in commercial breeder reactors (reactors that create more fissionable material than they consume), which Japan in particular has built recently—another source of fissionable material. In the 1990s, Japan shipped tons of plutonium home from separation plants in Europe by sea—creating a possible temptation for theft and a weapons-capable stockpile for Japan.(Thus, if it decided to do so in the future, Japan could build a formidable nuclear arsenal fairly quickly.)

Fission weapons were invented 50 years ago by scientists in a secret World War II science project in the U.S. known as the *Manhattan Project*. In 1945, one uranium bomb and one plutonium bomb were used to destroy Hiroshima and Nagasaki, killing 100 000 civilians in each city and inducing Japan to surrender unconditionally. By today's standards,

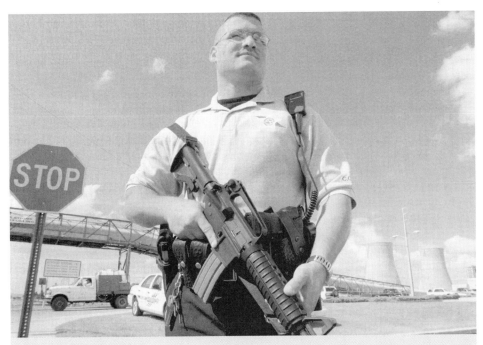

LIVING WITH NUKES
Nuclear weapons were invented during World War II. Tens of thousands of nuclear weapons have been built; eight or nine countries possess at least a few. Obtaining fissionable material is the main difficulty in making nuclear weapons. The worldwide nuclear industry—ranging from commercial plants to weapons facilities—is a key security concern since September 2001. Here a Florida sheriff guards a nuclear power plant, 2001.

those bombs were crude, low-yield weapons. But they are the kind of weapon that might be built by a relatively poor state or a nonstate actor.

Fusion weapons are extremely expensive and technically demanding; they provide leverage for only the richest, largest, most technologically capable states. In fusion weapons, two small atoms (variants of hydrogen) fuse together into a larger atom, releasing energy. This reaction occurs only at very high temperatures (the sun "burns" hydrogen through fusion). Weapons designers use fission weapons to create these high energies and trigger an explosive fusion reaction. The explosive power of most fission weapons is between 1 and 200 kilotonnes (each kilotonne is the equivalent of 1000 tonnes of conventional explosive). The power of fusion weapons is typically 1 to 20 megatonnes (a megaton is 1000 kilotonnes). In the post–Cold War era fusion weapons have become less important.

The effects of nuclear weapons include not only the blast of the explosion, but also heat and radiation. Heat can potentially create a self-sustaining firestorm in a city. Radiation creates radiation sickness, which at high doses kills people in a few days and at low doses creates long-term health problems, especially cancers. Radiation is most intense in the local vicinity of (and downwind from) a nuclear explosion, but some is carried up into the atmosphere and falls in more distant locations as nuclear fallout. Nuclear weapons also create an electromagnetic pulse (EMP) that can disrupt and destroy electronic equipment (some weapons are designed to maximize this effect). Using many nuclear weapons at once (as in a war) would also have substantial effects on global climate—possibly a nuclear winter in which years of colder and darker conditions would trigger an environmental catastrophe.

Ballistic Missiles and Other Delivery Systems

Delivery systems for getting nuclear weapons to their targets—much more than the weapons themselves—are the basis of states' nuclear arsenals and strategies (discussed shortly). Inasmuch as nuclear warheads can be made quite small—weighing a few hundred kilograms or even less—they are adaptable to a wide variety of delivery systems.

During the Cold War, nuclear delivery systems were divided into two categories. *Strategic* weapons were those that could hit an enemy's homeland, usually at long range (for instance, Moscow from Nebraska). Once carried on long-range bombers, they now are carried mainly on missiles. *Tactical* nuclear weapons were those designed for battlefield use in a theatre of military engagement. In the Cold War years, both superpowers integrated tactical nuclear weapons into their conventional air, sea, and land forces using a variety of delivery systems—gravity bombs, artillery shells, short-range missiles, land mines, depth charges, and so forth. As with all conventional forces, missiles assumed a greater role over time, and nuclear warheads were paired with short-range ground-to-ground missiles, ship-to-ship missiles, air-to-ground missiles, ground-to-air missiles, and so forth. Some conventional weapons systems were dual use, carrying either nuclear or conventional warheads.

The integration of nuclear weapons into conventional forces was meant to deter a conventional war, such as a Soviet invasion of Western Europe. In part, military planners simply found nuclear weapons cost-effective. From a strictly military view, if an enemy tank column were advancing, if an enemy airfield had to be neutralized, if an aircraft carrier had to be taken out of the picture, the result would be faster and more reliable using tactical nuclear weapons than it would using conventional weapons. However, the tens of thousands of nuclear warheads integrated into superpower conventional forces posed dangers such as theft or accident. Their actual use would have entailed grave risks of escalation to strategic nuclear war, putting home cities at risk. Thus, both superpowers phased out tactical nuclear weapons almost entirely when the Cold War ended. The tactical weapons deployed in the former Soviet republics were shipped back to Russia for storage and eventual disassembly.

The main strategic delivery vehicles are **ballistic missiles**; unlike airplanes, they are extremely difficult to defend against. Ballistic missiles carry a warhead up along a trajectory and let it drop on the target. A trajectory typically rises out of the atmosphere—at least 80 kilometres high—before descending. A powerful rocket is needed, and a guidance system adjusts the trajectory so that the warhead drops closer to the target. Various ballistic missiles differ in their range, accuracy, and throw weight (how heavy a warhead they can carry). In addition, some missiles fire from fixed sites, whereas others are mobile (making them hard to target).

Figure 6.2 Expanding Ranges of Indian and Pakistani Missiles, 1998–2003

Source: Washington Post 29 May 1999: A32, Table 6.3.

ballistic missiles The major strategic delivery vehicles for nuclear weapons; they carry a warhead along a trajectory (typically rising at least 80 kilometres high) and let it drop on the target.

intercontinental ballistic missiles (ICBMs) The longest-range ballistic missiles, able to travel 8000 kilometres.

The longest-range missiles are **intercontinental ballistic missiles (ICBMs)** with ranges over 8000 kilometres (the distance from Chicago to Moscow). Some carry up to ten warheads that can hit different targets. Most ICBMs are owned by the United States and Russia, a few by China. Intermediate- and medium-range missiles have ranges from about 1600 to a 5000 kilometres. They include most submarine-launched ballistic missiles (SLBMs) and most of the British, French, and Chinese missiles (and some U.S. and Russian ones). The U.S. and Soviet intermediate nuclear weapons deployed in Europe were eliminated under the 1987 Intermediate Nuclear Forces (INF) Treaty.

Of special interest today are short-range ballistic missiles (SRBMs) with ranges of well under 1600 kilometres. The modified scud missiles fired by Iraq at Saudi Arabia and Israel during the Gulf War were (conventionally armed) SRBMs. In regional conflicts, the long range of more powerful missiles may not be necessary. The largest cities of Syria and Israel are only 214 kilometres from each other; the capital cities of Iraq and Iran are less than 800 kilometres apart, as are those of India and Pakistan, as shown in Figure 6.2. All these states own ballistic missiles. Short-range and some medium-range ballistic missiles are cheap enough to be obtained and even home-produced by small middle-income states. Table 6.2 lists the capabilities of the 27 states with ballistic missiles.

Many short-range ballistic missiles, including those used by Iraq during the Gulf War, are highly inaccurate but still very difficult to defend against.[25] With conventional warheads they have more psychological than military utility (demoralizing an enemy population by attacking cities indiscriminately). With nuclear, chemical, or biological warheads, however, these missiles could be deadlier. A number of states now possess short-range ballistic missiles armed with weapons of mass destruction, but none has ever been used.

[25] Theodore A. Postol, "Lessons of the Gulf War Experience with Patriot," *International Security* 16.3 (1991–92): 119–71.

Table 6.2 Ballistic Missile Capabilities, 2004

Country	Range (Kilometres)		Potential Targets
United States[a]	21 000		(World)
Russia[a]	21 000		(World)
China[a]	21 000		(World)
Britain[a]	7 400		(World; submarine-launched)
France[a]	6 000		(World; submarine-launched)
North Korea[a]	1 290	[5 600]	South Korea, Russia, China [All Asia]
Iran[b]	480	[5 600]	Iraq, Kuwait, Afghanistan [Europe to Asia]
India[a,c]	2 400	[3 200]	Pakistan, China, Afghanistan, Iran, Turkey
Pakistan[a]	1 290	[3 200]	India [Russia, Turkey, Israel]
Saudi Arabia	2 700		Iran, Iraq, Syria, Israel, Turkey, Yemen, Egypt, Libya, Sudan
Israel[a,c]	1 450	[2 400]	Syria, Iraq, Saudi Arabia, Egypt
Libya	320	[965]	[Egypt, Sudan, Tunisia, Algeria]
Syria	480	[650]	Israel, Jordan, Iraq, Turkey
Egypt	480	[650]	Libya, Sudan, Israel
Yemen	320		Saudi Arabia
United Arab Emirates	320		Saudi Arabia, Iran
Afghanistan	320		Pakistan, Tajikistan, Uzbekistan
Kazakhstan	320		Uzbekistan, Tajikistan, Kyrgyzstan, Russia
Turkmenistan	320		Iran, Afghanistan, Uzbekistan, Tajikistan
Armenia	320		Azerbaijan
Azerbaijan	320		Armenia
Georgia	320		Russia, Armenia, Azerbaijan
Belarus	320		Russia, Ukraine, Poland
Ukraine	320		Russia, Belarus, Poland, Hungary, Romania
Slovakia	320		Czech Rep., Hungary, Poland, Ukraine
Democratic Congo	320		Congo Republic
South Korea	320		North Korea
Vietnam	320		China, Cambodia
Taiwan	130	[320]	China
Greece	160		Turkey
Turkey	160		Greece
Argentina	160		Brazil
Bahrain	[160]		[Saudi Arabia, Qatar]
Japan[c]	—		

Number of states with ballistic missiles: 33

[a] States that have nuclear weapons.
[b] States believed to be trying to build nuclear weapons.
[c] States developing space-launch missiles adaptable as long-range ballistic missiles.
[d] Iraq's missile capability was supposedly destroyed after the Gulf War.

Notes: Bracketed range numbers indicate missiles under development. List of potential targets includes both hostile and friendly states, and is suggestive rather than comprehensive. Missile ranges increase with smaller payloads. 320-km ranges (scud-B) and 480-km ranges (scud Mod-C) are approximate for a 0.7-tonne payload. Saudi range is for a 1.8-tonne payload; South Korean range is for a half-tonne payload.
Source: Carnegie Endowment for International Peace.

The accuracy of delivery systems of all ranges improves as one moves to great powers, especially the United States. After travelling thousands of kilometres, the best U.S. missiles can land within 15 metres of a target half of the time. The trend in the U.S. nuclear arsenal has been toward less-powerful warheads but more accurate missiles, for flexibility.

The newest capable class of delivery system is the **cruise missile.** This is a small, winged missile that can navigate across thousands of kilometres of previously mapped terrain to reach a particular target. Cruise missiles can be launched from ships, submarines, airplanes, or land. As a nuclear-weapon vehicle, it is owned only by the United States and Russia, but several states have developed conventionally armed versions. Argentina hit a British warship with a French-made cruise missile in the 1982 Falklands/Malvinas war. U.S. leaders have discovered that conventionally armed cruise missiles can attack distant targets without risking U.S. lives—a politically safe strategy used increasingly in recent years. In 1993, President Bill Clinton attacked the Iraqi intelligence headquarters with dozens of cruise missiles fired from hundreds of kilometres away—the first all-cruise-missile attack in history. The United States used cruise missiles extensively against Serbian forces in Bosnia in 1995, against Serbia in 1999, Iraq in 2003, and for smaller-scale strikes such as at terrorist Osama bin Laden's base in Afghanistan in 1998.

Conceivably, small states or substate groups that may acquire nuclear weapons in the future could deliver them through innovative means. Because nuclear weapons are small, one could be smuggled into a target state by car, by speedboat, or in diplomatic pouches, and then detonated like any terrorist bomb. One advantage of such methods would be the ease of concealing the identity of the perpetrator.

In all the world's nuclear arsenals, delivery systems include special provisions for command and control.[26] Because the weapons are so dangerous, control is highly centralized. In the United States and Russia, each president is accompanied everywhere by a military officer carrying a briefcase with the secret codes required to order such an attack. So far, at least, control procedures have succeeded in preventing any accidental or unauthorized use of nuclear weapons.

cruise missile A small, winged missile that can navigate across thousands of kilometres of previously mapped terrain to reach a particular target; it can carry either a nuclear or a conventional warhead.

Chemical and Biological Weapons

Several times during the 1991 Gulf War, most of the population of Israel—millions of people—spent nights huddled in special sealed-off rooms in their houses, wearing gas masks and putting infants into little tents. This action was caused by fear of chemical weapons on Iraqi missiles (which turned out to have only conventional warheads).

A *chemical weapon* releases chemicals that disable and kill people.[27] A variety of chemicals can be used, from lethal ones such as nerve gas to merely irritating ones such as tear gas. Different chemicals interfere with the nervous system, blood, breathing, or other body functions. Some can be absorbed through the skin; others must be inhaled. Some persist in the target area long after their use; others disperse quickly.

It is possible to defend against most chemical weapons by dressing troops in protective clothing and gas masks and following elaborate procedures to decontaminate equipment. But protective suits are hot, and antichemical measures reduce the efficiency of

[26] Scott D. Sagan, *The Limits of Safety: Organizations, Accidents, and Nuclear Weapons* (Princeton, NJ: Princeton UP, 1993). Janne E. Nolan, *Guardians of the Arsenal: The Politics of Nuclear Strategy* (NY: Basic, 1989). C. Kenneth Allard, *Command, Control, and the Common Defense* (New Haven, CT: Yale UP, 1990).

[27] Richard M. Price, *The Chemical Weapons Taboo* (Ithaca, NY: Cornell UP, 1997). Valerie Adams, *Chemical Warfare, Chemical Disarmament* (Bloomington: Indiana UP, 1990). Trevor Findlay, ed., *Chemical Weapons and Missile Proliferation: With Implications for the Asia/Pacific Region* (Boulder, CO: Rienner, 1991).

armies. Civilians are much less likely to have protection against chemicals than are military forces (the well-prepared Israeli civilians were an exception). Chemical weapons are by nature indiscriminate about whom they kill. Several times, chemical weapons have been deliberately used against civilians (most recently by the Iraqi government against Iraqi Kurds in the 1980s).

Use of chemical weapons in war has been rare. Mustard gas, which produces skin blisters and lung damage, was widely used (in artillery shells) in World War I. After the horrors of that war, the use of chemical weapons was banned in the 1925 Geneva protocol, a treaty that is still in effect. In World War II, both sides were armed with chemical weapons but neither used them, for fear of retaliation. Since then (with possibly a few unclear exceptions) only Iraq has violated the treaty—against Iran in the 1980s. Unfortunately, Iraq's actions not only breached a psychological barrier against using chemical weapons, but also showed such weapons to be cheap and effective against human waves of attacking soldiers without protective gear. This example stimulated more states to begin acquiring chemical weapons. Dozens now have them. During the Gulf War, Iraq deployed but apparently did not use chemical weapons. However, bombing of an Iraqi chemical weapons depot exposed thousands of U.S. troops to chemicals; a link to Gulf War Syndrome (mysterious illnesses affecting veterans of the war) has been suspected but not proven. In the 2003 Iraq War, again Iraq did not use chemical weapons, and neither were stockpiles of chemical weapons discovered.

Chemical weapons are a cheap way for states to gain weapons of mass destruction as potential leverage in international conflicts. Chemical weapons can be produced using processes and facilities similar to those for pesticides, pharmaceuticals, and other civilian products. It is difficult to locate chemical weapons facilities in suspect countries, or to deny those states access to the needed chemicals and equipment. In 1998, a U.S. cruise missile attack destroyed a suspected weapons facility in Sudan that apparently was only a pharmaceutical factory.

The 1925 treaty did not ban the production or possession of chemical weapons, and several dozen states built stockpiles of them. The United States and the Soviet Union maintained large arsenals of chemical weapons during the Cold War but have reduced them greatly in the past decade. In 1992, a new **Chemical Weapons Convention** to ban the production and possession of chemical weapons was concluded after years of negotiation; it has been signed by all but 14 states, including all the great powers (but not by Egypt, Syria, Libya, Iraq, or North Korea). The new treaty includes strict verification provisions and the threat of sanctions against violators including (an important extension) those who are nonparticipants in the treaty. It went into effect in 1997 and the U.S. Senate approved ratification at the last minute. Opponents argued that the treaty would be ineffective, but within months several states (including India, China, South Korea, France, and Britain) admitted to having secret chemical weapons programs, which will now be dismantled under international oversight. Russia still faces very costly and long-term work to destroy a 40 000-tonne arsenal of chemical weapons built during the Cold War. From 1997 to 2002, the treaty organization oversaw the elimination of about one-sixth of the world's chemical weapons.

Biological weapons resemble chemical ones, except that instead of chemicals they use micro-organisms or biologically derived toxins. Some use viruses or bacteria that cause fatal diseases, such as smallpox, bubonic plague, and anthrax. Others cause nonfatal, but incapacitating, diseases or diseases that kill livestock. Theoretically, a single weapon could spark an epidemic in an entire population, but this is considered too dangerous and use of less-contagious micro-organisms is preferred. Biological weapons have virtually never been used in war (Japan tried some on a few Chinese villages in World War II). Their potential strikes many political leaders as a Pandora's box that could let loose uncontrollable forces if opened.

Chemical Weapons Convention (1992) Treaty that bans the production and possession of chemical weapons, and includes strict verification provisions and the threat of sanctions against violators, including nonparticipants in the treaty.

VULNERABLE
Civilians are more vulnerable to chemical weapons than soldiers are. A 1992 treaty aims to ban chemical weapons worldwide. Here, Israeli kindergarteners prepare against a chemical warfare threat from Iraqi scud missiles during the Gulf War, 1991.

For this reason, the development, production, and possession of biological weapons are banned under the 1972 **Biological Weapons Convention,** signed by more than 100 countries including the great powers. The superpowers destroyed their stocks of biological weapons and had to restrict their biological weapons complexes to defensive research rather than the development of weapons. However, because the treaty makes no provision for inspection and because biological weapons programs are, like chemical ones, relatively easy to hide, several states—including Libya and Syria—remain under suspicion of having biological weapons. Evidence surfaced after the collapse of the Soviet Union that a secret biological weapons program had been under way there. UN inspections of Iraq in the mid-1990s uncovered an active biological weapons program. However, the invasion of Iraq in 2003 discovered no weapons of mass destruction.

Anthrax spores were one of the main biological weapons produced by the secret Soviet program, and the U.S. military also produced them (to work on defences). Iraq reportedly tried to convert crop-dusters to efficiently spread the spores, which can float over a large area, lodging in the lungs of victims and germinating into bacteria that are often lethal unless treated early with antibiotics. In 1997, the U.S. military began to vaccinate all 2.4 million U.S. soldiers against anthrax, and other countries such as Canada stockpiled vaccines. In 2001, soon after the September terrorist attacks against the United States, someone sent small amounts of anthrax spores through the U.S. mail to high government and media offices, killing several people and massively disrupting mail distribution. The attack remains unsolved, but reportedly originated from anthrax stolen from the U.S. military rather than foreign terrorists. However, the September terrorists had once shown a strong interest in crop-dusters, and Al Qaeda was known to have worked on biological weapons. The episode showed that deadly biological weapons are a real threat and not a futuristic worry.

Today the United States and perhaps a dozen other countries maintain biological weapons research (not banned by the treaty). Researchers try to ascertain the military implications of advances in biotechnology. Most states doing such research claim that

Biological Weapons Convention (1972) Treaty that prohibits the development, production, and possession of biological weapons, but makes no provision for inspections.

they are doing so only to deter another state from developing biological weapons. There is a security dilemma here (see pp. 72–73) with the potential for a future arms race. But so far such a race has been avoided.[28]

Proliferation

proliferation The spread of weapons of mass destruction (nuclear, chemical, or biological weapons) into the hands of more actors.

Proliferation is the spread of weapons of mass destruction—nuclear weapons, ballistic missiles, and chemical or biological weapons—into the hands of more actors. Some poor states and middle powers want ballistic missiles capable of delivering nuclear weapons—or if that is infeasible, then chemical or biological weapons. Such capability provides states with a potentially powerful means of leverage in international conflicts—a threat to cause extreme damage that is impossible to defend against. Because the only practical counter-leverage is a threat to retaliate in kind, states also want ballistic missiles with weapons of mass destruction in order to deter their use by others. This causes a security dilemma (as in the India-Pakistan example discussed on pp. 70–71).

The implications of proliferation for international relations are difficult to predict but evidently profound. Ballistic missiles with weapons of mass destruction remove the territorial protection offered by state borders and make each state vulnerable to others. Some realists, who believe in the basic rationality of state actions, are not so upset by this prospect, and some even welcome it. They reason that in a world where the use of military force could lead to mutual annihilation, there would be fewer wars—just as during the superpower arms race of the Cold War. Other IR scholars who put less faith in the rationality of state leaders are much more alarmed by proliferation. They fear that with more and more nuclear (or chemical/biological) actors, miscalculation or accident—or fanatical terrorism—could lead to the use of weapons of mass destruction on a scale unseen since 1945.[29] Some suggest that "rogue" states cannot be counted on to act rationally. Critics of this latter view often point out that only one state has ever actually used nuclear weapons on civilian targets—the United States, not normally characterized as a "rogue."

There is also a widespread fear that these weapons may fall into the hands of terrorists or other nonstate actors who would be immune from threats of retaliation (with no territory or cities to defend). Evidence captured during the 2001 war in Afghanistan showed that the Al Qaeda organization was trying to obtain weapons of mass destruction and would be willing to use them. Lax security at the vast, far-flung former Soviet nuclear complex in the 1990s has increased fears that fissionable materials could reach terrorists.[30]

---

[28] Joshua Lederberg, ed., *Biological Weapons: Limiting the Threat* (Cambridge, MA: MIT P, 1999). Jonathan B. Tucker, ed., *Toxic Terror: Assessing Terrorist Use of Chemical and Biological Weapons.* (Cambridge, MA: MIT P, 2000). Ken Alibek with Stephen Handelman, *Biohazard: The Chilling True Story of the Largest Covert Biological Weapons Program in the World—Told from Inside by the Man Who Ran It* (NY: Random House, 1999). Andrew T. Price-Smith, ed., *Plagues and Politics: Infectious Diseases and International Policy* (NY: Palgrave, 2001). Andrew T. Price-Smith, *The Health of Nations* (Cambridge, MA: MIT P, 2001).

[29] Devin T. Hagerty, *The Consequences of Nuclear Proliferation: Lessons from South Asia* (Cambridge, MA: MIT P, 1998). T. V. Paul, Richard J. Harknett, and James J. Wirtz, eds., *The Absolute Weapon Revisited* (Ann Arbor: U Michigan P, 1998). David Mutimer, *The Weapons State: Proliferation and the Framing of Security* (Boulder, CO: Rienner, 1999). Leonard S. Spector, Gregory P. Webb, and Mark G. McDonough, *Tracking Nuclear Proliferation: A Guide in Maps and Charts, 1998* (Washington, DC: Brookings/Carnegie Endowment for International Peace, 1998).

[30] Peter Finn, "Experts Discuss Chances of Nuclear Terrorism," *Washington Post* 3 Nov. 2001: A19. Steven Erlanger, "Lax Nuclear Security in Russia Is Cited as Way for bin Laden to Get Arms," *New York Times* 12 Nov. 2001: B1. Nadine Gur and Benjamin Cole, *The New Face of Terrorism: Threats from Weapons of Mass Destruction* (NY: Tauris, 2000). Richard A. Falkenrath, Robert D. Newman, and Bradley A. Thayer, *America's Achilles' Heel: Nuclear, Biological, and Chemical Terrorism and Covert Attack* (Cambridge, MA: MIT P, 1998).

However, states that sell technology with proliferation potential can make money doing so. For example, in the mid-1990s the United States pressured both Russia and China to stop selling nuclear technology to Iran (which the United States said was trying to build nuclear weapons). Russia and China would have to give up hundreds of millions of dollars in sales. Industrialized states have competed to sell technology and have simultaneously worked to restrain such sales by other states. This is another international collective-goods problem (see p. 91), in which states pursuing their individual interests end up collectively worse off.

Nuclear proliferation could occur simply by a state or nonstate actor's buying (or stealing) one or more nuclear weapons or the components to build one. The means to prevent this range from covert intelligence to tight security measures to safeguards preventing a stolen weapon from being used. But the economic crisis in Russia in the 1990s left vulnerable hundreds of tonnes of Russian fissile materials in the control of underpaid civilian workers and military officers at poorly funded facilities with lax security and recurrent corruption. In 2002, the G8 countries pledged US$20 billion to address the problem, but a 2003 study by 21 research groups found little had been spent and problems remained rampant. The study focused on 100 insecure research reactors with weapons-grade uranium in 40 countries.

A more lasting form of nuclear proliferation is the development by states of nuclear complexes to produce their own nuclear weapons on an ongoing basis.[31] Here larger numbers of weapons are involved, and there are strong potentials for arms races in regional conflicts and rivalries. The relevant regional conflicts are those between Israel and the Arab states, Iran and its neighbours, India and Pakistan,[32] the two Koreas, and possibly Taiwan and China. India and Pakistan both have exploded nuclear devices underground, and are moving forward to build arsenals and the missiles to deliver them. In addition, South Africa reported after the fact that it had built several nuclear weapons but then dismantled them in the 1980s (while still under white minority rule).

Israel has never test-exploded nuclear weapons or admitted it has them. It claims simply that "Israel will not be the first country to introduce nuclear weapons into the region" (which might imply that weapons hidden away have not been "introduced"). In fact, Israel is widely believed to have a hundred or more nuclear warheads on combat airplanes and medium-range missiles. Israel wants these capabilities to use as a last resort if it were about to be conquered by its neighbours.[33] By implicitly threatening such action, Israeli leaders hope to convince Arab leaders that a military conquest of Israel is impossible. But by keeping its weapons secret, Israel tries to minimize the provocation to its neighbours to develop their own nuclear weapons. To prevent Iraq from doing so, Israel carried out a bombing raid on the main facility of the Iraqi nuclear complex in 1981. Without this raid, Iraq probably would have had nuclear weapons by the time of the Gulf War.

Efforts to limit the development of nuclear complexes by these states hinge on stopping the flow of necessary materials and expertise—such as enriched uranium, enrichment equipment, electronic timers, and nuclear engineers. A particular fear in the 1990s

---

[31] Itty Abraham, *The Making of the Indian Atomic Bomb: Science, Secrecy, and the Post-Colonial State* (NY: Zed/St. Martin's, 1998). George Perkovich, *India's Nuclear Bomb: The Impact on Global Proliferation* (Berkeley: U California P, 1999). John Wilson Lewis and Xus Litai, *China Builds the Bomb* (Palo Alto, CA: Stanford UP, 1988).

[32] David Albright and Mark Hibbs, "India's Silent Bomb," *Bulletin of the Atomic Scientists* 48.7 (1992): 27–31. David Albright and Mark Hibbs, "Pakistan's Bomb: Out of the Closet," *Bulletin of the Atomic Scientists* 48.6 (1992): 38–43.

[33] Avner Cohen, *Israel and the Bomb* (NY: Columbia UP, 1998).

was that the nuclear complex of the former Soviet Union could be a source of fissionable material, equipment, or nuclear expertise. Since 1991, hundreds of attempts to smuggle uranium or plutonium from the former Soviet Union have been reported. We do not know whether any such attempts succeeded.

Non-Proliferation Treaty (NPT) (1968) Treaty that created a framework for controlling the spread of nuclear materials and expertise, including the International Atomic Energy Agency (IAEA), a UN agency based in Vienna that is charged with inspecting the nuclear power industry in NPT member states to prevent secret military diversions of nuclear materials.

The **Non-Proliferation Treaty (NPT)** of 1968 created a framework for controlling the spread of nuclear materials and expertise.[34] The International Atomic Energy Agency (IAEA), a UN agency based in Vienna, is charged with inspecting the nuclear power industry in member states to prevent secret military diversions of nuclear materials. However, a number of potential nuclear states (such as Israel) have not signed the NPT, and even those states that have signed may sneak around its provisions by keeping some facilities secret (as Iraq did). Under the terms of the Gulf War ceasefire, Iraq's nuclear program was uncovered and dismantled by the IAEA.[35]

North Korea withdrew from the IAEA in 1993, then bargained with Western leaders to get economic assistance, including safer reactors, in exchange for freezing its nuclear program. North Korea's leader died months later, but the compromise held up. In the late 1990s, North Korea's economic collapse and food crisis combined with the nuclear issue to make the country especially worrisome for Western leaders. Despite fears that its leaders were just playing for time and aid to prop up a failed regime, in 1999 North Korea allowed inspection of a disputed underground complex and agreed to suspend missile tests, in exchange for aid and partial lifting of U.S. trade sanctions.[36]

This hopeful picture was revealed as false, however, in 2002, when the United States confronted North Korea with evidence of a secret nuclear enrichment program and the North Koreans admitted it. As relations deteriorated, North Korea pulled out of the agreement and of the IAEA, restarted its nuclear reactor, and threatened to turn existing plutonium into a half dozen bombs within months. U.S. monitoring detected certain molecules indicative of plutonium reprocessing, and North Korea then announced it had finished. Although proof is lacking—unless or until North Korea tests a bomb—there is every reason to believe that North Korea is the world's ninth nuclear weapons power.

Nonetheless, nuclear proliferation has been less widespread than was feared decades ago. The five permanent members of the Security Council, who all had nuclear weapons by 1964, have continued to make up the nuclear club of states with large, openly acknowledged arsenals. A number of middle powers and two great powers (Japan and Germany) have the potential to make nuclear weapons but have chosen not to do so. The reasons for deciding against "going nuclear" include norms against using nuclear weapons, fears of retaliation, and practical constraints including cost. Several republics of the former Soviet Union have recently been added to the nonnuclear-by-choice category. Ukraine dragged its feet on commitments to get rid of strategic nuclear missiles—hoping to use them as bargaining chips to obtain Western aid and security guarantees—but ultimately came around.

At present, undeclared nuclear powers include Israel (with perhaps a hundred warheads) and North Korea (with perhaps a half dozen). Declared nuclear states are India and Pakistan (with dozens each, and growing). Iran has been singled out by the United States for trying to develop nuclear weapons (as it had begun to do under the shah in the 1970s),

---

[34] Richard Kokoski, *Technology and the Proliferation of Nuclear Weapons* (NY: Oxford UP/SIPRI, 1996). Ian Bellany, Coit D. Blacker, and Joseph Gallacher, eds., *The Nuclear Non-Proliferation Treaty* (Totowa, NJ: F. Cass, 1985).

[35] David Albright and Mark Hibbs, "Iraq's Nuclear Hide-and-Seek," *Bulletin of the Atomic Scientists* 47.7 (1991): 14–23.

[36] Leon V. Sigal, *Disarming Strangers: Nuclear Diplomacy with North Korea* (Princeton, NJ: Princeton UP, 1999).

but in 2003 agreed to suspend its uranium enrichment program and allow surprise IAEA inspections. Brazil and Argentina seemed to be headed for a nuclear arms race in the 1980s but then called it off as civilians replaced military governments in both countries.[37]

In 1995, the NPT came up for a 25-year review. In that period, the nonnuclear states were supposed to stay nonnuclear; they had largely done so, except for Israel, India, and Pakistan, which had never signed the treaty. The nuclear states were supposed to undertake serious nuclear disarmament; they had largely failed to do so until the 1990s, and still possessed far more potent nuclear arsenals than 25 years earlier. Despite these complaints, the 172 signers of the treaty agreed in 1995 to extend it indefinitely.

The proliferation of ballistic missiles has been more difficult to control.[38] There is a **Missile Technology Control Regime** through which industrialized states try to limit the flow of missile-relevant technology to states of the global South. One success was the interruption of an Egyptian-Argentinean-Iraqi partnership in the 1980s to develop a medium-range missile. West German companies were induced to stop selling technology secretly to the project. But, in general, the regime has been less successful. Short- and medium-range missiles (ranges up to about 3200 kilometres) apparently are being developed by Iran, Israel, Saudi Arabia, Pakistan, India, North Korea, and possibly Argentina and Brazil. Soviet-made short-range ballistic missiles are owned by a number of states in the global South. China has sold its missiles and technology to some countries of the South (bringing lower prices to buyers and hard currency to China)—a sore point in relations with the West.[39]

HOT STUFF

The most important hurdle in making nuclear weapons is access to fissionable materials (plutonium and uranium). In 2003, North Korea restarted its plutonium-producing reactor at Yongbyon, shut down since 1994, and apparently produced a half-dozen bombs from it, becoming the world's ninth nuclear-armed state. This 1996 photo, released in 2003, shows the nuclear fuel rods in a cooling pond at Yongbyon.

Missile Technology Control Regime A set of agreements through which industrialized states try to limit the flow of missile-relevant technology to states of the global South.

Nuclear Strategy

Certainly the decision to acquire or forgo nuclear weapons is the most fundamental aspect of a state's *nuclear strategy*. But the term generally is applied to states that have already decided to acquire nuclear weapons; it refers to their decisions about how many nuclear

---

[37] Paul L. Leventhal and Sharon Tanzer, eds., *Averting a Latin American Nuclear Arms Race: New Prospects and Challenges for Argentine-Brazil Nuclear Cooperation* (NY: St. Martin's, 1992).

[38] Aaron Karp, *Ballistic Missile Proliferation: The Politics and Technics*. (NY: Oxford UP/SIPRI, 1996). Steve Fetter, "Ballistic Missiles and Weapons of Mass Destruction: What Is the Threat? What Should Be Done?" *International Security* 16.1 (1991): 5–42. Janne E. Nolan, *Trappings of Power: Ballistic Missiles in the Third World* (Washington, DC: Brookings, 1991).

[39] Richard A. Bitzinger, "Arms to Go: Chinese Arms Sales to the Third World," *International Security* 17.2 (1992): 84–111.

THE RACE IS ON
India and Pakistan are building arsenals of nuclear-tipped missiles that could devastate each other's main cities. Their current arms race follows that of the superpowers during the Cold War. Superpower arms control agreements helped develop norms and expectations about the role of nuclear weapons, but did not stop a buildup of tens of thousands of nuclear weapons. Here, India shows off its new intermediate-range ballistic missile, 1999.

weapons to deploy, what delivery systems to put them on, and what policies to adopt regarding the circumstances in which they would be used.[40]

The reason for possessing nuclear weapons is almost always to deter another state from a nuclear or conventional attack by threatening ruinous retaliation. This should work if state leaders are rational actors wanting to avoid the huge costs of a nuclear attack. But it will work only if other states believe that a state's threat to use nuclear weapons is credible. The search for a credible deterrent by two or more hostile states tends to lead to an ever-growing arsenal of nuclear weapons. To follow this logic, start with Pakistan's deployment of its first nuclear missile aimed at India (the example also works with the countries reversed). Then India would not attack—that is, unless it could prevent Pakistan from using its missile. India could do this by building offensive forces capable of wiping out the Pakistani missile (probably using nuclear weapons, but that is not the key point here). Then the Pakistani missile, rather than deter India, would merely spur India to destroy the missile before any other attack. An attack intended to destroy—largely or entirely—a state's nuclear weapons before they can be used is called a *first strike*.

---

[40] Charles L. Glaser, *Analyzing Strategic Nuclear Policy* (Princeton, NJ: Princeton UP, 1990). Scott D. Sagan, *Moving Targets: Nuclear Strategy and National Security* (Princeton, NJ: Princeton UP, 1989). Joseph S. Nye, Graham T. Allison, and Albert Carnesdale, eds., *Fateful Visions: Avoiding Nuclear Catastrophe* (Cambridge, MA: Ballinger, 1988). Edward Rhodes, *Power and Madness: The Logic of Nuclear Coercion* (NY: Columbia UP, 1989). Robert Jervis, *The Meaning of the Nuclear Revolution: Statecraft and the Prospect of Armageddon* (Ithaca, NY: Cornell UP, 1989). Steven Kull, *Minds at War* (NY: Basic, 1988). Strobe Talbott, *The Master of the Game: Paul Nitze and the Nuclear Peace* (NY: Knopf, 1988).

Pakistan could make its missile survivable (probably by making it mobile). It could also build more nuclear missiles so that even if some were destroyed in an Indian first strike, some would survive with which to retaliate. Weapons that can take a first strike and still strike back give a state *second-strike* capabilities. A state that deploys the fewest nuclear forces needed for an assured second-strike capability (between tens and hundreds) has a minimum deterrent. Possession of second-strike capabilities by both sides is called **mutually assured destruction (MAD)** because neither side can prevent the other from destroying it. The term implies that the strategy, though reflecting "rationality," is actually insane (mad) because deviations from rationality could destroy both sides.

If India could not assuredly *destroy* Pakistan's missile, it would undoubtedly deploy its own nuclear missile(s) to *deter* Pakistan from using its missile. India, too, could achieve a second-strike capability. Now the question of credibility becomes important. In theory, India could launch a nonnuclear attack on Pakistan, knowing that rational Pakistani leaders would rather lose such a war than use their nuclear weapons and bring on an Indian nuclear response. The nuclear missiles in effect cancel each other out.

During the Cold War, this was the problem faced by U.S. war planners trying to deter a Soviet conventional attack on Western Europe. They could threaten to use nuclear weapons in response, but rational Soviet leaders would know that rational U.S. leaders would never act on such a threat and risk escalation to global nuclear war. Better to lose West Germany, according to this line of thinking, than lose both West Germany and New York. U.S. planners thus tried to convince the Soviets that such an attack would be too risky. They did this by integrating thousands of tactical nuclear weapons into conventional forces so that the escalation to nuclear war might happen more or less automatically in the event of conventional war. This was the equivalent of "throwing away the steering wheel" in a game of chicken (see p. 71). China currently uses a similar form of "rational irrationality" in its relations with Taiwan, trying to make credible the threat of war (which would be disastrous for China as well as Taiwan) if Taiwan declares independence (see p. 63).

Nuclear *warfighting,* or *counterforce,* specifically targets the other state's forces. Without such a capability, a state's only available lever is to blow up another state's cities—a countervalue capability (targeting something of value to the other side). The trouble with nuclear warfighting forces, however, is that they must be very accurate, powerful, and massive in order to successfully knock out the other side's nuclear weapons. This makes them effective first-strike weapons—very threatening to the other state and likely to provoke a further buildup of the other state's weapons in response. First-strike weapons are considered inherently unstable in a crisis because they are so threatening that the other side would be tempted to attack them quickly in a first strike of its own. Knowing that this could happen, the first state would itself be tempted to launch its weapons before such an attack—"use 'em or lose 'em."[41]

The problem is accentuated by the use of multiple warheads on a single missile (multiple independently targeted re-entry vehicles, or MIRVs). The more warheads on a missile, the more tempting a target it makes for the other side. (One successful strike can prevent multiple enemy strikes.) Thus, fixed land-based MIRVed missiles are considered destabilizing weapons. In the 1992 START II treaty (ratified in 2000), the United States and Russia agreed to phase them out.

Some of the language associated with nuclear weapons is also discussed by IR theorists. Particularly for critical theorists, calling strikes against cities and people a "counter-

> **mutually assured destruction (MAD)** The possession of second-strike nuclear capabilities, which ensures that neither of two adversaries could prevent the other from destroying it in an all-out war. See also *deterrence.*

[41] R. Harrison Wagner, "Nuclear Deterrence, Counterforce Strategies, and the Incentive to Strike First," *American Political Science Review* 85.3 (1991): 727–50.

value" attack (versus the "counterforce" targeting of military installations), or describing unintended strikes against civilian targets as "collateral damage," is a way to sanitize the impact of a nuclear attack. The use of even one nuclear weapon would be catastrophic; it would involve the incineration of tens of thousands of people and untold long-term suffering. Some critical theorists argue that the language used by strategic thinkers (and theorists) makes it easy to think about the possibility of nuclear war without really considering its actual consequences.[42]

Defence has played little role in nuclear strategy because no effective defence against missile attack has been devised. However, the United States is spending billions of dollars a year to try to develop defences that could shoot down incoming ballistic missiles. The program is called the **Strategic Defense Initiative (SDI),** "star wars," or "Ballistic Missile Defense" (BMD). It originated in President Ronald Reagan's 1983 call for a comprehensive shield that would make nuclear missiles obsolete.[43] However, the mission soon shifted to a (slightly) more realistic one of defending some U.S. missiles in a massive Soviet attack. After the Cold War the mission shifted again, to one of protecting U.S. territory from a very limited missile attack (at most a few missiles), such as might occur in an unauthorized launch, an accident, or an attack by a small state.

Current plans call for beginning within years to deploy ground-based, nonnuclear missiles to try to intercept incoming warheads. To proceed with this system, the Bush Administration in late 2001 formally signalled that it would withdraw from the Anti-Ballistic Missile Treaty with Russia (see p. 273), which it did in 2002. Allies such as Canada have expressed support for the U.S. project (also called National Missile Defense, or NMD).

Japan plans to spend $1 billion a year to build a U.S.-designed missile defence system by 2007, based on land and at sea. However, North Korea has more than 600 ballistic missiles capable of hitting Japan. In 2004, the United States began deploying both a prototype missile intercept system based in Alaska and a destroyer in the Sea of Japan, off North Korea, that could try to shoot down a North Korean missile in its boost phase after launch (when their engines make them easy to detect, and warheads and decoys have not yet deployed). It also moved to put in place—against the strong opposition of China—a missile-defence collaboration in Asia that would include Japan, Australia, possibly India, and Taiwan. Four Japanese destroyers are to join the U.S. one, and Patriot missiles based in Japan would try to shoot down incoming missiles.

Other technologies are also being tested, including lasers fired from either space or ships to disable ballistic missiles in the boost phase. Overall, no reliable defence against ballistic missiles exists, and experts disagree on whether such a defense is just a few or many years away.

In addition to the technical challenges of stopping incoming ballistic missile warheads, a true strategic defence would also have to stop cruise missiles and airplanes, if not more innovative delivery systems. Nobody has an answer to this problem.

States face complex choices regarding the configuration of their military forces in the post–Cold War era. Not only have the immediate contingencies and threats changed drastically, but the nature of threats in the new era is unknown. Perhaps most important,

Strategic Defense Initiative (SDI) A U.S. effort, also known as "star wars," to develop defences that could shoot down incoming ballistic missiles, spurred by President Ronald Reagan in 1983. Critics call it an expensive failure that would violate the ABM Treaty. See also *Anti-Ballistic Missile (ABM) Treaty.*

---

[42] Carol Cohn, "Sex and Death in the Rational World of Defense Intellectuals," *Signs: Journal of Women in Culture and Society* 12.4 (Summer 1987): 687–718.

[43] James M. Lindsay and Michael O'Hanlon, *Defending America: The Case for Limited National Missile Defense* (Washington, DC: Brookings, 2001). James Chace and Caleb Carr, *America Invulnerable: The Quest for Absolute Security from 1812 to Star Wars* (NY: Summit, 1988). David B. H. Denoon, *Ballistic Missile Defense in the Post–Cold War Era* (Boulder, CO: Westview, 1995).

world order itself is evolving even as military technologies do. The next chapter discusses the evolving structures and norms governing international political relations and how they are changing the nature of world order.

Thinking Critically

1. If you were the leader of, say, Vietnam, what size and kinds of military forces would you want your country to have? To meet what kinds of threats would you choose each type of capability?

2. Suppose that Libya turned out to have obtained three tactical nuclear warheads from the former Soviet arsenal and was keeping them in unknown locations. What, if anything, should the great powers do about this? What consequences might follow from their actions?

3. Imagine a world in which most of the states, rather than just a few, had nuclear weapons and long-range ballistic missiles. Would it be more peaceful or more war-prone? Why?

4. Most of the great powers are reconfiguring their military forces in the post–Cold War era. What kinds of capabilities do you think your own country needs in this period? Why?

5. World military spending is around US$800 billion every year. If you could redirect these funds, how would you use them? Would such uses be better or worse for the states involved? Do you think there is a realistic chance of redirecting military spending in the way you suggest?

Chapter Summary

- Military forces provide states with means of leverage beyond the various nonmilitary means of influence widely used in international bargaining.

- Political leaders face difficult choices in configuring military forces and paying for them. Military spending tends to stimulate economic growth in the short term but reduce growth over the long term.

- In the 1990s, military forces and expenditures of the great powers—especially Russia—were reduced and restructured.

- Military forces include a wide variety of capabilities suited to different purposes. Conventional warfare requires different kinds of forces than those needed to threaten the use of nuclear, chemical, or biological weapons.

- Except in time of civil war, state leaders—whether civilian or military—control military forces through a single hierarchical chain of command.

- Military forces can threaten the domestic power of state leaders, who are vulnerable to being overthrown by coups d'état.

- Control of territory is fundamental to state sovereignty and is accomplished primarily with ground forces.

- Air war, using precision-guided bombs against battlefield targets, proved extremely effective in the U.S. campaigns in Iraq in 1991, Serbia in 1999, and Afghanistan in 2001.

- Small missiles and electronic warfare are increasingly important, especially for naval and air forces. The role of satellites is expanding in communications, navigation, and reconnaissance.

- Weapons of mass destruction—nuclear, chemical, and biological—have been used only a handful of times in war.

- The production of nuclear weapons is technically within the means of many states and some nonstate actors, but the necessary fissionable material (uranium-235 or plutonium) is very difficult to obtain.

- Most industrialized states, and many poor ones, have refrained voluntarily from acquiring nuclear weapons. These states include two great powers, Germany and Japan.

- More states are acquiring ballistic missiles capable of striking other states from hundreds of kilometres away (or farther, depending on the missile's range). But no state has ever attacked another with weapons of mass destruction mounted on ballistic missiles.

- Chemical weapons are cheaper to build than nuclear weapons, they have similar threat value, and their production is harder to detect. More middle powers have chemical weapons than nuclear ones. A 1992 treaty bans the possession and use of chemical weapons.

- Several states conduct research into biological warfare, but by treaty the possession of such weapons is banned.

- Slowing the proliferation of ballistic missiles and weapons of mass destruction in the global South is a central concern of the great powers.

- The United States is testing systems to defend against ballistic missile attack, although none has yet proven feasible, and it withdrew from the ABM treaty with Russia to pursue this program.

- The United States and Russia have arsenals of thousands of nuclear weapons; China, Britain, and France have hundreds. Israel, India, and Pakistan each have scores. Weapons deployments are guided by nuclear strategy based on the concept of deterrence.

Key Terms

Weblinks

The following are a sampling of government departments, research centres, or advocacy groups that focus on different aspects of militaries and military force:

Canadian Defence and Foreign Affairs Institute:
http://www.cdfai.org

Canadian Department of National Defence:
http://www.dnd.ca

NATO:
http://www.nato.int

Nuclear Files.org:
http://www.nuclearfiles.org

Pearson Peacekeeping Centre:
http://www.peaceoperations.org

Project on Defense Alternatives:
http://www.comw.org/pda

Small Arms Survey (Geneva):
http://www.smallarmssurvey.org

International Law and Organization

7

UNHCR vehicles in Somalia, 1992.

WORLD ORDER

According to liberal pluralists (and even many realists), most international conflicts are not settled by military force. Despite the realist vision of an anarchic international system based on state sovereignty, the security dilemma does not usually lead to a breakdown in basic cooperation among states. States generally refrain from taking maximum short-term advantage of each other (such as by invading and conquering). States work *with* other states for mutual gain and take advantage of each other only "at the margin." Unfortunately the day-to-day cooperative activities of states often are less newsworthy than when states use force.

States work together by following rules they develop to govern their interactions. States usually *do* follow the rules. Over time, the rules become more firmly established and institutions grow up around them. States then develop the habit of working through those institutions and within the rules. They may do so because of self-interest; given the regulation of international interactions through institutions and rules, they can realize great gains, thereby avoiding the costly outcomes associated with a breakdown of cooperation (see pp. 91–93).

International anarchy thus does not mean a lack of order, structure, and rules. In many ways, actors in international society now work together as cooperatively as actors in domestic society—more so than some domestic societies. Today, most wars are civil, not interstate, wars; this change reflects the general success of international norms, organizations, and laws—in addition to the balance of power—in maintaining peace among states.

The Evolution of World Order

Over the centuries, international institutions and rules have grown stronger, more complex, and more important. For liberals, this means that while international order started out based largely on raw power, it has evolved to be based more on legitimacy and habit. *Domestic law,* too, was once enforced only by the most powerful for the most powerful. The first states and civilizations were largely military dictatorships. Law was what the top ruler decreed. International law and organization likewise began as terms imposed by powerful winners on losers after wars.

The international institutions and rules that operate today took shape especially during periods of hegemony (see "Hegemony" on pp. 80–83), when one state predominated in international power following a hegemonic war among the great powers. For realists, in fact, international organizations or alliances operate largely at the behest of the interests of powerful states, and when those states no longer find such institutions useful, they will be abandoned. The international organizations and agreements that today form the institutional framework for international interactions—such as the UN, NATO, the Organization of American States, and the World Bank—were created after World War II under U.S. leadership.

Rules of international behaviour have become established over time as norms and are often codified as international law. This is a more incremental process than the creation of institutions; it goes on between and during periods of war and of hegemony. But still the most powerful states, especially hegemons, have great influence on the rules and values that have become embedded over time in a body of international law.

For example, the principle of free passage on the open seas is now formally established in international law.[1] But at one time, warships from one state did not hesitate to seize the ships of other states and make off with their cargoes. This practice was profitable to the state that pulled off such raids, but of course their own shipping could be raided in return. Such behaviour made long-distance trade itself more dangerous, less predictable, and less profitable. The trading states could benefit more by getting rid of the practice. So over time a norm developed around the concept of freedom of navigation on the high seas. It became one of the first areas of international law developed by the Dutch legal scholar *Hugo Grotius* in the mid-1600s—a time when the Dutch dominated world trade and could benefit most from free navigation.

Dutch power, then, provided the backbone for the international legal concept of freedom of the seas. Later, when Britain was dominant, it enforced the principle of free seas through the cannons of its warships. As the world's main trading state, Britain benefited from a worldwide norm of free shipping and trade. And with the world's most powerful navy, it was in a position to define and enforce the rules for the world's oceans.

Likewise, twentieth-century world order depended heavily on the power of the United States (and, for a few decades, on the division of power between the United States and the Soviet Union). The United States at times came close to adopting the explicit role of "world police force." But in truth the world is too large for any single state—even a hegemon—to police effectively. Rather, the world's states usually go along with the rules established by the most powerful state without constant policing. Meanwhile they try to influence the rules by working through international institutions (to which the hegemon cedes some of its power). In this way, although states do not yield their sovereignty, they

---

[1] Ken Booth, *Law, Force and Diplomacy at Sea* (Winchester, MA: Allen & Unwin, 1985).

vest some power and authority in international institutions and laws and generally work within that framework.[2]

These kinds of observations begin to suggest a Gramscian vision of hegemony, which points to the way in which order is established through a combination of coercion and consent. Hegemony is "working," by the Gramscian view, when the relations of power that maintain any particular system are understood to be the natural order of things. From this more critical perspective, international law and organization are means through which those relations of power, and a particular world order, are maintained. This critical view thus does not see international law and organization in the benign or straight-forwardly positive way that liberals do; but neither does it see international institutions working simply at the behest of strong states, because the relations of power that sustain any world order are more complex than simple state interests (and can include, for example, the class interests associated with globalizing capitalism).[3]

International Norms

international norms
The expectations held by participants about normal relations among states.

The rules that govern most interactions in IR are rooted in norms. **International norms** are the expectations held by state leaders about normal international relations. For some observers of IR, the decisions of state leaders should have some basis in ethical or moral norms.[4] The invasion of Kuwait by Iraq was not only illegal, it was widely viewed as immoral—beyond the acceptable range of behaviour of states (that is, beyond the normal amount of cheating that states get away with). Political leaders in Canada and around the world drew on moral norms to generate support for a collective response to Iraq.

These norms, however, are often disputed. International morality is supposed to differ somewhat from morality within states, which is strongly influenced by the particular culture and traditions of the particular state. By contrast, international morality is presumed to be a more universal set of moral standards and rules applicable to the interactions of states themselves.

In practice, however, this is seldom the case. There is often no consensus about particular violations of international norms. While there may have been some broad agreement regarding Iraq's invasion of Kuwait, that agreement was not shared by all states (the leaders of Jordan and Yemen, for example, strongly disagreed). There was even less agreement about the U.S.-led invasion of Iraq in 2003 (with which many of the United States' allies did not agree), or NATO's bombing of the former Yugoslavia in 1999, or how to handle the Rwandan genocide in 1994. Sometimes a consensus emerges "after the fact" (particularly evident in the case of the Rwandan genocide), but that consensus is often very difficult to discern before or during an event or crisis.

The attempt to define universal norms nonetheless follows a centuries-long philosophical tradition. Philosophers such as Kant argued that it was natural for autonomous individuals (or states) to cooperate for mutual benefit because they could see that pursuing their narrow individual interests would end up hurting all. Sovereign states could work together through structures and organizations (like Kant's proposed world federation) that would respect each member's autonomy and not create a world government over them. In

[2] Richard Falk, *Explorations at the Edge of Time: The Prospects for World Order* (Philadelphia: Temple, 1992). Samuel S. Kim, *The Quest for a Just World Order* (Boulder, CO: Westview, 1984).

[3] Robert W. Cox, "Multilateralism and World Order," *Approaches to World Order*, ed. R.W. Cox and T. Sinclair (NY: Cambridge UP, 1996).

[4] Rosalind Irwin, ed., *Ethics and Security in Canadian Foreign Policy* (Vancouver: UBC P, 2001).

the nineteenth century, such ideas were embodied in practical organizations in which states participated to manage specific issues such as international postal service and control of traffic on European rivers.

Agreed norms of behaviour, institutionalized through such organizations, become *habitual* over time and gain *legitimacy*. State leaders become used to behaving in a normal way and stop calculating, for each action, whether violating norms would pay off. For instance, the U.S. president does not spend time calculating whether the costs of invading and plundering Canada would outweigh the benefits. The willingness to maintain normal behaviour has psychological roots in "satisficing" and in aversion to risk (see "Individual Decision-Makers" on pp. 131–136). Legitimacy and habit explain why international norms can be effective even when they are not codified and enforced, or when they are not universally held.

The end of the Cold War put basic expectations up for grabs even more. One problem with rapid change is that nobody knows what to expect; whatever prevailing norms do exist break down because leaders do not have common expectations.

Through a long process of coping with a sequence of cases, international leaders build up new understandings of the rules of the game.

These new norms remained unsettled in 2004. New expectations appeared to be emerging in such areas as human rights, UN peacekeeping,

The Information Revolution
Consolidating Norms

The post–Cold War era has created uncertainty about international norms—the shared expectations about how states should behave. The new rules are still being written and tested. One unsettled aspect of international norms is the changing view of when outsiders can interfere in states' internal affairs. Will technological change tear down walls and force states to accept international norms in such areas as human rights, nonproliferation, and environmental protection?

To explore this question, go to www.pearsoned.ca/goldstein.

humanitarian intervention
Armed intrusion into a state, without its consent, to prevent or alleviate widespread or severe human rights violations.

and **humanitarian interventions**. Though these too are sometimes contested (particularly by those who argue that there are real problems in the assumption that the only response to contemporary conflicts has to be a militarized response).[5] The 2001 terrorist attacks shifted international norms, bringing about greater cooperation among states (including among great powers) and curbing an isolationist streak in U.S. politics. Three factors had already combined to shake up international norms—the end of the Cold War, the shifts in economic position of various regions and states (such as China and the United States relative to Japan, Russia, and Africa), and the effects of technological change in creating a "small world." Domestic and local politics now play out on a global stage. In the coming years, international norms may settle down in a new configuration as these trends continue to evolve.

Roles of International Organizations

Especially in times of change, when shared norms and habits may not contribute to solving international dilemmas and achieve mutual cooperation, institutions play a key role. They are concrete, tangible structures with specific functions and missions. These institutions have proliferated rapidly in recent decades, and continue to play an increasing role in international affairs. **International organizations (IOs)** include *intergovernmental organizations (IGOs)* such as the UN, and *nongovernmental organizations (NGOs)* such as Médecins Sans Frontières or Amnesty International.

international organizations (IOs) Institutions including *intergovernmental organizations (IGOs)* such as the UN, and *nongovernmental organizations (NGOs)* such as Médecins Sans Frontières or Amnesty International.

The number of IOs has grown more than fivefold since 1945, reaching about five hundred IGOs and tens of thousands of NGOs (depending somewhat on definitions). New NGOs are created around the world daily. This weaving together of people across national boundaries through specialized groups reflects world interdependence (see "Interdependence" on pp. 308–310).[6]

Some IGOs are global in scope, others are regional or just bilateral (having only two states as members). Some are general in their purposes, others have specific functional purposes. Overall, the success of these IGOs has been mixed; the regional ones have had more success than the global ones, and those with specific functional or technical purposes have worked better than those with broad purposes (see pp. 369–371). IGOs hold together because they promote the national interests (or enhance the leverage) of their member states—not because of vague ideals.

Among *regional* IGOs, the European Union encompasses some of the most important (see Chapter 10), but it is not the only example. Others include the Association of South East Asian Nations (ASEAN), the Latin American Integration Association, and locust control organizations in Africa (on regional security alliances, see pp. 242–248). The functional roles of IOs are important to their overall effect on international relations, but those roles are taken up in Chapter 10 on international integration. Here, we will rely on the more general theoretical discussion of international institutions begun in Chapter 3.

---

[5] Nicholas J. Wheeler, *Saving Strangers: Humanitarian Intervention in International Society* (NY: Oxford UP, 2001). Alan J. Kuperman, *The Limits of Humanitarian Intervention* (Washington, DC: Brookings, 2001). Thomas G. Weiss, *Military-Civilian Interactions: Intervening in Humanitarian Crises* (Lanham, MD: Rowman & Littlefield, 1999).

[6] John Boli and George M. Thomas, eds., *Constructing World Culture: International Nongovernmental Organizations since 1875* (Palo Alto, CA: Stanford UP, 1999). David Armstrong, Lorna Lloyd, and John Redmond, *From Versailles to Maastricht: International Organization in the Twentieth Century* (NY: St. Martin's, 1996). Craig Murphy, *International Organization and Industrial Change: Global Governance since 1850* (NY: Oxford UP, 1994).

Global IGOs (aside from the UN) usually have functional purposes involving coordinating actions of some set of states around the world. The IGO called Intelsat, for example, is a consortium of governments and private businesses that operates communications satellites. Members of the Organization of Petroleum Exporting Countries (OPEC) are major oil producers who meet periodically in Vienna to set production quotas for members in an effort to keep world oil prices high and stable. The North Atlantic Treaty Organization (NATO) (discussed below, pp. 243–245) is an IGO created out of a military alliance.

NGOs tend to be more specialized in function than IGOs. For instance, someone wanting to meet political scientists from other countries can join the International Political Science Association. Many NGOs have economic or business-related functions. The International Air Transport Association coordinates the work of airline companies. Other NGOs have global political purposes—Amnesty International for human rights, Planned Parenthood for reproductive rights and family planning, or the Women's International League for Peace and Freedom for issues of women in conflict and peace. Still other NGOs have cultural purposes—for example, the International Olympic Committee.

Religious groups are among the largest NGOs—their memberships often span many countries. Both in today's world and historically, sects of Christianity, Islam, Buddhism, Judaism, Hinduism, and other world religions have organized themselves across state borders, often in the face of hostility from one or more national governments. Missionaries have deliberately built and nurtured these transnational links. The Catholic Church historically held a special position in the European international system, especially before the seventeenth century. NGOs with broad purposes and geographical scope often maintain observer status in the UN so that they can participate in UN meetings about issues of concern. For example, Greenpeace attends UN meetings about the global environment.

A web of international organizations and agreements of various sizes and types now connects people in all countries. The rapid growth of this network, and the increasingly intense communications and interactions that occur within it, are indicative of rising international interdependence. These organizations or agreements in turn provide the institutional mesh to hold together some kind of world order even when leaders and contexts come and go, and even when norms are undermined by sudden changes in power relations. Some agreements involve military coalitions between two or more states, called alliances.

ALLIANCES

An *alliance* is a coalition of states that coordinate their actions to accomplish some end. Some alliances are *formalized* in written treaties, concern a *common threat* and related issues of international security, *endure* across a range of issues and a period of time, and are institutionalized in an IGO. If actors' purposes in banding together are shorter-term, less formal, or more issue-specific (such as the current efforts to stop international terrorism), the association is usually called a *coalition* rather than an alliance. Informal but enduring strategic *alignments* in a region are discussed shortly. But all these terms are somewhat ambiguous. Two countries may have a formal alliance and yet be bitter enemies, such as the Soviet Union and China in the 1960s or NATO members Greece and Turkey today. Or, two countries may create the practical equivalent of an alliance without a formal treaty.

Purposes of Alliances

Alliances generally have the purpose of augmenting their members' power relative to other states. By pooling their power capabilities, two or more states can exert greater leverage in their bargaining with other states. For smaller states, alliances can be their most important power element, and for great powers the structure of alliances shapes the configuration of power in the system. Of all the elements of power, none can change as quickly and decisively as alliances.

Most alliances form in response to a perceived threat. When a state's power grows and threatens to overmatch that of its rivals, the latter often form an alliance to limit that power. Thucydides attributed the outbreak of the Peloponnesian Wars more than 2000 years ago to the growing power of Athens, and to the fear that caused in Sparta. Sparta turned to its neighbours in the Peloponnesian League, and that alliance managed to defeat Athens.

Alliances are an important component of the balance of power. Except in the rare circumstance of hegemony, every state is weaker than some combination of other states. If states overstep norms of international conduct they may face a powerful alliance of opposing states. This happened to Iraq when it invaded Kuwait in 1990, as it had to Hitler's Germany in the 1940s and to Napoleon's France in the 1800s.

Realists emphasize the fluidity of alliances. Because of the autonomy of states, alliances can be made or broken fairly easily. Alliances are not marriages of love; they are marriages of convenience. Alliances, for realists, are based on national interests, and can shift as national interests change. This fluidity helps the balance-of-power process to operate effectively.

As critics of realism point out, it is not simple or costless to break an alliance: one's reputation may suffer and future alliances may be harder to establish. There is an important norm that says that written treaties should be honoured—in Latin, *pacta sunt servanda*. So states often do adhere to alliance terms even when it is not in their short-term interest to do so. Nonetheless, because of the nature of international anarchy, there is no mechanism to enforce contracts in IR, so the possibility of turning against a friend is always present. Realists would agree with French president Charles de Gaulle (under whom France withdrew militarily from NATO and developed its own nuclear weapons in the 1960s) that "France has no permanent friends, only permanent interests."[7] One hears echoes of Napoleon, 150 years earlier: "Treaties are observed as long as they are in harmony with interests."[8]

Examples are many. Anticommunist Richard Nixon could cooperate with communist Mao Zedong in 1972. Joseph Stalin could sign a nonaggression pact with a fascist, Adolf Hitler, and then cooperate with the capitalist West against Hitler. The United States could back the Islamic militants in Afghanistan against the Soviet Union in the 1980s, then attack them in 2001. Every time history brings another such reversal in international alignments, many people are surprised or even shocked. Realists are not so surprised.

The fluidity of alliances deepens the security dilemma in a world of multiple actors. Recall that the dilemma is that one state's efforts to ensure its own security (building up military capabilities) reduce the security of another state. With only two states, it is possible to match capabilities so that both have adequate defence but cannot attack. But if one adds a third state, free to ally with either side, then each state has to build adequate defences against the potential alliance of its enemy with the third state. The threat is greater and the security dilemma is harder to escape.

The nightmare of being overpowered looms large when a state faces a potentially hostile alliance that could form overnight. For example, in a war Israel could defeat any of its

[7] *Time* 12 July 1963.

[8] Napoleon, *Maxims, 1804–1815*. See Rhoda Thomas Tripp, *The International Thesaurus of Quotations* (New York: Crowell, 1970).

neighbours alone. But Israeli leaders believe they must arm against the worst contingency—an attack by all their neighbours together. Because the neighbours are not very aligned (and the most important, Egypt and Jordan, are at peace with Israel), Israel's military capabilities appear excessive to those neighbours.

Alliance cohesion is the ease with which the members hold together an alliance.[9] Cohesion tends to be high when national interests converge and when cooperation within the alliance becomes institutionalized and habitual. When states with divergent interests form an alliance against a common enemy, the alliance may come apart if the threat subsides (as with the U.S.-Soviet alliance in World War II, for instance). Even when alliance cohesion is high, as in NATO during the Cold War, conflicts may arise over who bears the costs of the alliance (**burden sharing**).[10]

The credibility with which an alliance can deter an enemy depends on the alliance's cohesion as well as its total power capabilities. If an alliance is successful at displaying a common front and taking a unified line on issues, a potential enemy is more likely to believe that members will honour their alliance commitments (such as their promise to fight if an ally is attacked). An enemy may try to split the alliance by finding issues on which the interests of the members diverge. For instance, the United States subtly encouraged the Sino-Soviet split, and the Soviet Union subtly tried to turn European members of NATO away from the United States.

Great powers often form alliances with smaller states, sometimes called client states.[11] In the Cold War, each superpower extended a security umbrella over its allies. The issue of credibility in such an alliance is whether (and under what circumstances) the great power will assist its clients in a war. Extended deterrence refers to a strong state's use of threats to deter attacks on weaker clients—such as the U.S. threat to attack the Soviet Union if it invaded Western Europe.

Great powers face a real danger of being dragged into wars with each other over relatively unimportant regional issues if their respective clients go to war. If the great powers do not come to their clients' protection, they may lose credibility with other clients, but if they do, they may end up fighting a costly war.[12] The Soviet Union worried that its commitments to China in the 1950s, to Cuba in the 1960s, and to Syria and Egypt in the 1970s (among others) could result in a disastrous war with the United States.

NATO

By far the more powerful formal alliance at present (although with a somewhat uncertain future in the post–Cold War era), is the **North Atlantic Treaty Organization (NATO),** which encompasses Western Europe and North America. Using GDP as a measure of power, the 26 NATO members possess nearly half the world total (roughly twice the

alliance cohesion The ease with which the members hold together an alliance; it tends to be high when national interests converge and when cooperation among allies becomes institutionalized.

burden sharing The distribution of the costs of an alliance among members; the term also refers to the conflicts that may arise over such distribution.

North Atlantic Treaty Organization (NATO) A U.S.-led military alliance, formed in 1949 with mainly West European members, to oppose and deter Soviet power in Europe. It has recently expanded into the former Soviet bloc. See also *Warsaw Pact.*

---

[9] Charles W. Kegley and Gregory A. Raymond, *When Trust Breaks Down: Alliance Norms and World Politics* (Columbia: U South Carolina P, 1990).

[10] John R. Oneal, "The Theory of Collective Action and Burden Sharing in NATO," *International Organization* 44.3 (1990): 379–402. Glenn Palmer, "Corralling the Free Rider: Deterrence and the Western Alliance," *International Studies Quarterly* 34.2 (1990): 147–64.

[11] Steven R. David, *Choosing Sides: Alignment and Realignment in the Third World* (Baltimore: Johns Hopkins UP, 1991).

[12] Glenn H. Snyder, *Alliance Politics* (Ithaca, NY: Cornell UP, 1997). Randolph M. Siverson and Michael R. Tennefoss, "Power, Alliance, and the Escalation of International Conflict, 1815–1965," *American Political Science Review* 78.4 (1984): 1057–69.

power of the United States alone). Members are the United States, Canada, Britain, France, Germany, Italy, Belgium, the Netherlands, Luxembourg, Denmark, Norway, Iceland, Spain, Portugal, Greece, Turkey, Poland, the Czech Republic, Hungary, Bulgaria, Estonia, Latvia, Lithuania, Romania, Slovakia, and Slovenia. At NATO headquarters in Brussels, Belgium, military staffs from the member countries coordinate plans and periodically direct exercises in the field. NATO's Supreme Allied Commander Europe (SACEUR) and Supreme Allied Commander Atlantic (SACLANT) are both U.S. generals. In NATO, each state contributes its own military units—with its own national culture, language, and equipment specifications.

Warsaw Pact A Soviet-led Eastern European military alliance, founded in 1955 and disbanded in 1991. It opposed the NATO alliance. See also *North Atlantic Treaty Organization (NATO)*.

NATO was founded in 1949 to oppose and deter Soviet power in Europe. Its counterpart in Eastern Europe during the Cold War, the Soviet-led **Warsaw Pact,** was founded in 1955 and disbanded in 1991. During the Cold War, the United States maintained more than 300 000 troops in Europe, with advanced planes, tanks, and other equipment. After the Cold War ended, these forces were cut to about 100 000. But NATO stayed together because its members believed that NATO provided useful stability even though its mission was unclear.[13] Article V, considered the heart of NATO, asks members to come to the defence of a fellow member under attack. It was envisioned as a U.S. commitment to help defend Western Europe against the Soviet Union, but instead was invoked for the first time when Europe came to the defence of the United States after the terrorist attacks in 2001.

The first actual use of force by NATO was in Bosnia in 1994, in support of the UN mission there. A "dual key" arrangement gave the UN control of NATO's actions in Bosnia, and the UN feared retaliation against its lightly armed peacekeepers if NATO attacked the Serbian forces to protect Bosnian civilians. As a result, NATO made threats, underlined by symbolic air strikes, but then backed down after UN qualms; this waffling undermined NATO credibility. More extensive NATO air strikes in 1995, however, alarmed Russian leaders, who were already concerned by NATO's expansion plans. These problems, along with tensions between the American and European NATO members over Bosnia policy, dogged the first major NATO mission of the post–Cold War era. Later NATO actions in the Balkans (the air war for Kosovo in 1999 and peacekeeping in Macedonia in 2001) went more smoothly in terms of alliance cohesion.

In 2004, the European Union was trying to form its own rapid deployment force, outside NATO. The decision grew in part from European military weaknesses demonstrated in the 1999 Kosovo war, in which the United States contributed the most power by far. Although the European force will probably work *with* NATO in future operations, it also gives Europe a bit more independence from the United States. Despite other efforts in this direction earlier in the 1990s, currently NATO still dominates European security.

The biggest question for NATO is eastward expansion, beyond the East-West Cold War dividing line. In 1999, former Soviet-bloc countries Poland, the Czech Republic, and Hungary joined the alliance. In March 2004, seven new countries formally joined NATO: Bulgaria, Estonia, Latvia, Lithuania, Romania, Slovakia, and Slovenia. This was the fifth, and largest, round of enlargement in NATO's history. Albania, Croatia, and the former Yugoslav Republic of Macedonia are preparing to seek membership. Making the new members' militaries compatible with NATO is a major undertaking, requiring increased military spending by existing and new NATO members. Arms industries look forward to new sales as Eastern European countries restructure their military forces to meet NATO requirements.

---

[13] David S. Yost, *NATO Transformed: The Alliance's New Roles in International Security* (Washington, DC: U.S. Institute of Peace Press, 1999). George W. Grayson, *Strange Bedfellows: NATO Marches East* (Lanham, MD: UP America, 1999). James M. Goldgeier, *Not Whether But When: The Decision to Enlarge NATO* (Washington, DC: Brookings, 1999).

In 2003, the Iraq War bypassed NATO. Several members strongly opposed the war, and Turkey refused to let U.S. ground forces cross into Iraq. Also in 2003, the European Union sent military forces as peacekeepers to the Democratic Republic of the Congo—the first multinational European military operation to occur outside NATO.

Russian leaders oppose NATO's expansion into Eastern Europe as aggressive and anti-Russian. They view NATO expansion as reasserting dividing lines on the map of Europe, but pushed closer to Russia's borders. These fears strengthen nationalist and anti-Western political forces in Russia. To mitigate the problems, NATO created a category of symbolic membership—the Partnership for Peace—which almost all Eastern European and former Soviet states including Russia joined. However, the 1999 NATO bombing of Serbia heightened Russian fears regarding NATO's eastward expansion.

The U.S.-Japanese Security Treaty

Another important alliance is the **U.S.-Japanese Security Treaty,** a bilateral alliance. Under this alliance the United States maintains about 60 000 troops in Japan (with weapons, equipment, and logistical support). Japan pays the United States several billion dollars annually to offset about half the cost of maintaining these troops. The alliance was created in 1951 (during the Korean War) against the potential Soviet threat to Japan.

Because of its roots in the U.S. military occupation of Japan after World War II, the alliance is very asymmetrical. The United States is committed to defend Japan if it is attacked, but Japan is not similarly obligated to defend the United States. The United States maintains troops in Japan, but not vice versa. The United States belongs to several other alliances, but Japan's only major alliance is with the United States. The U.S. share of the total military power in this alliance is also far greater than its share in NATO.

Japan's constitution renounces the right to make war and maintain military forces, although interpretation has loosened this prohibition over time. Japan maintains military forces, called the Self-Defence Forces, strong enough for territorial defence but not for aggression. It is a powerful army by world standards but much smaller than Japan's economic strength could support. Japanese public opinion restrains militarism in general and precludes the development of nuclear weapons in particular after Japanese cities were destroyed by nuclear weapons in World War II. Even the dispatch of unarmed Japanese troops on a UN peacekeeping mission to Cambodia was barely approved in 1992 after a vigorous debate.

Japan is as dependent as ever on natural resources from foreign countries, but Japanese leaders generally believe that economic and diplomatic (rather than military) capabilities can best assure a smooth flow of resources to Japan and export markets for Japanese goods. The security alliance with the United States—Japan's largest trading partner—provides a stable security framework conducive to business. Nonetheless, some Japanese leaders believe that Japan's formal security role should now expand commensurate with its economic power. Japanese troops participated in the war in Afghanistan in 2001 and Iraq in 2004 (though not in combat roles), and Japan seeks a seat on the UN Security Council. The UN in turn is pressing Japan to participate fully in peacekeeping missions.

For its part, the United States has used the alliance with Japan as a base to project U.S. power in Asia, especially during the wars in Korea (1950–1953) and Vietnam (1965–1975) when Japan was a key staging area for U.S. war efforts. The continued U.S. military presence in Japan (as in Europe) symbolizes the U.S. commitment to remain

U.S.-Japanese Security Treaty A bilateral alliance between the United States and Japan, created in 1951 against the potential Soviet threat to Japan. The United States maintains troops in Japan and is committed to defend Japan if attacked, and Japan pays the United States to offset about half the cost of maintaining the troops.

engaged in Asian security affairs.[14] However, these U.S. forces have been drawn down somewhat in the past decade in response to high costs, reduced threats, and opposition by local residents (especially on Okinawa island, after the sexual assault of a Japanese schoolgirl by U.S. personnel).

NORAD

North American Aerospace Defense Command (NORAD) A binational military organization established in 1958 by Canada and the U.S. to monitor and defend North American Airspace.

The **North American Aerospace Defense Command (NORAD)** was established in 1958 through an agreement (not a formal treaty) between Canada and the United States. Both countries agreed to work together to monitor and defend North American airspace. The commander in chief of NORAD is appointed by and responsible to both the prime minister of Canada and the president of the United States. Normally, the commander of NORAD is appointed from the U.S. Air Force and the deputy commander from the Canadian Forces (these roles are reversed in Canada, where the deputy commander of the Canadian NORAD region is appointed from the U.S. while the commander of the Canadian region is Canadian). NORAD headquarters is located in Colorado, with its command and control centre buried deep in the Cheyene Mountains. Canada's NORAD headquarters is located in Winnipeg, with its command and control centre located in North Bay. The NORAD agreement has been renewed eight times since 1958, but in 2004, some commentators, both in Canada and the United States, insisted that NORAD would suffer if Canada did not agree to join plans for a U.S. missile defence shield.

The Former Soviet Republics

The 12 members of the *Commonwealth of Independent States (CIS)* comprise the former Soviet republics except the Baltic states (Estonia, Latvia, and Lithuania). Russia is the leading member and Ukraine the second largest. Officially, CIS headquarters is in the city of Minsk, in Belarus, but in practice there is no strong centre and meetings rotate around. After its first decade, the CIS remains a loose coordinating institution for states to solve practical problems in economic and (sometimes) military spheres.

When the Soviet Union disintegrated in 1991, a chaotic situation emerged. Power for several years had been shifting from the centre in Moscow to the 15 constituent Soviet republics. The Warsaw Pact had collapsed. The Soviet army itself began to break up, and several republics began forming their own military forces using Soviet forces, bases, and equipment located on their territories. At the same time, other former Soviet forces located outside Russia remained in a chain of command centred in Moscow, effectively under Russian control. For years until 1997, Russia and Ukraine debated ownership of the Black Sea fleet, whose port was in Ukraine but whose history was distinctly Russian. (The fleet will be split and Russia's basing rights maintained for 20 years.)

One reason for forming the CIS was simply to speed the death of the old Soviet Union and ease the transition to full independence for its republics. After the formation of the CIS at the end of 1991, the Soviet Union quickly dissolved. The extensive property of the Union (including state-owned industry and military forces) went to the individual republics, especially to Russia, which became the USSR's successor state.

The disposition of the Union's property and armed forces was negotiated by CIS members. Although some military coordination takes place through the CIS, plans for a

---

[14] Steven K. Vogel, "The 'Inverse' Relationship: The United States and Japan at the End of the Century," *Eagle Adrift: American Foreign Policy at the End of the Century,* ed. Robert J. Lieber (NY: Longman, 1997).

joint military force instead of 12 independent armies did not succeed. Among the largest CIS members, Kazakhstan and Belarus are the most closely aligned with Russia, while Ukraine is the most independent. In 1999, Russia and Belarus formed a confederation that might lead to future economic integration or even an anti-Western military alliance, but currently remains merely symbolic.

It is to the CIS's credit that in the post-Soviet chaos no major war erupted between major CIS member states. Substantial warfare did occur between some of the smaller members (notably Armenia and Azerbaijan), and there was civil violence within several other CIS states (Russia, Georgia, Moldova, and Tajikistan); CIS forces were drawn into a few small clashes. But the large members were not drawn into large wars. The outcome could have been much worse.

The most important relationship within the CIS is between its two largest members, Russia and Ukraine. They distrust each other somewhat but have managed to cooperate fairly effectively since becoming independent. Disputes over issues such as ownership of the Black Sea fleet have been negotiated step by step, often painfully but productively in the end.

One of the first problems facing CIS military forces was what position to take in inter-republic warfare, such as that between Armenia and Azerbaijan; secessionist wars as in Georgia; or civil wars to control republics' governments, as in Tajikistan. In the mid-1990s, the CIS operated a 24 000-person peacekeeping force in Tajikistan, generally supporting the government in a civil war there. A 1500-person force in Moldova and a 500-person force in Georgia, both acting as buffer forces to monitor ceasefires, operated under joint commands of Russia and the governments and rebel forces in each of those countries.

Another pressing military problem for the CIS was the disposition of the tens of thousands of nuclear weapons of the former Soviet Union. As the Soviet successor state, Russia assumed control of the weapons and within a year moved all the tactical nuclear weapons out of the other republics and into Russian territory. This was a very touchy operation because of the danger of theft or accident while so many weapons were in transit. Still, there were reports that nuclear materials (or perhaps even warheads) had been stolen and sold on the international market by corrupt CIS officers or officials (see pp. 226–229 on proliferation).

The strategic nuclear weapons—those on long-range missiles—presented another kind of problem. These weapons were located in four republics—Russia, Ukraine, Belarus, and Kazakhstan—under control of Russian commanders. They were not easily moved, and the three republic leaders expressed some ambivalence about losing them to Russia. At a minimum they wanted assurances that the nuclear weapons would be destroyed, not retargeted on their own republics. Ukraine toyed with using the missiles as bargaining chips in negotiations with Russia or with the Western powers. But in the end all the former Soviet republics except Russia agreed to become nonnuclear states.

Overall, the CIS is a marriage of convenience. For now the members find it a necessary marriage—especially because of the tight economic integration of the member states—if not always a happy one. A divorce could occur quickly.

Regional Alignments

Beyond the three alliances just discussed and the regional IGOs mentioned earlier, most international alignments and coalitions are not formalized in alliances. Among the great powers, a close working relationship (through the UN) developed among the United States, Western European powers, Japan, and Russia after the Cold War. By the mid-1990s new strains had appeared in great-power relations, including economic conflicts among the former Western allies, differences over policy in Bosnia and Kosovo, and Western alarm at Russia's war in the secession-minded Chechnya province. Of the great powers, China continues to be the most independent, but prudently avoids conflict with the others unless China's immediate security interests are at stake.

Many states of the global South (and some states from other regions of the world) joined a **nonaligned movement** during the Cold War, standing apart from the U.S.-Soviet rivalry. This movement, led by India and the former Yugoslavia, was undermined by the membership of states such as Cuba that were clearly clients of one superpower. In 1992, the nonaligned movement agreed to stay in business, though its future is unclear.

One vestige of past centuries is the Commonwealth—a group of countries with historical ties to Britain (including Canada and Australia) working together for mutual economic and cultural benefit. France also maintains ties (including regular summit meetings) with its former colonies in Africa. France had troops stationed in six African countries in the late 1990s. But France reduced its African ties in the 1990s, and in 1997 it stood by while friendly governments were overthrown. Meanwhile the 53-member Organization of African Unity, an IGO with few powers, is remaking itself as the African Union, a stronger organization with a continent-wide parliament, central bank, and court.

In Asia, China has had conflicts with most of its major neighbours. Between 1940 and 1979 it engaged in military hostilities with Japan, South Korea, the United States, India, Russia, and Vietnam. In 1965, China lost its only major regional ally (Indonesia) after a violent change of government there. China has long been loosely aligned with Pakistan in opposition to India. Vietnam slowly normalized relations with the West after the wars in Vietnam and Cambodia. The United States has 35 000 troops stationed in South Korea under terms of a formal bilateral alliance dating to the Korean War (North Korea is vaguely aligned with China). With Australia and New Zealand the United States has had since 1951 a formal military alliance called ANZUS, which formally invoked its mutual support provisions for the first time in response to the terrorist attacks in 2001.

In the Middle East, the Arab-Israeli conflict created a general anti-Israel alignment of the Arab countries for decades, but that alignment broke down as Egypt in 1978 and then the Palestine Liberation Organization (PLO) and Jordan in 1993–1994 made peace with Israel. As the Israeli-Palestinian peace process moves forward and backward year by year, Arab countries continue to express varying degrees of solidarity with each other and degrees of opposition to Israel. Meanwhile, Israel and Turkey formed a close military relationship that amplifies Israeli power and links it to the oil-rich Caspian see region.

It is unclear what new international alignments may emerge in the years to come. The fluidity of alliances makes them a wild card for scholars to understand and for policy-makers to anticipate. But the web of connections that bind states together today includes more than military alliances, it also includes international institutions, the most important of which is the United Nations.

THE UNITED NATIONS

The UN and other international organizations have both strengths and weaknesses in the anarchic international system. State sovereignty creates a real need for such organizations on a practical level, because no central world government performs the function of coordinating the actions of states for mutual benefit. However, state sovereignty also severely limits the power of the UN and other IOs, because governments reserve power to themselves and are stingy in delegating it to the UN or anyone else. The UN has had a mixed record with these strengths and weaknesses—in some ways providing remarkable global-level management and in other ways appearing helpless against the sovereignty of even modest-sized states (not to mention great powers).

The UN System

The UN is a relatively new institution, just approaching 60 years old. Even newer is the more prominent role that the UN has played in international security affairs since the Cold War ended. Despite this new prominence, the main purposes of the UN are the same now as when it was founded after World War II.[15]

Purposes of the UN The UN is the closest thing to a world government that has ever existed, but it is not a world government. Its members are sovereign states that have not empowered the UN to enforce its will within states' territories except with the consent of those states' governments. Thus, although the UN strengthens world order, its design acknowledges the realities of international anarchy and the unwillingness of states to surrender their sovereignty. Within these limits, the basic purpose of the UN is to provide a global institutional structure through which states can sometimes settle conflicts with less reliance on the use of force.

The **UN Charter** is based on the principles that states are *equal* under international law; that states have full *sovereignty* over their own affairs; that states should have full *independence* and *territorial integrity*; and that states should carry out their international *obligations*—such as respecting diplomatic privileges, refraining from committing aggression, and observing the terms of treaties they sign. The Charter also lays out the structure of the UN and the methods by which it operates.

The UN does not exist because it has power to force its will on the world's states; it exists because states have created it to serve their needs. A state's membership in the UN is essentially a form of indirect leverage. States gain leverage by using the UN to seek more beneficial outcomes in conflicts (especially on general multilateral issues where a global forum brings all parties together). The cost of this leverage is modest—UN dues and the expenses of diplomatic representatives, in addition to the agreement to behave in accordance with the Charter (most of the time).

States get several benefits from the UN. Foremost among these is the international stability (especially in security affairs) that the UN tries to safeguard; this allows states to realize gains from trade and other forms of exchange (see Chapter 8). The UN is a *symbol* of international order and even of global identity. It is also a *forum* where states promote their views and bring their disputes. And it is a *mechanism* for *conflict resolution* in international security affairs. The UN also promotes and coordinates development assistance (see Chapter 12) and other programs of *economic* and *social development* in countries of the global South. These programs reflect the belief that economic and social problems—above all, poverty—are an important source of international conflict and war. Finally, the UN is a coordinating system for *information* and planning by hundreds of internal and external agencies and programs, and for the publication of international data.

Despite its heavy tasks, the UN is still a small and fragile institution. Compare, for instance, what states spend on two types of leverage for settling conflicts—military forces and the UN. Every year, the world spends US$800 billion on the military and about US$10 billion in total on the UN, a ratio of 80:1.

Structure of the UN The UN's structure, shown in Figure 7.1, centres around the **UN General Assembly,** where representatives of all states sit together in a huge room, listen to speeches, and pass resolutions. The General Assembly coordinates a variety of

> **UN Charter** The founding document of the United Nations; it is based on the principles that states are equal, have *sovereignty* over their own affairs, enjoy independence and territorial integrity, and must fulfill international obligations. The Charter also lays out the structure and methods of the UN.

> **UN General Assembly** Comprised of representatives of all states, it allocates UN funds, passes nonbinding resolutions, and coordinates development programs and various autonomous agencies through the Economic and Social Council (ECOSOC).

---

[15] Evan Luard and Derek Heater, *The United Nations: How It Works and What It Does*, 2nd ed. (NY: St. Martin's, 1994). Chadwick F. Alger, Gene M. Lyons, and John E. Trent, eds., *The United Nations System: The Policies of Member States* (NY: United Nations UP, 1995).

Figure 7.1 The United Nations

development programs and other autonomous agencies through the *Economic and Social Council (ECOSOC)*. Parallel to the General Assembly is the **UN Security Council,** in which five permanent members and ten rotating member states make decisions about international peace and security. The Security Council has responsibility for the dispatch of peacekeeping forces to trouble spots. The administration of the UN takes place through the **UN Secretariat** (executive branch), led by the secretary-general of the UN. The *World Court* (International Court of Justice), which is discussed later in the chapter, is a judicial arm of the UN. (A *Trusteeship Council* oversaw the transition of a handful of former colonial territories to full independence; with the last trust territory's independence in 1994, the council suspended operations.)

National delegations to the UN, headed by ambassadors from each member state, work and meet together at UN headquarters in New York City. They have diplomatic status in the United States, which as host country also assumes certain other obligations to facilitate the UN's functioning. For example, the U.S. government has permitted people such as Fidel Castro—normally barred from entry to the United States—to visit New York long enough to address the UN.

A major strength of the UN structure is the *universality of its membership*. There were 191 members in 2004. Virtually every territory in the world is either a UN member or formally a province or colony of a UN member. (Switzerland, which traditionally maintains strict neutrality in the international system, joined in 2002.) Formal agreement on the Charter, even if sometimes breached, commits all states to a set of basic rules governing their relations. The old League of Nations, by contrast, was flawed by the absence of several important actors.

One way the UN induced all the great powers to join was to reassure them that their participation in the UN would not harm their national interests. Recognizing the role of power in world order, the UN Charter gave five great powers, the permanent members, each a veto over substantive decisions of the Security Council.

The UN Charter establishes a mechanism for *collective security*—the banding together of the world's states to stop an aggressor. Chapter 7 of the Charter explicitly authorizes the Security Council to use military force against aggression if the nonviolent means called for in Chapter 6 have failed. However, because of the great-power veto, the UN cannot effectively stop aggression by (or supported by) a great power. Thus Chapter 7 was used only once during the Cold War—in the Korean War when the Soviet delegation unwisely boycotted the proceedings (and when China's seat was held

UN Security Council A body of five great powers (that can veto resolutions) and ten rotating member states, which makes decisions about international peace and security including the dispatch of UN peacekeeping forces.

UN Secretariat The UN's executive branch, led by the secretary-general.

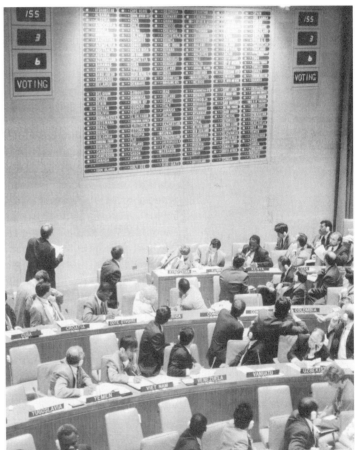

ASSEMBLY OF EQUALS
The universal membership of the United Nations is one of its strengths. All member states have a voice and a vote in the General Assembly. Here, it votes on a comprehensive test ban treaty, 1996. It passed 158–3, with India voting "no."

by the nationalists on Taiwan). It was under Chapter 7 of the Charter that the UN authorized the use of force to reverse Iraqi aggression against Kuwait in 1990 and to respond to the humanitarian disaster in Somalia in the early 1990s.

History of the UN The UN was founded in 1945 in San Francisco by 51 states. It was the successor to the League of Nations, which had failed to effectively counter aggression in the 1930s—Japan simply quit when the League condemned Japanese aggression against China. Like the League, the UN was founded to increase international order and the rule of law to prevent another world war.

There has long been a certain tension between the UN and the United States. The United States had not joined the League, and it was partly to assure U.S. interest that the UN headquarters was placed in New York. The UN in some ways constrains the United States by creating the one coalition that can rival U.S. power—that of all the states. A certain isolationist streak in U.S. foreign policy runs counter to the UN concept. At the same time, however, the UN can *amplify* U.S. power because the United States leads the global UN coalition. The U.S. regularly has refused to pay its dues to the UN, often in reaction to criticism it has faced, particularly by countries in the global South. At one point the U.S. stood in arrears of more than $1 billion; at the end of 2003 it was $762 million in arrears. But when it does pay its dues, the U.S. is the largest single contributor state to the United Nations. The United States is not rich or strong enough to keep order in the world by itself. And, as a great trading nation, the United States benefits from the stability and order that the UN helps to create.

Canada has long supported the United Nations. It was enthusiastically involved in its founding, and has been an active participant since. Canadian foreign policy has long viewed activity in multilateral organizations like the UN as a central element of achieving foreign policy goals, not least because multilateral efforts offset any lack of influence resulting from its middle power status in international relations. But Canadian foreign policy has also been informed by a liberal internationalist impulse, and a real faith that international organizations are the most effective means of managing global-level politics. Canada's long commitment to the United Nations means that it is highly regarded within UN and other IO circles. At the UN, for example, Canada's status is reflected in the number of times it has served as one of the ten rotating members on the Security Council—at six terms it is one of the highest "repeater" countries among the nonpermanent members.[16]

In the 1950s and 1960s, the UN's membership more than doubled as colonies in Asia and Africa won independence. This expansion changed the character of the General Assembly, where each state has one vote regardless of size. The new members had different concerns from the Western industrialized countries and in many cases resented having been colonized by Westerners. The General Assembly is one of the few international bodies in which countries from the global South hold a majority of seats and have the largest voice. Many new members (and a few of the original members) believed that the United States enjoyed too much power in the UN. They noticed that the UN is usually effective in international security affairs only when the United States leads the effort (which happens primarily when U.S. interests are at stake).

The growth in membership thus affected voting patterns in the UN. During the UN's first two decades, the Assembly had regularly sided with the United States, and the Soviet Union was the main power to use its veto in the Security Council to counterbalance that

---

[16] Michael Pearson, "Humanizing the UN Security Council," *Canada among Nations 2001: The Axworthy Legacy*, ed. Fen Osler Hampson, Norman Hillmer, and Maureen Appel Molot (Toronto: Oxford UP, 2001).

tendency. But as newly independent states began to predominate, the United States found itself in the minority on many issues, and by the 1970s and 1980s it had become the main user of the veto.[17]

Until 1971, China's seat on the Security Council (and in the General Assembly) was occupied by the nationalist government on Taiwan island, which had lost power in mainland China in 1949. The exclusion of communist China was an exception to the UN principle of universal membership, and in 1971 the Chinese seat was taken from the nationalists and given to the communist government. Today, the government of Taiwan—which functions autonomously in many international matters despite its formal status as a Chinese province—is not a member of the UN.

Throughout the Cold War, the UN had few successes in international security because the U.S.-Soviet conflict prevented consensus. The UN appeared somewhat irrelevant in a world order structured by two opposing alliance blocs. There were a few notable exceptions, such as agreements to station peacekeeping forces in the Middle East,

MAKING THE CASE
Collective security rests with the UN Security Council, which has authorized such military interventions as the Gulf War and the 2001 campaign in Afghanistan. Military actions not approved by the Council—such as the 1999 bombing of Serbia and the 2003 U.S.-British invasion of Iraq—tend to be controversial. Here, U.S. Secretary of State Colin Powell tries, unsuccessfully, to convince the Security Council to authorize military action against Iraq to eliminate Iraq's weapons of mass destruction, February 2003. Powell holds a vial representing the amount of anthrax spores (a substance Iraq had produced) that could kill thousands of people.

but the UN did not play a central role in solving international conflicts. The General Assembly concentrated on the economic and social problems of poor countries, and these became the main work of the UN.

After the Cold War, the bipolar world order gave way to one in which multilateral action was more important. The great powers could finally agree on measures regarding international security. Also, states of the global South could not hope to play off the superpowers against each other, so they cautiously avoided alienating the United States. In this context the UN moved to centre stage in international security affairs.[18]

The UN had several major successes in the late 1980s in bringing to an end violent regional conflicts (in Central America and the Iran-Iraq War). Ceasefires were negotiated under UN auspices, and peacekeeping forces were dispatched to monitor the situation. In Namibia (Africa), a UN force oversaw independence from South Africa and the nation's

[17] Robert W. Gregg, *About Face: The United States and the United Nations* (Boulder, CO: Rienner, 1993). Jack E. Vincent, *Support Patterns at the United Nations* (Lanham, MD: UP America, 1991).

[18] Thomas G. Weiss, ed., *The United Nations and Civil Wars* (Boulder, CO: Rienner, 1995). G. R. Berridge, ed., *Return to the U.N.: U.N. Diplomacy in Regional Conflicts* (NY: St. Martin's, 1991). Peter R. Baehr and Leon Gordenker, *The United Nations at the End of the 1990s*, 3rd ed. (NY: St. Martin's, 1999). Paul Taylor and A. J. R. Groom, eds., *Global Issues in the United Nations Framework* (NY: St. Martin's, 1989).

first free elections. By the 1990s, the UN had emerged as the world's most important tool for settling international conflicts. Between 1987 and 1993, Security Council resolutions increased from 15 to 78, peacekeeping missions from 5 to 17, peacekeepers from 12 000 to 78 000, and countries sending troops from 26 to 76.

The new missions ran into serious problems, however. Inadequate funding undermined peacekeeping efforts to some extent. In Angola, the UN sent only a few peacekeepers, and when the government won internationally observed elections in 1992, the rebels took to arms and the civil war resumed. Meanwhile in Somalia, the UN sided against one faction leader but could not defeat him and had to pull back. In Cambodia, the Khmer Rouge faction refused to disarm according to the UN-brokered peace plan it had signed. Later a coup interrupted Cambodia's transition to democracy.

Such problems were most dramatic in the former Yugoslavia, where the UN in 1993–1995 undertook its largest peacekeeping mission with nearly 40 000 foreign troops, costing more than $1 billion annually. The mission was deeply flawed by a mismatch between the types of forces sent (lightly armed, equipped for humanitarian operations) and the situation itself (territorial aggression by heavily armed forces). This unhappy combination was known as "peacekeeping where there is no peace to keep."

In response to these problems (and to the unpaid U.S. dues), the UN scaled back peacekeeping operations in 1995–1997 (from 78 000 to 19 000 troops) and carried out reductions and reforms in the UN Secretariat and UN programs. The changes grew out of a financial crisis in the mid-1990s that saw Secretary-General Boutros Boutros-Ghali declare at the UN's fiftieth anniversary that "practically, the United Nations is bankrupt." Overseeing reforms and reductions has occupied his successor, Kofi Annan, who took over in 1997. In Annan's first year, CNN founder Ted Turner gave him a boost with a $1 billion private contribution (pledged over 10 years).

For years the United States failed to pay its bills, even though the new secretary-general shrank budgets and jobs as the United States had demanded. Congress first refused to allocate funds, then attached abortion-related riders that triggered presidential vetoes. Congress also delayed confirming the new U.S. ambassador to the UN, Richard Holbrooke, leaving the position vacant for a year. The United States also fell behind in payments to other international organizations including the World Bank and the Food and Agriculture Organization. This U.S. free-riding shows that support of intergovernmental organizations presents a difficult collective goods problem (see p. 91).

However, a vigorous 1999 lobbying campaign by American UN supporters noted that "Great nations pay their bills." Close U.S. allies became outspoken in criticizing U.S. failure to honour its international commitments. Finally, a compromise was hammered out and the United States agreed to pay up, but not the entire outstanding amounts.

The 2001 terrorist attacks increased U.S. participation in the UN, where a decisive coalition of member states supported U.S. positions on terrorism. In 2003, however, the Security Council refused to support the U.S. plan to invade Iraq in search of weapons of mass destruction. The U.S. ignored UN efforts to prevent the invasion and attacked Iraq with what it called a "Coalition of the Willing." Canada, among other allies, did not join the U.S.-led coalition, in part because of its longstanding commitment to the United Nations, and in part because it opposed an invasion that appeared to be aimed primarily at regime change.

It is unclear what the impact of the 2003 Iraq war will be for the UN. For some observers, the fact that the U.S. ignored the Security Council signalled the death knell for the UN and underlined its irrelevance. Many people within the United States, both political leaders and average citizens, were angered at the UN's lack of support. The U.S. action seemed to lend some credence to the realist account of international organizations:

THE UN TARGETED
UN headquarters in Iraq was targeted by suicide bombers in August 2003, killing and injuring many people. The UN formally withdrew from Iraq after the attack.

useful when they support the foreign policy agendas of powerful states but disregarded when they do not.

Liberal commentators argued instead that the UN would have been shown to be irrelevant had it simply supported the U.S. position. It is true that the UN does not have the resources or enforcement capabilities to prevent an invasion by a powerful state such as the United States. However, according to liberals, the UN's divergence from the U.S. on Iraq signalled that neither does it act simply at the behest of powerful states. Instead, the UN charts an independent course based on a global calculation of international norms, rather than a state-based calculation of national interest.[19] The UN was also called upon immediately after the war had ended to help in the rebuilding of Iraq, and its Baghdad headquarters was targeted in a bomb attack in August 2003. The UN sustained significant casualties, including a number of Canadian UN workers as well as the loss of the UN's chief of mission, Sergio Vieira de Mello. The UN formally withdrew from Iraq after the attack, but its diplomats continued to contribute to plans that saw the turnover of power to Iraqi citizens in June of 2004.

---

[19] W. Andy Knight, "Don't Write off the UN Just Yet," *Japan Times* 24 March 2003.

The Security Council

The Security Council is responsible for maintaining international peace and security, and for restoring peace when it breaks down. Its decisions are *binding* on all UN member states. The Security Council has tremendous power to *define* the existence and nature of a security threat, to *structure* the response to such a threat, and to *enforce* its decisions through mandatory directives to UN members (such as to halt trade with an aggressor).

In nearly 60 years, the Council has passed about 1600 resolutions, with new ones being added by the week. In periods of crisis they can be added by the day. These resolutions represent the great powers' blueprints for resolving the world's various security disputes, especially in regional conflicts. (Because of the veto system the Council avoids conflicts among great powers themselves, such as on arms control.) The resolutions reflect what the great powers can all agree upon. This means that resolutions are sometimes criticized for being rather vague and imprecise. Resolutions with clear wording, or bold statements about an issue or event, reflect considerable consensus within the Security Council.

The five *permanent members* of the Council—the United States, Britain, France, Russia, and China—are the most important. The Council also has 10 *nonpermanent members* who rotate onto the Council for two-year terms. As noted above, Canada has served as a nonpermanent member on the Security Council six times since the UN was founded. Nonpermanent members are elected (five each year) by the General Assembly from a list prepared by informal regional caucuses. Usually there is a mix of regions and country sizes, though not by any strict formula. The Council's *chairperson* rotates among the Council members monthly. Sometimes this matters: in 1990 the United States pushed for action against Iraq before the chair passed from the United States to Yemen, which opposed the U.S. position.

Substantive Security Council resolutions require *nine* votes from among the 15 members. But a "no" vote by any permanent member defeats the resolution—the *veto* power. Many resolutions have been vetoed by the permanent members, and many more have never been proposed because they would have faced certain veto. During the Cold War, the United States and the Soviet Union used their vetoes most often, followed in distant third place by Britain. However, since the mid-1990s the use of the veto has dropped abruptly, to about once a year.

Members can *abstain* on resolutions, an option that some permanent members use to register misgivings about a resolution without vetoing. China abstains with regularity because it generally reserves its veto for matters directly affecting Chinese security. Its 1997 veto of a resolution on Guatemala (a country with strong ties to Taiwan) was its first veto in nearly 25 years. As a power with more regional than global interests, China avoids alienating other great powers by blocking their actions in distant parts of the world. (If the Security Council tried to condemn China, no such restraint would apply.) The United States has abstained several times on resolutions critical of Israel.

The Security Council meets in the UN's New York headquarters upon request of a UN member—often a state with a grievance regarding another state's actions. When Kuwait was invaded, and when Bosnia was being overrun, the victim called on the Security Council—a kind of 911 phone number for the world (but one without a standing police force). Because international security continues to be troublesome in many regions, and because these troubles often drag on for months or years, meetings of the Council are frequent.

The Security Council's *power is limited* in two major ways; both reflect the strength of state sovereignty in the international system. First, the Council's decisions depend entirely on the interests of its member states. The ambassadors who represent those states cannot change a Council resolution without authorization from their governments. Second, although Security Council resolutions in theory bind all UN members, member states in practice often try to evade or soften their effect. For instance, trade sanctions are difficult to enforce because it is tempting and relatively easy to cheat. A Security Council resolution can be enforced in practice only if enough powerful states care about it.

The Security Council has a formal mechanism for coordinating multilateral military action in response to aggression, called the *Military Staff Committee*. It is composed of military officers from the permanent Council members. But the United States opposes placing its forces under non-U.S. commanders, and the committee has never been used.

Instead, military forces responding to aggression under the auspices of Security Council resolutions have remained under national command. For example, U.S. forces in the Gulf War had the mission of enforcing UN resolutions but did not display UN insignia or flags, nor did U.S. soldiers sent to Somalia in late 1992 to restore humanitarian relief efforts disrupted by civil war. Similarly, NATO forces in the former Yugoslavia, the Australian-led force in East Timor, and the British-led force in Afghanistan all operate under national flag but were authorized by UN resolution.

In most *peacekeeping* operations, by contrast, UN forces operate under UN command, wear UN insignia (including blue helmets or berets), travel in UN-marked vehicles, and so forth.

Even when the Security Council cannot agree on means of enforcement, its resolutions shape the way disputes are seen and ultimately how they are resolved. Security Council Resolution 242 after the Arab-Israeli war of 1967 laid out the principles for a just peace in that conflict—primarily the right of all states in the region to live within secure and well-defined borders and the return by Israel of territories captured in the 1967 war. (The parties are still arguing about whether territories to be returned by Israel means "all" territories.) Reaffirmed in Resolution 338 after the 1973 war, these resolutions helped shape the 1978 Camp David agreement and later formed the basis for peace negotiations between Israel and its Arab neighbours that began in 1991.

After the end of the Cold War, the prestige of the Security Council rose and it became more active than before. The first *summit meeting* of Council members in 1992 brought together for the first time the leaders of the "big five." The summit reaffirmed the universal commitments of states to the security principles embodied in the UN Charter and to the Security Council as a structure for implementing those principles. However, in the second half of the 1990s, the Council lost influence or was marginalized in such hot spots as Iraq (weapons inspections blocked), Angola (war resumed, UN pulled out), Macedonia (renewing peacekeeping forces vetoed by China), and the large Ethiopia-Eritrea war (left to the Organization of African Unity). Most importantly, the 1999 NATO bombing campaign against Serbia proceeded without authorization from the Security Council, in contrast to most great-power military interventions in the 1990s. (After the fact, the Security Council authorized an international force for Kosovo because Serbia had agreed to it.)

The Security Council can also signal through its resolutions the kinds of concerns it wants UN personnel to be aware of, and the kinds of more general issues that it wants to address through its work. For example, in October 2000 the Security Council adopted Resolution 1325 on Women, Peace and Security and noted both the differential impact of armed conflict on women and men, and called for the greater presence of women on peacekeeping missions and in peace negotiations. In April 2004, the Security Council adopted resolution 1539 on Children and Armed Conflict, in which it condemned the use of child soldiers in conflict and indicated it might resort to trade sanctions against any state that continued to recruit children into armed forces. It also acknowledged the sexual exploitation that children can be subjected to during conflicts, in some cases even by the humanitarian workers and peacekeepers who have ostensibly come to assist them.

Proposed Changes The structure of the Security Council is not without its problems. Japan and Germany are great powers that contribute substantial UN dues (based on economic size) and make large contributions to UN programs and peacekeeping operations. Yet they have exactly the same formal representation in the UN as tiny states with less than one-hundredth of their populations: one vote in the General Assembly and the chance to rotate onto the Security Council (in practice they rotate on more often than the tiny states). As global trading powers, Japan and Germany have huge stakes in the ground rules for international *security* affairs, because a stable security climate is good for international business. The security rules are written in the Security Council. Naturally Japan and Germany would like seats at the table. In 2003, Japan decided to reduce its UN dues by one-quarter, in part because of unhappiness of the Security Council issue.

But including Japan and Germany as permanent Council members would not be simple. If Germany joined, three of the seven permanent members would be European, giving that region unfair weight (especially from the viewpoint of former European colonies in the global South). The three European seats could be combined into one (a rotating seat or one representing the European Union), but this would water down the power of Britain and France, which can veto any such change in the Charter. Also, if Japan or Germany were given a seat, then what about India, with 20 percent of the world's population? It, too, has only a lone vote in the General Assembly and so is badly underrepresented in the present scheme. But China (with a veto) would not welcome rival India onto the Council. Shouldn't an expanded Security Council include at least one predominantly Islamic country (such as Indonesia or Nigeria)? But which state could represent such a diverse set of countries? Finally, what about Latin America and Africa? One plan to overhaul the Security Council, proposed by Brazil in 1992, would give permanent seats, but without veto power, to Japan, Germany, India, Brazil, Nigeria, Egypt, and perhaps others—expanding the Council to around 25 members.

None of these plans has made much progress. Any overhaul of the Security Council would require a change in the UN Charter, possibly opening other issues of Charter reform on which member states disagree. Any change in membership would reduce the power of the current five permanent members, any one of which could veto the change. Thus, changes in the structure of the Security Council are difficult to achieve, barring a compelling reason to act.

Table 7.1 shows the recent rotations of members onto the Security Council. The system of nomination by regional caucuses has worked to keep the regional balance on the Council fairly constant as individual states come and go. Major regional actors, including those mentioned as candidates for possible new permanent seats (shown at right in the table), tend to rotate onto the Council more often than do less important states.

Peacekeeping Forces

Peacekeeping forces are not mentioned in the UN Charter. Secretary-General Dag Hammarskjöld in the 1960s joked that they were allowed under "Chapter Six and a Half"—somewhere between the nonviolent dispute resolution called for in Chapter 6 of the Charter and the authorization of force provided for in Chapter 7. The Charter requires member states to place military forces at the disposal of the UN, but such forces were envisioned as being used in response to aggression (under collective security). In

Table 7.1 Regional Representation on the UN Security Council

Region	Permanent Members[a]	NONPERMANENT MEMBERS[b]			Possible Contenders for New Permanent Seats[c]
		2004	2003	2002	
North America	United States				
W. Europe	Britain France	Germany Spain	Germany Spain	Norway Ireland	Germany
Japan/Pacific					Japan
Russia & E. Europe	Russia	Romania	Bulgaria	Bulgaria	
China	China				
Middle East		Algeria	Syria	Syria	Egypt?
Latin America		Brazil Chile	Mexico Chile	Mexico Colombia	Brazil, Mexico?
South Asia		Pakistan Philippines	Pakistan	Singapore	India, Indonesia?
Africa		Angola Benin	Angola Cameroon Guinea	Mauritius Cameroon Guinea	Nigeria?

[a] The five permanent members hold veto power.
[b] Nonpermanent members are elected for two-year terms by the General Assembly, based on nominations by regional caucuses.
[c] Possible new permanent seats might have fewer if any veto powers.

practice, when the UN has authorized force to reverse aggression—as in the Gulf War in 1990—the forces involved have been *national* forces not under UN command.

The UN's *own* forces—borrowed from armies of member states but under the flag and command of the UN—have been *peacekeeping* forces to calm regional conflicts, playing a neutral role between warring forces.[20] The first UN peacekeeping mission was established in the Suez in 1956 after Britain, France, and Israel invaded Egypt when the Nasser government nationalized the Suez Canal Company. That peacekeeping mission was aimed as much at allowing Britain and France—two Security Council members—to withdraw without losing face as it was at bringing the conflict to an end. The plan for the mission, United Nations Emergency Force I (UNEF I), was developed by Canada's then Ambassador to the UN, Lester B. Pearson, who would win a Nobel Peace Prize for his efforts. UN troops acted as a buffer between Israeli and Egyptian forces until 1967, and in large part, UNEF I was considered a success. It also set the principles that served as the basis of all subsequent peacekeeping missions: the importance of securing the consent of the parties to the dispute; the non-use of force, except for self-defence; and impartiality.[21]

---

[20] Michael W. Doyle, Ian Johnstone, and Robert C. Orr, eds., *Keeping the Peace: Multidimensional UN Operations in Cambodia and El Salvador* (NY: Cambridge UP, 1997). James Mayall, ed., *The New Interventionism, 1991–1994: United Nations Experience in Cambodia, Former Yugoslavia, and Somalia* (NY: Cambridge UP, 1996). William J. Durch, ed., *The Evolution of UN Peacekeeping: Case Studies and Comparative Analysis* (NY: St. Martin's, 1993). Steven R. Ratner, *The New UN Peacekeeping: Building Peace in Lands of Conflict after the Cold War* (NY: St. Martin's, 1995).

[21] Jocelyn Coulon, *Soldiers of Diplomacy: The United Nations, Peacekeeping, and the New World Order* (U Toronto P, 1998). A.B. Fetherston, *Towards a Theory of United Nations Peacekeeping* (Basingstoke, UK: Macmillan, 1994).

Throughout the Cold War, it was normally small or middle powers that contributed troops to peacekeeping missions, such as Ireland, India, Pakistan, Canada, Fiji, Indonesia, the Netherlands, Italy, and the Nordic countries. Large powers tended to make financial contributions but only rarely contributed troops. Though more large powers have begun to deploy troops on peace missions, peacekeeping remains largely a preserve of smaller and middle powers. Canada was not only actively involved in the creation of peacekeeping, it has been an active participant in most peacekeeping missions and is described by some observers as the peacekeeping country "par excellence."[22] By 2004, most of the largest troop-contributing countries were small and middle powers of the global South: Bangladesh, Ethiopia, Ghana, India, Jordan, Kenya, Nepal, Nigeria, Pakistan, Senegal, and Uruguay.

UN forces themselves won the Nobel peace prize in 1988 in recognition of their growing importance and success. As was learned in Bosnia, however, such neutral forces do not succeed well in a situation where the Security Council has identified one side as the aggressor—in short, when the UN departs from the principles upon which peace-keeping was based.

Peacekeeping Missions The secretary-general assembles a peacekeeping force for each mission, usually from a few states totally uninvolved in the conflict, and puts it under a single commander. The soldiers are commonly called **blue helmets** or blue berets. Peacekeeping forces serve at the invitation of a host government and must leave if that government orders them out (as Egypt did in 1967).

Authority for peacekeeping forces is granted by the Security Council, usually for a period of three to six months, that may be renewed—in some cases for decades. In the Suez crisis in 1956, the General Assembly authorized the forces under the "Uniting for Peace" resolution, allowing the Assembly to take up security matters when the Security Council was deadlocked (because of France and Britain's involvement in the conflict). In the Congo in 1960 it was the secretary-general who took the initiative. But today the Security Council controls peacekeeping operations, and they are authorized by Security Council resolutions.

Funds must be voted by the General Assembly, and lack of funds is today the single greatest constraint on the use of peacekeeping forces. Special assessments against member states pay for peacekeeping operations. With the expansion of peacekeeping in 1988–1994, the expenses of these forces (more than US$3 billion in 1993) came to exceed the rest of the UN budget by more than 2 to 1, but the sharp reduction in peacekeeping forces in 1994–1997 reduced costs to about US$1 billion annually. By 2003, peacekeeping costs had risen to US$2.6 billion annually, but by 2004 peacekeeping was growing again and the secretary-general predicted that the UN would need nearly US$4 billion to cover peace-keeping missions by the end of the year. Total unpaid contributions to peacekeeping, at mid-2004, was US$1.19 billion, what many observers described as a financial crisis within the UN. (See Global Policy Forum, http://www.globalpolicy.org)

Recent Missions In mid-2004, the UN maintained 58 862 troops, civilian police, and military observers from 97 countries in 16 separate peacekeeping or observing missions, spanning five world regions (see Table 7.2 on p. 262). (Missions change from year to year.) The size and cost of peacekeeping has nearly tripled since 1997 and is almost back to the peak levels of 1993.

blue helmets The UN peace-keeping forces, so called because they wear helmets or berets in the UN colour, blue, with UN insignia.

----

[22] Joseph T. Jockel, *Canada and International Peacekeeping* (Washington, DC: Center for Strategic and International Studies, 1994).

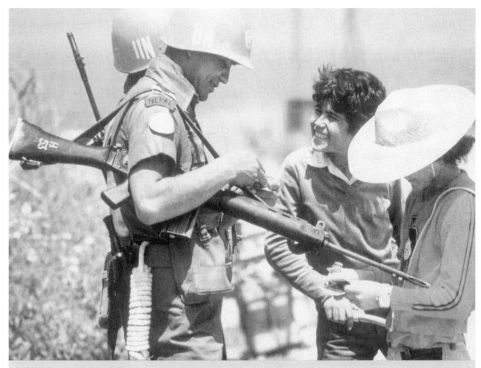

KEEPING THE PEACE
UN peacekeeping forces operate under authority of the Security Council with troops contributed voluntarily by an assortment of states. Peacekeeping grew rapidly in the early 1990s, declined in the late 1990s after several problem-plagued missions, and has grown again in recent years. Here, peacekeeping troops from Nepal patrol southern Lebanon, 1978.

The largest peacekeeping mission in early 2004 was in Liberia, where 16 000 peacekeepers disarmed militias and supervised elections after a civil war. The UN's other largest peacekeeping operations were in Sierra Leone (supporting a peace agreement and the disarmament, demobilization and reintegration, or DDR, plan) and the Democratic Republic of the Congo (assisting the parties in maintaining a ceasefire agreement). Both of these missions involved slightly fewer personnel than Liberia, but in the case of the mission to the Democratic Republic of the Congo, had a slightly larger budget. Other current missions include Kosovo (running the province pending resolution of its dispute with parent state Serbia), Lebanon (monitoring the war-torn Israeli border area), Ethiopia-Eritrea (monitoring a ceasefire after a recurrent border war), Haiti (support of the transitional government), Burundi (assistance in implementing a peace accord) and Côte d'Ivoire (facilitating implementation of a peace accord).

NATO-led forces largely replaced UN peacekeepers in Bosnia in the late 1990s (and, later, took military control of Kosovo). UN operations in these countries focus on civilian governmental functions, leaving security matters largely to UN-authorized but independently commanded international forces.

The same approach was used in East Timor, but with an Australian-led force replacing NATO. In 1999, the UN oversaw elections in which residents of East Timor—a former Portuguese colony occupied by neighbouring Indonesia for two decades—voted for

Table 7.2 UN Peacekeeping Missions as of Mid-2004

Location	Region	Size	Annual Cost (millions US$)	Role	Since
Liberia	Africa	15 985	$564.49	Assist transitional government	2003
Sierra Leone	Africa	11 960	$543.49	Help implement peace agreement	1999
Democratic Congo	Africa	11 407	$667.27	Observe ceasefire	1999
Côte d'Ivoire	Africa	3 189	$502.35	Facilitate implementation of a peace agreement	2004
Burundi	Africa	0 deployed (5770 authorized)	Under preparation	Assist implementation of Arusha peace agreement	2004
Ethiopia/Eritrea	Africa	4 247	$196.89	Monitor post-war border	2000
Western Sahara	Africa	369	$43.4	Organize referendum in territory	1991
Haiti	Americas	332 (8322 authorized)	Under preparation	Support transitional government	2004
East Timor	South Asia	2 003	$217.16	Peacekeeping; relief; administration	1999
India/Pakistan	South Asia	66	$7.25	Observe India-Pakistan ceasefire	1949
Kosovo	Russia/E. Eur.	4 366	$329.74	Civil administration; relief	1999
Georgia	Russia/E. Eur.	231	$32.10	Observe ceasefire in civil war	1993
Lebanon	Middle East	2 106	$94.06	Monitor ceasefire on Israeli border	1978
Cyprus	Middle East	1 288	$45.77	Monitor Greek-Turkish ceasefire	1964
Syria (Golan Heights)	Middle East	1 067	$41.81	Monitor Israel-Syria ceasefire	1974
Israel	Middle East	246	$27.69	Observe Arab-Israeli truce	1948
Total		58 862	$3 313.47		

independence. In response, the Indonesian army presided over a campaign of killing and burning by pro-Indonesian militias, evidently aimed at deterring provinces of Indonesia itself from pursuing separatism. Indonesia then withdrew, and an Australian-commanded international force under a UN mandate took control. The UN itself then began running a transitional administration, which led to statehood for East Timor in 2002.

At its peak in the early 1990s, the UN ran several other large peacekeeping operations in addition to those in the former Yugoslavia and in Lebanon. One of the most important was in *Cambodia*, called the United Nations Transitional Authority in Cambodia, or UNTAC. There, more than 15 000 peacekeepers were coupled with a large force of UN administrators, police, and volunteers who took over substantial control of the Cambodian government under a fragile pact that ended (for the most part) a long and devastating civil war. Despite difficulty in obtaining the cooperation of the Khmer Rouge faction (which refused to disarm as it had agreed), the UN pressed forward to hold elections in 1993 that chose a Cambodian government (though not a stable one).[23]

---

[23] Michael W. Doyle, *UN Peacekeeping in Cambodia: UNTAC's Civilian Mandate* (Boulder, CO: Lynne Rienner, 1995).

However, UNTAC also illustrated some of the other problems associated with large-scale peacekeeping missions. The arrival of over 20 000 UN troops and civilian personnel had an enormous social impact on Cambodia: prostitution increased exponentially, as did cases of HIV/AIDS and reports of sexual assaults against local women. The presence of these foreign personnel (most of whom earned more money in a single day than the average Cambodian earned in a year) also had disruptive economic effects, causing rampant inflation such that the cost of basic goods, food, and housing skyrocketed.[24]

Some of the lessons learned in Cambodia helped the UN accomplish a similar mission more easily in *Mozambique*. A peace agreement ended a long and devastating civil war there, setting up mechanisms for disarmament, the integration of military forces, and the holding of internationally supervised elections for a new government. However, reports of sexual exploitation of local women and children plagued that mission as well and similar charges emerged in 2004 regarding UN personnel on the peacekeeping mission to the Democratic Republic of the Congo.[25]

In 1992, the UN had tried to accomplish a similar mission in *Angola* with only 500 personnel. The peace process was on track until the government won the elections; the rebels refused to accept the results and resumed an even more destructive civil war. At the next opportunity, the UN sent a force to Angola 10 times larger than before. Results improved, but the war started again and the UN Security Council ended the mission in 1999. The UN Department of Peacekeeping Operations has created a Best Practices Unit in order to learn from experiences and respond more effectively, for example after civil wars in Sierra Leone, Côte d'Ivoire, and Liberia in 2002–2003.

The accomplishments of peacekeeping missions thus are quite mixed: sometimes they have made important contributions to keeping the peace, but they do not always achieve their goals, and sometimes the negative social impact on the country in which the mission has been deployed can be quite serious.

Observing and Peacekeeping   "Peacekeepers" actually perform two different functions—observing and peacekeeping. *Observers* are unarmed military officers sent to a conflict area in small numbers simply to watch what happens and report back to the UN. With the UN watching, the parties to a conflict are often less likely to break a ceasefire. Observers can *monitor* various aspects of a country's situation—ceasefires, elections, respect for human rights, and other areas. (Often this monitoring—such as certifying whether an election is fair—is organized by IGOs and NGOs outside the UN as well.) This kind of monitoring was useful in the transitions from war to democracy in Nicaragua and El Salvador in the 1990s.

The function of *peacekeeping* is carried out by lightly armed soldiers (in armoured vehicles with automatic rifles but without artillery, tanks, and other heavy weapons). Such forces play several roles. They can *interpose* themselves physically between warring parties to keep them apart (more accurately, to make them attack the UN forces in order to get to their enemy). UN peacekeepers often try to *negotiate* with military officers on both sides. This channel of communication can bring about tactical actions and

---

[24] Peter Utting, ed., *Between Hope and Insecurity: The Social Consequences of the Cambodian Peace Process* (Geneva: United Nations Research Institute for Social Development, 1994). Sandra Whitworth, *Men, Militarism and UN Peacekeeping: A Gendered Analysis* (Boulder: Rienner, 2004).

[25] Graça Machel, "The Impact of Armed Conflict on Children Report of the Expert of the Secretary-General, Ms. Graça Machel, Submitted Pursuant to General Assembly Resolution 48/157," United Nations General Assembly, A/51/306 (26 Aug. 1996). Kate Holt and Sarah Hughes, "SA soldiers fingered in DRC abuse scandal," *Pretoria News* 12 July 2004: 1.

understandings that support a ceasefire. But the UN forces in a war zone cannot easily get from one side's positions to those of the other to conduct negotiations.

Peacekeeping is much more difficult if one side sees the UN forces as being *biased* toward the other side. Israel feels this way about UN forces in southern Lebanon, for example. On occasion Israeli forces have broken through UN lines to attack enemies, and they allegedly have targeted UN outposts on occasion. In Cambodia and the former Yugoslavia in the early 1990s, one party deliberately attacked UN forces many times, causing a number of deaths. In general, when ceasefires break down, UN troops get caught in the middle. Nearly 1900 have been killed over the years—most of them in the Congo (Zaire) in 1960–1964, in Cyprus since 1964, in southern Lebanon since 1978, and in the former Yugoslavia in the 1990s. Canada has lost 106 peacekeeping personnel serving on UN missions. In some conflicts, peacekeepers organized outside the UN framework have been used instead of UN-commanded forces; CIS troops have played this role occasionally in the former Soviet Union, and U.S. forces have acted as peacekeepers in Egypt's Sinai desert since the 1970s.

Peacemaking In the past, peacekeeping forces have generally been unable to make peace, only to keep it. To go into a shooting war and suppress hostilities requires military forces far beyond those of past UN peacekeeping missions. Thus, peacekeepers are usually not sent until a ceasefire has been arranged, has taken effect, and has held up for some time. Often dozens of ceasefires are broken before one sticks—wars may simmer along for years, taking a terrible toll, before the UN gets its chance.

To address this problem, the secretary-general in 1992 proposed to create UN *peacemaking* (or *peace enforcement*) units that would not only monitor a ceasefire but enforce it if it broke down. These forces would be more heavily armed than peacekeeping forces because they would weigh into the battle. Also, they would be able to respond within a few days, rather than within several months as with past peacekeeping forces.[26] The secretary-general called for member states to make available, on a rapid deployment basis, 1000 soldiers each—specially trained volunteers—to create a standby UN army that could respond quickly to crises. Chapter 7 of the UN Charter allows the UN to draw on resources of member states in this way, but these provisions have not yet been used. Control over the deployment and operation of these forces would be held by the Security Council.

Not only did the member states refuse the request for soldiers, they shot down the idea of peacemaking and did not provide peace enforcement forces for Bosnia where the need was most pressing. In 1995, a more combat-ready "reaction force" was tried out briefly in Bosnia, but it was soon replaced when NATO-led forces took over from the UN there. Since then the UN has authorized member states to provide real military forces, not peacekeepers, when fighting may be required.

Peacekeeping missions themselves were scaled back drastically in the mid-1990s. In some cases, the great powers turned down the secretary-general when he urgently requested a peacekeeping mission to head off an impending disaster—for example, in Burundi in 1995, when the same Hutu-Tutsi conflict as in Rwanda threatened to erupt into another genocide.

In the late 1990s, as peacekeeping again expanded, seven countries—Denmark, Norway, Sweden, Poland, the Netherlands, Austria, and Canada—formed a 4000-troop UN Standby High Readiness Brigade. Headquartered in Denmark and available to deploy to conflict areas in two to four weeks rather than months as now, the brigade is controlled by the Security Council. It participated in the UN mission to Ethiopia-Eritrea in 2000–2001.

---

[26] Boutros Boutros-Ghali, *An Agenda for Peace: Preventive Diplomacy, Peacemaking and Peace-keeping* (NY: United Nations, 1992). Tom Woodhouse, Robert Bruce, and Malcolm Dando, eds., *Peacekeeping and Peacemaking: Towards Effective Intervention in Post–Cold War Conflicts* (NY: St. Martin's, 1998).

The Secretariat

The secretary-general of the UN is the closest thing to a "president or prime minister of the world" that exists. But the secretary-general represents member states—especially the five permanent Security Council members—and not the world's six billion people. The past secretary-general, Boutros Boutros-Ghali, was fond of calling himself just the "humble servant" of the member states. When the great powers do not have consensus, it is in fact hard for the secretary-general to be anything more than a humble servant.

The secretary-general is *nominated* by the Security Council—requiring the consent of all five permanent members—and must be *approved* by the General Assembly. The term of office is five years and may be renewed. Boutros-Ghali in 1996 fought for a second term, with the support of almost every UN member, but the United States opposed him and prevailed. Kofi Annan, the current secretary-general, finally emerged as a consensus choice. He has reinvigorated the UN,

WHOLE WORLD IN HIS HANDS
The UN secretary-general has a lofty mission but limited power and resources. Kofi Annan (1997) was the first to rise through the UN bureaucracy to the top position.

was re-elected in 2001 for five more years, and won the one-hundredth-anniversary Nobel Peace Prize. *Time* magazine said he "may well be the world's best-loved and most widely respected political figure."[27] Some critics of Annan, however, say that this support is centred more in the U.S. than the rest of the world.

The Secretariat of the UN is its executive branch, headed by the secretary-general. It is a bureaucracy for administering UN policy and programs, just as Foreign Affairs Canada is a bureaucracy for Canadian foreign policy. In security matters, the secretary-general personally works with the Security Council; development programs are coordinated by a second-in-command—the director-general for Development and International Economic Co-operation. The Secretariat is divided into functional areas, with undersecretaries-general and assistant secretaries-general.

The *UN staff* in these areas includes administrative personnel as well as technical experts and economic advisers working on various programs and projects in the member countries. The staff numbers about 15 000 people, and the total number of employees in the UN system is just more than 60 000. There is a concentration of UN-related agency offices in Geneva, Switzerland. Geneva is a frequent site of international negotiations and is seen by some as more neutral than New York. A few development programs are headquartered in cities of the global South.

One purpose of the UN Secretariat is to develop an *international civil service* of diplomats and bureaucrats whose loyalties are at the global level, not to their states of origin. The UN Charter sets the secretary-general and staff apart from the authority of national governments and calls on member states to respect the staff's "exclusively international character." The UN has been fairly successful in this regard; the secretary-general is

---

[27] *Time* 29 June 2001.

usually seen as an independent diplomat thinking about the whole world's interests, not a pawn of any state. Enthusiastic support by any one member of the Security Council can call a secretary-general's independence into question. For critics of Kofi Annan, this is true of his relationship with the U.S. (a criticism that became less compelling after the UN's refusal to authorize the U.S. attack on Iraq).

The secretary-general is more than a bureaucratic manager. He (it has not yet been a she) is a visible public figure whose personal attention to a regional conflict can move it toward resolution. The Charter allows the secretary-general to use the UN's "good offices" to serve as a neutral mediator in international conflicts—to bring hostile parties together in negotiations. For example, Boutros-Ghali was personally involved in trying to mediate conflicts in Somalia and the former Yugoslavia. Annan tried to talk Iraq into compliance with UN inspections in 1997, to which Iraq responded only in 2003. Annan used his position in 2001 to try to galvanize a stronger (and better funded) international program against AIDS (see p. 522).

The secretary-general also works to bring together the great-power consensus on which Security Council action depends—a much harder job than mere bureaucratic management. The secretary-general has the power under the Charter to bring to the Security Council any matter that might threaten international peace and security, and so to play a major role in setting the UN's agenda in international security affairs.

Boutros Boutros-Ghali was the secretary-general from 1992 through 1996. He was a "diplomat's diplomat" from Egypt, with decades of experience in foreign service and the UN. Boutros-Ghali tried to expand UN peacekeeping and peacemaking in local conflicts before they escalated and spread. But his assertiveness in the Security Council caused frictions with permanent members of the Council, especially the United States. He scolded members of the Security Council for giving him big mandates without adequate resources to carry them out.

By contrast, the current secretary-general, Kofi Annan (1997–2006), a U.S.-educated manager who knows the UN bureaucracy well, has concentrated on reforming the UN Secretariat's finances and operations and improving relations between the UN and the United States. Annan is the first secretary-general from sub-Saharan Africa (Ghana), and the first to rise through the UN civil service. He was previously undersecretary-general for peacekeeping operations, and gained a reputation for making the best of ill-conceived peacekeeping missions in Somalia and Bosnia in the early 1990s. But he was also the focus of criticism for the disaster in Rwanda, and for the Department of Peacekeeping Operation's failure to take the UN Commander General Roméo Dallaire's warnings of a coming genocide seriously.

Just as the Canadian prime minister can have tensions with Cabinet over foreign policy, the secretary-general sometimes has tensions with the Security Council. But the secretary-general is chosen by the Security Council and has less autonomy than the Canadian prime minister. When the secretary-general asks for authority for a peacekeeping mission for six months, the Security Council is likely to say "three months." If the secretary-general asks for $10 million, he might get $5 million. Thus the secretary-general remains, like the entire UN system, constrained by state sovereignty.

Past Secretaries-General have come from various regions of the world but never from a great power. They are Trygve Lie (from Norway, 1946–1952), Dag Hammarskjöld (Sweden, 1953–1961), U Thant (Burma, 1961–1971), Kurt Waldheim (Austria, 1972–1981), Javier Perez de Cuellar (Peru, 1982–1991), Boutros Boutros-Ghali (Egypt, 1992–1996), and Kofi Annan (Ghana, 1997–2006).

The General Assembly

The General Assembly is made up of all 191 member states of the UN, each with one vote. It usually meets every year, from late September through January, in *plenary session*. State leaders or foreign ministers, including the Canadian prime minister, generally come through one by one to address this assemblage. The Assembly sessions, like most UN deliberations, are simultaneously translated into dozens of languages so that delegates from around the world can carry on a single conversation. This global town hall is a unique institution and provides a powerful medium for states to put forward their ideas and arguments. Presiding over it is a president elected by the Assembly—a post without much power.

The Assembly convenes for *special sessions* every few years on general topics such as economic cooperation. The UN special session on disarmament in June 1982 provided the occasion for the largest political rally in U.S. history—a peace demonstration of a million people in New York. The Assembly has met in *emergency session* in the past to deal with an immediate threat to international peace and security, but this has happened only nine times and has now become uncommon.

The General Assembly has the power to accredit national delegations as members of the UN (through its Credentials Committee). For instance, in 1971 the delegation of the People's Republic of China was given China's seat in the UN (including on the Security Council) in place of the nationalists in Taiwan. For decades, neither North nor South Korea became members of the UN (because both claimed the whole of Korea), but they finally took seats as separate delegations in 1991. Some political entities that fall short of state status send *permanent observer missions* to the UN. These missions participate without a vote in the General Assembly. They include the Vatican (Holy See) and the Palestine Liberation Organization (PLO).

The General Assembly's main power lies in its *control of finances* for UN programs and operations, including peacekeeping. It also can *pass resolutions* on various matters, but these are purely advisory and not binding on member states. The Assembly also *elects members* of certain UN agencies and programs. Finally, the Assembly coordinates UN programs and agencies through its own system of committees, commissions, councils, and so forth.

The Assembly coordinates UN programs and agencies through the Economic and Social Council (ECOSOC), which has 54 member states elected by the General Assembly for three-year terms. ECOSOC manages the overlapping work of a large number of programs and agencies. Its *regional commissions* look at how UN programs work together in a particular region; its *functional commissions* deal with global topics such as population growth, narcotics trafficking, human rights, and the status of women; its *expert bodies* work on technical subjects that cut across various UN programs in areas such as crime prevention and public finances. Outside of ECOSOC, the General Assembly operates many *other specialized committees*. Standing committees ease the work of the Assembly in issue areas such as decolonization, legal matters, or disarmament.

Many of the activities associated with the UN do not take place under tight control of either the General Assembly or the Security Council. They occur in functional agencies and programs having various amounts of autonomy from UN control.

UN Programs

Through the Economic and Social Council, the General Assembly oversees more than a dozen major programs to advance economic development and social stability in poor

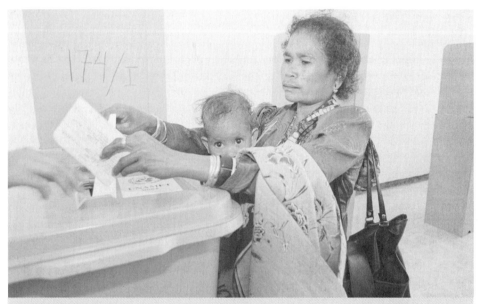

BIRTH OF A NATION
An array of UN programs, operating under the General Assembly, aim to help countries in the global South to overcome social and economic problems. Braving intimidation from pro-Indonesian militias, the population of East Timor voted overwhelmingly for independence in a 1999 UN-sponsored referendum. As a result, the former Portuguese colony, which had been occupied by Indonesia since 1975, came under UN administration in a transition to statehood—but not before the militias exacted violent revenge, burning and looting much of the territory. Indonesia eventually let an Australian-led international military force occupy East Timor, then turn over power to the interim UN administration. Full statehood arrived in 2002.

states of the global South. Through its programs, the UN helps to manage global North-South relations: it organizes a flow of resources and skills from the richer parts of the world to support development in the poorer parts.

The programs are *funded* partly by General Assembly allocations and partly by contributions that the programs raise directly from member states, businesses, or private charitable contributors. The degree of General Assembly funding, and of operational autonomy from the Assembly, varies from one program to another. Each UN program has a staff, a headquarters, and various operations in the field, where it works with host governments in member states.

Several of these programs are of growing importance. The *UN Environment Program (UNEP)* became more prominent in the 1990s as the economic development of the global South and the growing economies of the industrialized world took a toll on the world environment (see Chapter 13). UNEP grapples with global environmental strategies, guided by principles adopted at the Earth Summit (the UN Conference on Environment and Development) in Brazil in 1992. UNEP provides technical assistance to member states, monitors environmental conditions globally, develops standards, and recommends alternative energy sources.

UNICEF is the UN Children's Fund, which gives technical and financial assistance to developing countries for programs benefiting children. It is involved in research as well, for example in areas such as the use of child soldiers. Unfortunately, the needs of children in many countries are still urgent, and UNICEF is kept busy. Financed by voluntary contributions, UNICEF has for decades organized U.S. and Canadian children in an annual Halloween fund drive on behalf of their counterparts in poorer countries.

The *Office of the UN High Commissioner for Refugees (UNHCR)* has also been kept busy in recent years. UNHCR coordinates efforts to protect, assist, and eventually repatriate the many refugees who flee across international borders each year to escape from war and political violence. (The longer-standing problem of Palestinian refugees is handled by a different program, the *UN Relief Works Agency*, or *UNRWA*.)

The *UN Development Program (UNDP)*, funded by voluntary contributions, coordinates all UN efforts related to development in the global South. With about 5000 projects operating simultaneously around the world, UNDP is the world's largest international agency for technical development assistance. The UN also runs several development-related agencies for training and for promoting women's role in development.

Many developing countries depend on export revenues to finance economic development, making those countries vulnerable to fluctuations in commodity prices and other problems involved in international trade. The **UN Conference on Trade and Development (UNCTAD)** seeks to negotiate international trade agreements to stabilize commodity prices and promote development. Because countries of the global South do not have much power in the international economy, however, UNCTAD has little leverage with which to promote their interests in trade (see p. 474).

> **UN Conference on Trade and Development (UNCTAD)** A structure established in 1964 to promote development in the global South through various trade proposals.

Other UN programs manage problems such as disaster relief, food aid, housing, and population issues. Throughout the poorer countries, the UN maintains an active presence in economic and social affairs.

Autonomous Agencies

In addition to its own programs, the UN General Assembly maintains formal ties with about 20 autonomous international agencies not under its control. Most are specialized technical organizations through which states pool their efforts to address problems such as health care and labour conditions.

The only such agency in international security affairs is the *International Atomic Energy Agency (IAEA)*, headquartered in Vienna, Austria. It was established under the UN but is formally autonomous. Although the IAEA has an economic role in helping to develop civilian nuclear power plants, it mainly works to prevent nuclear proliferation (see p. 228). The IAEA was responsible for inspections in Iraq in 2002–2003, which found no evidence of a secret nuclear weapons program.

In the area of health care, the **World Health Organization (WHO)** based in Geneva provides technical assistance to improve conditions in the global South and conducts major immunization campaigns in poor countries. In the 1960s and 1970s, WHO led one of the great public health victories of all time—the worldwide eradication of smallpox. Today WHO is a leading player in the worldwide fight to control AIDS (see pp. 521–523). In 2003, Canadians became directly aware of WHO's work when it issued a travel advisory against Toronto due to the outbreak of severe acute respiratory syndrome (SARS) there.

> **World Health Organization (WHO)** Based in Geneva, an IO that provides technical assistance to improve health conditions primarily in the global South (but can address health concerns anywhere around the world) and conducts major immunization campaigns.

In agriculture, the Food and Agriculture Organization (FAO) is the lead agency. In labour standards, it is the International Labor Organization (ILO). UNESCO—the UN Educational, Scientific, and Cultural Organization—facilitates international communication and scientific collaboration. The UN Industrial Development Organization (UNIDO) promotes industrialization in the global South.

The longest-established IOs, with some of the most successful records, are specialized agencies dealing with technical aspects of international coordination, such as aviation and postal exchange. For instance, the *International Telecommunications Union (ITU)* allocates radio frequencies. The *Universal Postal Union (UPU)* sets standards for international mail. The *International Civil Aviation Organization (ICAO)* sets binding standards for international air traffic. The *International Maritime Organization (IMO)* facilitates international cooperation on shipping at sea. The *World Intellectual Property Organization (WIPO)* seeks world compliance with copyrights and patents, and promotes development and technology transfer within a legal framework that protects such intellectual property (see p. 317). Finally, the *World Meteorological Association (WMO)* oversees a world weather watch and promotes the exchange of weather information.

The major coordinating agencies of the world economy (discussed in Chapters 8, 9, and 12) are also UN-affiliated agencies. The World Bank and the International Monetary Fund (IMF) give loans, grants, and technical assistance for economic development (and the IMF manages international balance-of-payments accounting). The World Trade Organization (WTO) sets rules for international trade.

Overall, the density of connections across national borders, both in the UN system and through other IOs, is increasing year by year. In a less tangible way, people are also becoming connected across international borders through the meshing of ideas, including norms and rules. And gradually the rules are becoming international laws.

INTERNATIONAL LAW

IOs impinge on state sovereignty by creating new structures (both supranational and transnational) for regulating relations across borders. International law and international norms limit state sovereignty in another way. They create principles for governing international relations that compete with the core realist principles of sovereignty and anarchy.

International law, unlike national laws, derives not from actions of a legislative branch or other central authority, but from tradition and agreements signed by states. It also differs in the difficulty of enforcement, which depends not on the power and authority of central government but on reciprocity, collective action, and international norms.[28]

Sources of International Law

Laws within states come from central authorities—legislatures or dictators. Because states are sovereign and recognize no central authority, international law rests on a different basis. The declarations of the UN General Assembly are not laws, and most do not bind the members. The Security Council can compel certain actions by states, but these are commands rather than laws: they are specific to a situation. No body of international law has been passed by a legislative body. Where, then, does international law come from? Four sources of international law are recognized: treaties, custom, general principles of law (such as equity), and legal scholarship (including past judicial decisions).

---

[28] Michael Byers, ed., *The Role of Law in International Politics* (NY: Oxford UP, 2000). Malcolm N. Shaw, *International Law*, 4th ed. (Cambridge: Cambridge UP, 1998). Anthony D'Amato, *International Law: Process and Prospect*, 2nd ed. (Ardsley, NY: Transnational, 1995). Rosalyn Higgins, *Problems and Process: International Law and How We Use It* (NY: Oxford UP, 1994). Thomas M. Franck, *Fairness in International Law and Institutions* (NY: Oxford UP, 1995).

Treaties and other written conventions signed by states are the most important source.[29] International treaties now fill more than a thousand thick volumes, with tens of thousands of individual agreements. There is a principle in international law that treaties once signed and ratified must be observed (*pacta sunt servanda*). States violate the terms of treaties they have signed only if the matter is very important or the penalties for such a violation seem very small. In Canada, treaties are ratified by Cabinet. Implementing the treaty (if it requires changes to Canadian legislation, or the creation of new legislation) is charged to Parliament or, if appropriate, provincial legislatures.

Treaties and other international obligations such as debts are *binding on successor governments* whether the new government takes power through an election, a coup, or a revolution. After the revolutions in Eastern Europe around 1990, newly democratic governments were held responsible for debts incurred by their communist predecessors. Even when the Soviet Union broke up, Russia as the successor state had to guarantee that Soviet debts would be paid and Soviet treaties honoured. Although revolution does not free a state from its obligations, some treaties have built-in escape clauses that let states legally withdraw from them, after giving due notice, without violating international law. The United States in 2001, as discussed below, invoked the six-month opt-out provision of the ABM treaty.

Because of the universal commitment for all states to respect certain basic principles of international law, the UN Charter is one of the world's most important treaties. Its implications are broad and far-reaching, in contrast to more specific treaties, such as a fishery management agreement. The specialized agreements are usually easier to interpret and more enforceable than broad treaties such as the Charter.

Custom is the second major source of international law. If states behave toward each other in a certain way for long enough, their behaviour may become generally accepted practice with the status of law. Western international law (though not Islamic law) tends to be *positivist* in this regard—it draws on actual customs, the practical realities of self-interest, and the need for consent rather than on an abstract concept of divine or natural law.

General principles of law also serve as a source of international law. Actions such as theft and assault recognized in most national legal systems as crimes tend to have the same meaning in an international context. Iraq's invasion of Kuwait was illegal under treaties signed by Iraq (including the UN Charter and that of the Arab League) and under the custom Iraq and Kuwait had established of living in peace as sovereign states. Beyond treaty or custom, the invasion violated international law because of the general principle that one state may not overrun its neighbour's territory and annex it by force. (Of course, a state may still think it can get away with such a violation of international law.)

The fourth source of international law, recognized by the World Court as subsidiary to the others, is *legal scholarship*—the written arguments of judges and lawyers around the world on the issues in question. Only the writings of the most highly qualified and respected legal figures can be taken into account, and then only to resolve points not resolved by the first three sources of international law.

Often international law lags behind changes in norms; law is quite tradition-bound. Certain activities, such as espionage, are technically illegal but are so widely condoned that they cannot be said to violate international norms. Other activities are still legal but have come to be frowned upon and seen as abnormal. For example, China's shooting of student demonstrators in 1989 violated international norms but not international law.

---

[29] Paul Reuter, *Introduction to the Law of Treaties* (London: Pinter, 1992).

The Changing World Order
The Place of International Law

World orders encompass not only power relationships, but the rules and norms that shape behaviour on the international stage. International law provides an important and detailed guide to such behaviour, which states generally—though not perfectly—follow. In particular, great powers usually follow the laws of war (though less so in counter-guerrilla warfare, such as in Vietnam in the 1960s, Afghanistan in the 1980s, or Chechnya in the 1990s).

One feature of world order during the decade preceding 2001 was the increasing strength of international law. The UN convened tribunals to hear war-crimes cases from the former Yugoslavia and Rwanda, and many states worked to craft a new permanent International Criminal Court with powers to try such cases from anywhere in the world. International law began extending into new areas, such as human rights and humanitarian intervention. UN Secretary-General Kofi Annan even said after the 1999 Kosovo war that nations must not use the UN Charter as cover to commit genocide, and that human rights took "precedence over concerns of state sovereignty." However, he added, these norms were "evolving" and did not negate the continuing importance of sovereignty.

Clearly, terrorist attacks violate the laws of war, which concentrate heavily on maintaining a distinction between armed combatants and civilians. Combatants are to wear uniforms and insignia to identify themselves, and are to direct their attacks at other combatants and avoid, to the extent militarily feasible, attacking civilians. Violation of these principles earned Serbia's leader Slobodan Milosevic a trial for war crimes before a UN tribunal in 2002.

Will the war on terrorism deepen the trend towards stronger international law that characterized the evolving post–Cold War era before September 11? Or will it reverse that trend and reassert the primacy of raw power over the niceties of conventions and norms?

A number of early reference points for this question were the U.S. treatment of suspected Al Qaeda and Taliban fighters captured in battle in Afghanistan in 2001–2002, and the treatment of Iraqi prisoners after the U.S. invasion in 2003. In Afghanistan, the United States took hundreds of prisoners to a detention centre on the U.S. military base at Guantanamo Bay, Cuba. (Since the communist revolution in Cuba, the United States has maintained a military base on a corner of

Abu Ghraib Prison, Iraq, 2003–2004.

Cuba, separated from Cuban society.) By holding the prisoners outside U.S. territory, the U.S. government avoided restrictions that apply under U.S. law. The United States announced its intention to try the suspects in secret military tribunals, and at first said that the Geneva Conventions would not apply to them.

The 1949 Geneva Conventions extend special protections to prisoners of war (POWs) belonging to uniformed armies. These provisions reflect states' mutual interest in protecting their own soldiers if captured. They do not cover irregular forces who, by operating out of uniform, themselves violate the laws of war and blur the distinction between combatants and civilians. Thus, in World War II, allied soldiers were held as POWs by Germany, but French resistance fighters were often summarily executed upon capture.

In 2002, under prodding from the State Department and international opinion, President Bush agreed to deal with the Guantanamo Bay "detainees" (this term avoids the word "prisoner") according to provisions of the Conventions, but not as POWs. (While POWs must provide only name, rank, and serial number, the terrorist suspects were interrogated, and the plan for military tribunals proceeded.)

Questions arose again in Iraq when, in 2004, photographs emerged from the Abu Ghraib prison of systematic mistreatment of Iraqi prisoners. Photographs showed prisoners subjected to physical and sexual torture and humiliation. Some observers suggested that the interrogation techniques the U.S. had developed for suspected

Al Qaeda operatives at Guantanamo Bay had been trans-ferred to Iraq. While the U.S may have been able to make the case that they were not bound by the Geneva Conventions when dealing with suspected terrorists, it was harder to make this claim about prisoners captured in a more traditional warzone.*

What do these events tell us about international law? Is the argument that the U.S. government has a moral right and duty to do whatever it takes to destroy terrorists and protect the U.S. homeland from cata-strophic attack a persuasive one? Even if it means dis-pensing with international law?

* Peter Yost, "Geneva Code Too 'Quaint,' Bush Was Told," *Ottawa Citizen* 17 May 2004: A7. Seymour Hersh, "The Gray Zone: How a Secret Pentagon Program Came to Abu Ghraib," *The New Yorker* 24 May 2004: 38–44.

Treaties: The Case of Arms Control Agreements

Treaties are one source of international law, and in questions of international security, arms control agreements are one of the most important types of treaty. During the Cold War, the superpowers' nuclear forces grew and technologies developed. These evolving force structures were codified (more than constrained) by a series of arms control agree-ments. *Arms control* is an effort by two or more states to regulate by formal agreement their acquisition of weapons.[30] Arms control involves more than just nuclear weapons—for instance, after World War I the great powers negotiated limits on sizes of navies—but in recent decades nuclear weapons have been the main focus of arms control. Arms con-trol agreements typically require long, formal negotiations with many technical discus-sions, culminating in a treaty. Some arms control treaties are multilateral, but during the Cold War most were bilateral (U.S.-Soviet). Some stay in effect indefinitely; others have a limited term.

In the 1960s, the U.S. and Soviet Union began to use arms control agreements to regulate their relations. They gained confidence from these agreements that they could do business with each other and that they would not let the arms race lead them into a nuclear war—fear of which had increased after the Cuban Missile Crisis of 1962. Nuclear arms control talks and agreements did not stop either superpower from developing any weapon it wanted, but did *manage* the arms race and bring about a convergence of expect-ations about its structure.

For example, the first agreements, in the 1960s, banned activities that both sides could easily live without—testing nuclear weapons in the atmosphere and placing nuclear weapons in space. The Non-Proliferation Treaty (1968) built on the superpowers' com-mon fears of China and other potential new nuclear states. Other confidence-building measures were directed at the management of potential crises. The hot-line agreement connected the U.S. and Soviet heads of state by telephone. A later agreement on inci-dents at sea provided for efforts to control escalation after a hostile encounter or accident on the high seas. Eventually, the superpowers developed centres and systems for the exchange of information in a crisis.

Several treaties in the 1970s locked in the superpowers' basic parity in nuclear capabilities under MAD. The 1972 **Anti-Ballistic Missile (ABM) Treaty** prevented either side from using a ballistic missile defence as a shield from which to launch a first strike. However, as more states acquired ballistic missiles (see p. 221), the United States decided to try to develop a defensive system against ballistic missiles. To allow full-scale

Anti-Ballistic Missile (ABM) Treaty (1972) Treaty that pro-hibited either the United States or the Soviet Union from using a ballistic missile defence as a shield, which would have undermined mutually assured destruction and the basis of deterrence. See also *mutually assured destruction (MAD)* and *Strategic Defense Initiative (SDI)*.

---

[30] Emanuel Adler, ed., *The International Practice of Arms Control* (Baltimore: Johns Hopkins UP, 1992).

testing of missile-defence technologies, the United States withdrew from the ABM Treaty with six months' notice (as provided in the treaty itself), effective mid-2002. President Bush called the treaty a relic of the Cold War, but critics called U.S. missile defence a costly blunder that could induce China to greatly enlarge its minimal nuclear arsenal (which in turn could accelerate India's nuclear weapons production, and thus Pakistan's as well).

The **Strategic Arms Limitation Treaties (SALT)** put formal ceilings on the growth of both sides' strategic weapons. SALT I was signed in 1972 and SALT II in 1979—but SALT II was never ratified by the U.S. Senate (due to the subsequent Soviet invasion of Afghanistan). The U.S. arsenal peaked in the 1960s at more than 30 000 warheads; the Soviet arsenal peaked in the 1980s at more than 40 000.

More recent arms control agreements regulated the substantial reduction of nuclear forces after the end of the Cold War.[31] The **Intermediate Nuclear Forces (INF) Treaty** of 1987 banned an entire class of missiles that both sides had deployed in Europe—for the first time actually reducing nuclear forces instead of just limiting their growth. The 1991 **Strategic Arms Reduction Treaty (START I),** which took a decade to negotiate, called for reducing the superpowers' strategic arsenals by about 30 percent.[32] The final START I milestone was reached in 2001 as both sides reduced strategic nuclear weapons to below 6000. In 2002 they agreed on future cuts. Meanwhile the 1992 START II treaty was negotiated in less than a year, but ratified by Russia's parliament only after an eight-year delay. Under the U.S.-Russian Strategic Offensive Reductions Treaty, each side is to reduce deployed warheads from about 6000 to 2200 within a decade.(These reductions are in addition to the elimination of most tactical nuclear weapons.) The INF and START treaties provide for strict verification, including on-site inspection of facilities in the other side's nuclear complex. When coupled with satellite reconnaissance, these agreements create considerable transparency in nuclear matters.

A **Comprehensive Test Ban Treaty (CTBT)** to halt all nuclear test explosions was signed in 1996 after decades of stalemate. It aims to impede the development of new types of nuclear weapons. Technological advances—both in the design of weapons (without needing to actually explode one) and in verification that no tests are occurring—overcame the previous reluctance of the great powers to undertake this step. However, the treaty does not take effect until signed and ratified by all 44 states believed capable of building at least a crude nuclear weapon. India did not sign the CTBT, and defied it in 1998 with five nuclear tests. Pakistan followed suit with its own tests. The U.S. Senate voted in 1999 against ratifying the CTBT, and the Bush Administration opposes it. Russia ratified it in 2000.

Nuclear arsenals may be further reduced in the coming years. Perhaps Russia and the United States will find they need no more than the several hundred nuclear weapons in the arsenals of other great powers—Britain, France, and China. These arsenals provide a credible second-strike capability. Whether nuclear weapons can be eliminated altogether is a more difficult question, because in a nuclear-free world a handful of weapons of mass destruction might become all-powerful.

---

[31] Bennett Ramberg, ed., *Arms Control without Negotiation: From the Cold War to the New World Order* (Boulder, CO: Rienner, 1993). Michele A. Flournoy, ed., *Nuclear Weapons after the Cold War: Guidelines for U.S. Policy* (NY: HarperCollins, 1993). Charles L. Glaser, "Nuclear Policy without an Adversary: U.S. Planning for the Post-Soviet Era," *International Security* 16.4 (1992): 34–78.

[32] Spec. issue on START, *Bulletin of the Atomic Scientists* 47.9 (1991): 12–40. Brian Frederking, *Resolving Security Dilemmas: A Constructivist Explanation of the INF Treaty* (Burlington, VT: Ashgate, 2000).

Strategic Arms Limitation Treaties (SALT) SALT I (1972) and SALT II (1979) put formal ceilings on the growth of U.S. and Soviet strategic weapons. SALT II was never ratified by the U.S. Senate (due to the subsequent Soviet invasion of Afghanistan).

Intermediate Nuclear Forces (INF) Treaty (1987) Treaty that banned an entire class of missiles that both the Soviet Union and the United States had deployed in Europe.

Strategic Arms Reduction Treaties (START) START I (1991) called for reducing the superpowers' strategic arsenals by about 30 percent. START II (1992) proposes to cut the remaining weapons by more than half in the next decade. START III is under discussion.

Comprehensive Test Ban Treaty (CTBT) (1996) Treaty that bans all nuclear weapons testing, thereby broadening the ban on atmospheric testing negotiated in 1963.

Another convention aimed at the elimination of weapons of mass destruction is the Convention on the Prohibition of the Development, Production and Stockpiling of Bacteriological (Biological) and Toxin Weapons and on Their Destruction signed in 1972, which came into effect in 1975. Signatories to the Convention undertake never to develop, produce, stockpile, or otherwise acquire or retain biological or chemical weapons. Canada was an early signatory to the convention and has been actively involved in attempting to strengthen its effectiveness, in one small part by producing a website devoted to disseminating official information about the Convention to the widest possible audience (http://www.opbw.org).

Arms control efforts outside the area of nuclear arms have had mixed success. For decades the NATO and Warsaw Pact countries carried on the Mutual and Balanced Force Reduction (MBFR) talks aimed at limiting conventional military forces in Europe. Not until the last years of the Cold War was the **Conventional Forces in Europe (CFE) Treaty** signed; within two years it was virtually obsolete. The signatories have kept the treaty in effect as a guard against any future arms buildup in Europe, but relaxed limits on Russian forces deployed near southern Russia, a new conflict zone.

Conventional Forces in Europe (CFE) Treaty (1990) A U.S.-Soviet agreement that provided for asymmetrical reductions in Soviet forces in Europe and limited those of both sides.

Efforts to control the conventional arms trade through arms control treaties have been largely unsuccessful. After the Gulf War, the five permanent Security Council members tried to negotiate limits on the supply of weapons to the Middle East. The five participants account for most of the weapons sold in the Middle East. But no participant wanted to give up its own lucrative arms sales in the region, which each naturally saw as justified. At this point, no formal treaty has been developed to control the arms trade, but numerous countries have participated in the UN Programme of Action to Prevent, Combat and Eradicate the Illicit Trade in Small Arms and Light Weapons in All Its Aspects.

The Convention on Prohibitions or Restrictions on the Use of Certain Conventional Weapons Which May Be Deemed to Be Excessively Injurious or to Have Indiscriminate Effects, also known as the Certain Conventional Weapons Convention (CCW) or the Inhumane Weapons Convention, was signed in 1980 and came into effect in 1983. It covers weapons that leave undetectable fragments in the human body, mines, booby-traps, incendiary weapons, blinding laser weapons, and explosive remnants of war. As of 2004, only 94 states, including Canada, are parties to the convention.

As discussed in Chapter 4, Canada was the lead state in achieving a Convention to Ban Anti-personnel Landmines, signed in 1997. The Anti-personnel Landmines Ban elaborates a stronger set of restrictions for a weapon previously covered in the CCW. It is aimed at eliminating the use, stockpiling, production, and transfer of anti-personnel landmines.

Many of the disarmament treaties noted above are "deposited" with the United Nations, which means that the secretary-general is charged with overseeing new signatories, ratifications, and implementation. It also usually organizes, or helps to organize, review conferences and meetings for each convention. The UN's Department of Disarmament Affairs is the body within the United Nations most involved in this work.

Enforcement of International Law

Although the sources of international law distinguish it from national law, an even greater difference exists as to the *enforcement* of the two types of law. International law is much more difficult to enforce. There is no world police force. Enforcement of international law depends on the power of states themselves, individually or collectively, to punish transgressors.

Enforcement of international law depends heavily on practical reciprocity (see pp. 65–66). States follow international law most of the time because they want other states to do so. The reason neither side in World War II used chemical weapons was not that anyone could *enforce* the treaty banning use of such weapons. It was that the other side would probably respond by using chemical weapons, too, and the costs would be high to both sides. International law recognizes in certain circumstances the legitimacy of *reprisals:* actions that would have been illegal under international law may sometimes be legal if taken in response to the illegal actions of another state.

States also follow international law because of the general or long-term costs that could come from disregarding international law (rather than just immediate retaliation). If a state fails to pay its debts, it will not be able to borrow money on world markets. If it cheats on the terms of treaties it signs, other states will not sign future treaties with it. The resulting isolation could be very costly.

A state that breaks international law may also face a collective response by a group of states, such as the imposition of *sanctions*—agreements among other states to stop trading with the violator, or to stop some particular commodity trade (most often military goods) as punishment for its violation. Over time, a sanctioned state can become a *pariah* in the community of nations, cut off from normal relations with others. This is very costly in today's world, when economic well-being everywhere depends on trade and economic exchange in world markets. Libya, for example, suffered for decades from its isolated status in the international community, and decided in late 2003 to make a clean break and regain normal status. Libya admitted responsibility for past terrorism, began to compensate victims, and agreed to disclose and dismantle its nuclear, chemical, and biological weapons programs.

International law enforcement through reciprocity and collective response has one great weakness—it depends entirely on national power. Reciprocity works only if the aggrieved state has the power to inflict costs on the violator. Collective response works only if the collective cares enough about an issue to respond. Thus, it is relatively easy to cheat on small issues (or to get away with major violations if one has enough power).

If international law extends only as far as power reaches, what good is it? The answer lies in the uncertainties of power (see Chapter 2). Without common expectations regarding the rules of the game and adherence to those rules most of the time by most actors, power alone would create great instability in the anarchic international system. International law, even without perfect enforcement, creates expectations about what constitutes legal behaviour by states. Because violations or divergences from those expectations stand out, it is easier to identify and punish states that deviate from accepted rules. When states agree to the rules by signing treaties (such as the UN Charter), violations become more visible and clearly illegitimate. In most cases, although power continues to reside in states, international law establishes workable rules for those states to follow. The resulting stability is so beneficial that usually the costs of breaking the rules outweigh the short-term benefits that could be gained from such violations.

The World Court

World Court (International Court of Justice) The judicial arm of the UN; located in The Hague, it hears only cases between states.

As international law has developed, a general world legal framework in which states can pursue grievances against each other has begun to take shape. The rudiments of such a system now exist in the **World Court** (formally called the **International Court of Justice**), although its jurisdiction is limited and its caseload light.[33] The World Court is a branch of the UN.

ALL RISE
The World Court hears international disputes but with little power to enforce judgments.
Here, the judges assemble in December 2003 to hear Mexico's complaint that the U.S.
death penalty against Mexican citizens violates a 1963 treaty.

Only states, not individuals or businesses, can sue or be sued in the World Court.
When a state has a grievance against another, it can take the case to the World Court for
an impartial hearing. The Security Council or General Assembly may also request advisory court opinions on matters of international law.

The World Court is a panel of 15 judges elected for nine-year terms (five judges every
three years) by a majority of both the Security Council and General Assembly. The court
meets in The Hague, Netherlands. It is customary for permanent members of the Security
Council to have one of their nationals as a judge at all times. Ad hoc judges may be added
to the 15 if a party to a case does not already have one of its nationals as a judge.

The great *weakness* of the World Court is that states have not agreed in a comprehensive way to subject themselves to its jurisdiction or obey its decisions. Almost all states
have signed the treaty creating the court, but only about a third have signed the *optional
clause* in the treaty agreeing to give the court jurisdiction in certain cases—and even
many of those signatories have added their own stipulations reserving their rights and limiting the degree to which the court can infringe on national sovereignty. The United
States withdrew from the optional clause when it was sued by Nicaragua in 1986 (over

[33] Richard Falk, *Reviving the World Court* (Charlottesville: U Virginia P, 1986). Keith Highet, "The Peace Palace
Heats Up: The World Court in Business Again?" *American Journal of International Law* 85.4 (1991): 646–54.

the CIA's mining of Nicaraguan harbours).[34] Similarly, Iran refused to acknowledge the jurisdiction of the court when sued by the United States in 1979 over its seizure of the U.S. embassy in Iran. In such a case, the court may hear the case anyway, and usually rules in favour of the participating side—but has no means to enforce the ruling.

In one of its most notable successes, the World Court in 1992 settled a complex border dispute between El Salvador and Honduras. By mutual agreement, the two states had asked the court in 1986 to settle territorial disputes along six stretches of border, three islands, and territorial waters. The disputes dated from 1861 and had led to a war in 1969. The World Court drew borders that gave about two-thirds of the total land to Honduras and split the territorial waters among both countries and Nicaragua. Both countries abided by the decision. In 2002, the World Court settled a long-standing and sometimes violent dispute over an oil-rich peninsula on the Cameroon-Nigeria border, giving ownership to Cameroon. By mid-2004, however, Nigeria had requested a delay in the final settlement, and it remained unclear whether it would withdraw all troops as agreed. Also in 2004, the World Court ruled that Israel's 700-kilometre-long security barrier in the West Bank was a violation of international law and that parts of it should be torn down. Israel quickly declared that it would disregard the ruling.

An important use of the World Court now is to arbitrate issues of secondary importance between countries with friendly relations overall. The court has settled commercial disputes between Canada and the U.S., for example. Because security interests are not at stake, and because the overall friendly relations are more important than the particular issue, states have been willing to submit to the court's jurisdiction in these kinds of decisions.

There are other international forums for the arbitration of grievances (by mutual consent). Some regional courts, notably in Europe, resemble the World Court in function. Various bodies are capable of conducting arbitration—as when Israel and Egypt submitted their dispute about the tiny territory of Taba to binding arbitration after failing to reach a settlement. Arbitration can remove domestic political pressures from state leaders by taking the decision out of their hands. But for major disputes involving issues of great importance to states, there is still little effective international legal apparatus.

Because of the difficulty of winning enforceable agreements on major conflicts through the World Court, states have used the court infrequently over the years—a dozen or fewer cases per year (only 79 judgments and 25 advisory opinions since 1946). The number has been increasing, however, and by mid-2004, 20 cases were pending.

International Cases in National Courts

Most legal cases concerning international matters—whether brought by governments or by private individuals or companies—remain entirely within the legal systems of one or more states. National courts hear cases brought under national laws and can enforce judgments by collecting damages (in civil suits) or imposing punishments (in criminal ones).

A party with a dispute that crosses national boundaries gains several advantages by pursuing the matter through the national courts of one or more of the relevant states, rather than through international channels. First, judgments are enforceable. The party that wins a lawsuit in a national court can collect from the other party's assets within the state. Second, individuals and companies can pursue legal complaints through national courts (as can subnational governmental bodies), whereas in most areas of international

---

[34] David P. Forsythe, *The Politics of International Law: U.S. Foreign Policy Reconsidered* (Boulder, CO: Lynne Rienner, 1990).

law states must themselves bring suits on behalf of their citizens. (In truth, even national governments pursue most of their legal actions against each other through national courts.)

Third, there is often a choice of more than one state within which a case could legally be heard; one can pick the legal system most favourable to one's case. It is up to each state's court system to decide whether it has *jurisdiction* in a case (the right to hear it), and courts tend to extend their own authority with a broad interpretation. Traditionally, a national court may hear cases concerning any activity on its national territory, any actions of its own citizens anywhere in the world, and actions taken toward its citizens elsewhere in the world. Noncitizens can use the national courts to enforce damages against citizens, because the national court has authority to impose fines and if necessary seize bank accounts and property.

The United States is a favourite jurisdiction within which to bring cases for two reasons. First, U.S. juries have the reputation of awarding bigger settlements in lawsuits than juries elsewhere in the world (if only because the United States is a rich country). Second, because many people and governments do business in the United States, it is often possible to collect damages awarded by a U.S. court. For these reasons, U.S. courts in recent years have ruled on human-rights cases brought by Chinese dissidents over the 1989 Tiananmen massacre, Cuban exiles against the Cuban government, and a Paraguayan doctor suing a Paraguayan police official for torturing the doctor's son. Human rights activists have used the law against companies dealing with repressive governments, as when they sued U.S. oil companies Exxon Mobil and Unocal for aiding abusive regimes. The rapid extension of U.S. legal jurisdiction may bring a reciprocal response from European (and other) states, which may seek on occasion to extend their national laws to U.S. shores.[35]

Belgium's national courts also have become a favourite venue to bring international human rights cases, because a 1993 law gives Belgian courts jurisdiction over any violation of the Geneva Convention. In 2001, four people accused of war crimes in Rwanda in 1994 were sent to prison by a Belgian jury. (Rwanda is a former Belgian colony, and 10 Belgian soldiers had been killed at the outset of the genocide there.) But the Belgian government found itself on the spot later in 2001 when a judge began investigating the sitting Israeli prime minister, Ariel Sharon, for atrocities committed during the 1982 Israeli invasion of Lebanon.

There are important limits to the use of national courts to resolve international disputes, however. Most important is that the authority of national courts stops at the state's borders, where sovereignty ends. A court in Zambia cannot compel a resident of Thailand to come and testify; it cannot authorize the seizure of a British bank account to pay damages; it cannot arrest a criminal suspect (Zambian or foreigner) except on Zambian soil. To take such actions beyond national borders, states must persuade other states to cooperate.

To bring a person outside a state's territory to trial, the state's government must ask a second government to arrest the person on the second state's territory and hand him or her over for trial. Called *extradition*, this is a matter of international law because it is a legal treaty arrangement *between* states. If there is no such treaty, the individual generally remains immune from a state's courts by staying off its territory. Canada does not usually extradite suspects to countries in which they would face the death penalty, such as the United States (but will do so if agreement can be secured that the death penalty will not be imposed in a finding of guilt).

---

[35] William Glaberson, "U.S. Courts Become Arbiters of Global Rights and Wrongs around the World, *New York Times* 21 June 2001: A1.

Since 2001, the war on terrorism has expanded international legal and law-enforcement cooperation, but with sometimes quite controversial results. In 2004 an inquiry was underway into the role of Canadian authorities in the detention and deportation to Syria by the United States of a Syrian-born Canadian citizen travelling in the U.S. American authorities claimed the Canadian was suspected of terrorist links and deported him to his country of birth, where he was never formally charged and where he reported upon his release that he had been systematically tortured. Indeed, it took considerable time for his family in Canada to learn what had happened to him and where he had been sent, and then, eventually, to help secure his release. As of mid-2004, it remained unclear how much Canadian law enforcement officials had known, or assisted, the U.S. in the detention and deportation.

immigration law National laws that establish the conditions under which foreigners may travel and visit within a state's territory, work within the state, and sometimes become citizens of the state (naturalization).

The principle of territoriality also governs **immigration law.** When people cross a border into a new country, the decision about whether they can remain there, and under what conditions, is up to the new state. The state of origin cannot compel their return. National laws establish conditions for foreigners to travel and visit on a state's territory, to work there, and sometimes to become citizens (*naturalization*). Many other legal issues are raised by people travelling or living outside their own country—passports and visas, babies born in foreign countries, marriages to foreign nationals, bank accounts, businesses, taxes, and so forth. Practices vary from country to country, but the general principle is that *national laws prevail on the territory of a state*.

The former Chilean military dictator Augusto Pinochet was arrested in England in 1999 on a Spanish warrant, based on crimes committed against Spanish citizens in Chile during Pinochet's rule. His supporters claimed that he should have immunity for acts taken as head of state, but since he was not an accredited diplomat in England (where he had gone for medical treatment), and no longer head of state, the British courts held him on Spain's request to extradite him for trial there. Once on British soil without current diplomatic immunity, Pinochet was subject to British law, including its extradition treaties. However, the British government eventually let him return to Chile, citing his medical condition, and a Chilean court suspended his case on health grounds.

Despite the continued importance of national court systems in international legal affairs and the lack of enforcement powers of the World Court, it would be wrong to conclude that state sovereignty is supreme and international law impotent. Rather, there is a balance of sovereignty and law in international interactions.

LAW AND SOVEREIGNTY

The remainder of this chapter discusses particular areas of international law, from the most firmly rooted and widely respected, to newer and less-established areas. In each area, the influence of law and norms runs counter to the unimpeded exercise of state sovereignty. This struggle becomes more intense as one moves from long-standing traditions of diplomatic law to recent norms governing human rights.

Laws of Diplomacy

The bedrock of international law is respect for the rights of diplomats. The standards of behaviour in this area are spelled out in detail, applied universally, and taken very seriously. The ability to conduct diplomacy is necessary for all other kinds of relations among states, except perhaps all-out war. Since the rise of the international system five centuries ago, it has been considered unjustifiable to harm an emissary sent from another state as a means of influencing the other state. Such a norm has *not always existed*; it was once considered natural to kill the messenger who brought an unpleasant message, or to use another state's official as a hostage or bargaining chip. But today this kind of behaviour is universally condemned, though it still happens from time to time.

The status of embassies and of an ambassador as an official state representative is explicitly defined in the process of **diplomatic recognition.** Diplomats are *accredited* to each other's governments (they present "credentials"), and thereafter the individuals so defined enjoy certain rights and protections as foreign diplomats in the host country.

Diplomats have the right to occupy an *embassy* in the host country as though it were their own state's territory. On the grounds of the Canadian embassy in Kuwait, for instance, the laws of Canada, and not those of Kuwait, apply. Members of the Canadian Forces, RCMP, or military police occupy the embassy compound as though it were Canadian territory, and those of Kuwait may not enter without permission. This principle of international law explains why, when Iraq invaded Kuwait in 1990,

AGAINST THE LAW

International law prohibits attacks on diplomats. This fundamental principle, like others in international law, can ultimately be enforced only by applying the power of other states (through such leverage as imposing economic sanctions, freezing relations, or threatening military force). Here are U.S. diplomats on their first day as hostages in the U.S. embassy, Tehran, Iran, 1979.

it did not set foot inside most foreign embassy compounds even though it could have overrun them easily. Iraq claimed that since Kuwait no longer existed, the embassies there no longer enjoyed diplomatic status, but it was not willing to press the point.

A flagrant violation of the sanctity of embassies occurred in Iran after Islamic revolutionaries took power in 1979. Iranian students seized and occupied the U.S. embassy compound, holding the U.S. diplomats hostage for more than a year. The Iranian government did not directly commit this act but did condone it and refused to force the students out of the embassy. (Host countries are expected, if necessary, to use force against their own citizens to protect a foreign embassy.) Six of the American embassy staff escaped the embassy compound as it was being seized and were hidden at the Canadian embassy by Ambassador Ken Taylor until fake passports could be obtained to spirit the Americans safely out of Iran.

Diplomats enjoy **diplomatic immunity** even when they leave the embassy grounds. The right to travel varies from one country to another; diplomats may be restricted to one city or free to roam about the countryside. Alone among all foreign nationals, diplomats are beyond the jurisdiction of the host country's national courts. If they commit crimes, from jaywalking to murder, they may not be arrested and tried. All the host country can do is to take away a diplomat's accreditation and *expel* the person from the host country. However, strong countries can sometimes pressure weaker ones to lift immunity so that a diplomat may face trial for a crime. This happened twice in 1997, when the United States

diplomatic recognition The process by which the status of embassies and that of an ambassador as an official state representative are explicitly defined.

diplomatic immunity Refers to diplomats' activity being outside the jurisdiction of the host country's national courts.

and France were allowed to prosecute diplomats from Georgia and Zaire, respectively, for reckless driving that killed children. By contrast, in 2001 a Russian diplomat, allegedly driving drunk, struck two pedestrians in Ottawa, killing one of them. Despite local and national outrage over the incident, the diplomat quickly invoked his diplomatic immunity and returned to Russia, where he was tried in a Russian court.

U.S. commitments as host country to the UN include extending diplomatic immunity to the diplomats accredited to the UN. The UN delegates thus cannot be prosecuted under U.S. law. Given this immunity, delegates simply tear up thousands of parking tickets each year, for example. Occasionally, UN representatives are accused of more serious crimes (murder, in one case in the 1980s), but they cannot be brought to trial in the United States for those crimes, unless they or their country of origin agree to waive their diplomatic immunity.

Because of diplomatic immunity, it is common to conduct espionage activities through the diplomatic corps, out of an embassy. Spies are often posted to low-level positions in embassies, such as cultural attaché, press liaison, or military attaché. If the host country catches them spying, it cannot prosecute them, so it merely expels them. Diplomatic norms (though not law) call for politeness when expelling spies; the standard reason given is "for activities not consistent with his/her diplomatic status." If a spy operates under cover of being a businessperson or tourist, then no immunity applies: the person can be arrested and prosecuted under the host country's laws.

A *diplomatic pouch* is a package sent between an embassy and its home country. As the name implies, it started out historically as a small and occasional shipment, but today there is a large and steady volume of such shipments all over the world. Diplomatic pouches, too, enjoy the status of home country territoriality: they cannot be opened, searched, or confiscated by a host country. Although we do not know how much mischief goes on in diplomatic pouches (because they are secret), it is safe to assume that illicit goods such as guns and drugs regularly find their way across borders in diplomatic pouches.

To *break diplomatic relations* means to withdraw one's diplomats from a state and expel its diplomats from one's own state. This tactic is used to show displeasure with another government; it is a refusal to do business as usual. When a revolutionary government comes into power, some countries may withdraw recognition. The U.S. has not had diplomatic relations with Cuba since the 1959 revolution, for example.

When two countries lack diplomatic relations, they often do business through a third country willing to represent a country's interests formally through its own embassy. This is called an *interests section* in the third country's embassy. Thus, the practical needs of diplomacy can overcome a formal lack of relations between states. For instance, U.S. interests are represented by the Swiss embassy in Cuba, and Cuban interests are represented by the Swiss embassy in the United States. In practice, these interests sections are located in the former U.S. and Cuban embassies and staffed with U.S. and Cuban diplomats.

States register lower levels of displeasure by *recalling their ambassadors* home for some period of time; diplomatic norms call for a trip home "for consultations" even when everyone knows the purpose is to signal annoyance. Milder still is the expression of displeasure by a *formal complaint*. Usually the complaining government does so in its own capital city, to the other's ambassador.

The law of diplomacy is repeatedly violated in one context—terrorism (see pp. 189–193). Because states care so much about the sanctity of diplomats, the diplomats make a tempting target for terrorists, and because terrorist groups do not enjoy the benefits of diplomatic law (as states do), they are willing to break diplomatic norms and laws. An attack on diplomats or embassies is an attack on the territory of the state itself—yet can be carried out far from the state's home territory. Being a diplomat has become a dangerous occupation, and many have been killed in recent decades. In 1998, Al Qaeda terrorists bombed the U.S. embassies in Kenya and Tanzania, killing more than 200 people.

War Crimes

After the law of diplomacy, international law regarding war is one of the most developed areas of international law. Laws concerning war are divided into two areas—laws in war (*jus in bello*) and laws of war (*jus ad bellum*). Consider these in turn, beginning with laws in wartime, violations of which are considered **war crimes**.[36]

The Roman politician Cicero said: "Laws are silent in time of war."[37] This is no longer true. In wartime, international law is especially difficult to enforce, but there are extensive norms of legal conduct in war that are widely followed. After a war, losers can be punished for violations of the laws of war (war crimes).

In the 1990s, for the first time since World War II, the UN Security Council authorized an international war crimes tribunal, directed against war crimes in the former Yugoslavia. Similar tribunals were later established for genocide in Rwanda and Sierra Leone.[38] The tribunal on the former Yugoslavia, headquartered in The Hague, Netherlands, issued indictments against the top Bosnian Serb leaders and other Serbian and Croatian officers, and in 1999 against Serbian leader Slobodan Milosevic during the expulsion of Albanians from Kosovo. The tribunal was hampered by lack of funding and by its lack of power to arrest suspects who enjoyed the protection of Serbia and Croatia. A new Croatian government that won elections in 1999 began to cooperate with the tribunal, and after Milosevic lost power in Serbia, the new Serbian government turned him over to the tribunal in 2001. Following the civil war in Sierra Leone, the government there has run a war crimes tribunal jointly with the UN. In 2003, it indicted the sitting state leader in next-door Liberia, Charles Taylor, for his role in the war's extreme brutality. He fled for Nigeria shortly afterwards and had not been turned over to the tribunal as of mid-2004.

Following up on the UN tribunals for former Yugoslavia and Rwanda, in 1998 120 of the world's states signed the Rome Statute to create a permanent **International Criminal Court (ICC).** This is the first treaty-based court ever established and it will hear cases of genocide, war crimes, and crimes against humanity from anywhere in the world. The statute called for the establishment of the court upon ratification by 60 signatory states, which occurred in 2002. The court is located at The Hague in the Netherlands, and though it is currently functional with 18 judges sworn in from around the world, it will likely be a number of years before it hears its first cases. Some countries, like the United States, have not ratified the Rome Statute and are opposed to the court primarily because it infringes on sovereignty. The United States has also expressed opposition because the ICC might someday prosecute U.S. soldiers.

As with most international law, the enforcement of laws of war occurs mostly through practical reciprocity and group response, reinforced by habit and legitimacy. A state that violates laws of war can find itself isolated without allies and subject to reprisals.

war crimes Violations of the law governing the conduct of warfare, such as by mistreating prisoners of war or unnecessarily targeting civilians. See also *just war doctrine.*

International Criminal Court (ICC) Permanent tribunal for war crimes and crimes against humanity.

---

[36] Michael Howard, George J. Andreopoulos, and Mark R. Shulman, eds., *The Laws of War: Constraints on Warfare in the Western World* (New Haven, CT: Yale UP, 1994). Geoffrey Best, *War and Law Since 1945* (NY: Oxford UP, 1994).

[37] Pro Milone Cicero, *The Speeches of Cicero*, ed. and trans. N. H. Watts (Cambridge, MA: Harvard UP, 1931).

[38] Gary Jonathan Bass, *Stay the Hand of Vengeance: The Politics of War Crimes Tribunals* (Princeton, NJ: Princeton UP, 2000).

Thinking Theoretically

The United Nations Security Council can invoke Chapter 7 of the UN Charter to launch a peace enforcement mission in situations deemed to be a threat to international peace and security. Chapter 7 missions were launched only once during the Cold War (in Korea). Since 1989, the Security Council has interpreted "threats to the peace" quite broadly, and has authorized missions under Chapter 7 in the 1991 Gulf War, and to Somalia, Rwanda, Haiti, East Timor, Democratic Republic of the Congo, Sierra Leone, and Côte d'Ivoire. What might account for the dramatic increase in Chapter 7 missions?

A realist interpretation would likely focus on tensions between the Soviet Union and United States during the Cold War, which played out in the Security Council. Both used their vetoes to prevent any mission seen to impact on their interests. Thus the Security Council was held hostage to a great power conflict, but once that conflict dissipated the Security Council was able to do its work. For realists, state representatives to the Security Council will act based on a calculation of their national interest before any global interest. Members of the Security Council can agree now to deploy Chapter 7 missions because they do not, at this time, see those missions as threatening their own national interests. This means that if tensions emerge in future between any of the permanent members, or if any single member decides that supporting the UN is not in its interests, the Security Council's work could once again be slowed or effectively stopped.

A liberal might focus instead on the emergence of new international norms concerning human rights and humanitarian intervention. By this view, human rights advocates have been, until recently, limited to strategies of persuasion or "shaming" human rights abusers. But increasingly, states, individuals, human rights NGOs, and international organizations such as the UN have demanded that more be done, especially in the face of systematic atrocities. The Security Council's greater willingness to use Chapter 7, by this view, reflects a greater willingness to use force to prevent genocide, slaughter, and crimes against humanity. For some liberals, this represents a new era in human rights, in which military enforcement, alongside the use of judicial entities such as the International Criminal Court, will strengthen and give more meaning to the human rights regime. The more habitual such activities become, the greater legitimacy they will have and the harder it will be for states to ignore them.

For critical theorists, it is worth investigating the arguments used to authorize any intervention, including the current proliferation of Chapter 7 missions. By this view, imperialism was justified in part through the narratives told about "backward Third World peoples" desperately in need of the civilizing missions of colonialism. Colonizers were depicted as superior, indigenous people as barely human. Once understood in this way, the military, economic, cultural, and social domination of colonized lands and peoples was seen as justified. Critical theorists would argue that many of the same narratives are being deployed to justify current interventions: the international community is understood as the heroic saviour coming to the rescue of poor helpless victims trapped in conflict-prone Third World countries. Salvation comes in the form of Western systems of governance, free market capitalism, and militarized responses to conflict. For critical theorists, these narratives had tragic consequences when used to justify imperialism, and could have similarly tragic consequences today.*

* Anne Orford, *Rereading Humanitarian Intervention: Human Rights and the Use of Force in International Law* (Cambridge: Cambridge UP, 2003).

The most important principle in the laws of war is the effort to limit warfare to the combatants and to protect civilians when possible. It is illegal to target civilians in a war unless there is a compelling military utility in doing so. Even then the amount of force used must be *proportional* to the military gain, and only the *necessary* amount of force can be used.

To help separate combatants from civilians, soldiers must wear uniforms and insignia; for example, Canadian armed forces typically have a shoulder patch with a Canadian flag. This provision is frequently violated in guerrilla warfare, making that form of warfare particularly brutal and destructive of civilian life. If one cannot tell the difference between a bystander and a combatant, one is likely to kill both when in doubt (and in the "fog of war" soldiers are in doubt a lot). By contrast, in a large-scale conventional war such as the Gulf

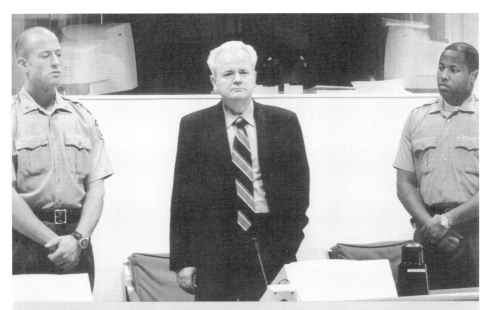

THE BIG FISH
War crimes include mistreatment of prisoners of war (POWs) and unnecessary targeting
of civilians. An international war-crimes tribunal is hearing cases from the former
Yugoslavia. The Serbian strongman Slobodan Milosevic was turned over for trial after losing power, and appeared here in 2001 before the start of his trial for war crimes, crimes
against humanity, and genocide. The top leaders of the Bosnian Serb forces, Radovan
Karadzic and Ratko Mladic, were indicted in 1996 for crimes including the execution of
7000 Muslim prisoners of war in 1995, but remained at large as of early 2004.

War, it is much easier to distinguish civilians from soldiers, although the effort is never
completely successful, and so-called friendly-fire casualties are still quite numerous.[39]

Soldiers who are captured or surrender abandon their status as combatants and
become **prisoners of war (POWs)**. POWs are provided protections under the laws of war,
and may not be killed, tortured, mistreated, or forced to disclose information beyond their
name, rank, and serial number. The law of POWs is enforced through practical reciprocity.
Once, late in World War II, German forces executed 80 POWs from the French partisan
forces (whom Germany did not recognize as legitimate belligerents). The partisans
responded by executing 80 German POWs.

The laws of war reserve a special role for the **International Committee of the Red
Cross (ICRC)**. The ICRC provides practical support—such as medical care, food, and
letters from home—to civilians caught in wars and to POWs. The ICRC works with
national societies of the Red Cross or Red Crescent from 178 countries. Exchanges of
POWs are usually negotiated through the ICRC. Armed forces must respect the neutrality of the ICRC, and most of the time they do so (again, guerrilla war is problematic).

The laws of warfare impose moral responsibility on individuals in wartime, as well as
on states. The Nuremberg Tribunal after World War II established that participants can
be held accountable for war crimes they commit. German officers defended their actions

prisoners of war (POWs)
Soldiers who are captured or
have surrendered (and who
thereby receive special status
under the laws of war).

**International Committee
of the Red Cross (ICRC)** An
organization based in Geneva
Switzerland that provides practical support, such as medical
care, food, and letters from
home, to civilians caught in
wars and to *prisoners of war
(POWs)*. The ICRC works with
national societies of the Red
Cross or Red Crescent in providing that support. Exchanges
of POWs are usually negotiated through the ICRC.

---

[39] Nicholas G. Fotion, "The Gulf War: Cleanly Fought," *Bulletin of the Atomic Scientists* 47.7 (1991): 24–29.
George A. Lopez, "The Gulf War: Not So Clean," *Bulletin of the Atomic Scientists* 47.7 (1991): 30–35.

as "just following orders," but this was rejected; the officers were punished, and some executed for their war crimes.

Not all Nuremberg defendants were found guilty, however. For example, laws of war limit the use of force against civilians to that which is necessary and proportional to military objectives. That can be a high limit in a total war. In World War II, the German army besieged the Russian city of Leningrad (St. Petersburg) for two years, and civilians in the city were starving. Sieges of this kind are permitted under international law if an army cannot easily capture a city. The impact of the use of nuclear weapons on civilian casualties was quite horrific, and it has always been understood that nuclear weapons will result in massive "collateral damage." Nonetheless, nuclear weapons remain a legitimate weapon of war.

Changing Context   The laws of warfare have been undermined by the changing nature of war. Conventional wars by defined armed forces on defined battlegrounds are giving way to irregular and "low-intensity" wars fought by guerrillas and death squads in cities or jungles. The lines between civilians and soldiers blur in these situations, and war crimes become more commonplace. In the Vietnam War, one of the largest problems faced by the United States was an enemy that seemed to be everywhere and nowhere. This led frustrated U.S. forces into attacking civilian villages seen as supporting the guerrillas. In one infamous case, a U.S. officer was court-martialled for ordering his soldiers to massacre hundreds of unarmed civilians in the village of My Lai in 1968 (he was convicted but given a light sentence). In today's irregular warfare, frequently inflamed by ethnic conflicts, the laws of war are increasingly difficult to uphold.

Another factor undermining laws of war is that states now rarely issue a *declaration of war* setting out whom they are warring against and the cause of their action. This practice, common until about 50 years ago, helped distinguish belligerents from bystanders, protecting neutral countries and invoking the rights and responsibilities of the warring states. Today, such declarations are seldom used because they bring little benefit to the state declaring war and incur obligations under international law. States just fight wars without declaring them. In many cases, such as revolutionary and counterrevolutionary civil wars in the global South, a declaration would not even be appropriate, because wars are declared only against states, not internal groups. In undeclared wars the distinctions between participants and nonparticipants are undermined (along with the protection of the latter). The Bush Administration called the 2001 terrorist attacks acts of war, and the response a war on terrorism, but Congress did not formally declare war (just as it had not during the Vietnam War). Likewise, the U.S. government also claimed that suspected Taliban and Al Qaeda prisoners taken from Afghanistan to Guantanamo Bay were not prisoners of war, and therefore not subject to protection under the Geneva Convention (to much criticism by ICRC and human rights organizations such as Amnesty International).

The laws of war have never been aimed at outlawing war, but rather signal the conditions under which a war may be conducted. Critics of the laws of war have thus noted the ways in which they actually facilitate war, setting the terms under which war is made possible. Anomalies can therefore occur, especially when determining whether an act was committed as part of armed conflict, or outside of that conflict. For example, recent clarifications about rape as a war crime effectively distinguish rape perpetrated as an act of war (which would therefore be prohibited under the laws of war) versus rape perpetrated under other circumstances (which would not be prohibited under the laws of war, though would presumably fall under other local legal standards).[40]

---

[40] Liz Philipose, "The Laws of War and Women's Human Rights," *Hypatia* 11.4 (1996): 46–62. Judith G. Gardam and Michelle J. Jarvis, *Women, Armed Conflict and International Law* (The Hague: Kluwer, 2001.)

Just War Doctrine

In addition to the laws about how wars are fought (war crimes), international law distinguishes **just wars** (which are legal) from wars of aggression (which are illegal). This area of law grows out of centuries-old religious writings about just wars (which once could be enforced by threats to excommunicate individuals from the church). Today, the legality of war is defined by the UN Charter, which outlaws aggression. Above and beyond the legal standing of just war doctrine, it has become a strong international norm, not one that all states follow but an important part of the modern intellectual tradition governing matters of war and peace that evolved in Europe.[41]

The idea of aggression, around which the doctrine of just war evolved, is based on a violation of the sovereignty and territorial integrity of states. It assumes recognized borders that are legally inviolable. Aggression refers to a state's use of force, or an imminent threat to do so, against another state's territory or sovereignty—unless the use of force is in response to aggression. Tanks swarming across the border constitute aggression, but so do tanks massing at the border if their state has threatened to invade. The lines are somewhat fuzzy. But for a threat to constitute aggression (and justify the use of force in response) it must be a clear threat of using force, not just a hostile policy or general rivalry.

In Iraq's invasion of Kuwait, Iraq's complaint that Kuwait had unfairly taken joint oil resources could not justify Iraq's invasion. Instead, Iraq justified its invasion on the grounds that Kuwait's territorial integrity had never existed, because it was historically a province of Iraq. However, Iraq and Kuwait had both signed the UN Charter binding them to respect each other's territorial integrity. The international community had little trouble determining that Iraq's invasion was aggression.

States have the right to respond to aggression in the only manner thought to be reliable—military force. Just war doctrine is not based on nonviolence. Responses can include both the *repelling* of the attack itself and the *punishment* of the aggressor. Responses can be taken by the victim of aggression or by other states not directly affected—as a way of maintaining the norm of nonaggression in the international system.

Response to aggression is the only allowable use of military force according to just war doctrine. The just war approach thus explicitly rules out war as an instrument to change another state's government or policies, or in ethnic and religious conflicts. In fact, the UN Charter makes no provision for "war" but rather for "international police actions" against aggressors. The analogy is with law and order in a national society, enforced by police when necessary. Because only aggression justifies military force, if all states obeyed the law against aggression there would be no international war.

Just war doctrine has been undermined, even more seriously than have laws of war crimes, by the changing nature of warfare.[42] In civil wars and low-intensity conflicts, the belligerents range from poorly organized militias to national armies, and the battleground is often a patchwork of enclaves and positions with no clear front lines (much less borders). It is harder to identify an aggressor in such situations, and harder to balance the relative merits of peace and justice.

just war doctrine A branch of international law and political theory that defines when wars can be justly started (*jus ad bellum*) and how they can be justly fought (*jus in bello*). See also *war crimes*.

---

[41] Michael Walzer, *Just and Unjust Wars: A Moral Argument with Historical Illustrations*, 2nd ed. (NY: Basic, 1992). *Twenty Years of Just and Unjust Wars* [symposium with articles by Michael Joseph Smith, David C. Hendrickson, Theodore J. Koontz, and Joseph Boyle], *Ethics & International Affairs* 11 (1997): 3–104.

[42] James Turner Johnson, *Can Modern War Be Just?* (New Haven, CT: Yale UP, 1984). Another change in the nature of warfare is the development of nuclear weapons. It is generally recognized that nuclear war could not be an adequate response to aggression. Thus, the use of nuclear weapons could never be just in the view of most scholars of the subject. Some scholars of just war theory argue that it is not just even to possess such weapons.

For a war to be *morally* just, it must be more than a response to aggression; it must be waged for the *purpose* of responding to aggression. The *intent* must be just. A state may not take advantage of another's aggression to wage a war that is essentially aggressive. Although the U.S.-led war effort to oust Iraq from Kuwait in 1990 was certainly a response to aggression, critics found the justness of the war to be compromised by the U.S. interest in obtaining cheap oil from the Middle East—not an allowable reason for waging war.

Human Rights

human rights Rights of all persons to be free from abuses such as torture or imprisonment for their political beliefs (political and civil rights), and to enjoy certain minimum economic and social protections (economic and social rights).

One of the newest and least developed areas of international law concerns **human rights**—the universal rights of human beings against certain abuses of their *own* governments.[43] The very idea of human rights flies in the face of the sovereignty and territorial integrity of states. Efforts to promote human rights are routinely criticized by governments with poor human rights records (including China and Russia) as "interference in our internal affairs." This charge puts human rights law on shaky ground.

Yet norms and even laws concerning human rights continue to develop, if only because what happens within one state can so easily spill over national borders. A prime example occurred when Iraq cracked down brutally on a Kurdish uprising in northern Iraq. The norm of noninterference in Iraq's internal affairs would dictate that the slaughter was Iraq's business alone. But when the Kurds fled in huge numbers across the Turkish border, they threatened to overwhelm Turkey's resources and perhaps inflame a Kurdish uprising in Turkey. The anti-Iraqi alliance therefore declared the matter an international concern and imposed its own armed forces within northern Iraq to provide security and coax the Kurds back home. Eventually the Kurdish groups gained virtual autonomy under foreign military cover, compromising Iraq's sovereignty. Because of Iraq's lack of military reach into the area, Turkey was able to invade several times in 1995–1998 to attack bases of the Kurdish guerrillas operating in Turkey.

Even in cases that do not so directly spill over national borders, the world is more interconnected and interdependent than ever. A government's abuses of its citizens can inflame ethnic conflicts, undermine moral norms of decency, and in other ways threaten the peace and stability of the international community. At least this is the rationale for treating human rights as a question of international law and norms. Human rights are also considered by some state leaders as a legitimate international concern because the presence or absence of democracy (including respect for rights) is thought to strongly influence states' foreign policies and propensities for violence (see "Democracy and Foreign Policy" on pp. 150–151).

Laws concerning human rights date back to the Nuremberg trials. Beyond the war crimes committed by German officers were their acts of *genocide* (attempts to exterminate a whole people) in which about 10 million civilians had been killed in death camps. Clearly this ranked among the most wicked crimes ever committed, yet it did not violate either international law or German law. The solution was to create a new category of legal offences—**crimes against humanity**—under which those responsible were punished. The category was not applied again until 1994–1995, when the tribunal for the

crimes against humanity A category of legal offences created at the Nuremberg trials after World War II to encompass genocide and other acts committed by the political and military leaders of the Third Reich (Nazi Germany). See also *dehumanization* and *genocide*.

---

[43] Richard A. Falk, *Human Rights Horizons* (NY: Routledge, 2000). Daniel Thomas, *The Helsinki Effect: International Norms, Human Rights, and the Demise of Communism* (Princeton, NJ: Princeton UP, 2001). Thomas Risse, Stephen C. Ropp, and Kathryn Sikkink, eds., *The Power of Human Rights: International Norms and Domestic Change* (NY: Cambridge UP, 1999). Cynthia Price Cohen, ed., *Human Rights of Indigenous Peoples* (Ardsley, NY: Transnational, 1998). Michael Perry, *The Idea of Human Rights: Four Inquiries* (NY: Oxford UP, 1998). Henry J. Steiner and Philip Alston, *International Human Rights in Context: Law, Politics, Morals* (Oxford: Clarendon, 1996).

former Yugoslavia handed down indictments for genocide.

Soon after the experience of World War II, in 1948, the UN General Assembly adopted the *Universal Declaration of Human Rights*. It does not have the force of international law, but it sets forth (hoped-for) international norms regarding behaviour by governments toward their own citizens and foreigners alike. At the root of the declaration is the principle that violations of human rights upset international order (causing outrage, sparking rebellion, etc.) and in the fact that the UN Charter commits states to respect fundamental freedoms. The declaration proclaims that "all human beings are born free and equal" without regard to race, sex, language, religion, political affiliation, or the status of the territory in which they were born. It goes on to promote norms in a wide variety of areas, from banning torture to guaranteeing religious and political freedom to the right of economic well-being.

Clearly this is a broad conception of human rights, and one far from today's realities. No state has a perfect record on human rights, and states differ as to which areas they respect or violate. When the

HUMAN RIGHTS AND SOVEREIGNTY

International norms concerning human rights conflict with state sovereignty, causing friction in relationships like Burma/Myanmar's with Japan. Here, Burmese residents in Japan hold pictures of their leader Aung San Suu Kyi, and protest Burma/Myanmar's military government for its human rights abuses. (Those opposed to the military regime also reject the name *Myanmar*, which was adopted by the military government in 1989, and use *Burma* instead. The United Nations and some other national governments, in deference to state sovereignty, use *Myanmar*).

United States criticizes China for prohibiting free speech, using prison labour, and torturing political dissidents, China notes that the United States has 40 million poor people, the highest ratio of prison inmates in the world, and a history of racism and violence.[44] Overall, despite the poor record of the world's states on some points, progress has been made on others. For example, legal slavery—once considered normal worldwide—has been abandoned in the past 150 years.

Today, human rights efforts focus on winning basic political rights—beginning with a halt to the torture, execution, and imprisonment of those expressing political or religious beliefs. The leading organization pressing this struggle is **Amnesty International,** an NGO that operates globally to monitor and try to rectify glaring abuses of human rights.[45] Amnesty International has a reputation for impartiality and has criticized abuses in many countries, including Canada and the United States. Other groups, such as Human Rights Watch, work in a similar way but often with a more regional or national focus. The UN also operates a Commission on Human Rights with a global focus.[46] In

Amnesty International An influential nongovernmental organization that operates globally to monitor and try to rectify glaring abuses of political (not economic or social) human rights.

---

[44] People's Republic of China, State Council, "America's 'Abominable' Human Rights Conditions," *Washington Post* 16 Feb. 1997: C3.

[45] Amnesty International, *Amnesty International Report* (London, annual). Ann Marie Clark, *Diplomacy of Conscience: Amnesty International and Changing Human Rights Norms* (Princeton, NJ: Princeton UP, 2000).

[46] Howard Tolley, Jr., *The UN Commission on Human Rights* (Boulder, CO: Westview, 1987).

1993, the General Assembly after 40 years of debate created the position of High Commissioner for Human Rights (whose powers do not, of course, include making states do anything, but do include publicizing their abuses). That position is currently held by a Canadian, Louise Arbour.

Enforcement of norms of human rights is difficult because it involves interference in a state's internal affairs. Cutting off trade or contact with a government that violates human rights tends to hurt the citizens whose rights are being violated by further isolating them (as with sanctions on Iraq and Taliban-ruled Afghanistan in recent years). The most effective method yet discovered is a combination of *publicity* and *pressure*. Publicity entails digging up information about human rights abuses, as Amnesty International does. The pressure of other governments, as well as private individuals and businesses, consists of threats to punish the offender in some way through nonviolent means. For instance, in Canada, proponents of human rights both inside government and without have argued that the terms of Canadian trade with China should be linked to China's human rights record. But inasmuch as most governments seek to maintain normal relations with each other most of the time, this kind of intrusive punishment by one government of another's human rights violations is rare—and not reliably successful.

A variety of covenants and conventions on human rights have been drawn up as legally binding (though not easily enforceable) treaties. These include a major covenant on civil and political rights and on economic, social, and cultural rights. More specific conventions cover genocide, racial discrimination, women's rights, torture, and the rights of the child. Human rights conventions must first be signed by state parties, and then ratified by their governments. Ratification indicates that the state agrees to be bound by the terms of the convention, and usually entails submitting reports to the relevant body within the United Nations outlining progress toward meeting commitments under the convention.

Some states will sign a treaty, but not ratify it. The United States, for example, may express its support for the principle of human rights protections by signing a convention, but then expresses its reluctance to be bound by an international human rights instrument by refusing to ratify. It has done this with the Convention on the Elimination of Discrimination Against Women. In other cases the U.S. expresses its resistance to certain types of rights by not signing: for example, the U.S. has both signed and ratified the Convenant on Civil and Political Rights, but has refused to sign the Covenant on Economic, Social, and Cultural Rights (because it disagrees that economic rights are human rights). Canada, in contrast, regularly both signs and ratifies and is a state party to all major human rights conventions.

Despite many limitations, concern about human rights is a force to be reckoned with in international relations. There are now widely held norms about how governments *should* behave, and someday governments may actually adhere to those norms as they have already begun to do in select areas, such as the abolition of legal slavery. With the downfall of many authoritarian and military governments in the former Soviet Union, Eastern Europe, Latin America, and Africa, a growing emphasis on human rights seems likely.

The concern of states for the human rights of individuals living in other states is a far cry from the realist concerns that have dominated the theory and practice of IR in the past. Indeed, the entire area of international law and organization runs counter to the fundamental assertions about international anarchy made by realists. The remaining chapters of this book move away from two other aspects of realism—its emphasis on military force above other forms of leverage, and its pessimism about the potentials for international cooperation as an outcome of bargaining.

Thinking Critically

1. Suppose you were asked to recommend changes in the structure of the UN Security Council (especially in permanent membership and the veto). What changes would you recommend, if any? Based on what logic?

2. The former UN Secretary-General Boutros-Ghali proposed (without success) the creation of a standby army of peacemaking forces loaned by member states (see p. 264). This would reduce state sovereignty a bit and increase supranational authority. Canada strongly supported this idea. Discuss this plan's merits and drawbacks.

3. Collective security against aggression depends on states' willingness to bear the costs of fighting wars to repel and punish aggressors. Sometimes states have been willing to bear such costs; at other times they have not. What considerations do you think should guide such decisions? Give examples of situations (actual or potential) that would and would not merit the intervention of foreign states to reverse aggression.

4. Given the difficulty of enforcing international law, how might the role of the World Court be strengthened in the future? What obstacles might such plans encounter? How would they change the court's role if they succeeded? Does the creation of an International Criminal Court strengthen the prospects for international law?

5. Although international norms concerning human rights are becoming stronger, many states continue to consider human rights an internal affair over which the state has sovereignty within its territory. Do you think human rights are a legitimate subject for one state to raise with another? If so, how do you reconcile the tensions between state autonomy and universal rights? What practical steps could be taken to get sovereign states to acknowledge universal human rights?

Chapter Summary

- International anarchy is balanced by world order—rules and institutions through which states cooperate for mutual benefit.

- World order has always been grounded in power, but order mediates raw power by establishing norms and habits that govern interactions among states.

- States follow the rules—both moral norms and formal international laws—much more often than not.

- International rules operate through agreements, such as military alliances, and institutions (IOs), such as the UN.

- States form alliances to increase their effective power relative to another state or alliance.

- Alliances can shift rapidly, with major effects on power relations.

- The world's main alliances, including NATO, the U.S.-Japanese alliance, NORAD and the CIS, face uncertain roles in a changing world order.

- The UN embodies a tension between state sovereignty and supranational authority. In its Charter and history, the UN has made sovereignty the more important principle. This has limited the UN's power.

- The UN particularly defers to the sovereignty of great powers, five of whom as permanent Security Council members can each block any security-related resolution binding on UN member states.

- In part because of its deference to state sovereignty, the UN has attracted virtually universal membership of the world's states, including all the great powers.

- Each of the 191 UN member states has one vote in the General Assembly, which serves mainly as a world forum and an umbrella organization for social and economic development efforts.

- The Security Council has 10 rotating member states and 5 permanent members: the United States, Russia, China, Britain, and France. Canada has been one of the highest "repeater" countries among the nonpermanent members, at 6 terms.

- The UN is administered by international civil servants in the Secretariat, headed by the secretary-general.

- The regular UN budget plus all peacekeeping missions together amount to less than 1 percent of what the world spends on military forces.

- Voting patterns and coalitions in the UN have changed over the years with the expanding membership and changing conditions. Some countries have refused to pay their dues to the UN. Currently the U.S. is catching up on more than US$1 billion in back payments to the UN.

- UN peacekeeping forces are deployed in regional conflicts in four world regions. Their main role is to monitor compliance with agreements such as ceasefires, disarmament plans, and fair election rules. They were scaled back dramatically in 1995–1997, then grew rapidly again in 1998–2004.

- UN peacekeepers operate under UN command and flag. Sometimes national troops operate under their own flag and command to carry out UN resolutions.

- IOs include UN programs (mostly on economic and social issues), autonomous UN agencies, and organizations with no formal tie to the UN. This institutional network helps to strengthen and stabilize the rules of IR.

- International law, the formal body of rules for state relations, derives from treaties (most importantly), custom, general principles, and legal scholarship—not from legislation passed by any government.

- Arms control agreements are a particularly important type of treaty in issues of international security.

- International law is difficult to enforce and is enforced in practice by national power, international coalitions, and the practice of reciprocity.

- The World Court hears grievances of one state against another but cannot infringe on state sovereignty in most cases. It is an increasingly useful avenue for arbitrating relatively minor conflicts.

- Most cases involving international relations are tried in national courts, where a state can enforce judgments within its own territory.

- A permanent International Criminal Court (ICC) was ratified and came into operation in 2002. Taking over from two UN tribunals, it will hear cases of genocide, war crimes, and crimes against humanity.

- In international law, the rights of diplomats have long had special status. Embassies are considered to be the territory of their home country.

- Laws of war are also long-standing and well established. They distinguish combatants from civilians, giving each certain rights and responsibilities. Guerrilla wars and ethnic conflicts have blurred these distinctions.

- Wars of aggression violate norms of just war—one waged only to repel or punish aggression. It is sometimes (but not always) difficult to identify the aggressor in a violent international conflict.

- International norms concerning human rights are becoming stronger and more widely accepted. However, human rights law is problematic because it entails interference by one state in another's internal affairs.

Key Terms

international norms   238

humanitarian intervention   240

international organizations (IOs)   240

alliance cohesion   243

burden sharing   243

North Atlantic Treaty Organization (NATO)   243

Warsaw Pact   244

U.S.-Japanese Security Treaty   245

North American Aerospace Defense Command (NORAD)   246

nonaligned movement   248

UN Charter   249

UN General Assembly   249

UN Security Council   251

UN Secretariat   251

blue helmets   260

UN Conference on Trade and Development (UNCTAD)   269

World Health Organization (WHO)   269

Anti-Ballistic Missile (ABM) Treaty   273

Strategic Arms Limitation Treaties (SALT)   274

Intermediate Nuclear Forces (INF) Treaty   274

Strategic Arms Reduction Treaties (START)   274

Comprehensive Test-Ban Treaty (CTBT)   274

Conventional Forces in Europe (CFE) Treaty   275

World Court (International Court of Justice)   276

immigration law   280

diplomatic recognition   281

diplomatic immunity   281

war crimes   283

International Criminal Court (ICC)   283

prisoners of war (POWs)   285

International Committee of the Red Cross (ICRC)   285

just war doctrine   287

human rights   288

crimes against humanity   288

Amnesty International   289

Weblinks

There are innumerable UN and other international organizations sites, as well as NGO sites. Here is a small sampling:

Amnesty International:

http://www.amnesty.org

International Criminal Court:

http://www.icc-cpi.int

The United Nations:

http://www.un.org

United Nations Department of Peacekeeping Operations:

http://www.un.org/Depts/dpko/dpko/index.asp

United Nations Office of the High Commissioner for Human Rights:

http://www.unhchr.ch/html/menu2/2/chr.htm

International Alert:

http://www.international-alert.org

International Committee of the Red Cross:

http://www.icrc.org/eng

Rights and Democracy (Montreal):

http://www.ichrdd.ca/frame00e.html

Women's International League for Peace and Freedom:

http://www.peacewomen.org

Trade

8

Trucks waiting to cross U.S. border
from Canada.

FROM SECURITY TO POLITICAL ECONOMY

We move now from security and international institutions to political economy. Scholars of *international political economy (IPE)* share a dissatisfaction with the way so much of the literature in international relations has emphasized questions of "high politics" and security. For IPE scholars, there has been a real absence of thinking through the relationship between domestic and international politics, and there has been an inappropriate and usually untenable separation of "politics" and "economics."

International political economists approach their work in a variety of ways. Some look to different actors (adding firms, international organizations, and social movements to the usual consideration of state behaviour). Others focus instead on the addition of new issues, arguing that trade, monetary, and international development are as important in their own right as military and strategic issues. Others still examine the array of social forces that sustain particular versions of world order, in particular the capitalist world order.[1]

This and the following chapters will examine some of the most frequently studied issues that are raised in IPE: trade, monetary relations, multinational corporations, and North-South relations (see this chapter and Chapters 9, 11, and 12). Two topics of special interest in recent years are the economic integration of Europe and other regions (Chapter 10) and the international politics of the global environment (Chapter 13).

---

[1] Richard Stubbs, and Geoffrey R. D. Underhill, *Political Economy and the Changing Global Order* (Toronto: Oxford UP, 2000). Stephen Gill and David Law, *The Global Political Economy: Perspectives, Problems and Policies* (Baltimore: Johns Hopkins UP, 1988).

The review of theoretical approaches to international relations (discussed in Chapters 2 and 3) noted that the different perspectives also had applications to questions of international political economy. This chapter will review the mercantilist and economic liberal approaches to IPE.

Economic Liberalism and Mercantilism

On a key assumption of realism—international anarchy—two major approaches within IPE differ.[2] One approach, called mercantilism (see p. 83), generally shares with realism the belief that each state must protect its own interests at the expense of others—not relying on international organizations to create a framework for mutual gains. Mercantilists therefore emphasize relative power (as do realists): what matters is not so much a state's absolute amount of well-being as its position relative to rival states.[3]

Economic liberalism (see p. 95) argues that states are only one among the many actors in the global political economy, which also includes individuals, households and firms. It holds that by building international organizations, institutions, and norms, and by conducting relations through the unfettered operations of the market, states can mutually benefit from economic exchanges. It matters little to liberals whether one state gains more or less than another—just whether the state's wealth is increasing in *absolute* terms. This concept parallels the idea that IOs allow states to relax their narrow, short-term pursuit of self-interest in order to realize longer-term mutual interests. (See pp. 88 and 237–238).

Economic liberalism and mercantilism are theories of political economy, but they also inform the position that some states take when developing policy. One of critical theory's most "developed" approaches to economics is Marxism. Marxist approaches are attuned to economic exploitation as a force in shaping political relations. We will explore these theories in depth in Chapter 12.

In IPE, contrary to international security, economic liberalism is the dominant tradition of scholarship and mercantilism is secondary. In truth, most international economic exchanges (as well as security relationships) contain some element of mutual interests—joint gains that can be realized through cooperation—and some element of conflicting interests. Game theorists call this a "mixed interest" game. For example, in the game of Chicken (see p. 71), the two drivers share an interest in avoiding a head-on collision, yet their interests diverge in that one can be a hero only if the other is a chicken. In international trade, economic liberals would argue that when two states trade, both will benefit (a shared interest), though one or the other will benefit more depending on the price of the transaction (a conflicting interest).

Liberalism places emphasis on the shared interests in economic exchanges, whereas mercantilism emphasizes the conflicting interests. Liberals see the most important goal of economic policy as the maximum creation of total wealth through achieving optimal *efficiency* (maximizing output, minimizing waste). Mercantilists see the most important goal as the creation of the most favourable possible *distribution* of wealth.

economic liberalism
An approach to IPE that emphasizes the gains that can be made through trade and which, in practice, is committed to free trade, free capital flows, and an "open" world economy See also *mercantilism* and *neoliberalism*.

---

[2] George T. Crane and Abla M. Amawi, eds., *The Theoretical Evolution of International Political Economy: A Reader*, 2nd ed. (NY: Oxford UP, 1997).

[3] Robert Gilpin, *Global Political Economy: Understanding the International Economic Order* (Princeton, NJ: Princeton, 2001). Joseph Grieco and John Ikenberry, *State Power and World Markets: The International Political Economy* (NY: Norton, 2002). Gregory P. Nowell, *Mercantile States and the World Oil Cartel, 1900–1939* (Ithaca, NY: Cornell UP, 1994). John A. Conybeare, *Trade Wars: The Theory and Practice of International Commercial Rivalry* (NY: Columbia UP, 1987). Brian M. Pollins, "Does Trade Still Follow the Flag?" *American Political Science Review* 83.2 (1989): 465–80.

Economic liberals would argue that in practice great gains have been realized from free trade. In any economic exchange that is not coerced by negative leverage, both parties gain. Both can gain because they place different values on the items being exchanged. Each party places less value on the item it starts with than the other party does. For instance, when a supermarket sells a head of cabbage, the consumer values the cabbage more than the cash paid for it, and the supermarket values the cash more than the cabbage. This simple principle is the basis for economic exchange.

Even though both parties gain in an exchange, they may not gain equally: the distribution of benefits from trade may not be divided equally among participating states. One party may benefit greatly from an exchange, whereas the other party benefits only slightly. Economic liberals are interested in maximizing the overall (joint) benefits from exchange—a condition called *Pareto-optimal* (after an economist named Pareto). They have little to say about how total benefits are distributed among the parties (see Figure 8.1).

Rather, the distribution of benefits is a matter for implicit or explicit bargaining, and hence a matter for politics and the use of leverage to influence the outcomes.[4] States as participants in the international economy try to realize the greatest overall gains for all states while simultaneously bargaining to maximize their own share of those gains. Power does matter in such bargaining, but the most relevant forms of leverage are positive (the prospect of gains by striking a deal) rather than negative. Because the exchange process creates much wealth, there is much room for bargaining over the distribution of that wealth.

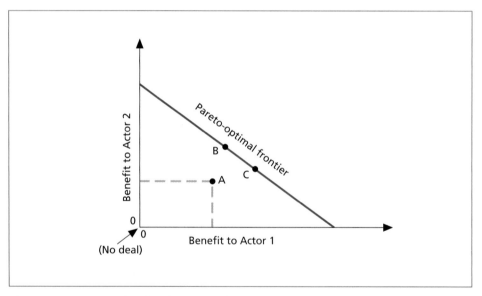

Figure 8.1 Joint and Individual Benefits

Any deal struck, such as at point A, yields certain benefits to each actor (dotted lines). Joint benefits are maximized at the Pareto-optimal frontier, but the distribution of those benefits, as between points B and C (both of which are better than A for both actors), is a matter for bargaining. Liberalism is more concerned with joint benefits, mercantilism more with the relative distribution.

---

[4] Joseph M. Grieco, *Cooperation among Nations: Europe, America, and Non-Tariff Barriers to Trade* (Ithaca, NY: Cornell UP, 1990). Joanne Gowa, *Allies, Adversaries, and International Trade* (Princeton, NJ: Princeton UP, 1993). S. Sideri, *Trade and Power* (Rotterdam: Rotterdam UP, 1970). Albert O. Hirschman, *National Power and the Structure of Foreign Trade* (Berkeley: U California P, 1945).

Economic liberalism sees individual households and firms as the key actors in the economy and views government's most useful role as one of noninterference in economics except to regulate markets in order to help them function efficiently (and to create infrastructure, such as roads, that also helps the economy function efficiently). Politics, in this view, should serve the interests of economic efficiency. With the hand of government removed from markets, the "invisible hand" of supply and demand can work out the most efficient patterns of production, exchange, and consumption (through the mechanism of prices). Because of the benefits of free trade, liberals disdain realists' obsession with international borders, because borders constrain the maximum efficiency of exchange.

For mercantilists, by contrast, economics should serve politics: the creation of wealth underlies state power. Because power is relative, trade is desirable only when the distribution of benefits favours one's own state over rivals. The terms of exchange shape the relative rates at which states accumulate power and thus shape the way power distributions in the international system change over time. As Japan and Germany, for instance, have achieved great prosperity, mercantilists saw them potentially overtaking the United States. Liberals, by contrast, thought Japanese and German wealth boosted the entire world economy and ultimately benefited all nations, including the United States.

Mercantilism achieved prominence several hundred years ago, and Britain used trade to rise in relative power in the international system around the eighteenth century. At that time mercantilism meant specifically the creation of a trade surplus (see "Balance of Trade" later in this chapter) in order to stockpile money in the form of precious metal (gold and silver), which could then be used to buy military capabilities (mercenary armies and weapons) in time of war.

Mercantilism declined in the nineteenth century as Britain decided it had more to gain from free trade than from protectionism. It returned as a major approach in the period between World Wars I and II, when liberal global trading relations broke down. Again in recent years, with the weakening of the liberal international economic order created after World War II, mercantilism has begun to become more prominent.[5]

The distinction between liberalism and mercantilism is reflected in the difference between hegemony and empire. Under hegemony (see p. 80), a dominant state creates an international order that facilitates free trade but does not try to control economic transactions by itself. An empire, by contrast, centrally controls economic transactions in its area. Historically, empires have a poor record of economic performance whereas hegemony has been much more successful in achieving economic growth and prosperity.[6] Of course, under hegemony, rival states also share (with the hegemon) in the overall growth and prosperity, which can ultimately erode the hegemon's relative power and end its hegemony.

Globalization

The ascendance of liberal over mercantilist economics in recent decades forms one strand of a complex mosaic of changes in the world political economy—changes that together are called **globalization**. This term refers to the increasing importance of the world level of analysis in economics, as the scope of economic activities expands worldwide.

Globalization encompasses many aspects, including expanded international trade, telecommunications, monetary coordination, multinational corporations, technical and scientific cooperation, cultural exchanges of new types and scales, migration and refugee

globalization The increasing integration of the world in terms of communications, culture, and economics; may also refer to changing subjective experiences of space and time accompanying this process.

---

[5] David J. Sylvan, "The Newest Mercantilism," *International Organization* 35.2 (1981): 375–81.

[6] Richard Rosencrance, *The Rise of the Virtual State: Wealth and Power in the Coming Century* (NY: Basic, 2000).

THINK GLOBALLY
As the world economy becomes more integrated, markets and production are becoming global in scope. This Chinese worker assembles sporting goods for export.

flows, and relations between the world's rich and poor countries. The coming chapters address this broad range of topics, each affected by globalization.[7]

However, although globalization clearly is very important, it is also rather vaguely defined and not well explained by any one theory. One popular conception of globalization is as "the widening, deepening and speeding up of worldwide interconnectedness in all aspects of contemporary social life ..."[8] At least three different conceptions of this process compete, however.

One view, informed by economic liberalism, sees globalization as the fruition of liberal economic principles. A global marketplace has brought growth and prosperity (not to all countries but to those most integrated with the global market). This economic process has made traditional states obsolete as economic units. States are thus losing authority to supranational institutions such as the IMF and EU, and to transnational actors such as MNCs and NGOs. The values of technocrats and elite educated citizens in liberal democracies are becoming global values, reflecting an emerging global civilization. The old North-South division is seen as less important, since the global South is moving in divergent directions depending on countries' and regions' integration with world markets.

A second perspective, informed by critical theorists, is sceptical of these claims about globalization. These observers doubt that regional and geographic distinctions such as the North-South divide are disappearing in favour of a single global market. Rather, they see the North-South gap as increasing with globalization, and they believe globalization is a process with long historical origins, not a recent phenomenon as economic liberals regularly suggest. This perspective is concerned also about the extent to which the idea of a "global civilization" is really a civilization based on the norms associated with the West, and the spread of a neoliberal market ideology around the world. This increasing homogeneity is in part offset by small, local moments of resistance, in which people try to identify along lines of language, religion, and other such cultural factors.

A third school of thought informed by mercantilism sees globalization as quite profound and is also uncertain of its positive connotations, though for different reasons than those outlined by critical theorists. Mercantilists see state sovereignty as being eroded by the EU, WTO, and other new institutions, so that sovereignty is no longer an absolute

---

[7] David Held, Anthony McGrew, David Goldblatt, and Jonathan Perraton, *Global Transformations: Politics, Economics and Culture* (Palo Alto, CA: Stanford UP, 1999). Anthony Giddens, *Runaway World: How Globalization Is Reshaping Our Lives* (London: Profile, 1999). John J. Kirton, Joseph P. Daniels, and Andreas Freytag, eds., *Guiding Global Order: G8 Governance in the Twenty-first Century* (Burlington, VT: Ashgate, 2001). Thomas L. Friedman, *The Lexus and the Olive Tree* (NY: Farrar Straus & Giroux, 1999). Jan Aart Scholte, *Globalization: A Critical Introduction* (UK: Palgrave, 2000).

[8] Held et al. (see footnote 7 above) 2.

but just one part of a spectrum of bargaining leverages held by states. The bargaining itself increasingly involves nonstate actors and nonterritorial organizations. Thus globalization diffuses authority. Whether or not state power is strengthened or weakened by globalization remains to be seen. It may be that state power will be transformed to operate in new contexts with new tools. However, the concern from this perspective is that states will be eclipsed by new, and more powerful, global actors.

While scholars debate these conceptions of globalization, popular debates focus on the growing power of large corporations operating globally, the disruptive costs associated with joining world markets (e.g., job loss and environmental impacts), the perception of growing disparities between the rich and the poor, and the collusion of national governments in these wrongs through their participation in IOs such as the WTO and IMF.[9]

Policies to expand free trade are a central focus of "antiglobalization" protesters (see "Resistance to Trade," pp. 326–328). At the 1999 Seattle WTO meeting (see p. 325), thousands of demonstrators from labour unions and environmental groups—often on opposite sides in the past—joined in street protests to demand that future trade agreements address their concerns. Anarchists "trashed" downtown Seattle to vent their anger with big corporations, while police blanketed the area with tear gas.

Street protests then turned host cities into besieged fortresses in Washington, DC (2000 IMF and World Bank meetings), Québec (2001 summit working toward a Free Trade Area of the Americas), and Genoa, Italy (2001 G8 summit), where some protesters and police engaged in battles that killed one person. The key 2001 WTO meeting to launch a new trade round was held in Qatar, where protesters had little access. The Canadian government followed suit and held the 2002 G8 Summit in Kananaskis, Alberta. Protestors could only get as close as Calgary, about 100 kilometres from the site. Hosts of subsequent summits have tried to find equally inaccessible locations to keep protestors at bay, as the U.S. did in 2004 by holding the annual G8 meeting on Sea Island, Georgia.

Just as scholars disagree on conceptions of globalization, so do protesters disagree on their goals and tactics. Union members from the global North want to stop globalization from shipping their jobs south. But workers in impoverished countries in the global South may desperately want those jobs as a first step toward decent wages and working conditions (relative to other options in their countries). Violence perpetrated by either protestors or police can steal media attention from some of the goals of the activists. Thus, neither globalization nor the backlash to it are simple. However you feel about the positive and negative effects of globalization, it is important to understand the interrelated processes that make up today's world political economy—trade, money, business, integration, communication, environmental management, and the economic development of poor countries. Trade is central to this list.

MARKETS

International exchanges of goods and services now occur in *global markets*. Liberal economics supports the use of market processes, relatively unhindered by political elements; mercantilism favours greater political control over markets and exchanges; and critical

---

[9] Walden Bello, *Deglobalization: Ideas for a New World Economy* (Blackwood, NS: Fernwood, 2002). Robin Broad, *Citizen Backlash to Economic Globalization* (Lanham, MD: Rowman & Littlefield, 2002). Jagdish Bhagwati, *The Wind of the Hundred Days: How Washington Mismanaged Globalization* (Cambridge, MA: MIT P, 2001). Brian Milani, *Designing the Green Economy: The Post-Industrial Alternative to Corporate Globalization* (Lanham, MD: Rowman & Littlefield, 2000).

theorists examine the inequalities inherent in market relations. The stakes in this debate are high because of the growing volume and importance of international trade.

Global Patterns of Trade

International trade amounts to about 20 percent of the total economic activity in the world. About US$6 trillion worth of trade crosses international borders each year.[10] This is a very large number, more than six times larger than the world's military spending, for example. The great volume of international trade reflects the fact that trade is profitable.

The role of trade in the economy varies somewhat from one region to another, but it is at least as important overall in the developing regions of the global South as in the industrialized regions of the world. Nonetheless, in the world economy as a whole, the global South accounts for a relatively small part of all trade, because its economic activity is only 40 percent of the world total (see pp. 14–22). This creates an asymmetrical dependence in North-South trade (see Chapters 11 and 12).

Overall, most political activity related to trade is concentrated in the industrialized West (North America, Western Europe, and Japan/Pacific), which accounts for about two-thirds of all international trade. Trade between these areas and the global South, although less in volume, is also a topic of interest to IPE scholars (see Chapter 11).[11] Of special interest currently are trade issues in the former communist transitional economies of Russia and Eastern Europe, which face formidable challenges as they try to join the capitalist world economy.

Two contradictory trends are at work in global trading patterns today. One trend is toward the integration of the industrialized regions with each other in a truly global market. The World Trade Organization (discussed later in this chapter) is especially important to this global integration process. The second trend is the emerging potential division of the industrialized West into three competing trading blocs, each internally integrated but not very open to the other two blocs. Regional free trade areas in Europe and North America, and perhaps in Asia in the future, raise the possibility of trading zones practising liberalism inwardly and mercantilism outwardly. However, as information technologies link the world across space, the integrating trend seems to have the upper hand and the more global vision of free trade is shaping the agenda.

Comparative Advantage

comparative advantage
The principle that states should specialize in trading those goods that they produce with the greatest relative efficiency and at the lowest relative cost (relative, that is, to other goods produced by the same state).

For economic liberals, the overall success of market economies is due to the substantial gains that can be realized through trade.[12] These gains result from the **comparative advantage** that different states enjoy in producing different goods (a concept pioneered by economists Adam Smith and David Ricardo 200 years ago). States differ in their abilities to produce certain goods because of differences in natural resources, labour force character-

---

[10] Data in this chapter are calculated from United Nations, *World Economic and Social Survey 2003: Trends and Policies in the World Economy* (NY: United Nations, 2003).

[11] Timothy J. McKeown, "A Liberal Trade Order? The Long-Run Pattern of Imports to the Advanced Capitalist States," *International Studies Quarterly* 35.2 (1991): 151–72.

[12] David A. Lake, ed., *The International Political Economy of Trade* (Brookfield, VT: Elgar, 1993). John S. Odell and Thomas D. Willett, eds., *International Trade Policies: Gains from Exchange between Economics and Political Science* (Ann Arbor: U Michigan P, 1990). Benjamin J. Cohen, "The Political Economy of International Trade," [review article] *International Organization* 44.2 (1990): 261–78.

istics, and other such factors. In order to max-imize the overall creation of wealth, by this view, each state should specialize in producing the goods for which it has a comparative advantage and then trade for goods that another state is better at producing. Of course, the costs of transportation and of processing the informa-tion in the trade (called *transaction costs*) must be included in the costs of producing an item. But frequently both of these are low relative to the differences in the cost of producing items in different locations.

The Information Revolution

Decentralizing Markets

Markets are said to be more efficient when participants have more information about each other. Information systems underlie the rapid growth of international trade. In a world where small producers and consumers meet in cyberspace instead of the village marketplace, how will the character of international trade change?

To explore this question, go to www.pearsoned.ca/goldstein.

Two commodities of great importance in the world are oil and cars. It is much cheaper to produce oil (or another energy source) in Saudi Arabia than in Japan, and much cheaper to produce cars in Japan than in Saudi Arabia. Japan needs oil to run its industry (includ-ing its car industry), and Saudi Arabia needs cars to travel its vast territory (including reaching its remote oil wells). Even with shipping and transaction costs, huge amount of money are saved by shipping Japanese cars to Saudi Arabia and Saudi oil to Japan, com-pared to the costs if each were self-sufficient.

A state need not have an absolute advantage over others in producing one kind of good in order to make specialization pay. It need only specialize in producing goods that are lower in cost than other goods relative to world market prices. Imagine that Japan dis-covered a way to produce synthetic oil using the same mix of labour and capital that it now uses to produce cars, and that this synthetic oil could be produced a bit more cheaply than what it cost Saudi Arabia to produce oil, but that Japan could still produce cars *much* more cheaply than could Saudi Arabia. From a strictly economic point of view, Japan should keep producing cars (its comparative advantage) and not divert capital and labour to make synthetic oil (where it had only a slight advantage). The extra profits Japan would make from exporting more cars would more than compensate for the slightly higher price it would pay to import oil.

Thus, international trade generally expands the Pareto-optimal frontier by increasing the overall efficiency of production. Free trade allocates global resources to states that have the greatest comparative advantage in producing each kind of commodity. As a result, prices are both lower overall and more consistent worldwide. Increasingly, produc-tion is oriented to the world market.

Trade is not without drawbacks, however, when seen from a political rather than purely economic vantage point (see "Resistance to Trade" at the end of this chapter). One drawback is familiar from the preceding discussions of international security—for liberals, long-term benefits may incur short-term costs. When a state begins to import goods that it had been producing domestically, there may be disruptions to its economy: workers may be fired or need to retrain and find new jobs, and capital may not be easy to convert to new uses.

Another problem is that the benefits and costs of trade tend not to be evenly dis-tributed *within* a state. Some industries or communities may benefit at the expense of oth-ers. For example, if a Canadian manufacturing company moves its factory to Mexico to take advantage of cheaper labour there, and exports its goods back to Canada, the work-ers at the old Canadian factory lose their jobs, but Canadian consumers enjoy cheaper goods. The costs of such a move fall heavily on a few workers, but the benefits are spread thinly across many consumers.

The Changing World Order
Trade versus Security?

World orders encompass rules and patterns of international political economy as well as security relationships. Historically, periods of hegemony have seen increasing trade, interdependence, and prosperity. The first post–Cold War decade of the 1990s fit that pattern. Corporations operated more globally, producing components in scattered locations and bringing them together into final products at the last minute ("just-in-time" inventory). By taking redundancies out of the global production system and facilitating the flow of goods and services across borders, these technical and managerial changes helped bring about a decade of unparalleled prosperity for much of the industrialized West, and parts of the global South.

The 2001 terrorist attacks on the United States exposed the "soft underbelly of globalization"—the vulnerability of a world without borders.* In the aftermath of September 11, tighter security slowed the movement of goods, services, and people across borders. Canadian truckers, for example, waited for hours—and in some cases days—at U.S. border crossings. Air traffic and business travel around the world became more difficult. Corporations waited for delayed materials coming from foreign sources, and governments worried that a terrorist attack could shut down an entire country.

Millions of shipping containers travel from port to port and disperse over road and rail networks throughout industrialized countries. Very few are searched. Doing so would be prohibitively costly—a drag on trade-based prosperity. Yet Al Qaeda reportedly owns as many as a dozen ocean-going cargo ships. Authorities worry that weapons of mass destruction could enter countries through ports, and that finding them would be like "finding a needle in a hay-stack." Customs agents now

New York, late 2003.

routinely wear radiation-detecting Geiger counters to sound the alarm if nuclear material is nearby (and not sufficiently shielded to pass undetected).

Economic liberals would argue that any impediments to the free flow of trade—including security measures—should be as minimal as possible, but mercantilists would argue that greater security measures are necessary in the post-9/11 world order, and that states should reduce their dependence on trade and aim for greater self-reliance.

In a world of heightened vulnerability, is it better for countries to rely more on their own resources and abilities, at a cost of slower economic growth and lower living standards? Or should they continue the openness of the 1990s, with increasing trade, economic growth, and interdependence, at the cost of higher military spending and risk of devastating attacks from time to time?

* William Booth, "Where Sea Meets Shore, Scenarios for Terrorists," *Washington Post* 3 Jan. 2002: A1.

Mercantilists might suggest the use of protectionist measures to try to save those jobs. Their argument would be that the loss of jobs (and greater dependence on foreign suppliers) potentially weakens the state. For liberals, protectionist measures benefit a few people greatly, and cost many people a bit. By one estimate, a 20 percent steel tariff being contemplated by the Bush Administration in 2002 would cost consumers US$7 billion and save 7300 U.S. jobs—a pricey US$326 000 per job.[13] Yet, those 7300 workers (and their

[13] Joseph Kahn, "U.S. Trade Panel Backs Putting Hefty Duties on Imported Steel," *New York Times* 8 Dec. 2001: C1, C3.

unions and companies) benefit greatly, whereas the roughly $20 cost per U.S. citizen goes unnoticed. This kind of unequal distribution of costs and benefits often creates political problems for free trade even when the *overall* economic benefits outweigh the costs.

Between states (as well as within each state) the distribution of benefits from trade can also be unequal. The new wealth created by international trade can be divided in any manner between the participants. For instance, it would be worthwhile for Saudi Arabia to import cars even at a price much higher than what it cost Japan to produce them, as long as the price was less than what it would cost Saudi Arabia to produce cars itself (or to buy them elsewhere). Similarly, Saudi Arabia would profit from selling oil even at a price just a bit above what the oil costs to produce (or what it can sell the oil for elsewhere). With so much added value from the exchange process, there is a great deal of room for bargaining over the distribution of benefits.

If there were only two states in the world, the bargaining over prices (that is, over the distribution of benefits from trade) would essentially be a political process entailing the use of leverage, possibly including military force. But in a world of many states (and even more substate economic actors, such as companies and households), this is less true. Prices are set instead by market competition. If Japan's cars are too expensive, Saudi Arabia can buy German cars; if Saudi oil is too expensive, Japan can buy Alaskan oil.

Prices and Markets

The *terms* of an exchange are defined by the price at which goods are traded. Often the *bargaining space*—defined by the difference between the lowest price a seller would accept and the highest price a buyer would pay—is quite large. For example, Saudi Arabia would be willing to sell a barrel of oil (if it had no better option) for as little as, say, $10 a barrel, and industrialized countries are willing to pay as much as $50 a barrel for the oil. (In practice, oil prices have fluctuated in this broad range in recent decades.) How are prices determined within this range? That is, how do the participants decide on the distribution of benefits from the exchange?

When there are multiple buyers and sellers of a good (or equivalent goods that can be substituted for it), prices are determined by market competition.[14] In terms of the above bargaining framework, sellers bargain for a high price, using as leverage the threat to sell to another buyer. Meanwhile buyers bargain for a low price, with the leverage being a threat to buy from another seller. In practice, free markets are supposed to (and sometimes do) produce stable patterns of buying and selling at a fairly uniform price. At this *market price*, sellers know that an effort to raise the price would drive the buyer to seek another seller, and buyers know that an effort to lower the price would drive the seller to seek another buyer. Because of this stability, the process of bargaining is greatly simplified and most economic exchanges take place in a fairly routine manner.

Buyers vary in the value they place on an item (like a barrel of oil); if the price rises, fewer people are willing to buy it, and if the price drops, more people are willing to buy it. This is called the *demand curve* for the item. Sellers also vary in the value they place on the item. If the price rises, more sellers are willing to supply the item to buyers; if the price drops, fewer sellers are willing to supply the item. This is called the *supply curve*.

In a free market, the price at which the supply and demand curves cross is the *equilibrium price*. At this price sellers are willing to supply the same number of units that buyers are willing to purchase. (In practice, prices reflect *expectations* about supply and

---

[14] Charles E. Lindblom, *The Market System: What It Is, How It Works, and What to Make of It* (New Haven, CT: Yale UP, 2001).

demand in the near future.) In a trade of Saudi oil for Japanese cars, for example, the prices would be determined by the world demand for, and supply of, oil and cars.

Thus, in liberal economics, *bilateral* relations between states are less important than they are in security affairs. The existence of world markets reduces the leverage that one state can exert over another in economic affairs (because the second state can simply find other partners). Imagine Japan trying to exert power by refusing to sell cars to Saudi Arabia. It would only hurt itself—Saudi Arabia would buy cars elsewhere. In IPE, then, power is more diffuse and involves more actors at once than in international security.

The currency in which world prices are expressed is somewhat arbitrary. Prices were once pegged to the value of gold or silver. Now prices are expressed in national currencies, most prominently the U.S. dollar, Japanese yen, and European euro. In practice, the conversion of money among national currencies is complex (see Chapter 9), but for the sake of simplicity we will proceed as if there were a common currency.

Centrally Planned Economies

centrally planned (command) economy An economy in which political authorities set prices and decide on quotas for production and consumption of each commodity according to a long-term plan.

One major alternative to a market economy is a **centrally planned** (or **command**) **economy,** in which political authorities set prices and decide on quotas for production and consumption of each commodity according to a long-term plan. This type of economy was for decades the standard in the communist states of the former Soviet Union, Eastern Europe, China, and several smaller countries—it is still in place in Cuba and North Korea. Within the Soviet economic bloc (which included Eastern Europe and Mongolia), international trade also took place at government-controlled prices.

The proponents of central planning claimed it would make economies both more rational and more just. By controlling the economy, governments could guarantee the basic needs of citizens (as in China's "iron rice bowl" policy under Chairman Mao) and could mobilize the state fully for war if necessary (as the Soviet Union did in World War II under Stalin). Proponents of central planning also hoped that governments' long-term view of resources and needs would smooth out the business cycles and avoid the recessions that periodically afflict capitalist economies.

Instead, communist economics has in recent years been discredited as hopelessly inefficient and discarded in whole or in part by virtually all of its former followers. The economies of Russia and Eastern Europe stagnated over the Cold War

DUSTBIN OF HISTORY

The unreliable, polluting East German Trabant car reflected the inefficiency of production in the centrally planned economies of the communist countries during the Cold War era. All those countries are now making transitions—by various routes and with various degrees of success—toward market-based economies. This Trabant in East Berlin was discarded as Germany unified, 1990.

decades while environmental damage and military spending both took an increasing economic toll. Now the former Soviet republics and Eastern Europe are almost all **transitional economies,** trying to make a *transition* to a market-based economy connected to the world capitalist economy.[15] This transition has proven very difficult. In the first half of the 1990s, the total GDP of the region *shrank* by about *35 percent*—a great depression worse than the one Canada experienced in the early 1930s (see p. 32). Living standards dropped dramatically for most citizens, and remained low for the rest of the decade. A program of *shock therapy*—a radical, sudden shift over to market principles—seemed to work in Poland despite short-term dislocation. But a similar program in Russia stalled after being effectively blocked by old-time communist officials. Through the final years of the Yeltsin administration, Russia's economy remained dysfunctional, owing to depression, corruption, tax delinquency, and the vast differences between the old communist and new capitalist models. President Putin brought new energy to economic reform, and progress in some areas, but the overall path of Russia's transition remains uncertain.

> **transitional economies**
> Countries in Russia and Eastern Europe that are trying to convert from communism to capitalism, with various degrees of success.

China, whose government continues to follow a Marxist *political* line (central control by the Communist party), has shifted substantially toward a market *economy*.[16] This transition dramatically increased China's economic growth in the 1980s, reaching a sustained annual rate of about 10 percent throughout the 1990s and slowing to more sustainable rates with the global recession of 2001 (see "The Chinese Experience" on pp. 449–453). Perhaps because China is not yet industrialized (and hence is more flexible about how it invests capital profitably), the introduction of market principles in China's economy has been less painful than in the "developed" (but actually maldeveloped) economies of Russia and Eastern Europe.

Today, the world's economic activity follows the principles of free markets more than central planning but often falls somewhere between the extremes. Many governments control domestic prices on some goods (for instance, subsidizing certain goods to win political support). Many states *own* (all or part of) industries thought to be vital for the national economy—**state-owned industries,** such as oil production companies or national airlines. For some types of goods, such as electricity service, it has traditionally been considered inefficient for competing suppliers to operate (each with its own transmission lines running along the street); in such cases governments sometimes supply the service themselves. Also, the government sector of the economy (military spending, road building, employment insurance, and so on) makes up a substantial fraction of the industrialized countries' economies. Because they contain both some government control and some private ownership, the economies of the industrialized West are called **mixed economies.**[17]

> **state-owned industries**
> Industries such as oil-production companies and airlines that are owned wholly or partly by the state because they are thought to be vital to the national economy.

> **mixed economies**
> Economies such as those in the industrialized West that contain both some government control and some private ownership.

Politics of Markets

A free and efficient market requires a fairly large number of buyers looking for the same item and a large number of sellers supplying it. It also requires that participants have fairly complete information about the other participants and transactions in the market. Also,

---

[15] Thane Gustafson, *Capitalism Russian-Style* (NY: Cambridge UP, 1999). Anders Aslund, *How Russia Became a Market Economy* (Washington, DC: Brookings, 1995). Leah A. Haus, *Globalizing the GATT: The Soviet Union's Successor States, Eastern Europe, and the International Trading System* (Washington, DC: Brookings, 1992).

[16] Lance L. P. Gore, *Market Communism: The Institutional Foundation of China's Post-Mao Hyper-Growth* (NY: Oxford UP, 1999). Harold K. Jacobson and Michael Oksenberg, *China's Participation in the IMF, the World Bank, and GATT: Toward a Global Economic Order* (Ann Arbor: U Michigan P, 1990).

[17] Carmelo Meso-Lago, *Market, Socialist, and Mixed Economies: Comparative Policy and Performance—Chile, Cuba, and Costa Rica* (Baltimore: Johns Hopkins UP, 2000).

the willingness of participants to deal with each other should not be distorted by personal (or political) preferences but should be governed only by price and quality considerations. Failures to meet these various conditions are called *market imperfections*: they reduce efficiency (to the dismay of liberal economists). Most political intrusions into economic transactions are market imperfections.

International trade occurs more often at world market prices than does *domestic* economic exchange. No world government owns industries, provides subsidies, or regulates prices. Nonetheless, world markets are often affected by politics. When states are the principal actors in international economic affairs, the number of participants is often small. When there is just one supplier of an item—a *monopoly*—the supplier can set the price quite high. For example, the South African company De Beers produces half the world supply and controls two-thirds of the world market for uncut diamonds. An *oligopoly* is a monopoly shared by just a few large sellers—often allowing for tacit or explicit coordination to force the price up. For example, OPEC members agree to limit oil production to keep prices up. To the extent that companies band together along national lines, monopolies and oligopolies are more likely.

Governments can use antitrust policies to break up monopolies and keep markets competitive. But home governments often *benefit* from the ability of their companies to distort international markets and gain revenue (whether they are state-owned or just taxed by the state). *Foreign* governments have little power to break up such monopolies.

Another common market imperfection in international trade is *corruption*; individuals may receive payoffs to trade at nonmarket prices. The government or company involved may lose some of the benefits being distributed, but the individual government official or company negotiator gets increased benefits (see pp. 462–464).

TRADE GETS THROUGH

Economic sanctions, such as the U.S. restrictions on trade with Iran, are among the most obvious ways that politics interferes in markets. But sanctions are hard to enforce because doing business is profitable, especially when competitors are restrained by sanctions. For example, European countries do not follow the U.S. lead on sanctions against Iran. Here, Lipton tea, owned by a British-Dutch company, is advertised in Iran's capital, 1993.

Politics provides a *legal framework* for markets—assuring that participants keep their commitments, that contracts are binding, buyers pay for goods they purchase, counterfeit money is not used, and so forth. In the international economy, lacking a central government authority, rules are less easily enforced. As in security affairs, such rules can be codified in international treaties, but enforcement depends on practical reciprocity (see pp. 275–276).

Taxation is another political influence on markets. Taxes are used both to generate revenue for the government and to regulate economic activity by incentives. For instance, a government may keep taxes low on foreign companies in hopes of attracting them to locate and invest in the country. Taxes applied to international trade itself, called tariffs, are a frequent source of international conflict (see "Protectionism," pp. 311–315).

Political interference in free markets is most explicit when governments apply *sanctions* against economic interactions of certain kinds or between certain actors. Political power then prohibits an economic exchange that would otherwise have been mutually beneficial.

Enforcing sanctions is always a difficult task, because there is a financial incentive to break the sanctions through parallel economies or other means.[18] For instance, despite UN sanctions against trading with Serbia in the early 1990s, many people and companies took risks to smuggle goods across Serbia's borders, because doing so was profitable. Without broad multilateral support for international sanctions, they generally fail. When the United States tried to punish the Soviet Union in the 1970s by applying trade sanctions against a Soviet oil pipeline to Western Europe, it did not stop the pipeline. It just took profitable business away from a U.S. company (Caterpillar) and allowed European companies to profit instead (because European states did not join in the sanctions). By contrast, when more and more states became involved in sanctions against apartheid-era South Africa, the impact is thought to have contributed to the transformation of that society in the early 1990s from white minority rule.

The difficulty of applying sanctions reflects a more general point made earlier—that power in IPE is more diffused among states than it is in security affairs. Canada rarely imposes economic sanctions unilaterally, and instead (through a federal piece of legislation called the United Nations Act) imposes them when the United Nations Security Council calls for members of the UN to impose sanctions. The Security Council has done this in recent years against Angola, Afghanistan, Iraq, Eritrea and Ethiopia, and the former Yugoslavia, but in all of these cases the sanctions have now been repealed. Arms embargoes (as of 2004) continue to exist against Liberia, Sierra Leone, and Rwanda, as do embargoes against the importation of timber or diamonds from Liberia and Sierra Leone. Canada can choose to impose sanctions in the absence of a Security Council Resolution (through the Special Economic Measures Regulations or the Export and Import Permits Act), but again, tends to do so only if called for by an international organization or if there is a perceived threat to international peace and security.

If one state tries to use economic means of leverage to influence another, other states can profitably take over. Refusing to participate in mutually profitable economic trade often harms oneself more than the target of one's actions, unless nearly all other states follow suit. This is one of the reasons Canada prefers to engage (when it engages in sanctions at all) in multilateral efforts.

---

[18] Daniel W. Drezner, *The Sanctions Paradox: Economic Statecraft and International Relations* (NY: Cambridge UP, 1999). Richard N. Haass and Meghan L. O'Sullivan, eds., *Honey and Vinegar: Incentives, Sanctions, and Foreign Policy* (Washington, DC: Brookings, 2000). George E. Shambaugh, *States, Firms, and Power: Successful Sanctions in United States Foreign Policy* (Albany: SUNY P, 2000). George A. Lopez, and David Cortwright, *The Sanctions Decade: Assessing UN Strategies in the 1990s* (Boulder, CO: Rienner, 2000). Lisa L. Martin, *Coercive Cooperation: Explaining Multilateral Economic Sanctions* (Princeton, NJ: Princeton UP, 1992).

Balance of Trade

Mercantilists favour political control of trade so that trade relations serve a state's political interests—even at the cost of some lost wealth that free markets might have created. Their preferred means of accomplishing this end is to create a favourable balance of trade. The **balance of trade** is the value of a state's imports relative to its exports.

balance of trade The value of a state's exports relative to its imports.

A state that exports more than it imports has a *positive balance of trade*, or *trade surplus*. Japan has run a trade surplus in recent years: it gets more money for cars and other goods it exports than it pays for oil and other imported goods. A state that imports more than it exports has a *negative balance of trade* (*trade deficit*). A trade deficit is different from a budget deficit in government spending. Canada has run an overall trade surplus for a number of years. This is a result of a large trade surplus with the United States. Canada consistently runs a trade deficit with almost all of its other trading partners.

The balance of trade must ultimately be reconciled, one way or another. It is tracked financially through the system of national accounts (see pp. 344–345). In the short term, a state can trade for a few years at a deficit and then a few years at a surplus. The imbalances are carried on the national accounts as a kind of loan. But a trade deficit that persists for years becomes a problem for the state. As noted above, Canada in recent years has run a trade surplus overall (and in Canada-U.S. bilateral trade), while the United States has run a deficit. To balance trade, the United States then "exports" currency (dollars) to Canada, which can use the dollars to buy such things as shares of U.S. companies, U.S. Treasury bills, or U.S. real estate. In essence (oversimplifying a bit), a state with a chronic trade deficit must export part of its standing wealth (real estate, companies, bank accounts, etc.) by giving ownership of such wealth to foreigners.

This is one reason mercantilists favour national economic policies to create a trade surplus. Then the state can "own" parts of other states, gaining power over them. Rather than being indebted to others, the state holds IOUs from others. Rather than being unable to find the money it might need to cope with a crisis or fight a war, the state sits on a pile of money representing potential power. Historically, mercantilism literally meant stockpiling gold (gained from running a trade surplus) as a fungible form of power (see Figure 8.2). Such a strategy is attuned to realism's emphasis on relative power. For one state to have a trade surplus, another must have a deficit.

There is a price for mercantilist-derived power. Often a trade surplus lowers the short-term standard of living. For instance, if Canadians cashed in their trade surplus each year for imported goods, they could enjoy those goods now instead of piling up money for the future. Mercantilists are willing to pay such short-term costs because they are more concerned with power than with standards of living.

Interdependence

When the well-being of a state depends on the cooperation of a second state, the first state is *dependent* on the second. When two or more states are simultaneously dependent on each other, they

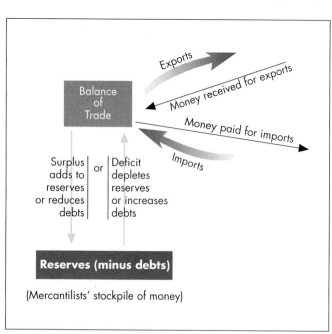

Figure 8.2 Balance of Trade

are *interdependent*. **Interdependence** is a political and not just an economic phenomenon. Economic liberals tend to see interdependence as mutually beneficial over the long term. Mercantilists are concerned about the risks to state power associated with interdependence. Critical theorists would say that interdependence is rarely a neutral condition, and usually involves relations of inequality.

States that trade become mutually dependent on each other's *political* cooperation in order to realize economic gains through trade. In IPE, interdependence refers less often to a bilateral mutual dependence than to a multilateral dependence in which each state depends on the political cooperation of most or all of the others to keep world markets operating efficiently. Most states depend on the world market, not on specific trading partners (though for large industrialized states each bilateral trade relationship is important as well).

The mutual dependence of two or more states does not mean that their degree of dependence is equal or symmetrical. Often one is more dependent than another. This is especially true because world markets vary in their openness and efficiency from one commodity and region to another. Saudi Arabia, for instance, has more power over the price of oil than Japan has over the price of cars.

The degree of a state's *short-term* dependence on another may differ from its *long-term* dependence. The short-term dislocation that is caused by disrupting exchange with another country is the *sensitivity* of supply. When oil prices rose sharply in the early 1970s, Japan and other industrialized states did not have policies to cope with the increases: they were *sensitive* to the disruption, and long lines formed at gas stations. Over the longer term, states may be able to change their policies to take advantage of alternatives that could substitute for disrupted trade. Japan then expanded nuclear power in response to oil price increases—a long-term strategy. A state that *cannot* adjust its policies to cope with disrupted trade, even over the long run, suffers from *vulnerability* of supply.[19]

Over time, as the world economy develops and technology advances, states are becoming *increasingly interdependent*. Some IR scholars point out that this is not entirely new. The great powers were very interdependent before World War I; for instance, international trade was about the same percentage of GDP then as now. But several other dimensions of interdependence show dramatic change. One is the extent to which individual *firms*, which used to be nationally based, now are international in their holdings and interests (becoming MNCs or transnational corporations, TNCs), and thus dependent on the well-being of other states in addition to their home state (making them tend to favour free trade).[20]

Another key aspect of interdependence is the tight integration of world markets through the ever-expanding flow of *information* and communication worldwide (see pp. 384–393). This facilitates the free competition of goods and services in global markets as well as the expanding volume of money (capital) that moves around the world every day. Yet another dimension of change is the expansion of *scope* in the global economy, from one based in Europe to a more diffuse network encompassing the world. Asian economic expansion, and the integration of Russia and Eastern Europe into the world market economy, are accelerating this trend.

Whether based on a specific bilateral trading relationship, an integrated global (or regional) market, or the international nature of corporate holdings, interdependence arises from comparative advantage—that is, from the greater absolute wealth that two or more states can produce by collaborating. This wealth depends on international political

[19] Robert O. Keohane and Joseph S. Nye, *Power and Interdependence*, 3rd ed. (NY: Longman, 2001).

[20] Helen V. Milner, *Resisting Protectionism: Global Industries and the Politics of International Trade* (Princeton, NJ: Princeton UP, 1988).

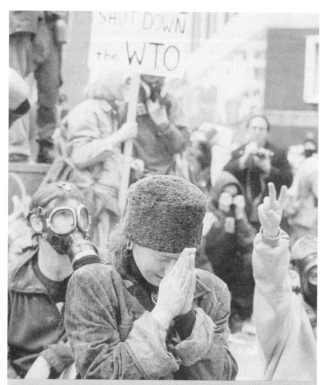

UNSETTLING CHANGES
Free trade creates both winners and losers. Backlash against free trade agreements led to a spectacular failure at the WTO summit meeting in Seattle, 1999. As environmentalists and labour unions led protests in the streets, the assembled states could not agree on an agenda for a new round of trade talks.

cooperation, which is therefore in the interests of all participants. Furthermore, violence is usually not an effective leverage in bringing about such cooperation. Thus, many liberal IR scholars argue that *interdependence inherently promotes peace*.[21] It alters the cost-benefit calculations of national leaders so as to make military leverage less attractive. (Some IR scholars saw similar trends in international interdependence just before World War I, but war occurred anyway.)

Despite the added wealth that states enjoy as a result of trade and the power that such wealth creates, interdependence does have drawbacks. The more a state gains from trade cooperation, the more its own well-being depends on other states, which therefore have power over it. In situations of asymmetrical interdependence, in particular, the economic benefits of cooperation may come with inherent vulnerabilities. The potential to take advantage of those vulnerabilities would be the kind of thing a mercantilist would caution against. For example, it is cheaper for Japan to import energy than to produce it domestically, but dependence on energy imports has historically put Japan at a disadvantage in power. In the 1930s, the United States cut off its oil exports to Japan to protest Japanese militarism. Exports as well as imports can create dependence (on those who buy the product); UN sanctions against Iraq's oil exports have deprived Iraq of revenue.

Interdependence thus ties the well-being of a state's population and society to policies and conditions in other states, outside its control. The price of trade-generated wealth (and the power it brings) is a loss of state autonomy and sovereignty. These problems are intensifying as world markets become more closely interwoven, especially in regional integration such as in Europe (see Chapter 10).

As states become more interdependent, power is becoming more, not less, important in IR. The intensification of linkages among states multiplies the number of issues affecting the relations of states and the avenues of influence by which outcomes are shaped. It is true that because power operates on multiple complex dimensions in a highly interdependent world, the importance of one dimension—military power—is gradually diminishing relative to other means of influence (diplomatic, economic, cultural, etc.). But the overall importance of international power on all dimensions combined is increasing as the world becomes more interdependent.

TRADE STRATEGIES

To manage the trade-offs of gains and losses in power and wealth, states develop economic strategies—trade strategies in particular—in order to maximize their own wealth while

---

[21] Edward D. Mansfield, *Power, Trade, and War* (Princeton, NJ: Princeton UP, 1994).

minimizing their vulnerability and dependence on others. Some strategies can be implemented by single states; most involve participation in some broader framework.

Autarky

One obvious way to avoid becoming dependent on other states, especially for a weak state whose trading partners would tend to be more powerful, is to avoid trading and instead to try to produce everything it needs by itself. Such a strategy is called *self-reliance* or **autarky.** As the theory of comparative advantage suggests, such a policy has proven ineffective. A self-reliant state pays a very high cost to produce goods for which it does not have a comparative advantage. As other states cooperate among themselves to maximize their joint creation of wealth, the relative power of the autarkic state in the international system tends to fall.

In practice, when states have relied on a policy of autarky they have indeed lagged behind others. A classic case in recent decades was the small state of Albania, next to the former Yugoslavia. A communist state that split from both the Soviet Union and China, Albania for decades did not participate in world markets but relied on a centrally planned economy designed for self-sufficiency. Few foreigners were allowed to visit, little trade took place, and Albania pursued autarky to prevent outsiders from gaining power over it. When this curtain of isolation finally fell in 1991, Albania was as poor as decades earlier. Little additional wealth had been generated; little economic development had taken place. This contributed to Albania's political instability, which affected conflicts in Kosovo and Macedonia that precipitated NATO military intervention.

China's experience also illustrates the problems with autarky. China's economic isolation in the 1950s and 1960s, resulting from an economic embargo imposed by the United States and its allies, was deepened during its own Cultural Revolution in the late 1960s when it broke ties with the Soviet Union as well. In that period, all things foreign were rejected. For instance, Chinese computer programmers were not allowed to use foreign software, such as Assembler language and Fortran—standards in the rest of the world. Instead they had to create all software from scratch. As a result, the computer industry lagged far behind, "reinventing the wheel," as the world's computer revolution unfolded.

When China opened up to the world economy in the 1980s, the pattern was reversed. The rapid expansion of trade, along with some market-oriented reforms in its domestic economy, resulted in rapid economic growth, which continued into the new century. By contrast, North Korea maintained a policy of self-reliance and isolation even after the Cold War. This policy (along with high military spending and other problems) led to mass starvation in the 1990s.

Protectionism

Although few states pursue strategies of autarky, many states try to manipulate international trade in such a manner so as to strengthen one or more domestic industries and shelter them from world markets. Such policies are broadly known as **protectionism**—protection of domestic industries from international competition. Although this term encompasses a variety of trade policies arising from various motivations, all are contrary to liberalism in that they seek to distort free markets to gain an advantage for the state (or for substate actors within it), generally by discouraging imports of competing goods or services.[22]

autarky (self-reliance) A policy of avoiding or minimizing trade and trying to produce everything one needs (or the most vital things) by oneself.

protectionism The protection of domestic industries against international competition, by trade tariffs and other means.

---

[22] Dominick Salvatore, ed., *Protectionism and World Welfare* (NY: Cambridge UP, 1993). Judith Goldstein, "The Political Economy of Trade: Institutions of Protection," *American Political Science Review* 801 (1986): 161–84.

Government policies discouraging imports can help domestic industries or communities avoid the costs inherent in full participation in world markets. Such costs often fall disproportionately on a small part of the population and lead that group to pressure the government for protection. The benefits of greater global efficiency, by contrast, are spread more broadly across the population and do not create similar domestic pressures (see p. 315).

A state's *motivation* to protect domestic industry can arise from several sources. Often governments simply cater to the political demands of important domestic industries and interests, regardless of the overall national interest. An industry may lobby or give campaign contributions in order to win special tax breaks, subsidies, or restrictions on competing imports (see "Industries and Interest Groups" later in this chapter).

States often attempt to protect an *infant industry* as it starts up in the state for the first time, until it can compete in world markets. For instance, when South Korea first developed an automobile industry, it was not yet competitive with imports, so the government gave consumers incentives to buy Korean cars. Eventually the industry developed and could compete with foreign producers and even export cars profitably. In a number of poor states, the *textile* trade has been a favoured infant industry (adding value without heavy capital requirements) that governments have protected.[23] Protection of infant industry is considered a relatively legitimate reason for (temporary) protectionism. Britain became a strong advocate of free trade by the eighteenth and nineteenth centuries, but mercantilists argued that it did so only after its own industries became strong enough to withstand foreign competition. This is one reason why mercantilists, as well as critical theorists, argue that free trade is a policy of the already rich and powerful.

Another motivation for protection is to give a domestic industry breathing room when market conditions shift or new competitors arrive on the scene. Sometimes domestic industry requires time to adapt and can emerge a few years later in a healthy condition. When gas prices jumped in the 1970s, U.S. auto producers were slow to shift to smaller cars, and smaller Japanese cars gained a great advantage in the U.S. market. The U.S. government used a variety of measures, including import quotas and loan guarantees, to help the U.S. industry through this transition.

Yet another motivation is the protection of industry considered vital to national security. In the 1980s U.S. officials sought to protect the U.S. electronics and computer industries against being driven out of business by Japanese competitors, because those industries were considered crucial to military production. A government-sponsored consortium of U.S. computer-chip companies called Sematech was formed to promote the U.S. capability to produce chips cheaply (ordinarily the government would discourage such a consortium as an antitrust violation). To ensure self-sufficiency in military goods, states are often willing to sacrifice some economic efficiency. Then, in the event of war the state will be less vulnerable.

In Canada, a common motivation for protectionism has been to protect industries considered vital to maintaining Canadian cultural diversity. Foreign content, in particular U.S. content, of Canadian radio, television, books, magazines, and feature films has long been considered a threat to the preservation of Canadian cultural industries. The government has sought a variety of ways to promote the development of Canadian culture, by funding such institutions as the Canadian Broadcasting Corporation (the CBC), arts councils, and the National Film Board; by providing tax incentives to domestically produced cultural products; and by regulating, through agencies such as the Canadian

---

[23] Vinod K. Aggarwal, *Liberal Protectionism: The International Politics of Organized Textile Trade* (Berkeley: U California P, 1985).

Radio Television and Telecommunications Commission (the CRTC), access to radio, television, and cable broadcasting.[24]

Any government support for cultural industries can be seen as providing an unfair trade advantage. In some cases, the Canadian government attempts simply to block foreign-owned cultural products. In 1994, for example, the CRTC revoked the broadcast license of Country Music Television (CMT), a U.S.-owned country music station, in order to facilitate a Canadian country music station, Canada's New Country Network. The CRTC regularly denied licenses (or as in this case, revoked them) to foreign-owned companies that were in direct competition with a Canadian-owned company. In this case, the U.S. threatened retaliatory trade sanctions, but in the end CMT bought a portion of Canada's New Country Network, renaming it CMT Canada and retaining access to the Canadian market.

Finally, protection may be motivated by a defensive effort to ward off predatory practices by foreign companies or states. *Predatory* generally refers to efforts to unfairly capture a large share of world markets, or even a near-monopoly, so that eventually the predator can raise prices without fearing competition. Most often these efforts entail **dumping** products in foreign markets at prices below the minimum level necessary to make a profit. The reason a state would want its companies to dump products in foreign markets is that money lost in the short term could lead to dominance of a market, which eventually lets the state's companies raise prices enough to recoup their losses and to profit more. In the 1980s and 1990s, the Canadian government sought to protect the domestic footwear industry, sometimes by claiming that foreign producers like Brazil and China were dumping low-priced shoes on the Canadian market. Critics argued that the Canadian government was inappropriately applying anti-dumping protections: the shoes were simply produced more cheaply by foreign producers, they were not being dumped. This is one of the concerns that generally arise in cases of dumping: is the product being intentionally undervalued by exporters seeking unfair access to a market (with the intention over time of establishing a monopoly), or has its price simply dropped by virtue of more efficient production techniques?

> **dumping** The sale of products in foreign markets at prices below the minimum level necessary to make a profit (or below cost).

Within a domestic economy, the government can use antitrust laws to break up an impending monopoly, but because no such mechanism exists in IR, governments try to restrict imports in such situations to protect their state's industries. Up to the late 1980s, it was generally industrialized countries such as Australia, Canada, the U.S., and members of the EU that accounted for most anti-dumping cases, but by the mid-1990s it was countries of the global South such as Argentina, Brazil, India, Mexico, South Korea, and South Africa that began to use anti-dumping laws to protect themselves against predatory trade practices.[25] These conflicts now generally are resolved through the WTO (see pp. 323–326).

Just as there are several motivations for protectionism, so too governments use several methods to restrict imports. The simplest is a **tariff** (or *duty*)—a tax imposed on certain types of imported goods, usually as a percentage of their value, as they enter the country. Tariffs not only restrict imports but also can be an important source of state revenues. If a state is going to engage in protectionism, international norms favour tariffs as the preferred method of protection because they are straightforward and not hidden (see

> **tariff** A duty or tax levied on certain types of imports (usually as a percentage of their value) as they enter a country.

[24] Steven Shrybman, *A Citizen's Guide to the World Trade Organization* (Toronto: Canadian Centre for Policy Alternatives and Lorimer, 1999).

[25] Thomas J. Prusa, "On the Spread and Impact of Antidumping," National Bureau of Economic Research Working Paper 7404, Cambridge.

COMPETITION AND PROTECTIONISM

Protectionism uses various means to keep foreign imports from competing with domestic products. U.S. tariffs on imported lumber from Canada were ruled illegal by the WTO and NAFTA.

nontariff barriers Forms of restricting imports other than tariffs, such as quotas (ceilings on how many goods of a certain kind can be imported).

pp. 323–326). Most states maintain a long and complex schedule of tariffs, based on thousands of categories and subcategories of goods organized by industry.

Other means to discourage imports are **nontariff barriers** to trade. Imports can be limited by a *quota*. Quotas are ceilings on how many goods of a certain kind can be imported; they are imposed to restrict the growth of such imports. The extreme version is a flat prohibition against importing a certain type of good (or goods from a certain country). The softwood lumber agreement of 1996 between Canada and the United States set quotas on Canadian exports to the U.S. of softwood lumber. Any exports above the quota were subject to steep tariffs. The agreement expired in March of 2001, and since that time, Canada and the U.S. have been engaged in ongoing disputes about softwood lumber exports. The U.S. argument is that Canadian lumber exporters are receiving unfair subsidies from the Canadian government and dumping softwood lumber on the U.S. market at below-market prices.[26] In 2004, the WTO and a North American Free Trade Agreement (NAFTA) panel found that the U.S. claims were flawed.

Related to the example above, a third way to protect domestic industry is providing *subsidies* to a domestic industry, which allows it to lower its prices without losing money. Subsidies can be funnelled to industries in a variety of ways. A state can give *tax breaks* to an industry struggling to get established or facing strong foreign competition. It can make *loans* (or guarantee private loans) on favourable terms to companies in a threatened industry. Sometimes governments buy goods from domestic producers at high *guaranteed prices* and resell them on world markets at lower prices; the European Community does this with agricultural products, to the dismay of U.S. farmers, as does the United States, to the dismay of European farmers.

---

[26] Gilbert Gagné, "The Canada-US Softwood Lumber Dispute," *International Journal* 58.3 (Summer 2003): 335–68.

Fourth, imports can be limited by *restrictions* and *regulations*, or sometimes simply different language requirements that make it hard to distribute and market a product even when it can be imported. Products that are produced in a foreign country must conform, for example in Canada, to the requirement that all products display at least both official languages, French and English. States that have different hygienic regulations in the production of a product can block imports that do not meet those same standards. The discovery of disease in agricultural exports, for example hoof and mouth disease in Britain in 2001, and mad cow disease in British cattle in 1986 and then in some Canadian cattle in 2003, led to restrictions on beef exports from both these countries.

Protectionism has both positive and negative effects on an economy, most often helping producers but hurting consumers. For instance, although the U.S. lumber industry has been aided somewhat by the restrictions imposed on Canadian imports, U.S. lumber consumers paid more as a result. By some U.S. estimates, for example, the cost of a new home in the United States was between US$800 and US$1300 higher than it would have been without trade restrictions.[27] As liberals argue, the costs to the consumers of lumber may be greater than the benefits to the producers of lumber; but those costs are spread among millions of households, whereas the benefits are concentrated on a few firms. This means that the firms most affected will be highly motivated to try to influence governments to act in their favour, more so than the many individuals and households who bear the costs of protectionism. Another problem with protectionism, for economic liberals, is that domestic industry may use protection to avoid needed improvements and may therefore remain inefficient and uncompetitive—especially if protection continues over many years.

Industries and Interest Groups

Industries and other domestic political actors often seek to influence a state's foreign economic policies (see "Interest Groups," pp. 143–144).[28] These pressures do not always favour protectionism. In the lumber example above, for instance, it was Home Builders Associations in the United States that used the estimates of increased new house prices to lobby the U.S. government to abandon restrictions on Canadian softwood lumber. In that industry's case, opening up free trade to Canadian softwood lumber would reduce the price its members pay for necessary inputs into home building. They did not want to pay the higher prices demanded by domestic producers.

Industries that are advanced and competitive in world markets often try to influence their governments to adopt free trade policies. This strategy promotes a global free trade system in which such industries can prosper. By contrast, industries that lag behind their global competitors tend to seek government restrictions on imports or other forms of protection.

Means to influence foreign economic policy include lobbying; forming coalitions, organizations, or agencies; paying bribes; even encouraging coups. Actors include industry-sponsored groups, companies, labour unions, and individuals. Within an industry, such

---

[27] Cato Institute, "Nailing the Homeowner? Assessing the Impact of Trade Restrictions on Softwood Lumber," Cato Institute Policy Forum, October 26, 2000, <http://www.freetrade.org/pubs/speeches/cf-102600.htm>.

[28] John M. Rothgeb, *U.S. Trade Policy: Balancing Economic Dreams and Political Realities* (Washington, DC: CQ Press, 2001). Beth A. Simmons, *Who Adjusts? Domestic Sources of Foreign Economic Policy during the Interwar Years* (Princeton, NJ: Princeton UP, 1994). I. M. Destler, *American Trade Politics*, 2nd ed. (Washington, DC: Institute for International Economics, 1992). G. John Ikenberry, David A. Lake, and Michael Mastanduno, eds., *The State and American Foreign Economic Policy*, spec. issue of *International Organization* 42.1 (1988). Daniel Verdier, *Democracy and International Trade: Britain, France, and the United States, 1860–1990* (Princeton, NJ: Princeton UP, 1994).

efforts usually work in a common direction because, despite competition among companies and between management and labour, all share common interests regarding the trade policies. However, a different industry may be pushing in a different direction. For instance, some Canadian industries supported the North American Free Trade Agreement (NAFTA); others opposed it.

A good example of how competing domestic interests can pull in opposite directions on state trade policy is U.S. tobacco exports. U.S. companies have a comparative advantage globally in producing cigarettes. As the U.S. market for cigarettes shrank in the 1980s (because of education about the dangers of smoking), manufacturers more aggressively marketed U.S. cigarettes overseas. They challenged regulations in foreign countries restricting cigarette advertising, claiming that these regulations were protectionist measures aimed at excluding a U.S. product from lucrative markets. In the late 1980s, the U.S. government sided with the U.S. tobacco companies and pressed foreign states to open their markets to U.S. cigarettes, threatening retaliatory trade measures if they refused. In 2001, U.S. pressure stopped South Korea from imposing tariffs on imported cigarettes. In 2002, Turkey met a U.S.-backed IMF demand to privatize the state tobacco monopoly, allowing foreign companies like Philip Morris to greatly expand their market in Turkey.

Health groups such as the American Cancer Society opposed such U.S. policies, which they saw as unethical. But with the U.S. government's help, the tobacco companies racked up high profits from rapidly growing sales in new foreign markets. The U.S. government was also criticized for putting up obstacles to negotiate an international tobacco-control agreement in 2001–2003.

In many countries, government not only responds to industry influence, but works actively with industries to promote their growth and tailor trade policy to their needs.[29] Such **industrial policy** is especially common in states where one or two industries are crucial to the entire economy (and of course where states own industries directly). But it is becoming a major issue in economic relations among great powers as well.[30] In Japan, the government coordinates industrial policy through the powerful Ministry of International Trade and Industry (MITI), which plans an overall strategy to take best advantage of Japan's strengths by directing capital and technology into promising areas. In Canada, the federal department Industry Canada focuses more on supporting innovation and investment and finding ways to enhance the global trading opportunities of Canadian companies than it does directing overall industrial decisions.

Interest groups not organized along industry lines also have particular interests in state trade policies. Canadian environmentalists, for example, do not want Canadian or U.S. companies to use NAFTA to avoid pollution controls by relocating to Mexico (where environmental laws are less strict). Canadian labour unions do not want companies to use NAFTA to avoid paying high wages.

Several industries are particularly important in trade negotiations currently. First is agriculture, which traditionally has been protected from foreign competition on grounds that self-sufficiency in food reduces national vulnerability (especially in time of war). Although such security concerns have now faded somewhat, farmers are well-organized and powerful domestic political actors in Japan, Europe, Canada, the United States, and other countries. In Japan, farmers are a key constituency in the Liberal Democratic Party

industrial policy The strategies by which a government works actively with industries to promote their growth and tailor trade policy to their needs.

---

[29] Susan Strange, *States and Markets: An Introduction to International Political Economy*, 2nd ed. (NY: St. Martin's, 1994).

[30] Lars S. Skalnes, *Politics, Markets, and Grand Strategy: Foreign Economic Policies as Strategic Instruments* (Ann Arbor: U Michigan P, 2000).

(LDP), which governed for decades. The farmers argue that Japan's rice-centred culture demands self-sufficiency in rice production. In France, farmers enjoy wide political support and have a huge stake in the trade policies of the European Union. Subsidies to farmers in France (and elsewhere in Europe) protect them against competition from U.S. farmers. In WTO negotiations in Doha, Qatar, in 2001, France bitterly resisted proposals to phase down the EU farm subsidies (compromise wording put the issue off).

Intellectual property rights are a second contentious area of trade negotiations. Intellectual property rights are the rights of creators of books, films, computer software, and similar products to receive royalties when their products are sold. The United States has had major conflicts with states such as China, Taiwan, India, Thailand, and Russia over piracy of computer software, music, films, and other creative works—products in which the United States has a strong comparative advantage globally. Infringement of intellectual property rights is widespread in many countries, on products ranging from videotaped movies to prescription drugs. In response, the international community has developed an extensive IGO with 178 member states, the World Intellectual Property Organization (WIPO), which tries to regularize patent and copyright law across borders. Most states have signed an important 1994 patent treaty and a 1996 copyright treaty.

EXPORT PRODUCT
Intellectual property rights have been an important focus of recent trade negotiations. As a new member of the WTO, China is to respect copyrights, for example, by paying royalties for showing a movie. In many countries, pirated copies of videos, music, and software sell on streets with no royalty payments. Here, the U.S. film *Titanic* is advertised in China, 1998.

The 2001 WTO meeting raised serious disputes about drug patents—especially expensive HIV/AIDS medications produced under patent in the West but available from India and Brazil in cheap generic versions (ignoring the patent). Canada's Stephen Lewis, serving as UN Special Envoy for HIV/AIDS, has called on Western countries to ease up on drug patent restrictions that make access to life-saving drugs practically impossible for most countries of the global South to afford. Patented HIV/AIDS medication, for example, costs on average $10 000 a year per patient, while the same drugs produced by generic manufacturers cost approximately $300. Canada is home to both generic drug manufacturers and brand-name companies. The Canadian government has sought changes in the patent act that would permit generic producers greater freedom to export drugs (to combat not only HIV/AIDS, but also tuberculosis and malaria), and at the same time maintain restrictions domestically to protect the interests of the brand name producers.[31]

Another key trade issue is the openness of countries to trade in the **service sector** of the economy. This sector includes many services, especially those concerning information, but the key focus in international trade negotiations is on banking, insurance, and related financial services. U.S. companies, and some in Asia, enjoy a comparative advan-

intellectual property rights The legal protection of the original works of inventors, authors, creators, and performers under patent, copyright, and trademark law. Such rights became a contentious area of trade negotiations in the 1990s.

service sector The part of an economy that concerns services (as opposed to the production of tangible goods); the key focus in international trade negotiations is on banking, insurance, and related financial services.

---

[31] Heather Scoffield and Steven Chase, "Ottawa Heeds Call on AIDS," *The Globe and Mail* 26 Sept. 2003.

tage in these areas because of their information-processing technologies and experience in financial management. The North American Free Trade Agreement (NAFTA) allows U.S. and Canadian banks and insurance companies to operate in Mexico. In general, as telecommunications become cheaper and more pervasive, services offered by companies in one country can be efficiently used by consumers in other countries. Canadian consumers phoning customer service at Canadian companies may not realize that the person at the other end is in Barbados, India, or another English-speaking country of the global South—a long-distance trade in services.

Another especially important industry in international trade is the arms trade, which operates largely outside of the framework of normal commercial transactions because of its national security implications.[32] Governments in industrialized countries want to protect their domestic arms industries rather than rely on imports to meet their weapons needs. And those domestic arms industries become stronger and more economically viable by exporting their products (as well as supplying their own governments). Governments usually participate actively in the military-industrial sector of the economy (see "The Military-Industrial Complex" on pp. 148–149). Even when arms-exporting countries agree in principle to try to limit arms exports to a region, they have found it extremely difficult to give up the power and profits that such arms exports bring.

Illicit Trade A different problem is presented by the "industry" of illicit trade, or *smuggling*. No matter what restrictions governments put on trading certain goods, someone is usually willing to risk punishment to make a profit in such trade. Smuggling exists because it is profitable to sell fake Taiwanese copies of MS-DOS in Germany, or Colombian cocaine in Canada, even though these products are illegal in those countries. Even with legal goods, profits can be increased by evading tariffs (by moving goods secretly, mislabelling them, or bribing customs officials), as for example by smuggling U.S. cigarettes into Canada.

Illegal goods, and legal goods imported illegally, often are sold in parallel markets—sometimes called secreted markets or black markets. Parallel markets are widespread, and flourish particularly in economies heavily regulated by government, such as centrally planned economies. In many countries of the global South, and in most of the transitional economies such as Russia, parallel markets are a substantial though hard-to-measure fraction of the total economic activity and deprive the government of significant revenue. Parallel markets also exist for foreign currency exchange (see Chapter 9).

The extent of illicit trade varies from one country and industry to another, depending on profitability and enforcement. Drugs and weapons are most profitable, and worldwide illegal trade networks exist for both. International illegal markets for weapons trade, beyond government controls, are notorious. A state with enough money can buy—although at premium prices—most kinds of weapons.

Different states have different interests in enforcing political control over illicit trade. In illegal arms exports, the exporting state may gain economically from the trade and the importing state gains access to the weapons; the losers are the other exporters that neither got the export revenue nor kept the weapons out of the hands of the importer (not to mention the people who then must live in highly weaponized societies). Thus, illicit trade often creates conflicts of interest among states and leads to complex political bargaining among governments, each looking after its own interests.

---

[32] Robert E. Harkavy and Stephanie G. Neuman, eds., *The Arms Trade: Problems and Prospects in the Post–Cold War World*, Annals of the American Academy of Political and Social Science, vol. 535 (Thousand Oaks, CA: Sage, 1994).

Cooperation in Trade

Successful trade strategies are those that achieve mutual gains from cooperation with other states. A global system of free trade is a collective good, according to economic liberals. Given the lack of world government, the benefits of trade depend on international cooperation—to enforce contracts, prevent monopolies, and discourage protectionism. A single state can profitably subsidize its own state-owned industries, create its own monopolies, or erect barriers to competitive imports as long as not too many other states do so. If other states also break the rules of free trade, the benefits of free exchange slip away from all parties involved.

As with international law generally, economic agreements between states depend strongly on

THE MEDIUM IS THE MESSAGE

Agriculture and trade in services are two issues high on the agenda of international trade negotiations. This British farmer combines a little of each: when an outbreak of mad cow disease halted exports of British beef in 1996, the farmer decided to use his location near a busy freeway to sell advertising space to a U.S. company—in effect, an export of services.

reciprocity for enforcement (see pp. 65–66, 275–276). If one state protects its industries, or puts tariffs on the goods of other states, or violates the copyright on works produced in other countries, the main resort that other states have is to apply similar measures against the offending state. The use of reciprocity to enforce equal terms of exchange is especially important in international trade, where states often negotiate complex agreements—commodity by commodity, industry by industry—based on reciprocity.[33]

Enforcement of fair trade is complicated by differing interpretations of what is fair. States generally decide what practices of other states they consider unfair (often prodded by affected domestic industries) and then take (or threaten) retaliatory actions to punish those practices. One disadvantage of reciprocity is that it can lead to a downward spiral of noncooperation, popularly called a trade war (the economic equivalent of the arms races discussed on p. 66). To prevent this, states often negotiate agreements regarding what practices they consider unfair. In some cases, third-party arbitration can also be used to resolve trade disputes. Currently, the World Trade Organization (see pp. 323–326) hears complaints and sets levels of acceptable retaliation.

Retaliation for unfair trade practices usually is based on an attempt to match the violation in type and extent. Under WTO rules, a state may impose retaliatory tariffs equivalent to the losses caused by another state's unfair trade practices (as determined by WTO hearings). In 2000, for example, the WTO permitted Canada to impose retaliatory trade sanctions of up to $344.2 million per year against Brazil as a result of Brazilian subsidies to its aircraft industry.

---

[33] Thomas O. Bayard, Kimberly Ann Elliott, Amelia Porges, and Charles Iceland, *Reciprocity and Retaliation in U.S. Trade Policy* (Washington, DC: Institute for International Economics, 1994). Carolyn Rhodes, "Reciprocity in Trade: The Utility of a Bargaining Strategy," *International Organization* 43.2 (1989): 273–300.

Thinking Theoretically

In 1957, newly elected Prime Minister John Diefenbaker returned from a meeting of Commonwealth heads of government and announced that in order to strengthen Commonwealth trade ties, he wanted to shift 15 percent of Canadian trade away from the United States to Britain. Analyses by his civil service indicated that in order to reach this goal, Britain would have to buy twice as many Canadian exports as they were purchasing at the time, and likewise, British exports to Canada would have to double. Critics pointed out also that Canadian consumers would suffer, not only by paying more for some goods, but also because the range and quality of goods available would become more limited. Would British cars, for example, be able to start on cold winter mornings?*

Diefenbaker's desire to shift trade in response to a political goal (closer ties with the Commonwealth) reflects a mercantilist orientation. What are some of the arguments in support of that position? Economic liberals, by contrast, would argue that trade does not (easily) respond to political imperatives and has negative consequences, both for consumers and overall growth. What might critical theorists say about Diefenbaker's plan?

* Michael Hart, "Lessons from Canada's History as a Trading Nation," *International Journal*, 58.1 (Winter 2002–2003): 25–42.

Trade disputes and retaliatory measures are common. States keep close track of the exact terms of trade. Large bureaucracies monitor international economic transactions (prices relative to world market levels, tariffs, etc.) and develop detailed policies to reciprocate any other state's deviations from cooperation.

Trade cooperation is easier to achieve under hegemony (see "Hegemony" on p. 80, and "Hegemonic Stability" on pp. 93–95). The efficient operation of markets depends on a stable political framework such as hegemony can provide. Political power can protect economic exchange from the distorting influences of violent leverage, of unfair or fraudulent trade practices, and of uncertainties of international currency rates. A hegemon can provide a world currency in which value can be universally calculated. It can punish the use of violence and can enforce norms of fair trade. Because its economy is so large and dominating, the hegemon has a potent leverage in the threat to break off trade ties, even without resort to military force. For example, to be denied access to U.S. markets today would be a serious punishment for export industries in many states, Canada in particular.

U.S. hegemony helped create the major norms and institutions of international trade in the post-1945 era. Now that U.S. hegemony seems to be giving way to a more multipolar world—especially in economic affairs among the great powers—institutions are even more important for the success of the world trading system. The role and operation of the major trade regimes and institutions occupy the remainder of this chapter.

TRADE REGIMES

Trade regimes are the common expectations governments have about the rules for international trade. A variety of partially overlapping regimes concerned with international trade have developed, mostly since World War II. The most central of these are bilateral and regional arrangements and the World Trade Organization.

Bilateral and Regional Agreements

Most international trade is governed by more specific international political agreements. These are of two general types: bilateral trade agreements and regional free trade areas.

Bilateral Agreements Bilateral treaties covering trade are reciprocal arrangements to lower barriers to trade between two states. Usually they are fairly specific. For instance, one country may reduce its prohibition on imports on product X (which the second country exports at competitive prices) while the second country lowers its tariff on product Y (which the first country exports).

Part of the idea behind the General Agreements on Tariffs and Trade (GATT) and the World Trade Organization (WTO) (discussed below) was to strip away the maze of bilateral agreements on trade and simplify the system of tariffs and preferences. This effort has only partially succeeded. Bilateral trade agreements continue to play an important role.[34] They have the advantage of reducing the collective goods problem inherent in multilateral negotiations and facilitating reciprocity as a means to achieve cooperation. When multilateral negotiations have bogged down, some state leaders will shift to bilateral agreements as more achievable than global agreements. Inasmuch as most states have only a few most-important trading partners, a few bilateral agreements can go a long way in structuring a state's trade relations.

Free-Trade Areas Regional free trade areas are also important in the structure of world trade. In such areas, groups of neighbouring states agree to remove the entire structure of trade barriers (or most of it) within their area. With outside countries, trade continues to be governed by bilateral treaties and the multilateral framework. (A free trade area resembles a "common market" or "customs union"; see p. 373.) The creation of a regional free trade area allows a group of states to cooperate in increasing their wealth without waiting for the rest of the world. In fact, from an economic nationalist perspective, a free trade area can enhance a region's power at the expense of other areas of the world.

The most important free trade area is in Europe; it is connected with the European Union but with a somewhat larger membership. Because Europe contains a number of small industrialized states living close together, the creation of a single integrated market allows these states to gain the economic advantages that come inherently to larger states. The European free trade experiment has been seen by many observers as a great success overall, contributing to Europe's accumulation of wealth since World War II (see Chapter 10).

The United States and Canada signed the Free Trade Agreement (FTA) in 1988 (which came into effect in January 1989) and followed this with the **North American Free Trade Agreement (NAFTA)** in 1994, between Canada, the U.S., and Mexico.[35] In Canada's early history, industrial development was based on such efforts as Sir John A. Macdonald's 1879 National Policy, which included high tariffs. From the end of World War II on, however, Canada had been involved in an increasingly open trading relationship with the United States. Different federal governments had attempted to diversify Canada's trading markets, but the United States by the 1980s was firmly, and remains, Canada's most important trading partner. Yet both the FTA and NAFTA were adopted by Canada for primarily defensive reasons. The FTA was an effort to ensure continued access to the American market, in the face of global competition from other

North American Free Trade Agreement (NAFTA) A free trade zone encompassing the United States, Canada, and Mexico since 1994.

[34] Beth V. Yarbrough and Robert M. Yarbrough, *Cooperation and Governance in International Trade: The Strategic Organizational Approach* (Princeton, NJ: Princeton UP, 1992). Kenneth A. Oye, *Economic Discrimination and Political Exchange: World Political Economy in the 1930s and 1980s* (Princeton, NJ: Princeton UP, 1992).

[35] Delal M. Baer and Sidney Weintraub, eds., *The NAFTA Debate: Grappling with Unconventional Trade Issues* (Boulder, CO: Rienner, 1994).

[36] Laura Macdonald, "Going Global: The Politics of Canada's Foreign Economic Relations," *Understanding Canada: Building on the New Canadian Political Economy*, ed. Wallace Clement (McGill-Queen's UP, 1997) 172–96.

CHEAP LABOUR

Labour, environmental, and human rights organizations have all criticized unrestricted free trade. They argue that free trade agreements encourage MNCs to produce goods under unfair and unhealthy conditions, including the use of child labour. This girl in Pakistan makes soccer balls, 1996.

countries as well as rising protectionist pressures within the United States, and Canada agreed to the NAFTA primarily to retain gains made under FTA.[36]

Opponents of the FTA and NAFTA included labour unions and environmental groups, who feared job losses, low wages, and declining labour standards. Some have noted that at the very least, the enormous gains that proponents of both FTA and NAFTA predicted never materialized: manufacturing wages remain stagnant, new investment has shifted outside of Canada, and unemployment levels remain largely unchanged. However, neither has free trade resulted in a massive movement of industry out of Canada, with the exception of a wave of plant closures in the early years of the FTA.[37] Environmentalists criticized Mexico's lax environmental laws (relative to the United States and Canada) and saw NAFTA as giving U.S. and Canadian corporations licence to pollute by moving into Mexico (see pp. 496–497).

Most of the same criticisms directed at the WTO (see pp. 325–326) are raised by critics about NAFTA. This should come as no surprise: as some observers have remarked, NAFTA served as the template for more global elements of the trade regime, such as the World Trade Organization.[38]

Many politicians in North and South America spoke in the 1990s of creating a single free trade area in the Western hemisphere, from Alaska to Argentina—the *Free Trade Area of the Americas (FTAA)*. Proponents of the FTAA included Canada and a number of South American countries, but it was a goal that increasingly lost favour within the United States, and without U.S. support, the future of the FTAA remains in doubt. Canada had also been interested in establishing more open relations between the countries of NAFTA and the European Union, but here too U.S. support was lukewarm and so progress is unlikely.[39]

Efforts to create a free trade area, or even a semi-free trade area, in Asia began in the late 1980s but moved slowly. Malaysia was the leading country promoting such an arrangement, which it hoped would boost its economic development (though economists expected Japan would benefit most). Unlike the European and North American arrangements, an Asian bloc would include very different kinds of states—rich ones such as Japan, poor ones such as the Philippines; democracies, dictatorships, and communist states. It is unclear how well such a diverse collection could coordinate their common interests, especially because their existing trade patterns are not focused on each other but are spread out among other states, including the United States and Canada (again in contrast to trade patterns existing before the creation of the European and North American free trade areas).

---

[37] Andrew Jackson, "The Free Trade Agreement—A Decade Later," *Studies in Political Economy* 58 (Spring 1999): 141–60.

[38] John N. McDougall, "National Differences and the NAFTA," *International Journal* 55.2 (Spring 2000): 281–91.

[39] Donald Barry, "Pursuing Free Trade: Canada, the Western Hemisphere, and the European Union." *International Journal*, 55.2 (Spring 2000): 292–300.

During the Cold War, the Soviet bloc maintained its own trading bloc, the Council for Mutual Economic Assistance (CMEA), also known as COMECON. After the Soviet Union collapsed, the members scrambled to join up with the world economy, from which they had been largely cut off. The Commonwealth of Independent States (CIS), formed by 12 former Soviet republics, may become an economic coordinating body and quite possibly a free trade area. The existing patterns of trade favour a CIS free trade area because the CIS was previously a free trade zone by virtue of being part of a single state, using transportation, communication, and other infrastructure links.

Other efforts to create free trade areas have had mixed results. The Southern Cone Common Market (Mercosur) tripled trade among its members—Brazil, Argentina, Uruguay, and Paraguay—in its first four years in the early 1990s. In the late 1990s, Chile and Bolivia had joined as associate members, and in 2001 Mercosur was negotiating a free trade agreement with the Andean countries. Nonetheless, Mercosur members trade twice as much with the United States as with each other. A Caribbean common market (CARICOM) was created in 1973, but the area is neither large nor rich enough to make regional free trade a very important accelerator of economic growth. Eleven countries created a Latin American Free Trade Association (LAFTA) in 1960 (changed in 1980 to the Latin American Integration Association), but the effort was held back by the different levels of poverty and wealth among the members and their existing patterns of trade (as in the Asian efforts just mentioned). Venezuela, Colombia, Ecuador, Peru, and Bolivia created the Andean Common Market in 1969; it had modest successes but not dramatic results, because trade within the bloc was not important enough (compared with, say, Venezuelan oil exports to the United States).

The World Trade Organization

The single most important international institution in the global trading regime is the **World Trade Organization (WTO).** The WTO is a global, multilateral IGO that promotes, monitors, and adjudicates international trade. Together with the regional and bilateral arrangements described above, the WTO is central to the overall expectations and practices of states with regard to international trade.[40] The WTO is the successor organization to the **General Agreement on Tariffs and Trade (GATT),** which was created in 1947 to facilitate freer trade on a multilateral basis. The GATT was more of a negotiating framework than an administrative institution. It did not actually regulate trade. Although the GATT was a regime with little institutional infrastructure until the mid-1990s, it did have a small secretariat with headquarters in Geneva, Switzerland. In addition to its main role as a negotiating forum, the GATT helped to arbitrate trade disputes, clarifying the rules and helping states observe them.

In 1995, the GATT became the WTO. The GATT agreements on manufactured goods were subsumed into the WTO framework and then extended to include trade in services and intellectual property. The WTO has some powers of enforcement and an international bureaucracy (more than 500 people from 60 countries), which monitors trade policies and practices in each member state and adjudicates disputes among members. It is unclear how much power over states the WTO will eventually be able to wield in practice. A growing public backlash against free trade (see below) reflects uneasiness about the potential power of a foreign and secretive organization to force changes in democratically

World Trade Organization (WTO) An organization begun in 1995 that expanded the GATT's traditional focus on manufactured goods, and created monitoring and enforcement mechanisms.

General Agreement on Tariffs and Trade (GATT) A world organization established in 1947 to work for freer trade on a multilateral basis; the GATT has been more of a negotiating framework than an administrative institution. It became the *World Trade Organization (WTO)* in 1995.

---

[40] Bernard Hoekman and Michel Kostecki, *The Political Economy of the World Trading System: From GATT to WTO*, 2nd ed. (NY: Oxford UP, 1999).

WINNERS AND LOSERS

Trade agreements create both winners and losers. This is nowhere truer than in the WTO's new member, China. As participation in the rules of international trade forces liberalization of China's economy, millions of people are getting relatively rich, and millions of others are losing their jobs and traditional safety net (state-provided housing, food, child care, and so on). Here, migrant workers pass a sparkling new shopping mall in Beijing, 2000.

most-favoured nation (MFN) concept The principle that one state, by granting another state MFN status, promises to give it the same treatment given to the first state's most-favoured trading partner.

Generalized System of Preferences (GSP) A mechanism by which some industrialized states began in the 1970s to give tariff concessions to global South states on certain imports; an exception to the most-favoured nation (MFN) principle.

enacted national laws. But the WTO is the central international institution governing trade and therefore one that almost all countries want to participate in and develop.

Over time, the membership of the WTO has grown, including some states from the former Soviet bloc. By 2004, almost all the world's major trading states except Russia had joined the WTO. In 2004, there were 147 members of the WTO, the most recent of which were Nepal and the former Yugoslav Republic of Macedonia. China and Chinese Taipei (Taiwan) joined in December of 2001 and January of 2002 respectively. The most notable remaining nonmember is Russia. Members of the WTO demand, as a condition of membership, liberalization of the trading practices of would-be members.

The WTO framework is based on the principles of reciprocity—that one state's lowering of trade barriers to another should be matched in return—and of nondiscrimination. The latter principle is embodied in the **most-favoured nation (MFN) concept,** which says that trade restrictions imposed by a WTO member on its most-favoured trading partner must be applied equally to all WTO members. If Australia applies a 20 percent tariff on auto parts imported from France, it is not supposed to apply a 40 percent tariff on auto parts imported from Canada. Thus, the WTO does not get rid of barriers to trade altogether but equalizes them in a global framework to create a level playing field for all member states. States are not prevented from protecting their own industries but cannot play favourites among their trading partners. States may also extend MFN status to others that are not WTO members.

An exception to the MFN system is the **Generalized System of Preferences (GSP),** dating from the 1970s, by which industrialized states give trade concessions to states of the global South to help the latter's economic development. Preferences amount to a promise by rich states to allow imports from poor ones under lower tariffs than those imposed under MFN.[41]

The WTO continues the GATT's role as a negotiating forum for multilateral trade agreements that lower trade barriers on a fair and reciprocal basis. These detailed and complex agreements specify the commitments of various states and regions to lower certain trade barriers by certain amounts on fixed schedules. Almost every commitment

---

[41] Akira Hirata and Ippei Yamazawa, eds., *Trade Policies towards Developing Countries.* (NY: St. Martin's, 1993). David J. Glover and Diana Tussie, eds., *The Developing Countries in World Trade: Policies and Bargaining Strategies* (Boulder, CO: Rienner, 1993). Jock A. Finlayson and Mark W. Zacher, *Managing International Markets: Developing Countries and the Commodity Trade Regime* (NY: Columbia UP, 1988).

entails domestic political costs because domestic industries lose protection against foreign competition. Even when other states agree to make similar commitments in other areas, lowering of trade barriers is often hard for national governments.

As a result, negotiations on these multilateral agreements are long and difficult. Typically they stretch on for several years or more in a *round of negotiations*; after it is completed the members begin a new round. Among the five rounds of GATT negotiations from 1947 to 1995, the Kennedy Round in the 1960s—so called because it started during the Kennedy administration—paid special attention to the growing role of the (increasingly integrated) European Economic Community (EEC). The Tokyo Round (begun in Tokyo) in the 1970s had to adjust rules to new conditions of world interdependence as, for instance, OPEC raised oil prices and Japan began to dominate the automobile export business.

The **Uruguay Round** started in 1986 in Uruguay. The Kennedy and Tokyo Rounds had been very successful in reducing tariff barriers on manufactured goods. The Uruguay Round tried to lower tariffs further, but also began to tackle the more difficult, and more politically sensitive, issues of nontariff barriers and agricultural trade. Although the rough outlines of a new GATT agreement emerged after a few years, closure eluded five successive G7 summit meetings in 1990–1994. As the round dragged on year after year, participants said the GATT should be renamed the "general agreement to talk and talk." A successful conclusion to the round could add more than US$100 billion to the world economy annually. But that money was a collective good, to be enjoyed both by states that made concessions in the final negotiations and by states that did not. Agreement was finally reached in late 1994.

From 1947 the GATT concentrated on manufactured goods and succeeded in substantially reducing the average tariffs, from 40 percent of the goods' value decades ago to 3 percent by 2002 (under the Uruguay Round agreement). Tariff rates in the global South are much higher, around 30 percent (reflecting the greater protection that industry in the developing world sees itself as needing).

Agricultural trade is politically more sensitive than trade in manufactured goods and was seriously addressed only in the Uruguay Round.[42] Trade in services, such as banking and insurance, is another current major focus of the WTO. Such trade approached one-quarter of the total value of world trade in the 1990s. Trade in telecommunications is a related area of interest. In 1997, 70 states (negotiating through the WTO) agreed on a treaty to allow telecommunications companies to enter each other's markets.

The problems in expanding into these and other sensitive areas became obvious in 1999. First, a North-South divide in the WTO emerged when the WTO could not agree on a new leader and split the five-year term between a New Zealander supported mostly by the North and a Thai politician supported mainly by the South (especially Asia).

Then the 1999 Seattle WTO conference, where trade ministers had hoped to launch a new round of trade negotiations, turned into a fiasco. Most industrialized countries wanted to include provisions on the negotiating agenda for the round, in areas such as environmental protection and labour laws, that poorer countries considered an attack on their sovereignty and a way to maintain the North's advantage in trade. The North's main advantage is technology, whereas the South's is cheap labour and natural resources. Economic liberals argue that these differences in comparative advantage are "givens," while critical theorists (and to some extent mercantilists) would suggest the world's trading system has both created and reinforced these unequal differences.

Uruguay Round A series of negotiations under the *General Agreement on Tariffs and Trade (GATT)* that began in Uruguay in 1986, and concluded in 1994 with agreement to create the World Trade Organization. The Uruguay Round followed earlier GATT negotiations such as the Kennedy Round and the Tokyo Round. See also *World Trade Organization (WTO)*.

---

[42] William P. Avery, ed., *World Agriculture and the GATT* (Boulder, CO: Rienner, 1992). Renee Elizabeth Marlin-Bennett, *Food Fights: International Regimes and the Politics of Agricultural Trade Disputes* (NY: Gordon & Breach, 1993).

326 Part III International Organizations and International Political Economy

Representatives of poorer countries argued that they needed trade to raise incomes, and could not meet the standards of industrialized countries (which had allowed low wages, harsh working conditions, and environmental destruction when *they* began industrializing). Environmental and labour activists, joined by anarchists, students, and citizen groups, staged street protests that delayed the conference opening. The trade ministers could not agree on a new agenda for trade talks, and the meeting ended in failure.

Recovering from Seattle, in 2001 trade ministers meeting in Doha, Qatar, agreed to launch a new round of trade negotiations, which began in 2003. The agenda includes agriculture, services, industrial products, intellectual property, WTO rules (including how to handle antidumping cases), dispute settlement, and some trade and environmental questions. The Doha Round is slated to conclude by January 2005, but whether it will keep to this timetable is open to question. At the 2003 meeting in Cancun, Mexico, states from the global South walked out after the industrialized countries would not agree to eliminate agricultural subsidies, which effectively shut out agricultural exports from the South.

In general, states continue to participate in the WTO because they consider the benefits, in terms of global wealth creation, to outweigh the costs, in terms of harm to domestic industries or painful adjustments in national economies. States try to change the rules in their favour during the rounds of negotiations (never with complete success), and between rounds they try to evade the rules in minor ways. But the overall benefits are seen as too great to jeopardize by nonparticipation or by allowing frequent trade wars to occur.

Resistance to Trade

The globalization of the world economy, which includes growing trade and other aspects (see Chapters 9–13), has created a backlash in many parts of the world, including Canada. Global-level integration has fuelled a countercurrent of growing nationalism in several world regions where people believe their identities and communities to be threatened by the penetration of foreign influences (see Chapter 5). Even more fundamental to the backlash against trade are the material dislocations caused by globalization, which directly affect the self-interests and sometimes the well-being of certain segments of a population.

Workers in industrialized countries in those industries—from steel and automobiles to electronics and clothing—that face increasing competition from low-wage countries in the global South, are among the most adversely affected by free trade. Inevitably, the competition from low-wage countries holds down wages in those industries in the industrialized countries. It also creates pressures to relax standards of labour regulation, such as those protecting worker safety, and it can lead to job losses if manufacturers close down plants in high-wage countries and move operations to the global South. Not surprisingly, labour unions have been among the strongest political opponents of unfettered trade expansion.

Human rights NGOs, international organizations, and social movement activists have joined labour unions in pushing for trade agreements to include requirements for improving working conditions in low-wage countries; these could include laws regarding a minimum wage, child labour, and worker safety. In June 2000, Canada ratified the International Labour Organization convention on Child Labour. Clothing manufacturers such as Nike and Reebok, meanwhile, stung by criticism of "sweatshop" conditions in their Asian factories, adopted a voluntary program to end the worst abuses. Critics claim it will make little difference, however, as much of the production for companies like Nike and Reebok has been "sourced" out to other manufacturers that continue to operate under the same unacceptable working conditions.[43] About 250 million children under age 14 are working in the global South, according to the UN-affiliated International Labour

---

[43] Naomi Klein, *No Logo: Taking Aim at the Brand Bullies* (Toronto: Knopf Canada, 2000).

Organization—about 20 percent of 10- to 14-year-olds in Latin America and Asia and 40 percent in Africa. In Côte d'Ivoire, the world's largest exporter of cocoa (for chocolate consumed in the global North), tens of thousands of children work for low wages, or even as slaves, on cocoa plantations.

Environmental groups also have actively opposed the unrestricted expansion of trade, which they see as undermining environmental laws in industrialized countries and promoting environmentally harmful practices worldwide (see p. 499). For example, U.S. regulations require commercial shrimp boats to use devices that prevent endangered species of sea turtles from drowning in shrimp nets. Indonesia, India, Malaysia, Thailand, and Pakistan, whose shrimp exports to the United States were blocked because they do not require use of such devices, filed a complaint with the World Trade Organization, arguing that the U.S. regulation unfairly discriminated against them. In 1998, the United States lost the WTO ruling and appeal. Sea turtles became a symbol of environmentalist opposition to the WTO. (In 2001, the WTO ruled the U.S. law acceptable after changes had made application of the law more even-handed.)

In 1997, Canada tried to limit shipments of gasoline containing the additive MMT. The Canadian federal government argued that MMT impaired onboard diagnostic systems designed to detect the emission of pollutants and therefore was a potential health hazard. A U.S. producer of MMT, the Ethyl Corporation, filed a complaint against the regulations through the North American Free Trade Agreement (NAFTA). NAFTA ruled in Ethyl Corporation's favour, imposed $19 million in damages, and eventually the Canadian government, under additional pressure from provincial producers of MMT, also repealed the legislation attempting to limit MMT shipments.[44]

In general, unrestricted trade tends to force countries to harmonize their regulations in a variety of areas not limited to labour and environmental rules, and the concern is that harmonization will always be directed toward more lax, rather than more stringent, standards. For example, the WTO ruled in 1997 that Europeans' fears about the use of growth hormones in beef were not scientifically warranted, and therefore EU regulations could not be used to exclude U.S. beef containing hormones. When the European Union persisted, the United States was allowed to impose trade restrictions on European exports worth approximately US$117 million a year. Meanwhile, U.S. consumers harbour fears about pesticide-laced produce grown in Mexico but at the same time, the U.S. has consistently blocked progress toward ratifying the Cartagena "Biosafety Protocol," part of the UN Convention on Biological Diversity aimed at governing trade in genetically modified food and organisms. Efforts to achieve a protocol became all the more important, according to environmental groups like Greenpeace, when genetic contamination was discovered in maize in Mexico in late 2001.

Canadians have also mobilized against free trade out of concern that it adversely impacts Canadian cultural industries (as discussed above, pp. 312–313). In an attempt to promote the Canadian magazine industry, the federal government in the 1990s subsidized domestically produced magazines through tax exemptions and a postal subsidy. U.S.-based Time Warner sought the same kinds of support for what are called "split-run" magazines: editions that retain the primarily U.S. content of the magazine but solicit Canadian advertisers and usually offer a few pages devoted to local stories. The Canadian government lost its case at the WTO, which ruled that both the made-in-Canada magazines and the U.S. split-run editions had to receive the same level of national treatment.[45]

---

[44] Chris Kukucha, "Domestic Politics and Canadian Foreign Trade Policy: Intrusive Interdependence, the WTO and NAFTA," *Canadian Foreign Policy* 10.2 (2003): 59–86.

[45] John Schofield, "Back to Square One: Washington Wins a Hotly Contested Trade Fight," *Maclean's* 14 July 1997: 36.

These examples illustrate the variety of sources of backlash against free trade agreements. Labour, environmental, nationalist, and consumer groups all portray the WTO and other elements of the trading regime, such as NAFTA, as secretive bureaucracies outside democratic control that serve the interests of big corporations at the expense of ordinary people in both the global North and South. Critics object to organizations like the WTO holding all major deliberations behind closed doors. More fundamentally, these critics distrust the corporate-driven "globalization" (see pp. 297–299) of which the WTO and NAFTA are a part. Street protests have become a regular feature of any major international meeting concerning economic policies.

Protests against free trade have made visible some of the arguments against trade liberalization. Prior to Seattle, few people knew about organizations like the WTO and most people probably did not think it was an organization that affected their lives. Few thought about what free trade or free trade agreements like NAFTA might mean, unless they were directly affected by job losses. Whether or not one agrees with antiglobalization protesters, their activism has opened up public debate about the costs and benefits of free trade.

States often have found it worthwhile to expand trade steadily, using a variety of regimes and institutions to do so—the WTO, free trade areas, and bilateral agreements. Stable political rules governing trade allow states to realize the great economic gains that can result from international exchange. This can come with a price, however, both in terms of job losses and some of the problems associated with harmonization of culture, services, and environmental and health standards. The kinds of political stability that are thought to be advantageous in trading relations are also important, especially for economic liberals, in international monetary and business relations. And like trade, much debate exists about some of the costs associated with that stability. Monetary and business relations are the subject of Chapter 9.

Thinking Critically

1. Suppose your state had a chance to reach a major trade agreement by making substantial concessions. The agreement would produce $5 billion in new wealth for your state, as well as $10 billion for each of the other states involved (which are political allies but economic rivals). What advice would a mercantilist give your state's leader about making such a deal? What arguments would support the advice? How would liberal advice and arguments differ? How would a critical theorist respond?

2. China seems to be making a successful transition to a market economy and is growing rapidly. It is emerging as the world's second-largest economy. Do you think this is a good thing or a bad thing for your state? Does your reasoning reflect mercantilist, critical, or liberal assumptions?

3. Before reading this chapter, to what extent did you have a preference for buying products made in your own country? Has reading this chapter changed your views on that subject? How?

4. NAFTA, the free trade agreement between Canada, Mexico, and the United States, is 10 years old. Given that wages in Mexico are lower and technology is less developed than in Canada, which Canadian industries do you imagine supported NAFTA? Specifically, do you think labour-intensive industries or high-technology industries were more supportive of the deal? Who was opposed? Why?

Chapter Summary

- Most international exchanges entail some conflicting interests and some mutual interests on the part of the states involved. Deals can be made because both sides benefit, but conflict over specific outcomes necessitates bargaining.

- Globalization is perceived differently by various scholars, but generally refers to the growing scope, speed, and intensity of connectedness worldwide. The process may be weakening, strengthening, or transforming the power of states. Antiglobalization activists oppose growing corporate power but disagree on goals and tactics.

- The volume of world trade is very large—about 15 percent of global economic activity—and is concentrated heavily in the states of the industrialized West (Western Europe, North America, and Japan/Pacific).

- Trade creates wealth, according to economic liberals, by allowing states to specialize in producing goods and services for which they have a comparative advantage (and importing other needed goods).

- The distribution of benefits from an exchange is determined by the price of the goods exchanged. With many buyers and sellers, prices are generally determined by market equilibrium (supply and demand).

- Communist states during the Cold War operated centrally planned economies in which national governments set prices and allocated resources. Almost all of these states are now in transition toward market-based economies, which seem to be more efficient in generating wealth. The transition has been very painful in Russia and Eastern Europe, less so in China.

- Politics intrudes into international markets in many ways, including the use of economic sanctions as political leverage on a target state. However, sanctions are difficult to enforce unless all major economic actors agree to abide by them.

- Mercantilists favour trade policies that produce a trade surplus for their own state. Such a positive trade balance generates money that can be used to enhance state power.

- States are becoming more and more interdependent, in that the well-being of states depends on mutual cooperation. Economic liberal scholars have long argued that rising interdependence makes military force a less useful form of leverage in international bargaining.

- States that have reduced their dependence on others, by pursuing self-sufficient autarky, have failed to generate new wealth to increase their well-being. Self-reliance, like central planning, has been largely discredited as a viable economic strategy.

- Through protectionist policies, many states try to protect certain domestic industries from international competition. Such policies tend to slow down the global creation of wealth but do help the particular industry in question.

- Protectionism can be pursued through various means, including import tariffs, quotas, subsidies, and other nontariff barriers.

- Industries often lobby their own governments for protection. Governments in many states develop industrial policies to guide their efforts to strengthen domestic industries in the context of global markets.

- Certain products—especially food, intellectual property, services, and military goods—tend to deviate more than others from market principles. Political conflicts among states concerning trade in these products are frequent.

- According to economic liberals, a world market based on free trade is a collective good (available to all members regardless of their individual contribution) inasmuch as states benefit from access to foreign markets whether or not they have opened their own markets to foreign products.

- Because there is no world government to enforce rules of trade, such enforcement depends on reciprocity and state power. In particular, states reciprocate each other's cooperation in opening markets (or punish each other's refusal to let in foreign products). Although it leads to trade wars on occasion, reciprocity has achieved substantial cooperation in trade.

- Over time, the rules embodied in trade regimes (and other issue areas in IR) become the basis for permanent institutions, whose administrative functions provide yet further stability and efficiency in global trade.

- Regional free trade areas (with few if any tariff or nontariff barriers) have been created in Europe, North America, and several other instances. NAFTA includes Canada, Mexico, and the United States.

- Free trade agreements have led to a backlash from politically active interest groups adversely affected by globalization; these include labour unions, environmental and human rights NGOs, and certain consumers.

- The World Trade Organization, formerly the GATT, is the most important multilateral global trade agreement. In successive rounds of GATT negotiations over nearly 50 years, states have lowered overall tariff rates (especially on manufactured goods).

- The Uruguay Round of the GATT, completed in 1994, focused on agricultural trade and nontariff barriers to trade. The Doha Round of the WTO began in 2003.

- The GATT was institutionalized in 1995 with the creation of the World Trade Organization (WTO), which expanded considerably the focus of free trade discussions.

- Although the WTO provides a global framework, states continue to operate under thousands of bilateral trade agreements specifying the rules for trade in specific products between specific countries.

Key Terms

economic liberalism   295
globalization   297
comparative advantage   300
centrally planned (or command)
    economy   304
transitional economies   305
state-owned industries   305
mixed economies   305
balance of trade   308
interdependence   309
autarky (self-reliance)   311
protectionism   311
dumping   313
tariff   313

nontariff barriers   314
industrial policy   316
intellectual property rights   317
service sector   317
North American Free Trade Agreement
    (NAFTA)   321
World Trade Organization (WTO)   323
General Agreement on Tariffs and Trade
    (GATT)   323
most-favoured nation (MFN) concept
    324
Generalized System of Preferences (GSP)
    324
Uruguay Round   325

Weblinks

The following are a sampling of research centres, government departments, and international organizations focused on trade:

Centre for Research on Globalization:
http://globalresearch.ca

International Trade Canada:
http://www.itcan-cican.gc.ca/menu-en.asp

The Council of Canadians:
http://www.canadians.org

NAFTA Secretariat:
http://www.nafta-sec-alena.org/DefaultSite/home/index_e.aspx

World Trade Organization:
http://www.wto.org/index.htm

Money and Business

9

International currencies.

ABOUT MONEY

This chapter summarizes the politics of the world monetary system and then discusses the role of private companies as nonstate actors in the world economy. The monetary system is just one aspect of the political environment governments create, an environment that shapes the rules for international business and the context for the actions of multinational corporations (MNCs).

Imagine a world *without* money. In order to conduct an economic exchange, the goods being exchanged would have to be brought together in one place and traded in quantities reflecting the relative values the parties placed on them. This kind of trade, involving no money, is called *barter*. It still occurs sometimes when monetary systems do not operate well. For example, during the Chinese-Soviet hostility of the 1960s and 1970s, Soviet money was worthless in China, and Chinese money was worthless in the Soviet Union. So traders brought goods to the border, agreed on their value (expressed nominally in Swiss francs), and traded the appropriate quantities.

The unit of currency used in an economy is arbitrary, but it must have roughly the same value for different people. With money, goods can move directly from sellers to buyers without having to meet in a central place. In a world economy, goods can flow freely among many states—the exchange of money keeps track of who owes whom for what. Money provides a single medium against which all goods can be valued. Different buyers and sellers place different values on goods, but all buyers and sellers place about the same value on money, so it serves as a standard against which other values can be measured.

Money itself has little or no inherent value. What gives it value is the widespread belief that it has value—that it can be exchanged for goods. Because it depends on the willingness of people to honour and use it, money's value rests on trust. Governments have the job of creating money and of maintaining public confidence in its value. For money to have stable value, the political environment must be stable. Political instability erodes public confidence that money today will be exchangeable for needed goods tomorrow. The result is inflation (discussed later in this chapter).

The international economy is based on national currencies, not a world currency, because of the nature of state sovereignty. One of the main powers of a national government is to create its own currency as the sole legal currency in the territory it controls. The national currencies are of no inherent value in another country, but can be exchanged one for another.[1] How can the value of goods or currencies be judged in a world lacking a central government and a world unit of money?

Traditionally, for centuries, the European state system used *precious metals* as a global currency, valued in all countries. *Gold* was most important, and *silver* second. These metals had inherent value because they looked pretty and were easily moulded into jewellery or similar objects. They were relatively rare, and the mining of new gold and silver was relatively slow. These metals lasted a long time, and they were difficult to dilute or counterfeit.

Over time, gold and silver became valuable *because* they were a world currency— because other people around the world trusted that the metals could be exchanged for future goods—and this overshadowed any inherent functional value of gold or silver. Bars of gold and silver were held by states as a kind of bank account denominated in an international currency. These piles of gold (literal and figurative) were the object of mercantilist trade policies in past centuries (see Chapters 2 and 8). Gold has long been a key power resource with which states could buy armies or other means of leverage.

In recent years the world has not used such a **gold standard** but has developed an international monetary system divorced from any tangible medium such as precious metal. Until recently, and still to some extent, private investors have bought stocks of gold or silver at times of political instability, as a haven that would reliably have future value. But gold and silver have now become basically like other commodities, with unpredictable fluctuations in price, and their role even as private havens is diminishing. The change in the world economy away from bars of gold to purely abstract money makes international economics more efficient; the only drawback is that without tangible backing in gold, currencies may seem less worthy of people's confidence.

gold standard A system in international monetary relations, prominent for a century before the 1970s, in which the value of national currencies was pegged to the value of gold or other precious metals.

THE CURRENCY SYSTEM

Today, national currencies are valued against each other, not against gold or silver. Each state's currency can be exchanged for a different state's currency according to an **exchange rate**—defining, for instance, how many Canadian dollars are equivalent to one U.S. dollar. These exchange rates are important because they affect almost every international economic transaction—trade, investment, tourism, and so forth.[2] We will consider first

exchange rate The rate at which one state's currency can be exchanged for the currency of another state. Since 1973, the international monetary system has depended mainly on flexible (or floating) rather than fixed exchange rates. See also *convertibility; fixed exchange rates; Exchange Rate Mechanism (ERM);* and *managed float.*

---

[1] Eric Helleiner, *The Making of National Money: Territorial Currencies in Historical Perspective* (Ithaca: Cornell UP, 2003). Robert Solomon, *Money on the Move: The Revolution in International Finance since 1980* (Princeton, NJ: Princeton UP, 1999). Robert A. Blecker, *Taming Global Finance: A Better Architecture for Growth and Equity* (Washington, DC: Economic Policy Institute, 1999). Benjamin J. Cohen, ed., *The International Political Economy of Monetary Relations* (Brookfield, VT: Elgar, 1993). Barry Eichengreen, *International Monetary Arrangements for the 21st Century* (Washington, DC: Brookings, 1995).

[2] Robert Z. Aliber, *The International Money Game,* 5th ed. (NY: Basic, 1987).

the mechanics by which exchange rates are set and adjusted, then the factors influencing the longer-term movements of exchange rates, and finally the banking institutions that manage these issues.

International Currency Exchange

Most exchange rates are expressed in terms of the world's most important currencies—the U.S. dollar, the Japanese yen, and the EU's euro. Thus, the rate for exchanging Danish kroner for Brazilian reals depends on the value of each relative to these world currencies. Exchange rates that most affect the world economy are those *within* the G7 states—U.S. dollars, euros, yen, British pounds, and Canadian dollars.

The relative values of currencies at a given point in time are arbitrary; only the *changes* in values over time are meaningful. For instance, in 2004, a Canadian dollar would trade for just over one-half a Euro. But if traded for the Japanese currency, a single dollar would buy over 80 yen. In itself this disparity says nothing about the desirability of these currencies or the financial positions of their states. However, when the value of yen rises (or falls) *relative* to dollars, because yen are considered more (or less) valuable than before, the yen is said to be strong (or weak).

Some states do not have **convertible currencies.** The holder of such money has no guarantee of being able to trade it for another currency. Such is the case in states cut off from the world capitalist economy, such as the former Soviet Union. Few such states remain, but a lingering challenge is to make the Russian ruble a fully convertible currency (see "The Position of Russia and Eastern Europe" later in this chapter). In practice, even nonconvertible currency can often be sold, in parallel markets or by dealing directly with the government issuing the currency, but the price may be extremely low.

Some currencies are practically nonconvertible because they are inflating so rapidly that holding them for even a short period means losing money (this was the biggest problem with the Russian ruble in the 1990s). Nobody wants to hold currency that is rapidly inflating—losing value relative to goods and services. So inflation reduces a currency's value relative to more stable (more slowly inflating) currencies.

The industrialized West has kept inflation relatively low—mostly below 5 percent annually—since 1980 (see Table 9.1). (The 1970s saw inflation of more than 10 percent per year in many industrialized economies, including Canada.) The global South has had less success with inflation, although the late 1990s were less inflationary than previously. Latin America brought inflation from 750 percent to less than 20 percent, while China and South Asia lowered inflation rates to below 10 percent. Most dramatically, in Russia and other former Soviet republics inflation rates of more than 1000 percent came down to less than 50 percent.

Extremely high, uncontrolled inflation—more than 50 percent per month, or 13 000 percent per year—is called **hyperinflation.** The 10-billion-dinar notes printed by Serbia in 1993 were worth only pennies after hyperinflation reached 100 trillion percent per year. Even at less extreme levels, currencies can lose 95 percent of their value in a year. In such conditions, money loses 5 percent of its value every week, and it becomes hard to conduct business domestically, let alone internationally.

In contrast with nonconvertible currency, **hard currency** is money that can be readily converted to leading world currencies (which now have relatively low inflation). For example, a Russian oil producer can export oil and receive payment in euros or another hard currency, which can then be used to pay for imported goods from outside Russia. But a Russian sausage producer selling products within Russia would be paid in rubles, which could not be used outside the country.

convertible currency The guarantee that the holder of a particular currency can exchange it for another currency. Some states' currencies are nonconvertible. See also *hard currency.*

hyperinflation An extremely rapid, uncontrolled rise in prices, such as occurred in Germany in the 1920s and some global South countries more recently.

hard currency Money that can be readily converted to leading world currencies. See also *convertible currency.*

Table 9.1 Inflation Rates by Region, 1993–2003

Region	Inflation Rate (percent per year)		
	1993	1996	2003*
Industrialized West	3	2	1
Russia and Eastern Europe	1 400	48	9
China	15	8	1
Middle East	27	34	12
Latin America	750	19	13
South Asia	6	6	4
Africa	112	37	12

* Data are estimates based on partial data for 2003.

Note: Regions are not identical to those used elsewhere in this book.

Source: Adapted from United Nations, *World Economic and Social Survey 2003* (New York: United Nations, 2003) 276–8.

reserves Hard-currency stockpiles kept by states.

fixed exchange rates The official rates of exchange for currencies set by governments; not a dominant mechanism in the international monetary system since 1973.

floating exchange rates The rates determined by global currency markets, in which private investors and governments alike buy and sell currencies.

States maintain **reserves** of hard currency. These are the equivalent of the stockpiles of gold in centuries past. National currencies are now backed by hard-currency reserves, not gold. Some states continue to maintain gold reserves as well. The industrialized countries have financial reserves roughly in proportion to the size of their economies.

One form of currency exchange uses **fixed exchange rates.** Here governments decide, individually or jointly, to establish official rates of exchange for their currencies. For example, the Canadian and U.S. dollars were for many years equal in value; a fixed rate of 1-to-1 was maintained (this is no longer true). States have various means for trying to maintain, or modify, such fixed rates in the face of changing economic conditions (see "Why Currencies Rise or Fall" later in this chapter).

Floating exchange rates are now more commonly used for the world's major currencies. Rates are determined by global currency markets in which private investors and governments alike buy and sell currencies. There is a supply and demand for each state's currency, with prices constantly adjusting in response to market conditions. Just as investors might buy shares of General Motors stock if they expected its value

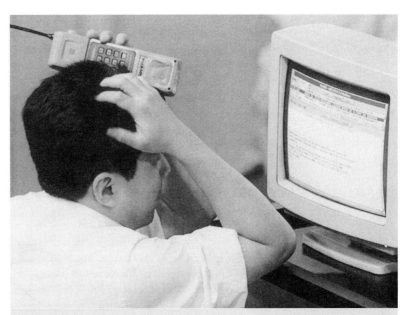

IT'S JUST MONEY
Money has value only because people trust its worth. Inflation erodes a currency's value if governments print too much money or if political instability erodes public confidence in the government. Brazil initially survived the loss of confidence in emerging markets that resulted from the 1997 Asian financial crisis. The next year, however, Brazil had to devalue its currency. This trader reacts to a stock market crash in 1998, after domestic politics threatened a $41 billion IMF agreement and shook investors' confidence in Brazil's economy.

to rise, so they would buy a pile of Japanese yen if they expected that currency's value to rise in the future. Through short-term speculative trading in international currencies, exchange rates adjust to changes in the longer-term supply and demand for currencies.

There are major international currency markets in a handful of cities—the most important being New York, London, Zurich, Tokyo, and Hong Kong—linked together by instantaneous computerized communications. These markets are driven in the short term by one question: What will a state's currency be worth in the future relative to what it is worth today? These international currency markets involve huge amounts of money— a trillion dollars every day—moving around the world (actually only the computerized information moves). They are private markets, not as strongly regulated by governments as are stock markets.[3]

managed float A system of occasional multinational government interventions in currency markets to manage otherwise free-floating currency rates.

National governments periodically *intervene* in financial markets, buying and selling currencies in order to manipulate their value. (These interventions may also involve changing interest rates paid by the government; see pp. 340–341.) Such government intervention to manage the otherwise free-floating currency rates is called a **managed float** system. The leading industrialized states often, but not always, work together in such interventions. If the price of the Canadian dollar, for instance, goes down too much relative to other important currencies (a political judgment), governments will step into the currency markets, side by side with private investors, and buy Canadian dollars. With this higher demand for Canadian dollars, the price may then stabilize and perhaps rise again. (If the price got too high, governments would step in to sell dollars, increasing supply and driving the price down.) Such interventions usually happen quickly, in one day, but may be repeated several times within a few weeks in order to have the desired effect.[4]

In their interventions in international currency markets, governments are at a disadvantage because even acting together they control only a small fraction of the money moving on such markets; most of it is privately owned. Governments do have one advantage in that they can work together to have enough impact on the market to make at least modest changes in price. Governments can also operate in secret, keeping private investors in the dark regarding how much currency governments may eventually buy or sell, and at what price. Only *after* a coordinated multinational intervention into markets does the public find out about it. (If speculators knew in advance they could make money at the government's expense.)

Group of 7 (G7) The world's seven largest industrial market economies: the United States, Japan, Germany, France, Britain, Italy, and Canada. The leaders of G7 countries meet in annual summits, and the finance ministers of G7 countries meet several times a year. When the group includes Russia, as it has done at summits since 1998, it is called the G8. On some issues, particularly monetary matters, the G7 acts without Russia (primarily because Russia's currency is not convertible).

Those interventions are often conducted by the world's major industrialized countries, or the **Group of 7 (G7).** The G7 consists of France, the United States, Britain, Germany, Japan, Italy, and Canada. Since 1998, The G7 has also included Russia in its annual summits of government leaders, and in this capacity operates as the G8. On some economic issues, particularly monetary and financial issues in which Russia is at a disadvantage because its currency is not convertible, the group still operates as the G7. In 2006, Russia is scheduled to host the G8 summit for the first time (see the weblink for the G8 Information Centre, at the end of this chapter).

A successful intervention can make money for the governments at the expense of private speculators. If, for example, the G7 governments step in to raise the price of dollars

---

[3] Richard O'Brien, "Who Rules the World's Financial Markets?" *Harvard Business Review* 73.2 (1995): 144–51.

[4] Randall D. Germain, *The International Organization of Credit: States and Global Finance in the World Economy,* (Cambridge: Cambridge UP, 1997). Jonathan Kirshner, *Currency and Coercion: The Political Economy of International Monetary Power* (Princeton NJ: Princeton UP, 1997). C. Randall Henning, *Currencies and Politics in the United States, Germany, and Japan* (Washington, DC: Institute for International Economics, 1994). Kathryn M. Dominguez and Jeffrey A. Frankel, *Does Foreign Exchange Intervention Work?* (Washington, DC: Institute for International Economics, 1993).

by buying them around the world (selling other hard currencies), and if they succeed, the governments can then sell again and pocket a profit. However, if the intervention fails and the price of dollars keeps falling, the governments will *lose* money and may have to keep buying and buying in order to stop the slide. In fact, the governments might run out of money before then and have to absorb a huge loss. Thus governments have to be realistic about the limited effects they can have on currency prices.

These limits were well illustrated in the *European currency crisis* of September 1992. The European Union (EU) tried to maintain the equivalent of a fixed exchange rate among the various European currencies while letting the European currencies as a whole float freely relative to the rest of the world (see "The Single European Act" on pp. 376–377). For 1992, the British pound was pegged at 2.95 German marks, and if it slipped from that rate, European governments were supposed to take various actions to bring it back into line. This was called the **Exchange Rate Mechanism (ERM),** and it was a step toward a single currency for Europe (see "Monetary Union" on pp. 379–380).

In September 1992, certain long-term forces were pushing apart the values of the German mark and British pound. Germans feared inflation due to the costs of reunifying their country and wanted to restrict money supply to prevent this. Britons were worried about recession and unemployment, and so wanted to loosen the money supply. As a result, currency speculators began to gamble that Britain would not be able to maintain the value of the British pound relative to the German mark.

As the pound began to fall, the British government intervened to buy pounds and drive the price back up. But speculators, who controlled far more money than the European governments, kept selling pounds. The speculators were convinced that the British government would be unable to prop up the pound's value, and they proved correct. With no way to stop the decline, Britain pulled out of the ERM and allowed the

Exchange Rate Mechanism (ERM) A system that established nearly fixed exchange rates among European currencies while letting them all float freely relative to the rest of the world.

BIG BUCKS
Private investors, not central banks, control most of the money traded internationally— over US$1.5 trillion every day. Here, a currency trader works from his home, 1992.

pound to float freely; it quickly fell in value. All the pounds that the British government had bought during its intervention were then worth less—a loss of billions of dollars. The government's loss was the private speculators' gain. One financial fund manager, George Soros, made a billion dollars for his clients in a few weeks. Although such large profits are rare—and although Soros later lost half a billion dollars in a week—the episode illustrates the problem governments have in controlling exchange rates when most money is privately owned.

The problems of the 1992 European currency crisis recurred spectacularly in the 2001 Argentine financial collapse. Argentina in the 1990s had pegged the value of its currency at a fixed rate to the U.S. dollar—a wonderfully effective way to stop runaway inflation that had recently wreaked devastation on Argentina's economy.

Tying the peso to the dollar, however, represented a loss of sovereignty over monetary policy, one of the key levers to control an economy. Just as Germany and Britain had different needs in 1992, so did Argentina and the United States in the late 1990s. As a historic U.S. expansion brought unprecedented prosperity (allowing interest rates to be kept relatively high), Argentina suffered four years of recession, but could not lower interest rates to stimulate growth. Argentina accumulated US$132 billion in foreign loans, and could not service its debts. IMF assistance in restructuring debt was contingent on a tight financial policy of tax increases and spending cuts—a mistake during a major multiyear recession, according to critics. In 2001, as the United States and IMF stood by, Argentina's economy collapsed, two presidents resigned in short order, and a populist took power, defaulted on foreign debts, and devalued the peso to create jobs—an embarrassing chapter for the IMF and a painful one for Argentina. In 2003, Argentina defaulted on a US$3 billion payment to the IMF, the largest default in IMF history. (Other countries to default on IMF debts are much smaller—Sudan, Somalia, Zimbabwe, and Liberia).

Why Currencies Rise or Fall

In the short term, exchange rates depend on speculation about the future value of currencies. But over the long term, the value of a state's currency tends to rise or fall relative to others because of changes in the long-term supply and demand for the currency. *Supply* is determined by the amount of money a government prints. Printing money is a quick way to generate revenue for the government, but the more money printed, the lower its price. Domestically, printing too much money creates inflation because the amount of goods in the economy is unchanged but more money is circulating to buy them with. *Demand* for a currency depends on the state's economic health and political stability. People do not want to own the currency of an unstable country because political instability leads to the breakdown of economic efficiency and of trust in the currency. Conversely, political stability boosts a currency's value. In 2001, when a new Indonesian president took office after a period of political and economic turmoil, the Indonesian currency jumped 13 percent in two days on expectations of greater stability.

A *strong* currency is one that increases its value relative to other currencies—not just in day-to-day fluctuations on currency markets, but in a longer-term perspective. A weak currency is the opposite. The strength of a state's currency tends to reflect that state's monetary policy and economic growth rate. Investors seek a currency that will not be watered down by inflation and that can be profitably invested in a growing economy.

To some extent, states have *common* interests—opposed to those of private investors—in maintaining stable currency exchange rates. This is hard to achieve. In 1990, the Canadian dollar traded for 134 Japanese yen, but by 1995 that had dropped to 61 yen. Canadian goods in Japan became cheaper and Japanese goods imported into Canada became more expensive. The Canadian trade deficit with Japan shrank a bit. By

PRICES SUBJECT TO CHANGE
Changes in exchange rates directly affect the prices of imported goods like these Apple computers for sale in Japan, 1992.

1997, the dollar rose to 86 yen, so the trade deficit widened again. By 1998 the dollar jumped to 92 yen, then down to 73 in 2000, then up to 82 in 2001, 84.5 in 2003, then down a little to 81 in 2004.

This kind of instability in exchange rates disrupts business in trade-oriented sectors since companies can face sudden and unpredictable changes in their plans for income and expenses. States also have a shared interest in currency stability because instability tends to be profitable for speculators at the expense of central banks—a direct cost to the governments involved.

Despite these shared interests in currency stability, states also experience *conflicts* over currency exchange, as we have seen in the example of Britain and Germany in the 1992 European currency crisis. States often prefer a *low* value for their own currency relative to others because a low value promotes exports and helps turn trade deficits into surpluses—as mercantilists especially favour (see "Balance of Trade" on pp. 308–310).

To some extent, exchange rates and trade surpluses or deficits tend to adjust automatically toward equilibrium (the preferred outcome for liberals). An *overvalued* currency is one whose exchange rate is too high, resulting in a chronic trade deficit. The deficit can be covered by printing more money, which in turn waters down the currency's value and brings down the exchange rate (assuming it is allowed to float freely).

Because they see adjustments as harmless, liberals are not bothered by exchange rate changes such as the fall of the dollar relative to the yen. These are viewed as mechanisms for allowing the world economy to work out inefficiencies and maximize overall growth.

A unilateral move to reduce the value of one's own currency by changing a fixed or official exchange rate is called a **devaluation.** Generally, devaluation is a quick fix for financial problems in the short term, but it can create new problems. It causes losses to foreigners who hold one's currency (which is suddenly worth less). Such losses reduce the trust people place in the currency—that it will be worth as much in the future as today. As a result, demand for the currency drops, even at the new lower rate. Investors become wary of future devalu-

devaluation A unilateral move to reduce the value of a currency by changing a fixed or official exchange rate. See also *exchange rate.*

ations, and indeed such devaluations often follow one after another in unstable economies. A currency may be devalued by allowing it to float freely, often bringing a single sharp drop in values. This is what Britain did in the European currency crisis just discussed.

The weakening of a currency, while encouraging exports, carries dangers. For example, the Mexican peso dropped 20 percent in one day (50 percent over several months) when allowed to float freely at the end of 1994. With imported goods shooting up in price, inflation jumped to a 45 percent annualized rate and standards of living fell. And with U.S. dollar-denominated loans suddenly becoming more expensive to service, corporate profits dropped. The Bank of Mexico had to offer 50 percent interest rates to attract capital. The resulting economic dislocations were a big setback to Mexico's economic growth and development, although Mexico eventually stabilized and paid back its loans in 1997. In general, any sharp or artificial change in exchange rates tends to disrupt smooth international trade and hence interfere with the creation of wealth.

Central Banks

Governments control the printing of money. In some states, the politicians or generals who control the government directly control the amounts of money printed. It is not surprising that inflation tends to be high in those states, because political problems can often be solved by printing more money to use for various purposes. But in most industrialized countries, politicians know they cannot trust themselves with day-to-day decisions about printing money. To enforce self-discipline and enhance public trust in the value of money, these decisions are turned over to a **central bank.**

central bank An institution common in industrialized countries whose major tasks are to maintain the value of the state's currency and to control inflation.

The economists and technical experts who run the central bank seek to maintain the value of the state's currency by limiting the amount of money printed and not allowing high inflation. Politicians appoint the people who run the bank, but generally for long terms that do not coincide with those of the politicians. The term for the Governor of the Bank of Canada, for example, is seven years. Thus, central bank managers try to run the bank in the national interest, a step removed from partisan politics. If a state leader orders a military intervention the generals obey, but if the leader orders an intervention in currency markets the central bank does not have to comply. In practice, the autonomy of central banks varies; the head of Thailand's central bank was fired by the prime minister in a dispute over interest rates in 2001.

In Canada, the central bank is the *Bank of Canada*. The Bank of Canada can affect the economy by releasing or hoarding its money. Internationally, it does this by intervening in currency markets (as described earlier). Multilateral interventions are usually coordinated by the heads of central banks and finance (treasury) ministries in the leading countries. The long-term, relatively nonpartisan perspective of central bankers makes it easier for states to achieve the collective good of a stable world monetary system.

discount rate The interest rate charged by governments when they lend money to private banks. The discount rate (called the bank rate in Canada) is set by countries' central banks.

Domestically, the Bank of Canada exercises its power mainly by setting the **discount rate,** in Canada called the *bank rate*—the interest rate the government charges when it loans money to private banks. (Central banks have only private banks, not individuals and corporations, as their customers.) In effect, this rate controls how fast money is injected into the economy. If the Bank of Canada sets the bank rate too low, too much money will come into circulation and inflation will result. If the rate is set too high, too little money will circulate and consumers and businesses will find it hard to borrow as much or as cheaply from private banks; economic growth will be depressed. Again, a state leader cannot order the central bank to lower the discount rate and inject more money into the economy but can only ask for such action. The central bankers will inject the money only if they are convinced that it will not be too inflationary.

Central bank decisions about the discount rate have important international consequences. If interest rates are higher in one state than another, foreign capital tends to be attracted to the state with the higher rate. And if economic growth is high in a foreign country, more goods can be exported to it. So states care about other states' monetary policies. The resulting international conflicts can be resolved only politically (such as at G8 summit meetings), not technically, because each central bank, although removed from domestic politics, still looks out for its own state's interests.

For example, in the unfolding global recession of 2001, the U.S. Federal Reserve (the Central Bank in the United States, also sometimes called "the Fed") worried more about slow economic growth than about inflation, so it lowered interest rates repeatedly. The European Central Bank, which controls the new euro currency, was more worried about inflation than about slow growth. Therefore the Europeans waited longer to lower their lending rates.

Although central banks control sizeable reserves of currency, they are constrained by the limited share of world money they own. Most wealth is controlled by private banks and corporations. As economic actors, states do not drive the direction of the world economy; in many ways they follow it, at least over the long run. However, states still have key advantages as actors in the international economy. Most important, states control the monopoly on the legal use of force (violent leverage) against which even a large amount of wealth usually cannot stand—leaders can jail corporate executives who do not follow the state's rules. Ultimately, then, political power is the state's trump card as an economic actor.

The World Bank and the IMF

Because of the importance of international cooperation for a stable world monetary system and because of the need to overcome collective goods problems, international regimes and institutions have developed around norms of behaviour in monetary relations. Just as the UN institutionally supports regimes based on norms of behaviour in international security affairs (see Chapter 7), the same is true in the world monetary regime.

As in security affairs, the main international economic institutions were created near the end of World War II. The **Bretton Woods system** was adopted at a conference of the winning states in 1944 (at Bretton Woods, New Hampshire). It established the *International Bank for Reconstruction and Development (IBRD)*, more commonly called the **World Bank,** as a source of loans to reconstruct the Western European economies after the war and to help states through future financial difficulties.(Later, the main borrowers were global South countries and, in the 1990s, Eastern European ones.) Closely linked with the World Bank was the **International Monetary Fund (IMF).** The IMF coordinates international currency exchange, the balance of international payments, and national accounts (discussed shortly). The World Bank and the IMF continue to be the pillars of the international financial system. (The roles of the World Bank and the IMF in global South development are taken up in Chapter 12.)

Bretton Woods set a regime of stable monetary exchange, based on the U.S. dollar and backed by gold, that lasted from 1944 to 1971.[5] During this period, the dollar had a fixed value equal to 1/35 of an ounce of gold, and the U.S. government guaranteed to buy dollars for gold at this rate (from a Fort Knox, Kentucky, stockpile). Other states' currencies

Bretton Woods system
A post–World War II arrangement for managing the world economy, established at a meeting in Bretton Woods, New Hampshire, in 1944. Its main institutional components are the *World Bank* and the *International Monetary Fund (IMF)*.

World Bank Formally the International Bank for Reconstruction and Development (IBRD), it was established in 1944 as a source of loans to help reconstruct the European economies. Later, the main borrowers were global South countries and, in the 1990s, Eastern European ones.

International Monetary Fund (IMF) An *intergovernmental organization (IGO)* that coordinates international currency exchange, the balance of international payments, and national accounts. Along with the *World Bank*, it is a pillar of the international financial system. See also *IMF conditionality*.

---

[5] Eric Helleiner, "The Evolution of the International Monetary and Financial System," *Global Political Economy*, ed. J. Ravenhill (Oxford: Oxford UP, forthcoming 2005). Harold James, *International Monetary Cooperation since Bretton Woods* (NY: Oxford UP, 1996). Barry Eichengreen, *Globalizing Capital: A History of the International Monetary System* (Princeton NJ: Princeton UP, 1996).

Thinking Theoretically

Monetary systems often entail a trade-off between international monetary stability and domestic political autonomy. When exchange rates are fixed either to gold or to the dollar, these systems provide considerable international monetary stability: states, firms, and individuals can be assured that exchange rates between currencies remain the same from day to day, week to week, often year to year. This is in contrast to a floating exchange rate system, in which exchange rates can fluctuate wildly, sometimes changing hourly, or even every few minutes.

But the stability of fixed rates usually comes at a price: the loss of some domestic political autonomy. This is because exchange rates do not stay "fixed" just because legislators order them to do so. Currencies are constantly traded one against the other and so their prices rise and fall. They are subject, like the trade in goods, to the rules of the market. To keep the market price of a currency in line with its fixed price, domestic monetary managers sometimes have to try to manipulate the market by adjusting the supply or demand of their currency (for example by buying or selling reserves or adjusting domestic interest rates). When currencies were pegged to gold, millions of dollars' worth of gold could flow from a country's reserves in order to bring the market value of a currency back in line with its fixed price.

For economic liberals, this is simply the price a state pays for the advantages that come with international monetary stability, for the certainty of knowing that the value between currencies will remain stable over time. For mercantilists, the loss of domestic political autonomy is too high a price: stores of wealth in the form of gold or other currencies might be needed for other domestic political goals, such as building up a military or investing in industry. Certainly, as a critical theorist might point out, a fixed rate system is based on the assumption that a country will have massive reserves of gold (in the case of the gold standard) or other convertible currencies available simply to maintain an exchange rate. It is a system, in other words, based on the assumption that a state is already enormously rich.*

* Robert Gilpin, *The Political Economy of International Relations* (Princeton, NJ: Princeton UP, 1987).

were exchanged at fixed rates relative to the dollar. These fixed exchange rates were set by the IMF based on the long-term equilibrium level that could be sustained for each currency (rather than short-term political considerations). The international currency markets operated within a narrow range around the fixed rate. If a country's currency fell more than 1 percent from the fixed rate, the country had to use its hard-currency reserves to buy its own currency back and thus shore up the price. (Or, if the price rose more than 1 percent, it had to sell its currency to drive the price down.)

The dollar standard was abandoned in 1971—an event sometimes called the "collapse of Bretton Woods." The term is not quite accurate: the institutions survived, and even the monetary regime underwent more of an adjustment than a collapse. The U.S. economy no longer held the overwhelming dominance it had in 1944—mostly because of European and Japanese recovery from World War II, but also because of U.S. overspending on the Vietnam War and other programs. Throughout the 1950s and 1960s, the U.S. had spent dollars abroad to stimulate world economic growth and fight the Cold War, but these had begun to far exceed the diminishing stocks of gold held by the Federal Reserve (called the dollar overhang: a situation in which there were more dollars in circulation than could be backed by gold). So successful were the efforts to reinvigorate the economies of Japan and Europe that the United States suffered a relative decline in its trade position.

As a result, the U.S. dollar became seriously overvalued. By 1971, the dollar was no longer worth 1/35 of an ounce of gold, and the United States had to abandon its fixed exchange rate—much as Britain did in its 1992 crisis. Without consulting any of the other signatories to the Bretton Woods Agreements, President Nixon announced in August

1971 that it would no longer convert gold for dollars. The dollar was allowed to float freely, and soon it had fallen to a fraction of its former value relative to gold.

The abandonment of Bretton Woods was good for the United States but bad for Canada, Japan, and Europe, where leaders expressed shock at the unilateral U.S. actions. The interdependence of the world capitalist economy, which had produced record economic growth for all the Western countries after World War II, had also created the conditions for new international conflicts.

The IMF had created a new world currency, the **Special Drawing Right (SDR)** in the late 1960s. After the dollar standard was abandoned in 1971, it was put to greater use to replace both gold and the U.S. dollar as a world standard. The SDR has been called "paper gold" because it is created in limited amounts by the IMF, is held as a hard-currency reserve by states' central banks, and can be exchanged for various international currencies. The SDR is today the closest thing to a world currency that exists, but it cannot buy goods—only currencies. And it is owned only by states (central banks), not by individuals or companies.

In the early 1970s, the value of the U.S. dollar was pegged to the SDR rather than to gold, at a fixed exchange rate (but one that the IMF periodically adjusted to reflect the dollar's strength or weakness). SDRs are linked in value to a basket of several key international currencies. When one currency rises a bit and another falls, the SDR does not change value much; but if all currencies rise (worldwide inflation), the SDR rises with them.

Since the early 1970s, the major national currencies have been governed by the managed float system. Transition from the dollar regime to the managed float regime was difficult. The United States was no longer dominant enough to single-handedly provide stability to the world monetary system. States had to bargain politically over the targets for currency exchange rates in the meetings now known as G7 summits.

The technical mechanisms of the IMF are based on each member state's depositing financial reserves with the IMF. Upon joining the IMF, a state is assigned a *quota* for such deposits, partly of hard currency and partly of the state's own currency (this quota is not related to the concept of trade quotas, which are import restrictions). The quota is based on the size and strength of a state's economy. A state can then borrow against its quota (even exceeding it somewhat) to stabilize its economy in difficult times, and repay the IMF in subsequent years.

Unlike the UN General Assembly or the Security Council, the IMF and the World Bank use a *weighted voting* system—each state has a vote equal to its quota. Thus the G7 states control the IMF, although nearly all the world's states are members. The United States has the single largest vote, and its capital city is headquarters for both the IMF and the World Bank.

Since 1944, the IMF and the World Bank have tried to accomplish three major missions. First, they sought to provide stability and access to capital for states ravaged by World War II, especially Japan and the states of Western Europe.

Special Drawing Right (SDR) A world currency created by the *International Monetary Fund (IMF)* to replace gold as a world standard. Valued by a "basket" of national currencies, the SDR has been called "paper gold."

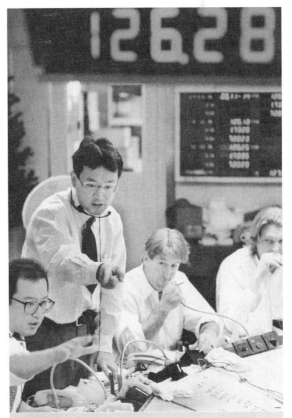

IT'S ALL RELATIVE
Gold historically served as a world currency but has now been largely replaced by the World Bank's SDRs ("paper gold"). Thus currencies are valued only against each other, not an external standard like gold. Here, dollar-yen trading in Tokyo, 1997.

This mission was a great success, leading to growth and prosperity in those states. Second, especially in the 1970s and 1980s but still continuing today, the Bank and the IMF have tried to promote economic development in countries of the global south. That mission was far less successful—as seen in the lingering (and even deepening) poverty in much of the global South (see Chapter 12). The third mission, in the 1990s, was the integration of Eastern Europe and Russia into the world capitalist economy. This effort posted a mixed record and the long-term outlook remains uncertain.

STATE FINANCIAL POSITIONS

As currency rates change and state economies grow, the overall positions of states relative to each other shift.

National Accounts

balance of payments
A summary of all the flows of money in and out of a country. It includes three types of international transactions: the current account (including the merchandise trade balance), flows of capital, and changes in reserves.

The IMF maintains a system of *national accounts* statistics to keep track of the overall monetary position of each state. A state's **balance of payments** is like the financial statement of a company: it summarizes all the flows of money in and out of the country. The system itself is technical, but it has important political implications. Essentially, three types of international transactions go into the balance of payments: the current account, flows of capital, and changes in reserves (see Table 9.2).

The *current account* is basically the balance of trade discussed in Chapter 8. Money flows out of a state to pay for imports and flows into the state to pay for exports. The goods imported or exported include both merchandise and services. For instance, money spent by a British tourist on Prince Edward Island is equivalent to money spent by a British consumer buying PEI lobsters in a London market; in both cases money flows into the Canadian current account. The current account includes two other items. *Government transactions* are military and foreign aid grants, as well as salaries and pensions paid to government employees abroad. *Remittances* are funds sent home by companies or individuals outside a country. For example, a Bombardier subsidiary in Britain may send profits back to Bombardier in Montreal. Conversely, a British citizen working in Quebéc City may send money to her parents in London.

Table 9.2 Balance of Payments Accounts, 2001
In Billions of 2001 US Dollars

	United States	Germany	Japan	Canada
Current Account				
Exports (goods and services)	998	658	448	304
− Imports (goods and services)	−1 356	−620	−422	−268
= Trade balance	−358	38	26	36
+ Government transactions and remittances	−35	−35	−8	−17
= Current account balance	−393	−3	88	19
Capital Flows (net money received)				
+ Foreign investment and loans received	398	−8	−150	−17
Changes in Reserves				
= Changes in reserves	+5	−5	−62	−2

Source: Data adapted from World Bank country data, Sept. 2003.

The second category in the accounts is *capital flows*, which are foreign investments in, and by, a country.[6] Capital flows are measured in *net* terms—the total investments and loans foreigners make *in* a country minus the investments and loans that country's companies, citizens, and government invest in *other* countries. Most of such investment is private, although some is by (or in) government agencies and state-owned industries. Capital flows are divided into **foreign direct investment** (or *direct foreign investment*)—such as building a factory, owning a company, or buying real estate in a foreign country—and indirect *portfolio investment*, such as buying stocks and bonds or making loans to a foreign company. These various kinds of capital flows have somewhat different political consequences (see "International Debt" and "Foreign Direct Investment" later in this chapter), but they are basically equivalent in the overall national accounts picture.

The third category, *changes in foreign exchange reserves*, makes the payments balance in the national accounts. Any difference between the inflows and outflows of money (in the current account and capital flows combined) is made up by an equal but opposite change in reserves. These changes in reserves consist of the state's purchases and sales of SDRs, gold, and hard currencies other than its own, and changes in its deposits with the IMF. If a state has more money flowing out than in, it takes that money from its reserves. If it has more money flowing in than out, it puts the money in its reserves.

Thus, national accounts always balance in the end. At least, they almost balance; there is a residual category—errors and omissions—because even the most efficient and honest government (many governments are neither) cannot keep track of every bit of money crossing its borders. But basically the payments balance.

An important issue raised by some political observers is that systems of national accounts determine value based exclusively on transactions that pass through a market. This means that any productive activity that does not pass through the market does not appear in national accounts measures: for example, anything produced for subsistence (growing or preparing food for one's own consumption), and unpaid child care or elder care. Feminists and other critical theorists point out that this makes the work of much of the world's women invisible. This has an impact on people's lives: political and economic agendas flow from the kinds of statistics kept in the system of national accounts. Anyone who does not "appear" within those statistics will not see their interests and concerns represented in political and economic agendas.

These same critics point out further anomalies in a system that values only that which passes through a market. Other things that remain invisible in national accounts are elements of the natural world: trees and forests, plant species, animals, and insects. If someone does not want to buy or sell a particular tree or animal or insect, then it has no value. Yet many people today would argue that animal, plant, and insect species do have an inherent value (see Chapter 13). An important implication of the system of national accounts is that if plant or animal species do not have value, then neither does their disappearance through extinction reflect a loss or a debit in the national accounts.[7]

International Debt

In one sense, an economy is constantly in motion, as money moves through the processes of production, trade, and consumption. But economies also contain *standing wealth*. The

foreign direct investment
The acquisition by residents of one country of control over a new or existing business in another country. Also called direct foreign investment.

---

[6] Charles P. Kindleberger, *International Capital Movements* (NY: Cambridge UP, 1987).

[7] Marilyn Waring, *Counting for Nothing: What Men Value and What Women are Worth*, 2nd ed. (Toronto: U Toronto P, 1999).

hard-currency reserves owned by governments are one form of standing wealth, but not the most important. Most standing wealth is in the form of homes and cars, farms and factories, ports and railroads. In particular, *capital* goods (such as factories) are products that can be used as inputs for further production. Nothing lasts forever, but standing wealth lasts for enough years to be treated differently from goods that are quickly consumed. The main difference is that capital can be used to create more wealth: factories produce goods, railroads support commerce, and so forth. Standing wealth creates new wealth, so the economy tends to grow over time. As it grows, more standing wealth is created. In a capitalist economy, money makes more money.

Interest rates reflect this inherent growth dynamic. *Real* interest rates are the rates for borrowing money above and beyond the rate of inflation (for instance, if money is loaned at an annual interest rate of 8 percent but inflation is 3 percent, the real interest rate is 5 percent). Businesses and households borrow money because they think they can use it to create new wealth faster than the rate of interest on the loan.

Borrowing and lending are like any other economic exchange; both parties must see them as beneficial. The borrower values the money now more than the promise of more money in the future, whereas the lender values the promise of more money in the future more than the money now. The distribution of benefits from the exchange is, as usual, subject to bargaining. Imagine that a profitable business can use a loan to generate 10 percent annual profit (above the inflation rate). At one extreme, the business could pay 1 percent real interest and keep 9 percent for itself; at the other, it could pay 9 percent interest and keep 1 percent.

The actual split, reflected in prevailing interest rates, is determined by the market for money. Lenders seek out businesses profitable enough to pay high interest; businesses seek out lenders with enough idle cash to lend it at low interest rates. In an imperfect but workable way, the supply and demand for money determine interest rates.

Imagine now that the business borrowing the money is an entire state—the government, companies, and households. If the state's economy is healthy, it can borrow money from foreign governments, banks, or companies and create enough new wealth to repay the debts a few years later. But states, like businesses, sometimes operate at a loss; then their debts mount up. In a vicious circle, more and more of the income they generate goes to paying interest, and more money must be borrowed to keep the state in operation. If its fortunes reverse, a state or business can create wealth again and over time pay back the principal on its debts to climb out of the hole. If not, it will have to begin selling off part of its standing wealth (buildings, airplanes, factories, and the like). The *net worth* of the state or business (all its assets minus all its liabilities) will decrease.

When a state's debts accumulate, the standing wealth of the state is diminished as assets are sold off to pay the debts. Yet failure to repay debts makes it hard to borrow in the future, a huge impediment to economic growth. In the 1970s and 1980s, debts accumulated in some countries of the global South to the point of virtual national bankruptcy. The debts became unpayable, and the lenders (banks and governments) had to write them off the books or settle them at a fraction of their official value. In 2001, Argentina defaulted on over $100 billion of debt accumulated over the prior decade—in the process undergoing street riots and two changes of president within a week.[8] (All amounts in this section are in U.S. dollars.)

The industrialized states, by contrast, have enough standing wealth that even in their most indebted times they have substantial net worth. Still, rising debts are encumbrances

---

[8] William R. Cline, *International Debt Reexamined* (Washington, DC: Institute for International Economics, 1994).

against the future creation of wealth, and foreign lenders come to own a greater share of the state's total standing wealth. Naturally, such a situation horrifies mercantilists. National debt to them represents a loss of power. It is the opposite of the pile of reserves that mercantilists would like to be sitting on.[9]

Why do states go into debt? One major reason is a trade deficit. In the balance of payments, a trade deficit must somehow be made up. It is common to borrow money to pay for a trade deficit. A second reason is the income and consumption pattern among households and businesses. If people and firms spend more than they take in, they must borrow to pay their bills. The credit card they use may be from a local bank, but that bank may be getting the money it lends to them from foreign lenders. As will be discussed in more detail in Chapter 12, consideration of the accumulation of massive amounts of private debt by developing countries, especially during the 1980s, must also take into account the aggressive lending policies of northern banks.[10]

Another reason for national debt is government spending relative to taxation. Under the principles of **Keynesian economics** (named for economist John Maynard Keynes), governments sometimes spend more than they take in—*deficit spending*—to stimulate economic growth. If this strategy works, increased economic growth eventually generates higher tax revenues to make up the deficit. The government lends money to the nation and recovers it later from a healthier economy. Where does the government get this money? It could print more money, but this step would be inflationary so central banks try to prevent it. So the government often borrows the money, from both domestic and foreign sources.

Government decisions about spending and taxation are called **fiscal policy**; decisions about printing and circulating money are called **monetary policy**.[11] These are the two main tools available for government to manage an economy. There is no free lunch: high taxation chokes off economic growth, printing excess money causes inflation, and borrowing to cover a deficit places a mortgage on the state's standing wealth. Thus, for all the complexities of governmental economic policies and international economic transactions, a state's wealth and power ultimately depend more than anything on the underlying health of its economy—the education and training of its labour force, the amount and modernity of its capital goods, the morale of its population, and the skill of its managers. In the long run, international debt reflects these underlying realities.

Keynesian economics The principles articulated by British economist John Maynard Keynes, used successfully in the Great Depression of the 1930s, including the view that governments should sometimes use deficit spending to stimulate economic growth.

fiscal policy A government's decisions about spending and taxation, and one of the two major tools of macroeconomic policy-making (the other being *monetary policy*).

monetary policy A government's decisions about printing and circulating money, and one of the two major tools of macroeconomic policy-making (the other being *fiscal policy*).

The Position of the United States

The United States is an extraordinarily wealthy and powerful state. Its most *unique* strengths may be in the area of international security—as the world's only superpower—but its economic strengths are also striking. It is not only the world's largest economy but also the most technologically advanced one in such growth sectors as computers, telecommunications, aviation and aerospace, and biotechnology. The U.S. position in scientific research and higher education is unparalleled in the world.

The U.S. position in the international economy, however, has shifted over the decades. U.S. hegemony peaked after World War II, then gradually eroded as competitors

---

[9] Ethan B. Kapstein, *Governing the Global Economy: International Finance and the State* (Cambridge, MA: Harvard UP, 1994). Eric Helleiner, *States and the Reemergence of Global Finance: From Bretton Woods to the 1990s* (Ithaca, NY: Cornell UP, 1994).

[10] Susan George, *A Fate Worse than Debt* (NY: Grove Press 1988).

[11] Jeffry A. Frieden, "Invested Interests: The Politics of National Economic Policies in a World of Global Finance," *International Organization* 45.4 (1991): 425–52.

gained relative ground (especially in Western Europe and Asia). In the early 1950s, the U.S. economy (GDP) was about twice the size of the next six advanced industrial states *combined*. By the 1980s, its relative share of world GDP had dropped almost by half. In 1950, the United States held half of the world's financial reserves; by 1980 it held less than 10 percent. This long-term decline after the extraordinary post–1945 U.S. hegemony was a natural and probably unavoidable one.

In the 1980s, however, a rapidly worsening U.S. financial position caused great alarm within the United States.[12] The U.S. national debt had increased dramatically as the government financed a military buildup while reducing taxes—without stimulating faster growth. In the private sector, the United States started the 1980s with well more than $100 billion more invested in foreign countries than foreigners had invested in the United States. By 1988, foreigners had more than $500 billion more invested in the United States than U.S. investors had in foreign countries.[13]

The country slipped into *recession* (a shrinking GDP) in the early 1990s. The U.S. government continued to slide further into debt by hundreds of billions of dollars each year. The United States was losing net worth and having to sell off its standing wealth to pay the bills. Where the United States had once sat on a pile of gold, it now sat under a pile of debt.

In the early 1980s, the trade deficit (exports minus imports) grew from near zero to $200 billion in just a few years. The trade deficit shrank back, but then grew to $500 billion a year by 2003. The budget deficit meanwhile jumped to $300 billion per year in the early 1980s, then closed in the 1990s and became a large surplus, only to return to $500 billion by 2004 as a result of war spending, tax cuts, and recession.

The U.S. economy showed remarkable resiliency in the mid- to late-1990s, as those of other industrialized countries (notably Japan) stumbled. Technological change and restructuring created strong growth of productivity, especially as computer networks took on more of the work. The United States ended the 1990s with all-time low unemployment, low inflation, robust growth, and stock market gains. The budget deficit turned to a surplus. Despite these successes, the U.S. expansion eventually ran out of steam, the bubble of internet investment burst, and the United States was again in recession by 2001—this time joined by all the world's major economies, and hammered painfully home by the economic disruptions that followed the September 2001 attacks. By 2004, global economic recovery was well established.

The accumulated debt from 20 years of deficit spending remains. The U.S. government's **national debt** grew from about $1 trillion at the beginning of the 1980s to $3 trillion by the end of that decade, and nearly the equivalent of one year's GDP by the mid-1990s. The interest payments were equivalent to what would otherwise be a healthy rate of economic growth. Not long ago, the United States was the world's leading lender state; now it is the world's leading debtor state.

These U.S. financial trends have profound implications for the entire world political economy. They first undermined (in the 1980s) and then reconstructed (in the 1990s) the leading U.S. role in stabilizing international trade and monetary relations, in assuring the provision of collective goods, and in providing capital for the economic development of other world regions. In a more decentralized, more privatized world economy with an

national debt The amount a government owes in debt as a result of deficit spending.

---

[12] Kenneth W. Dam, *The Rules of the Global Game: A New Look at U.S. International Economic Policy Making* (Chicago: U Chicago P, 2001). Paul A. Volcker and Toyoo Gyohten, *Changing Fortunes: The World's Money and the Threat to American Leadership* (NY: Random House, 1992).

[13] Edward M. Graham and Paul R. Krugman, *Foreign Direct Investment in the United States*, 3rd ed. (Washington, DC: Institute for International Economics, 1994).

uncertain U.S. role, collective goods problems would be harder to solve and free trade harder to achieve.

The Position of Canada

Canada is considered a "middle power" on questions of security, and in some ways its position economically reflects a similarly mixed location. On the one hand, Canada is a member of the G7, a reflection of its status as one of the world's most important economies. Canada was also a strong supporter of the establishment in 1999 of the **Group of 20 (G20)**, which is comprised of the G7, Australia, Argentina, Brazil, China, India, Indonesia, Mexico, Korea, Russia, Saudi Arabia, South Africa, and Turkey, along with the European Union, International Monetary Fund, and the World Bank. Members of the G7 had realized that even acting together, they were not sufficient in number to manage world financial markets. G20 finance ministers and central bank governors meet annually.

Group of 20 (G20) The G20 comprises the G7, Australia, Argentina, Brazil, China, India, Indonesia, Mexico, Korea, Russia, Saudi Arabia, South Africa, and Turkey, along with the European Union, International Monetary Fund, and World Bank. Members of the G7 realized that even acting together, they were not sufficient in number to manage world financial markets.

Despite Canada's role in the G7 and G20, economic trends within Canada do not have the kind of impact on the rest of the world as does the U.S. economy. In general terms, the Canadian economy tends to follow trends in the rest of the world (most particularly in the U.S.) than it does lead them. The Canadian dollar floats (or more accurately, is a managed float), and its value is usually given in relation to the U.S. dollar. Canada's enormous balance of trade surplus (see Chapter 8) with the United States—which grew from approximately $17 billion in 1994 to nearly $90 billion by 2004—was largely the result of the strong economic performance of the U.S. over that period (and therefore rising demand for Canadian exports). It was also related to Canada's declining exchange rate relative to the U.S. dollar, making Canadian exports more attractive to U.S. consumers.

Canada's position as a country that is more affected by the global political economy than affects it explains its enthusiasm for formal and informal multilateral efforts, such as the G7. Canada can exert more influence through these kinds of initiatives than its economy can alone.

The Position of Russia and Eastern Europe

At the end of World War II, the United States provided considerable capital and aid to stimulate new growth in Western Europe and Japan, but the U.S. did not repeat those efforts to help get the Russian and Eastern European region on its feet again after the Cold War.

Instead, states in this region face daunting challenges as they try to convert from centrally planned to capitalist economies and to join the world capitalist economy. These challenges include integration into the world trading system (membership in the WTO, bilateral trade agreements, and so forth) and attracting foreign investment. Among the most difficult tasks are the attempts of states in this region to join the international monetary system. These matter greatly because having a stable and convertible currency is a key element in attracting foreign business and expanding international trade.

Most of the states of the former Soviet bloc became members of the IMF and were assigned financial reserves quotas. But the IMF and the World Bank would not make loans available freely to these states until their governments took strong action to curb inflation, balance government budgets, and assure economic stability. Such stability would have been easier to achieve with the foreign loans, however, creating a chicken-and-egg problem.

All the economies of the region experienced a deep depression (shrinking GDP) in 1989–1991. By 1992, only Poland had resumed economic growth—a 1 to 4 percent annual growth of GDP following a 20 percent shrinkage in 1990–1991. The rest of Eastern Europe (except Bulgaria and Slovakia) stopped shrinking by 1994. But the states of the former Soviet Union continued downward, until by 1996 the total economic activity of those states had been cut by half over seven years (see Table 9.3).

In general, the Eastern European countries have stabilized their economies more effectively than have the former Soviet republics. Among the latter, Russia was better off than some others; it had inherited much of the Soviet Union's economic infrastructure and natural resources and was large enough to gain the attention of the West. But internal power struggles created political instability in Russia, discouraging foreign investment. The costs of wars in Chechnya made matters worse. Russia was not a WTO member as of 2004. Inflation reached 1500 percent in 1992 but was brought down to less than 10 percent by 2003. Russia's future remains uncertain.

Ukraine had even more severe economic woes (as did some other former Soviet republics). Ukraine's 1992 inflation rate was 2700 percent, and almost two-thirds of its economy operated on a barter basis. Inflation was tamed, but political zigzags slowed economic reform and Ukraine suffered eight straight years of negative GDP growth. In next-door Belarus, democratic reforms evaporated and the transition from a centrally planned economy stalled.

Thus, the states of Eastern Europe had varying experiences, ranging from Poland's relative speed in making the transition away from communism to Belarus's slowness. Russia was somewhere in between—itself a mix of successes and failures. During the transition, the gold reserves of the former Soviet Union—previously among the world's largest—were sold off to make ends meet.

The region's financial problems were similar to those facing the global South countries trying to stabilize their economies (see Chapter 11), but they were compounded by special problems resulting from the breakup of the Soviet Union. First, some states printed their own currency while others kept using the Russian ruble (through the framework of the CIS). In other former Soviet republics—Azerbaijan, Armenia, Georgia, and Tajikistan—devastating wars wrecked economies and further fuelled inflation.

Table 9.3 Economic Collapse in Russia and Eastern Europe

Country	Cumulative (10-Year) Change in GDP, 1990–1999
Former Soviet Republics[a]	−50%
Former Yugoslavia	−35%
Estonia, Latvia, and Lithuania	−29%
Bulgaria	−29%
Romania	−28%
Albania	−12%
Czech Republic	−11%
Slovakia	−1%
Hungary	−1%
Poland	+21%

[a] Russia, Ukraine, and 10 other CIS members.

Source: Author's estimates based on United Nations, *World Economics and Social Survey 1999* (New York: United Nations, 1999) 263.

BITTER FRUITS
Inflation and unemployment in Russia and other former Soviet republics in the 1990s
have cut the GDP about in half and created political turmoil. These women in Moscow try
to make ends meet by selling pickled vegetables grown in their yards, 1999.

The soaring inflation and general economic collapse throughout the region made it
much harder to resolve all these problems and arrive at a stable political and economic
environment in which IMF and World Bank assistance would be useful. In any case, the
amounts of money available for such assistance were limited because of the economic
recession of the early 1990s in the world's leading economies. Nonetheless, the former
Soviet republics joined the IMF after negotiating reform plans. In 1996, creditor states
renegotiated (to a longer-term basis) $40 billion in previous Russian debts; this reduced
interest payments but did not address the underlying causes of the debts.

Several billion dollars were collected from the major economic powers in the early
1990s to create a "ruble-convertibility fund" that could be used to intervene in currency
markets to shore up the value of the Russian ruble if necessary. This fund, combined with
other forms of economic assistance (mostly loans rather than grants), made about $20 bil-
lion available for the task of helping the region through its transition. Such a sum, however, was inadequate for such a massive, historic, and unprecedented transition of an
entire economic system. By way of comparison, international bail-outs of much smaller
countries with less severe financial problems, such as Mexico and South Korea in the
1990s, each required tens of billions of dollars.

To get access to these assistance funds, Russia had to take steps to control inflation
and government spending, sell off state-owned industry, and institute a market system
throughout its economy. The attempt to implement such measures turned out to be even
more painful than expected. Russian President Boris Yeltsin found himself challenged by
a coalition of former communists and industry leaders, who demanded continuing state
subsidies of major industries. To stop the subsidies risked alienating those political forces,

deepening the shrinkage of GDP, and throwing more people out of work. But continuing the subsidies risked widening the budget deficit and triggering high inflation.

Organized crime emerged as a major problem in the 1990s. Politicians, journalists, and business people in particular have been targeted; for example, in 1996 a U.S. entrepreneur was killed gangland-style in Moscow (this did not encourage foreign investment), and the chairman of Russia's central bank had his apartment windows shot out. In 2004, the U.S.-born editor of the Russian edition of *Forbes*, a business magazine, was killed by gunmen. "Plutocrats" seized formerly state-owned companies and drained their wealth into private bank accounts. The chaos of transition also provided fertile ground for corruption among government officials.

The economic and financial problems of the region have been compounded by security problems—ethnic and national conflicts along the southern rim of the former union—which disrupted trade and monetary relations. For example, rail traffic from Russia was disrupted by separatists in Georgia, and Azerbaijan cut off energy supplies to Armenia. The main oil pipeline from Azerbaijan went right through the bombed-out capital of Chechnya, and was shut down for years.

It appears that for some years to come, Russia and Eastern Europe will struggle to find the economic and political stability that will allow them to integrate into the world capitalist economy. Until then, most of these states remain largely cut off from the potential benefits that could result from stable convertible currencies, expanded trade, and increased foreign investment.

The Position of Asia

Financial positions in the leading economies of Asia in some ways were reversed from the Canadian and U.S. path in the 1980s and 1990s. Whereas the Canadian and U.S. positions deteriorated in the 1980s and early 1990s but strengthened in the late 1990s, the main Asian economies enjoyed a tremendous boom in the 1980s and early 1990s but serious financial deterioration in the late 1990s (except in China). Only in the 2001 recession did Asia and North America find synchrony, along with Europe.

Japan has led Asia up and down. Following decades of robust growth since the devastation of World War II, Japan by the 1980s seemed to be emerging as a possible rival to the United States as the world's leading industrial power. Japanese auto manufacturers gained ground on U.S. rivals when smaller cars became popular after the oil-price shocks of the 1970s. In electronics and other fields, Japanese products began to dominate world markets, and Japanese capital became a major economic force in nearby developing economies (such as China and Thailand) and even in the United States where Japanese creditors financed much of the growing U.S. national debt.

These successes masked serious problems. The go-go economic growth of the 1980s drove prices of stocks and real estate to unrealistic levels based on speculation rather than inherent value. When these collapsed at the end of the 1980s, many banks were left with bad loans backed by deflated stocks and real estate. These losses were covered up, and the underlying problems—lax banking regulation, political cronyism, and outright corruption and fraud—persisted through the 1990s. A reform-oriented prime minister (Junichiro Koizumi) took office in 2001, but Japan now also faces a worldwide recession that will depress exports.

Despite the example of Japan's financial system, these mistakes were repeated almost exactly in the 1990s by the newly industrializing countries (NICs, see pp. 447–449) of East and Southeast Asia. Real estate and stocks became overvalued as rapid economic growth led to speculation and ever-rising expectations. Banks made massive bad loans based on the overvalued assets and got away with it because of political corruption and cronyism. In 1997, these economies suffered a serious financial crisis, which jumped across international borders and sent shock waves around the globe that reverberated for two years.

The *1997 Asian financial crisis* began when currency speculators began selling off the currencies of Southeast Asian countries. Thailand, the Philippines, Malaysia, and Indonesia were forced to let their currencies be devalued. Such pressure on currencies creates pressure on prospects for economic growth—because governments will have to cut back money supplies (raise interest rates) in response. The reduced prospects for economic growth in turn put pressure on stock prices, since companies will be less profitable. Also, currency devaluation reduces foreign investment (because investors lose confidence) and makes foreign loans harder to repay (since more local currency is needed to repay each unit of foreign currency). Thus, the currency problems of Asian countries led to stock market crashes in several of them. Other so-called *emerging markets* around the world—notably Brazil—suffered as investors generalized the problems in Asia.

The Philippines addressed the problem in the manner that international agencies and foreign investors preferred. After losing $1 billion unsuccessfully defending its currency's value, the Philippines let its currency float and then asked the IMF for a $1 billion stabilization loan, which the IMF approved in a week. In return for the IMF loan, the Philippines' government agreed to keep interest rates high and budget deficits low (to reduce inflation), to pass a tax reform law, and to tighten control of banks that had made bad real estate loans. These kinds of tough measures create political problems, especially when banks are politically connected or when governments are corrupt. The Philippines, by addressing such problems, won international approval.

Thailand promised, in return for a $16 billion IMF bailout, to close dozens of indebted banks, raise taxes, cut government deficits, and lower economic growth rates by more than half. The government of Thailand, a shaky coalition based on political patronage, soon collapsed as street protests vented anger at the economic downturn. A reform-minded prime minister was appointed and the situation stabilized.

Other Asian countries did not act decisively. In Malaysia, the prime minister annoyed foreign investors by accusing currency speculators, including George Soros (see p. 338), of political motives in undermining Asian economies, because of racism and differences regarding human rights. He said that currency speculation should be illegal. (Soros in fact has used his wealth to support programs in transitional countries to foster an "open society." But there is no reason to doubt that the speculators' motive in Malaysia was making money.) Malaysian controls on capital and currency had success in this case.

The currency speculators, meanwhile, moved on to attack Indonesia, which had to let its currency fall, raise interest rates, and let its stock market drop. Within months, Indonesia too sought tens of billions of dollars in IMF loans, with the usual conditions attached. Indonesia resisted implementing the promised reforms, however, and its economy continued to slide (as did its political stability) in 1998. Riots and student protests eventually forced Indonesia's President Suharto to resign after 30 years of dictatorship. Megawati Sukarnoputra, the daughter of Suharto's arch-rival, became president in 2001.

Overall in Thailand, Malaysia, and Indonesia, stock markets lost about half their value and currencies about a quarter of their value in the first nine months of 1997. Observers declared the "Asian economic miracle" to be at an end. The impact on people's lives was devastating, with massive job losses and increased costs for basic goods and services. Despite healthy resurgence in many of these economies since 1997, the go-go years appear to be gone for good.

China escaped harm from the 1997 crisis, for several reasons: Its economic growth had been less speculative (although rapid), its currency was not freely convertible, it held

IS MY MONEY SAFE?
The Asian financial crisis of 1997 led to currency devaluations, bank failures, and stock market crashes in a
number of fast-growing Asian economies. Ordinary
people faced hardships as a result, and financial analysts worried that the effects could seriously impact
international financial markets. Here, depositors gather
outside a Hong Kong bank after a rumour of a run on
the bank during the 1997 crisis.

massive reserves of hard currency, and its government had
shown the discipline necessary to bring inflation under
control. Lowering the economic growth rate from 14 to
10 percent annually, the government reduced inflation
from 20 percent to less than 4 percent in 1995–1997. The
engineer of this tight-money policy, Zhu Rongji, became
the Chinese prime minister in 1998, just as successful
inflation-fighters became presidents of Brazil and
Argentina in the 1990s. China then rode out the Asian
crisis without devaluing its currency, by further lowering
growth to 7 percent by 1999, still a very strong pace.

Hong Kong, like China, did not devalue in 1997. Just
months after coming under Chinese control, Hong Kong
became the central target of currency speculators. To
maintain the Hong Kong dollar, which was (and still is)
pegged at a fixed rate per U.S. dollar, the Hong Kong government had to raise interest rates drastically and watch
the stock market lose a third of its value in weeks. The
Hong Kong stock crash triggered a huge global sell-off, but
the Hong Kong government remained firm in maintaining
its currency's value—which it saw as critical to foreign
investors' long-term confidence—despite the costs of
financial collapse and economic slowdown. In the first test
of China's "one country, two systems" formula, the
Chinese government allowed the Hong Kong administration to manage the crisis.

When South Korea caught the "Asian flu," however,
the stakes increased. South Korea is the largest of the NICs,
an economic power in the region ranking behind only
Japan and China. Yet by the end of 1997, South Korea's currency was down 20 percent, its stock markets collapsing,
and its banks saddled with $50 billion in bad loans. The
IMF stepped in with a $60 billion international bail-out—
the largest ever—and the Korean government adopted
stringent austerity measures. Some nationalist South
Koreans called signing the IMF agreement a Day of
National Humiliation, but Koreans elected a new reformist president, Kim Dae Jong—a former political prisoner. He convinced South Koreans that foreign investment was positive;
they accepted the IMF and even started using it as a face-saving way to reduce the costs of
extravagant status-oriented weddings and funerals.[14] Thus in South Korea, as in Thailand
and Indonesia, the financial crisis brought about democratization and reform as well as pain.

The Asian crisis suddenly dried up huge sums of capital that had poured into
Southeast Asia, doubling every two years and reaching nearly $100 billion annually. In
1997 and 1998, about $10 billion annually moved *out* of Southeast Asia. The capital
flight also hit other so-called emerging markets in other regions. Brazil in particular was
the recurrent target of currency speculators because Brazil found it hard to pass legislation
to stem a $50 billion government deficit. Every time the Brazilian political system

---

[14] Sandra. A Sugawara, "'Xenophobic' Nation Is Sold on Aid from Foreigners," *Washington Post* 24 Feb 1998:
A15.

The Changing World Order

The IMF—Playing Favourites?

International financial institutions play an important part in world order, regulating the complex flows of money that sustain the global economy. The main international monetary institutions—the IMF and World Bank—survived the end of the Cold War and played active and controversial parts in the 1990s boom, with its winners and losers. In particular, the IMF repeatedly used its cash to rescue large middle-income countries unable to pay huge foreign debts after years of irresponsible or inept policies (including lax bank regulation, cronyism, and politically expedient quick fixes that created lasting problems). In 1997–1998, the IMF provided tens of billions of dollars each to Indonesia, South Korea, and Russia (as new, long-term loans on favourable terms). The IMF demands reforms as the condition for such loans, but in these cases it was unclear how many reforms would actually materialize. It seemed these big countries would not be allowed to fail because Western powers feared that contagion and panic could bring down the world's banking system and possibly set back the whole world economy. In effect, the prosperous economies underwriting the IMF would carry a collective-goods burden by funding bailouts to protect the benefits they received from a stable world financial system.

The Bush Administration came into office in 2001 wanting to change this policy and allow market forces to correct wrong policies in large middle-income countries. As Argentina slid toward disaster in 2001 (see p. 338), the United States discouraged an IMF bailout. In December 2001, when Argentina's economy collapsed and it was forced to devalue its currency and default on its debt, the IMF refused to provide loans. Because Argentina's default had been widely anticipated for months, it did not produce panic or destabilize the world banking system.

Yet, within weeks in early 2002, the IMF offered Turkey a $16 billion bailout package, added to $15 billion in loans in 1999–2001. Why did Turkey but not Argentina receive massive aid? IMF officials claimed that Turkey had faithfully adhered to its IMF conditionality agreement, whereas Argentina had not carried out the promised reforms. (Turkey's conditions included propping up banks, reducing corruption, and ending the state's tobacco monopoly.) However, this may not be the whole story. After all, Turkey's reforms had not succeeded: Turkey's economy shrank by 8 percent in 2001, with

Beggar and child, Argentina, December 2001.

68 percent inflation eroding both the currency and living standards. And the new Bush Administration had warned Turkey early in 2001 that it would oppose further loans if Turkey's economy did not pick up. The United States reversed this stand and supported the $16 billion IMF package only after September 11.

Apparently, Turkey could not be allowed to fail because it is an extremely important ally in the war on terrorism. Turkish air bases host U.S. planes that bomb Iraq and patrol the region. Turkey provides a model of secular government in an Islamic country. Turkey is a "pivotal state" located between Europe and Asia; between the turbulent Middle East and the unsettled, newly independent former Soviet republics; and between the Caspian Sea oil rush and energy-hungry European consumers. An economic and financial collapse in Turkey could destabilize the region and provide a giant opening for terrorist organizations to extend their reach and power.

The 1990s norm of bailing out large middle-income countries—treating them as too big to fail—clearly has changed, as Argentina demonstrates. It appears that the new pattern of IMF bailouts will be more discriminating and more political. Traditionally, central banks and the IMF itself have been most successful in providing stability when removed a step from politics. What do you think about taking political and security considerations into account in future IMF bailout decisions? Are you comfortable with the influence of national power on international economic institutions, or do you believe in minimizing political intrusions into the management of world finance?

The Information Revolution

Liquid Capital

Technology has allowed electronic transfer of money around the world. As a result, more than $1 trillion crosses borders daily in international currency exchanges, and international investment capital can quickly bail out of emerging markets in crises. Currency speculators can drive foreign governments and economies into ruin, but in so doing may stimulate needed reforms. Will the liquidity of international capital ultimately prove destabilizing to the global economy?

To explore this question, go to www.pearsoned.ca/goldstein.

stumbled in making promised reforms, Brazil's stock market fell and its currency came under attack. It devalued in 1999.

In theory, the instant free flow of capital around the world—a result of global communications technologies and an important feature of globalization—should stabilize economies. Investors can shift money quickly, and thus incrementally, as conditions indicate shifting strength and weakness of different currencies and economies. Instead of waiting for governments to devalue or revalue currencies when problems are far along, markets can gradually adjust values day by day. In practice, however, the global liquidity of capital has also shown a destabilizing tendency, as small events can be amplified and reverberate in distant locations. Thus the problems of Thailand became an Asian crisis and then an emerging-markets crisis, as liquid capital fled for cover at the speed of light.

The Asian financial crisis of 1997 illustrates the importance of currency exchange rates in overall economic stability and growth. Governments face a dilemma in that politically desirable policies—from stimulating growth and keeping taxes low to supporting banks and businesses owned by friends and relatives—tend to undermine currency stability. If allowed to continue, such policies may lead to an economic collapse and the loss of foreign investment, but tough policies to maintain currency stability may cause a government to lose power.

Overall, troubling signs of economic instability have shadowed the past decade—in the turbulent, recession-plagued years that followed the end of the Cold War, in the financial collapses in Asia and Russia in the late 1990s, in Japan's decade-long stagnation, in the U.S. technology sector's bursting stock bubble, and in the synchronized global recession of 2001–2002.

In all the regions just discussed—North America, Asia, and especially Russia and Eastern Europe—the role of private businesses is expanding relative to that of the state. Throughout the world, private business plays a role in the economy that exceeds that of the state. The remainder of this chapter considers the international political issues related to the operation of private businesses across state borders.

MULTINATIONAL BUSINESS

Although states are the primary rule makers for currency exchange and other international economic transactions, those transactions are carried out mainly by private firms and individuals, not governments. Most important among these private actors are multinational corporations.

Multinational Corporations

multinational corporations (MNCs) Companies based in one state with affiliated branches or subsidiaries operating in other states. See also *home country* and *host country*.

Multinational corporations (MNCs) are companies based in one state with affiliated branches or subsidiaries operating in other states. There is no exact definition, but the clearest case of an MNC is a large corporation that operates on a worldwide basis in many countries simultaneously, with fixed facilities and employees in each. With no exact definition, there is also no exact count of the total number of MNCs, but most estimates are in the tens of thousands worldwide.

Most important are *industrial corporations*, which make goods in factories in various countries and sell them to businesses and consumers in various countries. The automobile, oil, and electronics industries have the largest MNCs. Almost all of the largest MNCs are based in G7 states, and the largest of all, based on their revenues, are American or Japanese.

Financial corporations (the most important being banks) also operate multinationally—although often with more restrictions than industrial MNCs. Canada's six major domestic banks operate internationally in the United States and various countries of Latin America, the Caribbean, and Asia. Approximately one-third of their revenues is derived from international operations, but none figure among the top financial institutions in the world. The U.S. for a long time did not hold a leading position among the largest commercial banks worldwide—reflecting the traditional U.S. antitrust policy that limits banks' geographic expansion and restricts them from certain financial services (such as stock brokerage and insurance). But with legislative changes in 1999, U.S. banks expanded globally and two took up positions among the top 10, which include banks from Japan, Germany, Switzerland, the U.K., and France.

The growing international integration of financial markets was spectacularly illustrated in 1995, when a single 28-year-old trader in Singapore lost $1 billion speculating on Japanese stock and bond markets and bankrupted his employer, a 200-year-old British investment bank. The 1997 stock market crash in Hong Kong created a wave of sell-offs across international time zones as markets opened in Europe and then North America. Money moves across borders at the rate of $1.5 trillion per day. In this context, financial corporations are becoming more internationalized.

Some MNCs sell *services*.[15] McDonald's fast-food chain and Nortel are good examples. So are the international airlines, which sell tickets in dozens of states (and currencies) for travel all over the world.

The role of MNCs in international political relations is complex and in some dispute.[16] Some scholars see MNCs as virtually being agents of their home national governments. This view resonates with mercantilism, in which economic activity ultimately serves political authorities; thus MNCs have clear national identities and act as members of their national society under state authority. A variant of this theme (from a more critical world view) considers national governments as being agents of their MNCs; state interventions (economic and military) serve private, monied interests. MNCs are, by this view, contemporary agents of imperialism.

Others see MNCs as citizens of the world beholden to no government, a view congruent with economic liberalism. The head of Dow Chemical once said he dreamed of buying an island beyond any state's territory and putting Dow's world headquarters there. In such a view, MNCs act globally in the interests of their (international) stockholders

---

[15] Jonathan D. Aronson, "The Service Industries: Growth, Trade, and Development Prospects," *Growth, Exports and Jobs in a Changing World Economy: Agenda 1988*, ed. John W. Sewell and Stuart K. Tucker (New Brunswick, NJ: Transaction [for the Overseas Development Council], 1988).

[16] Paul N. Doremus, William W. Keller, Louis W. Pauly, and Simon Reich, *The Myth of the Global Corporation* (Princeton, NJ: Princeton UP, 1998). David J. Saari, *Global Corporations and Sovereign Nations: Collision or Cooperation?* (Westport, CT: Quorum/Greenwood, 1999). Razeen Sally, *States and Firms: Multinational Enterprises in Institutional Competition* (NY: Routledge, 1995). Robert Gilpin, *U.S. Power and the Multinational Corporation* (NY: Basic, 1975).

and owe loyalty to no state. In any case, MNCs are motivated by the need to maximize profits, and managers who fail to do so are likely to be fired. Only in the case of state-owned MNCs—an important exception but a small minority of the total companies worldwide—do MNC actions reflect state interests. Even then, managers of state-owned MNCs have won greater autonomy to pursue profit in recent years (as part of the economic reforms instituted in many countries), and in many cases state-owned enterprises are being sold off (privatized).

As independent actors in the international arena, MNCs are increasingly powerful. Dozens of industrial MNCs have annual sales of tens of billions of dollars each (hundreds of billions for the top corporations, such as Wal-Mart, GM, and Exxon Mobil). Only 30 states have more economic activity per year (GDP) than did the largest MNC in 2003, Wal-Mart. A more apt comparison might be between MNCs and IOs as nonstate actors operating in the international arena. MNCs more than match most such organizations in size and financial resources. The largest IGO (the UN) has about $2 billion a year in revenue, compared to more than $200 billion for the largest MNC. However, the largest *government* (the United States) has government revenues of $2 trillion—nearly 10 times larger than Exxon Mobil. Canadian government revenues are closer to that of Exxon's, at just under $200 billion in 2003; but Canada's gross domestic product is $1.2 trillion. Thus the power of MNCs does not rival that of the largest states but exceeds that of many poorer states and many IOs; this affects MNC operations in the global South (see pp. 464–467).

Giant MNCs contribute to global interdependence. They are so deeply entwined in so many states that they have a profound interest in the stable operation of the international system—in security affairs as well as in trade and monetary relations. MNCs prosper in a stable international atmosphere that permits freedom of trade, of movement, and of capital flows (investments)—all governed by market forces with minimal government interference. Thus MNCs are, overall, a strong force for economic liberalism in the world economy, despite the fact that particular MNCs in particular industries do push for certain mercantilist policies to protect their own interests.

Most MNCs have a world management system based on *subsidiaries* in each state in which they operate. The operations within a given state are subject to the legal authority of that state's government. But the foreign subsidiaries are owned (in whole or in substantial part) by the parent MNC in the home country. The parent MNC hires and fires the top managers of its foreign subsidiaries.

Corporations that do business internationally and the states that host them have created a global *infrastructure* of facilities, services, communication links, and the like, that facilitate the conduct of business. The business infrastructure is a key aspect of *transnational relations*—linkages among people and groups across national borders.

In addition to the direct connections among members of a single MNC, the operations of MNCs support a global business infrastructure connecting a transnational community of businesspeople. A Canadian manager arriving in Seoul, South Korea, for instance, does not find a bewildering scene of unfamiliar languages, locations, and customs. Rather, she or he moves through a familiar sequence of airport lounges, telephone calls and faxes, international hotels, business conference rooms, and CNN broadcasts—most likely hearing English spoken in all.

Foreign Direct Investment

MNCs do not just operate in foreign countries, they also own capital (standing wealth) there—buildings, factories, cars, and so forth. For instance, Canadian and German MNCs own some of the capital located in Japan, and Japanese MNCs own capital located in

Canada and Germany. *Investment* means exchanging money for ownership of capital (for the purpose of producing a stream of income that will, over time, more than compensate for the money invested). Investments in foreign countries are among the most important, and politically sensitive, activities of MNCs.

Unlike portfolio investment (on paper), *foreign direct investment* involves tangible goods such as factories and office buildings (including ownership of a sizeable fraction of a company's total stock, as opposed to a portfolio with little bits of many companies). Paper can be traded on a global market relatively freely, but direct investments cannot be freely moved from one state to another when conditions change. Direct investment is long term, and it is more visible than portfolio investment. Investments in the manufacturing sector usually entail the greatest investment in fixed facilities, which are difficult to move, and in training workers and managers. Investments in the extraction of minerals or fuels are less expensive, but even less moveable. Investments in the service sector tend to be less expensive and easier to walk away from if conditions change.

Mercantilists tend to view foreign investments in their own country suspiciously. In countries of the global South, foreign direct investment often causes concerns about a loss of sovereignty, because governments may be less powerful than the MNCs that invest in their country. These fears also reflect the historical fact that most foreign investment in the global South used to come from colonizers. Furthermore, although such investments create jobs, they also bring dislocations of traditional ways of life and cultures. For example, in 2001, villagers in Thailand tried to block a planned $500 million gas pipeline in their area, fearful that it would destroy their way of life and attract problems ranging from industrial pollution to AIDS.[17]

But because many poor and transitional states also desperately need capital from any source to stimulate economic growth, foreign direct investment is generally welcomed and encouraged despite the fears of economic nationalists.[18] (North-South investment is discussed further in Chapter 12, pp. 464–467.) Most foreign direct investment (like most portfolio investment) is not in the developing world, however, but in industrialized countries.

Economic nationalists in industrialized countries also worry about losing power and sovereignty due to foreign investment. In Canada, for instance, mercantilists are alarmed that U.S. firms own more than half of Canada's manufacturing industry and more than two-thirds of Canada's oil and gas industry. Canada is much smaller than the United States, and it depends heavily on U.S. trade. In this asymmetrical situation, some Canadians worry that they are being turned into an annex of the United States—economically, culturally, and ultimately politically—losing their own national culture and control of their economy.

Meanwhile, U.S. economic nationalists have similar concerns over foreign direct investment in the United States. Partly this reflects alarm over the accumulation of U.S. debts. Mercantilists see a loss of power when foreign investors buy up companies and real estate in a debtor country. Such concerns seem to be stronger when a foreign MNC buys an existing company or building than when it builds a new factory or other facility. For example, when Japanese investors bought Columbia movie studios in Los Angeles and (temporarily) Rockefeller Center in New York, many Americans saw these properties as

---

[17] Wayne Arnold, "A Gas Pipeline to World Outside." *New York Times* 26 Oct. 2001: C1.

[18] Ben Gomes-Casseres and David B. Yoffie, eds., *The International Political Economy of Direct Foreign Investment* (Brookfield, VT: Elgar, 1993). Thomas J. Biersteker, *Distortion or Development? Contending Perspectives on the Multinational Corporation* (Cambridge, MA: MIT, 1978). Margaret M. Pearson, *Joint Ventures in the People's Republic of China: The Control of Foreign Direct Investment under Socialism* (Princeton, NJ: Princeton UP, 1992).

somehow representative of the American spirit, and their sale was seen as a U.S. loss. But when Honda built a new car factory in Ohio, adding jobs and facilities to the U.S. economy, no such loss was perceived.

Critical theorists share some of the concerns raised by mercantilists, and would claim also that MNCs pull wealth out of countries, rather than bring it in. They do this through various mechanisms, such as transfer prices and licensing agreements. This is particularly true, critical theorists argue, when MNCs locate in countries of the global South. Their arguments will be explored in more detail in Chapter 12.

Liberals do not agree with such arguments. Economic liberals emphasize that global efficiency and the increased generation of wealth result from the ability of MNCs to invest freely across international borders. Investment decisions should be made solely on economic grounds, not nationalistic ones. U.S. investments in Canadian manufacturing or resource extraction generate economic growth, by this view: they create employment and benefit Canadian consumers. While some profits may return to the home country of the MNC, much of it is re-invested locally. Liberals also point out a glaring inconsistency in the U.S. public's preoccupation with Japanese investment in the United States in the late 1980s: more than half of all foreign investment in the United States was from Western Europe, and only a third as much was from Japan. Yet there was little outcry about a loss of U.S. sovereignty to Europe. Presumably this disparity reflects either racism or a lingering shadow of World War II in the U.S. public's perceptions. The tables were turned in the late 1990s when financial crises in Japan made Americans worry that Japanese investors would pull out of the United States, not that more would come in.

Host and Home Government Relations

host country A state in which a foreign *multinational corporation (MNC)* operates.

home country The state where a *multinational corporation (MNC)* has its headquarters.

A state in which a foreign MNC operates is called the **host country**; the state where the MNC has its headquarters is called its **home country.** MNC operations create a variety of problems and opportunities for both the host and home countries' governments. Conflicts between the host government and the MNC may spill over to become an interstate conflict between the host government and home government. For example, if a host government takes an MNC's property without compensation or arrests its executives, the home government may step in to help the MNC.[19]

Because host governments can regulate activities on their own territories, in general an MNC cannot operate in a state against the wishes of its government. Conversely, because MNCs have many states to choose from, a host government cannot generally force an MNC to do business in the country against the MNC's wishes. At least in theory, MNCs operate in host countries only when it is in the interests of both the MNC and the host government. Common interests result from the creation of wealth in the host country by the MNC. Both the MNC and the host government benefit—the MNC from profits, the government directly by taxation and indirectly through economic growth (generating future taxes and political support).

However, there are also conflicts in the relationship. One obvious conflict concerns the distribution of new wealth between the MNC and host government. This distribution depends on the rate at which MNC activities or profits are taxed, as well as on the ground rules for MNC operations. Before an MNC invests or opens a subsidiary in a host country, it sits down with the government to negotiate these issues. Threats of violent leverage are largely irrelevant. Rather, the government's main leverage is to promise a favourable

---

[19] Kenneth A. Rodman, *Sanctity versus Sovereignty: U.S. Policy toward the Nationalization of Natural Resource Investments in the Third World* (NY: Columbia UP, 1988).

IT'S A JOB
Foreign direct investment is often sought by host governments because it stimulates employment and economic growth, though at wages that home countries would not tolerate. Here, Muslim women in Indonesia assemble Barbies at a Mattel factory. Note that along with investment, a host country imports certain cultural trappings of the MNC's activity—such as Mattel's rendition of femininity in its doll. (This is a literal case of what postmodern feminists call the social construction of gender roles.)

climate for doing business and making money; the MNC's main leverage is to threaten to take its capital elsewhere. In an increasingly globalized economy, this threat is more frequently invoked.

Governments can offer a variety of incentives to MNCs to invest. Special terms of taxation and of regulation are common. In cases of resource extraction, negotiations may revolve around the rates the government will charge to lease land and mineral rights to the MNC. National and local governments may offer to provide business infrastructure—such as roads, airports, or phone lines—at the government's expense. (An MNC could also offer to build such infrastructure if allowed to operate on favourable terms in the country.) Over time, certain locations may develop a strong business infrastructure and gain a comparative advantage in luring MNCs to locate there. This has been particularly in Export Processing Zones, which are established specifically to attract MNCs. Critics, however, point out that the concessions by host country governments are so large that little direct benefit flows to the host state.

These issues all concern the distribution of the new wealth that will be created by MNC operations. MNCs seek host governments that will let the MNC keep more of that wealth; governments seek MNCs that will let the government keep more. With many MNCs and quite a few governments involved in such negotiations, there is a market process at work in the worldwide investment decisions of MNCs.

In addition to questions of distribution, MNC relations with host governments contain several other sources of potential conflict. One is the potential for governments to break their agreements with MNCs and change the terms of taxes, regulations, or other conditions. The extreme case is nationalization, in which a host government takes ownership of MNC facilities and assets in the host country (with or without compensation). Once an MNC has invested in fixed facilities, it loses much of its leverage over the government because it cannot move to another country without incurring huge expenses. However, governments hesitate to break their word with MNCs because then other MNCs may not invest in the future. Nationalization of foreign assets is rare now. It is more common for MNCs to break their agreements and pull up stakes and move out.

Another source of conflict is the trade policies of the host government. Government restrictions on trade seldom help foreign MNCs; more often they help the host country's own industries—which often directly compete with foreign MNCs. Ironically, although they favour global free trade, MNCs may funnel direct investment to states that restrict imports, because MNCs can avoid the import restrictions by producing goods in the host country (rather than exporting from the home country). Trade restrictions are thus another form of leverage that states have in luring foreign direct investment.

Trade regulations often seek to create as many jobs and as much taxable income as possible within the host country. If Toyota assembles cars at a factory in Canada (perhaps to avoid Canadian import restrictions), the Canadian government tends to pressure Toyota to use more Canadian parts in building the cars (such "domestic content" rules were part of the 1992 North American Free Trade Agreement). MNCs generally want the freedom to assemble goods anywhere from parts made anywhere; governments by contrast want to maximize the amount of wealth created on their own territories. With parts and supplies now routinely converging from many countries to go into a product completed in one country, it is very difficult to say exactly where the product was made. The question is a complex one that entails long negotiations between MNCs and host governments.

Monetary policy also leads to conflicts between MNCs and host governments. When a state's currency is devalued, imports suddenly become more expensive. A foreign MNC selling an imported product (or a product assembled from imported parts) in the host country can be devastated by such a change. For example, if the Canadian dollar falls relative to the yen, Toyota Canada may have to charge more Canadian dollars for its cars in order to pay for the parts it brings in from Japan. Therefore, an MNC making a long-term investment in a host country wants the country's currency to be reasonably stable.

Finally, MNCs may conflict with host governments on issues of international security as well as domestic political stability. When an MNC invests in a country, it puts much effort into political **risk assessment** before making international investments. It wants to determine the probability that political conditions in future years (during which the investments will be paid back) will change so radically that the flow of income is disrupted. If a war or revolution takes away the MNC's facility, the company loses not just income but capital—the standing wealth embodied in that facility. In 2001, Exxon Mobil suspended operations at gas fields in Aceh province of Indonesia for three months until the Indonesian government—which earns $1 billion a year from the operation—brought in military forces to suppress armed separatists who had been attacking Exxon Mobil.

MNCs thus depend on host country governments to provide security domestically for business operations. If Toyota builds a factory in Italy, it wants the Italian government to apprehend criminals who kidnap Toyota executives or steal Toyota payrolls, not to mention terrorists who might plant bombs to protest Toyota's presence. Many corporations have their own security personnel, and independent companies provide security services to businesses. But such capabilities do not compare with those of the armed forces maintained by states, so MNCs ultimately rely on host and sometimes their home governments to provide a secure environment for business.

risk assessment The pre-investment efforts by corporations (especially banks) to determine how likely it is that future political conditions in the target country will change so radically as to disrupt the flow of income.

In negotiating over these various sources of conflict, MNCs use a variety of means to influence host governments. These generally follow the same patterns as those used by domestic corporations (see "Interest Groups" on pp. 143–144, and "Industries and Interest Groups" on pp. 315–318). MNCs hire lobbyists, use advertisements to influence public opinion, and offer incentives to host-country politicians (such as locating facilities in their districts). Such activities are politically sensitive because host country citizens and politicians may resent foreigners' trying to influence them. If Toyota Canada ran television ads supporting a Canadian prime ministerial candidate who supported free trade, Canadian voters might react negatively to this foreign intrusion into Canadian politics.

Domestic political stability also means that MNCs regularly resist trade union activity within their subsidiary operations, and often seek support from host country governments in limiting, or eliminating, trade union activism. In some of the most egregious examples of MNC interference in host country political affairs, MNCs have actively used their home country governments to assist in the overthrow of political candidates. This occurred in Chile in 1973, when democratically elected Salvador Allende was overthrown in a military coup after he planned to nationalize the U.S.-based International Telegraph and Telegraph's local subsidiary. In 1995 the Nigerian government executed poet and political activist Ken Saro-Wiwa after his protests against environmental and human costs of Shell Oil activities in southern Nigeria. Though Royal Dutch Shell did not have a direct hand in the execution, it was accused of contributing to the repressive activities of the Nigerian government by ignoring the economic and environmental costs of its operations.[20]

Canadian companies have not been immune from these kinds of accusations. A number of Canadian mining companies have been associated with the repression of local protests against mining operations, for example in Suriname in 1995 and in Chile in 1996. One question that arises in these cases is whether the firm is directly involved in quashing local protests (usually it is not) or whether the presence of the company increases the repressive activities of domestic regimes eager to attract foreign investment. The Canadian oil company Talisman Energy has also faced these kinds of accusations as a result of its activities in Sudan, where UN and Amnesty International reports indicate that police and military forces had violently displaced civilian populations to clear a 100 kilometre area around Talisman's oilfields and that roads constructed for the company were also used by the military to launch attacks against civilians.[21]

Corruption is another means of influence over host governments that cannot be overlooked. Nobody knows the full extent to which MNCs use payoffs, kickbacks, gifts, and similar methods to win the approval of individual government officials for policies favourable to the MNC. Certainly this occurs frequently with host governments in the global South (where government officials may be more desperate for income), but corruption also occurs regularly in rich, industrialized countries. For example, in the early 1990s the Bank of Commerce and Credit International (BCCI) was found to have operated a vast illegal worldwide network of money laundering, fraud, and corruption.[22]

As these kinds of criticism toward MNCs have emerged, a variety of responses have been generated. If the activities are clearly illegal, MNCs can be prosecuted. In some cases, MNCs have agreed to adopt a voluntary code of conduct (though compliance is

---

[20] Thomas D. Lairson and David Skidmore, *International Political Economy: The Struggle for Power and Wealth*, 3rd ed. (Florence, KY: Wadsworth, 2003).

[21] Craig Forcese, "'Militarized Commerce'in Sudan's Oilfields: Lessons for Canadian Foreign Policy," *Canadian Foreign Policy* 8.3 (Spring 2001): 37–56.

[22] James Ring Adams and Douglas Frantz, *A Full Service Bank: How BCCI Stole Billions around the World* (NY: Pocket, 1992).

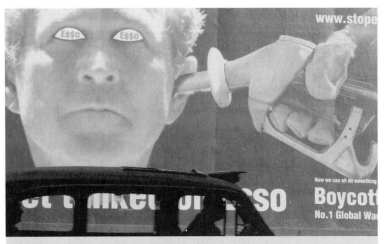

UNWELCOME CORPORATIONS

International business prospers in stable political environments in host countries, but the relationship of a host country with an investing MNC can be complex. Foreign investors are wary of putting money into business environments marked by inflation, crime, corruption, and especially armed violence that could hit their facilities and employees. Mere political criticism is less serious but can sting, like this billboard outside Exxon Mobil (Esso) headquarters in London attacking the company for fighting the Kyoto Treaty on global warming, 2001.

difficult to determine). In other cases, sanctions can be imposed or, as in the Talisman case, activists have lobbied for shareholders to divest themselves of questionable stocks. Home country governments usually do little to reign in their own companies, out of concern that it will result in financial (and employment) losses for a domestic firm.

MNCs also have a range of conflicts with their home governments (where their headquarters are located), just as they do with their host states.[23] Because MNCs are not foreigners but citizens in their home states, they have somewhat more freedom of action in influencing their home governments than they do in influencing host governments. For instance, U.S. MNCs routinely contribute to U.S. politicians' campaigns in hopes that those politicians will support policies favourable to the MNCs' global operations. In Canada, strict limitations came into effect in 2004 to limit the amount of campaign contributions corporations (and trade unions) can make to politicians in any given year.

Some MNC conflicts with home governments resemble the conflicts with host governments. Taxation is an important one. Trade policies are another. A recurrent complaint of MNCs against home governments is that policies adopted to punish political adversaries—economic sanctions and less extreme restrictions—end up harming the home-country MNCs more than the intended target. Usually, a competing MNC from another country is able to step into the gap when a government restricts its own MNCs. Unless ordered to do so, MNCs tend to go on doing business wherever it is profitable, with little regard for the political preferences of their governments. True to the wealth-maximizing principles of liberalism, MNCs generally prefer to keep politics from interfering with business.

For example, the U.S.-based oil company Unocal described as "positive" the 1996 capture of Afghanistan's capital by the fundamentalist Taliban faction, whose treatment of women Secretary of State Albright called "despicable." The oil company hoped that if any faction, of whatever political or religious beliefs, could capture all of Afghanistan and end a civil war, then a multibillion dollar natural gas pipeline crossing Afghanistan could be built.

The location of an MNC's headquarters determines its home nationality. The shareholders and top executives of an MNC are mostly from its home country. But as the world economy becomes more integrated, this is becoming less true. Just as MNCs are increasingly doing business all over the world and assembling products from parts made in many countries, so are shareholders and managers becoming more international in composition.

---

[23] Louis W. Pauly, *Who Elected the Bankers? Surveillance and Control in the World Economy* (Ithaca, NY: Cornell UP, 1997). Benjamin J. Cohen, *In Whose Interest? International Banking and American Foreign Policy* (New Haven, CT: Yale UP, 1986).

We do not yet live in a world without national borders—by a long shot—but the international activities of MNCs are moving us in that direction. Chapter 10 explores some of the ways in which people, companies, and ideas are becoming globally integrated across states.

Thinking Critically

1. Find a recent newspaper article about a change in currency exchange rates (usually located in the business section). Analyze the various influences that may have been at work in the change of currency values—monetary policies, the underlying state of national economies, the actions of central banks (separately or in coordination), and factors such as political uncertainty that affect investors' confidence in a currency.

2. Many scholars and politicians alike think private international investment is the best hope for the economies of Russia and Eastern Europe. Given the current economic and political disarray in that region, what kinds of investors from the industrialized West might be willing to invest there? What actions could the governments of Western states take to encourage such investment? What pitfalls would the governments and investors have to watch out for?

3. If you were representing an MNC such as Toyota in negotiations over building an automobile factory in a foreign country, what kinds of concessions would you ask the host government for? What would you offer as incentives? In your report to Toyota's top management regarding the deal, what points would you emphasize as most important? If instead you were representing the host state in the negotiations and reporting to top state leaders, what would be your negotiating goals and the focus of your report?

4. If you were representing a trade union or human rights organization over allegations that a foreign-owned MNC had acted improperly within your country, what kinds of arguments do you think would be most effective? Who do you want to speak to most? Governments? The public in your country? The public in the MNC's home country? What kinds of networks might be usefully employed to get your message out?

Chapter Summary

- Each state uses its own currency. These currencies have no inherent value but depend on people's belief that they can be traded for future goods and services.

- Gold and silver were once used as world currencies that had value in different countries. Today's system is more abstract: national currencies are valued against each other through exchange rates.

- The most important currencies—against which most other states' currencies are compared—are the U.S. dollar, euro, and Japanese yen.

- Inflation, most often resulting from the printing of currency faster than the creation of new goods and services, causes the value of a currency to fall relative to other currencies. Inflation rates vary widely but are generally much higher in the global South and former Soviet bloc than in the industrialized West.

- States maintain reserves of hard currency and gold. These reserves back a national currency and cover short-term imbalances in international financial flows.

- Fixed exchange rates can be used to set the relative value of currencies, but more often states use floating exchange rates driven by supply and demand on world currency markets.

- Governments cooperate to manage the fluctuations of (floating) exchange rates but are limited in this effort by the fact that most money traded on world markets is privately owned.

- Over the long term, the relative values of national currencies are determined by the underlying health of the national economies and by the monetary policies of governments (how much money they print).

- Governments often prefer a low (weak) value for their own currency, as this promotes exports and discourages imports, and hence improves the state's balance of trade. However, a sudden unilateral devaluation of the currency is a risky strategy because it undermines confidence in the currency.

- To ensure discipline in printing money—and to avoid inflation—industrialized states turn monetary policy over to semi-autonomous central banks, such as the Bank of Canada. By adjusting interest rates on government money loaned to private banks, a central bank can control the supply of money in a national economy.

- The World Bank and the International Monetary Fund (IMF) work with states' central banks to maintain stable international monetary relations. From 1945 to 1971, this was done by pegging state currencies to the U.S. dollar and the dollar in turn to gold (backed by gold reserves held by the U.S. government). Since then the system has used Special Drawing Rights (SDRs)—a kind of world currency controlled by the IMF—in place of gold.

- The IMF operates a system of national accounts to keep track of the flow of money into and out of states. The balance of trade (exports minus imports) must be balanced by capital flows (investments and loans) and changes in reserves.

- International debt results from a protracted imbalance in capital flows—a state borrowing more than it lends—in order to cover a chronic trade deficit or government budget deficit. The result is that the net worth of the debtor state is reduced and wealth generated is diverted to pay interest (with the creditor state's wealth increasing accordingly).

- The U.S. financial position declined naturally from an extraordinary predominance immediately after World War II. The fall of the dollar-gold standard in 1971 reflects this decline.

- In the 1980s, the U.S. position worsened dramatically. A chronic budget deficit and trade deficit expanded the country's debt burden. Economic growth in the mid-1990s helped bring the budget deficit back down.

- Canada's position in the global political economy is somewhat mixed. On the one hand, it is a member of the G7, and therefore is considered one of the seven strongest industrialized economies in the world. At the same time, Canada's economy is more affected by economic conditions in the rest of the world than it affects those conditions; in particular, the Canadian economy is affected by the U.S. economy

- The positions of Russia and the other states of the former Soviet bloc have declined drastically in the past decade as they have tried to make the difficult transition from communism to capitalism. Though the uncontrolled inflation of the early 1990s has subsided, the economies of the former Soviet republics are about half their former size. Western states have not extended massive economic assistance to Russia and Eastern Europe.

- Multinational corporations (MNCs) do business in more than one state simultaneously. The largest are based in the leading industrialized states, and most are privately owned. MNCs are increasingly powerful in international economic affairs.

- MNCs contribute to international interdependence in various ways. States depend on MNCs to create new wealth, and MNCs depend on states to maintain international stability conducive to doing business globally.

- MNCs try to negotiate favourable terms and look for states with stable currencies and political environments in which to make direct investments. Governments seek such foreign investments on their territories so as to benefit from the future stream of income.

- MNCs try to influence the international political policies of both their headquarters state and the other states in which they operate. Generally MNCs promote policies favourable to business—low taxes, light regulation, stable currencies, and free trade. They also support stable international security relations, because war generally disrupts business.

Key Terms

gold standard   333
exchange rate   333
convertible currency   334
hyperinflation   334
hard currency   334
reserves   335
fixed exchange rates   335
floating exchange rates   335
managed float   336
Group of 7 (G7)   336
Exchange Rate Mechanism (ERM)   337
devaluation   339
central bank   340
discount rate   340
Bretton Woods system   341
World Bank   341

International Monetary Fund (IMF)   341
Special Drawing Right (SDR)   343
balance of payments   344
foreign direct investment   345
Keynesian economics   347
fiscal policy   347
monetary policy   347
national debt   348
Group of 20 (G20)   349
multinational corporations (MNCs)   356
host country   360
home country   360
risk assessment   362

Weblinks

The following are a sampling of research centres, government departments, and international organizations focused on money and business:

Bretton Woods Project:
http://www.brettonwoodsproject.org/index.shtml

Finance Canada:
http://www.fin.gc.ca/fin-eng.html

The Globalization Website:
http://www.emory.edu/SOC/globalization/index.html

G8 Information Centre at the University of Toronto:
http://www.g7.utoronto.ca

International Monetary Fund:
http://www.imf.org

World Bank:
http://www.worldbank.org

Integration

Houses and satellite dish, Nepal, 1996.

SUPRANATIONALISM

This chapter and the next continue to develop a theme from the discussion of MNCs—that of nonstate actors in interaction with state actors. Although MNCs are *substate* actors in the formation of state foreign policy (see pp. 142–147), they are also *transnational* actors bridging national borders and creating new avenues of interdependence among states.[1] This chapter discusses transnational and international nonstate actors whose roles and influences are **supranational**—they subsume a number of states within a larger whole.

The UN, as we have seen, has some supranational aspects, though they are limited by the UN Charter, which is based on state sovereignty. On a regional level, the European Union (EU) is a somewhat more supranational entity than the UN; other regional organizations have tried to follow Europe's path as well, but with only limited success. These IOs all contain a struggle between the contradictory forces of *nationalism* and *supranationalism*—between state sovereignty and the higher authority (in level but not yet in power or legitimacy) of supranational structures.

Formal IGOs such as the UN and EU are not the only way that supranationalism is developing. Even more far-reaching in many ways are the effects of information technologies that operate globally and regionally across state boundaries without formal political structures. Here, too, supranational influences compete for influence with the sovereign

supranationalism The subordination of state authority or national identity to larger institutions and groupings, such as the European Union.

---

[1] Joseph S. Nye, Jr., and Robert O. Keohane, eds., *Transnational Relations and World Politics* (Cambridge, MA: Harvard UP, 1972).

state. This chapter considers these various supranational influences on international politics, from the formal structures of the EU to the globalizing effects of information.

INTEGRATION THEORY

The theory of international integration can help to explain these developments, which challenge once again the foundations of realism (state sovereignty and territorial integrity). **International integration** refers to the process by which supranational institutions replace national ones—the gradual shifting upward of sovereignty from state to regional or global structures. The ultimate expression of integration would be the merger of several (or many) states into a single state—or ultimately into a single world government. Such a shift in sovereignty to the supranational level would probably entail some version of federalism, in which states or other political units recognize the sovereignty of a central government while retaining certain powers for themselves. This is the form of government adopted in Canada through the BNA Act.

> **international integration**
> The process by which supranational institutions come to replace national ones; the gradual shifting upward of some sovereignty from the state to regional or global structures.

Today one hears some calls for a "United States of Europe"—or even of the world—but in practice the process of integration has never gone beyond a partial and uneasy sharing of power between state and supranational levels. States have been unwilling to give up their exclusive claim to sovereignty and have severely limited the power and authority of supranational institutions. The UN, certainly, falls far short of a federal model (see Chapter 7). It represents only a step in the direction of international integration. Other modest examples of the integration process have been encountered in previous chapters—for example, NAFTA and the WTO. Monetary regimes and MNCs are also examples of integration.

The most successful example of the process of integration by far—though even that success is only partial—is the European Union. Although we can observe aspects of international integration at work elsewhere in the world, these processes have gone much further in Europe than anywhere else. The regional coordination now occurring in Western Europe is a new historical phenomenon achieved only since World War II.[2]

Until 50 years ago the European continent was the embodiment of national sovereignty, state rivalry, and war. For 500 years until 1945, the states of Europe were locked in chronic intermittent warfare; indeed, it was in Europe that the idea (and practice) of the Westphalian state system was born. In the twentieth century alone two world wars left the continent in ruins. The European states have historical and present-day religious, ethnic, and cultural differences. The 25 members of today's EU speak 20 different official languages. If ever there were a candidate for the failure of integration, Europe would appear to be it. Even more surprising, European integration began with the cooperation of Europe's two bitterest enemies over the previous 100 years, enemies in three major wars since 1870—France and Germany (references to "Germany" refer to West Germany from 1944 to 1990, and unified Germany since).

That Western European states began forming supranational institutions and creating an economic community to promote free trade and coordinate economic policies caught the attention of IR scholars, who used the term *integration* to describe what they observed. Seemingly, integration challenged the assumption of realism that states were strictly autonomous and would never yield power or sovereignty.

---

[2] Andrew Moravcsik, *The Choice for Europe: Social Purpose and State Power from Messina to Maastricht* (Ithaca, NY: Cornell UP, 1998). Robert O. Keohane and Stanley Hoffman, eds., *The New European Community: Decisionmaking and Institutional Change* (Boulder, CO: Westview, 1991). Miles Kahler, *International Institutions and the Political Economy of Integration* (Washington, DC: Brookings, 1995).

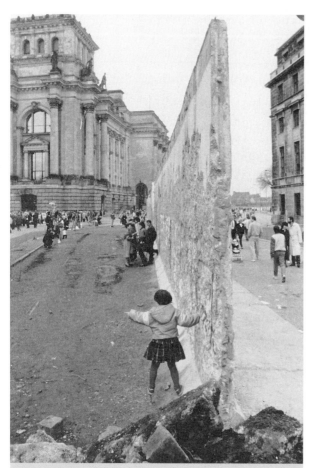

TEAR DOWN THE WALLS

Integration processes in Europe and elsewhere are making state borders more permeable to people, goods, and ideas—increasing interdependence. The European Union is deepening economic integration while contemplating eastward expansion. Here, the opening of the Berlin Wall makes integration very tangible, 1989.

neofunctionalism The theory that holds that economic integration (functionalism) generates a "spillover" effect, resulting in increased political integration.

security community A situation in which low expectations of interstate violence permit a high degree of political cooperation—as, for example, among NATO members.

These scholars proposed that European moves toward integration could be explained by *functionalism*—growth of specialized technical organizations that cross national borders.[3] According to functionalists, technological and economic development lead to more and more supranational structures as states seek practical means to fulfill necessary *functions*, such as delivering mail from one country to another or coordinating the use of rivers that cross borders. Some IR scholars tried to measure the extent of functional connections in Europe, for instance, by counting flows of mail and other communications among countries.[4] As these connections became denser and the flows faster, functionalism predicted that states would be drawn together into stronger international economic structures.

The European experience, however, went beyond the creation of specialized agencies to include the development of more general, more political supranational bodies, such as the European Parliament. **Neofunctionalism** is a modification of functional theory by IR scholars to explain these developments. Neofunctionalists argue that economic integration (functionalism) generates a *political* dynamic that drives integration further. Closer economic ties require more political coordination in order to operate effectively and eventually lead to political integration as well—a process called *spillover*.

Some scholars focused on the less-tangible *sense of community* ("we" feeling) that began to develop among Europeans, running parallel to nationalist feelings that still existed as well. The low expectation of violence among the states of Western Europe created a **security community** in which such feelings could grow.[5] The emergence of a European identity was also assisted by such efforts as the textbook revision project (see p. 177).

Elsewhere in the world, economies were becoming more interdependent at both the regional and global levels. The Andean Common Market, begun in 1969, promoted a limited degree of regional integration in the member states of Venezuela, Colombia, Ecuador, Peru, and Bolivia. In Asia, the Association of South East Asian Nations (ASEAN) chalked up some successes in pro-

[3] David Mitrany, *The Functional Theory of Politics* (London: London School of Economics/Robertson, 1975). Ernst B. Haas, *Beyond the Nation-State: Functionalism and International Organization* (Palo Alto, CA: Stanford UP, 1964). Ernst B. Haas, *When Knowledge Is Power: Three Models of Change in International Organizations* (Berkeley: U California P, 1989). Eugene B. Skolnikoff, *The Elusive Transformation: Science, Technology, and the Evolution of International Politics* (Princeton, NJ: Princeton UP, 1994).

[4] Claudio Cioffi-Revilla, Richard L. Merritt, and Dina A. Zinnes, eds., *Communication and Interaction in Global Politics* (Newbury Park, CA: Sage, 1987).

[5] Emanuel Adler and Michael Barnett, eds., *Security Communities* (Cambridge: Cambridge UP, 1998). Karl W. Deutsch, *Political Community and the North Atlantic Area: International Organization in the Light of Historical Experience* (Princeton, NJ: Princeton UP, 1957). Richard H. Ullman, *Securing Europe* (Princeton, NJ: Princeton UP, 1991).

moting regional economic coordination over several decades.[6] Most recently, the countries of Africa in 2002 formed the African Union, an ambitious plan to coordinate economic and foreign policies, elect an African parliament, and create a stronger infrastructure than the predecessor Organization of African Union (OAU).

Interest in integration theory among IR scholars has waxed and waned with the uneven pace of European integration. In the 1960s and 1970s, European integration seemed to slow down; regional efforts elsewhere in the world also failed to develop as hoped. For most of the Cold War decades, integration took a secondary position among IR scholars (and policy-makers) to the concerns of East-West conflict, nuclear weapons, and related security issues. Then, in the 1980s, Europe accelerated its progress toward integration again, the Cold War ended, and the North American Free Trade Agreement took form; the scholarly interest in integration expanded again.

Costs of Integration Ironically, the new wave of integration in Europe and elsewhere is encountering limits and setbacks just as scholars are reinvigorating the theory of integration. Integration reduces states' ability to shield themselves and their citizens from the world's many problems and conflicts. For example, in the early 1990s Venezuela found that its open border with Colombia brought in large trans-shipments of cocaine bound for the United States.

Integration can mean greater centralization at a time when individuals, local groups, and national populations demand more say over their own affairs. The centralization of political authority, information, and culture as a result of integration can threaten both individual and group freedom. Ethnic groups want to safeguard their own cultures, languages, and institutions against the bland homogeneity that a global or regional melting pot would create. As a result, many states and citizens, in Europe and elsewhere, responded to the new wave of integration with resurgent nationalism over the past decade.

Indeed these forces have set in motion a wave of *disintegration* of states running counter to (though simultaneous with) the integrating tendencies in today's world. The wave of disintegration in some ways began with the decolonization of former European empires in Africa, Asia, and the Middle East after World War II. After the Cold War, disintegration was most pronounced in Russia and Eastern Europe—especially in the former Soviet Union and former Yugoslavia. States in other regions—for example Somalia and Democratic Republic of the Congo—appear in danger of breaking into pieces, in practice if not formally. A challenge to integration theorists in the future will be to account for these new trends running counter to integration.

Throughout the successful and unsuccessful efforts at integration runs a common thread—the tension between nationalism and supranational loyalties (regionalism or globalism). In the less-successful integration attempts, nationalism stands virtually unchallenged, and even in the most successful cases nationalism remains a potent force locked in continual struggle with supranationalism. This struggle is a central theme even in the most successful case of integration—the European Union.

THE EUROPEAN UNION

Like the UN, the **European Union (EU)** was created after World War II and has developed since. But whereas the UN structure has changed little since the Charter was adopted,

European Union (EU) The official term for the European Community (formerly the European Economic Community) and associated treaty organizations. The EU has 25 member states and is negotiating with other states that have applied for membership. See also *Maastricht Treaty*.

---

[6] Walter Mattli, *The Logic of Regional Integration: Europe and Beyond* (NY: Cambridge UP, 1999). Kenneth P. Thomas and Mary Ann Tétrault, eds., *Racing to Regionalize: Democracy, Capitalism, and Regional Political Economy* (Boulder, CO: Rienner, 1999). Gordon Mace, and Louis Belanger, eds., *The Americas in Transition: The Contours of Regionalism* (Boulder, CO: Rienner, 1999).

the EU has gone through several waves of expansion in its scope, membership, and mission over the past 50 years.[7]

The Vision of a United Europe

Europe in 1945 was decimated by war. Most of the next decade was spent recovering, with help from the United States through the Marshall Plan. But already two French leaders, Jean Monnet and Robert Schuman, were developing a plan to implement the idea of functionalism in Europe—that Europe could be saved from future wars by creating economic linkages that would eventually bind states together politically.

In 1950, Schuman as French foreign minister proposed a modest first step—the merger of the French and German steel (iron) and coal industries into a single framework that could most efficiently use the two states' coal resources and steel mills. Coal and steel were key to European recovery and growth. The Schuman plan gave birth in 1952 to the *European Coal and Steel Community (ECSC)*, in which France and Germany were joined by Italy (the third large industrial country of continental Europe) and by three smaller countries—Belgium, Netherlands, and Luxembourg (together called the Benelux countries). These six states worked through the ECSC to reduce trade barriers in coal and steel and to coordinate their coal and steel policies. The ECSC also established a High Authority that to some extent could bypass governments and deal directly with companies, labor unions, and individuals. The United Kingdom did not join, however.

If coal and steel sound like fairly boring topics, that was exactly the idea of functionalists. The issues involved were matters for engineers and technical experts, and did not threaten politicians. Since 1952, technical experts have served as the leaders of the integration process in other aspects of European life and outside Europe. As mentioned in Chapter 7, technical IOs such as the Universal Postal Union came before political ones such as the UN.

International scientific communities deserve special mention in this regard. If German and French steel experts had more in common than German and French politicians, this is even truer of scientists. Today the European scientific community is one of the most internationally integrated areas of society. For example, the EU operates the European Space Agency and the European Molecular Biology Laboratory.

Although technical cooperation succeeded in 1952, political and military cooperation proved much more difficult. In line with the vision of a united Europe, the six ECSC states signed a second treaty in 1952 to create a European Defence Community to work toward integrating Europe's military forces under one budget and command. But the French Parliament failed to ratify the treaty, and the United Kingdom refused to join such a force. The ECSC states also discussed formation of a European Political Community in 1953, but could not agree on its terms. Thus, in economic cooperation the supranational institutions succeeded but in political and military affairs state sovereignty prevailed.

---

[7] Dusan Sidjanski, *The Federal Future of Europe: From the European Community to the European Union* (Ann Arbor: U Michigan P, 2000). James A. Caporaso, *The European Union: Dilemmas of Regional Integration* (Boulder, CO: Westview, 2000). Stanley Henig, *The Uniting of Europe: From Discord to Concord* (NY: Routledge, 1997). Desmond Dinan, ed., *Encyclopedia of the European Union* (Boulder, CO: Rienner, 1998). Brent F. Nelsen and Alexander C. Stubb, eds., *The European Union: Readings on the Theory and Practice of European Integration* (Boulder, CO: Rienner, 1994).

The Treaty of Rome

In the **Treaty of Rome** in 1957, the same six states (France, Germany, Italy, Belgium, Netherlands, and Luxembourg) created two new organizations. One extended the coal-and-steel idea into a new realm, atomic energy. **Euratom,** the European Atomic Energy Community, was formed to coordinate nuclear power development by pooling research, investment, and management. It continues in operation today with an expanded membership. The second organization was the *European Economic Community (EEC)*, later renamed the *European Community (EC)*. After its founding in 1957, the EEC was often called simply the *Common Market*. Actually a common market was not immediately created but was established as a goal, which has since largely been realized.

In Chapter 8, the terms *free trade area, customs union,* and *common market* were not distinguished; let us now define them more precisely. Creating a **free trade area** meant lifting tariffs and restrictions on the movement of goods across (EEC) borders, as was done shortly after 1957. Today the *European Free Trade Association (EFTA)* is an extended free trade area associated with the EU; its members are Norway, Iceland, Liechtenstein, and Switzerland. (All but Switzerland became, with the EU, the European Economic Area, participating in the "Europe 1992" single market described below.)

A **customs union** means that participating states adopt a unified set of tariffs with regard to goods coming in from outside the free trade area. Without this, each type of good could be imported into the state with the lowest tariff and then re-exported (tariff-free) to the other states in the free trade area; this would be inefficient. The Treaty of Rome committed the six states to creating a customs union by 1969. A customs union creates free and open trade within its member states, bringing great economic benefits. Thus, the customs union remains the heart of the EU and the one aspect widely copied elsewhere in the world.

A **common market** means that in addition to the customs union, member states allow labour and capital (as well as goods) to flow freely across borders. For instance, a Belgian financier can invest in Germany on the same terms as a German investor. Although the Treaty of Rome adopted the goal of a common market, even today it has been only partially achieved.

One key aspect of a common market was achieved, at least in theory, in the 1960s when the EU (then the EC) adopted a **Common Agricultural Policy (CAP)**. In practice, the CAP has led to recurrent conflicts among member states and tensions between nationalism and regionalism. Recall that agriculture has been one of the most difficult sectors of the world economy in which to achieve free trade (see pp. 315–318). To promote national self-sufficiency in food, many governments give subsidies to farmers. The CAP was based on the principle that a subsidy extended to farmers in any EC country should be extended to farmers in all EC countries. That way, no EC government was forced to alienate politically powerful farmers by removing subsidies, yet the overall policy would be equalized throughout the community in line with the common-market principle. As a result, subsidies to farmers today absorb about two-thirds of the total EU budget and are the single greatest source of trade friction between Europe and the rest of the world (see pp. 319–320).

The fourth step in the plan for European integration (after a free trade area, customs union, and common market) was an *economic and monetary union (EMU)* in which the overall economic policies of the member states would be coordinated for greatest efficiency and stability. In this step, a single currency would replace separate national currencies (see "Monetary Union," pp. 379–380). A future fifth step would be the supranational coordination of economic policies, such as budgets and taxes.

Treaty of Rome (1957) The founding document of the European Economic Community (EEC) or Common Market, now subsumed by the European Union.

Euratom Created in the Treaty of Rome in 1957 to coordinate nuclear power development by pooling research, investment, and management.

free trade area A zone in which there are no tariffs or other restrictions on the movement of goods and services across borders.

customs union A common external tariff adopted by members of a free trade area; that is, participating states adopt a unified set of tariffs with regard to goods coming in from outside.

common market A zone in which labour and capital (as well as goods) flow freely across borders.

Common Agricultural Policy (CAP) A European Union policy based on the principle that a subsidy extended to farmers in any member country should be extended to farmers in all member countries.

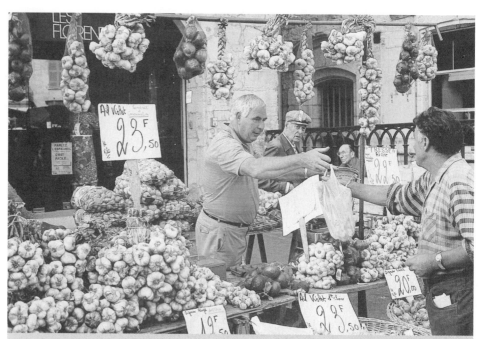

POLITICS AND MARKETS
Under the free-trade area first created by the 1957 Treaty of Rome, goods can move freely across European borders to reach consumers in any member country. In agriculture, creating an integrated free market in Europe has not been easy; the EC adopted a Common Agricultural Policy in the 1960s to address the problem. Prices in this French marketplace are affected by subsidies to French farmers, 1991.

To reduce state leaders' fears of losing sovereignty, the Treaty of Rome provides that changes in its provisions must be approved by all member states. For example, France vetoed the United Kingdom's application for membership in the EEC in 1963 and 1967. However, in 1973 the U.K. did finally join, along with Ireland and Denmark.

In 1981, Greece was admitted, and in 1986 Portugal and Spain joined. In May 2004, 10 new members joined, including Poland, the Czech Republic, Slovakia, Hungary, Latvia, Lithuania, Estonia, Malta, Slovenia, and Cyprus. Romania and Bulgaria are set to join in 2007, and it is assumed that Croatia, and other Balkan countries, will not be far behind. The EU may open talks on Turkey's membership in 2005. Inclusion of poorer countries with less industry and lower standards of living has created difficulties in effectively integrating Europe's economies. Richer European states give substantial aid to the poorer ones in hopes of strengthening the weak links. But the richer states also expect new EU members to undergo rapid liberalization of their economies, which some critics argue will have negative effects, especially in social programs and prices for basic goods and services. Popular reaction to expansion has also been mixed, with alarming expressions of xenophobia alongside celebrations welcoming the new members, many of which were under communist rule little more than a decade before.[8]

---

[8] Ed Vulliamy, "In From the Cold," *Guardian Unlimited* 11 April 2004 <http://www.guardian.co.uk/eu/story/0,7369,1189613,00.html>

Structure of the European Union

The structure of the EU reflects its roots in technical and economic cooperation. The coal and steel experts have been joined by experts on trade, agriculture, and finance at the heart of the community. The EU headquarters and staff have the reputation of being colourless bureaucrats—sometimes called *Eurocrats*—who care more about technical problem-solving than about politics. These supranational bureaucrats are balanced in the EU structure by provisions that uphold the power of states and state leaders.

Although the rule of Eurocrats follows the functionalist plan, it has created problems as the EU has progressed. Politicians in member states have qualms about losing power to the Eurocrats. Citizens in those states have become more uncomfortable in recent years with the growing power of faceless Eurocrats over their lives. Citizens can throw their own political leaders out of office in national elections, but the Eurocrats seem less accountable.

The EU's structure is illustrated in Figure 10.1. The Eurocrats consist of a staff of some 24 000, organized under the **European Commission** at EU headquarters in Brussels, Belgium. The commission has 30 individual members—one or two from each member state—who are chosen for four-year renewable terms. Their role is to identify problems and propose solutions to the Council of the European Union. They select one of their members as the commission president. These individuals are supposed to represent the interests of Europe as a whole (supranational interests), not their own states, but this goal has been only imperfectly met.

The European Commission lacks formal autonomous power except for day-to-day EU operations. Formally the commission reports to, and implements policies of, the **Council of the European Union** (formerly known as the *Council of Ministers*). The council is the main legislative and decision-making body in the EU and comprises relevant ministers from the 25 member countries. Agenda items for workshop meetings of the council dictate

European Commission
A European Union body whose members, while appointed by states, are supposed to represent EU interests. Supported by a multinational civil service in Brussels, the commission's role is to identify problems and propose solutions to the Council of the European Union.

Council of the European Union (Formerly known as the *Council of Ministers*.) The Council is the main legislative and decision-making body in the European Union and comprises relevant ministers (foreign, economic, agriculture, finance, etc.) from the 25 member countries. When a meeting takes place among the state leaders it is called the "European Council."

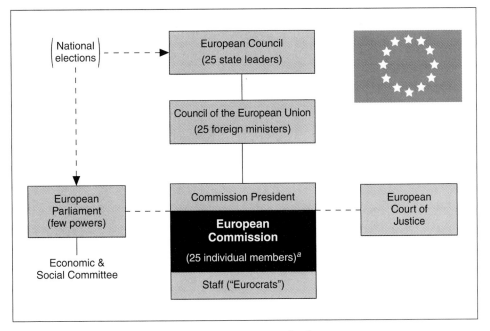

Figure 10.1 Structure of the European Union (EU)

[a] The commission will have 30 members until November 2004, then a maximum of 26, with one per country.

which ministers will attend (foreign, economic, agriculture, finance, etc.). When policy decisions must be made, the council includes elected leaders such as presidents or prime ministers. This structure means that the individuals making up the council vary from one meeting to the next, and that technical issues tend to receive priority over political ones.

The Council of the European Union in theory has a weighted voting system based on each state's population, but in practice it operates by consensus on major policy issues (all 25 members must agree). On other issues, decisions can be made by qualified majorities, overriding national sovereignty. The council's presidency rotates every six months and has limited power. The Council of the European Union must approve the policies of the European Commission and give it general directions.[9]

In the 1970s, state leaders (prime ministers or presidents) created a special place for themselves in the EC, to provide input into the direction of the community. The *European Council* refers to the regular meetings of the 25 heads of state or of government of all EU members. The European Council meets at least twice a year with the European Commission president.

European Parliament
A quasi-legislative body of the European Union that operates mainly as a watchdog over the *European Commission* and has little real legislative power.

There is a **European Parliament,** which might someday operate as a true legislature passing laws for all of Europe.[10] At present it operates more as a watchdog over the commission, with little power to legislate. The parliament must approve the commission's budget but cannot control it item by item. The parliament serves mainly as a debating forum and a symbol of European unity. However, in 1999 an independent commission created by the parliament found waste and fraud in the commission, leading all of the then 20 commissioners to resign. Since 1979, voters throughout Europe have directly elected their representatives to the European Parliament, according to population. As of May 2004, the European Parliament was composed of 788 members. Political parties are organized across national lines, with all Christian Democrats from all 25 countries, for instance, sitting together. But many of the most heated debates are between national delegations *within* a party—reflecting the continuing influence of nationalism.

An *Economic and Social Committee* discusses continent-wide issues that affect particular industries or constituencies. This committee is purely advisory; it lobbies the commission on matters it deems important. It is designed as a forum in which companies, labour unions, and interest groups can bargain transnationally.

European Court of Justice
A judicial arm of the European Union, based in Luxembourg. The court has actively established its jurisdiction and its right to overrule national law when it conflicts with EU law.

A **European Court of Justice** in Luxembourg adjudicates disputes on matters covered by the Treaty of Rome—which covers many issues. Unlike the World Court (see pp. 276–278), the European Court has actively established its jurisdiction and does not merely serve as a mechanism of international mediation. The court can overrule national law when it is in conflict with EU law—giving it unique powers among international courts. It hears cases brought by individuals, not just governments. In hundreds of cases, the court has ruled on matters ranging from discrimination in the workplace to the pensions of commission staff members.

The Single European Act

European integration has proceeded in a step-by-step process that produces tangible successes, reduces politicians' fears of losing sovereignty, and creates pressures to continue the process. Often major steps forward are followed by periods of stagnation or even reversals

---

[9] Emil Joseph Kirchner, *Decision Making in the European Community: The Council Presidency and European Integration* (Manchester, UK: Manchester UP, 1992).

[10] Richard Corbett, *The European Parliament's Role in Closer EU Integration* (NY: Palgrave, 2001). Julie Smith, *Voice of the People: The European Parliament in the 1990s* (Washington, DC: Brookings, 1995).

in integration. The first major revision of the Treaty of Rome—the 1985 **Single European Act**—began a new phase of accelerated integration. The EU set a target date of the end of 1992 for the creation of a true common market in Europe.[11] This comprehensive set of changes was nicknamed *Europe 1992*.

The 1992 process focused on about 300 directives from the European Commission, aimed at eliminating nontariff barriers to free trade in goods, services, labour, and capital within the EC. The issues tended to be complex and technical. For instance, professionals licensed in one state should be free to practise in another; but Spain's licensing requirements for, say, physical therapists, may have differed from those of the United Kingdom. The commission bureaucrats worked to smooth out such inconsistencies and create a uniform set of standards. Each national government had to pass laws to implement these measures.

For example, a dispute raged for decades over the definition of chocolate. Belgium—famous for its chocolates—requires the exclusive use of cocoa butter for a product to be called chocolate; the United Kingdom and other countries use a cheaper process that partially substitutes other vegetable oils. With deepening integration and seamless trade, Belgium worried that it would lose its competitive advantage in the US$30 billion world-wide chocolate market (half of which came from Europe). The United Kingdom and six other EU countries that joined the EU since 1973 won an exemption from the all–cocoa butter rule that applies to the other eight EU members. Under the pressure of integration, however, the EU is moving to unify standards such as food regulations. The chocolate wars illustrate that the seemingly simple concept of economic integration sets in motion forces of change that reach into every corner of society and affect the daily lives of millions of people.

The Single European Act also gave a new push to the creation of a European Central Bank (in Frankfurt, Germany), and a single currency and monetary system—longstanding goals that have now been accomplished for many EU members. As long as the economies of the EU members were tied to separate states (with separate central banks), efforts to maintain fixed exchange rates were difficult. For example, British politicians in 1992 were reluctant to deepen a recession in order to save German politicians from inflation.

The 1992 process moved economic integration into more political and controversial areas, eroding sovereignty more visibly than before. It also deepened a trend toward the EU's dealing directly with provinces rather than the states they belong to—thus beginning to "hollow out" the state from below (stronger provincial governments) as well as from above (stronger Europe-wide government). However, Europe 1992 continued to put aside for the future the difficult problems of political and military integration.

The Maastricht Treaty

The **Maastricht Treaty,** signed in the Dutch city of Maastricht in 1991, renamed the EC as the EU and committed it to further progress in three main areas. The first is monetary union (discussed shortly), in which the existing national currencies were to be abolished and replaced by a single European currency. A second set of changes, regarding justice and home affairs, created a European police agency and responded to the new reality that borders were opening to immigrants, criminals, sex traffickers, and contraband alike. It also expanded the idea of citizenship, so that, for example, a French citizen living in Germany can vote in local elections there. A third goal of Maastricht is even more controversial—political and military integration. The treaty commits European states to work toward a

Single European Act (1985) It set a target date of the end of 1992 for the creation of a *true common market* (free cross-border movement of goods, capital, people, and services) in the European Community (EC).

Maastricht Treaty Signed in the Dutch city of Maastricht and ratified in 1992, the treaty commits the European Union to monetary union (a single currency and European Central Bank) and to a common foreign policy. See also *European Union (EU)*.

---

[11] Andrew Moravcsik, "Negotiating the Single European Act: National Interests and Conventional Statecraft in the European Community," *International Organization* 45.1 (1991): 19–56.

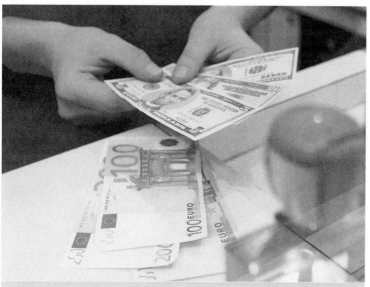

INTEGRATION MARCHES ON
The Maastricht Treaty called for a monetary union with a common currency. Despite unexpected public resistance in several European countries, the euro currency came into effect smoothly in 11 countries by 2002. Here, a teller exchanges dollars for euros in Paris, 2003.

common foreign policy with a goal of eventually establishing a joint military force. All three of these areas of change infringe on state sovereignty.

The Maastricht Treaty encountered problems soon after its signing. One problem was the fractious response of EU members to the war in the former Yugoslavia—next door on the European continent. Efforts by the EU to mediate the conflict failed repeatedly, as the war spread and a humanitarian and refugee crisis deepened. In 1992, French President Mitterrand secretly flew straight from an EU summit meeting to the embattled Bosnian capital, Sarajevo; this unilateral initiative reflected the EU's inability to act in unison. Members of the EU also diverged sharply over support for the U.S.-led invasion of Iraq, with the U.K. one of the strongest supporters and France one of the strongest opponents.

Closer to home, some citizens of Europe began to react strongly against the loss of national identity and sovereignty implicit in Maastricht.[12] Through the years of European integration, public opinion has been largely supportive. In recent years, polls have shown a strong majority of European citizens in favour of greater political and military integration, and of expanding the powers of the European Parliament—although support for political union is weak in Denmark and the United Kingdom. Perhaps the Eurocrats took public support too much for granted, for a substantial and growing minority was having second thoughts—as with the backlash against free trade discussed at the end of Chapter 8.

As an amendment to the Treaty of Rome, Maastricht had to be ratified by all (then 12) members. The ratification process stirred up strong public feelings against closer European union in several countries. British politicians had already received assurances that allowed the United Kingdom to stay outside a monetary union and a unified European social policy, if it so chose. In other EU states, however, political leaders and citizens had not fully anticipated the public reactions to Maastricht before signing it. Suddenly, citizens and leaders in several countries seemed to realize that the faceless Eurocrats in Brussels were stripping away their national sovereignty.

In a 1992 referendum, Danish voters narrowly rejected the treaty despite the support of the major political parties, industries, and labor unions (in a second 1993 vote Danes approved the treaty, with provisions like the United Kingdom's). A referendum in Ireland passed easily, but one in France just barely passed. As a result, EU leaders had to admit that public opinion in several countries reflected deep reservations about a closer European union. Although the EU implemented the Maastricht treaty, it did so more slowly and with fewer participating countries than originally hoped. Nonetheless, eco-

---

[12] Sieglende Gstohl, *Reluctant Europeans: Norway, Sweden, and Switzerland and the Process of Integration* (Boulder, CO: Rienner, 2002). Carl Lankowski, ed., *Europe's Emerging Identity: Opposition Movements vs. Regional Integration in the European Community* (Boulder, CO: Rienner, 1993).

nomic and technical integration, including the monetary union among 12 of the then 15 members, has maintained momentum.

Political and military integration have been much more problematic. The EU decided in 1999 to develop a 60 000-troop military force (see p. 244), which is still under development, but NATO will continue to be more important and may even subsume the new force in practice.[13] The struggle between nationalism and supranationalism seems precariously balanced between the two; the transition to supranationalism has not yet been accomplished regarding sovereignty and foreign and military policy. Even after 50 years of preparation, spillover is elusive.

Monetary Union

A European currency, the **euro,** has replaced national currencies in 12 of the 25 EU members, as mandated in the Maastricht process. After several years as an abstract unit like the IMF's SDR (see p. 343), used by national governments and for international exchange, the euro came into full circulation in 2002 and the national currencies ceased to exist. A European Central Bank took over the functions of states' central banks.[14]

Monetary union is difficult for both economic and political reasons. In participating states, fundamental economic and financial conditions must be equalized. One state cannot stimulate its economy with low interest rates while another cools inflation with high interest rates. This is a problem because in a monetary union the EU will not be able to handle differences across countries well, such as a recession in one country while another is booming. For example, in 2001 the unemployment rate was 13 percent in Spain but 2 percent in the Netherlands. The 2000 inflation rate was below 2 percent in France but above 5 percent in Ireland. (Recall that Argentina's divergence from the United States during the dollar-peso peg period led to a political and economic crisis; see p. 338.)

In an integrated economy that is also politically centralized, the central government can reallocate resources, as the Canadian federal government might do if British Columbia were booming and New Brunswick were in recession. But the EU does not have centralized powers of taxation or control of national budgets. This split of fiscal and monetary policy is unusual and makes establishing the monetary union more difficult.

One solution is to work toward equalizing Europe's economies. For example, to reduce the disparity between rich and poor EU states, the Maastricht Treaty increased the EU budget by US$25 billion annually to provide economic assistance to the poorer members. But the richer EU members pay the cost for this aid, and it is insufficient to truly equalize the rich and poor countries.

The main solution adopted at Maastricht was to restrict membership in the monetary union, at least in the first round, to only those countries with enough financial stability not to jeopardize the union. To join the unified currency, a state had to achieve certain benchmarks: a budget deficit less than 3 percent of GDP, a national debt less

euro Also called the *ECU (European currency unit)*, the euro is a single European currency used by 12 members of the *European Union (EU)*.

---

[13] Simon Duke, *The Elusive Quest for European Security: From EDC to CFSP* (NY: St. Martin's, 2000). Sophie Vanhoonacker, *The Bush Administration and the Development of a European Security Identity* (Brookfield, VT: Ashgate, 2001). Brian White, *Understanding European Foreign Policy* (NY: Palgrave, 2001).

[14] Paul Grauwe, *The Economics of Monetary Integration*,. 4th ed. (NY: Oxford UP, 2000). Randall Henning and Pier Carlo Padon, *Transatlantic Perspectives on the Euro* (Washington, DC: Brookings, 2000). Barry Eichengreen and Jeffry Frieden, The *Political Economy of European Monetary Unification* (Boulder, CO: Westview, 2000). Kenneth Dyson and Kevin Featherstone, *The Road to Maastricht: Negotiating Economic and Monetary Union* (NY: Oxford UP, 1999). Steven Weber, *Globalization and the European Political Economy* (NY: Columbia UP, 2001).

than 60 percent of GDP, an inflation rate no more than 1.5 percentage points above the average of the three lowest-inflation EU members, and stable interest rates and national currency values.

These targets proved difficult to meet for many EU members. There was talk of loosening the standards for admission, but EU leaders believed this to be a dangerous course that could undermine the ultimate stability of the euro. Instead, the leaders of states wanting to participate agreed to buckle down and try to meet the standards. This meant hard choices by governments in France, Spain, Italy, and other countries, to cut budgets and benefits and to take other politically unpopular moves. French workers responded with massive strikes on several occasions. Governments fell to opposition parties in several countries, but the new leaders generally kept to the same course. As a result of their new-found fiscal discipline, all 12 EU members that wanted to participate in the euro ultimately qualified. The United Kingdom, Denmark, and Sweden opted to retain their national currencies, although Britain may join soon. In a 2003 referendum, a strong majority of Swedes opposed adopting the euro. The 10 newest members as of May 2004 do not yet participate in the euro.

Germany's participation was central because the mark was the strongest European currency. In a sense, the euro replaced the mark and the other countries tagged along. (This is why the European Central Bank is in Frankfurt, where the German central bank was located.) Proponents of monetary union hope that Germany's sacrifice of its own respected currency, the mark, will help reassure Europe that German reunification (see pp. 36–37) does not threaten other European countries.

Money is more political than steel tariffs or chocolate ingredients. A monetary union infringes on a core prerogative of states—the right to print currency. Because citizens use money every day, a European currency along these lines could deepen citizens' sense of identification with Europe—a victory for supranationalism over nationalism. When the euro went into circulation in 2002, people for the first time could "put Europe in their pocket." However, precisely for this reason, some state leaders and citizens resisted the idea of giving up the symbolic value of their national currencies. These problems were reflected in the task of designing euro banknotes and coins. How could any country's leaders or monuments become Europe-wide symbols? The solution was to put generic architectural elements (not identifiable by country) on the front of the banknotes and a map of Europe on the back. Coins come in various member-state designs (all valid throughout the euro zone).

The EU met its timetable to launch the euro in 2002. Production of euro banknotes and coins began in 1998. Currency exchange rates were frozen in 1999, and a transition to European Central Bank control began. International currency markets began trading the euro instead of the national currencies. Cash registers across Europe were reprogrammed, and prices were displayed in both euros and national currencies for the transition years. The circulation of euros as legal tender, and the cancellation of national currencies, came in 2002. On E-day, January 1, 2002, 300 million Europeans met US$600 billion in freshly printed money in a surprisingly smooth process. But in 2003, Germany and France ran budget deficits higher than allowed under the euro rules, raising conflicts within the euro zone. In 2004, the European Commission sued the EU member states for voting to let France and Germany break the euro rules.

The EU still faces uncharted waters in actually making a monetary union work without political unification. Before even going into circulation, the value of the euro slumped (from US$1.17 to US$0.88) as investor confidence in the experiment proved shaky. Having survived its birth, the euro gained back its value, to US$1.25 by early 2004. Because the creation of a European currency is arguably the largest financial overhaul ever attempted in history, nobody knows how it will work in practice.

Expanding the European Union

Despite the resistance encountered in the Maastricht process, the EU has been successful enough to attract neighbouring states that want to join. In fact, the larger and more integrated the EU becomes, the less attractive is the prospect of remaining outside it for any state in the vicinity of Europe.

Spain and Portugal were admitted in 1986 as the eleventh and twelfth members, and in 1995, Austria, Sweden, and Finland joined the EU, bringing the total to 15. Norway applied to join and was accepted, but its citizens voted down the idea in a referendum in 1994. By 1995, all but two of the main states of Western Europe were members of the EU. (Switzerland's plans to join were, like Norway's, halted by a popular referendum in the early 1990s; citizens preferred to maintain their traditional strict neutrality even at a cost to the Swiss economy.)

On May 1, 2004, Poland, the Czech Republic, Slovakia, Hungary, Latvia, Lithuania, Estonia, Malta, Slovenia, and Cyprus joined the EU, its single biggest expansion in history. The EU's population is now some 455 million, its borders range from the former Soviet Union to the Middle East and North Africa, and its GDP nearly equals that of the U.S. economy.

 Thinking Theoretically

Over the years, the membership of the European Union has expanded, from 6 members to 25. Further expansion is planned, and it is likely the EU will have at least 30 members within the decade. According to collective goods theory (see p. 91), the expanding membership should make it easier to free-ride on the community's larger, richer members without being so visible and without disrupting the overall provision of collective goods by the community. This approach could help to explain the difficulties faced by the EU in the decade since the 1992 Maastricht Treaty—popular resistance and razor-thin referendum margins, disunity over foreign affairs such as in Bosnia, the United Kingdom's shunning of the euro, squabbles over future directions, and so forth.

However, other theories could explain these outcomes as well. A realist could simply point to differences in national interests as creating a natural barrier to integration beyond a certain point. In this view, it was the gradual infringement of national sovereignty (hitting some natural limit) rather than the expansion of membership that explains the problems of EU integration in the 1990s. Critical theorists might argue that support for integration (which in the EU was shared not only by business elites, but by many trade unionists and social democrats as well) will decline as these social classes recalculate the costs associated with EU membership as the EU expands.

We can judge these theories in part by how well they predict the effects of EU expansion in the next few years.

The number-of-actors theory would predict increasing difficulties in holding the EU together as the number of actors keeps growing. Institutional structures and rules would have to change as a result. In particular, the unanimity rule, giving each member state a veto, would have to be much more narrowly restricted. (The EU is in fact exploring these and other structural changes through a constitutional commission, which began in 2002. By May of 2004 a draft constitution was in place but had yet to be accepted by EU members). Eventually, a smaller core group might emerge—perhaps even a German-French duopoly or German hegemony—to dictate policy and enforce cooperation in order to overcome collective goods problems.

If public protests and riots increase as EU membership expands, this might be a sign that the critical theorists are correct. By contrast, realism should predict little effect of the expansion in membership, since the problem is the level of infringement on sovereignty (which does not change when more members are added). Indeed, by one logic, the expansion of membership is slowing down the deepening of ties among today's EU members. In that case, expansion would actually smooth out the EU's problems by slowing the assault on national sovereignty.

Theories play different roles, but one important feature of a theory is the ability to improve projections of future possibilities. By watching the effects of EU expansion in the coming years, we can see which theory best explained the outcome.

WE'RE IN!
The European Union added 10 members, mostly from Eastern Europe, in 2004. Here, Latvia's president and prime minister sign the treaty of accession, 2003.

More members are set to join the EU (Rumania and Bulgaria) and others will likely begin negotiations about accession in the near future (such as Turkey). A number of Balkan states, including Croatia, are also expected to join soon.

Discussions about expansion usually hinge on a choice between deepening the community through a monetary union and other measures envisioned by Maastricht, or broadening it by adding members. States that favour deepening the EU—France especially—argue that an enlarged membership would prove unwieldy and would endanger the gains the EU has made. Those that favour broadening (such as the United Kingdom) argue that the ideal of a united Europe requires the EU to take in those who want to join, even though progress toward economic integration would be slowed down. The United Kingdom is less eager to deepen the European Union and favours expansion partly because it would slow down such deepening.

Perhaps as a result of these pressures, the EU in the last decades shows signs of dividing into "inner" and "outer" layers—those states such as France and Germany joining a currency union and deepening their integration, and those such as the U.K. and perhaps the new members operating at the edges of the EU with more autonomy. This division of the EU was illustrated in 1995, when seven countries from Portugal to Germany established what has been called the Schengen area (after the town in Luxembourg in which the agreement was originally signed in 1985). The Schengen area abolished border controls and the need for passports but in turn tightened border controls between themselves and the eight other EU members that did not join the free-movement zone (though most did join later). Suddenly, Germans who crossed into Denmark (a nonparticipant) on Sunday mornings to buy bread (because German bakeries were closed on Sunday) began to need identification at the border; formerly they had just waved their bags of bread at the border guards as they crossed back into Germany.

Beyond the EU itself, Europe is a patchwork of overlapping structures with varying memberships. Despite the Single European Act, there are still many Europes. Around the edges are the EFTA states participating in the European Economic Area. NATO membership overlaps partly with the EU. More distantly, a number of countries seek closer ties to the EU, including Canada. The European Union is Canada's second-largest trade and investment partner, and Canada signed a Framework Agreement for Commercial and Economic Cooperation with the (then) European Community in 1976, following that up with an Action Plan in 1996, both intended to enhance further Canada-EU commercial, trade, and investment relations.

One truly universal intergovernmental organization exists in Europe—the *Organization for Security and Cooperation in Europe (OSCE)*. Operating by consensus, with a large and expanding universal membership of 55 states, the OSCE has little actual power except to act as a forum for multilateral discussions of security issues. (The name was upgraded in 1994 from "Conference" to "Organization"—CSCE to OSCE.) In the late 1990s, the OSCE shifted into new tasks such as running elections and helping political parties in Bosnia and Kosovo, as well as providing various forms of monitoring and assistance in a half dozen Eastern European countries.

A NORTH AMERICAN MONETARY UNION?

With increasing economic integration between Canada and the United States through the FTA and then NAFTA, it was natural that there would also be some consideration given to creating a **North American Monetary Union (NAMU).** Since 1999 the idea of a currency union has become a regular feature in some policy discussions, especially in the media and conservative think-tanks such as the Vancouver-based Fraser Institute. No federal political party, however, has officially endorsed the idea of a monetary union.

North American Monetary Union (NAMU) A proposed currency union between Canada and the U.S. The NAMU has become a regular feature in some policy discussions but has never been endorsed by a federal political party.

Some of the discussions about NAMU have proposed the creation of a new single currency, not unlike the euro. Most advocates realize that such a scenario is unlikely, given U.S. reluctance to give up sovereignty to a supranational institution such as a North American Central Bank (which would need to be created, as in Europe, to manage the new currency). Thus most of the discussions have focused instead on the adoption of the U.S. dollar within Canada, what is also called "dollarization."

Those who favour NAMU suggest that it is practically inevitable, especially given the integrative measures already undertaken with NAFTA. They argue that a monetary union would increase efficiency between the U.S. and Canada, result in price stability, and stabilize wages. The idea has also received support from sovereigntists within Québec, who partly support it for the symbolic value associated with abandoning the Canadian dollar, but also see it as an obvious choice for a province that trades more with the United States than it does with the rest of Canada.

A number of observers, however, point to a series of problems associated with the idea of a monetary union. One, and perhaps the most difficult from a political perspective, is a surprising lack of support from financial and business elites within Canada for such a proposition. Unlike the EU, where support for a monetary union was relatively strong among business classes, there is no such widespread consensus within Canada. Canadian business associations, such as the Conference Board of Canada and the Canadian Chamber of Commerce, have indicated support for the existing currency system, and some of the strongest opposition to NAMU comes from Canadian banks. The C.D. Howe Institute, another conservative think-tank in Canada, was originally a supporter of NAMU but published a study in 2000 that argued against it. Opponents from the business and financial community are joined by trade union members, social movement activists, and social democrats in arguing against a currency union.

Some of those opposed to NAMU argue that it will accomplish little and cost a lot: Canadian business transactions are often conducted using the U.S. dollar already, by this view, and there is little need to formalize it by creating new structures and institutions. Others insist that maintaining a separate monetary system provides Canadian monetary authorities with greater flexibility (and sovereignty) to adjust to economic disruptions that may result from fluctuations within the U.S. economy. Others note that the Canadian and U.S. economies are far too different to be integrated successfully through a monetary union, and that manufacturing growth in Canada since the late 1990s has been facilitated in part by an undervalued Canadian dollar (making our exports cheaper for foreign buyers). Abandoning that difference, in other words, will result in job losses, not economic gains.

A North American Monetary Union is not as inevitable as its proponents like to suggest, but neither is it something that has been completely dismissed. Discussion and debate about NAMU will undoubtedly continue for years to come.[15]

These examples of integration illustrate that it is not a matter of a single group or organization, but more a mosaic of structures tying states together. The various structures of the European political system, centred on the EU, are IGOs composed of states as members. Such would be the case also if a North American Monetary Union was ever created. But as was mentioned at the outset of this chapter, a more diffuse, less tangible aspect of integration also deserves attention. That is the sense of identity that develops over time as economic (and other functional) ties bring people closer together across borders. Supranational identity, culture, and communication are also aspects of international integration. The remainder of this chapter considers how information technologies are bypassing states and bringing about this kind of integration globally.

THE POWER OF INFORMATION

Global telecommunications are profoundly changing how information and culture function in international relations.[16] Information is now a vital tool of national governments in their interactions with each other. Yet technology is at the same time undermining and disempowering those governments and shifting power to substate actors and individuals. Those newly empowered individuals and groups have begun to create new transnational networks worldwide, bypassing states.

Wiring the World

New international political possibilities are based on technological developments.[17] Just a hundred years ago, the idea of instant global communication was incomprehensible. It would have seemed unthinkable that anyone could push a dozen buttons on a handheld instrument and be able to talk with any of billions of people anywhere in the economically developed areas of the world (and many of the poorer areas). Equally ridiculous was the idea that you could look at a box no bigger than a suitcase and see in it moving pictures of things happening at that moment in distant lands. For most of the history of the international system, until about 150 years ago, the fastest way to send information was to write it down and bring it to the recipient by horse or sailing ship.

---

[15] This material is drawn from Jim Stanford, "Future for the Loonie? Introduction to Forum on North American Monetary Integration"; Eric Helleiner, "The Strange Politics of Canada's NAMU Debate"; and Mario Seccareccia, "Is Dollarization a Desirable Alternative to the Monetary Status Quo? A Critical Evaluation of Competing Currency Arrangements for Canada," in the "Forum on Dollarization," *Studies in Political Economy* 71/72 (Autumn 2003/Winter 2004): 59–108. See also H. Grubel, *The Case for the Amero: The Economics and Politics of a North American Monetary Union* (Vancouver: Fraser Institute, 1999); and D. Laidler and F. Poschmann, *Leaving Well Enough Alone: Canada's Monetary Order in a Changing International Environment* (Toronto: C.D. Howe Institute, 2000).

[16] Edward A. Comor, ed., *The Global Political Economy of Communication: Hegemony, Telecommunication and the Information Economy* (NY: St. Martin's, 1994). Cees J. Hamelink, *The Politics of World Communication* (Thousand Oaks, CA: Sage, 1994). Howard H. Frederick, *Global Communication and International Relations* (Belmont, CA: Wadsworth, 1993).

[17] Craig Warkentin, *Reshaping World Politics: NGOs, the Internet, and Global Civil Society* (Lanham, MD: Rowman & Littlefield, 2001). Ithiel de Sola Pool, *Technologies without Boundaries: On Telecommunications in a Global Age*, ed. Eli M. Noam (Cambridge, MA: Harvard UP, 1990). William J. Drake, ed., *The New Information Infrastructure: Strategies for U.S. Policy* (Washington, DC: Brookings, 1995).

The media over which information travels—telephones, television, films, magazines, and so forth—shape the way ideas take form and spread from one place to another. The media with the strongest political impact are radio and (especially) television. There are about one and a half billion TV sets and two and a half billion radio receivers in the world (roughly one-third are in North America, one-third in Western and Eastern Europe and Russia, and the rest in the global South and Japan/Pacific).[18] The power of these media is to take a single source of information (a moving picture or a voice) and reproduce it in many copies in many locations.

Radio, and increasingly TV, reaches the poorest rural areas of the global South. Peasants who cannot read can understand radio. Shortwave radio—typically stations such as the Canadian Broadcasting Corporation (CBC), the British Broadcasting Corporation (BBC), and Radio Moscow—is very popular in remote locations.

TV is especially powerful. The combination of pictures and sounds affects viewers emotionally and intellectually. Viewers can experience distant events more fully. As technology has developed, some viewers have an even wider range of channels and information from which to choose—from the local city council meeting, to simultaneous translation of the Russian evening news (in the United States), to MTV music videos (in Russia). Some argue that this makes television a less passive medium than it once was: less and less frequently are millions of TV viewers all forced to march to the beat of the same drummer; rather, the global TV audience is being fragmented into many small pieces, often not along national lines. Even with more channels to choose from, however, television itself remains a very passive medium.

Ordinary over-the-air TV and radio signals are radio waves carried on specific frequencies. Frequencies are a limited resource in high demand, which governments regulate and allocate to users. Because radio waves do not respect national borders, the allocation of frequencies is a subject of interstate bargaining. International regimes have grown up around the regulation of international communications technologies.[19]

Cable TV does not use the airwaves of the radio spectrum and can carry hundreds of signals at once. Cable also has the potential to carry signals *from* viewers. Satellite transmissions also bypass the normal over-the-air radio spectrum and transmit signals over a huge area to dish-shaped antennas.

The Qatar-based all-news satellite TV network, Al Jazeera, begun in 1996, has become a force in Middle East politics. It reaches an influential audience across the region and world. (Reportedly only 10 to 15 percent of Arab peoples have satellite dishes, but that fraction still amounts to millions of viewers.) It is considered one of the few media that does not stick narrowly with a government line. Criticized by Western governments for airing Osama bin Laden videos and anti-American propaganda generally, Al Jazeera also occasionally broadcasts interviews with top U.S. and other Western officials. The only foreign network allowed to report regularly from Taliban-ruled Afghanistan during the 2001 U.S. bombing, its office there was destroyed by a U.S. missile. When photographs emerged of U.S. physical and sexual abuse against Iraqi prisoners in the Abu Ghraib prison facility in 2004, Al Jazeera quickly broadcast the photos to audiences in the Middle East. When President George W. Bush delivered his televised apology to the Iraqi people for the abuse, he intentionally chose a U.S. supported network in Iraq rather than

[18] UNESCO, *UNESCO Yearbook* (NY: United Nations, annual).

[19] Marcus Franda, *Governing the Internet: The Emergence of an International Regime* (Boulder, CO: Rienner, 2001). Stephen D. Krasner, "Global Communications and National Power: Life on the Pareto Frontier," *World Politics* 43.3 (1991): 336–66. Peter F. Cowhey, "The International Telecommunications Regime: The Political Roots of Regimes for High Technology," *International Organization* 44.2 (1990): 169–200.

WIRED
Global communication, a very new capability on the time scale of the international system, is changing the rules of IR and empowering nonstate transnational actors. This internet café in Tehran (2000) plays a part in Iran's vibrant though embattled democratization movement.

Al Jazeera on which to make his address. Though the sentiment that Al Jazeera only inflamed local sentiment by broadcasting the photographs likely informed President Bush's decision to snub the network, the credibility of his apology may have been enhanced had he chosen to be interviewed by Al Jazeera.

Images and sounds are being recorded, reproduced, and viewed in new ways through audiotapes and videotapes. Videocassette recorders (VCRs) have proliferated in many countries in recent years. Audio- and videotapes can be played repeatedly and passed from person to person, again giving the listener and viewer more control. Video cameras are empowering ordinary citizens to create their own visual records, such as videos of political demonstrations in one country that end up on the TV news in another country.

Even more empowering of ordinary citizens is the telephone. Unlike TV and radio, phones are a two-way medium through which users interact without any centralized information source. Phones are becoming more powerful, with the advent of fibre-optic cables, communication satellites, cellular phones, satellite phones, fax machines, and modems. In Africa, cheap cell phones with cheap prepaid calling cards have let millions of relatively poor individuals bypass the lack of infrastructure previously needed to communicate. (Sub-Saharan Africa in total has fewer phone lines than Manhattan alone.) Telephones, perhaps more than any other technology, make individuals international actors.

These forms of communication do not slow down for one second when they cross an international border. The increased flows of information from state to state reflect the growing functional interdependence of states in today's world.

Information technologies have security implications. Capabilities such as fibre-optic cables or satellite communications serve governments in conducting their foreign and military policies (see "Evolving Technologies" on pp. 215–217). Because fibre-optic cables facilitate military command and control, the United States tried to prevent the sale of such cables to Russia even after the Cold War ended.

In a subtle but pervasive way, communication technologies may be diffusing power away from governments and toward ordinary people and other nonstate actors.[20] New communications technologies may be empowering ordinary citizens relative to governments and political parties.

Information as a Tool of Governments

Not all aspects of the information revolution work against governments. With more information travelling around the world than ever before, information has become an important instrument of governments' power (domestic and interstate).[21] Above all, governments want *access to information*. In 1992, U.S. Secretary of State James Baker made his first visit to the newly independent Asian republics of the former Soviet Union (the poorest and most remote CIS members). At each stop, one of the first questions Baker was asked by the state leader was, "How do I get CNN?"[22] CNN, state leaders hoped, would tie them directly to the Western world and symbolize their independence from Russia.

U.S. military leaders recognized the importance of playing to a global audience when, during the bombing of Bosnian Serb forces in 1995, they designated an ammunition dump close to Sarajevo the "CNN site" because they knew the explosion would make good footage for Sarajevo-based TV cameras. During the Gulf War, the U.S. military fed TV networks pictures of precision weapons striking their targets, hoping to "sanitize" the bombing campaign.

Governments spend large amounts of money and effort trying to gain information about what is happening both inside and outside their territories. They keep files on their citizens ranging from social security records to secret police files. They compile economic statistics to chart their own economic health and make estimates of the economic health of other states. Most operate intelligence-gathering agencies.

With today's information technologies, it is easier for governments to gather, organize, and store huge amounts of information. In this respect, the information revolution empowers governments more than ever. In the past, a wanted criminal, drug lord, or terrorist could slip over the border and take refuge in a foreign country. The terrorists who attacked the United States in 2001 demonstrated how easy this was. Today, however, it is just as likely that a routine traffic ticket in the foreign country could trigger an instant directive to arrest the person. Information technologies give repressive governments more power to keep tabs on citizens, spy on dissidents, and manipulate public opinion. Those technologies are now also being mobilized in force to strengthen international counterterrorism, in sometimes equally repressive ways.

Just as citizens and terrorists find it harder to hide from governments, so are state governments finding it harder to hide information from each other. The military importance of satellite reconnaissance has been cited (see p. 215). A powerful state such as the United

[20] James N. Rosenau, *Turbulence in World Politics: A Theory of Change and Continuity* (Princeton, NJ: Princeton UP, 1990). James N. Rosenau and Ernst-Otto Czempiel, eds., *Governance without Government: Order and Change in World Politics* (NY: Cambridge UP, 1992).

[21] Karl W. Deutsch, *The Nerves of Government: Models of Political Communication and Control* (NY: Free Press, 1969).

[22] *New York Times* 2 Feb. 1992: A10.

The Changing World Order

Big Brother is Watching

One outcome of the Cold War was the victory of "free" countries over those whose governments tried to know about and control all aspects of their citizens' lives. In communist societies like East Germany, the ruthless secret police kept files on everyone, had informers on every block, and monitored the streets with video cameras. George Orwell's futuristic novel, *1984,* published in 1948, envisioned a totalitarian state so powerful that it watched everything and everyone through two-way TVs in every room. Signs proclaimed, "Big Brother Is Watching You!" to intimidate citizens. However, the year 1984 passed, and such extreme totalitarian societies did not develop. Instead, both the Soviet Union and China (in different ways) relaxed the state's control over personal spaces. With right-wing totalitarianism having been defeated in World War II, it seemed that free societies were the rule. See-all-and-know-all government was a thing of the past.

Yet, the information revolution delivered into the hands of governments tremendous new power to extend the reach of government surveillance both horizontally (to every square metre of distant countries) and vertically (peering into what had been private places in citizens' lives).

The changes in world order since September 11, 2001, have changed this balance between the state's responsibility to provide security and individuals' rights to not have the government constantly looking over their shoulders. In response to the threat of terrorism, law-enforcement agencies around the world began to expand and network together surveillance systems.

New video surveillance centre, Washington, DC, 2002.

Privacy and human rights advocates argue that these governmental intrusions into traditionally private areas of life undermine the very values that Western democracies were founded on. We live in an age when authorities employ video cameras and face recognition software in public locations, listen to phone calls and emails in volume, peer behind walls with infrared detectors, examine bodily fluids by using drug tests, scan carry-on luggage with X-rays, and require fingerprint identification for international travel. Since September 11, governments have used these powers more freely, and citizens have largely acquiesced.

How should privacy rights change in a time of terrorism? Do you think governments should be free to use new technologies to monitor all aspects of social life in hopes of finding terrorists? Or should government powers be limited? Where would you draw the line?

States can increase its power through information technologies. It can and does monitor the phone calls, faxes, data transmissions, and radio conversations in foreign countries.

As the cost of information technology decreases, it comes into reach of more states. The great powers have always been able to maintain a worldwide presence and gather information globally. Now small states can gain some of the same capabilities electronically. Even sophisticated information is becoming more available and cheaper—high-resolution satellite photos are now available commercially within the price range of most states. These images can be used for both military purposes and natural-resource management—knowing what states (including one's own) have such resources as minerals, forests, and farmland, and the rate at which they are being used.

The very nature of interstate interactions is affected by changes in information technology. The risks of surprise in IR are reduced by the information revolution. The security dilemma is less severe as a result (states do not need to arm against unknown

TELLING THE WORLD
Control of television news and other mass media has become an important instrument of political power, one that states often seek to control. Independent journalists are often directly or indirectly targeted in this effort. Here, 28-year-old American photographer Cynthia Elbaum works to show the world the effects of Russia's war in Chechnya (1994). She was killed an hour later in a Russian air raid on the site.

potential threats since they know what the "real" threats are). Similarly, the ability to monitor performance of agreements makes collective goods problems easier to resolve. (Collective goods are more easily maintained when cheaters and free riders can be identified; see p. 91).

The ability of governments to bargain effectively with each other and to reach mutually beneficial outcomes is enhanced by the availability of instant communications channels. The "hot line" connecting Washington with Moscow is a classic example.

In addition to gaining access to information, governments use information as a power capability by disseminating it internationally and domestically. In today's information-intensive world, TV transmitters may be more powerful than tanks. Even in war itself, propaganda plays a key role. For instance, in the Gulf War, pamphlets and loudspeakers were used to appeal to Iraqi soldiers, which probably contributed to their mass surrenders. Dropping leaflets and pamphlets, however, can also backfire. The United Nations Mission to Somalia in the early 1990s used written leaflets to explain to Somalis the goals of the mission, even though the Somali people are an overwhelmingly oral culture. To make matters worse, due to a translation error, the first leaflets announced that "slave nations have come to help you."[23]

---

[23] Tamara Duffey, "Cultural Issues in Contemporary Peacekeeping," *International Peacekeeping* 7.1 (Spring 2000): 142–68.

The information disseminated by a government often crosses international borders, intentionally and otherwise. The government of Jordan, for example, is well aware that its Arabic programs are received by Arab citizens of Israel and that its English programs are watched by Israeli Jews. When Jordanian TV broadcasts, say, a Canadian documentary about social movement activism in the West (with Arabic subtitles), the message influences Israeli-Palestinian relations across the border.

Most governments create explicit channels of information dissemination to influence domestic and international audiences. Stations such as Radio Moscow broadcast radio programs in dozens of languages aimed at all the world's regions. The United States operates the Voice Of America (VOA) shortwave radio network, which is picked up in many regions of the global South where it may be one of the few outside information sources. The United States also beams specialized programming into Cuba (TV/Radio Marti) and China (Radio Free Asia, which includes programs in the minority Tibetan and Uighur languages), among others. During the 2001 U.S.-Chinese crisis regarding a U.S. reconnaissance plane that crash-landed in China, the Chinese government heavily jammed broadcasts into China of VOA and Radio Free Asia.

Governments spread false as well as true information as a means of international influence. This is called *disinformation*. In the 1930s, the Nazis discovered that the "big lie," if repeated enough times, would be accepted as truth by most people. It is harder to fool international audiences these days, but domestic ones can still respond to propagan-

LET'S TALK
Information, which easily crosses state borders, has become a major factor in both international and domestic politics and may even be laying technological foundations for a global identity. Telecommunications could change the path of development in poor countries, possibly bypassing traditional infrastructure like phone lines and leapfrogging to a wireless networked economy. Cheap phones and prepaid calling cards are putting cell phones in reach of a growing segment of Africa's population. This shop does a brisk business in Abidjan, Ivory Coast, 2001.

distic misinformation. Anyone who follows international events should remember that even stories reported in the Western news as fact are sometimes disinformation.

Most governments own and operate at least one main TV station (in Canada, the CBC), and many hold a monopoly on TV stations. Thus TV signals often rank with military equipment and currency as capabilities so important to a government that it must control them itself. Indeed, in a military coup d'état, usually one of the first and most important targets seized is the television broadcasting facility. When power is up for grabs in a state, it is now as likely that fighting will occur in the government TV studios or at the transmitting antenna as at the legislature or presidential offices. As the Soviet Union broke up in the early 1990s, TV towers were the scene of confrontations in several republics. In Lithuania, a crowd of Lithuanian nationalists surrounded the TV tower, and Soviet troops killed a dozen people shooting their way in.

Information as a Tool against Governments

Information can be used against governments as well, by foreign governments or by domestic political opponents.[24] Some governments fear the free flow of information, for good reason. When they are allowed to circulate among a population, ideas become a powerful force that can sweep aside governments, as when the idea of democracy swept away the white-rule system of apartheid in South Africa in the early 1990s. New information technologies have become powerful tools of domestic opposition movements and their allies in foreign governments. Television coverage fed popular discontent regarding the U.S. war in Vietnam in the 1960s and 1970s, and the Russian war in Chechnya in 1995. Television and film coverage of antiglobalization activists have made available some of their critiques of neoliberalism to people not active in the movement.

In Iran in the 1970s, the government was brought down in part by audiotapes containing speeches and sermons by Ayatollah Khomeini, who spoke against the inequalities and harsh repression of the pro-Western government of the Shah of Iran. Khomeini advocated a revolution to create an Islamic state. The power of his sermons could never have been captured in newspapers and pamphlets. In today's Iran, millions of people use the internet to talk about politics and other taboo subjects, though the Iranian government does try to filter some internet service providers. Similarly in China, people have increasing access to service providers, and an estimated 50 million Chinese use the internet. The Chinese government, however, has been accused of monitoring internet use and shutting down controversial sites. The governments of both China and Iran want the economic benefits of information on the internet, but still attempt to control some of that information. An important new area of research in IR explores government surveillance of internet use (see Citizen Lab under Weblinks at the end of this chapter).

In Thailand in 1992, military leaders lost power in what some Thais called "the cellular phone revolution." Students protesting against the military government were joined by newly affluent Thais with access to cellular phones and fax machines. When the government shot the demonstrators in the streets, arrested them, and cut off their phone lines, the protesters stayed organized by using mobile phones and fax machines. In the Philippines in 2001, huge protests that swept a president from office were organized through text messages on cell phones (sent to entire lists at a time). The phones are used

---

[24] Adam Jones, "Wired World: Communications Technology, Governance, and the Democratic Uprising," *The Global Political Economy of Communication: Hegemony, Telecommunication and the Information Economy*, ed. Edward A. Comor (NY: St. Martin's, 1994).

THE WHOLE WORLD IS WATCHING

States do not control the global flow of information, which has become a potent force in world politics. State leaders are becoming just another set of players in a worldwide competition to reach audiences and markets and to "spin" stories a certain way. For example, Israeli-Palestinian conflicts play out regionally and globally in the media, making the Palestinian issue a top priority even for citizens of Arab countries not materially affected by the conflict. This TV footage of a 12-year-old Palestinian being fatally shot as his father pleaded with Israeli soldiers to stop shooting, was replayed repeatedly on Arab TV and deepened anti-Israeli sentiment as the second Intifada (uprising) gathered steam in Palestine, September 2000.

by two million Filipinos, including some homeless people. The harsh military government in Burma (Myanmar) faced the power of shortwave radio broadcasts by the opposition movement, made using a transmitter owned by the government of Norway. In Ghana, very popular talk shows on private FM radio programs—allowed after 1995—gave voice to ordinary people who then threw out the ruling party in 2000. Organizers of the global antiwar demonstrations preceding the invasion of Iraq in 2003 used information technology to turn out millions of people in dozens of countries on short notice. One U.S. group (moveon.org) used a website to schedule protester's phone calls to their Congressional representatives every minute of the day, the kind of coordinated action that would have required a large staff and budget in the past (moveon.org had a staff of four).[25]

To counteract such uses of information, governments throughout the world try to limit the flow of unfavourable information—especially information from foreign sources. For example, China and several other developing countries have channelled all access to the internet (and the World Wide Web) through a few state-controlled service providers This system lets the government monitor and control who can have access to the mass of information available through the internet.[26] During and after the 1989 Tiananmen protests, before the internet was a factor, the Chinese government tried desperately to suppress the flow of information into and out of China. It stationed police at every fax machine in the country to screen incoming faxes after foreigners in Hong Kong, North America, and Europe began faxing in reports of the shooting of hundreds of protesters in Beijing.

In an extreme case, the Soviet Union during the Cold War prohibited all but a few photocopy machines. Dissidents' writings were passed from hand to hand and recopied on

---

[25] Fathi Nazila and Erik Eckholm, "Taboo Surfing: Click Here for Iran ... and Click Here for China," *New York Times* 4 Aug. 2002. Philip Shenon, "Mobile Phones Primed, Affluent Thais Join Fray," *New York Times* 20 May 1992: A10. Uli Schmetzer, "Cellphones Spurred Filipinos' Coup," *Chicago Tribune* 22 Jan. 2001. Barbara Crossette, "Burmese Opposition Gets Oslo Radio Service," *New York Times* 19 July 1992: A11. Thomas L. Friedman, "Low-Tech Democracy," *New York Times* 1 May 2001: A27.

[26] Ron Deibert, "Dark Guests and Great Firewalls: Chinese Internet Security Policy," *Journal of Social Issues.* 58.1 (2001): 143–58.

typewriters. In 1987 the Soviet Union had only 16 international long-distance circuits in and out of the country, all routed through Moscow. This helped the government to reduce the influence of foreign ideas and to closely monitor foreigners—but at a huge cost in economic efficiency. When the Soviet Union broke up there were still only 91 circuits. A decade later Russia had 50 000.[27]

Efforts by one government to project power through media broadcasts often bring counter-efforts by other governments to block such broadcasts. The VOA, the BBC, and other foreign media were routinely jammed by the Soviet Union during the Cold War. But Soviet efforts to control information did not prevent collapse of that society. To the contrary, the effort to run a modern economy without photocopy machines, international phone lines, computers, and other information technologies clearly contributed to the economic stagnation of the country.

All in all, the tide of technology seems to be running against governments (though not all scholars would agree with this assessment). Information gets through, and no political power seems capable of holding it back for long. As more and more communication channels carry more information to more places, governments become just another player in a crowded field.

As the information revolution continues to unfold, it will further increase international interdependence, making actions in one state reverberate in other states more strongly than in the past. Information is thus slowly undermining the assumptions of state sovereignty and territorial integrity held dear by realists. At the same time, by empowering substate and transnational actors, information technology is undermining the centrality of states themselves in world affairs.

INTERNATIONAL CULTURE

As the information revolution increases the power and importance of transnational actors, it puts into motion two contradictory forces. One we have just discussed—the empowering of substate actors. This force was a factor in the disintegration of the Soviet Union and Yugoslavia. As substate groups gain power, they demand their own national rights of sovereignty and autonomy. Nationalism reasserts itself in smaller but more numerous units.

The second force, however, is the forging of transnational communities and supranational identities—a process alluded to earlier with reference to the EU. Here regionalism or globalism asserts itself as an internationalized culture resting on communication links among people in different states. This second force, perhaps more than the first, challenges the realist emphasis on national borders and territorial integrity.

Telecommunications and Global Culture

Not only can people in one part of the world communicate with those elsewhere, they can also now find common interests to talk about. Riding the telecommunications revolution, a **global culture** is beginning to develop, notwithstanding the great divisions remaining in culture and perspective (especially between the rich and poor regions of the world; see Chapter 11). In the global village, distance and borders matter less and less. Across dozens of countries, people are tuned in to the same news, the same music, the same sports

global culture Worldwide cultural integration based on a massive increase in satellite television, radio, and internet communication.

[27] Anthony Ramirez, "Dial Direct to Moscow and Beyond," *New York Times* 20 May 1992: D1. United States, *CIA World Factbook*, 2001.

events. Along with international politics, these activities now take place on a world stage with a world audience. The process might be seen as a form of cultural integration, similar to economic and technical integration.

Cultures, languages, and locations interact more quickly as the unfinished process of cultural integration proceeds. For example, in a rural town in Massachusetts, the local cable TV channel on weekends carries live news broadcasts from around the world (without translation), downloaded from a satellite consortium. One weekend, the Brazilian TV news on this broadcast included an ad for a U.S. film set in the Brazilian rain forest, dubbed in Portuguese. Information is bouncing around the world—Brazilian rain forest to Hollywood movie production to Brazilian movie theatres to Massachusetts cable TV. Such trends clearly undermine assumptions of state autonomy.

Ultimately, transnational cultural integration might lead to the emergence of supranational identities, including a global identity. If citizens in EU states can begin to think as Europeans, will citizens in UN member states someday begin to think as human beings and residents of Planet Earth? The answer is unclear. As we have seen, group identity is an important source of conflict between in-groups and out-groups (see "Ethnic Conflict" on pp. 173–178). Nationalism has tapped into the psychological dynamics of group identity in a powerful way that has legitimized the state as the ultimate embodiment of its people's aspirations and identity. Now the information revolution may aid the development of supranational identity. So far, nationalism continues to hold the upper hand. Global identity has not yet come to rival national identity in any state.

For a fleeting moment at the turn of the millennium such a global identity seemed almost possible. The feared "Y2K" computer bug, which would cause old software to think time had jumped back 100 years, was fixed in a massive technology upgrade that "leveraged the resources of the whole planet," in the words of an IBM executive. On December 31, 1999, as each time zone passed midnight, people around the world watched to see whether fears of computer failures, terrorist attacks, or riots would materialize. UN Secretary-General Annan said that "each city seemed to be rooting for cities in the next time zone to get through Y2K without any problems. It was like, 'O.K., Tokyo is through, now how about Beijing?' And then, 'Moscow is through, how about New York?' For one brief moment there was a pulling together all over the planet."[28] As the feared problems did not materialize, the world was left with a 24-hour moment of good feeling broadcast live on television stations like CNN and CBC and the internet.

Cultural Imperialism Like international integration generally, global culture has its down side. The emerging global culture is primarily the culture of white Europeans and their descendants in rich areas of the world (mixed slightly with cultural elements of Japan and local global South elites). For many people, especially in the global South, the information revolution carrying global culture into their midst is, despite its empowering potential, an invasive force in practice. Because cultures are being subsumed, half of the world's nearly 7000 languages risk extinction this century, according to UNESCO.

Above all, the emerging global culture is dominated by the world's superpower, the United States; this dominance has been referred to as **cultural imperialism.**[29] U.S. cultural influence is at least as strong as U.S. military influence. If there is a world language,

cultural imperialism A critical term for Western (especially U.S.) dominance of the emerging global culture.

---

[28] Thomas L. Friedman, "The Spirit of Y2K," *New York Times* 7 Jan. 2000.

[29] Richard Maxwell, *Culture Works: The Political Economy of Culture* (Minneapolis: U Minnesota P, 2001). Karin Gwinn Wilkins, *Redeveloping Communication for Social Change: Theory, Practice, Power* (Lanham, MD: Rowman & Littlefield, 2000). Thomas L. Friedman, *The Lexus and the Olive Tree* (NY: Farrar Straus & Giroux, 1999). Benjamin R. Barber, *Jihad vs. McWorld* (NY: Times Books, 1995). John Tomlinson, Cultural Imperialism: A Critical Introduction. Johns Hopkins, 1991.

it is English. If there is a "president of the world," it is more likely the U.S. president than the UN secretary-general.

U.S. films and TV shows dominate world markets. For instance, U.S. movies predominate in countries from Europe to Asia to Latin America (although top music titles, and most top TV shows, tend to be national, not American).[30] Culture may be just another economic product, to be produced in the place of greatest comparative advantage, but culture also is central to national identity and politics. France held up the GATT agreement in 1994 until it could protect its film industry from U.S. competition.

Industrialized countries have responded in various ways to U.S. cultural dominance. As discussed in Chapter 8, Canada has long resisted American cultural influence, but critics worry that Canada is more inundated than ever by American magazines, books, films, and television broadcasts. In English Canada, the most popular television shows and music are generally from the U.S. In some ways, Québec's efforts to maintain its cultural heritage vis-à-vis the rest of Canada, coupled with the difference in language, has permitted it more leverage to insulate itself from an overwhelming U.S. cultural influence. Québec television viewers are more likely to tune in to Radio-Canada for French-language programming than they are an American broadcast, and popular music fans regularly hear Québecois performers on local radio stations. By contrast, France has been especially wary of U.S. influence; commissions periodically try to weed English expressions out of the French language (not an easy task). However, Japan seemingly incorporated whole segments of U.S. culture after World War II, from baseball to hamburgers, yet retained distinctively Japanese cultural practices as well.

Global culture and cultural imperialism shape the news that is reported by the TV, radio, and print media. To an increasing extent, everyone in the world follows the same story line of world news from day to day. To some extent, there is now a single drama unfolding at the global level, and the day's top international story on CNN very likely will also be reported by Canadian television networks, the national TV news in France, Japan, Russia, and most other states, and the world's radio and print media. The fact that everyone is following the same story reflects the globalizing influence of world communications. Cultural imperialism is reflected in the fact that the story often revolves around U.S. actions, reflects U.S. values, or is reported by U.S. reporters and news organizations. The attack on Iraq in 1991 illustrates in the extreme how the whole world watches one story—a story shaped by U.S. perspectives. When the bombing of Baghdad began, Saddam Hussein reportedly sat in his bunker watching the war unfold on CNN.

Transnational Communities

Although a global culture is both nascent and, in some ways, problematic, people have begun to participate in specific communities that bridge national boundaries. International journalists, for example, are members of such a community. They work with colleagues from various countries and travel from state to state with each other. Though a journalist's identity *as* a journalist rarely takes precedence over his or her national identity, the existence of the transnational community of journalists creates a new form of international interdependence. Part of that interdependence results from their shared vulnerability covering news stories that states or other groups or organizations do not wish to become public. In some cases journalists risk imprisonment, persecution and death in the course of their work. In Canada, the Canadian Journalists for Free Expression make annual

---

[30] Philip Shenon, "Indonesian Films Squeezed Out by U.S. Giant," *New York Times* 29 Oct. 1992: A17. "The Media Business: What Is Playing in the Global Village?" *New York Times* 26 May 1997: D4–D5.

awards to journalists from around the world who have faced such persecution, and also lobby on behalf of imprisoned journalists.

Like journalists, scientists and church members work in communities spanning national borders. So do members of transnational movements, such as those linking women from various countries, or environmentalists, or human rights activists. The effect once again is to undermine the state's role as the primary actor in international affairs. More important, the links forged in such transnational communities may create a new functionalism that could encourage international integration on a global scale.

International sports competition is one of the broadest-based transnational communities, especially strong at the regional level. Millions of fans watch their teams compete with teams from other countries. Of course, international sports competition can stir up animosities between neighbours, as when English soccer hooligans rampage through another European country after their team loses a game. But sports also create a sense of participation in a supranational community. This is especially true of world-level sports events in which a global athletic community participates. The Olympic Games (sponsored by the International Olympic Committee, an NGO) are a global event broadcast to a worldwide audience.[31] Some people, in particular liberal pluralists, view sports as a force for peace. Sports events bring people from different countries together in shared activities. Citizens of different states share their admiration of sports stars, who become international celebrities.

By contrast, critical theorists argue that competitive sport is a lucrative multibillion dollar industry with established corporate links to institutions like the IOC. By this view, the IOC is a closed institution that makes decisions behind closed doors and has been mired in controversy in recent years, as a result of payoffs to members of the IOC by host cities, its failure to adequately address the use of performance-enhancing drugs, and judging scandals such as occurred in figure skating competitions against Canadian athletes in 2002. Rather than bring people together, Olympic games have usually been preceded by a sweep of homeless people in host cities, and in some cases, cities have been bankrupted after staging the games.[32]

Most communication over the world's broadcasting networks is neither news nor sports, but drama—soap operas, films, situation comedies, documentaries, and so forth. Here U.S. cultural imperialism is particularly strong, because so many films and TV shows watched around the world originate in Hollywood (home of the U.S. movie industry). The entertainment industry is a strong export sector of the U.S. economy. Large global South countries such as Brazil and India have concentrated their TV production efforts in an area where local contexts can gain viewers' interest and where production costs are modest— soap operas. They are immensely popular in these and other global South countries.

The popularity of Brazilian soap operas notwithstanding, many international viewers see less of their own experiences than of dramas set in the United States. These dramas, of course, give a distorted view of U.S. life, such as the impression that all Americans are rich. Recall that "deconstruction" of such TV shows, according to postmodernists, reveals hidden political subtexts (see pp. 118–120).

Both live performances and recordings of music have become increasingly internationalized. In the world of classical music, a great conductor or violinist can roam the world in search of great orchestras and appreciative audiences, with almost complete dis-

[31] Christopher R. Hill, *Olympic Politics* (Manchester, UK: Manchester UP, 1992). Lincoln Allison, *The Changing Politics of Sports* (NY: St. Martin's, 1993). John Bale and Joseph McGuire, eds., *The Global Sports Arena: Athletic Talent Migration in an Interdependent World* (Ilford, UK: Cass, 1994). Hugh Dauncey and Geoff Hare, eds., *France and the 1998 World Cup: The National Impact of a World Sporting Event* (Ilford, UK: Cass, 1999).

[32] Varda Burstyn, *The Rites of Men: Manhood, Politics and the Culture of Sport* (Toronto: U Toronto P, 1999).

regard for national borders. International tours are a central element in rock music and jazz as well. Some genres of music are essentially more international than national, spanning several continents and explicitly global in outlook. Even highly specialized national music forms—such as Bulgarian chants or Mongolian throat singing—are gaining worldwide audiences. It is significant that people who cannot understand each other's languages can understand each other's music.

Advertising is crucial to the emerging international culture. Advertising links the transnational products and services of MNCs with the transnational performances and works of actors, athletes, and artists. Most global broadcasts and performances—from the Olympic Games to reruns of *Dallas*—are paid for by advertising. Advertising often carries subtle (or not so subtle) messages about culture, race, gender roles, and other themes. In Europe and Japan, international advertising may contain a subtext of U.S. superiority. In Eastern Europe and Russia, the advertising of products from Europe, Japan, and the United States may imply the superiority of the West, whereas in the global South advertising may promote the values of the industrialized world over local and native cultures. For example, ads for cosmetics may portray stereotypical images of white Euro-American women as the ideal of beauty, even on billboards or TV shows in Asia or Latin America.

Finally, tourism also builds transnational communities, and is also controversial.[33] International tourists cross borders 500 million times a year. Tourism ranks among the top export industries worldwide. People who travel to other countries often develop both a deeper understanding and a deeper appreciation for them. Person-to-person contacts and friendships maintained across borders make it harder for nationalism to succeed in promoting either war or protectionism. For example, a Canadian citizen who has visited Japan may be more likely to favour expanded Canada-Japanese trade; a Greek who has visited Turkey and made friends there may be more likely to oppose a Greek-Turkish military confrontation. At the same time, tourism can distort economies, and depends

MAC ATTACK
Some call it "global community;" others, "cultural imperialism." The power of information, opening up a wave of globalization in international business, is bringing together cultures in sometimes incongruous ways. Chinese leaders seemed unsure for years about whether McDonald's brought Western-style prosperity or spiritual pollution—maybe a bit of each.

in part on presentations of places (and peoples) as "exotic." It can also direct scarce resources into tourism rather than serving direct developmental needs. After a UN peacekeeping mission to Cambodia in the early 1990s, for example, foreign investors poured capital into Cambodia to build hotels and casinos but there was little available to support de-mining operations, or to build hospitals or schools.

The internet now allows transnational dialogues to take place at a global level. The World Wide Web allows people to move seamlessly from site to site around the world. Significantly, the Web creates organizing structures and communities that can be almost totally divorced from physical location, bringing together people with common cultural or economic interest from anywhere in the world. In the 1990s, the Web quickly gained acceptance as a key infrastructure for business, and increasingly for governments (which

[33] Patricia Goldstone, *Making the World Safe for Tourism* (New Haven, CT: Yale UP, 2001).

control country-coded domain names). This textbook's Companion Website at **http://www .pearsoned.ca/goldstein** contains resources such as practice tests not included in the book.

The transnational connections forged by various communities—sports, music, tourism, and so forth—deepen the international interdependence that links the well-being of one state to that of other states. This may promote peace, because a person who knows more about a foreign country and has developed empathy for its culture is likely to reject political conflict with that country and support positive cooperation with it. But they also raise troubling questions about the way, for example, sport and tourism are integrated into the global political economy.

Furthermore, as the internet wires parts of the world into a tight network centred on the United States, other regions are largely left out. Poor countries and poor people cannot afford computers—the equivalent of eight years' wages for a typical Bangladeshi, for example. Users of the World Wide Web in 2001 made up 26 percent of the population in the United States, 7 percent in Russia, and 1 percent in South Asia, the Middle East, and Africa. In Canada, 73 percent of Canadian adults have internet access from at least one location.[34] The worldwide community of web users in 2001 was 40 percent North American, with Europeans and Asia-Pacific splitting most of the remainder. English is the language of a strong majority of websites worldwide, even though non-English speakers now make up a slight majority of web users. Even the architecture of cyberspace assumes the United States as the default in such domain names as .gov (U.S. government), .mil (U.S. military), and .edu (U.S. universities). Elsewhere on the web, domain names signal country of origin, such as .ca in Canada. Just from 1999 to 2001, internet users increased from 150 million to 400 million worldwide (with China going from 7 million to 16 million). This explosive growth is mainly occurring among the richest strata of the world's people, however.[35]

Some activists hope that the internet can transform poor villages in the global South, partly by letting them produce traditional goods locally and market them globally. The UN ECOSOC (see p. 267) hopes to place an internet computer within a mile of most of the world's villages, to be funded by US$1 billion in hoped-for contributions (that seem unlikely to materialize in full).

A model project in Cambodia in 2001 helped revive a village silk-weaving industry by marketing locally made scarves on a village website. However, critics noted that the project was feasible only because a satellite company owned by the Thai prime minister donated US$18 000 per year of link time. A U.S. aid organization provided the computers, training, website design, and credit-card processing required to sell scarves from the village. The reality is that most poor villages cannot afford the internet, cannot read the language of most websites, and cannot maintain computers and websites without extensive training.[36]

The internet in many ways empowers small fringe groups relative to states, and leaves states vulnerable in new ways. Hackers have taken over control of government computers (155 times in the U.S. in 2000) and have unleashed costly viruses against businesses and people worldwide.

These cyberattacks by small-scale actors may target foreign countries. Thousands of Israeli teenagers attacked websites in the Arab world, and Arab hackers knocked out Israeli sites in return, during the violent "Intifada II" of fall 2000. During the U.S.-China "spy plane" standoff in 2001, nationalistic Chinese hackers claimed to have put pro-Chinese

---

[34] Ispos-Reid data (2003).

[35] United Nations Development Program, *Human Development Report 1999* (NY: United Nations, 1999).

[36] Rajiv Chandrasekaran, "Cambodian Village Wired to Future," *Washington Post,* 13 May 2001: A1.

graffiti on 1000 U.S. websites, and U.S. hackers returned the favour. After September 11, however, the U.S. government worried that real terrorists could use the internet to cause massive disruptions in U.S. economic life. The Al Qaeda network had already used the internet extensively to help coordinate its worldwide operations.[37]

These supranational cultural influences are still in their infancy. Over the coming years and decades their shape will become clearer, and scholars will be able to determine more accurately how they are influencing world politics and state sovereignty. We need not wait as long to see the effects of a different kind of supranational influence, however. Issues of North-South development both transcend national borders, and lead to activism and the development of policies that are necessarily supranational. These issues occupy Chapter 11.

The Information Revolution
World Wide Web

The internet-based World Wide Web grew explosively in the late 1990s, becoming a ubiquitous element in corporate and cultural life, as well as increasingly a business venue. Will the web create new transnational communities and interest groups that redraw international politics by empowering non-state actors?

To explore this question, go to www.pearsoned.ca/goldstein.

Thinking Critically

1. Functional economic ties among European states have contributed to the emergence of a supranational political structure, the EU, which has considerable though not unlimited power. Do you think the same thing could happen in North America? Could the U.S.-Canadian-Mexican NAFTA develop into a future North American Union like the EU? What problems would it be likely to face?

2. Suppose you happened to be chatting with the president of the European Commission, who is complaining about the public reaction in European states against the growing power of the commission's Eurocrats. What advice would you give? What steps could the commission take to calm such fears without reversing the process of integration? How would your suggestions address the resentments that many European citizens or governments feel against Brussels?

3. Suppose the government of Turkey hired you as a consultant to help it develop a presentation to the EU about why Turkey should be admitted as a member. What arguments would you propose using? What kinds of rebuttals might you expect from the present EU members? How would you recommend responding?

4. Information technologies are strengthening transnational and supranational communications and identity. However, they are also providing states with new instruments of power and control. Which aspect do you find predominant now? Are these new capabilities helpful or harmful to state governments? Why? Do you expect your answer will change in the future, as technology continues to develop?

5. What are the good and bad effects, in your opinion, of the emergence of global communications and culture? Should we be cheering or lamenting the possibility of one world culture? Does the answer depend on where one lives in the world? Give concrete examples of the effects you discuss.

---

[37] Lee Hockstader, "Pings and E-Arrows Fly in Mideast Cyber-War," *Washington Post* 27 Oct. 2000: A1. Ariana Eunjung Cha, "Chinese Suspected of Hacking U.S. Sites," *Washington Post* 13 April 2001: A13.

Chapter Summary

- Supranational processes bring states together in larger structures and identities. These processes generally lead to an ongoing struggle between nationalism and supranationalism.

- International integration—the partial shifting of sovereignty from the state toward supranational institutions—is considered an outgrowth of international cooperation in functional (technical and economic) issue areas.

- Integration theorists thought that functional cooperation would spill over into political integration in foreign policy and military issue areas. Instead, powerful forces of disintegration are tearing apart previously existing states in some regions (especially in the former Soviet Union and Yugoslavia).

- The European Union (EU) is the most advanced case of integration. Its 25 member states have given considerable power to the EU in economic decision making and 12 have adopted a common currency, the euro. However, national power still outweighs supranational power even in the EU.

- Since the founding of the European Coal and Steel Community (ECSC) in 1952, the mission and membership of what is now the EU have expanded continually.

- The most important and most successful element in the EU is its customs union (and the associated free trade area). Goods can cross borders of member states freely, and the members adopt unified tariffs with regard to goods entering from outside the EU.

- Under the EU's Common Agricultural Policy (CAP), subsidies to farmers are made uniform within the community. Carrying out the CAP consumes two-thirds of the EU's budget. EU agricultural subsidies are a major source of trade conflict with the United States.

- The EU has a new monetary union with a single European currency (the euro) in 12 of the 25 EU states. It is the biggest experiment with money in history. Such a union requires roughly comparable inflation rates and financial stability in participating states.

- In structure, the EU revolves around the permanent staff of "Eurocrats" under the European Commission. The commission's president, individual members, and staff all serve Europe as a whole—a supranational role. However, the Council of the European Union (also called by its former name, the Council of Ministers) representing member states (in national roles) has power over the commission.

- The European Parliament has members directly elected by citizens in EU states, but it has few powers and cannot legislate the rules for the community. The European Court of Justice also has limited powers, but has extended its jurisdiction more successfully than any other international court, and can overrule national laws.

- The Single European Act, or "Europe 1992," created a common market throughout the EU, with uniform standards, open borders, and freedom of goods, services, labour, and capital within the EU.

- The 1991 Maastricht Treaty on closer European integration (monetary union and political-military coordination) provoked a public backlash in several countries. Some citizens began to resent the power of EU bureaucrats over national culture and daily life. The treaty was ratified despite these difficulties, however.

- The EU took in three new members in 1995—Austria, Finland, and Sweden—but Norwegians voted not to join. Ten others, mostly in Eastern Europe, joined in 2004. The EU faces challenges in deciding how far to expand its membership. To some extent the broadening of membership conflicts with the deepening of ties among the existing members.

- In addition to the EU and the associated European Free Trade Association (EFTA), there are a variety of overlapping groupings, formal and informal, that reflect the process of integration in Europe.

- There has been some discussion in Canada about a currency union with the United States, called a North American Monetary Union; such a union is much debated within Canada, and though its proponents describe it as inevitable, no political party has officially endorsed the idea

- A different type of international integration can be seen in the growing role of communication and information operating across national borders. Supranational relationships and identities are being fostered by new information technologies—especially mass media such as TV, radio, and the internet—although such a process is still in an early stage.

- Greater access to information increases government power both domestically and internationally. Governments also use the dissemination of information across borders as a means of influencing other states. Thus information technologies can serve national and not just supranational purposes.

- Government access to information increases the stability of international relationships. The security dilemma and other collective goods problems are made less difficult in a transparent world where governments have information about each others' actions.

- The greater and freer flow of information around the world can undermine the authority and power of governments as well. It is now extremely difficult for authoritarian governments to limit the flow of information in and out of their states. Information technologies can empower ordinary citizens and contribute to transnational and supranational structures that bypass the state.

- Telecommunications are contributing to the development of global cultural integration. This process may hold the potential for the development of a single world culture. However, some people worry about cultural imperialism—that such a culture would be too strongly dominated by the United States.

- Transnational communities are developing in areas such as sports, music, and tourism, but these too are problematic. Sports, for example, is a multibillion dollar industry with strong corporate ties.

Key Terms

supranationalism   368
international integration   369
neofunctionalism   370
security community   370
European Union (EU)   371
Treaty of Rome   373
Euratom   373
free trade area   373
customs union   373
common market   373
Common Agricultural Policy (CAP)   373

European Commission   375
Council of the European Union   375
European Parliament   376
European Court of Justice   376
Single European Act   377
Maastricht Treaty   377
euro   379
North American Monetary Union (NAMU)   383
global culture   393
cultural imperialism   394

Weblinks

The following are a sampling of some of the world's regional organizations and research centres involved in media, specifically the internet and world politics:

African Union:
http://www.africa-union.org

Association of South East Asian Nations (ASEAN):
http://www.aseansec.org/home.htm

Citizen Lab, at the Munk Centre for International Studies, University of Toronto:
http://www.citizenlab.org

The Economic Community of West African States (ECOWAS):
http://www.ecowas.int

The European Union (EU):
http://europa.eu.int

Organization of American States (OAS):
http://www.oas.org

POVERTY

THEORIES OF ACCUMULATION
Economic Accumulation
Capitalism
Socialism
Economic Classes

IMPERIALISM
The Globalization of Class
The World-System
European Colonialism
Anti-Imperialism
Postcolonial Dependency

THE STATE OF THE SOUTH
Basic Human Needs

World Hunger
Rural and Urban Populations
Women in Development
Migration and Refugees

REVOLUTION
Revolutionary Movements
Islamic Revolutions
Postrevolutionary Governments

Ethiopian refugees, 2000.

POVERTY

This and the following chapter concern the world's poor regions—the global South—where most people live. States in these regions are called by various names: Third World countries, less-developed countries (LDCs), *underdeveloped countries* (UDCs), or **developing countries.**[1] This chapter discusses the gap in wealth between the industrialized regions, mostly located in the North, and the global South. Chapter 12 discusses international aspects of economic development in the South.

Poverty can be viewed from several theoretical perspectives. IR scholars do not all agree on the causes or implications of poverty, or on solutions (if any) to the problem. Thus, they also disagree about the nature of relations between rich and poor states (North-South relations).[2] Everyone agrees, however, that much of the global South is extremely poor.[3]

developing countries
States in the global South, the poorest regions of the world—also called Third World countries, less-developed countries, and undeveloped countries.

[1] Larry A. Swatuk and Timothy M. Shaw, eds., *The South at the End of the Twentieth Century: Rethinking the Political Economy of Foreign Policy in Africa, Asia, the Caribbean and Latin America* (NY: St. Martin's, 1994). Manochehr Dorraj, ed., *The Changing Political Economy of the Third World* (Boulder, CO: Rienner, 1995).

[2] Sarah Owen and Paris Yeros, eds., *Poverty in World Politics: Whose Global Era?* (NY: St. Martin's, 1999). Stephan Haggard, ed., *The International Political Economy and the Developing Countries* (Brookfield, VT: Elgar, 1994). Zaven N. Davidian, *Economic Disparities among Nations: A Threat to Survival in a Globalized World* (NY: Oxford UP, 1994). Mitchell A. Seligson and John T. Passe-Smith, eds., *Development and Underdevelopment: The Political Economy of Inequality.* (Boulder, CO: Rienner, 1993). Robert O. Slater, Barry M. Schutz, and Steven R. Dorr, eds., *Global Transformation and the Third World* (Boulder, CO: Rienner, 1993). Frances Stewart, *North-South and South-South: Essays on International Economics* (NY: St. Martin's, 1991).

[3] UN Development Program, *Human Development Report* (NY: Oxford UP, annual). World Bank, *World Development Report* (NY: Oxford UP, annual).

Such poverty is difficult for North Americans to grasp. It is abject poverty; the extreme on the scale is starvation. As conveyed in pictures from places such as Somalia and Sudan, starvation is dramatic and horrible. Starvation is generally caused by war or extreme drought or both. In most places, people who die from poverty do not starve but succumb to diseases after being weakened by malnutrition. A lack of adequate quality of nutrition kills many more people than outright starvation does—but less dramatically because people die in many locations day in and day out rather than all at once in one place. Hunger and malnutrition are sometimes caused by war but more often by other factors that displace people from farmable land to cities, where many are unable to find other income (see "World Hunger" later in this chapter).

People who die from malnutrition do not die because of a lack of food in the world, or usually even a lack of food in their own state, but because they cannot *afford* to buy food. Likewise, people lack water, shelter, health care, and other necessities because they cannot afford them. The widespread, grinding poverty of people who cannot afford necessities is more important than the dramatic examples of starvation triggered by war or drought, because chronic poverty affects many more people.

Of all the world's people, about half are without adequate supplies of safe drinking water. About half live in substandard housing or are homeless altogether. About a third are malnourished, and one in seven is chronically undernourished (unable to maintain body weight). Nearly half are illiterate, and 99 percent do not have a university education. Multiplied by six billion people, these percentages add up to a staggering number of extremely poor people.

DIRT POOR
Nearly a billion people in the global South live in abject poverty; the majority lack such basic needs as safe water, housing, food, and the ability to read. China still contains large areas of impoverished countryside, despite rapid economic development in the coastal cities. Here, a peasant moves dirt in a Chinese village where the average income is below $100 per year, 1997.

Globalization in the 1990s increased the gap between the world's richest and poorest countries. The number of people living on less than $1 per day—about 1.2 billion—has grown since the mid-1980s. The greatest setbacks have been in Africa, where 29 of the 34 lowest-ranked countries are located, and where the AIDS epidemic is worsening a bad situation (see pp. 521–523). Dozens of countries are worse off than 20 years ago, even while other countries in the South rise gradually out of poverty.[4] Environmental disasters linked to deforestation, climate change, and urbanization have also contributed to the dire situation of the poorest countries in recent years, driving 25 million people from their homes in 1998, for example. The El Niño weather shift triggered drought in Indonesia, ultimately leading to both massive forest fires and food riots.[5]

Globalization has sharpened inequality within both the North and the South, as well as between the North and the South. As North America and Western Europe enjoy unprecedented prosperity, incomes in Russia and Eastern Europe have shrunk by about half. As China and parts of Southeast Asia, along with much of Latin America, climb gradually out of poverty, much of Africa slips further into it. In the global South as a whole, some trends, such as environmental degradation, are alarming, while others, such as reduced warfare and slow reductions in hunger, are encouraging. Clearly, globalization creates both winners and losers, with the world's poorest billion people mostly among the losers.

In all, about a billion people live in utter, abject poverty, without access to basic nutrition or health care. They are concentrated in the densely populated states of South Asia and in Africa.[6] The average income per person in South Asia—home to nearly two billion people—is only $2050 per year, and in Africa less than $1300 (even after adjusting for the lower costs of living in these regions compared to richer ones). In fact, half of all people globally have incomes of less than $2 a day.[7]

If these statistics are difficult to digest, consider the bottom line. Every five seconds, somewhere in the world, a child dies as a result of malnutrition. That is 700 every hour, 16 000 every day, 6 million every year. The world produces enough food to nourish these children and enough income to afford to nourish them, but their own families or states do not have enough income. They die, ultimately, from poverty. Consider that in the same five seconds in which another child dies this way, the world spends US$125 000 on military forces. A thousandth of that amount could save the child's life. This reality shadows the moral and political debates about North-South relations.

THEORIES OF ACCUMULATION

How do we explain the enormous gap between income levels in the world's industrialized regions and those in the global South? What are the implications of that gap for international politics? There are several very different approaches to these questions; we will concentrate on two contrasting theories of wealth accumulation, based on more liberal and more critical world views.

---

[4] United Nations Development Program, *Human Development Report 1999* (NY: United Nations, 1999). Paul Lewis, "World Bank Says Poverty Is Increasing," *New York Times* 3 June 1999: C7.

[5] International Committee of the Red Cross, *World Disasters Report 1999* (Geneva: Red Cross, 1999).

[6] Thomas M. Callaghy and John Ravenhill, eds., *Hemmed In: Responses to Africa's Economic Decline* (NY: Columbia UP, 1993). David L. Lindauer and Michael Roemer, eds., *Asia and Africa: Legacies and Opportunities in Development* (San Francisco: ICS, 1994).

[7] United Nations, *Human Development Report 1996* (NY: United Nations, 1996).

Economic Accumulation

A view of the problem from the perspective of capitalism is based on economic liberalism—stressing overall efficiency in maximizing *economic growth*. This view sees the global South as merely lagging behind the industrialized North. More wealth creation in the North is a good thing, as is wealth creation in the South—the two are not in conflict.

A more critical view is concerned with the distribution of wealth as much as the absolute creation of wealth. It sees the creation of wealth in the North most often coming at the expense of the South. Advocates of a socialist perspective would give politics (the state) more of a role in redistributing wealth and managing the economy than does capitalism. Socialism thus parallels mercantilism in some ways. But socialists see economic classes rather than states as the main actors in the political bargaining over the distribution of the world's wealth. And mercantilism promotes the idea of concentrating wealth (as a power element), whereas socialism promotes the broader distribution of wealth.

For socialists, and other critical scholars of development studies, international exchange is shaped by capitalists' exploitation of cheap labour and cheap resources—using states to help create the political conditions for this exploitation. (Some focus on workers in countries of the global South, some on workers in richer industrialized countries, and some on both.) Thus, whereas mercantilists see political interests (of the state) as driving economic policies, socialists see economic interests (of capitalists and of workers) as driving political policies.

capital accumulation The creation of standing wealth (capital) such as buildings, roads, factories, and so forth; such accumulation depends on investment and the creation of an economic surplus.

economic surplus Made by investing money in productive capital rather than using it for consumption.

Economic development is based on **capital accumulation**—the creation of standing wealth (capital) such as buildings, roads, factories, and so forth. In order for human populations and their capital to grow, they must produce an **economic surplus** by using capital to produce more capital. This is done by investing money in productive capital rather than using it for consumption. The more surplus an economy produces, the more resources are available for investment above the minimum level of consumption needed to sustain human life.

Early human societies had a very simple stock of capital—mostly clothes and hand tools—and produced little surplus. Then came the discovery of agriculture about 10 000 years ago. A group of people could produce a surplus—more grain than they could eat—decade after decade. The extra grain could feed specialists who made tools from metals, built houses, and constructed irrigation works. Ever since, the human species has been on an uninterrupted growth cycle based on economic surplus. More and more wealth has accumulated, and the human population has grown larger and larger.

The Industrial Revolution of several centuries ago greatly accelerated the process of world accumulation, drawing on large amounts of energy from fossil fuels. But industrialization has occurred very unevenly across the world regions. The North has accumulated vast capital. Though the South produces spurts of wealth and has pockets of accumulation, in most areas it remains a preindustrial economy—the reason why the North consumes nearly 10 times as much commercial energy per person as the South does (see Table 13.1 on p. 509).

Information technology now is making a fuel-burning infrastructure relatively less important in the advanced economies. The countries of the global South may need to pass through a phase of heavy industrialization, as countries in the North did, or perhaps they can develop economically along different paths, using new technology from the start. The problem is that, just as industrial infrastructure is located mostly in the North, so is the world's information infrastructure (see pp. 387–388). While a generation of students in industrialized countries go online, poorer countries still struggle to extend literacy to rural populations.

Nonetheless, neither the absolute size of GDP nor its size relative to other countries indicates whether a national economy is growing or shrinking. Accumulation, or profit, in a national economy corresponds with the *economic growth rate*. States that operate profitably grow from year to year; those that operate at a loss shrink. (GDP and related concepts refer here to real values after adjusting for inflation.)

A state's economic growth rate does not indicate how much wealth it has accumulated in the past. In recent years, countries like Canada have grown only slowly—even shrinking a bit at times of recession (see "The Position of Canada" on p. 349). But Canada has a considerable amount of standing wealth amassed over the previous 150 years. By contrast, Mexico may have stronger economic growth, but because it does not have the accumulated wealth it still lags far behind in total wealth. On a global scale, the South will continue to lag behind the North in GDP (income), even if its economic growth rate continues to be higher than the North's, as it has been in the last few years. The concentration of surplus in the world economy—in the North—tends to be self-reinforcing for

The Information Revolution
Sharpening Disparities?

The concentration of surplus tends to be self-reinforcing: the rich get richer. The information revolution is no exception, in that richer countries and individuals tend to have much greater access to information technologies than do poorer ones. Will the information revolution give the industrialized West more power than ever, and increase the North-South gap in wealth?

To explore this question, go to www.pearsoned.ca/goldstein.

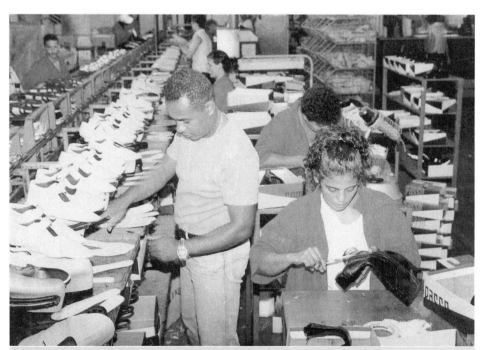

LOW-TECH
Production in the global South uses relatively little capital and much labour (at low wages), reflecting an early stage of industrialization. To develop economically, poor countries must generate self-sustaining capital accumulation. Shoes and textiles, as here in Pakistan (2002), are classic export products from the global South, relatively low-capital and labour-intensive.

two reasons. First, concentrating wealth allows it to be invested more efficiently, which generates more wealth. Second, the more wealth is concentrated, the more power its own- ers gain. With 60 percent of the world's wealth, the North dominates world politics. Because critical theorists see a conflict of interest between rich and poor, they see the North's political power as oppressive to the South.

Ultimately, the distribution of the benefits of world accumulation is an issue for inter- national bargaining, just as the distribution of benefits from trade is (see Chapter 8, pp. 295–297). In the bargaining between rich and poor regions over the process of world accumulation, the two sides have very unequal power.[8]

Capitalism

Earlier chapters referred to capital in a general way as standing wealth. More precisely, *cap- ital* is the set of goods that are used in producing other goods. Thus, a warehouse full of refined tin is capital, as is a tin can or a canning factory—all these goods go into produc- ing further goods. But a stamp collection, a set of Lego toys, and a pleasure boat are not capital in this sense, even though they have value; they are **consumption goods.** Their consumption does not contribute directly to the production of other goods and services.

A cycle of accumulation depends on capital goods more than consumption goods. Mines, factories, oil refineries, railroads, and similar goods contribute directly to the cycle of surplus production by which more factories and oil refineries are produced.

Investment competes with consumption. Forgoing consumption for investment is another case where short-term costs produce long-term benefits (as in aspects of trade, environmental, and population policies).

Capitalism is a system of *private ownership of capital* that relies on market forces to govern distribution of goods. Under capitalism, the cycle of accumulation is largely con- trolled by private individuals and companies. When a surplus is produced, it is profit for the owners of the capital that produced the surplus (after taxes). Private ownership encourages reinvestment of surplus because private individuals and companies seek to maximize their wealth. The concentration of capital ownership in few hands also allows investment to be shifted easily from less productive sectors and technologies to more pro- ductive ones. Capitalism concentrates wealth, promoting efficient and rapid accumula- tion; it does not seek an equitable distribution of benefits.

In reality, no state is purely capitalist. Almost all have some form of mixed economy that includes both private and state ownership.[9] Also, in most capitalist countries the government balances the inhuman side of capitalism by redistributing some wealth down- ward (and regulating capitalists). A "welfare state" provides education, certain health benefits, welfare for the poor, and so forth. The post–World War II period was one of a vastly expanding welfare state in many countries of the global North. However, scholars who examine capitalism in industrialized states now tend to focus on erosions in welfare state provisions, especially over the last two decades.

The principles of capitalism underlie the global economy, with its great disparities of wealth. The concentration of capital in the global North furthers the development of global trade, of technology, and of reinvestment for maximum profit (overall growth). The private ownership of companies and of currency makes international markets oper- ate more efficiently. Capital can be moved around from less productive to more productive

consumption goods Goods whose consumption does not contribute directly to pro- duction of other goods and services, unlike some forms of investment.

investment Putting surplus wealth into capital-producing activities rather than consum- ing it, to produce long-term benefits.

capitalism An economic sys- tem based on private owner- ship of capital and the means of production (standing wealth and other forms of property). See also *socialism*.

---

[8] David A. Lake, "Power and the Third World: Toward a Realist Political Economy of North-South Relations" [review article], *International Studies Quarterly* 31.2 (1987): 217–34.

[9] John R. Freeman, *Democracy and Markets: The Politics of Mixed Economies* (Ithaca, NY: Cornell UP, 1989).

countries and economic sectors. If wealth were distributed equally across world regions, these efficiencies might be lost and world economic growth might be slower.

Socialism

Socialism—the idea that workers should have political power—favours the *redistribution of wealth* toward the workers who produce that wealth. Because such redistribution does not happen naturally under capitalism, socialism generally endorses the use of the state for this purpose. It favours *governmental planning* to manage a national economy rather than leaving such management entirely to market forces. Often, socialists advocate *state ownership* of capital, rather than private ownership, so that the accumulation of wealth is controlled by the state, which can distribute it equitably.

Socialism includes many political movements, parties, and ideologies, both historical and present-day. In Canada, the New Democratic Party has its roots in social democratic politics, and has held power in some provincial governments and held the balance of power in a number of minority governments at the federal level. Elsewhere in the global North, socialist or social democratic parties have also held important roles in recent years as governing parties (Britain, France), parts of governing coalitions (Germany, Japan), or main opposition parties (Russia). In the global South, where great poverty and disparities of wealth make the idea of redistributing wealth popular, most revolutionaries and many reformers consider themselves socialists of some sort.

Communist governments, including in China (and the former Soviet Union), base their political philosophy on socialism as well. In practice, however, they tend to extract wealth toward the centre and have thus been called a form of state capitalism. For example, in the Soviet Union under Stalin in the 1930s there was a tremendous concentration of capital, which allowed rapid industrialization but starved millions of people. This took place under dictatorial political control rather than workers' control. The term *democratic socialism* in part emerged out of a critique of policies like those of Stalin, and advocates instead the economic principles of socialism joined to democratic rather than authoritarian political principles.

Marxism is a theoretical and political approach that views capitalism as exploitative and advocates forms of governance based on socialism and communism. (Not all socialists, however, are Marxist.) In the mid-nineteenth century, *Karl Marx* emphasized labour as the source of economic surplus. At that time, the Industrial Revolution was accompanied by particular hardship among industrial workers (including children) in Europe. Marxists still believe that the surplus created by labour should be recaptured by workers through political struggle. Today, Marxism is most influential in countries where capital is scarce and labour conditions are wretched, most particularly in the global South. Some of the differences among Marxists and socialists focus on how political and economic transformation will be accomplished. For most Marxists, capitalism contains within itself the seeds of its own destruction—the transition to socialism and then communism is, in a sense, inevitable. For other Marxists, and many socialists, the transition will need to be achieved through other means, for example by capturing state power and adopting policies that are socialist in principle and purpose.

Like capitalism, socialism does not exist anywhere in a pure form. There is an element of socialism in mixed economies. China now calls its economic system "market socialism"—a combination of continuing state ownership of many large industries, capitalism at the local level, and openness to international investment and trade.

Some socialist theories argue that state ownership of industry increases efficiency by avoiding problems that arise from the fragmentation of decision-making under capitalism.

socialism A term encompassing many political movements, parties, economic theories, and ideologies, historical and present-day. With its idea that workers should have political power (or a larger share of power), socialism favours the redistribution of wealth toward the workers who produce it. In economic policy, socialists have favoured different combinations of planning and reliance on market forces, as well as various patterns of ownership.

Marxism A theoretical and political approach that views capitalism as exploitative and emphasizes class struggle; includes both socialism and communism and other approaches to social transformation.

In theory, central planners are supposed to use resources in a rational way that maximizes overall efficiency. But after decades of experimentation, it is clear that whatever its benefits in equity, state ownership is not very efficient. State planners who set quotas for production at each factory cannot adjust to economic conditions as efficiently as market-based prices can. State ownership is still promoted in many countries in order to redistribute wealth, to coordinate development of key industries, or to maintain self-sufficiency in military production—but not because it is more efficient in general.

Russia and Eastern European states are now in a difficult transition to market economies because of the failure of centrally planned economies. Many countries are also moving to sell off large state-owned industries—*privatization*—in hopes of increasing growth. Phone companies, oil companies, railroads—all are going on the auction block. This is happening a great deal in countries of the global South, but also in countries such as Canada, where some provinces have moved to privatize hydro companies and the federal government has sold off its interests in some companies, such as Petro-Canada.

Privatization has gone quickly in several Eastern European and former Soviet republics, where the state owned virtually the whole economy during decades of communism. Before Czechoslovakia split in two, citizens received coupons representing a small bit of stock in state-owned companies. They could sell the coupons for cash or invest them in any of several new mutual funds established by entrepreneurs. The mutual fund managers pooled the coupons and bought up state-owned companies they thought would be profitable. Lured by promises of large profits, most Czechoslovak citizens as new capitalists invested in this way. But when a similar scheme was tried in Russia, citizens weary from economic depression did not put much value in the coupons. Many Russians invested in a leading mutual fund that promised high profits but then went bankrupt.

Thus, in the region of Russia and Eastern Europe, communism had collapsed under the weight of inefficiency, but the beginning stages of capitalism were even more inefficient, leading to a reduction of economic activity by roughly half over several years. Some countries, including Russia, slowed the pace of reforms in response, while reformists argued that what was needed was a speedup to get through the transition. Some countries democratically threw out the reformers and brought back the old communist leaders. In coming years, it is likely that the various experiments being tried by the different countries of Eastern Europe and the former Soviet Union will sort themselves out, making clearer the best routes of transition for former communist economies.

In any event, the collapse of Soviet communism has closed the books on a historic experiment in one type of socialism that failed—old-style **Stalinism** as articulated and practised by *Joseph Stalin*, which was marked by totalitarian state control under the Communist party. But the failures of state-owned enterprises do not mean that socialism is dead. Rather, other types of socialism are now more salient. And new mixes of socialism and capitalism are being created.

Economic Classes

Socialists and Marxists argue that IR and domestic politics alike are structured by unequal relationships between **economic classes.** (This emphasis on classes denies the realist dichotomy between domestic and international politics.) The more powerful classes oppress and exploit the less powerful by denying them their fair share of the surplus they create. The oppressed classes try to gain power, in order to seize more of the wealth for themselves. This process, called **class struggle,** is one way of looking at the political relationships between richer and poorer people, and between richer and poorer world regions.

Stalinism The system that prevailed during Stalin's rule in the Soviet Union (1924–1953), which was marked by totalitarian state control under the Communist party and the ruthless elimination of the regime's opponents on a massive scale.

economic class A categorization of individuals based on economic status (which for Marxists is determined by one's relationship to the means of production, for example, as either owners of capital or workers).

class struggle The process in which the more powerful classes oppress and exploit the less powerful by denying them their fair share of the surplus they create, and the oppressed classes try to gain power, to rebel, and to organize in order to seize more of the economic surplus for themselves.

RICH AND POOR
Disparity of wealth is a central aspect of global North-South relations. Marxists see international relations and domestic politics alike as being shaped by a class struggle between the rich and poor. In Sao Paulo, Brazil, rich and poor neighbourhoods sit side by side.

Marx used a particular language to describe the different classes in an industrial economy. The **bourgeoisie** is the class of owners of capital—people who make money from their investments rather than from their labour. Under capitalism they are also the ruling class (sometimes in concert with politicians, military officers, or other powerful allies). The *petty bourgeoisie* are small-time owners of capital, such as shopkeepers. They tend to think like owners and to identify with the bourgeoisie. *Intellectuals* (including university professors and students) are treated ambiguously in most Marxist analyses; they often see the world from the perspective of the rich, yet they sometimes are radicalized and side with the oppressed.

The **proletariat**—industrial factory workers—are considered potentially the most powerful class because their labour is necessary for the production of surplus. They are supposed to lead the revolution against the bourgeoisie. But factories have changed since the time of Marx: they are more capital-intensive, and workers in them are better paid. Various Marxist theories try to come to terms with these changes. Marxists also do not agree on how to categorize increasingly important classes such as technical workers and managers. Some Marxist theorists describe them as a class unto themselves (a technical managerial class). The class of economically unproductive people at the bottom of society is the *lumpenproletariat*—prisoners, criminals, drug addicts, and so forth. They are so down-and-out that they seldom become effective political revolutionaries.

One very important class in revolutions during the past century (contrary to Marxist expectations) has been *peasants*.[10] Marxists traditionally consider peasants backward,

bourgeoisie In Marxist terminology, the class of owners of capital—people who make money from their investments rather than from their labour.

proletariat In Marxist terminology, the class of workers who must sell their labour power to capitalists in order to survive and whose labour is needed to produce surplus value; more specifically, industrial factory workers. It was considered the class that would spearhead the socialist revolution.

[10] Barrington Moore, *Social Origins of Dictatorship and Democracy: Lord and Peasant in the Making of the Modern World* (1966; Boston: Beacon, 1993). James C. Scott, *Weapons of the Weak: Everyday Forms of Peasant Resistance* (New Haven, CT: Yale UP, 1986).

ignorant, individualistic, and politically passive as compared to the well-educated and class-conscious proletariat. But in practice the successful revolutions of the global South have been primarily peasant rebellions (often led by Marxists talking about the proletariat). The largest was the Chinese revolution in the 1930s and 1940s.

According to Marxism, capitalism is just one stage of social evolution, preceded by feudalism and followed by socialism (when workers seize the state and use it to redistribute wealth) and eventually by communism (when everyone would be equal and the state would wither away). Each stage has its own forms of politics and culture, which make up society's **superstructure.** This superstructure is shaped by the **economic base** of society—its mode of production, such as slavery, feudalism, or capitalism.

superstructure In Marxist terminology, the forms of politics and culture that are shaped by the economic base or mode of production (slavery, feudalism, capitalism).

economic base A society's mode of production, such as slavery, feudalism, or capitalism.

In their particulars, Marxist analyses have been insightful about the operation and effect of capitalist relations of production, though not always successful in their predictions about the stages of social development, about class alliances, and about the results of revolutions. Marxist revolutions have occurred in many states of the global South, and Marxism (along with other forms of socialism) remains a force in development and North-South relations.

IMPERIALISM

Marx's theories of class struggle were oriented toward *domestic* society in the industrializing countries of his time, not toward poor countries or international relations. Traditional Marxists looked to the advanced industrialized countries for revolution and socialism, which would grow out of capitalism. In their view, the global South would have to develop through its own stages of accumulation from feudalism to capitalism before taking the revolutionary step to socialism. What actually happened was the opposite. Proletarian workers in industrialized countries enjoyed rising standards of living and did not make revolutions. Meanwhile, in the less-developed global South, oppressed workers and peasants have staged a series of revolutions, successful and failed, over the past 90 years.

The Globalization of Class

Why did revolutions occur in less-developed rather than industrialized countries? The answer largely shapes how one sees North-South relations today.[11] Marxists have mostly (but not exclusively) followed a line of argument developed by V. I. *Lenin*, founder of the Soviet Union, before the Russian Revolution of 1917.[12] Russia was then a relatively backward state, and most Marxists considered a revolution there unlikely (looking instead to Germany).

imperialism The acquisition of colonies by conquest or otherwise. Lenin's theory of imperialism argued that European capitalists were investing in colonies where they could earn big profits, and then using part of those profits to buy off portions of the working class at home.

Lenin's theory of **imperialism** argued that European capitalists were investing in colonies where they could earn big profits and then using part of these to *buy off* the working class at home. The only limit Lenin saw was that after the scramble for colonies in the 1890s, few areas of the world were left to be colonized. Imperialist expansion could occur only at the expense of other imperialist states, leading to inter-imperialist competition and wars, such as World War I. Seizing on Russia's weakness during that war, Lenin led the first successful communist revolution there in 1917.

---

[11] Anthony Brewer, *Marxist Theories of Imperialism: A Critical Survey* (Boston: Routledge, 1980). Vendulka Kubálková and Albert Cruickshank, *Marxism and International Relations* (Oxford: Clarendon, 1985).

[12] V. I. Lenin, "Imperialism the Highest Stage of Capitalism," *Essential Works of Lenin* (1916; (NY: Bantam, 1966) 177–270.

Lenin's general idea still shapes a major approach to North-South relations—the idea that industrialized states exploit poor countries (through both formal and informal colonization) and buy off their own working classes with the profits. Through this *globalization of class relations*, world accumulation concentrates surplus toward the rich parts of the world and away from the poor ones. Revolutions, then, would be expected in poor regions.

Many revolutionaries of the global South have sought to break loose from exploitation by the European colonizers. After European colonization ended, the United States as the world's richest country (with large investments in the global South and a global military presence) became the target of revolutionaries agitating against exploitation in poor countries. In a number of countries, imperialists were thrown out (often violently, sometimes not) and revolutionary nationalists took power.

One of the most important such revolutions was in China, where Mao Zedong's communists took power in 1949 on a Leninist platform adapted to the largely peasant-based movement they led. Mao declared that "China has stood up"—on its own feet, throwing off foreign domination and foreign exploitation. In India at the same time, the movement led by Gandhi used a different means (nonviolence) to achieve similar ends—national independence from colonialism. Indonesia threw out the Dutch. Lebanon threw out the French. Cuba threw out the Americans. This pattern was repeated, with variations, in dozens of countries.

According to the revolutionaries in these countries, exploitation of countries in the global South by rich countries takes away the economic surplus of the South and concentrates the accumulation of wealth toward the rich parts of the world. By breaking free of such exploitation, developing states can then retain their own surplus and begin to accumulate their own wealth. Eventually they can generate their own self-sustaining cycles of accumulation and lift themselves out of poverty.[13]

In reality such an approach has not worked well. A policy of autarky fosters growth for only a limited period of time, and then reaches a plateau (see p. 311). And within a single poor country, trade-offs arise between concentrating or distributing wealth. For former colonies, the realities of economic development after independence have been complex.

Not all Marxist approaches favour a policy of self-reliance after revolution. *Leon Trotsky*, a Russian revolutionary, believed that after the 1917 revolution Russia would never be able to build socialism alone and should make its top priority the spreading of revolution to other countries to build a worldwide alliance. Trotsky's archrival Stalin wanted to build "*socialism in one country*" and he prevailed (and had Trotsky killed).[14] Most revolutions since then, including China's, have had a strongly nationalist flavour.

The World-System

The global system of regional class divisions has been seen by some IR scholars as a **world-system** or a *capitalist world economy*.[15] This view is an elaboration of Marxist thinking

world-system theory
A view of the world in terms of regional class divisions, with industrialized countries as the *core*, poorest global South countries as the *periphery*, and other areas (for example, some of the newly industrializing countries) as the *semiperiphery*.

[13] J. Ann Tickner, *Self-Reliance Versus Power Politics* (NY: Columbia UP, 1987). Samir Amin, "Self-Reliance and the New International Economic Order," *Monthly Review* 29.3 (1977).

[14] Ernest Mandel, *From Stalinism to Eurocommunism: The Bitter Fruits of "Socialism in One Country"* trans. Jon Rothschild (London: NLB, 1978). Irving Howe, *Leon Trotsky* (NY: Viking, 1978).

[15] Immanuel Wallerstein, *The Modern World-System*, 3 vols. (NY: Academic, 1974, 1980, 1989). Samir Amin, Giovanni Arrighi, André Gunder Frank, and Immanuel Wallerstein, *Dynamics of Global Crisis* (NY: Monthly Review Press, 1982). André Gunder Frank, *World Accumulation, 1492–1789* (NY: Monthly Review Press, 1978). Sing C. Chew and Robert A. Denemark, eds., *The Underdevelopment of Development: Essays in Honor of André Gunder Frank* (Thousand Oaks, CA: Sage, 1996).

(focusing on economic classes) and relies on a global level of analysis. In the world-system, class divisions are regionalized. Regions of the global South mostly extract raw materials (including agriculture)—work that uses much labour and little capital, and pays low wages. Industrialized regions mostly manufacture goods—work that uses more capital, requires more skilled labour, and pays workers higher wages. The manufacturing regions are called the **core** (or *centre*) of the world-system; the extraction regions are called the **periphery.**

core The manufacturing regions of the world-system.

periphery The global South regions of the world-system that mostly extract raw materials from their area.

The most important class struggle today, in this view, is that between the core and the periphery of the world-system.[16] The core uses its power (derived from its wealth) to concentrate surplus from the periphery, as it has done for about 500 years. Conflicts among great powers, including the two world wars and the Cold War, basically result from competition among core states over the right to exploit the periphery.

The core and periphery are not sharply delineated. Within the periphery, there are also centres and peripheries (for instance, the city of Rio de Janeiro compared to the Amazon rain forest) as there are within the core (such as New York City compared to the Mississippi Delta or Toronto compared to the coastal towns and villages of Newfoundland). The whole global structure is one of overlapping hierarchies. The concentration of capital and the scale of wages each form a continuum rather than a sharp division into two categories.[17]

semiperiphery The area in the world-system in which some manufacturing occurs and some capital concentrates, but not to the extent of the core areas.

In world-system theory, the **semiperiphery** is an area in which some manufacturing occurs and some capital concentrates, but not to the extent of the most advanced areas in the core. Eastern Europe and Russia are commonly considered to be semiperipheral, as are some of the newly industrializing countries (see pp. 447–449), such as Taiwan and Singapore. The semiperiphery acts as a kind of political buffer between the core and periphery because poor states can aspire to join the semiperiphery instead of aspiring to rebel against domination by the core.

Over time, membership in the core, the semiperiphery, and the periphery changes somewhat, but the overall global system of class relations remains.[18] Areas that once were beyond the reach of Europeans, such as the interior of Latin America, become incorporated as periphery. Areas of the periphery can become semiperiphery and even join the core, as North America did. And core states can slip into the semiperiphery if they fall behind in accumulation, as Spain did in the late sixteenth to early seventeenth centuries. Because world-system theory provides only general concepts but not firm definitions of what constitutes the core, semiperiphery, and periphery, it is hard to say exactly which states belong to each category.[19]

The actual patterns of world trade support world-system theory to some extent. Table 11.1 shows the net exports (exports minus imports) of each world region for several types of goods. As the boxed numbers indicate, different regions specialize in exporting different kinds of goods. The core (industrialized West) exports US$82 billion more than

---

[16] Terry Boswell, ed., *Revolution in the World-System* (NY: Greenwood, 1989).

[17] Terry Boswell and Christopher Chase-Dunn, *The Spiral of Capitalism and Socialism: Toward Global Democracy* (Boulder, CO: Rienner, 1999). Christopher Chase-Dunn, *Global Formation: Structures of the World-Economy* (Cambridge, MA: Blackwell, 1989).

[18] Edward Friedman, ed., *Ascent and Decline in the World-System* (Beverly Hills, CA: Sage, 1982). James M. Goldgeier and Michael McFaul, "A Tale of Two Worlds: Core and Periphery in the Post–Cold War Era," *International Organization* 46.2 (1992): 467–92.

[19] William R. Thompson, ed., *Contending Approaches to World System Analysis* (Beverly Hills, CA: Sage, 1983). Terence K. Hopkins and Immanuel Wallerstein, *The Age of Transition: Trajectory of the World-System, 1945–2025* (London: Zed, 1996). Albert Bergesen, ed., *Studies of the Modern World-System* (NY: Academic, 1980).

Table 11.1 Commodity Structure of World Trade by Region
Net Exports (Exports Minus Imports) for 2001, in Billions of 2001 US Dollars

| Region[a] | Manufactured Goods | | Raw Materials | |
	Machinery/Chemicals[b]	Textiles	Agriculture and Minerals	Energy
North America/Western Europe/Japan	11	−116	−54	−250
Russia and Eastern Europe	−21	1	−4	34
Middle East	−104	6	−7	181
Latin America	−43	5	50	27
Asia[c]	229	117	3	−1
Africa	−13	0	12	10

[a] Regions do not exactly match those used elsewhere in this book. World total imports do not equal exports owing to discrepancies in data from national government.

[b] Machinery, metal manufactures, and chemicals.

[c] China, Taiwan, Hong Kong, and South Korea are here included in Asia.

Source: Calculated from data in United Nations. *World Economic and Social Survey 2003* (New York: United Nations, 2003) 285–88.

it imports in machinery, chemicals, and similar heavy manufactured goods. All the other regions import more than they export in such goods.

Asia—here including China, Taiwan, Hong Kong, and South Korea (but not Japan)—has a niche in light manufacturing including textile production; it exports US$96 billion more of these goods than it imports. Such a pattern fits the semiperiphery category.

The Middle East and Africa (including North Africa) specialize in exporting oil (net exports of energy are US$45 billion and US$9 billion, respectively). This is an extraction role typical of the periphery. Latin America has net exports of US$52 billion in food, agricultural products, and minerals—also typical of the periphery. These regions' patterns of specialization must be kept in perspective, however: all regions both import and export all these types of goods, and the net exports listed in the table amount to only a small part of the world's US$6 trillion in trade.

European Colonialism

For most countries of the global South, the history of having been colonized by Europeans is central to their national identity, foreign policy, and place in the world. For these states—and especially for those within them who favour socialist perspectives—international relations revolves around their asymmetrical power relationships with industrialized states. Economic liberal approaches tend to pay less attention to history and to focus on present-day problems in the South, such as unbalanced economies, unskilled work forces, and corrupt governments. Their focus, in other words, looks at problems *internal* to Southern states to explain underdevelopment. More critical approaches look to more *global* and *historical* explanations. For critical approaches in particular, the North plays a central role in creating, maintaining, and perhaps someday helping to solve poverty in the South.

Today's global disparities did not exist until a few centuries ago. Eight hundred years ago there were a variety of relatively autonomous, independent civilizations in the world, none of which held power over each other—the Sung dynasty in China, the Arab empire in the Middle East, the Aztecs and Incas in Central America, the African kingdoms near present-day Nigeria, the shoguns in Japan, Genghis Khan's society in Siberia, and the feudal society of Europe (see pp. 22–25).

Europe between the twelfth and fifteenth centuries saw the rise of capitalism, a merchant class, science, and stronger states. Technological improvements in agriculture, industry, and the military gave Europe an edge over other world civilizations for the first time. European states conquered and colonized different world regions at different times (see "Imperialism, 1500–the Present" on pp. 28–29). Decolonization in some regions (such as the United States in 1776) overlapped with new colonizing in other regions.[20] But most of the world's territory was colonized by Europe at one time or another (see Figure 11.1).

Decolonization occurred only 25 to 50 years ago in most of Asia, Africa, and the Middle East. In Asia, the most important British colony was India (which included today's Pakistan and Bangladesh). Hong Kong was until 1997 a British colony serving as the gateway to China. British possessions also included Malaysia, Singapore, New Guinea, Australia, New Zealand, and others. Almost all the Asian colonies became independent around the time of World War II and the two decades afterward.

In Africa, European colonizers included Portugal, the Netherlands, Britain, France, Belgium, Germany, and Italy. In the late nineteenth century, European states rushed to grab colonies there (with France and Britain gaining the most territory). Africa then became a patchwork collection of colonies without coherent ethnic or geographic foundations.

The Middle East came under European influence as the Ottoman Empire disintegrated in the late nineteenth and early twentieth centuries—and as oil became a key fuel. Britain and France were most prominent there as well. Present-day Israel and Jordan were British-run until 1948. Syria and Lebanon were French. Iraq's claims on Kuwait stem from Britain's creation of Kuwait as an independent territory. The Arab-Israeli conflict also is strongly influenced by the history of British rule.

European conquerors treated their colonies as possessions that could be traded, seized as booty in wars, or given as mandates to new rulers. For instance, the island of Guam in the Pacific was once Spanish territory, then German, then Japanese, and then American.

Being colonized has a devastating effect on a people and culture. Foreigners overrun a territory with force and take it over. They install their own government, staffed by their own nationals. The inhabitants are forced to speak the language of the colonizers, to adopt their cultural and religious practices, and to be educated at schools run under their guidance. The inhabitants are told that they are inherently, racially inferior to the foreigners.

White Europeans in the colonies of Africa and Asia were greatly outnumbered by native inhabitants but maintained power by a combination of force and (more important) psychological conditioning. After generations under colonialism, most native inhabitants either saw white domination as normal or believed that nothing could be done about it. This is another way in which the Gramscian notion of hegemony (see p. 80) was exercised. The whites often lived in a "bubble world" separated from the lives of the local inhabitants.

Colonialism also had negative *economic* implications. The most easily accessible minerals were dug up and shipped away. The best farmland was planted in export crops rather than subsistence crops, and was sometimes overworked and eroded. The infrastructure that was built served the purposes of imperialism rather than the local population—for instance, railroads going straight from mining areas to ports. The education and skills needed to run the economy were largely limited to whites. As a result, when colonies attained independence

---

[20] David Strang, "Global Patterns of Decolonization, 1500–1987," *International Studies Quarterly* 35.4 (1991): 429–54.

Figure 11.1 Conquest of the World
Former colonial territories of European states.

B = British   **G** = German   **N** = Netherlands

Belg = Belgian   **I** = Italian   **P** = Portuguese

F = French   **J** = Japanese   **S** = Spanish

and many of the whites departed, what remained was an undereducated population with a distorted economic structure and valuable natural resources depleted.

For economic liberals, the economic effects were not all negative. Colonialism often fostered local economic accumulation (although controlled by whites). Cities grew. Mines were dug and farms established. It was in the colonial administration's interest to foster local cycles of capital accumulation. Much of the infrastructure that exists today in many countries of the global South was created by colonizers. In some cases, colonization combined disparate communities into a cohesive political unit with a common religion, language, and culture, thus creating more opportunities for economic accumulation. In some cases, the local political cultures replaced by colonialism were themselves oppressive to the majority of the people. So, for economic liberals, colonialism established important economic infrastructure. Critical theorists see little positive coming out of colonialism. Mining and large-scale agriculture, for example, usually resulted in environmental degradation and massive displacement of local peoples.

Anti-Imperialism

Wherever there were colonizers, there were anti-colonial movements. Independence movements throughout Africa and Asia gained momentum during and after World War II, when the European powers were weakened. Through the 1960s, a wave of successful independence movements swept from one country to the next, as people stopped accepting imperialism as normal or inevitable (see Figure 11.2 on African decolonization).

MY DOLL, MY SELF?
European colonialism worldwide promoted values and norms implying that the colonizer's culture was superior to the indigenous culture. Lingering effects remain in postcolonial societies. Here, mixed-race girls play with a European-featured doll, Lima, Peru, 1992.

Figure 11.2 Areas of White Minority Rule in Africa, 1952–1994

Formal colonialism was swept away over 40 years. However, postcolonial dependency lingers on in many former colonies.

Source: Adapted from Andrew Boyd, *An Atlas of World Affairs,* 9th ed. (NY: Routledge, 1992) 91.

Although many colonized countries gained independence around the same time, the methods by which they did so varied. In India, the most important colony of the largest empire (Britain), Gandhi led a movement based on nonviolent resistance to British rule (see "Nonviolence" on pp. 106–107). However, nonviolence broke down in the subsequent Hindu-Muslim civil war, which split India into two states—India mostly with Hindus, and Pakistan (including what is now Bangladesh) mostly with Muslims.

Some colonies—for example, Algeria and Vietnam—won independence through warfare to oust their European colonizers; others won it peacefully by negotiating a transfer of power with weary Europeans. In Algeria, France abandoned its colonial claims in 1962 only after fighting a bitter guerrilla war. Some colonial liberation movements fought guerrilla wars based on communist ideology. The Viet Minh, for instance, defeated the French occupiers in 1954 and established communist rule in all of Vietnam by 1975 after its war with the United States.

Across the various methods and ideologies of liberation movements in the global South, one common feature was reliance on nationalism for strong popular support. Nationalism was only one idea that these movements took from Europe and used to undermine European control; others included democracy, freedom, progress, and Marxism. Leaders of liberation movements often had gone to European universities. Under European control many states also developed infrastructures, educational and religious institutions, health care, and military forces on the European model. Europe's conquest of the global South thus contributed tools to undo their conquest.[21]

Postcolonial Dependency

If imperialism concentrated the accumulation of wealth in the core and drained economic surplus from the periphery, one might expect that accumulation in the South would take off once colonialism was overthrown. Generally this has not been the case. A few states, such as Singapore, have accumulated capital successfully since becoming independent. But others, including many African states, seem to be slipping even further behind, with little new capital accumulating to replace the old colonial infrastructure. Most former colonies are making only slow progress in accumulation. Political independence has not been a cure-all for poor countries.

---

[21] Geoffrey Barraclough, *An Introduction to Contemporary History* (NY: Penguin, 1964), chap. 6.

One reason for these problems is that under colonialism the training and experience needed to manage the economy were often limited to white Europeans. A few native inhabitants went to Europe for university training, but most factory managers, doctors, bankers, and so forth were whites. Often the white Europeans fled the country at the time of independence, leaving a huge gap in technical and administrative skills.

Another problem faced by newly independent states was that, as colonies, their economies had been narrowly developed to serve the needs of the European home country. Many of these economies rested on the export of one or two primary products, called commodity concentration. For Zambia, it was copper ore; for El Salvador, coffee; for Botswana, diamonds; and so forth.

Such a narrow export economy would seem well suited to use the state's comparative advantage to specialize in one niche of the world economy. But it leaves the state vulnerable to price fluctuations on world markets. Given North-South disparity in power, the raw materials exported by developing countries do not tend to receive high prices (oil, from the mid-1970s to the mid-1980s, was an exception). The liberal free trade regime based around the WTO corrected only partially for the North's superior bargaining position in North-South trade. And the GATT/WTO has allowed agriculture (exported by the periphery) to remain protected in core states (see pp. 326–327).

It is not easy to restructure an economy away from the export of a few commodities. Nor do state leaders generally want to do so, because the leaders benefit from the imports that can be bought with hard currency (including weapons). In any case, coffee plantations and copper mines take time and capital to create, and they represent capital accumulation—they cannot just be abandoned. In addition, local inhabitants' skills and training are likely to be concentrated in the existing industries. Furthermore, infrastructure such as railroads most likely was set up to serve the export economy. For instance, in Angola and Namibia the major railroads lead from mining or plantation districts to ports (see Figure 11.3). Political borders also may follow lines dictated by colonial economies. For example, an Angolan enclave (surrounded by Democratic Republic of the Congo) contains the area's most profitable oil wells. A South African enclave, surrounded by Namibia, controls the best port in the area.

The newly independent states inherited borders that were drawn in European capitals by foreign officers looking at maps. As a result, especially in Africa, the internal rivalries of ethnic groups and regions made it very difficult for the new states to implement coherent economic plans. In a number of cases, ethnic conflicts within countries of the global South contributed to civil wars, which halted or reversed capital accumulation.

In quite a few cases, the newly independent countries of Africa were little more than puppet governments serving their former colonizers. According to a recent memoir by a

Figure 11.3 Borders, Railroads, and Resources in Angola and Namibia

Despite the independence of Angola and Namibia, colonial times shaped the borders and infrastructure in the region.

French official, France in the 1960s punished and even helped assassinate African leaders who opposed French policies. Those supporting France gave France open-ended permission for military intervention. French officials auditioned a potential president of Gabon before allowing him to take office, and the self-declared emperor of the Central African Republic (later accused of cannibalism) called President de Gaulle of France "Papa."[22]

Finally, governments of many postcolonial states did not function very effectively, creating another obstacle to accumulation. In some cases, corruption became much worse after independence (see "Corruption" on pp. 462–464). In other cases, governments tried to impose central control and planning on their national economy, based on nationalism, mercantilism, or socialism.

In sum, liberation from colonial control did not change underlying economic realities. The main trading partners of newly independent countries were usually their former colonizers. The main products were usually those developed under colonialism. The administrative units and territorial borders were those created by Europeans. The state continued to occupy the same peripheral position in the world-system after independence as it had before. And in some cases it continued to rely on its former colonizer for security.

For these reasons, the period after independence is sometimes called **neocolonialism**—the continuation of colonial exploitation without formal political control (see p. 28). This concept also covers the relationship of the global South with the United States, which (with a few exceptions) was not a formal colonizer. And it covers the North-South international relations of Latin American states, independent for almost two centuries.

neocolonialism The continuation, in a former colony, of colonial exploitation without formal political control.

Dependency Marxist IR scholars have developed **dependency theory** to explain the lack of accumulation in the global South.[23] They noticed that after World War II, Latin American states seemed on the verge of self-sustaining growth, in which a country's own capital would produce goods for its own markets. But this did not happen. These scholars define dependency as a situation where accumulation of capital cannot sustain itself internally. A dependent country must borrow capital to produce goods; their debt payments then reduce the accumulation of surplus. (Dependency is a form of international interdependence—rich regions need to loan out their money just as poor ones need to borrow it—but it is an interdependence with an extreme power imbalance.)

dependency theory A Marxist-oriented theory that explains the lack of capital accumulation in the global South as a result of the interplay between domestic class relations and the forces of foreign capital.

Dependency theorists focus not on the overall structure of the world-system (core and periphery) but on how a peripheral state's own internal class relationships play out. The development (or lack of development) of a state depends on its local conditions and history, though it is affected by the same global conditions as other countries located in the periphery. Recall that within the global South there are local centres and local peripheries. There are capitalists and a national government within the state in addition to the external forces such as MNCs and governments of industrialized countries. These various forces can take on different configurations.

One historically important configuration of dependency is the **enclave economy,** in which foreign capital is invested in a country to extract a particular raw material in a particular place—usually a mine, oil well, or plantation. Here the cycle of capital accumulation is primed by foreign capital, is fuelled by local resources, and completes itself with the

enclave economy An historically important form of dependency in which foreign capital is invested in a global South country to extract a particular raw material in a particular place—usually a mine, oil well, or plantation.

---

[22] Howard W. French, "French Held the Strings in Africa," *New York Times*, 28 Feb. 1995: A14.

[23] Fernando Henrique Cardoso and Enzo Faletto, *Dependency and Development in Latin America*, trans. Marjory Mattingly Urquidi (Berkeley: U California P, 1979). Robert A. Packenham, *The Dependency Movement: Scholarship and Politics in Dependency Studies* (Cambridge, MA: Harvard UP, 1992). Mary Ann Tétreault and Charles Frederick Abel, eds., *Dependency Theory and the Return of High Politics* (NY: Greenwood, 1986). James Painter, *Bolivia and Coca: A Study in Dependency* (Boulder, CO: Rienner, 1994). Peter Evans, *Dependent Development: The Alliance of Multinational, State, and Local Capital in Brazil* (Princeton, NJ: Princeton UP, 1979).

sale of products on foreign markets. Such an arrangement leaves the country's economy largely untouched except to give employment to a few local workers in the enclave and to provide taxes to the state (or line the pockets of some state officials). Over time, it leaves the state's natural resources depleted.

Angola's Cabinda province, located up the coast from the rest of Angola, is a classic enclave economy. Chevron pumps oil from a large field of offshore wells, with the money going to Angolan government officials who spend some on weapons for the civil war there and pocket large sums in flagrant acts of corruption. The people of Cabinda, aside from a tiny number who work for Chevron, live in poverty with crumbling infrastructure, few government services, few jobs, and recurrent banditry by unpaid soldiers. Inside the Chevron compound, however, U.S. workers drive on paved roads, eat American food, and enjoy an 18-hole golf course. They spend 28 days there, working 12-hour days, then fly back to the United States for 28 days of rest. Travelling the 19 kilometres to the airport by helicopter, the Americans rarely leave the fenced compound, which Chevron is believed to have surrounded with land mines.

 Thinking Theoretically

Let us return to the example of genocide in Rwanda in 1994. We have discussed the theory that ethnic groups develop in-group biases that can lead to dehumanization of a rival group. Conservative realists might even say that violence of this type between ethnic groups is inevitable and natural, if deplorable. Since these conflicts are driven by "ancient ethnic hatreds," there is little the international community can do about them. Similar arguments were used, as we saw earlier, to justify the international community's feeble response in Bosnia as well.

Critical approaches provide different perspectives on the violence in Rwanda, pointing us to different kinds of explanations and evidence. For starters, the position of a peripheral country such as Rwanda in the world-system can help explain violence and social upheaval there. Rwanda is one of the world's poorest countries, with a dense, fast-growing, and extremely poor population, more than 90 percent rural. Typically for a peripheral state, Rwanda's main exports are tea and coffee; it imports machinery, fuel, and other manufactured goods. But income from its exports pays less than half the costs of its imports. Before its recent troubles, the annual GDP was only US$1000 per person, and the land is depleted. Naturally such poverty drives a desperate struggle to survive.

Furthermore, dependency theories point to specific colonial histories as sources of explanation for the current problems of former colonies. Rwanda was colonized by Germany in the scramble for colonies by European powers at the end of the nineteenth century, and then grabbed by Belgium as Germany lost World War I. Although the minority Tutsi group (about 10 percent of the population) had ruled the majority Hutu group for several centuries before colonialism, it was under Belgian rule that large-scale Hutu violence against Tutsis first erupted.

It might be hypothesized that Belgium's interest would be to undermine the strongest political powers in a colony and support rival political forces that would be dependent on Belgium. Ultimately, among other things, keeping Rwanda down in this way could keep coffee prices low for Belgian consumers (who would then, according to Lenin's theory, live more comfortable lives and not make trouble for their bosses and politicians). In 1959, the Tutsi king and hundreds of thousands of Tutsis were driven into exile (from where they fought back for 35 years). Rwanda under Hutu rule was then granted independence from Belgium in 1962. In the following decade, the government repeatedly used massacres of Tutsis to respond to efforts of the Tutsi rebels in exile to return to power. As late as 1990, when Tutsi rebels advanced back into Rwanda, it was the Belgian army that showed up to save the Rwandan government—demonstrating the lasting nature of colonial ties. Ultimately, the government of Hutu extremists that perpetrated genocide against the Tutsis in 1994 must be understood in the context of Rwanda's colonial history. (This telling is of course highly simplified, but the point is that the colonial element, while not necessarily determinative of outcomes, must be a part of any useful explanation.)

A different historical pattern is that of nationally controlled production, in which a local capitalist class controls a cycle of accumulation based on producing export products. The cycle still depends on foreign markets, but the profits accrue to the local capitalists, building up a powerful class of rich owners within the country. This class—the local bourgeoisie—tends to behave in a manner consistent with the interests of rich industrialized countries (on whose markets the class depends). They are not unpatriotic, but their interests tend to converge with those of foreign capitalists. For instance, they want to keep local wages as low as possible, to produce cheap goods for consumers in the rich countries. The local capitalists, in alliance with political authorities, enforce a system of domination that ultimately serves the foreign capitalists. This is another form of dependency.

After World War II a third form of dependency became more common—penetration of national economies by MNCs. Here the capital is provided externally (as with enclaves), but production is for local markets. For instance, a GM factory in Brazil would produce cars mostly for sale within Brazil. To create local markets for such manufactured goods, income must be concentrated enough to create a middle class that can afford such goods. This sharpens disparities of income within the country (most people remain poor). The cycle of accumulation depends on local labour and local markets, but because MNCs provide the foreign capital they take out much of the surplus as profit.

According to dependency theory, the particular constellation of forces within a country determines which coalitions form among the state, the military, big landowners, local capitalists, foreign capitalists (MNCs), foreign governments, and middle classes such as professionals and skilled industrial workers. On the other side, peasants, workers, and sometimes students and the church, form alliances to work for more equal distribution of income, human and political rights, and local control of the economy. These class alliances and the resulting social relationships are not determined by any general rule but by concrete conditions and historical developments in each country. Like other Marxist theories, dependency theory pays special attention to class struggle as a source of social change.

Some people think that under conditions of dependency, economic development is almost impossible. Others think that development is possible under dependency, despite certain difficulties. We will return to these possibilities in Chapter 12.

THE STATE OF THE SOUTH

In the postcolonial era, some states of the global South have made progress toward accumulation; some have not. Some (though not all) are caught in a cycle of abject poverty. Until incomes rise, the population will not move through the demographic transition (see pp. 516–518); population growth will remain high and incomes low.

Basic Human Needs

In order to put accumulation on a firm foundation, and to move through the demographic transition, the **basic human needs** of most of the population must be met.[24] People need food, shelter, and other necessities of daily life in order to feel secure.

Children are central to meeting a population's basic needs. In particular, education allows a new generation to meet other basic needs and move through the demographic

basic human needs The fundamental needs of people for adequate food, shelter, health care, sanitation, and education. Meeting such needs may be thought of as both a moral imperative and a form of investment in "human capital" essential for economic growth.

[24] Paul Streeten et al., *First Things First: Meeting Basic Human Needs in the Development Countries* (NY: Oxford UP, 1981). Joshua S. Goldstein, "Basic Human Needs: The Plateau Curve," *World Development* 13 (1985): 595–609.

DO THE MATH
Children are a main focus of efforts to provide basic human needs in the global South. Education is critical to both economic development and the demographic transition. Girls worldwide receive less education than boys, and in Afghanistan under the Taliban, they were banned from schools altogether. This math class in Kandahar, Afghanistan, in 2002 followed the Taliban's fall.

transition.[25] Literacy—which UNESCO defines as the ability to read and write a simple sentence—is the key component of education. A person who can read and write can obtain a wealth of information about farming, health care, birth control, and so forth. Some countries of the global South have raised literacy rates substantially; others lag behind. Nearly half the adults in South Asia, Africa, and the Middle East are illiterate, compared with fewer than 10 percent in some middle-income developing countries, and fewer than 5 percent in the industrialized West.

There is also great variation in schooling. Primary school attendance is fairly high in most poor states, which bodes well for future literacy. Secondary education—middle and high school—is another matter. In the North, about 90 percent are enrolled, but in most of the South, fewer than half are enrolled. University is available to only a small fraction of the population.

Effective health care in poor countries is not expensive—just $4 per person per year for primary care. For instance, UNICEF has promoted four inexpensive methods that together are credited with saving the lives of millions of children each year. One method is growth monitoring. It is estimated that regular weighing and advice could prevent half of all cases of malnutrition. A second method is oral rehydration therapy (ORT), which stops diarrhea in children before they die from dehydration. A facility that produced 300 packets per day of the simple sugar-salt remedy, at a cost of 1.5 cents each, was built in Guatemala for just $550. Child deaths from diarrhea were cut in half in one year. The third method is immun-

---

[25] Abdun Noor, *Education and Basic Human Needs* (Washington, DC: World Bank, 1981).

ization against six common deadly diseases: measles, polio, tuberculosis, tetanus, whooping cough, and diphtheria. In the past 25 years, the number of children immunized in countries of the global South has risen from 5 percent to more than 50 percent.

The fourth method is the promotion of breast-feeding rather than the use of infant formula. Many mothers consider baby formula more modern and better for a baby—a view promoted at times by unethical MNCs eager to market formula to large countries of the global South. In the worst cases, salespeople dressed like nurses gave out free samples to new mothers. But once mothers started using formula, their own milk dried up and they had to continue with the costly formula, which is inferior to breast milk and can be dangerous when water supplies are unsafe and means of sterilization and refrigeration are lacking. After a consumer boycott of a well-known MNC (Nestlé), formula producers agreed in the 1980s to abide by WHO guidelines for selling formula in poor countries.

Globally, the disparities in access to health care are striking. The 75 percent of the world's people living in the South have about 30 percent of the world's doctors and nurses. In medical research, less than 5 percent of world expenditures are directed at problems in developing countries, according to the WHO. The biggest killers are acute respiratory infections, diarrhea, TB, malaria, and hepatitis. More than 600 million people are infected with tropical diseases—300 to 500 million with malaria alone. Yet, because the people with such diseases are poor, there is often not a large enough market for drug companies (MNCs) in the industrialized world to invest in medicines for them. And when poor countries need medicines developed for rich markets, the drugs may be prohibitively expensive—as with the AIDS drugs discussed in Chapter 13 (see pp. 522–523).

In one case, the U.S. Army created a lotion that can protect against infection by snail-borne worms that carry schistosomiasis, which the WHO considers the second-worst public health problem in the world. Soldiers who serve in tropical areas can now be protected, but the drug company that produces the lotion has no plans to make it available to ordinary people because the market cannot afford the product. In another case, a drug used against "river blindness" disease was profitably marketed by a drug company as a veterinary medicine in the North but was not profitable as a human medicine in the South. After the company began donating the drug, an international campaign gave it annually to 25 million people and largely eliminated river blindness in West Africa.[26]

Safe water is another essential element of meeting basic human needs. In many rural locations, people (usually women and girls) must walk kilometres every day to fetch water. Access to water is not running water in every house, but a clean well or faucet for a village. Unfortunately, many people in the global South lack such access—half or more of the population in India, Bangladesh, and Pakistan; two-thirds in Nigeria and Indonesia; one-quarter in relatively well-off Brazil and Mexico. Even among those with access to safe drinking water, many lack sanitation facilities (such as sewers and sanitary latrines). Half the world's population does not have access to sanitation, and as a result suffers from recurrent epidemics and widespread diarrhea, which kill millions of children each year.

For shelter, like water, the needs are minimal—safe structures that keep weather out and do not collapse on the inhabitants. It is taken for granted that large families live in a single room. Even so, in shantytowns shelter is inadequate and unsafe—especially in potential areas of earthquakes or hurricanes. Refugees from war also lack shelter unless they are able to reach a well-equipped refugee camp.

In theory, providing for basic needs should give poor people hope of progress and should ensure political stability. However, it is not always the result. In Sri Lanka, a

[26] *Science* 246, 8 Dec. 1989: 1242. David Brown, "Blindness Prevention Expanded in Africa," *Washington Post* 15 Dec. 2001: A24.

progressive-minded government implemented one of the world's most successful basic needs strategies, addressing nutrition, health care, and literacy. The policy showed that even a very poor country could meet basic needs at low levels of per capita income. Then a civil war broke out. The war became more and more brutal—with death squads and indiscriminate reprisals on civilians—until it consumed the progress Sri Lanka had made.

War in the global South—both international and civil war—is a leading obstacle to the provision of basic needs and political stability.[27] War causes much greater damage to society than merely the direct deaths and injuries it inflicts. In war zones, economic infrastructure such as transportation is disrupted, as are government services such as health care and education. Wars drastically reduce the confidence in economic and political stability on which investment and trade depend.

Almost all the wars of the past 40 years have taken place in the global South (see pp. 185–187). The shadow of war stretches from Central America through much of Africa, the Middle East, and South Asia. These wars may be the single greatest obstacle to economic development in the South. War is often part of a vicious circle for states unable to rise out of poverty. As of 2002, for example, the war in Sudan was the only obstacle to eradicating Guinea worm disease, which once afflicted millions worldwide but is now concentrated in Sudan.

There is a trade-off for most governments between spending funds on the military or on people. Many governments in the South import expensive weapons—whether because of real security conflicts with their neighbours, to put down internal challenges, or just as status symbols. These military forces are so expensive that even if they are never used they may deplete a state's ability to pursue basic needs and economic development. In the 1990s, despite these problems (and the HIV/AIDS epidemic), public health in the global South registered some important gains. Polio was nearly eliminated, infant tetanus deaths halved, and access to safe water extended to nearly a billion more people.[28]

World Hunger

malnutrition The lack of needed foods, including protein and vitamins; about 10 million children die each year from malnutrition-related causes.

undernourishment The lack of needed foods; a lack of calories.

Of all the basic needs of people in the global South, the most central is *food*. **Malnutrition** (or malnourishment) refers to the lack of needed foods, including protein and vitamins. The term *hunger* refers broadly to malnutrition or outright **undernourishment**—a lack of calories. Hunger does not usually kill people through outright starvation, but it weakens them and leaves them susceptible to infectious diseases that would not ordinarily be fatal.[29]

Some 820 million people—about one in eight worldwide—are chronically undernourished (see Table 11.2). Their potential contribution to economic accumulation is wasted because they cannot do even light work. They cannot forgo short-term consumption for long-term investment. And they are a potential source of political instability—including international instability—as long as they stay hungry. At a World Food Summit

[27] William J. Dixon and Bruce E. Moon, "Domestic Political Conflict and Basic Needs Outcomes: An Empirical Assessment," *Comparative Political Studies* 22.2 (1989): 178–98.

[28] Milton J. Esman and Ronald J. Herring, eds., *Carrots, Sticks and Ethnic Conflict: Rethinking Development Assistance* (Ann Arbor: U Michigan P, 2001). Caroline Thomas and Paikiasothy Saravanamuttu, eds., *Conflict and Consensus in South/North Security* (NY: Cambridge UP, 1989). Marc Lacey, "Sudan's War Bars Cure for Disease Eradicated in Other Parts of Africa," *New York Times* 10 March 2002. *New York Times* 9 May 2002: A8.

[29] Jean Dréze, Amartya Sen, and Athar Hussain, eds., *The Political Economy of Hunger: Selected Essays* (NY: Oxford UP, 1995). Vaclav Smil, *Feeding the World: A Challenge for the Twenty-First Century* (Boston, MA: MIT, 2000). Phillips Foster, *The World Food Problem: Tackling the Causes of Undernutrition in the Third World* (Boulder, CO: Rienner, 1992).

Table 11.2 Who's Hungry?
Chronically Undernourished People by Region, c. 2001

Region	Number (millions)	Percentage of Population	20 Years Earlier
Asia	500	16%	32%
Africa	200	33%	37%
Latin America	50	10%	13%
Middle East	40	10%	9%
Russia / E. Europe	30	8%	n.a.
Total World	820	13%	20%

Note: Data are from 1999–2001 and 1979–1981. Chronic undernourishment means failing to consume enough food on average over a year to maintain body weight and support light activity.

Source: Based on FAO. *The State of Food Insecurity in the World 2003* (Rome: FAO, 2003).

in 1996, world leaders adopted a goal to cut hunger in half by 2015. By 1999, with the number of undernourished people falling but only by 8 million a year and only in selected countries, the FAO stated that "there is no hope of meeting that goal."[30]

The world has the potential to produce enough food to feed all the world's people. The problem is not so much that there is an absolute shortage of food (though that condition does exist in some places) but that poor people do not have money to buy food.

Traditionally, rural communities have grown their own food—**subsistence farming.** Colonialism disrupted this pattern, and the disruption has continued in postcolonial times. States of the global South have shifted from subsistence to commercial agriculture, often at the insistence of international institutions such as the IMF or World Bank. Small plots have been merged into big plantations, often under the control of wealthy landlords. By concentrating capital and orienting the economy toward a niche in world trade, this process is consistent with liberal economics. But it displaces subsistence farmers from the land. Wars displace farmers even more quickly, with similar results.

subsistence farming Rural communities growing food mainly for their own consumption rather than for sale in local or world markets.

Commercial agriculture relies on machinery, commercial fuels, and artificial fertilizers and pesticides, which must be bought with cash and often must be imported. To pay for these supplies, big farms grow **cash crops**—agricultural goods produced for export to world markets.[31] Such crops typically provide little nutrition to local peasants; examples include coffee, tea, and sugar cane. When a plantation is built or expanded, subsistence farmers end up working in the plantation at very low wages or migrating to cities in search of jobs. Often they end up hungry.

cash crops Agricultural goods produced as commodities for export to world markets.

Many governments support commercial agriculture with loans, subsidies, irrigation projects, or technical help. This government support reflects both the political power of the big landowners and the government's ability to obtain hard-currency revenues from export crops, but not from subsistence crops.

---

[30] Food and Agriculture Organization, *The State of Food Insecurity in the World 1999* (Rome: FAO, 1999).

[31] David Barkin, Rosemary L. Batt, and Billie R. DeWatt, *Food Crops vs. Feed Crops: Global Substitution of Grains in Production* (Boulder, CO: Rienner, 1990).

[32] Peter Uvin, "Regime, Surplus, and Self-Interest: The International Politics of Food Aid," *International Studies Quarterly* 36.3 (1992): 293–312.

International food aid itself can sometimes contribute to these problems.[32] Agricultural assistance may favour mechanized commercial agriculture. And if an international agency floods an area with food, prices on local markets drop, which may force even more local farmers out of business and increase dependence on handouts from the government or international community. Also, people in a drought or famine often have to travel to feeding centres to receive the food, halting their work on their own land.

Rural and Urban Populations

urbanization A shift of population from the countryside to the cities that typically accompanies economic development and is augmented by displacement of peasants from *subsistence farming*.

The displacement of peasants from subsistence farming contributes to a massive population shift that typically accompanies the demographic transition. More and more people move to the cities from the countryside—**urbanization.** This is hard to measure exactly; there is no standard definition of when a town is considered a city. But industrialized states report that about 70 to 90 percent of their populations live in cities. By contrast, China is only 20 percent urbanized—a level typical of Asia and Africa. Most Middle Eastern states are a bit more urban (40 to 50 percent), and South American ones are 70 to 85 percent urban.

Urbanization is not caused by higher population growth in cities than in the countryside. In fact, the opposite is true. In cities, the people are generally better educated, with higher incomes. They are further along in the demographic transition, and have lower growth rates than people in the countryside. Rather, the growth of urban population is caused by people moving to the cities from the countryside. They do so because of the higher income levels in the cities—economic opportunity—and the hope of more chances for an exciting life. They also move because population growth in the countryside stretches available food, water, arable land, and other resources—or because they have been displaced from subsistence farming as land is turned to commercial cultivation, or have been displaced by war.

Capital accumulation is concentrated in cities. To some extent this makes urban dwellers more politically supportive of the status quo, especially if the city has a sizeable middle class. Governments extend their influence more readily to cities than to the countryside—Chinese government policies adopted in Beijing often have little bearing on village life. But urban dwellers can also turn against a government: they are better educated and have rising expectations for their futures. Often rebellions arise from frustrated expectations rather than from poverty itself.

land reform Policies that aim to break up large land holdings and redistribute land to poor peasants for use in *subsistence farming*.

In many cities, the influx of people cannot be accommodated with jobs, housing, and services. In slums, basic human needs often go unmet. Many states have considered policies to break up large land holdings and redistribute land to poor peasants for use in subsistence farming—**land reform.**[33] Socialists and other critical theorists almost always favour land reform, and some economic liberals also favour it in moderation. The standards of moderation change over time; for instance, the El Salvadoran land reform favoured by the United States in the 1980s was more sweeping than a program that U.S. officials considered a sign of communism in Guatemala when the United States intervened there militarily in 1954.

The main opponents of land reform are large landowners, who often wield great political power because of their wealth and international connections to markets, MNCs, and other sources of hard currency. Landowners have great leverage in bargaining with

---

[33] Peter Dorner, *Latin American Land Reform in Theory and Practice* (Madison: U Wisconsin P, 1992). John D. Montgomery, ed., *International Dimensions of Land Reform* (Boulder, CO: Westview, 1984).

peasants—from using the legal system to having virtual private armies.

Women in Development

Economic accumulation in poor countries is closely tied to the status of women in those societies.[34] This is a relatively recent revelation; most attention in the past was focused on men as supposedly the main generators of capital. Governments and international reports concentrated on work performed by male wage earners. Women's work, by contrast, often is not paid for in money and does not show up in financial statistics. But as studies in the 1970s onward began to show, women in much of the world work harder than men and contribute more to the economic well-being of their families and communities. Women are key to efforts to improve the lot of children and reduce birthrates. In nutrition, education, health care, and shelter, women are central to providing the basic needs of people in poor countries.

Yet women hold inferior social status to men in the countries of the South

LANDLESS
Subsistence farmers displaced from their land risk chronic hunger and sometimes starvation. In Sudan (1993), famine and war forced this starving girl to set out for a feeding centre, stalked by a vulture at one point. She survived the incident, but the South African photographer committed suicide the next year, haunted by the photo (which had won a Pulitzer prize).

(sometimes even more so than in the North). For instance, when food is in short supply, men and boys often eat first, with women and girls getting what is left. Because of this practice, of the world's malnourished children, 80 percent are female, according to Oxfam America.

Discrimination against girls is widespread in education and literacy. Worldwide, nearly twice as many women as men are illiterate. Across the global South, only in Latin America do women's literacy rates approach those of men. In Pakistan, 50 percent of boys but fewer than 30 percent of girls receive primary education. Throughout Asia, Africa, and the Middle East (though not in Latin America), more boys receive education, especially at the secondary level. At university level, only 30 percent of students are women in China and the Middle East, a bit more than 20 percent in South Asia and Africa (but 45 percent in Latin America). During the Taliban regime in Afghanistan (1996–2001), extreme measures were taken against women's education, with all girls banned from school and all women from work.

---

[34] Ester Boserup, *Women's Role in Economic Development* (London: Allen & Unwin, 1970). Martha Nussbaum and Jonathan Glover, eds., *Women, Culture, and Development: A Study of Human Capabilities* (NY: Oxford UP, 1996). Valentine M. Moghadam, ed., *Patriarchy and Economic Development: Women's Positions at the End of the Twentieth Century* (NY: Oxford UP, 1996). Irene Tinker and Gale Summerfield, eds., *Women's Rights to House and Land: China, Laos, Vietnam* (Boulder, CO: Rienner, 1999). Catherine V. Scott, *Gender and Development: Rethinking Modernization and Dependency Theory* (Boulder, CO: Rienner, 1994). Joycelin Massiah, ed., *Women in Developing Economies: Making Visible the Invisible* (NY: Berg, 1992).

BRIDE AVAILABLE
The status of women in countries of the global South affects their prospects for economic development. Women are central to rural economies, to population strategies, and to the provision of basic human needs, including education. This Asian 12-year-old, a prostitute's daughter, wears a wedding dress to invite a marriage proposal.

States and international agencies have begun to pay attention to ending discrimination in schooling, assuring women's access to health care and birth control, educating mothers about prenatal and child health, and generally raising women's status in society (allowing them a greater voice in decisions). These issues occupied the 1995 UN women's conference in Beijing, China, attended by tens of thousands of state and NGO representatives. The United Nations also organized the Beijing +5 meetings in 2000 to review progress toward the Plan of Action adopted at Beijing.

International agencies help women organize small businesses, farms, and other income-producing activities. For example, UNICEF has helped women get bank loans on favourable terms to start up small businesses in Egypt and Pakistan, and cooperative farms in Indonesia. Women have organized cooperatives throughout the global South, often in rural areas, to produce income through weaving and other textile and clothing production, retail stores, agriculture, and so forth.[35] In the slums of Addis Ababa, Ethiopia, women heads of household with no land for subsistence farming had been forced into begging and prostitution. Women taking part in the Integrated Holistic Approach Urban Development Project organized income-producing businesses from food processing to cloth weaving and garment production. These profitable businesses earned income for the women and helped subsidize health and sanitation services in the slums.

---

[35] Jill Bystydzienski, ed., *Women Transforming Politics: Worldwide Strategies for Empowerment* (Bloomington: Indiana UP, 1992). Amrita Basu, *Two Faces of Protest: Contrasting Modes of Women's Activism in India* (Berkeley: U California P, 1992). Helen Todd, *Women at the Center: Grameen Bank Borrowers After One Decade* (Boulder, CO: Westview, 1996).

Migration and Refugees

The processes just outlined—basic-needs deprivation, displacement from land, urbanization—culminate in one of the biggest political issues affecting North-South relations—**migration** from poorer to richer states.[36] Millions of people from the global South have crossed international borders, often illegally, to reach the North.

Someone who moves to a new country in search of better economic opportunities, a better professional environment, or better access to their family, culture, or religion is engaging in migration (emigration from the old state and immigration to the new state). Such migration is considered voluntary. The home state is not under any obligation to let such people leave, and, more important, no state is obligated to receive migrants. As with any trade issue, migration creates complex patterns of winners and losers. Immigrants often provide cheap labour, benefiting the host economy overall, but also compete for jobs with (poor) citizens of the host country.

Most industrialized states try to limit immigration from the global South. Despite border guards and fences, many people migrate anyway, illegally. In the United States, such immigrants come from all over the world, but mostly from nearby Mexico, Central America, and the Caribbean. In Western Europe, they come largely from North Africa, Turkey, and (increasingly) Eastern Europe.[37] Some Western European leaders worry that the loosening of border controls under the process of integration (see pp. 376–379) will make it harder to keep out illegal immigrants. Indeed, fear of immigration is one reason why Swiss voters rejected membership in the EU. Canada is considered a country that is relatively open to foreign immigration. In 2002, the largest number of immigrants to Canada came from China, followed by India, Pakistan, and the Philippines. However, even in Canada the arrival of illegal immigrants has been met with the same kind of xenophobia witnessed elsewhere in the world.

International law and custom distinguish migrants from **refugees,** people fleeing to find refuge from war, natural disaster, or political persecution.[38] (Fleeing from chronic discrimination may or may not be grounds for refugee status.) International norms obligate countries to accept refugees who arrive at their borders. Refugees from wars or natural disasters are generally housed in refugee camps temporarily until they can return home (though their stay can drag on for years). Refugees from political persecution may be granted asylum to stay in the new state. Acceptance of refugees—and the question of which states must bear the costs—is a collective goods problem.

The number of international refugees in the world grew from 3 million in 1976 to 12 million in 2002. In addition, 8 million more people are currently displaced within their own countries. The majority of refugees and internally displaced people have been displaced by wars (see Table 11.3).

migration Movement between states, usually emigration from the old state and immigration to the new state.

refugees People fleeing their countries to find refuge from war, natural disaster, or political persecution. International law distinguishes them from migrants.

---

[36] Caroline Brettell and James Hollifield, eds., *Migration Theory: Talking across Disciplines* (NY: Routledge, 2000). Peter Stalker, *Workers without Frontiers: The Impact of Globalization on International Migration* (Boulder, CO: Rienner, 2000). Myron Weiner, *The Global Migration Crisis: Challenge to States and to Human Rights* (NY: HarperCollins, 1995).

[37] Alexander Aleinikoff and Douglas Klusmeyer, eds., *From Migrants to Citizens: Membership in a Changing World* (Washington, DC: Carnegie Endowment for International Peace, 2000). Stephen Castles and Alastair Davidson, eds., *Citizenship and Migration* (NY: Routledge, 2000). Mark J. Miller, ed., "Strategies for Immigration Control: An International Comparison," *Annals of the American Academy of Political and Social Science* 534 (July 1994).

[38] UN High Commissioner for Refugees, *The State of the World's Refugees* (NY: Oxford UP, annual). Gil Loescher, *The UNHCR and World Politics: A Perilous Path* (NY: Oxford UP, 2001). Aristide Zolberg, Astri Suhrke, and Sergio Aguayo, *Escape from Violence: Conflict and the Refugee Crisis in the Developing World* (NY: Oxford UP, 1989). Leon Gordenker, *Refugees in International Politics* (NY: Columbia UP, 1987).

Table 11.3 Refugee Populations, 2002

Region	Millions	Main Concentrations
Middle East and Asia	8	Afghanistan, Iran, Pakistan, and Sri Lanka
Africa	4	Tanzania, Liberia, Dem. Congo, Sudan
Latin America	1	Columbia
Western and Eastern Europe	6	Former Yugoslavia, Russia, Germany*
North America	1	United States*
World total	20	

* Various regions of origin.

Note: Includes refugees, asylum-seekers, returned refugees, and internally displaced people. Excludes 4 million Palestinians under UNRWA, not UNHCR.

Source: UNHCR.

The political impact of refugees has been demonstrated repeatedly in recent years. After the Gulf War, Iraq's persecution of rebellious Iraqi Kurds sent large numbers of Kurdish refugees streaming to the Turkish border, where they threatened to become an economic burden to Turkey. Turkey closed its borders, and the hungry Iraqi Kurds were left stranded in the mountains. The United States and its allies then sent in military forces to protect the Kurds and return them to their homes in Iraq—violating Iraq's territorial integrity but upholding the Kurds' human rights. When the Kurdish-controlled area of Iraq became a base for Kurdish guerrillas in Turkey, the Turkish Army in 1995 invaded the area (another violation of Iraqi sovereignty). The close connection of economics and international security is clear from this episode—a security-related incident (the war) caused an economic condition (starving Kurds) that in turn led to other security ramifications (U.S. military protection of Kurdish areas of Iraq; Turkish invasion of the area).

The connection of economics and security appears in other refugee questions as well. The Palestinian refugees displaced in the 1948 and 1967 Arab-Israeli wars (and their children and grandchildren) live in "camps" that have become long-term neighbourhoods, mainly in Jordan and Lebanon. Economic development is impeded in these camps because the host states and Palestinians insist that the arrangement is only temporary. The poverty of the refugees in turn fuels radical political movements among the camp inhabitants. The question of Palestinian refugees' right to return to what is now Israel was one of two issues that blocked agreement at the failed Camp David II summit in 2000.

It is not always easy to distinguish a refugee fleeing war or political persecution from a migrant seeking economic opportunity. Illegal immigrants may claim to be refugees in order to be allowed to stay, when really they are seeking better economic opportunities. At the same time, legitimate refugees may be subject to intense scrutiny and denied refugee status when in fact they should receive it. In recent decades this issue has become a major one throughout the North.

In Germany, France, Austria, and elsewhere, resentment of foreign immigrants has fuelled upsurges of right-wing nationalism in domestic politics. Germany, with lax regulations for asylum seekers (they could live for years at state expense while applications for refugee status were processed), became a favoured destination for growing numbers of immigrants—most of whom were not political refugees. At a time of economic difficulty following German reunification, around 1992, neo-Nazi youths staged violent attacks on

HUMAN CARGO
Refugees are both a result of international conflicts and a source of conflict. In addition to those fleeing war and repression, and those seeking economic opportunity, hundreds of thousands of people each year cross borders as sex and labour slaves. This truck X-rayed entering Mexico from Guatemala in 1999 may have held Central American migrants seeking work in Mexico or, equally well, sex slaves from Asia or Eastern Europe en route to the United States.

foreigners and forced the government to tighten restrictions on immigration. (Hundreds of thousands of Germans then demonstrated against the neo-Nazis.) In 1999, Austria alarmed its EU partners by including a far-right party in a coalition government.

After a 1991 coup in Haiti deposed the elected (socialist) president, tens of thousands of poor people set off for U.S. shores in small boats. Were they fleeing from persecution or just looking for better economic opportunities (especially plausible given the U.S.-led economic sanctions that had damaged Haiti's economy)? The U.S. government screened the Haitians, granted asylum to a few, and shipped most back to Haiti. As the numbers grew, the United States began intercepting boats on the high seas and returning them directly to Haiti—a response that violated international law. President Clinton promised to change the U.S. policy if elected, but he reversed himself when thousands of Haitians prepared to set sail on his inauguration day. Evidently the only solution to the Haitian problem was to seek a political solution within Haiti itself (and then drop the U.S. sanctions). Thus, the United States ultimately intervened militarily to restore Haiti's president to power, but the country remained poor, the U.S.-supported president was accused of widespread corruption, and a coup in 2004 eventually ousted him, leading to even more instability.

Trafficking   In addition to migration and refugees, a growing number of persons—estimated at 900 000 annually—are trafficked across international borders against their will. They include both sex slaves and labour slaves, with each category including both females and males, adults and children. An estimated half million women and children are thought to be trafficked into Western Europe each year, and some 50 000 women are trafficked to the United States annually, as part of the sex trade alone.[39]

In general, migration of all types creates problems that, it seems, can only be solved by addressing the problems of the South itself. To the extent that these problems remain unaddressed, people in the South may turn to other solutions, which often include revolutionary strategies.

REVOLUTION

Poverty and lack of access to basic human needs are prime causes of revolutions, especially when poor people see others living much better.[40] Most revolutionary movements espouse egalitarian ideals—a more equal distribution of wealth and power. Political revolutions seek to change the form of government; social revolutions also seek changes in the structure of society, such as class relations. Most countries of the global South have had active revolutionary movements at some time since their independence.

Revolutionary Movements

During the Cold War years, the classic revolutionary movement was a communist insurgency based in the countryside. Such a revolution typically was organized by disenchanted students, professionals, and educated workers—usually committed to some variant of Marxist ideology—who won support from labourers and peasants. Its targets were the state, the military forces backing up the state, and the upper classes whose interests the state served. Usually "U.S. imperialism" or another such foreign presence was viewed as a friend of the state and an enemy of the revolution.[41]

Sometimes the U.S. government gave direct military aid to governments facing such revolutionary movements; in a number of countries, U.S. military advisers and combat troops were sent to help put down the revolutions and keep communists from taking power, thus reinforcing the analysis offered by revolutionaries. For its part, the Soviet Union often armed and helped train revolutionaries. If a revolution won power, then it was the Soviet Union that armed the new government and sent military advisers, and the United States that supported antigovernment rebels.

Thus, the domestic politics of countries of the global South became intertwined with great-power politics in the context of the North-South gap. In reality, many of these governments and revolutions had little to do with global communism, capitalism, or imperialism. They were local power struggles—sometimes between the haves and the have-nots, sometimes between rival ethnic groups—into which great powers asserted themselves.

---

[39] Joni Seager, *The Penguin Atlas of Women in the World*, rev. ed. (NY: Penguin, 2003). Barbara Ehrenreich and Arlie Russell Hochschild, eds, *Global Woman: Nannies, Maids, and Sex Workers in the New Economy* (NY: Holt, 2002).

[40] Theda Skocpol, *Social Revolutions in the Modern World* (NY: Cambridge UP, 1994). Theda Skocpol, *States and Social Revolutions: A Comparative Analysis of France, Russia, and China* (NY: Cambridge UP, 1979). Barry M. Schutz and Robert O. Slater, eds., *Revolution and Political Change in the Third World* (Boulder, CO: Rienner, 1990). Ted Robert Gurr, *Why Men Rebel* (Princeton, NJ: Princeton UP, 1970). Mark Irving Lichbach, "An Evaluation of 'Does Economic Inequality Breed Political Conflict?' Studies," *World Politics* 41.4 (1989): 431–70.

[41] Michael Parenti, *The Sword and the Dollar: Imperialism, Revolution, and the Arms Race* (NY: St. Martin's, 1988).

Some revolutions succeeded in taking power: they gained strength, captured some cities, and (often following the defection of part of the government army) marched on the capital city and took control. New foreign policies quickly followed (see "Postrevolutionary Governments" later in this chapter).

Elsewhere, and more frequently, revolutions failed: ever-smaller numbers of guerrillas were forced ever farther into the countryside with dwindling popular support. A third outcome became more common in recent years—a stalemated revolution in which after 10 or 20 years of guerrilla warfare neither the revolutionaries nor the government defeats the other. In these cases, the international community may step in to negotiate a ceasefire and the reincorporation of the revolutionaries, under some set of reforms in government practices, into peaceful political participation. This happened successfully in El Salvador, and elsewhere with varying degrees of success.

The Chinese revolution of the 1930s and 1940s was the model of a successful communist revolution for decades thereafter. In Southeast Asia, communist guerrillas ultimately took power in South Vietnam, Cambodia, and Laos, but lost in Thailand, Burma, and Malaysia. In Latin America, Fidel Castro's forces took power in Cuba in 1959 after years of guerrilla war. But when Castro's comrade-in-arms, Che Guevara, tried to replicate the feat in Bolivia, Guevara failed and was killed.[42]

By the early 1990s, these communist revolutions seemed to have played themselves out—winning in some places, losing in others, and coming to a stalemate in a few countries. The end of the Cold War removed superpower support from both sides, and the collapse of the Soviet Union and the adoption of capitalist-oriented economic reforms in China undercut some of the ideological appeal of communist revolutions.

Several Marxist revolutionary movements in Peru lingered after the Cold War, using brutal tactics of terrorism, which were answered with harsh repression by Peru's government. One group seized the Japanese embassy during a reception in 1996, and held hundreds of foreign hostages for months until a military attack ended the occupation.[43]

Islamic Revolutions

Although revolutions in the global South almost always advocate for the poor versus the rich and for nationalism versus imperialism, the particular character of these movements varies across regions and time periods. In Africa, where colonialism left behind state boundaries at odds with ethnic divisions, many revolutionary movements have a strong tribal and provincial base; this may fuel secessionism by a province (such as Eritrea from Ethiopia). Asian revolutionary movements tapped into general anticolonial sentiments, as when Vietnamese communists fought to oust the French colonizers and then saw the war against the United States as a continuation of the same struggle. In Latin America, where national independence was won long ago, revolutions tended to be couched in terms of class struggle against rich elites and their foreign allies (states and MNCs).

In the post–Cold War era, some of the most potent revolutionary movements are Islamic, not communist. Islam is now a key focal point of global North-South conflict. Islamic political activists in Middle Eastern countries, like revolutionaries elsewhere, derive

---

[42] Cynthia McClintock, *Revolutionary Movements in Latin America* (Washington, DC: U.S. Institute of Peace, 1998). Jorge Dominguez, *To Make a World Safe for Revolution: Cuba's Foreign Policy* (Cambridge, MA: Harvard UP, 1989). Forrest D. Colburn, *The Vogue of Revolution in Poor Countries* (Princeton NJ: Princeton UP, 1994).

[43] Ward Stavig, *The World of Túpac Amaru: Conflict, Community, and Identity in Colonial Peru* (Lincoln: U Nebraska P, 1999). Ellenbogen Gustavo Gorriti, *The Shining Path: A History of the Millenarian War in Peru* (Chapel Hill: U North Carolina P, 1999).

their main base of strength from championing the cause of poor and disenfranchised masses against rich elites. Like other revolutionaries throughout the global South, Islamic movements in countries such as Turkey and Egypt draw their base of support from poor slums, where the revolutionaries sometimes provide basic services unmet by the government. The Lebanese radical group Hezbollah (or Hizbollah), for example, runs hundreds of schools, hospitals, and other charities, and holds 12 seats in Lebanon's parliament (as of 2001).

Islamic revolutionary movements often criticize the Westernized ways of the ruling elite. For example, in Iran the shah had been armed by the United States as a bulwark against Soviet expansion into the Middle East. The Islamic revolutionaries who overthrew him in 1979 (led by Ayatollah Khomeini) declared the United States, as the leading political and cultural force in the industrialized West, to be the world's "great Satan." (Later, reformers in Iran offered other, less confrontational, interpretations of Islam.)

Some Islamic perspectives reject the cultural practices of the West, which can sometimes include a rejection of Western human rights norms (including extending rights to women and to sexual minorities). In 1989 Ayatollah Khomeini offered a large reward to anyone who killed Anglo-Indian author Salman Rushdie, whose book Khomeini considered blasphemous. However, Islam encompasses a broad spectrum of political practices and forms of government, most of which are neither revolutionary nor based on anti-Western sentiments.

Whereas Iran's revolution was directed against a U.S.-backed leader, an Islamic guerrilla war in Afghanistan showed that similar ideas could prevail against a Soviet-backed leader. There it was communism and Soviet domination, rather than capitalism and Western domination, that Islamic revolutionaries overthrew. After a decade of destructive civil war (in which U.S. aid helped the revolutionaries), the Islamic forces took power in 1992, but in-fighting resulted in further conflict. The fundamentalist Taliban faction (see pp. 180–181) seized control of the capital and most of Afghanistan in 1996, but the war continued. The Al Qaeda terrorist network used Taliban-controlled territory as a global base from which they planned their attacks against the U.S in 2001. Thus the U.S. had provided resources to the very groups that later attacked them. Some observers describe this as "blowback": the unintended consequences of distant actions.[44] The United States then supported the Northern Alliance in 2001, another fundamentalist Islamic faction, in an effort to topple the Taliban.

The defeat of the Taliban in Afghanistan, however, put pressure on its much larger next-door neighbour, nuclear-armed Pakistan. By allying with the United States, Pakistan's military ruler has struggled to smother Islamic extremists as well as popular discontent. As some observers have noted, nowhere is the possibility of "blowback" more visible than in Pakistan, which devotes 85 to 90 percent of its state budget to paying interest on it debt and to maintaining its military and police forces, with little left over to support domestic infrastructure or services. Although the poor in Pakistan do not vote for fundamentalist parties in large number, they do send their sons to the religious *madrasas*, where they learn the doctrines of fundamentalism.[45]

Bombings and other terrorist actions continued in Asia and elsewhere. Documents uncovered in Afghanistan in 2001 uncovered a plot in Singapore to blow up the U.S. embassy. In 2002, a nightclub bombing in Bali, Indonesia, killed hundreds, as did bombings in Spain, Morocco, Saudi Arabia, Russia, the Philippines, Indonesia, Iraq, and Turkey. In 2004, an Ottawa man was arrested in connection with plans to bomb a num-

---

[44] Chalmers Johnson, *Blowback: The Costs and Consequences of American Empire* (NY: Metropolitan, 2000).

[45] Leo Panitch, "The Meaning of 11 September for the Left," *Studies in Political Economy* 67 (Spring 2002): 47–54.

ber of London targets (a charge he and his family denied). An attack on Westerners in Saudi Arabia in 2004 resulted in over 20 deaths.

In Algeria, Islamic revolutionaries organized against the ruling party that itself had kicked out the French colonizers in 1962 but was now seen as corrupt, inept, and not revolutionary enough. The Islamic parties won preliminary parliamentary elections in 1991 and were assured of coming to power in the final elections. Instead, the military took over, cancelled the elections, and touched off eight years of violence before a new president reached a peace agreement with the main rebel faction.

Elsewhere in the Middle East, Islamic movements are particularly active in Tunisia, Jordan, and Tajikistan. In Jordan, Islamic parties for years controlled the largest bloc of seats in the parliament. In the former Soviet republic of Tajikistan they are a major faction in civil strife (since the Soviet Union's demise). Middle Eastern Islamic revolutionaries also took a keen interest in the fate of Muslims targeted for genocide in Bosnia from 1992 on. They saw this conflict as part of a broad regional (or even global) struggle of Western, Christian imperialism against Islam—a struggle dating back to the Crusades almost a thousand years ago. In the 1990s, Muslim civilians were indeed targeted by Christians in wars in Bosnia, Azerbaijan, and Chechnya.

Overall, Islamic-based movements around the world vary widely.

Postrevolutionary Governments

When revolutionaries succeed in taking power, their state's domestic and international politics alike are affected. This occurred in China in 1949; Cuba in 1959; Algeria in 1962; South Vietnam, Cambodia, Angola, and Mozambique in 1975; Nicaragua and Iran in 1979; and Afghanistan in 1992.

Even though revolutionaries advocate the broad distribution of wealth, they tend to find after taking power that centralizing accumulation is more practical: it gives the state more control of wealth and power (with which to meet the needs of the masses, or line the pockets of the new leaders, as the case may be). Over time, the new elite may come to resemble the old one, although individuals change places. Similarly, revolutionaries often advocate improving women's status, but after taking power male revolutionaries have tended to push aside their female comrades, and traditional sex roles have reappeared.[46]

More relevant to international relations are the problems that beset successful revolutionaries due to violence—usually backed directly or indirectly by foreign states. After many revolutions, the meeting of basic human needs has been severely impeded by continuing political violence and even civil war. For example, the socialist government that took power in Angola in 1975 wanted to improve the lot of poor people, but instead civil war ravaged the country for more than 15 years and the poor ended up much hungrier than ever. In Vietnam, the war that brought the communists to power was so fierce that it left the country devastated.

Such problems reached an extreme under the communist Khmer Rouge faction that took power in Cambodia in 1975. They sought to radically alter the society by destroying economic classes, destroying concentrations of capital, destroying ideas that ran contrary to the revolution, abolishing money, and rebuilding the entire nation on the basis of agrarian socialism. To implement this plan, the Khmer Rouge executed almost everyone associated with government, business, or universities, or who had independent ideas. They then evacuated the populations of cities into the countryside, where hundreds of

---

[46] Stephanie Urdang, *And Still They Dance: Women, War and the Struggle for Change in Mozambique* (NY: Monthly Review Press, 1989)

The Changing World Order

Engaging the South

Global poverty has become a problem of enormous concern within international relations. When the Cold War ended, it became easier to raise issues that previously had been submerged under the framework of "First World–Second World conflict." Today scholars of IR can engage with questions of poverty in its own right, though some will still link poverty to questions of security. For some observers, the attacks against the United States on September 11, 2001, demonstrated the increased interdependence of the global North and South. By this view (largely one shared by realist/mercantilists and some liberals), the extreme disparities of wealth and power between North and South create conflicts and resentments that can reach out of the South to punish the privileged citizens of the North who had been oblivious to the problems of poor countries. To let a continent or even a country descend into despair may no longer be practical in the era of terrorism, by this view. Their fate ultimately may be the fate of the North that ignores them. This is the century in which desperate African states may be able to press their demands with weapons of mass destruction, and in which fanatics may destroy cities with nuclear weapons. To combat terrorism may require addressing poverty, repression, and war throughout the poorest world regions. The need to address "root causes" of terrorism may draw the United States and other Northern countries into close cooperation with the UN and other international institutions such as the IMF and World Bank in the years to come.

Others would argue that poverty needs to be addressed for its own sake, not simply because it is "impractical" to ignore because of the risk that "fanatics" will emerge bent on destroying the North. Poverty needs to be addressed because it destroys human potential and human lives, and normally also has a devastating effect on local culture and the environment. This view results from an analysis of poverty in the global South that sees it as inextricably related to the accumulation of wealth in the North. So, simply working with existing international institutions—especially those like the IMF and World Bank—will not by itself alleviate poverty. Many of the prescriptions suggested by these institutions may actually exacerbate poverty.

It is unclear how these views will play out in practice. Elites tend to emphasize the more instrumental approach to poverty (we want to address poverty in the South to ensure it does not come back to haunt the North). But that very attitude may be part of the perceived arrogance that critics in both the South and North insist is part of the problem of global poverty and inequality.

thousands starved to death. After losing power in 1979, the Khmer Rouge continued for more than a decade to wage guerrilla war. A UN-administered peace plan was implemented in the early 1990s (though against continuing Khmer Rouge resistance), but the country had been decimated. The Khmer Rouge disaster showed that merely destroying concentrations of capital does not help meet poor people's basic needs.

Violence and war—both international and civil war—are tremendous obstacles to economic accumulation and the provision of basic human needs. It is a great contradiction of violent revolutions that they rely on the methods of war to gain power, supposedly to redistribute wealth and meet people's basic needs. Yet rich and poor alike are often caught in a downward spiral of indiscriminate violence and destruction. And after taking power, violent revolutionaries often face continuing civil or international war in the struggle to keep power. Successful revolutions often induce neighbouring states either to contain the revolution or to take advantage of the new government's instability. For example, within a year of the 1979 revolution in Iran, Iraq had attacked in hopes of conquering Iran while it was weak. (European states did much the same to France after the French Revolution of 1789.)

In foreign policy, revolutionary governments often start out planning radically different relationships with neighbours and great powers. The pattern of international alliances often shifts after revolutions, as when a Cold War client of one superpower shifted to the other after a change of government.

But the new government usually discovers that, now that it holds power, it has the same interest as other states in promoting national sovereignty and territorial integrity. The rules of the international system now work for the revolutionaries instead of against them, once they control a state. Their state also has the same geographical location as before, the same historical conflicts with its neighbours, and the same ethnic ties. So it is not unusual over time to find similar foreign policies emanating from a revolutionary government as from its predecessor.

Capitalism also exerts an enormous force on revolutionary governments. The democratic transition in South Africa that eliminated white minority rule brought to power a government, the African National Congress (ANC), with a strong commitment to socialist principles. It did not take long, however, for even the ANC to begin to commit itself to economic liberalism. Some of the ANC's strongest supporters, trade union movements and Marxist scholars both inside and outside of South Africa, soon became some of its loudest critics.

Violent revolutions often lead to authoritarian rule (for fear that counterrevolutionaries will retake power), not to multiparty democracy. Thus the revolutionary party has a monopoly on power, year after year, which leads to a certain conservatism. These tendencies are illustrated in the experiences of Algeria and China. The young revolutionaries

MIXED SUCCESS
South Africa's former president Nelson Mandela (shown here at a march of the African National Congress in Boipatong, 1992) had considerable success in making the difficult transition from revolutionary to state leader, and then leaving office peacefully. Critics of Mandela's successor, however, argue that the ANC has abandoned its more revolutionary ideas and embraced economic liberalism, to the detriment of South Africa's poorer communities.

of the National Liberation Front drove the French colonialists out of Algeria in 1962. Twenty years later, these revolutionaries were moderate enough to be intermediaries between revolutionary Iran and the United States in the hostage crisis of 1980. And 10 years later, the old revolutionaries were the entrenched rulers against whom young Islamic revolutionaries rose up. Similarly, in China the revolutionaries who took power in 1949 were able to make common cause with the U.S. by 1971, and by 1989 they were the conservative rulers shooting down student protesters in the streets of Beijing.

Thus, although revolutions create short-term shifts in foreign policy, over the longer term the pressures of global politics have tended to triumph over revolutionary challenges. Likewise, though revolutions promise great economic change, the overall state of economic conditions and relations—especially between North and South—has been resistant to change.

Overall, North-South relations show how difficult it has become to separate political economy from international security. The original political relations contained in European imperialism led to economic conditions in the South—from high population growth to urbanization and concentrations of wealth—that in turn led to political movements for independence, and later to revolutions. The various aspects of the North-South gap considered in this chapter—from hunger and refugees to the structure of commodity exports—all contain both economic and political-military aspects.

Economic liberals argue that problems internal to countries of the global South explain their underdevelopment: corrupt governments, high government expenditures, poor educational systems, and insufficient production geared toward the export market, among others. Critical theorists argue that it is the way in which Southern countries have been inserted into the global political economy that explains their underdevelopment, and in particular it is the legacies of colonialism that still shape what is possible in the global South. Chapter 12 turns to some of the practical strategies, suggested by both critical theorists and economic liberals, as a way to promote development in the global South.

Thinking Critically

1. In what ways does the North American Free Trade Agreement (NAFTA) discussed in Chapter 8 reflect the overall state of North-South relations as described in this chapter? How would economic liberalism and critical theory as general approaches to the theory of wealth accumulation differ in their views of the agreement?

2. The zones of the world economy as described by world-system theorists treat the North as a core and the South as largely a periphery. Can you think of exceptions to this formula? How seriously do such exceptions challenge the overall concept as applied to North-South relations generally? Be specific about why the exceptions do not fit the theory.

3. In North and South America, independence from colonialism was won by descendants of the colonists themselves. In Asia and Africa, it was won mainly by local populations with a long history of their own. How do you think this aspect has affected the post-colonial history of one or more specific countries from each group?

4. Suppose you lived in an extremely poor slum in the global South and had no money or job—but retained all the knowledge you now have. What strategy would you adopt for your own survival and well-being? What strategies would you reject as infeasible? Would you adopt or reject the idea of revolution? Why?

Chapter Summary

- Most of the world's people live in poverty in the global South. About a billion live in extreme poverty, without access to adequate food, water, and other necessities.

- Moving from poverty to well-being requires the accumulation of capital. Capitalism and socialism take different views on this process. Capitalism emphasizes overall growth with considerable concentration of wealth, whereas socialism emphasizes a fair distribution of wealth.

- Most states have a mixed economy, with some degree of private ownership of capital and some degree of state ownership. However, state ownership has not been very successful in accumulating wealth. Consequently, many states have been selling off state-owned enterprises (privatization), especially in Russia and Eastern Europe.

- Marxists view international relations, including global North-South relations, in terms of a struggle between economic classes (especially workers and owners) that have different roles in society and different access to power.

- Since Lenin's time, many Marxists have attributed poverty in the South to the concentration of wealth in the North. In this theory, capitalists in the North exploit the South economically and use the wealth thus generated to buy off workers in the North. Revolutions thus occur in the South and are ultimately directed against the North.

- IR scholars in the world-system school argue that the north is a core region specializing in producing manufactured goods and the south is a periphery specializing in extracting raw materials through agriculture and mining. Between these are semiperiphery states with light manufacturing.

- Today's North-South gap traces its roots to the colonization of the countries of the global South by Europe over the past several centuries. This colonization occurred at different times in different parts of the world, as did decolonization.

- Because of the negative impact of colonialism on local populations, anticolonial movements arose throughout the global South at various times and using various methods. These culminated in a wave of successful independence movements after World War II in Asia and Africa. (Latin American states gained independence much earlier.)

- Following independence, states of the global South were left with legacies of colonialism, including their basic economic infrastructures, that made wealth accumulation difficult in certain ways. These problems still remain in many countries.

- Wealth accumulation (including the demographic transition discussed in Chapter 13) depends on the meeting of basic human needs such as access to food, water, education, shelter, and health care. States of the global South have had mixed success in meeting their populations' basic needs.

- War has been a major impediment to meeting basic needs, and to wealth accumulation generally, in poor countries. Almost all the wars of the past 50 years have been fought in the global South.

- Hunger and malnutrition are rampant in the global South. The most important cause is the displacement of subsistence farmers from their land because of war, population pressures, and the conversion of agricultural land into plantations growing export crops to earn hard currency, often at the insistence of international financial institutions like the IMF and World Bank.

- Urbanization is increasing throughout the global South as more people move from the countryside to cities. Huge slums have grown in the cities as poor people arrive and cannot find jobs.

- Women's central role in the process of accumulation has begun to be recognized. International agencies based in the North have started taking women's contributions into account in analyzing economic development in the South.

- Poverty in the South has led huge numbers of migrants to seek a better life in the North; this has created international political frictions. War and repression in the South have generated millions of refugees seeking safe haven. Under international law and norms, states are generally supposed to accept refugees but do not have to accept migrants.

- Many people throughout the global South have turned to political revolution as a strategy for changing economic inequality and poverty. Often, especially during the Cold War, states in the North were drawn into supporting one side or the other during such revolutions.

- Today the most potent revolutions in the global South are the Islamic revolutions in the Middle East. Even more than the communist revolutions of the past, Islamic revolutions are directed against the North and reject the Western values on which the international system is based. Like communist ones, Islamic revolutions draw support and legitimacy from the plight of poor people.

- When revolutionaries succeed in taking power, they usually change their state's foreign policy. Over time, however, old national interests and strategies tend to reappear.

- North-South relations, although rooted in a basic economic reality—the huge gap in accumulated wealth—reflect the close connections of economics with international security.

Key Terms

Weblinks

The following are a sampling of research centres, government departments, and international organizations focused on North-South issues:

International Secretariat for Human Development and Democratic Governance:
http://www.yorku.ca/hddg

Maquila Solidarity Network:
http://www.maquilasolidarity.org

Mining Advocacy Network:
http://www.jatam.org/english/index.html

Third World Network:
http://www.twnside.org.sg/index.htm

United Nations Development Programme:
http://www.undp.org

New Delhi bus stop, 2000.

WHAT IS DEVELOPMENT?

Economic development refers to the combined processes of capital accumulation, rising per capita incomes (with consequent falling birthrates), increasing skills in the population, adoption of new technologies, and other related social and economic changes.[1] The most central aspect, especially for economic liberals, is the accumulation of capital (with its ongoing wealth-generating potential). Critical theorists would emphasize instead the distribution of wealth, and quality of life indicators such as educational levels, nourishment, access to housing, clean water, and the like.

The concept of development has a subjective side that cannot be measured statistically—the judgment of whether a certain pattern of wealth creation and distribution is good for a state and its people. One simple measure of economic development is the per capita GDP—the amount of economic activity per person. By this measure, most of the global South made progress on economic development in the 1970s, with real per capita GDP growth of almost 3 percent annually. This rate was a bit higher than in the global North (despite the higher population growth in the South, which pulls down per

economic development The combined processes of capital accumulation, rising per capita incomes (with consequent falling birthrates), the increasing of skills in the population, the adoption of new technological styles, and other related social and economic changes.

---

[1] Joseph Stiglitz, and Gerald Meier, *Frontiers in Development* (NY: Oxford UP, 2000). Diane Stone, *Banking on Knowledge: The Genesis of the Global Development Network* (NY: Routledge, 2001). Robert H. Bates, *Prosperity and Violence: The Political Economy of Development* (NY: Norton, 2001). Uma Kothari and Martin Minogue, eds.. *Development Theory and Practice: Critical Perspectives* (NY: Palgrave, 2002). Santosh Mehrota and Richard Jolly, eds., *Development with a Human Face: Experiences in Social Achievement and Economic Growth* (NY: Oxford, 1997). Robert J. Barro, *Determinants of Economic Growth: A Cross-Country Empirical Study* (Cambridge, MA: MIT P, 1997).

capita GDP). However, in the 1980s this economic development came to a halt except in Asia. Per capita GDP *decreased* from 1981 to 1991 in Latin America, Africa, and the Middle East.[2] By contrast, China had 7.5 percent annual growth. In the 1990s, real economic growth returned across much of the South—about 5 to 6 percent annual growth for the South as a whole, and even higher for China, compared to 2 to 3 percent in the global North. The 1997 Asian crisis curbed growth there, and the 2001 recession slowed growth globally, but China continued to grow rapidly, merely slowing somewhat during hard economic times. Thus, China stands out among the regions of the South as making rapid progress in economic development. All the other regions of the global South showed much slower progress, if any, and faced serious problems moving development forward.

Growth varies greatly across regions and countries, as well as within countries. The gap between rich and poor—both within countries and globally—is widening, according to a 1996 UN report. In countries with the greatest internal disparities in income, such as Brazil and Guatemala, the poorest fifth of the population lives on incomes one-tenth of the national average. The same is true in some Northern countries: in the United States, the income of the top 1 percent of families was 23 times that of median family income in 1995.[3]

In the decade of the 1990s, so prosperous for much of the North, 21 countries experienced declines according to the United Nations; half of Latin America either stagnated or declined over the decade. In 2003, declines occurred in Eastern Europe and Central Asia, especially Russia, Ukraine, Moldova, and Tajikistan. These conditions lead some observers to wonder if the global South is dividing into two parts, one moving forward and one stalled.[4]

Regarding how income is distributed and spent, the perspectives and prescriptions of economic liberalism and critical theory again diverge (see pp. 408–410). Economic liberals tend to favour the concentration of capital as a way to spur investment rather than consumption (and to realize economies of scale and specialization). In line with liberalism, capitalists favour development paths that tie states of the global South closely to the world economy and international trade.[5] They argue that although they defer equity, such development strategies maximize efficiency. Once a developing state has a self-sustaining cycle of accumulation under way, it can better redress poverty in the broad population. To do so too early would choke off economic growth, in this view.

An alternative measure of development to per capita GDP is called the **Human Development Index (HDI).** The HDI measures a country's achievements in the areas of: life expectancy at birth (as a measure of a long and healthy life); knowledge (including adult literacy and enrolment levels in primary, secondary, and tertiary education); and standard of living, based on per capita GDP. The United Nations Development Programme (UNDP) publishes annual Human Development Reports that compare national HDI rankings. Using a broader scale than simply per capita GDP addresses some of the concerns raised by critical theorists about the distribution of wealth and quality of life indicators. While Nordic countries tend to be ranked high and most African countries quite low,

Human Development Index (HDI) The HDI is an alternative measure of development to the gross domestic product (GDP) alone. It measures a country's achievements in the areas of: life expectancy at birth (as a measure of a long and healthy life); knowledge (including adult literacy and enrolment levels in primary, secondary, and tertiary education); and standard of living, based on per capita GDP.

---

[2] South and East Asia here includes South Korea, Taiwan, and Hong Kong. United Nations, *World Economic and Social Survey* (annual).

[3] United Nations Development Program, *Human Development Report 2002* (NY: Oxford UP, 2002).

[4] United Nations, *Human Development Report 2003* (NY: United Nations, 2003). Paul Kennedy, *Preparing for the Twenty-First Century* (NY: Random House, 1993).

[5] William Easterly, *The Elusive Quest for Growth: Economists' Adventures and Misadventures in the Tropics* (Cambridge, MA: MIT P, 2001). Arthur McEwan, *Neo-Liberalism or Democracy? Economic Strategy, Markets, and Alternatives for the 21st Centur.* (NY: Zed/St. Martin's, 1999). Christopher Colclough and James Manor, eds., *States or Markets? Neo-Liberalism and the Development Policy Debate* (NY: Oxford UP, 1991).

many countries of the Middle East belong to high or medium human development categories (countries such as Kuwait and Qatar have high HDI meausures; Libya, Saudi Arabia, and Iran are in the middle categories). Others such as Cuba and Sri Lanka, with high literacy and life expectancy rates, compare favourably to countries such as the United States (which despite high GDP per capita has enormous inequality between rich and poor, with some 32.9 million people living in absolute poverty in 2001).[6]

The same kinds of disagreement between critical theorists and economic liberals apply broadly to the world's development as a whole. From an economic liberal perspective, the North-South gap is a stage of world development in which capital accumulation is concentrated in the North. This unequal concentration creates faster economic growth, which ultimately will bring more wealth to the South as well (a "trickle-down" approach). There is no practical way, in this view, to shift wealth from the North to the South without undermining the free market economics responsible for global economic growth.

Critical theorists by contrast argue that meaningful development should improve the position of the whole population and of the poor—sooner rather than later. Thus, critical theorists tend to advocate a more equitable distribution of wealth; they dispute the idea that greater equity will impede efficiency or slow down economic growth. Rather, by raising incomes among the poorer people, a strategy based on equity will speed up the demographic transition and lead more quickly to sustained accumulation. Such a strategy seeks to develop a state's economy from the bottom up instead of the top down.

On a global level, critical theorists do not see the North-South disparities as justified by global growth benefits. They favour political actions to shift income from North to South in order to foster economic growth in the South. Such a redistribution, in this view, would create faster, not slower, global economic growth—as well as more balanced and stable growth.

In reality, most states in the South use a mix of the two strategies in their economic policies, as do the industrialized states in shaping their roles in development. Welfare capitalism, such as most industrialized states practice, distributes enough wealth to meet the basic needs of many while letting most wealth move freely in capitalist markets. Such a mix is harder to achieve in a state of the global South, where the smaller total amount of wealth may force a choice between welfare and capitalism.

The economic liberal theory that unequal income distributions are related to higher economic growth is only weakly supported by empirical evidence. Many states with fairly equitable income distributions have high growth rates (including South Korea, Taiwan, Singapore, and Hong Kong); many with unequal distributions have grown slowly if at all (Zambia, Argentina, and Ghana). But there are also cases of relatively equitable countries that grow slowly (India) and inequitable ones that grow rapidly (Malaysia).

EXPERIENCES

Although much of the global South went backward in the 1980s, some Asian states continued to develop and China began to raise its GDP per capita rapidly, though from a low starting level (see Figure 12.1). This difference indicates that a single, simplified model of the South does not apply to all countries. One must consider the various experiences of different countries as they try different approaches to development.[7]

---

[6] Ananya Mukherjee-Reed, "Human Development," *International Encyclopedia of Public Policy: Governance in a Global Age* (Routledge: London & New York, 2004). See also A.K. Sen, *Development as Freedom* (NY: Anchor, 1999).

[7] Guy Arnold, *The End of the Third World* (NY: St. Martin's, 1993).

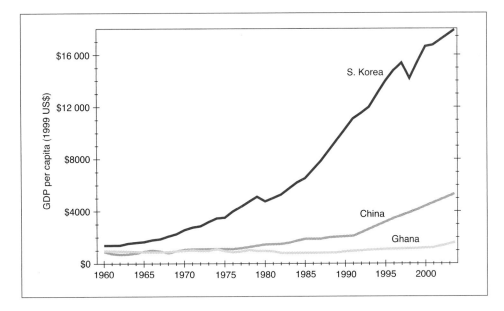

Figure 12.1 Per Capita GDP of South Korea, China, and Ghana

Source: Based on Penn World Tables and World Bank and IMF data.

The Newly Industrializing Countries

Given the extent of poverty in the global South, is it even possible for a developing country to lift itself out of poverty? The answer is yes, at least for some countries. A handful of poor states—called the **newly industrializing countries (NICs)**—have achieved self-sustaining capital accumulation, with impressive economic growth.[8] These semiperiphery states, which export light manufactured goods, posted strong economic growth in the 1980s and early 1990s (see "The World-System" on pp. 413–415). They ran into serious problems in the late 1990s because growth had been pushed too fast, with overly idealistic loans, speculative investments, and corrupt deals (the 1997 financial crisis is described on pp. 353–356). Notwithstanding these setbacks, the NICs resumed growth and have developed much further and faster than most of the global South.

The most successful NICs are the **"four tigers"** or **"four dragons"** of East Asia: South Korea, Taiwan, Hong Kong, and Singapore. Each has succeeded in developing particular sectors and industries that are competitive on world markets.[9] These sectors and industries can create enough capital accumulation within the country to raise income levels not just among the small elite but across the population more broadly. However, income is not equitably distributed, and the NICs also tended to depend on quite authoritarian forms of government, which sometimes took a direct role in business decisions and imposed severe restrictions on trade union activity and any forms of protest against the state.

Many countries of the global South have tried to apply the model of the NICs, but so far few have succeeded. Most poor states remained mired in poverty, with as many failures as successes. Scholars do not know whether the success of the NICs can eventually

newly industrializing countries (NICs) States of the global South that have achieved self-sustaining capital accumulation, with impressive economic growth.

"four tigers"/"four dragons" The most successful newly industrialized areas of East Asia: South Korea, Taiwan, Hong Kong, and Singapore.

[8] Alice Amsden, *The Rise of the "Rest": Challenges to the West from Late-Industrializing Economies* (NY: Oxford UP, 2001). Stephan Haggard, *Pathways from the Periphery: The Politics of Growth in the Newly Industrializing Countries* (Ithaca, NY: Cornell UP, 1990). Stephan Haggard, *Developing Nations and the Politics of Global Integration* (Washington, DC: Brookings, 1995).

[9] Ryoshin Minami, Kwan S. Kim, and Malcolm Falkus, eds., *Growth, Distribution, and Political Change: Asia and the Wider World* (NY: St. Martin's, 1999). Robert Wade, *Governing the Market: Economic Theory and the Role of Government in East Asian Industrialization* (Princeton, NJ: Princeton UP, 1992).

be replicated throughout the world. An important unanswered question has been whether authoritarianism is a necessary feature of their success.

South Korea, with iron and coal resources, developed competitive steel and automobile industries that export globally, creating a trade surplus (see "Balance of Trade" on p. 308). For example, Hyundai cars and trucks, sold in Canada and other countries, are produced by the giant South Korean MNC, Hyundai. The state has been strongly involved in industrial policy, trying to promote and protect such industries. By the mid-1990s, South Korea had an income level per capita equivalent to that of Spain; Korean companies began to move manufacturing operations to Britain where production costs were lower.

Taiwan too has a strong state industrial policy. It specializes in the electronics and computer industries, in which Taiwanese products are very successful worldwide, and in other light manufacturing. Taiwan holds one of the world's largest hard-currency reserves.

Hong Kong—controlled by China since 1997—also has world-competitive electronics and other light industries, but its greatest strengths are in banking and trade—especially trade between southern China and the rest of the world. Hong Kong is a small territory with some of the world's highest real estate prices and great internal disparities of wealth. Its rich neighbourhoods are jammed with high-rise office buildings and expensive apartments, and Hong Kong is a financial centre for much of Asia.

Singapore is a trading city located at the tip of the Malaysian peninsula—convenient to the South China Sea, the Indian Ocean, and Australia. Singapore has developed niches in light manufacturing and has (like Hong Kong) attracted MNCs to locate headquarters there.

For different reasons, each of these states holds a somewhat unusual political status in the international system. South Korea and Taiwan are hotspots of international conflict.

South Korea and North Korea are separate states in practice, but have not recognized each other since fighting the Korean War in 1950–1953. Taiwan is formally part of China, but in practice operates independently. Both South Korea and Taiwan came under the U.S. security umbrella during the Cold War. Both were militarized, authoritarian states intolerant of dissent, although they later became democratic. U.S. spending in East Asia during the Cold War benefited South Korea and Taiwan. In these cases military conflict did not impede development, in fact their geo-strategic significance to the United States benefited them significantly.

Hong Kong and Singapore have a different political profile. They are both former British colonies. They are more city-states than nation-states, and their cities are trading ports and financial centres. Although not as repressive or as militarized as South Korea and Taiwan during the Cold War era, Hong Kong and Singapore were not democracies either. Hong Kong was ruled by a British governor (and since 1997 by the government in Beijing), Singapore by a dominant individual (who once banned sales of the *Asian Wall Street Journal*, hardly a radical newspaper, after it criticized him). Criticisms against state policy by citizens of both Hong Kong and Singapore is still highly restricted.

Thailand has been suggested as a potential "fifth tiger." It received enormous foreign investment in the 1980s (mostly from Japan) and created a sizeable middle class. But its growth masked serious problems that put Thailand at the centre of the 1997 financial crisis in Asia. Nonetheless, Thailand recovered and posted strong growth (until the 2001 world recession), despite continuing problems with bad loans.

Malaysia is also trying to follow closely in the footsteps of the tigers. Again, it is too soon to say whether this will succeed. *Indonesia* set itself a goal in 1969 to become an NIC by 1994. It fell short of that goal, but has made some progress in attracting foreign investment. With 200 million people, Indonesia's major assets are cheap labour (an average wage of about 25 cents per hour) and exportable natural resources, including oil. All of these Asian countries were caught in the 1997 financial downturn, which slowed their growth. Since 2001 several countries have also had to address problems of terrorism within their borders, and Indonesia faced simmering ethnic unrest in several islands. These factors dimmed the economic prospects of the would-be NICs of Southeast Asia.

Israel has developed economically in an unusual manner. It received sustained infusions of outside capital from several sources—German reparations, U.S. foreign aid, and contributions from Zionists in foreign countries. This outside assistance was particular to the history of German genocide against Jews during World War II and the efforts of Jews worldwide to help build a Jewish state afterward. Few if any countries of the global South could hope to receive such outside assistance (relative to Israel's small size). In common with the other NICs, however, Israel has a strong state involvement in key industries, and it has carved out a few niches for itself in world markets (notably in cut diamonds and military technology).

Thus, it is unclear whether there are general lessons to be learned from the success of the "four tigers." Hong Kong and Singapore are small trading cities located at the intersection of industrialized and developing regions (Japan/Pacific, South Asia, and China). There are no equivalents elsewhere in the global South. South Korea and Taiwan came of age while enmeshed in security relationships with the United States that no longer apply to most countries, if they ever did.

The Chinese Experience

Very few people of the global South live in NICs. The largest, South Korea, has fewer than 50 million people. China's population is more than 20 times its size. Size alone

CHINA BOOTS UP

China's rapid economic growth has raised incomes dramatically, especially for a growing middle class. These successes followed China's opening to the world economy and adoption of market-oriented reforms. China's leaders hope to use information technology to further these economic trends without undermining their political rule. China's new WTO membership allows foreign investment in internet businesses in China. Here, police officers surf the internet at a Beijing computer fair, 2000.

free economic zones The southern coastal provinces of China that were opened to foreign investment and run on capitalist principles with export-oriented industries, in the 1980s and 1990s.

makes China's efforts to generate self-sustaining accumulation worthy of study. But China has also had one of the fastest-growing developing economies in recent years.

Between the communist victory of 1949 and the Cultural Revolution of the late 1960s, Chinese economic policy emphasized national self-sufficiency and communist ideology. The state controlled all economic activity through central planning and state ownership. An "iron rice bowl" policy guaranteed basic food needs to all Chinese citizens (at least in theory).

After Mao died in 1976, China under Deng Xiaoping instituted economic reforms and transformed its southern coastal provinces (near Hong Kong and Taiwan) into **free economic zones** open to foreign investment and run on capitalist principles. Peasants work their own fields, instead of collective farms, and "get rich" (by Chinese standards) if they do well. Entrepreneurs start companies, hire workers, and generate profits. Foreign investment has flooded into southern China, taking advantage of its location, cheap labour, and relative political stability. Other areas of China have gradually opened up to capitalist principles as well. The state now requires more industries to turn a profit and gives more initiative to managers to run their own companies and spend the profits as they see fit.

Economic growth has been rapid since these policies were instituted. Standards of living are rising substantially. However, China is also recreating some of the features of capitalism that Mao's revolutionaries had overturned. New class disparities are emerging, with rich entrepreneurs driving fancy imported cars while poor workers find themselves unemployed (earlier, socialism guaranteed everyone employment despite reduced efficiency). Unprofitable state-owned industries laid off 10 million workers in the 1990s, with more coming each year. In the countryside, areas bypassed by development still contain 200 million desperately poor Chinese peasants. Social problems such as prostitution have returned, as have economic problems such as inflation. Most frustrating for ordinary Chinese is the widespread official corruption accompanying the get-rich atmosphere.

MNCs continue to shift production to China year by year because China's labour force is vast, low-paid, and disciplined (strikes are not allowed). Of the US$700 billion in foreign direct investment (see pp. 358–360) in Asia in 1990–2000, nearly half was in mainland China. The largest investor, Motorola, has put in more than US$3 billion, and General Motors has built a US$1.5 billion plant near Shanghai. Some 40 000 Taiwanese companies have invested US$60 billion. These foreign investments have primed rapid growth in Chinese exports—to US$250 billion in 2000 and US$400 billion in 2003. In the next few years, China may join the United States, Japan, and Germany as a major automobile exporter. China's new WTO membership should accelerate these trends.[10]

---

[10] Clay Chandler, "A Factory to the World," *Washington Post* 25 Nov. 2001: A1, A30.

Popular resentment over such problems as inflation and corruption led industrial workers and even government officials to join students in antigovernment protests at Beijing's Tiananmen Square in 1989. Authorities used the military to violently suppress the protests, killing hundreds of people and signalling its determination to maintain tight political control while economic reform proceeded. This policy of combining economic reform with political orthodoxy was reaffirmed at the Party Congress in 1992 and again in 1997.

China's leaders felt vindicated by subsequent economic performance. Foreign investors returned quickly after the political disruption of 1989, and economic growth roared ahead at 12 percent per year in 1992–1994. Inflation returned, however, reaching 22 percent in 1994 as a result of what the government called "mistakes." The government then devalued the Chinese currency and successfully tamed inflation by trimming growth back to 10 percent annually—a difficult task requiring both economic skill and political will. By 1997, with inflation in check and growth proceeding rapidly, Shanghai's mayor estimated that his city alone was using 18 percent of the world's construction cranes.[11]

After the death of Deng Xiaoping in 1997, Chinese President Jiang Zemin consolidated power and reaffirmed Deng's principles, while the government's chief inflation-fighter was named prime minister. Hong Kong joined China in 1997 under the "one country, two systems" formula.

At that moment of Chinese strength, the Asian financial crisis introduced new doubts about China's prospects. China was guilty of many of the excesses of the Asian growth economies—debt, bad bank loans, money-losing state industries, real estate over-building, speculative investment, and corruption. Since China's currency was not freely traded on world markets, however, China was immune in the short term to the "Asian flu" that led to currency and market crashes in neighbouring countries targeted by international currency speculators (see pp. 352–356).

Nonetheless, the 1997 financial crisis affected China in several ways. First, Hong Kong's dollar was convertible, and China (which had just taken control of Hong Kong) wanted to prop up its value. Doing so required measures that led to stock market and real estate crashes there. Second, the devaluation of neighbouring states' currencies made Chinese exports less competitive, but if China in turn devalued its currency, a new round of devaluations by the neighbouring states might follow—leading to a downward spiral of competitive devaluations such as happened in the Great Depression of the 1930s. Therefore, China maintained both its own and Hong Kong's exchange rates. Although growth slowed to about 7 percent, China weathered the Asian flu in good health.

By 2003, as a new generation of Chinese leaders began taking charge—led by President Hu Jintao—China had continued rapid economic growth year by year with the help of large government infrastructure expenditures. President Hu's top priority is to address the growing inequality between the country's new newly rich strata and the

The Information Revolution

China and the Net

China is emerging as a more globally oriented great power, one that can put astronauts in space, stabilize Asian financial crises, and join the World Trade Organization. China's leaders need the internet as a connecting point with the world economy, yet fear its political impacts. Can China open to the world as a great trading power without letting information in and out freely? Will new information channels affect China's form of government?

To explore this question, go to www.pearsoned.ca/goldstein.

---

[11] Nicholas R. Lardy, *China's Unfinished Economic Revolution* (Washington, DC: Brookings, 1998). Kenneth Lieberthal, *Governing China* (NY: Norton, 1995). Robert G. Kaiser, "China Rising: Is America Paying Attention?" *Washington Post* 26 Oct. 1997: C1.

Thinking Theoretically

China's economic growth in the 1980s and 1990s stands out (along with a few other East Asian countries) from the pattern of sluggish development (if any) elsewhere in the global South. Several different explanations can be offered for China's success. One explanation is that China's traditional Confucian culture (shared to some extent by its East Asian neighbours) provides the discipline and social cohesion that allow rapid economic development and relative political stability. (China's path, then, would not apply to other areas of the global South.) The trouble with this explanation is that China's cultural traditions have been fairly fixed from decade to decade, yet China's politics have careened from civil war to totalitarian stability to Cultural Revolution to reformism, and its economic development has varied from the disaster of the Great Leap Forward in the 1950s to the success of market socialism since the 1980s.

A more liberal approach—and the dominant one now for explaining China's success—emphasizes the effect of market-oriented reforms in opening the way for rapid growth and rising incomes. Since liberals tend to favour open economies and free trade, they make much of the fact that when China moved its economic system in these directions, growth picked up rapidly. This explanation is appealing in that it can be applied widely to other countries of the South. However, the evidence that it actually works well across the board is not very strong. After all, economic reforms similar to China's have been imple-

mented in many other countries, yet China's performance far exceeds most of those other cases. This line of thinking then suggests avenues for further refinement of this theoretical approach. For example, one could tease apart the various elements of China's economic reforms—ranging from agricultural reforms to privatization to allowing foreign investment and so forth—and see which ones coincide with other successful cases in the global South.

A different explanation can be found in world-system theory, a more critical approach. China can be seen as moving from the periphery zone of the world economy to the semiperiphery (along with some East Asian neighbours). As we have seen, China's exports of light-industrial products support this characterization. In this theory, however, such a movement between zones does not change the overall structure of the world-system. Some regions such as China move up a zone; others such as Russia and Eastern Europe move down a zone (from core to semiperiphery). But the periphery itself must remain, and only a small part of the world can ever belong to the core. Thus, China's economic rise does not provide lessons or a viable path for states elsewhere in the global South. This theoretical approach, as compared to the liberal one, is a bit vague on its predictions ("some move up, some move down"). But its main conclusion—that the success of one region does not indicate any overall convergence of the South with the North—is borne out by the data in Chapter 11. China is, so far, the exception to a persistent (even growing) North-South gap.

---

hundreds of millions left in poverty in the countryside or laid off from jobs in state-owned industries in the cities.

China's new membership in the WTO raises new questions about how the ongoing Chinese opening of its economy to the world can coexist with continued political authoritarianism under communist rule. For example, 50 million Chinese are internet users, and hundreds of millions more may join them within a few years. They will be able to communicate with overseas partners, monitor shipments, and follow economic trends globally. They will also be able to bypass government-controlled sources of political information. Some observers expect economic integration in an information era to inexorably open up China's political system and lead to democratization, whereas other experts think that as long as Chinese leaders deliver economic growth, the population will have little appetite for political change.

It is unclear what lessons China's economic success over the past decade holds for the rest of the global South, but as Figure 12.2 suggests, economic development within China may have an enormous impact on its neighbours. The shift away from central planning and toward private ownership was clearly a key factor in its success, yet the state continued to play a central role in overseeing the economy (even more than in the NICs). These topics are being debated vigorously as China navigates the post-Deng era and as other poor states look to China's experience for lessons.

Other Experiments

Other sizeable states of the global South have pursued various development strategies, with mixed successes and failures. *India,* like China, deserves special attention because of its size. Its economy was until recently based loosely on socialism and state control of large industries but on private capitalism in agriculture and consumer goods. The state subsidizes basic goods and gives special treatment to farmers. Unlike China, India has a relatively democratic government, but a fractious one, with various autonomy movements and ethnic conflicts. Recent elections have forced out of government the long-standing ruling party, the Hindu-nationalist Bharatiya Janata Party, widely considered corrupt.

Indian state-owned industries, like those elsewhere, are largely unprofitable. The new prime minister, Manmohan Singh, has pledged increasing privatization of state-owned enterprises and growth rates of 7–8 percent per year. Privatization and steady growth will likely also attract more foreign investment, which has lagged behind other large countries of the global South. In the 1990s, China received many times the foreign investment that India did.

Figure 12.2 China's Neighbourhood

China's continuing growth is the leading success of economic development in the global South. China's future path will affect all of Asia.

The 1991 collapse of the Soviet Union—India's major trading partner—threw India into a severe economic crisis that nearly caused it to default on its international debts. India sought help from the IMF and the World Bank and committed itself to far-reaching economic reforms such as reducing bureaucracy and selling money-losing state-owned industries (see "IMF Conditionality," pp. 471–473). India saw robust economic growth in the late 1990s and early 2000s, and developed special strength in the export of computer software services.

Among other sizeable Asian countries, *Indonesia* and *Thailand* are trying, with some limited success, to follow a Pacific Rim NIC strategy like that of South Korea or Taiwan. Thailand's military government followed China's example in 1992 by shooting student demonstrators, but this did not silence critics. Afterward, some military commanders were forced off lucrative positions on the boards of directors of state-owned enterprises.

Other large Asian states—*Bangladesh, Pakistan, Vietnam,* and the *Philippines*—are more deeply mired in poverty and have dimmer prospects for capital accumulation in the coming years. All have problems with state bureaucracies and corruption. Vietnam is a communist state trying to follow a reform model parallel to China's. The Philippines is trying to overcome a rebellion in the countryside and a history of political instability that discourages foreign investment. It has not fully recovered from the looting of its economy and treasury under the Marcos dictatorship in the 1970s and early 1980s. Pakistan also faces political instability and a chronic danger of war with India. Bangladesh is just extremely poor, with no apparent foothold to get accumulation started.

Brazil and *Mexico* are the largest states of the global South in the Western hemisphere. Brazil built up a sizeable internal market by concentrating income in a growing middle and upper class, especially after a military coup in 1964. However, its cities are still ringed with huge slums filled with desperately poor people. In the 1980s, Brazil returned to democratic civilian rule and began economic reforms, such as selling off unprofitable state-owned enterprises, promoting free markets, and encouraging foreign investment.

Nonetheless, by the early 1990s, Brazil remained well more than US$100 billion in debt (the largest foreign debt in the South). It had annual inflation of 200 percent and more, causing the currency's value to fall drastically. The president was impeached in a corruption scandal. The positive side of this embarrassing episode for Brazil was a constitutional, civilian transfer of power. With faster economic growth and foreign investment, a bigger grain harvest, and a substantial trade surplus, Brazil's main problem by 1993 was inflation. The anti-inflation plan of finance minister Fernando Cardoso was so successful that he was elected president in 1995, and other countries tried to copy his methods. In the 1997 currency crisis, Cardoso was able to scare off currency speculators, though at the cost of a dramatic slowdown in Brazil's economy. Brazil received a US$41 billion IMF package in 1998, devalued its currency in 1999, and felt waves from next-door Argentina's financial meltdown in 2001. In 2002, the IMF provided a US$30 billion bailout loan, with few requirements for domestic reform because of worries that a financial collapse in Brazil would damage the world economy in a way that Argentina could not. The election of a leftist president, Lula da Silva, raised fears that free spending on social programs would undermine Brazil's financial position, but instead he reined in spending, brought down inflation, and stabilized Brazil's financial position in 2003 at the short-term cost of economic recession.

In Mexico, similar economic reforms were undertaken in the 1980s. Like Brazil, Mexico had pockets of deep poverty and a sizeable foreign debt. Unlike Brazil, Mexico had oil to export (a good source of hard currency, despite fluctuating world prices). Mexico has also enjoyed relative political stability, though corruption is a problem. Leaders hoped NAFTA would accelerate foreign investment, creating jobs and export opportunities. Mexico also sold off more than US$20 billion of state-owned companies (sparing the strategic oil industry) to help lower its debt and bring down inflation. But assassinations and other political upheaval, including an armed rebellion in Chiapas that broke out in response to the NAFTA accord, complicated Mexico's development problems. In 1994–1995, Mexico's currency collapsed and standards of living for many consumers took a sharp drop. With help from the United States, Mexico undertook new economic reforms and began to rebuild the economy and restore international and domestic confidence. A reformist president, Vicente Fox, was elected from outside the long-standing ruling party in 2000.[12] But by NAFTA's tenth anniversary in 2003, these upheavals had brought Mexico neither a breakthrough nor a disaster.

In Africa, *Nigeria* is the largest country and, with oil to export, one of the less impoverished. In 1980, when oil prices were high, Nigeria began building a huge, Soviet-style steel plant, which leaders hoped would serve as the cornerstone of Nigerian economic development. Twelve years and US$5 billion later, the plant was ready to start producing steel. It is the biggest industrial project in sub-Saharan Africa. But because its products will not be competitive in the world steel industry, government subsidies may be required indefinitely. By 2003, with the steel complex still not producing steel, the Nigerian government signed an agreement with a U.S. company to take over management and provide billions of dollars in new foreign investment. The government brought in hundreds of Russian and Ukrainian experts to help, but the prospects for competitive steel production remain doubtful in the short term.

Meanwhile, as world oil prices fell drastically in the 1980s, the country went in debt by US$35 billion. Corruption took a steady toll on the economy. This pattern of centralized industrialization under Nigeria's military government faces uncertain prospects at best, although oil exports provide continuing income.[13] Nigeria cancelled a planned experiment in democracy in the early 1990s, and a military dictatorship continued in power. African Americans began an unusual campaign to press for democracy in Nigeria, in order to move Africa's largest country forward in both human rights and overall development. In 1995 Nigeria ignored international pleas and executed a popular leader of an oil-rich but impoverished region, Ken Saro-Wiwa. Finally, the dictator died and his successor held elections in which a civilian president took power in 1999. Nigeria has enjoyed some political stability since then, but new ethnic conflicts broke into violence. Nigeria's economic condition remains fragile, though rising oil prices in 2004 may contribute to economic recovery.

In the Middle East, the small countries with large oil exports—such as *Saudi Arabia, Kuwait,* and *Bahrain*—have done well economically. But they are in a special class; their experience is not one that global South states without oil can follow. *Iran* and *Iraq* are somewhat larger countries that have also benefited from oil exports. After the Iran-Iraq War ended in 1988, Iran began to grow robustly and to attract foreign investment. A reformist president of Iran has opened new avenues to Western powers and their investment capital, although U.S. sanctions remain. Iraq used oil revenues on military assaults against Iran and Kuwait. Its economic development was set back enormously by the bombing of its infrastructure during the Gulf War and 2003 Iraq war.

Turkey has been fairly successful in developing its economy without oil revenues, a rare case. Like South Korea and Taiwan, Turkey was an authoritarian state for many years

---

[12] Nancy Neiman Auerbach, *States, Banks, Markets: Mexico's Path to Financial Liberalization in Comparative Perspective* (Boulder, CO: Westview, 2000).

[13] Kenneth B. Noble, "Nigeria's Monumental Steel Plant: Nationalist Mission or Colossal Mistake?" *New York Times* 11 July 1992: 3.

but has allowed political liberalization since the 1990s. It has developed under a Western security umbrella (NATO) and has received considerable U.S. foreign aid. Like Mexico, Turkey is trying to join its richer neighbours—the EU. Turkey also hopes to develop strong ties with the five former Soviet Asian republics. Unlike Iran, Turkey formally espouses secular politics, with Islam relegated to the religious and cultural sphere. A small but growing minority of Turks favours a more explicitly Islamic, less secular basis for Turkish society. A long-standing violent conflict hinders development in Turkey's Kurdish region. Turkey suffered recession in 2000–2001 and received a US$30 billion IMF bailout.

Egypt is mired in poverty despite substantial U.S. aid since the late 1970s. The state owns 70 percent of industry, operates the economy centrally, imposes high import tariffs, and provides patronage jobs and subsidized prices in order to maintain political power. A major portion of Egypt's foreign debt was forgiven after it helped the anti-Iraq coalition in the Gulf War, but Egypt remains about US$30 billion in debt. Reforms in the 1990s brought economic growth, but remaining problems include high unemployment, a trade deficit, and widespread corruption. Islamic militants have disrupted Egypt's economy (especially tourism) and politics in the past decade.

These examples illustrate the many approaches toward economic development that states of the global South have tried and the mixed success they have met. Such experiences have been generalized into "lessons" for economic development.

LESSONS

Clearly, the largest states of the global South are following somewhat different strategies with somewhat different results. But several common themes recur. These themes concern trade, the concentration of capital, authoritarianism, and corruption.

Import Substitution and Export-Led Growth

Throughout the global South, states are trying to use international trade as the basis of accumulation. For the reasons discussed in Chapter 8, a policy of self-reliance or autarky is at best an extremely slow way to build up wealth. But through the creation of a trade surplus, a state can accumulate hard currency and build industry and infrastructure.

One way to try to create a trade surplus, used frequently a few decades ago, is through **import substitution**—the development of local industries to produce items that a country had been importing. These industries may receive state subsidies or tariff protection. This might seem to be a good policy for reducing dependency—especially on the former colonial centre—while shrinking a trade deficit or building a trade surplus. But it tends to produce growth rates that then plateau fairly quickly. Some scholars think that import substitution is a policy useful only at a very early phase of economic development, after which it becomes counterproductive. Others think it is never useful.

More and more states have shifted to a strategy of **export-led growth,** a strategy used by the NICs. This strategy seeks to develop industries that can compete in specific niches in the world economy. These industries may receive special treatment, such as subsidies and protected access to local markets. Exports from these industries generate hard currency and create a favourable trade balance. The state can then spend part of its money on imports of commodities produced more cheaply elsewhere.

Such a strategy has risks, especially when a state specializes in the export of a few raw materials (see "Postcolonial Dependency" on pp. 419–421). It leaves poor countries vulnerable to sudden price fluctuations for their exports. For example, when world copper prices fell from US$3000 to US$1300 per ton in 1974, income fell accordingly in Zambia,

import substitution A strategy of developing local industries, often conducted behind protectionist barriers, to produce items that a country had been importing.

export-led growth An economic development strategy that seeks to develop industries capable of competing in specific niches in the world economy.

which got 94 percent of export earnings from copper. It had to cut back imports of needed goods drastically and suffered a 15 percent decline in its (already low) GDP.[14]

The overall relationship between the prices of exported and imported goods—called the **terms of trade**—affects an export strategy based on raw materials. There is evidence that in the 1950s and 1960s, and again in the 1980s, the terms of trade eroded the value of raw materials, also called the declining terms of trade in raw materials and commodities. A state trying to create trade benefits by exporting such goods would have to export more and more over time in order to import the same amount of manufactured goods— a major obstacle to accumulation.

terms of trade The overall relationship between prices of imported and exported goods.

Because of both terms of trade and price fluctuations, states have looked to exporting manufactured goods, rather than raw materials, as the key to export-led growth. However, in seeking a niche for manufactured goods, a state of the global South must compete against industrialized countries with better technology, more educated work forces, and much more capital. For example, Nigeria's steel exports are unlikely to provide the desired trade surplus (although South Korean steel did so). Thus, countries of the global South need to be selective in developing export-oriented industrial strategies. It is not enough to subsidize and protect an industry until it grows in size; someday it has to be able to stand its own ground in a competitive world or it will not bring in a trade surplus.

Concentrating Capital for Manufacturing

Manufacturing emerges as a key factor in both export-led growth and self-sustaining industrialization (home production for home markets). It is not surprising that states of the global South want to increase their own manufacturing base and change the global division of labour based on manufacturing in the core and resource extraction in the periphery. One great difficulty in getting manufacturing started is that capital is required to build factories. Competitive factories in technologically advanced industries can require large amounts of capital—such as the US$5 billion for Nigeria's steel plant. Nigeria obtained much of the money from oil exports, but most states in the South lack such a source of funds.

To invest in manufacturing, these countries must *concentrate* what surplus their economies produce. They face the familiar trade-off between short-term consumption and long-term investment. Money spent building factories cannot be spent subsidizing food prices or building better schools. Thus the concentration of capital for manufacturing can sharpen disparities in income. A political price must often be paid in the short term for reducing public consumption, even in industrialized states. In states of the global South there is little margin for reducing consumption without causing extreme hardship. The result may be crowds rioting in the streets or guerrillas taking over the countryside.

The problem is compounded by the need to create domestic markets for manufactured goods. Because it is unlikely that a manufacturing industry in a poor country will be immediately competitive on world markets, one common strategy is to build up the industry with sales to the home market (protected by tariffs and subsidies) before pursuing world markets. But home markets for manufactured goods do not come from poor peasants in the countryside or the unemployed youth in city slums. Rather, wealth must be concentrated in a *middle class* that has the income to buy manufactured goods.

The growing disparity of income in such a situation often triggers intense frustration on the part of poorer people, even those whose income is rising. (Political rebellion is fuelled by relative deprivation as much as by absolute poverty.) A common way states respond to such problems is to crack down hard with force to stamp out the protests of the poor and of

---

[14] Willy Brandt et al., *North-South: A Programme for Survival* (Cambridge, MA: MIT P, 1980) 145.

CAPITAL INTENSIVE
Foreign investment, international debt, and domestic inequality all can help concentrate the necessary capital for manufacturing. In recent years, microcredit—very small loans made directly to very poor people—has provided a way to use capital more diffusely. These women in Bangladesh (1997) bought a cell phone with a loan and rented time on it to villagers.

informal sector Those modes of business, such as shadow markets and street vendors, operating beyond state control; some scholars see this sector as the core of a new development strategy.

microcredit The use of very small loans to small groups of individuals, often women, to stimulate economic development.

other political opponents of the government (see "Authoritarianism and Democracy" later in this chapter).

Such problems might be minimized by reducing the amount of capital that needs to be squeezed from a state's domestic economy. Capital for manufacturing can come from foreign investment or foreign loans, for instance. This strategy reduces short-term pain, but it also reduces the amount of surplus (profit) available to the state in the long term. Another way to minimize the capital needs of manufacturing is to start out in low-capital industries. These industries can begin generating capital, which can in turn be used to move into somewhat more technologically demanding and capital-intensive kinds of manufacturing. A favourite starter industry is *textiles*. The industry is fairly labour-intensive, giving an advantage to countries with cheap labour, and does not require huge investments of capital to get started. Many states in the South have built their own textile industries as a step toward industrialization. For this reason, many states impose high tariffs on textiles, which are among the least freely traded commodities.

There are some problems with concentrating capital for manufacturing. One is that it creates conditions ripe for corruption (discussed shortly). The problem is especially severe when authoritarian political control is used to enforce compliance with hardships that may accompany the concentration of wealth—an issue currently for China.

An approach that received international attention in the 1980s is based on a Peruvian entrepreneur's analysis of the **informal sector** in Lima's economy—black markets (also called parallel markets or shadow markets), street vendors, and other private arrangements.[15] These modes of business are often beyond state control and may not even show up in state-compiled economic statistics. Markets operate rather freely, and some scholars have begun to see such markets, rather than large manufacturing industries, as the core of a new development strategy.

A related approach to capitalization in very poor countries, growing in popularity in recent years, is **microcredit** (or *microlending*). Based on a successful model in Bangladesh (the Grameen Bank), microcredit uses small loans to poor people, especially women, to support economic self-sufficiency. The borrowers are organized into small groups and take responsibility for each other's success, including repaying the loans. Repayment rates have been high, and the idea is spreading rapidly in several regions. In one high-tech twist, village women have begun using small loans to start businesses offering cellular phone booths (or huts) where people pay to make domestic or international calls. Rural farmers used the phone time to find out market conditions before making a long trek to sell their products. Thus, bringing the information revolution to isolated villages raised incomes for the farmers and the women alike, and the bank got its loans repaid. Microcredit is now being applied on a macroscale. By 2002, 40 million families had received loans from 2500 institutions worldwide. Microcredit is the opposite of a trickle-down approach, instead

[15] Hernando De Soto, *The Other Path: The Invisible Revolution in the Third World* (NY: HarperCollins, 1989).

injecting capital at the bottom of the economic hierarchy. A loan to buy a goat or cell phone may do more good, dollar for dollar, than a loan to build a dam.

Cartels

A **cartel** is an association of producers (or more rarely consumers, or both), of a certain product—formed to manipulate its price on the world market. It is an unusual but interesting form of trade regime, and one that has been used with some limited success by developing countries in an effort to control the impact of fluctuating commodity prices on their economies, and to gain the most from their commodity exports. Producers are able to coordinate their actions so as to keep prices high. Cartels can use a variety of means to affect prices; the most effective is to coordinate limits on production by each member so as to lower the supply, relative to demand, of the good.

The most prominent cartel in the international economy is the **Organization of Petroleum Exporting Countries (OPEC).** Its member states together control hundreds of billions of dollars in oil exports annually—about 60 percent of the world total and enough to significantly affect the price. (A cartel need not hold a monopoly on production of a good to be able to affect its price.) At OPEC's peak of strength in the 1970s, the proportion was even higher. OPEC maintains a headquarters in Vienna, Austria (which is not a member), and holds negotiations several times a year to set quotas for each country's production of oil in order to keep world oil prices in a target range. Members and their export levels are shown in Table 12.1. Saudi Arabia is by far the largest oil exporter, and therefore occupies a unique position in the world economy.

OPEC illustrates the potential that a cartel creates for serious collective goods problems. Individual members of OPEC can (and do) cheat a bit by exceeding their production quotas while still enjoying the collective good of high oil prices. The collective good breaks down when too many members exceed their quotas, as has happened repeatedly to OPEC. Then world oil prices drop. (Iraq's accusations that fellow OPEC member Kuwait was exceeding production quotas and driving oil prices down was one factor in Iraq's invasion of Kuwait in 1990.)

OPEC may work as well as it does because one member, Saudi Arabia, has enough oil to unilaterally manipulate supply enough to drive prices up or down. Saudi Arabia can take up the slack from some cheating in OPEC (cutting back its own production) and keep prices up. Or if too many OPEC members are cheating on their quotas, it can punish them by flooding the market with oil and driving prices down until the other OPEC members collectively come to their senses.

Even with Saudi predominance, high oil prices in the 1970s led non-OPEC states to increase production and importing states to improve energy conservation, so that by the 1980s OPEC could not prevent a severe decline in world oil prices, to around US$20 per barrel. But by mid-2004, oil prices were back up again, at over US$40 per barrel. In this case, market forces (rising demand in China and other Asian markets), the impact of the Iraq War, and the declining value of the U.S. dollar pushed up prices by 42 percent in a single year. Saudi Arabia pledged to increase production to bring prices back down to around US$30 a barrel, but other OPEC members resisted. Those producing at nearly full capacity, such as Libya and Venezuela, have little to gain from increased production (they cannot sell any more than before if they are already at capacity, but will be hit by the lower prices once Saudi production increases). Some economic analysts also suggested that this new mini "oil shock" might be a precursor to a global recession.[16]

cartel An association of producers or consumers (or both) of a certain product, formed for the purpose of manipulating its price on the world market.

Organization of Petroleum Exporting Countries (OPEC) The most prominent cartel in the international economy; its members control over half the world's total oil exports, enough to significantly affect the world price of oil.

---

[16] J. Srinivasan, "Is an Oil Peak upon the World?" *The Hindu Business Line* 2 June 2004, <http://www.thehindubusinessline.com/2004/06/02/stories/2004060200171100.htm>.

Table 12.1 OPEC Members and Oil Production, August 2003	
Member State	**Millions of Barrels/Day**
Saudi Arabia	8.6
Iran	3.7
Venezuela	2.4
United Arab Emirates	2.2
Nigeria	2.2
Kuwait	2.1
Libya	1.4
Algeria	1.2
Iraq	1.1
Indonesia	1.0
Qatar	0.7
Total OPEC	26.6
Percentage of World	38%

Note: Major oil exporters not in OPEC include Russia, Kazakhstan, Mexico, China, Canada, Britain, and Norway. Ecuador and Gabon, minor exporters, left OPEC in 1992 and 1995, respectively. The United States, until several decades ago a major oil exporter, is now a major importer.

Source: Data adapted from United States Dept. of Energy, Energy Information Administration.

Consumers usually do not form cartels. However, in response to OPEC, the major oil-importing states formed their own organization, the *International Energy Agency (IEA)*, which has some of the functions of a cartel. The IEA coordinates the energy policies of major industrialized states—such as the maintenance of oil stockpiles in case of a shortage on world markets—in order to keep world oil prices low and stable. The largest importers of oil are the members of the G8 (large industrialized states).

For a few commodities that are subject to large price fluctuations on world markets—detrimental to both producers and consumers—joint producer-consumer cartels have been formed. In order to keep prices stable, producing and consuming states use the cartel to coordinate the overall supply and demand globally. Such cartels exist for coffee, several minerals, and some other products. In the coffee cartel, Colombia argued in the late 1980s for a higher target price for coffee, so that Colombian peasants would have an incentive to switch from growing coca (for cocaine production) to coffee. But the United States, as the major coffee-consuming state, would not agree to the proposal for higher prices.[17]

In general, the idea of cartels runs counter to liberal economics because cartels are deliberate efforts to distort free markets. However, for countries of the global South that rely on commodity exports, and suffer price fluctuations or declining terms of trade, the creation of a cartel can be a means to take control of the impact of market forces on commodity prices. Cartels usually are not as powerful as market forces in determining overall world price levels: too many producers and suppliers exist, and too many substitute goods

---

[17] Robert H. Bates, *Open-Economy Politics: The Political Economy of the World Coffee Trade* (Princeton, NJ: Princeton UP, 1997).

can replace ones that become too expensive, for a cartel to corner the market. The exceptions, such as OPEC, are rare.

Authoritarianism and Democracy

Several decades ago, many scholars expected that states of the global South would follow the European and North American states in economic and political development. The gradual accumulation of capital would be accompanied by the gradual extension of literacy and education, the reduction of class and gender disparities, and the strengthening of democracy and political participation.

In reality, democracy has not accompanied economic development in a systematic or general way. In fact, the fastest-growing states have generally been authoritarian states, not democracies. This observation has led to the theory that economic development is incompatible with democracy. Accordingly, political repression and the concentration of political control are necessary to maintain order during the process of concentrating capital and to start accumulation. Demands by poor people for greater short-term consumption must be refused. Class disparities must be sharpened. Labour discipline must be enforced at extremely low wage levels. Foreign investors must be assured of political stability—above all, that radicals will not take power and that foreign assets will not be nationalized in a revolution. A democracy may be inherently incapable of accomplishing these difficult and painful tasks, according to this theory.

The NICs did not achieve their success through free and open democratic politics, but through firm state rule permitting little dissent. Chinese leaders, for example, contrast their recent economic successes, achieved under tight political control, with the failed Soviet efforts under Gorbachev to promote economic reform by first loosening political control.

It has been suggested that a strong state facilitates capital accumulation.[18] Only a strong state, in this view, has the power to enforce and coordinate the allocations of wealth required to start accumulation going. But scholars do not agree on the definition of a strong state; some refer to the size of the state bureaucracy or its ability to extract taxes, others to its legitimacy or its ability to enforce its will on the population. The idea of a strong state is often connected with economic nationalism, or mercantilism (see pp. 311–315).

In reality, the theory that authoritarianism leads to economic development does not hold up, just as the theory that democracy automatically accompanies economic development does not hold up. Many authoritarian states have achieved neither political stability nor economic development. Others have realized political stability but have failed at economic accumulation. The many military dictatorships in Africa are among the least successful models in the global South. In Latin America, the poorest country, Haiti, had the most authoritarian government for decades.

Furthermore, authoritarian states can lead to greater political instability, not less. The harder the state cracks down, the more resentment the population feels. Instead of peaceful protests, violent insurgencies often grow out of such resentments. In Guatemala, a military government harshly repressed rural revolutionaries and their peasant sympathizers for decades, until a peace agreement was reached in 1996. Since the 1960s, in this country of 9 million, repression and war killed 100 000 people, and another 45 000 "disappeared"; most were killed and buried in mass graves.[19] Guatemala's government at times

[18] Peter B. Evans, Dietrich Rueschemeyer, and Theda Skocpol, eds., *Bringing the State Back In* (NY: Cambridge UP, 1985). Stephen D. Krasner, *Structural Conflict: The Third World Against Global Liberalism* (Berkeley: U California P, 1985).

[19] Human Rights Watch World Report 1990. Cited in *Science* 257 (24 July 1992): 479.

received substantial U.S. aid (based on "anticommunism") and at other times was banned from receiving such aid (based on violations of human rights). But its decades of authoritarian rule did not stop dissent, bring political stability, attract much foreign investment, or create much economic accumulation.

Meanwhile, elsewhere in Latin America a wave of civilian governments replaced military ones in the late 1980s.[20] Economic conditions there have improved, not worsened, as a result. In states such as South Korea and Taiwan, which began industrializing under authoritarianism but have since shifted toward democracy, economic progress was not harmed. Relatively free elections and some limited tolerance of dissent signalled greater stability and maturity, and did not discourage investment or slow economic growth.

It has been suggested that authoritarian rule and the concentration of income in few hands represent a phase in the development process. First, capital must be concentrated to get accumulation started, and tight political control must be maintained during this painful phase. Later, more wealth is generated, income spreads to more people, the middle class expands, and political controls can be relaxed.

But again, the empirical reality does not support such a theory as a general rule. There is no guarantee that, even in early phases of accumulation, authoritarian control leads to economic development. In fact, flagrant human rights abuses seem to cause political instability at any stage of economic development. Some successful accumulators, such as China and Saudi Arabia, have maintained tight political control throughout the process. Others, such as South Korea and Turkey, have started with authoritarian rule and evolved into democracies. Still others, such as Costa Rica and Malaysia, have achieved good economic results while maintaining relative democracy and little repression. Others however, such as Singapore, retain tight domestic control. Similarly, among the countries that have done poorly in economic accumulation are both authoritarian regimes and democratic ones. Therefore, a state's form of political governance does not determine its success in economic development.

Corruption

Corruption is an important negative factor in economic development in many states; corruption also plays a role in some of the theories just discussed about various strategies for using trade, industry, and government to promote economic development. In the past decade, high-level corruption cases have become high-profile international news, knocking governments from power in Brazil, Italy, India, Pakistan, Indonesia, and elsewhere, and sending two former South Korean presidents to jail.

Analyses of corruption look first and foremost to the governments of particular states, and to their relationship with foreign economic actors such as MNCs. Through foreign policy, the government mediates the national economy's relationship to the world economy. It regulates the conditions under which MNCs operate in the country. It enforces worker discipline—calling out the army if necessary to break strikes or suppress revolutions. It sets tax rates and wields other macroeconomic levers of control over the economy. And in most states of the global South, it owns a sizeable stake in major industries—a monopoly in some cases.

---

[20] Guillermo O'Donnell, Phillipe C. Schmitter, and Lawrence Whitehead, eds., *Transitions from Authoritarian Rule: Prospects for Democracy* [series] (Baltimore: Johns Hopkins UP, 1986). Charles A. Reilly, ed., *New Paths to Democratic Development in Latin America: The Rise of NGO-Municipal Collaboration* (Boulder, CO: Rienner, 1995). Adam Przeworski, *Democracy and the Market: Political and Economic Reforms in Eastern Europe and Latin America.* (NY: Cambridge UP, 1991).

CORRUPTION STINKS

Corruption is a major impediment to development. In South Korea in 1997, two former presidents were jailed for corruption, and the ruling party lost power. Officials had taken bribes in exchange for granting government loans; these bad loans were a major factor in the 1997 financial crisis. Here, South Korean students, demanding the president's resignation for corruption, run from riot police, early in 1997.

Corruption is a kind of privatization of politics in that it concerns the distribution of benefits from economic transactions (exchange and capital accumulation). For example, when a foreign MNC comes into a country to drill for oil, the surplus produced will be shared among the MNC (through profits), the state (through taxation and fees), the local capitalists who make money supplying the operation, the local workers who earn wages, and the foreign consumers who use the oil (which, because of the added supply, will be slightly cheaper on world markets).

State officials will decide whether to let the MNC into the country, which MNC to give the drilling rights to, and what terms to insist on (leasing fees, percentages of sales, etc.). These are complex deals struck after long negotiations. Corruption merely adds another player, the corrupt official, to share the benefits. For instance, a foreign oil company can pay off an official to award a favourable contract, and both can profit. In 2003, U.S. prosecutors indicted a Mobil Oil executive and a New York banker for paying US$78 million to two senior officials in Kazakhstan—with a kickback of $2 million for the Mobil executive—to secure Mobil's billion-dollar stake in a huge oil field there.

Corruption is by no means limited to the global South. But for several reasons corruption has a deeper effect in poor countries. First, there is simply less surplus to keep economic growth going; accumulation is fragile. Another difference is that in those countries dependent on exporting a few products, the revenue arrives in a very concentrated form—

large payments in hard currency. This presents a greater opportunity for corruption than in a more diversified economy with more (smaller) deals. Furthermore, in developing countries incomes are often so low that corrupt officials are more tempted to accept payments, and redirection of services from the poor (who cannot pay bribes) has a devastating effect. Corruption can have a significant environmental impact also: the World Bank estimates that some 80 percent of timber harvests in the Amazon are illegal.[21]

Corruption in the global South presents a collective goods problem for states and MNCs in the global North: individually, MNCs and their home states can profit by clinching a deal with a private payoff, but collectively the MNCs and states of the North lose money by having to make these payoffs. Therefore, there is an incentive to clamp down on corruption only if other industrialized states do likewise. More often, governments will try to support their MNCs, even when convicted of corruption charges. For example, the Canadian multinational engineering company Acres International was convicted in the African country of Lesotho on bribery charges in a $12 billion water project (a conviction that was upheld on appeal). The Canadian government did not sanction Acres International, and also came to its defence at the World Bank. World Bank anti-corruption efforts entail barring companies engaged in corrupt or fraudulent practices from receiving World Bank contracts. Most companies that have been barred have been based in the South. The Acres case is considered an important test of World Bank resolve in addressing corruption committed by companies based in the global North.[22]

Transparency helps solve collective goods problems (see p. 91). A Berlin-based NGO called Transparency International pushed successfully for action to stem corruption in international business deals. The group publishes annual surveys showing the countries that business executives considered most corrupt. The top five on the list in 2003 were Bangladesh, Nigeria, Haiti, Paraguay, and Burma.

In 1997 the world's 29 leading industrialized states agreed to forbid their companies from bribing foreign officials (payments to political parties were not forbidden, however). The effect has been limited in practice. The IMF meanwhile vowed to crack down on corruption. It suspended a US$220 million IMF loan to Kenya (triggering a stock market crash) when Kenya failed to take promised steps against corruption in 1997.

Occasionally, government officials serve not their own private interests but those of a foreign state. Such a government is called a *puppet government*. The officials of such a government are bought off to serve the interests of a more powerful state (which may have installed the government through military conquest). For example, during the Cold War, both superpowers justified installing friendly governments by reference to global power politics. Critics, however, believed the puppet governments served business interests of the controlling state, not security interests. This and other issues concern the role of international business in the global South.

NORTH-SOUTH BUSINESS

Given the importance of international trade and investment to economic development, not only governments but private banks and MNCs from the North are also major par-

---

[21] World Bank, *World Development Report 2004: Making Services Work For Poor People* (Washington DC: World Bank, 2004). World Bank, "How the Bank Helps Countries Fight Corruption" 8 April 2004, <http://web .worldbank.org/WBSITE/EXTERNAL/NEWS/>.

[22] Lawrence Solomon, "Martin's Problem: Corruption at Home and Abroad," *National Post* 27 March 2004. Emad Mekay, "Activists Prod World Bank on Canadian Corruption Case," *Inter Press Service* (23 Mar. 2004).

ticipants in the economies of the South. Several large developing country states have also created their own MNCs, though these play a fairly minor role compared to MNCs from the North.

Foreign Investment

Poor countries have little money available to invest in new factories, farms, mines, or oil wells. Foreign investment—investment in such capital goods by foreigners (most often MNCs)—is one way to get accumulation started (see "Foreign Direct Investment" on pp. 358–360). Foreign investment has been crucial to the success of China and other Asian developing countries. Overall, private capital flows to the global South totalled more than US$150 billion in 2003—triple the amount given in official development assistance.

Foreigners who invest in a country then own the facilities; the investor by virtue of its ownership can control decisions about how many people to employ, whether to expand or shut down, what products to make, and how to market them. Also, the foreign investor can usually take the profits from the operation out of the country (repatriation of profits). However, the host government can share in the wealth by charging fees and taxes, or by leasing land or drilling rights (see "Host and Home Government Relations" on pp. 360–365).

Because of past colonial experiences, many governments in the global South have feared the loss of control that comes with foreign investments by MNCs. Sometimes the presence of MNCs was associated with the painful process of concentrating capital and the sharpening of class disparities in the host state. In other instances domestic legislation, tax rules, and service provision are expected to adapt in order to attract foreign investment. The World Bank, for example, recommends that countries seeking foreign investment in the mining sector reduce or eliminate import taxes, release all land reserved for exploration by state-owned enterprises to foreign investors, and reform the public service to enable administration of mining rights for foreign investors.[23] Part of the argument of the World Bank, and others informed by an economic liberal perspective, is that any loss of sovereignty is counterbalanced by the ability of foreign investors to infuse capital and generate more surplus. By the 1980s and 1990s, as models based on autarky or state ownership were discredited and the NICs gained success, many poor states rushed to embrace foreign investment.

One way in which states have sought to soften the loss of control is through *joint ventures*, companies owned partly by a foreign MNC and partly by a local firm or the host government itself. Sometimes foreign ownership in joint ventures is limited to some percentage (often 49 percent), to ensure that ultimate control rests with the host country even though a large share of the profits go to the MNC. The percentage of ownership is usually proportional to the amount of capital invested; if a host government wants more control it must put up more of the money. Joint ventures work well for MNCs because they help ensure the host government's cooperation in reducing bureaucratic hassles and ensuring success (by giving the host government a direct stake in the outcome).

MNCs invest in a country because of some advantage of doing business there. In some cases, it is the presence of natural resources. Sometimes it is cheap labour. Sometimes geographical location is a factor. Some states have better *absorptive capacity* than others—the ability to put investments to productive use—because of more highly

---

[23] World Bank, *A Mining Strategy for Latin America and the Caribbean*, World Bank Technical Paper No. 345 (1996).

GM MOVES IN
Foreign investment is an important source of capital for economic development in the global South. The relationship of foreign investors and host countries transcends economics and draws in culture, politics, and identity. General Motors built this US$1.5 billion Buick assembly line in Shanghai, the historical (and perhaps future) centre of foreign economic penetration in China, 1998.

developed infrastructure and a higher level of skills among workers or managers. As these are most often middle-income states, the funnelling of investments to states with high absorptive capacity tends to sharpen disparities *within* the global South.

MNCs also look for a favourable *regulatory environment* in which a host state will facilitate, rather than impede, the MNC's business. For example, Motorola had decided to invest more than $1 billion in new facilities in India in the 1990s, but changed its mind after encountering India's bureaucracy and shifted its investments toward China instead.[24]

MNC decisions about foreign investment also depend on prospects for *financial stability*, especially for low inflation and stable currency exchange rates. If a currency is not convertible into hard currency, an MNC will not be able to take profits back to its home state or reinvest them elsewhere.

Beyond these financial considerations, a foreign investor producing for local markets wants to know that the host country's *economic growth* will sustain demand for the goods being produced. For example, automobile producers who built factories in Thailand and other Southeast Asian countries in the 1990s to meet the demands of a growing middle class were burned by the 1997 financial crash; some pulled up stakes and left. Similarly, whether producing for local consumption or export, the MNC wants the local *labour* supply—whether semi-skilled labour or just cheap—to be stable. This means in part that the MNC is reluctant to invest in countries with strong legislation protecting worker's rights, or active trade union activity. Foreign investors often look to international financial institutions, such as the World Bank and the IMF, and to private analyses, to judge a state's economic stability before investing in it.

Of equal importance in attracting investment is *political stability* (see pp. 362–363). Banks and MNCs conduct *political risk analyses* to assess the risks of political disturbances in global South states in which they might invest. Host countries for their part seek to assure potential foreign investors that they have stable political environments in which investments will not be at risk.

Beyond their usual role in providing foreign investment, technology transfer, and loans (in the case of banks), MNCs also sometimes participate in more broadly conceived development projects in a host state. Such participation is a way of investing in political goodwill as well as helping provide political stability by improving the condition of the population. The attitude of the government and the goodwill of the population affect the overall business prospects of the MNC. However, the people most adversely affected by MNC activities (for example, peasant farmers displaced from their land in order to make

[24] Edward A. Gargan, "India's Rush to a Free Market Economy Stumbles," *New York Times* 15 Aug. 1992: 2.

way for bauxite mining) often have little influence with either the MNC or their own government. It is usually the middle classes, who benefit more immediately from enhanced economic growth, who are more willing to embrace MNCs.

Technology Transfer

The productive investment of capital depends on the knowledge and skills—business management, technical training, higher education, as well as basic literacy and education—of workers and managers. Of special importance are the management and technical skills related to the key industries in a state's economy. In many former colonies, whites with such skills left after independence (see "Postcolonial Dependency" on pp. 419–423). In other states, the skills needed to develop new industries have never existed. A few states in the Persian Gulf with large incomes and small populations have imported a whole work force from foreign countries. But this practice is rare.

Most states of the global South seek to build up their own educated elite with knowledge and skills to run the national economy. One way to do so is to send students to industrialized states for higher education. This entails some risks, however. Students may enjoy life in the North and fail to return home. In most developing countries, every student talented enough to study abroad represents a national resource and usually a long investment in primary and secondary education, which is lost if the student does not return. The same applies to professionals (for example, doctors) who emigrate later in their careers. The problem of losing skilled workers to richer countries, called the **brain drain,** has impeded economic development in states such as India, Pakistan, the Philippines, and China. It is even a concern in countries such as Canada, which has seen many professionals leave for careers in the United States.

brain drain Poor countries' loss of skilled workers to rich countries.

Technology transfer refers to a state's acquisition of technology (knowledge, skills, methods, designs, and specialized equipment) from foreign sources, usually in conjunction with foreign direct investment or similar business operations. A state in the South may allow an MNC to produce certain goods in the country under favourable conditions, provided the MNC shares knowledge of the technology and design behind the product. The state may try to get its own citizens into the management and professional work force of factories or facilities created by foreign investment. Not only can physical capital accumulate in the country, so can the related technological base for further development. But MNCs are sometimes reluctant to share proprietary technology.

technology transfer Global South states' acquisition of technology (knowledge, skills, methods, designs, specialized equipment, etc.) from foreign sources, usually in conjunction with *direct foreign investment* or similar business operations.

Technology transfer sometimes encounters difficulty when the technological abilities of the source country does not fit the needs of the recipient country. A good fit has been called *appropriate technology*.[25] In particular, the Soviet Union was fond of creating the "world's largest" factory of some type, and it tended to apply the same overly centralized approach to its investments and development projects in the global South—such as the huge Nigerian steel plant mentioned earlier. Furthermore, technology that seemed useful to bureaucrats in Moscow might not be appropriate to a recipient country; in 1960 the Soviets sent snowplows to the tropical country of Guinea.[26]

The **green revolution**—a massive transfer of agricultural technology coordinated through international agencies—deserves special mention.[27] This effort, which began in

green revolution The massive transfer of agricultural technology, such as high-yield seeds and tractors, to countries of the global South that began in the 1960s.

---

[25] Matthew J. Betz, Pat McGowan, and Rolf T. Wigand, eds., *Appropriate Technology: Choice and Development* (Durham, NC: Duke UP, 1984). Nicolas Jequier, ed., *Appropriate Technology: Problems and Promises* (Paris: OECD, 1976).

[26] Robert Legvold, *Soviet Policy in West Africa* (Cambridge, MA: Harvard UP, 1970) 124.

[27] Mohammed Alauddin and Clement Tisdell, *The "Green Revolution" and Economic Development: The Process and Its Development in Banglades*.(NY: St. Martin's, 1991).

the 1960s, transplanted a range of agricultural technologies from rich countries to poor ones—new seed strains, fertilizers, tractors to replace oxen, and so forth. The green revolution increased crop yields in a number of states, especially in Asia, and helped food supplies keep up with growing populations.

However, it did have drawbacks. Critics noted that the green revolution made recipients dependent on imported technologies such as tractors and oil, that it damaged the environment with commercial pesticides and fertilizers, and that it disrupted traditional agriculture (driving more people off the land and into cities). Environmental reactions to the green revolution—including the emergence of pesticide resistance in insect populations—have led to recent declines in crop yields, forcing changes.[28] For example, in Indonesia pesticides introduced in the green revolution created resistant strains of a rice parasite and killed off the parasite's natural predators. The pesticides also polluted water supplies. Recognizing the need to adapt imported technologies to local needs, the Indonesian government banned most pesticides in 1986 and adopted organic methods instead. In recent years, the Food and Agriculture Organization (FAO) has spread information about organic pest control through traditional village theatre plays. Pesticide usage has declined sharply while rice production has increased.

The green revolution also replaced local expertise with that of foreigners. On the Indonesian island of Bali, "water priests" traditionally controlled the allocation of scarce water resources to agriculture. In the green revolution, such practices were often dismissed as superstitious nonsense and replaced with modern water-allocation schemes. But the water priests actually had more experience with local conditions over many years, and more legitimacy with the local farmers, than did the foreign experts. Over time, some attempts have been made to re-focus on local expertise and return, at least in part, to indigenous agricultural practices.

In the 1990s, states in the North also began to focus on technology transfer that promotes *environmentally sustainable development* (see pp. 492–494). Japan's MITI-funded International Center for Environmental Technology Transfer geared up to train 10 000 people from developing countries, over 10 years, in energy conservation, pollution control, and other environmental technologies. Japan also hosts the International Environmental Technology Centre, a project of the UN Environment Program (UNEP). However, among other motives, Japan hopes these projects will encourage developing countries to choose Japanese technology and products.[29]

Debt

Borrowing money is an alternative to foreign investment as a way of obtaining funds to prime a cycle of economic accumulation. If accumulation succeeds, it produces enough surplus to repay the loan and still make a profit. Borrowing has several advantages. It keeps control in the hands of the state (or other local borrower) and does not impose painful sacrifices on local citizens, at least in the short term.

Debt has disadvantages too. The borrower must service the debt—making regular payments of interest and repaying the principal according to the terms of the loan. **Debt service** is a constant drain on whatever surplus is generated by investment of the money. With foreign direct investment, a money-losing venture is the problem of the foreign MNC; with debt, it is the problem of the borrowing state, which must find the money

debt service An obligation to make regular interest payments and repay the principal of a loan according to its terms, which is a drain on many economies of the global South.

---

[28] *Science* 256 (22 May 1992): 1140. *Science* 256 (29 May 1992): 1272.

[29] *Science* 256 (22 May 1992): 1145.

elsewhere. Often, a debtor must borrow new funds to service old loans, slipping further into debt. Debt service has created a net financial outflow from South to North in recent years, as the South has paid billions more in interest to banks and governments in the North than it has received in foreign investment or development aid.

The failure to make scheduled payments, called a **default,** is considered a drastic action because it destroys lenders' confidence and results in cutoff of future loans. Rather than defaulting, borrowers attempt **debt renegotiation**—a reworking of the terms on which a loan will be repaid. By renegotiating their debts with lenders, borrowers seek a mutually acceptable payment scheme to keep at least some money flowing to the lender. If interest rates have fallen since a loan was first taken out, the borrower can refinance. Borrowers and lenders can also negotiate to restructure a debt by changing the length of the loan (usually to a longer payback period) or the other terms. Occasionally state-to-state loans are written off altogether—forgiven—for political reasons, as happened with U.S. loans to Egypt after the Gulf War. In recent years, activists and NGOs have called for extensive debt forgiveness for the poorest countries. A movement called Jubilee 2000 sought debt cancellation in honour of the millennium, and claimed credit for write-offs of more than US$30 billion in debt owed by the poorest countries (they still owe more than US$200 billion, however). Critics said such cancellations just put more money in the hands of corrupt, inept governments. The IMF has begun an initiative to reduce debt burdens in about 40 very poor countries, mostly in Africa.

Debt encompasses several types of lending relationships, all of which are influenced by international politics. The *borrower* may be a private firm or bank in a developing country, or it may be the government itself. Loans to the government are somewhat more common because lenders consider the government less likely to default than a private borrower. The *lender* may be a private bank or company, or a state (both are important). Usually banks are more insistent on receiving timely payments and firmer in renegotiating debts than are states. Some state-to-state loans are made on artificially favourable *concessionary* terms, in effect subsidizing economic development in the borrowing state.

In the 1970s and 1980s, many states of the global South borrowed heavily from banks and states in the North, which engaged in sometimes quite aggressive lending policies, offering very favourable interest rates to borrowers. For banks, lending to a country was considered a good risk (countries do not normally disappear). But growth began to falter. In oil-exporting states such as Venezuela and Mexico, for instance, price declines reduced export earnings with which states planned to repay the loans. Other exporting states found

default The failure to make scheduled debt payments.

debt renegotiation A reworking of the terms on which a loan will be repaid; frequently negotiated by global South debtor governments in order to avoid default.

GLOBALIZE THIS
Globalization is creating winners and losers while sharpening income disparities. Debt, currency crises, IMF conditionality, and the privatization of state-owned enterprises are among the sources of upheaval and poverty in many countries in the global South. These unemployed workers in Buenos Aires were among four million people living in poverty in the Argentine capital, 2001.

that protectionist measures in the North, combined with a global economic slowdown, limited their ability to export. Sometimes borrowed funds were simply not spent wisely and produced too little surplus to service the debt.

As a result, by the 1980s a *debt crisis* had developed, particularly in Latin America.[30] Many states in the South could not generate enough export earnings to service their debts, much less to repay them—not to speak of retaining some surplus to generate sustained local accumulation. Major states of the global South, such as Brazil, Mexico, and India, found foreign debt a tremendous weight on economic development. Although the "crisis" passed, and many debts were renegotiated to a longer-term basis, the weight of debt remains (see Table 12.2). The world banking system rode out the 1980s crisis, and some made sizeable profits during the worst of the debt crisis, even when writing off a portion of the uncollectible debts each year.

Debt renegotiation has become a perennial occupation of states in the global South. Such renegotiations are complex international bargaining situations, like international trade or arms control negotiations but with more parties. The various lenders—private banks and states—try to extract as much as they can, and the borrower tries to hold out for more favourable terms. If a borrowing government accepts terms that are too burdensome, it may lose popularity at home; the local population and opposition politicians may accuse it of selling out to foreigners, neocolonialists, and so on. But if the borrowing state does not give enough to gain the agreement of the lenders, it might have to default and lose out on future loans and investments, which could greatly impede economic growth.

For the lenders, debt renegotiations involve a collective goods problem: all of them have to agree on the conditions of the renegotiation but each really cares only about getting its own money back. To solve this problem, state creditors meet together periodically as the **Paris Club,** and private creditors as the **London Club,** to work out their terms.

Paris Club A group of global North governments that have loaned money to global South governments; it meets periodically to work out terms of debt renegotiations. Private creditors meet as the **London Club**.

Table 12.2 Global South Debt, 2003

Region	Foreign Debt		Annual Debt Service	
	Billion US$	% of GDP[a]	Billion US$	% of Exports
Latin America	800	44%	150	41%
Asia	700	25	110	12
Africa	300	49	30	15
Middle East	500	55	40	12
Total "South"	2 300	38	330	18

[a] GDP not calculated at purchasing-power parity.

Notes: Regions do not exactly match those used elsewhere in this book. Africa here includes North Africa. Asia includes China.

Source: IMF, Statistical Appendix to World Economic Outlook (Sept. 2003) 228–29.

---

[30] Antonio Jorge and Jorge Salazar-Carrillo, eds., *The Latin American Debt* (NY: St. Martin's, 1992). Jeffry A. Frieden, *Debt, Development, and Democracy: Modern Political Economy and Latin America, 1965–1985* (Princeton, NJ: Princeton UP, 1992). Miles Kahler, ed., *The Politics of International Debt* (Ithaca, NY: Cornell UP, 1986). York W. Bradshaw, and Ana-Maria Wahl, "Foreign Debt Expansion, the International Monetary Fund, and Regional Variation in Third World Poverty," *International Studies Quarterly* 35.3 (1991): 251–72. Robert E. Wood, *From Marshall Plan to Debt Crisis: Foreign Aid and Development Choices in the World Economy* (Berkeley: U California P, 1986).

Through such renegotiations and the corresponding write-offs of debts by banks, developing countries have largely avoided defaulting on their debts. Some large states threatened to default—or even to lead a coalition of states all defaulting at once—but backed off from such threats. However, in 2001, Argentina in effect defaulted on its debts. By then, financial institutions had adjusted psychologically to the reality that Argentina could not pay its debt, so the default did not cause a wider panic. Default is a risky course because of the integrated nature of the world economy, the need for foreign investment and foreign trade to accumulate wealth, and the risks of provoking international confrontations. Lenders too have generally proven willing to absorb losses rather than push a borrower over the edge and risk financial instability.

Despite stabilization, states of the global South have not yet solved the debt problem. As shown in Table 12.2, the South owes US$2 trillion in foreign debt, and pays about US$330 billion a year to service that debt. The debt service (in hard currency) absorbs nearly a third of the entire hard-currency export earnings in Latin America—the region most affected. Africa's debt is equal to two-thirds of the annual GDP of the region. Many states in Asia are vulnerable to debt problems as well.

IMF Conditionality

The International Monetary Fund (IMF) and the World Bank have a large supply of capital from their member states (see "The World Bank and the IMF" on pp. 341–344). This capital plays an important role in funding early stages of accumulation in developing countries and in helping them get through short periods of great difficulty. And, as a political entity rather than a bank, the IMF can make funds available on favourable financial terms (though normally with significant political and economic strings attached).

The IMF does not give away money indiscriminately. Indeed, it scrutinizes states' economic plans and policies, withholding loans until it is satisfied that the right policies are in place. Then it makes loans to help states through the transitional process of implementing the IMF-approved policies. The IMF also sends important signals to private lenders and investors. Its approval of a state's economic plans is a "seal of approval" bankers and MNCs use to assess the wisdom of investing in that state. Thus, the IMF wields great power to influence the economic policies of states in the global South.

An agreement to loan IMF funds on the condition that certain government policies are adopted is called an **IMF conditionality** agreement; implementation of these conditions is referred to as a *structural adjustment program*.[31] Dozens of developing states have entered into such agreements with the IMF in the past two decades. The terms insisted on by the IMF, called austerity measures, are usually painful for the citizens (and hence for national politicians). The IMF demands that inflation be brought under control, which requires reducing state spending and closing budget deficits. These measures often spur unemployment and require that subsidies of food and basic goods be reduced or eliminated. Short-term consumption is curtailed in favour of longer-term investment. Surplus must be concentrated to service debt and invest in new capital accumulation. The IMF wants to ensure that money lent to a country is not spent for politically popular but economically

IMF conditionality
An agreement to loan IMF funds on the condition that certain government policies are adopted. Dozens of global South states have entered into such agreements with the IMF in the past two decades. See also *International Monetary Fund (IMF)*.

[31] Biplab Dasgupta, *Structural Adjustment, Global Trade, and the New Political Economy of Development* (NY: Zed/St. Martin's, 1999). David E. Sahn, Paul A. Dorosh, and Stephen D. Younger, *Structural Adjustment Reconsidered: Economic Policy and Poverty in Africa* (NY: Cambridge UP, 1997). Jacques J. Polak, *The Changing Nature of IMF Conditionality*, Princeton Essays in International Finance, no. 184. (Princeton, NJ: Dept. of Economics, Princeton University, 1991). Erik Denters, *Law and Policy of IMF Conditionality* (The Hague and Boston: Kluwer, 1996).

MIRACLE OF LOAVES

IMF conditionality agreements often called for reducing subsidies for food, transportation, and other basic needs. In Egypt, bread prices are heavily subsidized, forcing the government to use hard currency to import wheat. But public resistance to bread price increases is so strong that the government has not brought itself to cut the subsidy. Here, bread is delivered by bicycle in Cairo, 1996.

unprofitable purposes (such as subsidizing food). It wants to ensure that inflation does not eat away all progress and that the economy is stable enough to attract investment. In addition, it demands steps to curtail corruption.

Because of the pain inflicted by a conditionality agreement—and to some extent by any debt renegotiation agreement—such agreements are often politically unpopular in the global South, as they would be anywhere.[32] On quite a few occasions, a conditionality agreement has brought rioters into the streets demanding the restoration of subsidies for food, gasoline, and other essential goods. Sometimes governments have backed out of the agreement or have broken their promises under such pressure. Occasionally, governments have been toppled. In a country such as Peru, which in the early 1990s faced a violent leftist guerrilla war that fed on mass poverty, such a choice was especially difficult.

In Egypt, where the same word is used for bread as for life, cheap bread is vital to political stability, at least in the government's view. State-owned flour mills, and an annual subsidy of US$750 million, ensure a supply of bread at one-third its real cost, for Egypt's large and poor population. For economic liberals, these costs distort the free market, encouraging Egyptians to eat (and waste) more bread than they otherwise would, and driving the need for imported wheat to more than US$1 billion per year. But when the government tried to raise the price of bread in 1977, street riots forced a reversal. Instead, the government has subtly changed the size and composition of loaves, and in 1996 began secretly mixing cheaper corn flour into state-milled wheat flour. This example illustrates the political difficulties that many governments face in implementing typical IMF conditionality requirements.

The IMF formula for stability and success is remarkably universal from one country to the next. When the IMF negotiated terms for economic assistance to Russia and the former Soviet republics in the early 1990s, the terms were similar to those for any state in the global South: cut inflation, cut government spending, cut subsidies, crack down on corruption.

Critics of the IMF argue that it does not adapt its program adequately to account for differences in the local cultural and economic conditions in different states. The United States in the 1980s and early 1990s, for example, would not have qualified for IMF assistance because of government deficits, but did not have to submit to IMF austerity meas-

---

[32] Stephan Haggard and Robert R. Kaufman, eds., *The Politics of Economic Adjustment: International Constraints, Distributive Conflicts, and the State* (Princeton, NJ: Princeton UP, 1992). Fredoline O. Anunobi, *The Implications of Conditionality: The International Monetary Fund and Africa* (Lanham, MD: UP America, 1992).

ures because of an otherwise strong economy. More importantly, critics argue that the IMF prescription is an approach derived from another time and another place, which may no longer apply to current problems of development and inequality. The IMF was created to assist the countries of Europe and Japan in their post–World War II recovery. In that case, short-term austerity measures made sense, and were quite effective. The developing world today does not suffer from short-term imbalances, but rather long-term structural conditions, resulting in part from the historical legacies of colonialism. By this view, the IMF diagnosis, and its prescriptions, are both misplaced and sometimes only exacerbate difficult economic conditions even further.[33]

The South in International Economic Regimes

Because of the need for capital and the wealth created by international trade, most states of the global South nonetheless see their future economic development as resting on a close interconnection with the world economy, not on national autarky or regional economic communities. Thus states of the global South must play by the rules embedded in international economic regimes (see Chapters 8 and 9).

The WTO trading regime tends to work against developing states relative to industrialized ones. A free trade regime makes it harder for poor states to protect infant industries in order to build self-sufficient capital accumulation. It forces competition with more technologically advanced states. A poor state can be competitive only in low-wage, low-capital niches—especially those using natural resources that are scarce in the North, such as tropical agriculture, extractive (mining and drilling) industries, and textiles.

Yet just these economic sectors in which Southern states have comparative advantages on world markets—agriculture and textiles in particular—were largely excluded from the free trade rules of the GATT (see pp. 323–325). The GATT instead concentrated on free trade in manufactured goods, in which states in the North have comparative advantages. As a result, some states of the global South found that they were expected to open their home markets to foreign products, against which home industries are not competitive, yet see their own export products shut out of foreign markets.

In part to address this inequity and to help developing countries use trade to boost their economic growth, the GATT created the Generalized System of Preferences (p. 324). These and other measures—such as the Lomé conventions in which EU states relaxed tariffs on goods from the global South—are exceptions to the overall rules of trade, intended to ensure that participation in world trade advances rather than impedes global South development.[34] Nonetheless, critics claim that states of the global South are the losers in the overall world trading regime.

In the past decades, critics have accused the World Bank of supporting authoritarian regimes and underwriting huge infrastructure projects that displaced poor people and had devastating environmental effects. Critics allege that the Bank's portfolio of loans in the global South, totalling more than US$100 billion, is more a hindrance than a help to true development. Bank officials respond that despite a few mistakes, the Bank and its mission are sound.

The tenuous position of the global South in international economic regimes reflects the role of power in IR. The global North, with nearly two-thirds of the world's wealth,

---

[33] Joseph E. Stiglitz, *Globalization and Its Discontents* (NY: Norton, 2003).

[34] Diana Tussie and David J. Glover, eds., *The Developing Countries in World Trade: Policies and Bargaining Strategies* (Boulder, CO: Rienner, 1993). John Ravenhill, *Collective Clientelism: The Lomé Conventions and North-South Relations* (NY: Columbia UP, 1985).

clearly has more power—more effective leverage—than the South. The global disparity of power is accentuated by the fact that the South is split up into more than a hundred actors whereas the North's power is concentrated in eight large states (the G8 members). Thus, when the rules of the world economy were created after World War II, and as they have been rewritten and adjusted over the years, the main actors shaping the outcome have been a handful of large industrialized states.

States in the South have responded in several ways to these problems with world economic regimes. In the 1970s, OPEC shifted the terms of trade for oil—bringing huge amounts of capital into the oil-exporting countries. Some states hoped such successes could be repeated for other commodities, resulting in broad gains for the global South, but these did not occur (see "Cartels" on pp. 459–461, and "Minerals, Land, Water" on pp. 511–514).

Also in the 1970s, developing country states tried to form a broad political coalition to push for restructuring the world economy so as to make North-South economic transactions more favourable to the South. A summit meeting of the nonaligned movement (see p. 248) in 1973 first called for a **New International Economic Order (NIEO)**.[35] Central to the NIEO was a shift in the terms of trade to favour primary commodities relative to manufactured goods. The NIEO proposal also called for the promotion of industrialization in the global South, and for increased development assistance from the North.

The NIEO never became much more than a rallying cry for the global South, partly because of the South's lack of power and partly because disparities within the South created divergent interests among states there. In the 1980s, the terms of trade further deteriorated for raw material exporters, and economic development slowed down in much of the developing world. But in China and some other Asian countries, development accelerated.

States of the global South continue to pursue proposals to restructure world trade to benefit the South. These efforts now take place mainly through the *UN Conference on Trade and Development (UNCTAD)*, which meets periodically but lacks power to implement major changes in North-South economic relations.[36] Attempts to promote South-South trade (reducing dependence on the North) have proven largely impractical. Efforts continue, however, to boost cooperation and solidarity among developing countries through a variety of groups such as the nonaligned movement and the UN.[37] Nonetheless, such efforts have done little to change the South's reliance on assistance from the North.

FOREIGN ASSISTANCE

Foreign assistance (or *overseas development assistance*) is money or other aid made available to developing countries to help them speed up economic development or simply

---

New International Economic Order (NIEO) A global South effort begun in the mid-1970s, mainly conducted in UN forums, to advocate restructuring of the world economy so as to make North-South economic transactions less unfavourable to the South.

foreign assistance Money or other aid made available to developing countries to help them speed up economic development or meet humanitarian needs. Most foreign assistance is provided by governments and is called official development assistance (ODA). See also *Development Assistance Committee (DAC)*.

[35] R.W.Cox, "Ideologies and the New International Economic Order: Reflections on Some Recent Literature," *International* Organization 332 (Spring 1979): 257–302. Craig N. Murphy, *The Emergence of the NIEO Ideology* (Boulder, CO: Westview, 1984). Johan Galtung, *The North/South Debate: Technology, Basic Human Needs, and the New International Economic Order* (NY: Institute for World Order, 1980).

[36] Marc Williams, *Third World Cooperation: The Group of 77 in UNCTAD* (NY: St. Martin's, 1991). Thomas G. Weiss, *Multilateral Development Diplomacy in UNCTAD* (NY: St. Martin's, 1986).

[37] Sheila Page, *Regionalism among Developing Countries* (NY: Palgrave, 2000). Steen Folke, Niels Fold, and Thyge Enevoldsen, *South-South Trade and Development: Manufacturers in the New International Division of Labour* (NY: St. Martin's, 1993). Donald Bobiash, *South-South Aid: How Developing Countries Help Each Other* (NY: St. Martin's, 1992). H. Michael Erisman, *Pursuing Postdependency Politics: South-South Relations in the Caribbean* (Boulder, CO: Rienner, 1992).

meet basic humanitarian needs.[38] Along with the commercial economic activities just discussed (investments and loans), foreign assistance is a second major source of money for development. It covers a variety of programs—from individual volunteers lending a hand to massive government packages.

Different kinds of development assistance have different purposes. Some are humanitarian, some are political, and others are intended to create future economic advantages for the giver (these purposes often overlap). The state or organization that gives assistance is called a *donor*; the state or organization receiving the aid is the *recipient*. Foreign assistance creates, or extends, a relationship between donor and recipient that is simultaneously political and cultural as well as economic.[39] Foreign assistance can be a form of power in which the donor seeks to influence the recipient, or it can be a form of interdependence in which the donor and recipient create a mutually beneficial exchange.

Patterns of Foreign Assistance

The majority of foreign assistance comes from governments in the North. Private donations provide a smaller amount, although sometimes a significant one. In 1997, for instance, Ted Turner pledged US$1 billion for UN programs, George Soros contributed or pledged nearly US$2 billion in aid to Russia and other countries (see p. 338), and Bill Gates's foundation contributed millions to world health campaigns.

Table 12.3 lists the major donors toward the US$65 billion in governmental foreign assistance provided in 2000. More than 90 percent of government assistance comes from members of the **Development Assistance Committee (DAC)**, consisting of states from Western Europe, North America, and Japan/Pacific. Several oil-exporting Arab countries provide some foreign development assistance as well. Three-quarters of the DAC countries' government assistance goes directly to governments in the global South as state-to-state **bilateral aid**; the rest goes through the UN or other agencies as **multilateral aid.**

The DAC countries have set themselves a goal to contribute 0.7 percent of their GNPs in foreign aid. But overall they give less than half this amount. Only Norway, Sweden, Denmark, the Netherlands, and Luxembourg are close to the target.

The United States gives the lowest percentage of GNP—about one-eighth of 1 percent—of any of the 29 states of the industrialized West that make up the Organisation for Economic Co-operation and Development (OECD). In total economic aid given (US$9 billion), the United States has slipped behind Japan (US$15 billion). Germany, Britain, and France each give $3 to $6 billion. Canada gives $1.5 billion. U.S. foreign assistance dropped by nearly half from 1992 to 1995 and has never returned to former levels.

Types of Aid Bilateral aid takes a variety of forms. *Grants* are funds given free to a recipient state, usually for some stated purpose. *Technical cooperation* refers to grants given in the form of expert assistance in some project rather than just money or goods. *Credits* are grants that can be used to buy certain products from the donor state. For instance,

Development Assistance Committee (DAC) A committee whose members—consisting of states from Western Europe, North America, and Japan/Pacific—provide 95 percent of official development assistance to countries of the global South. See also *foreign assistance*.

bilateral aid Government assistance that goes directly to the global South governments as state-to-state aid.

multilateral aid Government foreign aid from several states that goes through a third party, such as the UN or another agency.

---

[38] Michael O'Hanlon, and Carol Graham, *A Half Penny on the Federal Dollar: The Future of Development Aid* (Washington, DC: Brookings, 1997). Steven W. Hook, *National Interest and Foreign Aid* (Boulder, CO: Rienner, 1995). Anne O. Krueger, Constantine Michalopoulos, and Vernon W. Ruttan, *Aid and Development* (Baltimore: Johns Hopkins UP, 1989). Brian H. Smith, *More Than Altruism: The Politics of Private Foreign Aid* (Princeton, NJ: Princeton UP, 1990).

[39] Margee M. Ensign, *Doing Good or Doing Well? Japan's Foreign Aid Program* (NY: Columbia UP, 1992). Davis B. Bobrow and Mark A. Boyer, "Bilateral and Multilateral Foreign Aid: Japan's Approach in Comparative Perspective," *Review of International Political Economy* 3.1 (1996): 95–121.

Table 12.3 Who's Helping?
Foreign Assistance, 2001

Donor	Assistance Given	
	Billion US$	**% of GNP**[a]
World total	53.2	0.2%
Total G7	38.1	0.2%
United States	11.4	0.1%
Japan	9.8	0.2%
Germany	5.0	0.3%
Britain	4.6	0.3%
France	4.2	0.3%
Italy	1.6	0.2%
Canada	1.5	0.2%
Netherlands	3.2	0.8%
Sweden	1.7	0.8%
Denmark	1.6	1.0%
Norway	1.3	0.8%
Other "North"	6.7	
Arab Countries	0.6	

[a] GDP not calculated at purchasing-power parity.

Source: United Nations, *World Economic and Social Survey 2003* (NY: United Nations, 2003) 299. UN estimates based on OECD data; governmental aid only.

Canada gives credits that can be used for purchases of Canadian grain. This is sometimes called "tied" aid. If people in a recipient country become accustomed to products from the donor state, they are likely to buy those same products in the future.

Loans are funds given to help in economic development, which must be repaid in the future out of the surplus generated by the development process (they too are often tied to the purchase of products from the donor state). Unlike commercial loans, government-to-government development loans are often on concessionary terms, with long repayment times and low interest rates. Although still an obligation for the recipient country, such loans are relatively easy to service.

Loan guarantees, which are used only occasionally, are promises by the donor state to back up commercial loans to the recipient. If the recipient state services such debts and ultimately repays them, there is no cost to the donor. But if the recipient cannot make the payments, the donor has to step in and cover the debts. A loan guarantee allows the recipient state to borrow money at lower interest from commercial banks (because the risk to the bank is much lower).

Military aid is not normally included in development assistance, but in a broad sense belongs there. It is money that flows from North to South, from government to government, and it does bring a certain amount of value into the developing country economy. If a country is going to have a certain size of army with certain weapons, getting them free from a donor state frees up money that can be used elsewhere in the economy. However,

of all the forms of development assistance, military aid is certainly one of the least efficient and most prone to impede rather than help economic development. It is also geared
almost exclusively to political alliances rather than actual development needs.

The main agency dispensing foreign economic assistance in Canada (but not military
aid) is the Canadian International Development Agency (CIDA). It supports projects in
more than 100 countries and focuses on supporting sustainable development. Canada's
Official Development Assistance (ODA) program emphasizes six priority areas: meeting
basic human needs; gender equality; infrastructure support; human rights, democracy and
good governance; private sector development; and the environment. CIDA normally
works with international and local partners in a wide range of projects, which include the
promotion of women and girl's literacy, HIV/AIDS awareness programs, desertification
projects (planting trees with maize crops to prevent soil erosion), the provision of safe
water and sanitation facilities, capacity-building in human rights monitoring and the
criminal justice systems, microcredit programs, and many others.

Canada has other publicly funded agencies involved in development issues. For
example, the International Development Research Centre (IDRC) was created by an Act
of Parliament in 1970 and is mandated to support and conduct policy-relevant research
into problems faced by people in the global South. IDRC is innovative in that it aims
primarily to support research (scientific and social scientific) that is produced by peoples
in the South for the South. So, rather than bring in northern "experts," IDRC attempts
to support research capacity in the South itself. The aim is to fund research into issues
deemed relevant by the very people the research aims to assist.

Canada also has a number of nongovernmental organizations that are involved in
development assistance and are mandated to provide opportunities for Canadians to work
in the field of international development. **World University Service of Canada
(WUSC)**, for example, is involved in development assistance projects in over 50 countries and also coordinates professional and volunteer positions in many of those projects.

In the United States, foreign assistance is administered through the State Department's
Agency for International Development (USAID), which works mainly through the U.S.

**World University Service
of Canada (WUSC)** Agency
involved in development assistance projects in over 50 countries that also coordinates
professional and volunteer positions in many of those projects.

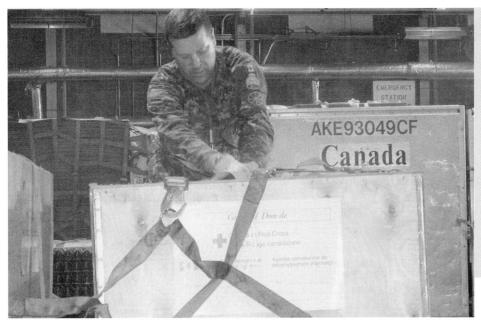

JOINT EFFORT
Governments provide
$55 billion annually in
foreign assistance, and
private donors over
$10 billion more (1999
data). Here, Canadian
Corporal helps load
more than 20 000 kg
of humanitarian relief
supplies to be sent to
Iran following a devastating earthquake that
left more than 20 000
dead and another
30 000 injured.

embassy in each recipient country. The major recipients of U.S. foreign aid are its import-ant strategic allies in the Middle East, including Israel, Egypt, and Turkey. The U.S., more than Canada, uses the promise of aid, or the threat of cutting it off, as a leverage in political bargaining with recipients. For example, when Pakistan proceeded in the late 1980s with a nuclear weapons program, despite U.S. warnings, a sizeable flow of U.S. aid was terminated. Then when Pakistan supported U.S. military action in next-door Afghanistan in 2001, U.S. aid was restored.

UN Programs   Most of the multilateral development aid goes through *UN programs*. The place of these programs in the UN structure is described in Chapter 7 (see pp. 249–252). The overall flow of assistance through the UN is coordinated by the **UN Development Programme (UNDP)**, which manages 5000 projects at once around the world (focusing especially on technical development assistance). Other UN programs focus on concentrating capital, transferring technology, and developing work force skills for manufacturing. UNIDO works on industrialization, UNITAR on training and research. But most UN programs—such as UNICEF, UNFPA, UNESCO, WHO, and others—focus on meeting basic needs.

UN programs have three advantages in promoting economic development. One is that governments and citizens tend to perceive the UN as a friend of the South, not an alien force, a threat to sovereignty, or a reminder of colonialism. The UN can sometimes mobilize technical experts and volunteers from other developing countries so that people who arrive to help do not look like white European colonialists. A team of Egyptian med-ical workers under a UN program may be more easily accepted in an African country than French or British workers, however well intentioned.

Second, UN workers may be more likely to make appropriate decisions because of their backgrounds. UN workers who come from the global South or have worked in other poor countries in a region may be more sensitive to local conditions and to the pitfalls of development assistance than are aid workers from rich countries.

A third advantage is that the UN can organize its assistance on a global scale, giving priority to projects and avoiding duplication and the reinvention of the wheel in each state. For some issues—such as the fight against AIDS or the integration of development objectives with environmental preservation—there is no substitute for global organiza-tion linked to specific local circumstances.

A major disadvantage faced by UN development programs is that they are funded largely through voluntary contributions by rich states. Each program has to solicit con-tributions to carry on its activities, so the contributions can be abruptly cut off if the program displeases a donor government—a strategy used regularly by the United States (see pp. 519–520).

The Disaster Relief Model

The remainder of this chapter discusses three models of development assistance, which are distinguished by the type of assistance rather than the type of donor (all three models encompass both government and private aid).

First is the disaster relief model. It is the kind of foreign assistance given when poor people are afflicted by famine, drought, earthquakes, flooding, or other such natural dis-asters. (War is also a disaster and can compound naturally occurring disasters.) When dis-aster strikes a poor state, many people are left with no means of subsistence and often without their homes. **Disaster relief** is the provision of short-term relief to such people in the form of food, water, shelter, clothing, and other essentials.

UN Development Programme (UNDP)
UN agency that coordinates the flow of multilateral development assistance and manages 5000 projects at once around the world (focus-ing especially on technical development assistance).

disaster relief The provision of short-term relief in the form of food, water, shelter, clothing, and other essentials to people facing natural disasters.

Disaster relief is very important because disasters can wipe out years of progress in economic development in a single blow. Generally, the international community tries to respond with enough assistance to get people back on their feet. The costs of such assistance are relatively modest, the benefits visible and dramatic. Having a system of disaster relief in place provides the global South with a kind of insurance against sudden losses that could otherwise destabilize economic accumulation.

Disasters generally occur quickly and without much warning. Rapid response is difficult to coordinate. International disaster relief has become more organized and better coordinated in the past decade but is still a complex process that varies somewhat from one situation to the next. Contributions of governments, private charitable organizations, and other groups and agencies are coordinated through the *UN Office of the Disaster Relief Coordinator (UNDRO)* in Geneva. Typically, international contributions make up no more than about one-third of the total relief effort, the remainder coming from local communities and national governments in the affected states.

Disaster relief is something of a collective good because the states of the North do not benefit individually by contributing, yet they benefit in the long run from greater stability in the South. Disaster relief is generally a positive example of international cooperation to get a job done. Food donated by the World Council of Churches may be carried to the scene in Canadian military aircraft and then distributed by the International Committee of the Red Cross (ICRC). Embarrassing failures in the past—of underresponse or overresponse, of duplication of efforts or agencies working at cross-purposes—became rarer in the 1990s, and in the new century groups try to coordinate their actions more effectively.[40]

The relationship of disasters with economic development is complex, and appropriate responses vary according to location, type and size of disaster, and phase of recovery. For instance, refugees displaced from their home communities have different needs from those of earthquake or hurricane victims whose entire communities have been damaged. Different resources are needed in the emergency phase (for example, food and medical supplies) than in the reconstruction phase (for example, earthquake-resistant housing designs). Responses that are too small in scale or too short-term may fail to meet critical needs, but those that are too large or prolonged can overwhelm the local economy and create dependency (reducing incentives for self-help). Thus, appropriate disaster relief can promote local economic development, whereas inappropriate responses can distort or impede such development.[41]

When the disaster is *war*, the lead role often falls to the *International Committee of the Red Cross (ICRC)*, based in Switzerland. International norms and traditions treat the ICRC as an agency with special protected status (see p. 285). Red Cross societies in each country (called Red Crescent societies in Islamic countries and the Red Star of David in Israel) are autonomous agencies that also participate in disaster relief efforts.

International norms regarding states' legal obligations to assist others in time of natural disaster and to accept such assistance if needed are changing.[42] In the 1990s—designated by the UN as the International Decade for Natural Disaster Reduction—a new international regime in this area began solidifying.

---

[40] Kimberly A. Maynard, *Healing Communities in Conflict: International Assistance in Complex Emergencies* (NY: Columbia UP, 1999).

[41] Mary B. Anderson and Peter J. Woodrow, *Rising from the Ashes: Development Strategies in Times of Disaster* (Boulder, CO: Westview, 1989). Frederick C. Cuny, *Disasters and Development* (NY: Oxford UP, 1983).

[42] Jiri Toman, "Towards a Disaster Relief Law: Legal Aspects of Disaster Relief Operations," *Assisting the Victims of Armed Conflict and Other Disasters*, ed. Frits Kalshoven (Dordrecht, Netherlands: Martinus Nijhoff, 1989).

The Missionary Model

Beyond disaster relief, many governments and private organizations provide ongoing development assistance in the form of projects administered by agencies from the North in local communities in the South to help meet basic needs. Although such efforts vary, one could call the approach a *missionary* model because it resembles the charitable works performed by missionaries in poor countries in past centuries. In fact, many of these private programs are still funded by churches and carried out by missionaries. Often such assistance is considered "God's work."

Such charitable programs are helpful though not without problems. They are a useful means by which people in the North funnel resources to people in the South. Even during the colonial era, missionaries did some good despite often perpetuating stereotypes of European superiority and native inferiority. Today's efforts to help poor people in the global South are helpful in giving local individuals and communities some resources with which they may better contribute to national economic development.

However, most handout programs provide only short-term assistance and do not create sustained local economic development. They do not address the causes of poverty, the position of poor countries in the world economy, or the local political conditions such as military rule or corruption.

One version of "missionary" assistance—advertised widely in Canada—lets citizens in rich countries "adopt" poor children in the global South. Photos of a hungry child stare at the reader from a magazine page while the accompanying text notes that a few cents a day can "save" the child. Although such programs raise awareness in the North of the extent of poverty in the South, at worst they tend to be exploitive and to reinforce racist and paternalistic stereotypes of the helplessness of people in the developing world.

There is a danger in the missionary model that people from the North may provide assistance inappropriate for a developing state's local conditions and culture. This danger is illustrated by an experience in Kenya in the 1970s. Nomadic herders in the area of Lake

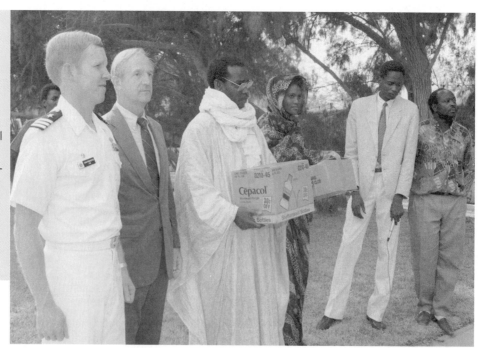

MOUTHWASH FOR MAURITANIA
The missionary model of foreign assistance contributes goods to economies of the global South, but often with little understanding of local needs or long-term strategies. Here, free supplies including cartons of mouthwash are delivered by the U.S. ambassador and the captain of a U.S. Navy ship participating in Project Handclasp, 1989.

Turkana near the Sahara desert—the Turkana tribe—were poor and vulnerable to periodic droughts. Northern aid donors and the Kenyan government decided that the herders' traditional way of life was not environmentally sustainable and should be replaced by commercial fishing of the abundant tilapia fish in Lake Turkana. Norway, with long experience in fishing, was asked to teach fishing and boat-building methods to the Turkana. To create a commercially viable local economy, Norwegian consultants recommended marketing frozen fish fillets to Kenya and the world. Thus in 1981 Norway finished building a $2 million, state-of-the-art fish freezing plant on the shores of Lake Turkana and a US$20 million road connecting the plant to Kenya's transportation system.

There were only three problems. First, with temperatures of 38 degrees Celsius outside (a contrast with Norway), the cost of operating the freezers exceeded the income from the fillets. So after a few days the freezers were turned off and the facility became a dried-fish warehouse. Second, Turkana culture viewed fishing as the lowest-status profession, suitable only for those incompetent at herding. Third, every few decades Lake Turkana shrinks as drought reduces the inflow of water. Such a drought in 1984–1985 eliminated the gulf where the fishing operations were based. The Norwegians might have foreseen these problems by doing more homework instead of just transplanting what worked in Norway. When the drought hit, the 20 000 herders who had been brought to the lake to learn fishing were left in an overcrowded, overgrazed environment in which every tree was cut for firewood and most cattle died. Instead of becoming self-sufficient, the Turkana became totally dependent on outside aid.[43]

The NGO Model

A third model of development assistance can be found in the approach taken by nongovernmental organizations devoted to development aid, such as Oxfam and CARE. Originally devoted to short-term aid to famine victims, and still active in that effort, many development NGOs realized that over the longer term people needed not just handouts of food but the means to feed themselves—land, water, seed, tools, and technical training.

The distinctive aspect of the NGO model is that it relies on local communities to determine the needs of their own people and to carry out development projects. NGOs such as Oxfam, for example, do not operate projects themselves but provide funding to local organizations. NGOs do not normally describe themselves as donors and these organizations as recipients. Rather, they call both sides "project partners"—working together to accomplish a task. In this model, a little outside money can go a long way toward building sustained local economic development. Furthermore, projects help participants empower themselves by organizing to meet their own needs.

For example, Oxfam America helped the Ethiopian women's cooperative mentioned in Chapter 11 (see p. 430). Oxfam did not design or organize the project; women in Addis Ababa did. But when their garment-making workshop became profitable and was ready to expand and employ twice as many women, Oxfam gave the group a US$15 000 grant to build a new building. This small grant helped to consolidate a new centre of accumulation in one of the world's poorest neighbourhoods.

CARE Canada (with assistance from CIDA) supported a charcoal stoves project in Zambia. Charcoal is the most common cooking and heating fuel among Zambia's poor and sometimes consumes as much as 90 percent of a family's income to acquire it. The charcoal stoves project supported the manufacture and sale of a fuel-efficient stove based

---

[43] Blaine Harden, *Africa: Dispatches from a Fragile Continent* (NY: Norton, 1990).

on a model developed in Kenya. The stove itself resulted in savings of almost 50 percent of fuel costs and were produced and marketed by Zambians, eventually becoming a self-sustaining and profit-making enterprise. (See http://carezambia.org)

The NGO approach seeks to reconceptualize development assistance to focus on long-term development through a bottom-up basic needs strategy. The measure of development adopted by most NGOs is similar to the Human Development Index (p. 445). Genuine development, in Oxfam's view, enables people to meet their essential needs. This means extending beyond food aid and emergency relief, and instead attempting to reverse the process of impoverishment. Genuine development also enhances democracy; strikes a balance between populations and resources; aims at improving the well-being and status of women; respects local cultures; is environmentally sustainable; involves change, not just charity; requires the empowerment of the

The Changing World Order

Foreign Aid

In late 2001, Britain urged the United States to double global foreign aid from the North to the South, by spending US$50 billion more per year. The increase would almost equal, in inflation-adjusted terms, the Marshall Plan by which the United States helped rebuild Western Europe after World War II. The idea of a massive increase in foreign aid globally has some support from Canada and the United Nations. It would mark a shift in the North-South dimension of world order, in which the North would more seriously engage the task of progressively reducing poverty and despair in the South. This shift would also depart from the trend of the 1990s, which saw foreign aid fall sharply even as Northern countries got richer.

Britain's finance minister used the "instrumental" argument described in the Changing World Order box in Chapter 11 (p. 438) and argued that the terrorist attacks demonstrated that the safety of people in the North depends in part on the well-being of people in the South. "Today what happens to the poorest person in the poorest country can affect the richest person in the richest country."*

The United States resisted the British proposal at first. U.S. critics of foreign aid say that programs are wasteful and even counterproductive. Bush Administration officials say that market forces and foreign investment should drive development, not handouts.

The U.S. share of GDP spent on foreign aid, one-tenth of 1 percent, is the lowest of industrialized coun-

tries. (Denmark gives a full 1 percent.) Just as UN peace-keeping dropped sharply in the 1990s and grew again in recent years, so foreign aid dropped in the mid-1990s and had begun to increase again before September 2001. Despite the recent partial recovery in funding and longstanding criticisms of U.S. stinginess in foreign aid, major increases were not expected even after the terrorist attacks. The U.S. government hardly seemed inclined to radically increase foreign aid, especially to countries that did not pose a terrorist-related threat, at a time of sharp increases in military spending and other kinds of new expenditures in the war on terrorism.

In March 2002, however, President Bush proposed a 50 percent increase in U.S. foreign aid, US$10 billion spread over three years. Although it would still leave the United States near the bottom of the list in foreign aid as a share of GDP, this initiative seems to signal that U.S. foreign aid will grow, not shrink, despite its earlier criticisms about aid ineffectiveness.

What do you think? Should Canada, the United States, and other rich countries dramatically increase foreign aid? Is threat of terrorist attacks the only argument that will persuade rich countries to finally begin to meet their foreign aid commitments? What is your view of the prospects of sustainable support for the South when it is justified on the basis of fear?

* Joseph Kahn, "Britain Urges U.S. to Expand Global Antipoverty Programs," *New York Times*, 18 Dec. 2001: A10.

PARTNER IN DEVELOPMENT
The Oxfam model of foreign assistance emphasizes support for local groups that can stimulate self-sustaining economic development at a local level. A mutually beneficial North-South partnership is the global goal of such projects. These women show off a mill they purchased with microcredit from an Oxfam-affiliated group in Gambia, 2001.

poor; and promotes the interests of the majority of people worldwide, in the global North as well as the South.[44]

The general goals of the NGO model of foreign aid are consistent with a broader movement in the global South toward grassroots **empowerment.** Efforts such as those of Oxfam and CARE are organized by poor people to gain some power over their situation and meet their basic needs—not by seizing control of the state in a revolution but by means that are more direct, more local, and less violent. The key to success is getting organized, finding information, gaining self-confidence, and obtaining needed resources to implement action plans.

empowerment In the development context, it refers to the grassroots efforts of poor people to gain power over their situation and meet their basic needs.

For example, women in Bangladesh have a very low status in rural society (see "Women in Development" on pp. 429–430). Often they cannot own property, participate in politics, or even leave their houses without their husbands' permission. Now some women in rural Bangladesh have organized women's groups to raise women's self-esteem, promote their rights, and mobilize them to change conditions. One woman reported: "Our husbands used to beat us—now they don't. They used to not let us in the fields— now we go with them. They used to not help us at home—now they do. . . . We now can do all this thanks to the group and the support it has given us."[45] In this example,

[44] *Oxfam America News* (Boston: Oxfam America).

[45] Oxfam America, *Community,* video (Boston: Oxfam, 1995).

economic development and the satisfaction of basic needs have been furthered not by violence or revolution, nor by the actions of the state, foreign governments, or international agencies, but directly at the community level.

In India, local women's groups, using only the power of persuasion and logic, have convinced some landowners to give them land for cooperative income-generating projects such as vegetable farming and raising silkworms. Elsewhere in India, women working as gatherers of wood and other forest products got organized to win the legal minimum wage for 250 000 female forest workers—three times what they had been paid before. In this case, government action was necessary, but the pressure for such action came from local organizing. The women took their case to the public and the press, staging protest marches and getting an art exhibit relating to their cause displayed in the provincial capital.

Such examples do not mean that national and foreign governments are unimportant. On the contrary, government policies affect millions of people more quickly and more widely than do grassroots efforts. Indeed, grassroots organizing often has as an ultimate goal the restructuring of national political and social life so that policies reflect the needs of poor people. But the successes of grassroots empowerment show that poor communities are not simply victims of poverty waiting to be saved or passive bystanders in North-South relations.

The NGO model has the advantage of promoting this trend toward grassroots empowerment, thereby overcoming the dangers of externally run programs under the disaster relief and missionary models. However, the NGO model to date has been tested on only a very small scale. Although the model may be effective in the local communities it reaches, it would have to be adopted widely and replicated on a much larger scale in order to influence the overall prospects for development in the global South. It is unclear whether the principles the model embodies, from a reliance on local community organizers to an avoidance of government involvement, would work on a massive scale.

Confronting the North-South Gap

It is imperative that people in affluent countries such as Canada become knowledgeable about questions of poverty and the different arguments and policies that are developed both to explain poverty and respond to it. It is increasingly difficult for citizens in rich countries to turn their backs and just try to live their own lives. North-South relations have become a part of everyday life. The integrated global economy brings to the North products and people from the South. The information revolution puts images of poverty on TV sets in comfortable living rooms. The growing role of the UN brings North and South together in a worldwide community. Security relations and political economy alike have shifted in the post–Cold War era to give new prominence to the global South.

The environment is another issue that impacts all regions of the world, and raises questions of both political economy and security. Responses to environmental problems also cross many boundaries and range from efforts conducted at the local, national, and global levels. These issues are the subject of Chapter 13.

Thinking Critically

1. How might the strong economic growth of the Asian NICs and of China affect proposals for an Asian free trade area similar to NAFTA and the EU? What would be the interests and worries of Japan, of China and the NICs, and of the poor states of the region, in such an arrangement?

2. Past successes in economic development have depended heavily on developing a manufacturing base, which requires access to scarce capital. How do you think the information revolution and the increasing role of services in the world economy might change this pattern? Might any countries of the global South find a niche in these growing sectors of the world economy and bypass manufacturing? What states or regions might be candidates for such an approach, and why?

3. How does the debt problem compare with debt accumulated in countries such as Canada or the United States? Do the two debt problems arise from similar causes? Which of them do you consider the more serious problem, and why?

4. Some scholars criticize the IMF for imposing harsh terms in its conditionality agreements with poor states. Others applaud the IMF for demanding serious reforms before providing financial resources. If you were a leader of a developing country negotiating with the IMF, what kinds of terms would you be willing to agree to and what terms would you resist? Why?

5. If the states in North America, Western Europe, and Japan/Pacific all met the target of providing 0.7 percent of GNP in foreign assistance, what might the effects be? How much additional aid would be made available? To whom would it likely go? What effects might it have on the recipient states and on global South economic development overall?

Chapter Summary

- Economic development in the global South has been uneven; per capita GDP increased in the 1970s but, except in Asia, decreased in the 1980s. Growth in the 1990s was brisk in Asia but slow elsewhere, with parts of Africa sliding backwards. The 2001 recession created further obstacles for development.

- Evidence does not support a strong association of economic growth either with internal equality of wealth distribution or with internal inequality.

- The newly industrializing countries (NICs) in Asia—South Korea, Taiwan, Hong Kong, and Singapore—show that it is possible to rise out of poverty into sustained economic accumulation. Other states are trying to emulate these successes, but it is unclear whether these experiences can apply elsewhere, and whether authoritarianism is a necessary element of the NICs success.

- China has registered strong economic growth in the past 20 years of market-oriented economic reforms. Though still quite poor, China may be emerging as a leading success story in economic development.

- Economic development in other large countries of the global South, such as India, Brazil, and Nigeria, has been slowed by the inefficiency of state-owned enterprises, by corruption, and by debt.

- Import substitution has been largely rejected as a development strategy in favour of export-led growth. This reflects both the experiences of the NICs and the theory of comparative advantage.

- Most poor states want to develop a manufacturing base, but this is a difficult thing to do. Even when focused on low-capital industries, states have generally had to sharpen income disparities in the process of concentrating capital for manufacturing.

- The theory that democratization would accompany and strengthen economic development has not been supported by the actual experiences of developing countries. But the opposite theory—that authoritarian government is necessary to maintain control while concentrating capital for industrialization—has also not been supported or refuted.

- Debate exists about the causes of underdevelopment. Liberals emphasize internal problems (such as government corruption); critical theorists emphasize historical and global conditions (such as the structural relations of inequality that resulted from colonialism and continue to this day).

- Given the shortage of local capital in most poor states, foreign investment by MNCs is often courted as a means of stimulating economic growth. MNCs look for favourable local conditions, including political and economic stability, in deciding where to invest. Critics argue that MNCs take more out of a developing country than they bring in.

- States in the global South seek the transfer of technology to support their future economic development. Technology transfer can be appropriate or inappropriate to local needs depending on the circumstances of each case.

- The green revolution of the 1960s was a massive North-South transfer of agricultural technology, which had both good and bad effects. Today's "green" technologies being transferred to the South are techniques for environmentally sustainable development.

- Debt, resulting largely from overborrowing in the 1970s and early 1980s, is a major problem. Through renegotiations and other debt management efforts, the North and South have improved the debt situation in recent years. However, the South remains almost $2 trillion in debt to the North, and annual debt service consumes about one-sixth of all hard-currency earnings from exports of the South (much more in some regions and states).

- The IMF makes loans to states in the South conditional on economic and governmental reforms. These conditionality agreements often necessitate politically unpopular measures such as cutting food subsidies.

- The WTO trading regime works against the global South by allowing richer nations to protect sectors in which the South has advantages—notably agriculture and textiles. The Generalized System of Preferences (GSP) tries to compensate by lowering barriers to global South exports.

- Efforts to improve the South's solidarity, cooperation, and bargaining position relative to the North—such as the New International Economic Order (NIEO)—have had little success.

- Foreign assistance, most of it from governments in the North, plays an important part in the economic development plans of the poorer states of the South.

- Only a few states in the North meet the goal of contributing 0.7 percent of their GNPs as foreign assistance to the South. The United States, at 0.1 percent of its GNP, contributes the smallest share of any industrialized state, and its contributions decreased sharply in the past decade.

- Most foreign aid consists of bilateral grants and loans from governments in the North to specific governments in the South. Such aid is often used for political leverage, and promotes the export of products from the donor state.

- About one-fifth of foreign aid is not bilateral but is funnelled through multilateral agencies—mostly UN programs.

- Disaster relief provides short-term aid to prevent a natural disaster from reversing a poor state's economic development efforts. Disaster relief generally involves cooperation by various donor governments, local governments, the UN, and private agencies.

- Handouts to poor communities to meet immediate needs for food and supplies outside times of disaster—here called the missionary model—can be helpful but also have several drawbacks. Such aid can be inappropriate to local needs and can encourage dependence.

- Efforts to support local organizations working to empower poor people and generate community economic development—here called the NGO model—are promising but have been tried only on a small scale.

Key Terms

economic development   444
Human Development Index (HDI)   445
newly industrializing countries (NICs)   447
"four tigers"/"four dragons"   447
free economic zones   450
import substitution   456
export-led growth   456
terms of trade   457
informal sector   458
microcredit   458
cartel   459
Organization of Petroleum Exporting Countries (OPEC)   459
brain drain   467
technology transfer   467
green revolution   467
debt service   468

default   469
debt renegotiation   469
Paris Club, London Club   470
IMF conditionality   471
New International Economic Order (NIEO)   474
foreign assistance   474
Development Assistance Committee (DAC)   475
bilateral aid   475
multilateral aid   475
World University Service of Canada (WUSC)   477
UN Development Programme (UNDP)   478
disaster relief   478
empowerment   483

Weblinks

The following are a sampling of research centres, government departments, and international organizations focused on international development:

Canadian International Development Agency:
http://www.acdi-cida.gc.ca/index-e.htm

CARE Canada:
http://www.care.ca/care_e.asp

International Development Research Centre:
http://web.idrc.ca/en/ev-1-201-1-DO_TOPIC.html

Oxfam Canada:
http://www.oxfam.ca

United Nations Development Fund for Women:
http://www.unifem.org/

Women in Development Network:
http://www.focusintl.com/widnet.htm

Environment and Population

Windmill and nuclear power plant, Britain, c. 1984.

INTERDEPENDENCE AND THE ENVIRONMENT

As we have seen, world industrialization and technological development have increased international interdependence through functional economic integration and transnational communication. Industrialization has also intensified international interdependence in another way, through its impact on the world's natural environment. Actions taken by one state now routinely affect other states' access to natural resources and to the benefits of a healthy environment.[1] The global threats to the natural environment are thus a major new source of interdependence.

Because environmental effects tend to be diffuse and long term and because such effects easily spread from one location to another, international environmental politics creates difficult collective goods problems (see p. 91). A sustainable natural environment is a collective good, and states bargain over how to distribute the costs of providing that good. The technical, scientific, and ethical aspects of managing the environment are complex, but the basic nature of states' interests is not. The collective goods problem arises in each issue area concerning the environment, natural resources, and population.

For example, the world's major fisheries in international waters are not owned by any state; they are a collective good. The various fishing states must cooperate (partly by regulating nonstate actors, such as MNCs) to avoid depleting the stocks of fish. If too many states fail to cooperate, the fish populations are wiped out and everyone's catch is much reduced. In fact, this has already happened in many of the world's largest fisheries, such as Canada's. Fish catches worldwide dropped sharply in the early 1990s and the global

---

[1] Jyrki Käkönen, ed., *Perspectives on Environmental Conflict and International Politics* (London: Pinter, 1992).

fishing industry started losing more than $50 billion a year, and relied increasingly on government subsidies. Cod in North American waters were wiped out in the early 1990s, with the North Sea cod likely to follow. The EU cut quotas for cod fishing by 80 percent in 1998–2003, after long political negotiations, but scientists do not expect stock to recover short of a total ban. Worldwide, according to a 2003 study, the oceans' population of large fish including cod has dropped by 90 percent in the past 50 years.[2]

This depletion has occurred because each additional fishing boat—and its owners as well as its state of origin—gains by catching an additional fish. The benefits of that fish go entirely to the one catching it, whereas the eventual costs of depleted stocks will be shared by all who fish there. But what is a state's fair quota of fish? There is no world government to decide such a question, so states must enter into multilateral negotiations, agreements, and regimes. Such efforts create new avenues for functionalism and international integration, but also new potentials for conflict and "prisoner's dilemmas."

States negotiate complex agreements to try to manage the fisheries dilemma. In 1999, a UN-sponsored agreement among all the world's major fishing states set goals to reduce fleet overcapacity. (There are 4 million fishing boats worldwide, of which 40 000 are ships larger than 90 tonnes.) Participating nations are capping the size of fishing fleets and then scaling them back gradually, while reducing subsidies. The pain of unemployment and economic adjustment would thus be shared. However, the agreement is voluntary, and its effect on collapsing fisheries probably too little, too late.

tragedy of the commons
A collective goods dilemma that is created when common environmental assets (such as the world's fisheries) are depleted or degraded through the failure of states to cooperate effectively. One solution is the *enclosure of the commons* (splitting them into individually owned pieces); international regimes can also be a (partial) solution.

enclosure of the commons
The splitting of a common area or good into privately owned pieces, giving individual owners an incentive to manage resources responsibly.

This type of collective goods dilemma has been called the **tragedy of the commons.**[3] Centuries ago, the commons was shared grazing land in Britain. As with fisheries, if too many people kept too many sheep, the commons would be overgrazed. Yet adding one more sheep was profitable to that sheep's owner. Britain solved the problem (although creating other problems) by **enclosure of the commons**—splitting it into privately owned pieces on each of which a single owner would have an incentive to manage resources responsibly. The world's states are gradually taking a similar approach to fisheries by extending territorial waters to put more fish under the control of single states (see "Minerals, Land, Water" later in this chapter). The *global commons* refers to the shared parts of the earth, such as the oceans and outer space.

The solution of environmental collective goods problems is based on achieving shared benefits that depend on overcoming conflicting interests.[4] *Regimes* are an important part of the solution, providing rules to govern bargaining over who gets the benefits and bears the costs of environmental protection. So are functional IOs that specialize in technical and management aspects of the environment.[5]

---

[2] Ransom A. Myers and Boris Worm, "Rapid Worldwide Depletion of Predatory Fish Communities," *Nature* 423 (15 May 2003): 280–283.

[3] Garrett Hardin, "The Tragedy of the Commons," *Science* 162 (16 Dec. 1968): 1243–48. Elinor Ostrom, *Governing the Commons: The Evolution of Institutions for Collective Action* (NY: Cambridge UP, 1991). Robert O. Keohane and Elinor Ostrom, eds., *Local Commons and Global Interdependence: Heterogeneity in Two Domains* (Thousand Oaks, CA: Sage, 1995).

[4] Dimitris Stevis and Valerie J. Assetto, eds., *The International Political Economy of the Environment: Critical Perspectives* (Boulder, CO: Rienner, 2001). Miranda A. Schreurs and Elizabeth Economy, eds., *The Internationalization of Environmental Protection* (NY: Cambridge UP, 1997). Benedict Kingsbury and Andrew Hurrell, eds., *The International Politics of the Environment* (NY: Oxford UP, 1992).

[5] Oran R. Young, ed., *The Effectiveness of International Environmental Regimes: Casual Connections and Behavioral Mechanisms* (Cambridge, MA: MIT P, 1999). Lynne M. Jurgielewicz, *Global Environmental Change and International Law: Prospects for Progress in the Legal Order* (Lanham, MD: UP America, 1996). Robert O. Keohane, Marc A. Levy, and Peter M. Haas, *Institutions for the Earth: Sources of Effective International Environmental Protection* (Cambridge, MA: MIT P, 1993).

TOO MANY COOKS
Management of environmental issues is complicated by the large numbers of actors involved, which make collective goods problems hard to resolve (individuals may be more tempted to free-ride). Here is the negotiating table at the 1992 "Earth Summit" (UN Conference on Environment and Development) in Rio de Janeiro, Brazil. It was the largest gathering of state leaders in history.

Increasingly, these IOs overlap with broader communities of experts from various states that structure the way states manage environmental issues; these have been called **epistemic communities** (knowledge-based communities). For example, the transnational community of experts and policy-makers concerned with pollution in the Mediterranean is an epistemic community.[6]

In global environmental politics, it is hard to manage collective goods problems because of the large number of actors. Collective goods are easier to provide in small groups, where individual actions have more impact on the total picture and where cheating is more noticeable. The opposite is true with the environment. The actions of nearly 200 states (albeit some more than others) aggregate to cause indirect but serious consequences throughout the world. This large number of actors was seen in the 1992 *UN Conference on Environment and Development* (the *"Earth Summit"*) in Rio de Janeiro, Brazil; it was the largest summit meeting of state leaders ever, 153 in all.

With a few exceptions, only in the last two decades has the global environment become a major subject of international negotiation and of IR scholarship.[7] Interest in the environment has grown rapidly since the first "Earth Day" was held by environmental activists in 1970. The energy crises of the 1970s seemed to underline the issue in

epistemic communities
Transnational communities of experts who help structure the way states manage environmental and other issues.

[6] Peter M. Haas, "Introduction: Epistemic Communities and International Policy Coordination," spec. issue of *International Organization* 46.1 (1992): 1–36. Peter M. Haas, *Saving the Mediterranean: The Politics of International Environmental Cooperation* (NY: Columbia UP, 1990).

[7] Elizabeth R. DeSombre, *Domestic Sources of International Environmental Policy* (Cambaridge, MA: MIT P, 2000). Harold Sprout and Margaret Sprout, *The Ecological Perspective on Human Affairs, with Special Reference to International Politics* (Princeton, NJ: Princeton UP, 1965).

industrialized regions. Oil spills, urban air pollution, pesticide residues, and difficulties at nuclear power plants elevated the environment on the international agenda.

The first UN conference on the international environment took place in Stockholm, Sweden, in 1972. It adopted general principles—that one state's actions should not cause environmental damage to another, for instance—and raised awareness about international aspects of environmental damage. A second conference was held, with less publicity, in 1982 in Nairobi, Kenya (headquarters of the UN Environment Programme). The larger and more ambitious 1992 Earth Summit was the third conference. The fourth was held in Johannesburg, South Africa, in 2002.

Sustainable Economic Development

At the 1992 Earth Summit, the major theme was *sustainable* economic development. This refers to economic growth that does not deplete resources and destroy ecosystems so quickly that the basis of that economic growth is itself undermined. The concept applies to both the industrialized regions and the global South.[8]

In the past, the growth of population, industry, energy use, and the extraction of natural resources on the planet has been exponential—growing faster and faster over time. Such exponential growth cannot continue indefinitely, almost by definition. Several possibilities emerge. First, new technologies may allow *unabated economic growth*, but will shift the basis of that growth away from the ever-increasing use of energy and other resources. This is what optimists with faith in technology expect. Goods and services would continue to multiply, raising the global standard of living, but would do so more efficiently to reduce strains on the environment.

carrying capacity The limits of the planetary ecosystem's ability to absorb continual growth of population, industry, energy use, and extraction of natural resources.

A second possibility is a *collapse* of population and living standards in the world, as excessive growth leads to ecological disaster. Pessimists worry that the present course will overshoot the **carrying capacity** of the planetary ecosystem and cause ecosystems to break down because of long-term environmental problems, such as species depletion and global warming. By the time such problems produced severe short-term effects, it would be too late to correct them. In effect, what happened to the world's largest fisheries off the coast of Peru would happen on a global scale—overuse and collapse.

During the past 30 years scholars have produced computer models of the world—population, economic activity, pollution, and other key variables—which show that a finite earth cannot sustain infinite growth and that we are already reaching the "limits to growth."[9] These models are controversial, however. A variety of computer simulations have been developed to try to analyze the carrying capacity of the planet, given available resources and the demands of industrialization and population growth.[10] Some of these models explicitly consider international politics as a factor.[11]

---

[8] Paul Harrison, *The Third World Revolution: Population, Environment, and a Sustainable World* (NY: Penguin, 1994). Lester R. Brown, et al., *State of the World* (NY: Norton/Worldwatch Institute, annual). Richard N. Cooper, *Environment and Resource Policies for the World Economy* (Washington, DC: Brookings, 1995).

[9] Donella H. Meadows et al., *The Limits to Growth: A Report for the Club of Rome's Project on the Predicament of Mankind* (NY: Universe, 1972). Donella Meadows, John Richardson, and Gerhart Bruckmann, *Groping in the Dark: The First Decade of Global Modelling* (Chichester, NY: Wiley, 1982).

[10] Amilcar O. Herrera et al., *Catastrophe or New Society? A Latin American World Model* (Bariloche, Arg.: International Development Research Center, 1976).

[11] Stuart A. Bremer and Barry B. Hughes, *Disarmament and Development: A Design for the Future?* (Englewood Cliffs, NJ: Prentice Hall, 1990). Stuart A. Bremer, ed., *The GLOBUS Model: Computer Simulation of Worldwide Political and Economic Developments* (Boulder, CO: Westview, 1987). Michael Don Ward, ed., *Theories, Models, and Simulations in International Relations: Essays in Honor of Harold Guetzkow* (Boulder, CO: Westview, 1985).

NOT SUSTAINABLE
China's growth has brought serious air pollution in its cities, creating an obstacle to sustaining growth. In response, China must shift away from coal toward oil and gas, as it has begun doing. Earlier, pollution from Soviet industrialization caused great environmental damage, contributing to the stagnation and collapse of the Soviet economy—an unsustainable path. Today's developing countries will have to industrialize along cleaner lines to realize sustainable development. Here, clean bicycles pass a dirty coal-burning train in Shenyan, 1990.

A third possibility is that the past curve of exponential growth will flatten out to form an *S-curve*. The curve rises from a fairly flat slope to an exponential growth curve and then levels off back to a flat slope (at a higher level). Instead of overshooting the planet's limits of human population and energy (triggering collapse), human beings would adapt to those limits in time to achieve a *steady-state* economy in which population, food production, energy use, and other key processes are stable from year to year. It has been argued that our generation is the "hinge of history," just past the middle point of the S-curve. If so, we are experiencing the most rapid change of any generation in the past *or* the future.[12] In this scenario, the key task of our generation would be to adapt our economics and our politics, including IR, to level out into a sustainable long-term relationship with the environment.

The Earth Summit produced an overall plan, called *Agenda 21*, whereby large states of the global South promise to industrialize along cleaner lines (at a certain cost to economic growth) and industrialized states promise to funnel aid and technology to them to assist in that process.[13]

The Earth Summit established the **Commission on Sustainable Development**, which monitors states' compliance with the promises they made at the Earth Summit and hears

Commission on Sustainable Development
An organization established at the 1992 UN Earth Summit that monitors states' compliance with their promises and hears evidence from environmental *nongovernmental organizations (NGOs)*.

---

[12] John R. Platt, "The Step to Man," *Science* 149 (6 Aug. 1965): 607–13.

[13] Tim O'Riordan and Heather Voisey, eds., *Sustainable Development in Europe: Coming to Terms with Agenda 21* (Ilford, UK: Cass, 1997). Marian A. L. Miller, *The Third World in Global Environmental Politics* (Boulder, CO: Rienner, 1995).

evidence from environmental NGOs such as Greenpeace. But it lacks powers of enforcement over national governments—again reflecting the pre-eminence of state sovereignty over supranational authority (see pp. 368–371). Of the 53 commission members, as of 2004, 16 are from the global North, 9 from Africa, 11 from Latin America, and 17 from the Middle East, South Asia, and China combined. It was hoped that the commission's ability to monitor and publicize state actions would discourage states from cheating on the Earth Summit plan.[14] But the commission's first meeting, two years after the Earth Summit, found the states of the global North providing only half of the level of financial support pledged for sustainable development in the South. Funding for sustainable development in the global South—a collective good—continued to lag throughout the 1990s.

In 2002, the Johannesburg World Summit on Sustainable Development involved 22 000 participants, including 100 heads of state and government. The summit also had 8000 NGO representatives and 4000 members of the media in attendance. The 2002 summit resulted in the Johannesburg Plan of Implementation, which attempted to outline concrete actions and measures to achieve the goals outlined in Agenda 21. For example, the Plan of Implementation calls for countries to implement the globally harmonized system for the classification and labelling of chemicals as soon as possible, with a view to having the system fully operational by 2008. It also promotes the idea of supporting sustainable tourism, in particular eco-tourism, and suggests ways to provide technical support for countries of the global South that are attempting a transition into more sustainable forms of tourism.

China and other developing countries in Asia stood at the centre of the debate over sustainable development. In the drive for rapid economic growth, these countries have cut corners environmentally, resulting in the world's worst air pollution and other serious problems. China is building the Three Gorges Dam, which will be the world's largest hydroelectric station, with 26 separate generators on line when it becomes fully operational in 2009. It provides a clean source of energy in a coal-burning country, but environmentalists fear it will damage a large river ecosystem, and human rights advocates have been concerned about the massive resettlement of people resulting from the 600-kilometre long reservoir created by the dam. Because of China's size, any success in developing its economy along Northern industrialized lines (for example, with widespread ownership of automobiles) could create massive shocks to the global environment. Yet no practical alternative has been taken seriously. In recent years, however, China has begun to switch away from dirty coal, helping ease the pollution caused by sustained rapid economic growth.

Rethinking Interdependence

We have thus far treated international environmental issues as problems of interstate bargaining, an approach that reflects a neoliberal theoretical orientation. This approach has been challenged in recent years by an emerging theoretical framework that is more critical in orientation, seeking more fundamental change in the nature of the international community's approach to environmental problems. This approach is well reflected in the grassroots activism of Greenpeace and other environment-related NGOs. Environmentalists object to free trade provisions that weaken environmental standards by empowering international bureaucrats who care more about wealth generation than eco-preservation (see p. 500). Similarly, environmental groups have objected to management of economic development in the global South by international institutions, in particular the World Bank.

---

[14] Paul Lewis, "UN Implementing the Earth Summit," *New York Times* 1 Dec. 1992: A16.

Thus the more critical theoretical perspective rejects the liberal goal of maximizing wealth (see pp. 295–297). Although liberal concepts of rationality are longer-term than realist ones (see p. 88), environmentalists take an even broader and longer-term view. From this perspective, the collective goods problem among states is not the problem; it is the growth of industrial civilization out of balance with the planetary ecosystem that must ultimately support it. True rationality, for environmentalists, must include very long-term calculations about how the self-interest of humanity itself is undermined by a greedy drive to exploit nature—that is, interdependence and the collective goods problem are broadened to include humanity versus nature, not just state versus state.

The remainder of this chapter will focus primarily on interstate bargaining processes concerning the environment, but will include the broader forces of concern to environmentalists. As these forces shape the contexts for interstate bargaining, they must be of concern even to liberals and conservatives.

MANAGING THE ENVIRONMENT

In discussing the issue areas in which states are bargaining over environmental problems, we begin with the most global problems—those that are collective goods for all states and people in the world. Later sections consider more localized conflicts over pollution and natural resources.

The Atmosphere

Preserving the health of the earth's atmosphere is a benefit that affects people throughout the world without regard for their own state's contribution to the problem or its solution. Two problems of the atmosphere have become major international issues—global warming and depletion of the ozone layer.

Global Warming Global climate change, or **global warming,** is a slow, long-term rise in the average world temperature. Scientists are not certain that such a rise is occurring, or if so how fast, but there is growing evidence that global warming is a real problem, that it is caused by the emission of carbon dioxide and other gases, and that it will get worse in the future. Many scientists believe it prudent to address the problem soon, because once the symptoms become obvious it will be too late to prevent disaster. The time frame is unclear: 1998 and 2001 were the two warmest years on record, but this may or may not indicate a rapid onset of serious global warming.

It is not easy to guess who will be harmed and how soon. But over the next 50 years, according to most estimates, global temperatures may rise by between one degree and five degrees Celsius if nothing is done. The high end of this temperature range corresponds with the difference between today's climate and that of the last ice age; it is a major climate change. Possibly within a few decades the polar ice caps would begin to melt and cause the sea level to rise by as much as a few feet. Such a rise could flood many coastal cities and devastate low-lying areas, such as the heavily populated coastal areas of Bangladesh and China. Urgent calls for action to avert global warming come from island states in the Pacific that are likely to disappear this century.

Global climate change could also change weather patterns in many regions, causing droughts, floods, and widespread disruption of natural ecosystems. It is also possible that climate changes (at least mild ones) could *benefit* some regions and make agriculture more productive. Nobody knows for sure, but sudden environmental changes are usually much more destructive than helpful.

global warming A slow, long-term rise in the average world temperature caused by the emission of greenhouse gases produced by burning fossil fuels—oil, coal, and natural gas. See also *greenhouse gases.*

The Information Revolution

Silicon versus Fossil Fuels?

The industrial revolution, which harnessed fossil fuels to power machinery, changed IR profoundly (see pp. 32–34). Now, perhaps, a comparable revolution in technology is driving world events in new directions. Some call information- and service-based economies "postindustrial." Is the information revolution the endpoint of industrialization and, if so, can the global South bypass industrialization and the global North decrease its energy use, thus reducing global warming?

To explore this question, go to www.pearsoned.ca/goldstein.

fossil fuels Oil, coal, and natural gas, burnt to run factories, cars, tractors, furnaces, electrical generating plants, and other things that drive an industrial economy.

greenhouse gases Carbon dioxide and other gases that, when concentrated in the atmosphere, act like the glass in a greenhouse, holding energy in and leading to *global warming*.

It is very difficult to reduce the emissions of gases—mainly carbon dioxide—that cause global warming. These gases result from the broad spectrum of activities that drive an industrial economy. They are a by-product of burning **fossil fuels**—oil, coal, and natural gas—to run cars, tractors, furnaces, factories, and so forth. These activities create **greenhouse gases**—so named because when concentrated in the atmosphere these gases act like the glass in a greenhouse: they let energy in as short-wavelength solar radiation but reflect it back when it tries to exit again as longer-wavelength heat waves. The greenhouse gases are *carbon dioxide* (responsible for two-thirds of the effect), *methane gas*, *chlorofluorocarbons* (CFCs), and *nitrous oxide*. The concentration of these gases in the global atmosphere is slowly increasing, though the rates and processes involved are complicated (carbon is exchanged among the atmosphere, oceans, and trees).

Thus the costs of reducing the greenhouse effect are high, because the solutions entail curbing economic growth or shifting it onto entirely new technological paths.[15] The political costs of such actions—which would likely increase unemployment, reduce corporate profits, and lower personal incomes—could be severe. For example, in Canada, the government of Alberta, Canada's largest energy-producing province, and representatives from industry, have argued that efforts to address global warming will have a detrimental impact on the Canadian economy. Not only will industry bear the burden of the costs of reducing the emissions, but because Canada's largest trading partner, the United States, has refused to set limits on greenhouse gas emissions, Canadian industry would be at a distinct disadvantage vis-à-vis U.S. exporters.

For individual states, the costs of reducing greenhouse emissions are almost unrelated to the benefits of a solution. If one state reduces its industrial production or makes expensive investments in new technologies, this will have little effect on the long-term outcome unless other states do likewise. And if most states took such steps, a free rider that did not go along would save money and still benefit from the solution.

Global warming thus presents states with a triple dilemma. First, there is the dilemma of short-term (and predictable) costs to gain long-term (and less predictable) benefits. Second, specific constituencies such as oil companies and industrial workers pay the costs, whereas the benefits are distributed more generally across domestic society. Third, there is the collective goods dilemma among states: benefits are shared globally but costs must be extracted from each state individually.

This third dilemma is complicated by the North-South divide, which creates divergent expectations about fair allocation of costs. Specifically, how can the industrialization of today's poor countries take place without pushing greenhouse emissions to unacceptable levels? Greenhouse gases are produced by each state roughly in proportion to its industrial activity. Eighty percent of greenhouse gases now come from the industrialized countries—25 percent from the United States alone. (U.S. carbon dioxide emissions

---

[15] Urs Luterbacher and Detlef F. Sprinz, *International Relations and Global Climate Change* (Cambridge, MA: MIT P, 2001). Ian H. Rowlands, *The Politics of Global Atmospheric Change* (NY: St. Martin's, 1995). Matthew Paterson, *Global Warming and Global Politics* (NY: Routledge, 1996). Edward S. Rubin, et al., "Realistic Mitigation Options for Global Warming," *Science* 257 (10 July 1992): 148.

amount to 18 tonnes per person annually, about twice the European rate and ten times China's.) Yet the most severe impacts of global warming are likely to be felt in the global South. Thus, serious international conflicts exist over who should pay the bills to avert global warming.[16]

All of these elements make for a difficult multilateral bargaining situation, one not yet resolved. The *Framework Convention on Climate Change* adopted at the 1992 Earth Summit set a nonbinding goal, to limit greenhouse emissions to 1990 levels by the year 2000; that goal was not met. The treaty did not commit the signatory states to meet target levels of greenhouse emissions by a particular date, owing to U.S. objections to such a commitment.

Western Europe and Japan have been more willing to regulate greenhouse emissions than is the United States (which burns more fossil fuel per person). Europe and Japan later proposed a binding treaty requiring all states to stabilize their emissions at 1990 levels by the year 2000, and then reduce them 15 percent further by 2010. The United States modified its position in 1996, supporting a binding treaty, but with a target date of 2010 to reach 1990 levels and no subsequent targets.

The 1997 *Kyoto Protocol* adopted a complex formula for reducing greenhouse emissions to 1990 levels in the global North over about a decade.[17] Countries in the global South received preferential treatment, however, since their levels (per capita) were much lower. Yet China is the world's second-largest producer of carbon dioxide (after the United States), and India the sixth largest (after Russia, Japan, and Germany). Objecting to this "free ride," the U.S. Congress promptly declared that it would not ratify the treaty. President Bush then dropped out of follow-up negotiations to Kyoto, declaring the treaty "dead." China meanwhile began lowering its carbon emissions, independently of the treaty, as it began switching away from its predominant fuel, coal.

Moving forward without U.S. support, 160 countries in 2001 agreed to implement the Kyoto Protocol. Canada ratified in 2002. The agreement now calls for 40 industrialized countries to reduce emissions to 5 percent below 1990 levels by 2012, with binding penalties for failure. States will be able to buy and sell carbon emission credits, and will get credit for forests that absorb carbon dioxide. The EU pledged US$400 million per year to help the global South reduce its emissions. The treaty requires 55 ratifications from states totalling 55 percent of world emissions before it will come into force. As of April 2004, it had received 84 ratifications, but carbon dioxide emissions from those states amounted to only 44 percent of the world total. It is unclear whether Kyoto will be able to come into effect without ratification by a large carbon emission–producing country like the United States, or how effective it would be without U.S. participation.

More broadly, the dilemma of global warming remains fundamentally unsolved, and with no enforcement mechanism it is questionable whether states that signed the Kyoto Protocol will in fact meet their targets on schedule, if ever.

Technology may help to make the bargaining a bit easier in the future. Many technical experts now argue that dramatic gains can be made through energy efficiency measures and other solutions that do not reduce the amount of economic activity but do make it cleaner and more efficient. Although costly, such investments would ultimately pay for themselves through greater economic efficiency. If this approach succeeds, international conflicts over global warming will be reduced.

---

[16] James K. Sebenius, "Designing Negotiations Toward a New Regime: The Case of Global Warming," *International Security* 15.4 (1991): 110–48.

[17] David G. Victor, *The Collapse of the Kyoto Protocol and the Struggle to Slow Global Warming* (Princeton, NJ: Princeton UP, 2001). Michael Grubb and Duncan Brack, eds., *The Kyoto Protocol: A Guide and Assessment* (London: Royal Institute of International Affairs, 1999).

MELTING AWAY
International treaties have been much more successful at addressing ozone depletion than global warming, mostly because the costs of the latter are much higher and the results are further in the future. A 1997 conference in Kyoto, Japan, set goals for industrialized countries to reduce their output of carbon dioxide and related gases modestly over the next decade, but the goals probably will not be met. If global warming melts polar ice caps in the new century, sea levels could rise and devastate many cities. This crack in the Antarctic ice shelf in 1997 suggests that this process is underway.

Japanese leaders think their country can profit by gaining a comparative advantage in environmental technologies. The government- and industry-funded *Research Institute of Innovative Technology for the Earth (RITE)*, with 300 employees in 2001, is developing methods to filter carbon dioxide out of industrial exhausts.[18] RITE is part of a MITI (see p. 316) campaign called *New Earth 21*, to coordinate a movement of Japanese industry into environmental technologies.

The **UN Environment Programme (UNEP)**, whose main function is to monitor environmental conditions, works with the World Meteorological Organization to measure changes in global climate from year to year. Since 1989 the UN-sponsored *Intergovernmental Panel on Climate Change* has served as a negotiating forum for this issue.

Ozone Depletion A second major atmospheric problem being negotiated by the world's governments is the depletion of the world's **ozone layer**.[19] Ozone high in the atmosphere screens out harmful ultraviolet rays from the sun. Chemicals expelled by some industries float up to the top of the atmosphere and interact with ozone in a way that breaks it down. The chief culprits are CFCs, widely used in refrigeration and in aerosol sprays. (Unfortunately, ozone produced by burning fossil fuels does not replace the high-level ozone but only pollutes the lower atmosphere.)

As the ozone layer thins, more ultraviolet radiation is reaching the earth's surface. Over Antarctica, where the ozone is thinnest, a hole in the ozone appears to be growing larger and lasting longer year by year. Depleted ozone levels over North America were detected in the early 1990s, and people have been warned to limit exposure to the sun to lower the risk of skin cancer. Eventually, the increased radiation could begin to kill off vegetation, reduce agricultural yields, and disrupt ecosystems.

Clearly, this is another collective goods problem in that one state benefits from allowing the use of CFCs in its economy, provided that most other states prohibit their use. But the costs of replacing CFCs are much lower than the costs of addressing global warming: CFCs can be replaced with other chemicals at relatively modest costs. Furthermore, the consequences of ozone depletion are both better understood and more immediate than those of global warming.

Therefore, states have had more success in negotiating agreements and developing regimes to manage the ozone problem. In the 1987 **Montreal Protocol**, 22 states agreed to reduce CFCs by 50 percent by 1998. In 1990, the timetable was accelerated and the

UN Environment Programme (UNEP)
UN agency that monitors environmental conditions and, among other activities, works with the World Meteorological Organization to measure changes in global climate.

ozone layer The part of the atmosphere that screens out harmful unltraviolet rays from the sun. Certain chemicals used by some industries, in particular chlorofluorocarbons (CFCs), break the ozone layer down.

Montreal Protocol (1987)
An agreement on protection of the ozone layer in which states pledged to reduce and then eliminate use of chlorofluorocarbons (CFCs). It is the most successful environmental treaty to date.

---

[18] "Japan Bids for Global Leadership in Clean Industry," *Science* 256 (22 May 1992): 1144.

[19] Richard Elliot Benedick, *Ozone Diplomacy* (Cambridge, MA: Harvard UP, 1991). Karen Litfin, *Ozone Discourses: Science and Politics in Global Environmental Cooperation* (NY: Columbia UP, 1993).

signatories expanded: 81 states agreed to eliminate all CFCs by 2000. In 1992, as evidence of ozone depletion mounted, the schedule was again accelerated, with major industrial states phasing out CFCs by 1995. The signatories agreed in principle to establish a fund (of unspecified size and source) to help countries of the global South pay for alternative refrigeration technologies not based on CFCs. Without such an effort, developing-country states would be tempted to free-ride and could ultimately undermine the effort. These countries were also given until 2010 to phase out production. Rich countries stopped making CFCs in 1996, and poor countries began to reduce emissions—helped somewhat by the global North's contribution of more than US$1 billion during the 1990s to 110 countries in the South. However, even the reduced levels of global CFC emissions further damage the ozone layer (since they take decades to break down). The ozone hole continues to grow larger. With payments by rich countries lagging, and a parallel market in cheap CFCs, it is unclear whether countries in the global South will succeed in eliminating CFCs by 2010 as agreed.

The Montreal Protocol on CFCs is the most important success yet achieved in international negotiations to preserve the global environment. It showed that states can agree to take action on urgent environmental threats, can agree on targets and measures to counter such threats, and can allocate the costs of such measures in a mutually acceptable way. Recent measurements of CFCs in the atmosphere show that the yearly rate of increase has slowed down—a promising start.[20] But the international cooperation on the ozone problem has not been widely repeated on other environmental issues.

Biodiversity

Biodiversity refers to the tremendous diversity of plant and animal species making up the earth's (global, regional, and local) ecosystems.[21] Biologists believe that the 1.4 million species they have identified and named are only a small fraction of the total number of species in existence (most of which are micro-organisms). Some species, such as humans, are distributed broadly around the world, whereas others live in just one locale.

Because of humans' destruction of ecosystems, large numbers of species are already *extinct* and others are in danger of becoming so. Extinct species cannot return. The causes of their extinction include overhunting, overfishing, and introducing nonnative species that crowd out previous inhabitants. But the most important cause is *loss of habitat*—the destruction of rain forests, pollution of lakes and streams, and loss of agricultural lands to urban sprawl. Because ecosystems are based on complex interrelationships among species, the extinction of a few species can cause deeper changes in the environment. For example, the loss of native micro-organisms can lead to chronic pollution of rivers or to the transformation of arable land into deserts.

Because ecosystems are so complex, it is usually impossible to predict the consequences of a species' extinction or of the loss of a habitat or ecosystem. Generally the activities that lead to habitat loss are economically profitable, so there are real costs associated with limiting such activities. For example, logging in the U.S. Northwest has been restricted to save the northern spotted owl from extinction. Less extensive restrictions have been attempted in British Columbia, and by some estimates there are fewer than 50 spotted owls remaining in Canada. Nobody can be sure what effect the owl's extinction would have, but the costs to loggers are clear and immediate.

biodiversity The tremendous diversity of plant and animal species making up the earth's (global, regional, and local) ecosystems.

---

[20] *Science* 256 (22 May 1992): 1109.

[21] Timothy M. Swanson, ed., *The Economics and Ecology of Biodiversity Decline: The Forces Driving Global Change* (NY: Cambridge UP, 1998).

Species preservation is thus a collective good resembling global warming; the costs are immediate and substantial but the benefits are long term and ill defined. As to biodiversity, the effects of policies tend to be more local than those of global warming, so the problem to some degree can be enclosed within the purview of states. But to a surprising extent the biodiversity in one state affects the quality of the environment in other states. Topsoil blown away in Africa is deposited in South America; monarch butterflies that failed to breed in Mexico in 1991 did not appear in Ontario in 1992.

It has been difficult to reach international agreement on sharing the costs of preserving biodiversity. A UN convention on trade in endangered species has reduced but not eliminated such trade. At the 1992 Earth Summit, a treaty on biodiversity was adopted that committed signatories to preserving habitats, and got rich states to pay poor ones for the rights to use commercially profitable biological products extracted from rare species in protected habitats (such as medicines from rain forest trees). However, because of fears that it could limit U.S. patent rights in biotechnology, the United States did not sign the treaty. It signed in 1993, with stipulations, but did not ratify the treaty. As of 2001, parties to the biodiversity treaty include all UN member states, including Canada, with the exception of the United States and nine small countries.

Many environmentalists have a special concern for whales and dolphins, which like humans are large-brained mammals. In the past 20 years, environmental activists have persuaded states to agree to international regimes to protect whales and dolphins. The **International Whaling Commission** (an IGO) sets quotas for hunting certain whale species; participation is voluntary, and Norway dropped out in 1992 when it decided unilaterally that it could increase its catch without endangering the species. The *Inter-American Tropical Tuna Commission* (another IGO) regulates methods used to fish for tuna, aiming to minimize dolphin losses.

International Whaling Commission An *intergovernmental organization (IGO)* that sets quotas for hunting certain whale species; states' participation is voluntary.

The United States, which consumes half the world's tuna catch, has gone further and unilaterally requires—in the Marine Mammal Protection Act—that "dolphin-safe" methods be used for tuna sold in U.S. territory. Under this law, the United States in 1990 banned imports of tuna from Mexico and Venezuela. These countries, which could not comply with the U.S. law as easily as the U.S. tuna industry could, took their case to the GATT (see pp. 323–325) and won. Species protection lost out to free trade in the GATT ruling. But the United States did not comply with the GATT ruling, despite appeals from the EC and dozens of other states, including Canada.[22]

Such conflicts portend future battles between environmentalists and free trade advocates.[23] Free traders argue that states must not use domestic legislation to seek global environmental goals. Environmentalists do not want to give up national laws that they worked for decades to enact, over the opposition of industrial corporations. Canadian efforts to prohibit the gasoline additive MMT (see p. 327) was rejected by NAFTA and the restriction was eventually abandoned by the Canadian government. Environmentalists adopted the sea turtle as a symbol of their opposition to the WTO after the WTO overturned U.S. regulations that required shrimp to be caught in nets from which sea turtles (an endangered species) can escape. NAFTA and the WTO's actions in cases such as the

[22] James Brooke, "America—Environmental Dictator?" *New York Times* 3 May 1992: F7.

[23] W. Bradnee Chambers, ed., *Inter-Linkages: The Kyoto Protocol and the International Trade and Investment Regimes* (Washington, DC: Brookings, 2001). Dani Rodrik, *Has Globalization Gone Too Far?* (Washington, DC: Institute for International Economics, 1997). Daniel C. Esty, *Greening the GATT: Trade, Environment and the Future* (Washington, DC: Institute for International Economics, 1994). H. Jeffrey Leonard, *Pollution and the Struggle for the World Product: Multinational Corporations, Environment, and International Comparative Advantage* (NY: Cambridge UP, 1988). Thomas J. Schoenbaum, "International Trade and Protection of the Environment: The Continuing Search for Reconciliation," *American Journal of International Law* 91.2 (1997): 268–313.

gasoline or shrimp disputes are based on unfair *application* of environmental rules to domestic versus foreign companies. In practical terms, however, the effect is negative from environmentalists' perspective.

In recent years, most spectacularly at the WTO's failed 1999 Seattle summit, a coalition of environmental groups campaigned against the "faceless bureaucrats" at the WTO who override national laws such as the tuna act; these bureaucrats are portrayed as agents of the MNCs, out to increase profits with no regard for the environment. (Note the similarity to earlier popular European resistance to "faceless Eurocrats.") Recent conflicts have arisen over U.S. laws restricting imports of foods with pesticide residues, and over European laws on imports of genetically engineered agricultural and pharmaceutical products, which the United States wants to export worldwide. Environmentalists fear that the successful Montreal Protocol on ozone protection (see p. 498), which relies on trade sanctions for enforcement, could be threatened by WTO agreements.

Thus, unilateral approaches to biodiversity issues are problematic because they disrupt free trade; multilateral approaches are problematic because of the collective goods problem. It is not surprising that the international response to species extinction has been fairly ineffective to date.

Forests and Oceans

Two types of habitat—tropical rain forests and oceans—are especially important to biodiversity *and* the atmosphere. Both are also reservoirs of commercially profitable resources, such as fish and wood. They differ in that forests are located almost entirely within state territory, but oceans are largely beyond any state territory, in the global commons.

Rain Forests As many as half the world's total species live in *rain forests*; they replenish oxygen and reduce carbon dioxide in the atmosphere—slowing down global warming. Rain forests thus benefit all the world's states; they are collective goods.

International bargaining on the preservation of rain forests has made considerable progress, probably because most rain forests belong to a few states. These few states have the power to speed up or slow down the destruction of forests—and international bargaining amounts to agreements to shift costs from those few states onto the broader group of states benefiting from the rain forests. This collective goods problem is simpler and has fewer actors than the global warming problem.

Although some rich states (including Canada) have large forests, most of the largest rain forests are in poor states, such as Brazil, Indonesia, Malaysia, and Madagascar. Such states can benefit economically from exploiting the forests—freely cutting lumber, clearing land for agriculture, and mining.[24] Until recently (and still to an extent), leaders of rich states have been most interested in encouraging maximum

DEVELOPMENT OR DESTRUCTION?
Some environmentalists criticize the World Bank and other international institutions promoting economic development in poor countries, for interfering destructively in local ecosystems such as rain forests. The Green Revolution increased yields but shifted patterns of agriculture in complex ways, such as by increasing pesticide and fertilizer runoff. Now genetically engineered crops promise further increases in agricultural productivity—more food on the table—but with environmental consequences that are not fully understood. This corporate president holds a genetically modified seedling, 2001.

economic growth in poor states so that foreign debts could be paid—with little regard for environmental damage. The World Bank, for example, has been criticized by environmentalists for providing technical assistance and investment to build large dams in environmentally sensitive areas in the global South.

Now that rich states have an interest in protecting rain forests, they are using money and development assistance as leverage to induce poorer states to protect their forests rather than exploiting them maximally. Under international agreements of the early 1990s, rich countries are contributing hundreds of millions of dollars in foreign aid for this purpose. In some countries of the global South, burdened by large foreign debts, environmentalists and bankers from rich countries have worked out "debt-for-nature swaps" in which a debt is cancelled in exchange for the state's agreement to preserve forests.

Brazil in particular has responded to these agreements with significant steps. A major government-sponsored drive to settle and exploit the Amazon basin had begun in the 1960s. In the early 1990s, the government adopted sweeping new policies to balance economic exploitation of the Amazon basin with the needs of environmental preservation and the rights of indigenous peoples. However, a 1999 study found the forest disappearing twice as fast as previously estimated.

Oceans   The *oceans*, covering 70 percent of the earth's surface, are (like the rain forest) a key to regulating climate and preserving biodiversity. Oceans, like forests, are attractive targets for short-term economic uses that cause long-term environmental damage. Such uses include overfishing, dumping toxic and nuclear waste (and other garbage), and long-distance oil shipments with their recurrent spills. Unlike rain forests, oceans belong to no state but are a global commons.[25] This makes the collective goods problem more difficult because no authority exists to enforce regulations. Preserving the oceans depends on the cooperation of more than a hundred states and thousands of nonstate actors.

Free riders have great opportunities to profit. For example, *drift nets* are huge fishing nets, kilometres long, that scoop up everything in their path. They are very profitable but destructive of a sustainable ocean environment. Most states have now banned their use (under pressure from the environmental movement). However, no state has the authority to go onto the **high seas** (nonterritorial waters) and stop illegal use of these nets.

One solution that states have pursued involves "enclosing" more of the ocean. Territorial waters have expanded to hundreds of kilometres off the coast (and around islands), so that state sovereignty encloses substantial resources (fisheries and offshore oil and mineral deposits). This solution has been pursued in the context of larger multilateral negotiations on ocean management.

The **UN Convention on the Law of the Sea (UNCLOS)**, negotiated from 1973 to 1982, governs the uses of the oceans. The UNCLOS treaty established rules on territorial waters—12 nautical miles (22.2 kilometres) for shipping and 200 nautical miles (370.4 kilometres) for economic activities, such as fishing and mining. The 200–nautical mile limit placed a substantial share of the economically profitable ocean resources in the control of about a dozen states (see Figure 13.1).

high seas That portion of the oceans considered common territory, not under any kind of exclusive state jurisdiction. See also *territorial waters.*

UN Convention on the Law of the Sea (UNCLOS) A world treaty (1982) governing use of the oceans. The UNCLOS treaty established rules on territorial waters and a 200–nautical mile exclusive economic zone (EEZ). See also *territorial waters.*

[24] Peter Dauvergne, *Shadows in the Forest: Japan and the Politics of Timber in Southeast Asia* (Cambridge, MA: MIT P, 1997). Roberto P. Guimãraes, *The Ecopolitics of Development in the Third World: Politics and Environment in Brazil* (Boulder, CO: Rienner, 1991.

[25] Elisabeth Mann Borgese, *The Oceanic Circle: Governing the Seas as a Global Resource* (NY: UN UP, 1999). Giulio Pontecorvo, ed., *The New Order of the Oceans* (NY: Columbia UP, 1986).

Figure 13.1 State-Controlled Waters

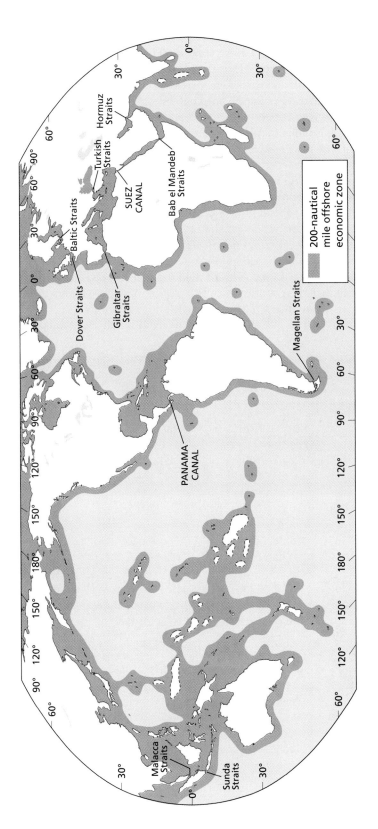

Overfishing and similar problems of managing the "commons" of world oceans have been addressed by enclosing the most important ocean areas under the exclusive control of states. Shaded areas are within the 200-nautical mile economic zones controlled by states under terms of the UNCLOS treaty.

Source: Adapted from Andrew Boyd, *An Atlas of World Affairs,* 9th ed. (NY: Routledge, 1992).

A conflict developed over a small piece of the continental shelf off Newfoundland that was just beyond the 200–nautical mile range controlled by Canada. The Canadian Navy harassed Spanish fishing ships there, which the Canadians claimed were overfishing and thus endangering fish populations that were mostly within the 200–nautical mile limit. Although the European Union accused Canada of "piracy" on the high seas, the two sides in 1995 reached an agreement on fishing levels and practices. The agreement in turn stimulated progress in UN talks that had been trying to develop global rules and norms for ocean fishing. (These talks reached no quick breakthrough, however.) In 1994, Russian warships drove away dozens of foreign fishing ships in the Sea of Okhotsk (where the 200–nautical mile limit leaves a small hole of high seas in the centre). Similar conflicts may develop near Norway, West Africa, the South Pacific, and the Indian Ocean.

UNCLOS also developed the general principle that the oceans are a common heritage of humankind. A mechanism was created, through an International Sea-Bed Authority, for sharing some of the wealth that rich states might gain from extracting minerals on the ocean floor (beyond 200 nautical miles).

The UNCLOS treaty faced uncertain prospects when the United States decided not to sign the treaty, believing that their country bore too great a share of the costs in the plan. The United States is the dominant naval power with de facto military control in much of the world's ocean space. It is also the state most likely to benefit from unilateral

Thinking Theoretically

In 1995, Canada began unilaterally enforcing fishing rules just outside its 200–nautical mile exclusive economic zone, using military force several times to threaten Spanish fishing ships, once even seizing one. The actions seemed to set the stage for a nasty confrontation between allies (Canada and the European Union). Instead, an agreement was reached that limited fishing methods and catches in the area, as Canada had wanted. How might we explain this episode in theoretical terms?

Realism would note the effectiveness of Canada's resort to military leverage, which drove the cost of European resistance way up and made it worthwhile for the EU to come to terms with Canadian demands. Since treaties such as UNCLOS are viewed with some skepticism by realists, they would attribute Canada's success to its proximity—the greater ease with which its navy could deploy to the disputed area—and its stronger will to prevail (reflecting the fact that the issue affected Canada's national interests much more than those of the EU).

Liberals could note, however, that the EU is far more powerful than Canada overall, so sheer power politics does not provide a very good starting point for explaining the outcome. Rather, liberals might emphasize the collective goods problem involved in overfishing, and note that Canada's willingness to unilaterally take on the enforcement costs effectively resolved the dilemma. It remained only to negotiate the terms of what was being enforced (the specific rules for fishing), and there the conflicts of interest were small compared to the overall range of mutual benefits produced by the close economic cooperation of Canada and the EU. The idea that unilateral enforcement could resolve collective goods dilemmas is supported by the comments of the chairman of a UN conference working on an international fishing treaty. He noted that the Canadian-EU agreement "will help our discussions here because it establishes the principle that there can be boarding and monitoring on the high seas."

Critical theorists would be less concerned about the question of enforcing norms, and might ask instead why "enforcement" became the important question when thinking about overfishing. Focusing on enforcement, as liberals and realists do, redirects our attention away from larger questions such as the role of global capitalism in species depletion. Critical theorists are concerned that problem-solving responses such as the creation of treaties, and questions of their enforcement, keep us from applying a deeper analysis and considering more radical solutions. Most critical theorists, for example, do not think that capitalism can be "managed" to produce better environmental outcomes; rather, capitalism would need to be transformed in order to get to the root causes of environmental degradation.

deep-sea mining. It was not willing to underwrite the costs of providing the collective good of ocean management. After more than a decade's delay and renegotiation of some of the deep-sea mining aspects, the United States signed UNCLOS in 1994.

Private environmental groups have been active players on oceans, as in rain forests—pressuring governments and MNCs to change policies and activities. Tactics include direct action (such as Greenpeace ships shadowing garbage barges), lobbying, lawsuits, and public education. These tactics have effectively used global communications (see Chapter 10, pp. 387–391)—a dramatic event videotaped in a remote location on the high seas can be seen on millions of TV sets.

Antarctica   Like the oceans, *Antarctica* belongs to no state.[26] The continent's strategic and commercial value are limited, however, and not many states care about it. Thus, states have been successful in reaching agreements on Antarctica because the costs were low and the players few. The **Antarctic Treaty of 1959**—one of the first multilateral treaties concerning the environment—forbids military activity as well as the presence of nuclear weapons or the dumping of nuclear waste in Antarctica. It sets aside territorial claims on the continent for future resolution and establishes a regime under which various states conduct scientific research in Antarctica. The treaty was signed by all states with interests in the area, including both superpowers. By 1991, Greenpeace had convinced the treaty signatories to turn the continent into a "world park." Antarctica is largely a success story in international environmental politics.

Antarctic Treaty of 1959 One of the first multilateral treaties concerning the environment, it forbids military activity in Antarctica as well as the presence of nuclear weapons or the dumping of nuclear waste there, sets aside territorial claims on the continent for future resolution, and establishes a regime for the conduct of scientific research.

Pollution

Pollution generally creates a collective goods problem, but one that is not often global in scale. Pollution is more often a regional or bilateral issue. With some exceptions—such as dumping at sea—the effects of pollution are limited to the state where it occurs and its close neighbours—U.S. industrial smokestack emissions affect acid rain in Canada but do not directly affect distant states. Even when pollution crosses state borders, it often has its strongest effects closest to the source. This localized effect makes for a somewhat less intractable collective goods problem, because a polluting state can seldom get an entirely free ride, and there are a limited number of actors. The effects of pollution also are more tangible than global warming or the ozone hole.

In several regions—notably Western and Eastern Europe and the Middle East—states are closely packed in the same air, river, or sea basins. In such situations, pollution controls must often be negotiated multilaterally. In Europe during the Cold War, the international pollution problem was exacerbated by the inability of Western European states to impose any limits on Eastern ones, whose pollution was notorious. These problems are only now being addressed.

Several regional agreements seek to limit **acid rain,** caused by air pollution. Acid rain often crosses borders. European states—whose forests have been heavily damaged—have agreed to limit air pollution and acid rain for their mutual benefit. In 1988, 24 European states signed a treaty to limit nitrogen oxide emissions to 1988 levels by 1995. After long negotiations, the United States and Canada have signed bilateral agreements to limit such pollution as well. These regional agreements have worked fairly well.

acid rain Rain that contains acids caused by air pollution; it damages trees and often crosses borders. Limiting acid rain (via limiting nitrogen oxide emissions) has been the subject of several regional agreements.

Water pollution often crosses borders as well, especially because industrial pollution, human sewage, and agricultural fertilizers and pesticides all tend to run into rivers and seas.

---

[26] Olav Schram Stokke and Davor Vidas, eds., *Governing the Antarctic: The Effectiveness and Legitimacy of the Antarctic Treaty System* (NY: Cambridge UP, 1997). Gail Osherenko and Oran R. Young, *The Age of the Arctic: Hot Conflicts and Cold Realities* (NY: Cambridge UP, 1989).

Long-standing international regional agencies that regulate shipping on heavily used European rivers now also deal with pollution. The Mediterranean basin is severely polluted, and difficult to manage because so many states border it.[27] The Great Lakes on the U.S.-Canadian border had become heavily polluted by the 1970s. But because the issue affected only two countries, it was easier to address through the Great Lakes Water Quality Agreement of 1978, which is monitored by the International Joint Commission (IJC)—a binational body established in 1909 to monitor and resolve transboundary water issues between Canada and the U.S. As a result of IJC efforts—as well as those of federal, provincial, and state governments on both sides of the border—water quality in the Great Lakes has improved in recent years.

Sometimes water pollution results not from industrial effluent, but from accidents. One of the worst occurred in 1989 when the Exxon Valdez, a supertanker carrying over a million barrels of crude oil, rammed a reef and dumped its cargo into Prince William Sound, Alaska, destroying local habitat, animal and sea life. Blame was soon laid with the ship's captain who was not on the bridge at the time of the accident and had allegedly been drinking. Critical theorists point out that that the Exxon Valdez is also a good illustration of the way in which, given the nature of the corporate drive for profit, environmental "accidents" are inevitable. Investigations into the accident showed that years of cost-cutting efforts by large oil companies had resulted in personnel reductions on oil tankers (with a corresponding increase in stress levels and a persistent problem of alcoholism); the use of ever-larger supertankers (which made them increasingly difficult to manoeuvre); and a refusal, on the part of oil companies, to switch to double-hulled ships to transport oil (which would have reduced the amount of the Alaska spill by as much as 60 percent according U.S. Coast Guard estimates). In the drive to be more efficient, and earn larger profits, corporate decisions, according to critical theorists, set the stage for environmental catastrophes.[28]

In other cases, it is not accidents that result in environmental damage and adverse health effects, but simply the production of particular products. Canada, for example, is a large producer of asbestos—a known carcinogen. Because of restrictions on its use, most of Canada's asbestos (between 95 and 97 percent) is exported. In recent years, a number of European countries have banned asbestos imports (bans that have been supported by the WTO). Thus, most of Canada's asbestos is exported to countries of the global South. The Canadian government promotes asbestos use abroad because asbestos manufacturing is an important and profitable industry (especially to the province of Québec). It argues that safe handling can eliminate the health effects of asbestos. Critics argue that safe handling of asbestos is possible only with the most advanced protective measures—often unavailable in poorer countries where health and safety regulations also tend to be more lax. Critics, in other words, point out that profit takes precedence over the known adverse health effects of a product destined for the global South.[29]

Toxic and *nuclear wastes* are a special problem because of their long-term dangers. States occasionally try to ship such wastes out of the country. International agreements now ban the dumping of toxic and nuclear wastes at sea (an obvious collective goods problem). But such wastes have been sent to countries of the global South for disposal, for a fee. For instance, toxic ash from Pennsylvania became material for bricks in Guinea, and Italian nuclear waste was shipped to Nigeria.

---

[27] Peter M. Haas, *Saving the Mediterranean* (see footnote 6 in this chapter).

[28] Joni Seager, *Earth Follies: Coming to Feminist Terms with the Global Environmental Crisis* (NY: Routledge, 1993).

[29] Department of Foreign Affairs and International Trade, "Canada Disappointed with WTO Appellate Body's Decision" (news release), 12 March 2001, <http://webapps.dfait-maeci.gc.ca/minpub/Publication.asp?FileSpec=/Min_Pub_Docs/103981.htm>.

Norms have developed in recent years against exporting toxic wastes—a practice seen as exploitive of the receiving country. In 1989, 100 states signed a treaty under UN auspices to regulate shipments of toxic and nuclear wastes and prevent their secret movements under corrupt deals. Forty more countries, in Africa, did not sign the treaty but called for a complete halt to toxic waste shipments to Africa. In one famous case in the 1980s, a ship carrying 12 700 tonnes of toxic waste from Philadelphia's trash incinerator spent three years travelling from continent to continent in search of a state that would take its cargo, which eventually was illegally dumped at sea and on a beach in Haiti, where it remains. The ship's owners were jailed for perjury.

In the 1950s, atmospheric nuclear tests created radioactive fallout that travelled thousands of kilometres before falling back to the ground. After milk drunk by U.S. schoolchildren was found to contain radioactive iodine, alarm over fallout led to the 1963 limited test ban, which stopped nuclear tests above ground.

In 1986, a meltdown at the Soviet nuclear power plant at **Chernobyl,** in Ukraine, created airborne radioactivity that spread over much of Europe, from Italy to Sweden. The accident exemplified the new reality—that economic and technical decisions taken in one state can have grave environmental consequences for other countries. Soviet leaders made matters worse by failing to notify neighbours promptly of the accident.

Chernobyl A city in Ukraine that was the site of a 1986 meltdown at a Soviet nuclear power plant.

On the various issues of water and air pollution, both unilateral state actions and international agreements have often been feasible and effective. In recent decades, river water quality has improved in most industrialized regions. Market economies have begun to deal with pollution as just another cost of production that should be charged to the polluter instead of to society at large. Some governments have begun to allocate "pollution rights" that companies can buy and sell on a free market.

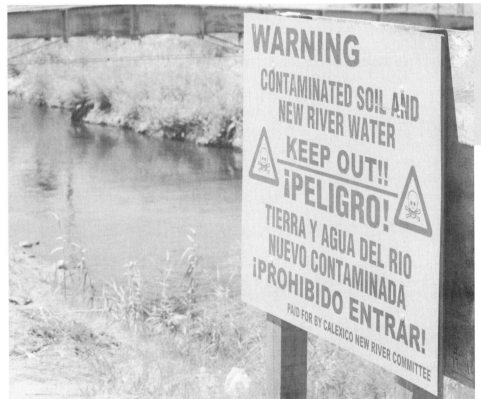

POISONED WATERS
Pollution easily crosses national borders. For example, here industrial waste and sewage in the New River crosses from Mexico into California, 2003.

In the former Soviet bloc, decades of centrally planned industrialization have created more severe environmental problems, which may prove more intractable.[30] With staggering environmental damage and human health effects, the economically strapped former Soviet republics now must bargain over limiting pollution and repairing the damage. For example, the severely polluted Aral Sea, formerly contained within one state, the Soviet Union, is now shared by two, Kazakhstan and Uzbekistan. Once the world's fourth largest inland sea, it shrank in half, its huge fisheries destroyed, after a Soviet-era mega-irrigation project to grow cotton in the desert diverted the Aral Sea's inlet rivers and polluted them with pesticides. Former fishing towns found themselves dozens of kilometres away from the shoreline. In the 1990s, environmentalists gave up efforts to save the Aral Sea, after local and international political leaders failed to implement plans to address the problem. Local populations suffered from widespread health effects of the disaster. Decisions by the former Soviet republics to keep operating old and unsafe nuclear power reactors, as well as the problems associated with dismantling nuclear weapons, also add to the region's long environmental agenda.

NATURAL RESOURCES

The natural environment is not only a delicate ecosystem requiring protection; it is also a repository of natural resources. Because the extraction of resources brings states wealth (and hence power), these resources regularly become a source of international conflicts.[31] Because they are mostly located within individual states, they do not present a collective goods problem. Rather, states bargain (with leverage) as to these vital resources.

Three aspects of natural resources shape their role in international conflict. First, they are required for the operation of an industrial economy (sometimes even an agrarian one). Second, their sources—mineral deposits, rivers, and so forth—are associated with particular territories over which states may fight for control. Third, natural resources tend to be unevenly distributed, with plentiful supplies in some states and an absence in others. These aspects mean that trade in natural resources is extremely profitable; much additional wealth is created by such trade. They also mean that trade in resources is fairly politicized—creating market imperfections such as monopoly, oligopoly, price manipulation, and so on (see "Politics of Markets" on pp. 305–307).

World Energy

Of the various natural resources required by states, energy resources (fuels) are central. The commercial fuels that power the world's industrial economies are oil (about 40 percent of world energy consumption), coal (30 percent), natural gas (25 percent), and hydroelectric and nuclear power (5 percent). The fossil fuels (coal, oil, gas) thus account for 95 percent of world energy consumption. Some energy consumed as electricity comes from hydroelectric dams or nuclear power plants, but most of it comes from burning fossil fuels in electric-generating plants.

Imagine a pile of coal weighing 11 tonnes (about the weight of ten automobiles). The energy released by burning that much coal is equivalent to the amount of energy North

---

[30] Murray Feshbach, *Ecological Disaster: Cleaning Up the Hidden Legacy of the Soviet Regime* (Washington, DC: Brookings, 1995). Klaus Schleicher, ed., *Pollution Knows No Frontiers: A Reader* (NY: Paragon, 1992). Joan DeBardeleben, ed., *To Breathe Free: Eastern Europe's Environmental Crisis* (Baltimore: Johns Hopkins UP, 1991). Fred Singleton, ed., *Environmental Problems in the Soviet Union and Eastern Europe* (Boulder, CO: Rienner, 1987).

[31] Mark W. Zacher, ed., *The International Political Economy of Natural Resources* (Brookfield, VT: Elgar, 1993). Lim Teck Ghee and Mark J. Valencia, eds., *Conflict over Natural Resources in South-East Asia and the Pacific* (NY: Oxford UP, 1991). Ronnie D. Lipschutz, *When Nations Clash: Raw Materials, Ideology, and Foreign Policy* (NY: Ballinger, 1989). Dennis Pirages, *Global Technopolitics: The International Politics of Technology and Resources* (Pacific Grove, CA: Brooks/Cole, 1989).

Americans use per person each year. Wealthier people, of course, consume more energy per person than do poorer people, but 11 tonnes is the average.

Table 13.1 shows energy consumption per person in the nine world regions. The four industrialized regions of the North use much more energy per person than those of the South. Because Asia and Africa have little industry, North America uses 30 times as much as Asia or Africa. Among industrialized countries there are differences in the *efficiency* of energy use—GDP produced per unit of energy consumed. The least efficient are Russia and Eastern Europe (even before that region's current economic depression); North America is also rather inefficient; Europe and Japan are the most energy efficient.

International trade in energy plays a vital role in the world economy. As Table 13.1 shows, the regions of the industrialized West are all net importers of energy (though considered alone, Canada is a net exporter of energy). Together the industrialized West imports from the rest of the world, each year, energy equivalent to more than a billion tonnes of coal. The other six world regions are net exporters of energy.

Although all forms of energy are traded internationally, the most important by far is oil, the cheapest to transport over long distances. Russia and Eastern Europe receive vital hard currency earnings from exporting oil. Venezuela and Mexico (in Latin America) and Nigeria and Angola (in Africa) are important oil exporters, as is Canada. But by far the largest source of oil exports is the Middle East—especially the countries around the Persian Gulf (Saudi Arabia, Kuwait, Iraq, Iran, and the small sheikdoms of United Arab Emirates, Qatar, Bahrain, and Oman). Saudi Arabia is the largest oil exporter and sits atop the largest oil reserves (see Table 12.1 on p. 460). The politics of world energy revolve around Middle East oil shipped to Western Europe, Japan/Pacific, and North America.

The importance of oil in the industrialized economies helps to explain the political importance of the Middle East in world politics.[32] Iraq's 1990 invasion of Kuwait (and the

Table 13.1 Per Capita Energy Consumption and Net Energy Trade, 1999

	Per Capita Consumption (million BTU)	Total Net Energy Exports[a] (quadrillion BTU)
North America	360	–20
Western Europe	150	–26
Japan/Pacific	160	–20
Russia & Eastern Europe	125	+10
China	30	–5
Middle East	70	+45
Latin America	50	+7
South Asia	15	–1
Africa	10	+8
World as a whole	65	

[a] Net exports refers to production minus consumption. Net exports worldwide do not equal net imports for technical reasons.

Source: Calculated from data in U.S. Dept. of Energy. Energy Information Administration. See www.eia.doe.gov/emeu/iea.

[32] Ethan B. Kapstein, *The Insecure Alliance: Energy Crises and Western Politics since 1944* (NY: Oxford UP, 1990). Daniel Yergin, *The Prize: The Epic Quest for Oil, Money, and Power* (NY: Simon & Schuster, 1991). G. John Ikenberry, *Reasons of State: Oil Politics and the Capacities of American Government* (Ithaca, NY: Cornell UP, 1988). Joshua S. Goldstein, Xiaoming Huang, and Burcu Akan, "Energy in the World Economy, 1950–1992," *International Studies Quarterly* 41.2 (1997): 241–66.

mere possibility that Iraq's army could move into Saudi Arabia) threatened the West's access to stable, inexpensive supplies of oil. World oil prices immediately more than doubled. But Saudi Arabia could increase its own rate of oil exports massively enough to compensate for both Kuwaiti and Iraqi exports cut off by the invasion and the UN sanctions against Iraq (see Table 12.1 on p. 460). When it became clear that Saudi exports would not be disrupted, the price of oil dropped again on world markets. Thus, not only is energy a crucial economic sector (on which all industrial activity depends), but it is also one of the most politically sensitive (because of the dependence of the West on energy imported from the Middle East and other regions of the global South).

To secure a supply of oil in the Middle East, Britain and other European countries colonized the area early in the twentieth century, carving up territory into protectorates in which European power kept local monarchs on their thrones. (Iraq, for instance, argues that Kuwait is part of Iraq, that it was cut off and made into a separate state by the British.) The United States did not claim colonies or protectorates, but U.S. MNCs were heavily involved in the development of oil resources in the area from the 1920s through the 1960s—often wielding vast power. Local rulers depended on the expertise and capital investment of U.S. and European oil companies. The "seven sisters"—a cartel of Western oil companies—kept the price paid to local states low and their own profits high.

After World War II the British gave up colonial claims in the Middle East, but the Western oil companies kept producing cheap oil there for Western consumption. Then in 1973, during an Arab-Israeli war, the oil-producing Arab states of the region decided to punish the United States for supporting Israel. They cut off their oil exports to the United States and curtailed their overall exports. This supply disruption sent world oil prices skyrocketing. OPEC realized its potential power and the high price the world was willing to pay for oil. After the war ended, OPEC agreed to limit production to keep oil prices high.

oil shocks The two sharp rises in the world price of oil that occurred in 1973–1974 and 1979.

The 1973 **oil shock** had a profound effect on the world economy and on world politics. Huge amounts of hard currency accumulated in the treasuries of the Middle East oil-exporting countries, which in turn invested them around the world (these were called *petro-dollars*). High inflation plagued the United States, Canada, and Europe for years afterward.

In 1979, the revolution in Iran led to another major increase in oil prices. This second oil shock further weakened the industrialized economies. But these economies were already adjusting to the new realities of world energy. Higher oil prices led to the expansion of oil production in new locations outside of OPEC—in the North Sea (Britain and Norway), Alaska, Angola, Russia, and elsewhere. By the mid-1980s, the Middle East was rapidly losing its market share of world trade in oil. At the same time, industrialized economies learned to be more *energy efficient*. With supply up and demand down, oil prices dropped in the late 1980s to historic lows below US$20/barrel, and stayed low into the new century except for a price surge around 2000 and again in 2004. Because of the market adjustments that followed high oil prices, the industrialized West is now somewhat less dependent on Middle East oil and the power of OPEC has been greatly reduced. Still, energy continues to be a crucial issue in which the Middle East plays a key role.

In the late 1990s, the Caspian Sea region beckoned as a new and largely untapped oil source (see Figure 13.2). However, international politics and geography hampered the development of this zone. The oil must travel overland by pipeline to reach world markets (the Caspian is an inland sea). But the main pipeline from oil-producing Azerbaijan to the Black Sea (where tanker ships can load) travels through war-torn Chechnya in southern Russia. The pipeline reopened in 1997, but in 2000 it still carried only a fraction of its capacity. Russia meanwhile built a bypass route around Chechnya that carries a large and growing amount of Caspian oil for export through the Black Sea.

FIGURE 13.2 Dividing the Caspian Sea

The Caspian Sea is the world's largest inland body of water. It could be defined under international law as either a lake or a sea. The middle of a *lake* (beyond territorial waters) is a joint area (see left panel), which can be exploited only if the countries agree on terms. In a *sea* less than 644 kilometres (400 miles) wide, the bordering countries' Exclusive Economic Zones (EEZs) split up the whole sea (right panel).

     After a 1912 treaty, the Soviet Union and Iran treated the Caspian as a lake and made agreements on fishing. Later, substantial oil deposits were found offshore. When the Soviet Union broke up a decade ago, the Caspian was suddenly bordered by five countries instead of two, with most of the oil and gas in or near Azerbaijan and Turkmenistan, not Russia. Under the "lake" interpretation, however, Russia could share in revenues from some of the offshore oil. In the past few years, more oil and gas has been discovered, including some potentially big fields near Russia. This makes Russia more inclined to accept a "sea" interpretation and begin drilling, without waiting to negotiate a complex deal with contentious neighbours.[a] The negotiations dragged on into 2002, and Iran sent a warship in 2001 to drive away an Azerbaijan-based oil exploration ship (owned by British Petroleum) from disputed waters.

[a]Elaine Sciolino, "It's a Sea! It's a Lake! No. It's a Pool of Oil!" *New York Times* 21 June 1998.

     Low oil prices help the industrialized economies, but they have two major drawbacks. First, burning oil contributes to global warming, and low prices make it profitable to burn more oil and be less energy efficient. Second, low oil prices reduce the export earnings of oil-producing countries. Those like Saudi Arabia, with huge financial reserves and plenty of oil, feel only modest pain. But countries such as Venezuela and Mexico had counted on oil revenues in their economic development plans and had borrowed foreign money to be repaid from future oil earnings. Some of these countries faced major debt problems as a result.

Minerals, Land, Water

To build the infrastructure and other manufactured goods that create wealth in a national economy, states need other raw materials in addition to energy. These include metals, other minerals, and related materials extracted through mining.

     The political economy of minerals—iron, copper, platinum, and so forth—differs from that of world energy. The value of international trade in oil is many times greater than that of any mineral. Mineral production is distributed more evenly than is oil production—supply is not so concentrated in one region of the world. Industrialized countries have also reduced their vulnerability by stockpiling strategic minerals (easier to do with minerals than with energy because of smaller quantities and values).

Nonetheless, industrialized countries do have certain vulnerabilities with regard to mineral supply, and these do affect international politics. Among the industrialized regions, Japan and Europe are most dependent on mineral imports; Canada and the United States are more self-sufficient. The former Soviet Union was a leading exporter of key minerals—a role that Russia may continue in the future. Despite its economic problems, one great strength of the Russian economy is being self-sufficient in both energy and mineral resources.

Another major exporter of key minerals is South Africa. For a few strategic minerals, notably manganese and chromium, South Africa controls three-quarters or more of the world's reserves. Western leaders worried that political instability in South Africa (where the black majority struggled for years under white minority rule) could disrupt the supply of these minerals. This is one reason why the industrialized countries were reluctant to impose trade sanctions on South Africa over human rights issues. South Africa's leading position in supplying diamonds, gold, and platinum to world markets gave South Africa a valuable source of income, but in the end the West did apply economic sanctions that hurt the South African economy and helped end apartheid.

Most important to industrialized economies are the minerals that go into making industrial equipment. Traditionally most important is iron, from which steel is made. The leading producers of steel are China, Japan, the United States, Russia, and South Korea, followed by Germany, Ukraine, India, and Brazil. As of 2003, Canada ranked fifteenth among major steel-producing countries (producing 15.9 tonnes of crude steel annually). Thus, major industrialized countries as well as some large developing countries produce their own steel (as of 2002, Russia and Japan were the leading exporters worldwide). To preserve self-sufficiency in steel production, the United States and others have used trade policies to protect domestic steel industries.

Some industrialized countries, notably Japan, depend heavily on importing iron ore for their steel industry. Unlike oil, iron ore is not concentrated in a "Persian Gulf" but is exported from both global South and industrialized countries around the world. There is an *Association of Iron Ore Exporting Countries (AIOEC)*, but it is limited to consultation, and the United States, Canada, and the former Soviet Union are exporters that are not among the 12 members.

For other important industrial minerals such as copper, nickel, and zinc, the pattern of supply and trade is much more diffuse than for oil, and the industrialized countries are largely self-sufficient. Even when states of the global South are the main suppliers, as with tin and bauxite, they have not gained the power of OPEC. There is a producer cartel in some cases (copper), a producer-consumer cartel in some (tin), and separate producer and consumer cartels in others (bauxite).

Certain agricultural products have spawned producer cartels, such as the Union of Banana Exporting Countries (UBEC) and the African Groundnut Council. Like minerals, some export crops come mainly from just a few countries. These include sugar (Cuba), cocoa (Ivory Coast, Ghana, Nigeria), tea (India, Sri Lanka, China), and coffee (Brazil, Colombia). Despite the concentrations, producer cartels have not been very successful in boosting prices of these products, which are less essential than energy.

Water Disputes In addition to energy and minerals, states need water. Need of water increases as a society industrializes, as it intensifies agriculture, and as its population grows. World water use is 35 times higher than just a few centuries ago, and grew twice as fast as population in the twentieth century. Yet water supplies are relatively unchanging, and are becoming depleted in many places. One-fifth of the world's population lacks safe drinking water, and 80 countries suffer water shortages. Water supplies—rivers and water tables—often cross international boundaries; thus access to water is increasingly a source of international conflict. Sometimes—as when several states share access to a single water table—these conflicts are collective goods problems.

Canada has an abundance of fresh water reserves, by some estimates some 20 percent of the world's total supply. An issue that has arisen in Canada concerns bulk water exports. On the one hand, it would make some sense for Canada to export water, in particular to the United States, which has a demand for fresh water. But the bulk export of water from Canada would have a number environmental impacts, such as altering ecosystems and changing groundwater levels. Critics of bulk

WATER, WATER EVERYWHERE

As population growth and economic development increase the demand for water, more international conflicts arise over water rights. Many important rivers pass through multiple states, and many states share access to seas and lakes. The Aral Sea, once part of the Soviet Union but now shared between Kazakhstan and Uzbekistan, was among the world's largest lakes until it was decimated by the diversion of its water sources to irrigate cotton. This scene shows the former seabed, now 113 kilometres from shore, in 1997.

water exports also point out that exporting water would result in it being treated as a commodity rather than a natural resource under trade agreements such as NAFTA or the WTO. This would mean that Canada could lose control of its water supplies: for example, in times of shortage, or if exports seriously depleted reserves, Canada's obligations to export water would be determined by its trade commitments and not national policies (Canada would be required, for example, to treat signatories to NAFTA in the same manner it treats domestic users of Canadian water). In order to retain control over fresh water, amendments to the International Boundary Waters Treaty Act (IBWTA) between Canada and the U.S. came into force in 2002 prohibiting water exports. (See Environment Canada's Freshwater website: http://www.ec.gc.ca/water/e_main.html)

Water problems are especially important in the Middle East. For instance, the Euphrates River runs from Turkey through Syria to Iraq before reaching the Persian Gulf. Iraq objects to Syrian diversion of water from the river, and both Iraq and Syria object to Turkey's diversion.

The Jordan River originates in Syria and Lebanon and runs through Israel to Jordan. In the 1950s, Israel began building a canal to take water from the Jordan River to "make the desert bloom." Jordan and its Arab neighbours complained to the UN Security Council, but it failed in efforts to mediate the dispute, and each state went ahead with its own water plans (Israel and Jordan agreeing, however, to stay within UN-proposed allocations). In 1964, Syria and Lebanon tried to build dams and divert water before it reached Israel, rendering Israel's new water system worthless. Israeli air and artillery attacks on the construction site forced Syria to abandon its diversion project, and Israel's 1967 capture of the Golan Heights precluded Syria from renewing such efforts.[33]

---

[33] Miriam L. Lowi, *Water and Power: The Politics of a Scarce Resource in the Jordan River Basin* (NY: Cambridge UP, 1993). United Nations, *Comprehensive Assessment of the Freshwater Resources of the World* (NY: United Nations, 1997).

Water also contains other resources, such as fish and offshore oil deposits. The UNCLOS treaty enclosed more of these resources within states' territory—but this enclosure creates new problems. Norms regarding territorial waters are not firmly entrenched; some states disagree on who owns what. Also, control of small islands now implies rights to surrounding oceans with their fish, offshore oil, and minerals. A potentially serious international dispute has been brewing in the Spratly Islands, where some tiny islands are claimed by China, Vietnam, and other nearby countries (see p. 166). With the islands come nearby oil drilling rights and fisheries. China has invited a U.S. company to explore for oil there, promising protection by the Chinese navy. For similar reasons, Iran and the United Arab Emirates dispute control of several small islands in the Persian Gulf.

A common theme runs through the conflicts over fuels, minerals, agricultural products, and territorial waters. They are produced in fixed locations but traded to distant places. Control of these locations gives a state both greater self-sufficiency (valued by mercantilists) and market commodities generating wealth (valued by liberals). But the exploitation of these products can have severe environmental impacts (a concern raised by critical theorists).

International Security and the Environment

In recent years, IR scholars have expanded their studies of environmental politics to systematically study the relationship of military and security affairs with the environment.[34] One side of this relationship is the role of the environment as a source of international conflict. We have seen how environmental degradation can lead to collective goods problems among large numbers of states, and how competition for territory and resources can create conflicts among smaller groups of states.

The other side of the environment-security relationship concerns the effect of activities in the international security realm on the environment. Military activities—especially warfare—are important contributors to environmental degradation, above and beyond the degradation caused by economic activities such as mining and manufacturing.

These damaging effects were spotlighted during the Gulf War. Iraqi forces spilled large amounts of Kuwaiti oil into the Persian Gulf—either to try to stop an amphibious invasion, or simply to punish Saudi Arabia (in whose direction the currents pushed the oil). Then, before retreating from Kuwait, the Iraqis blew up hundreds of Kuwaiti oil wells, leaving them burning uncontrollably and covering the country with thick black smoke. Air pollution and weather effects lasted more than a year and were felt in other countries around the Gulf. Iraq's environment also suffered tremendous damage from the massive bombing campaign. (Since the war, Iraq has built a giant canal to drain marshes used for refuge by rebels—another potential environmental disaster.)

The deliberate environmental destruction seen in the Gulf War is not without precedent. Armies sometimes adopt a "scorched earth policy" to deny sustenance to their adversaries. Fields are burned, wells poisoned, and villages levelled. In World War II, the Soviets left a scorched earth behind as they retreated before the Nazi invasion. Japan used incendiary devices carried in high-altitude balloons to start forest fires in the U.S. Northwest. The United States sprayed defoliants massively in Vietnam to destroy jungles in an attempt to expose guerrilla forces. The Vietnamese countryside still shows effects from these herbicides, as do U.S. veterans and Vietnamese citizens who suffer lingering

---

[34] Daniel H. Deudney and Richard A. Matthew, eds., *Contested Grounds: Security and Conflict in the New Environmental Politics* (Albany: SUNY P, 1999). Thomas F. Homer-Dixon, "On the Threshold: Environmental Changes as Causes of Acute Conflict," *International Security* 16.2 (1991): 76–116.

health effects due to contact with chemicals such as *Agent Orange*.

Military activity short of war also tends to damage the environment. Military industries pollute. Military forces use energy less efficiently than civilians do. Military aircraft and missiles contribute to ozone depletion. Military bases contain many toxic-waste dumps.

The greatest *potential* environmental disaster imaginable would be a large nuclear war. Ecosystems would be severely damaged throughout the world by secondary effects of nuclear weapons alone—radioactive fallout and the breakdown of social order and technology. Some scientists also think that global climate changes, leading to famine and environmental collapse, could result—the "nuclear winter" mentioned on page 220.

WAR IS NOT GREEN
Wars often bring environmental destruction, sometimes deliberately and sometimes as a by-product. Military operations in peacetime also contribute to environmental problems. Hundreds of Kuwaiti oil wells, set on fire by retreating Iraqi troops in 1991, burned for months.

POPULATION

The international system is having to cope with increasing conflict and complexity in managing the global environment. The problem is increasing over time because human demands on the environment keep growing but the environment tends to remain static. The growing demands have two causes—economic growth (higher GDP per person) and a growing number of people.

We have so far focused on the first cause—world industrialization as a source of demands. This cause is the more important one in the industrialized regions. But in the global South, with less industry and more people, population pressures are more important.

World Population Trends

Global population reached a record high today, as it does every day. World population, 6.2 billion in 2002, is growing by 75 million each year—more than 200 000 additional people per day.

Forecasting future population is easy in some respects. Barring a nuclear war or an environmental catastrophe, today's children will grow up and have children of their own. The projected world population in 25 years will be 7 to 8 billion people, and there is little anyone can do to change that projection.

Of the increase in population in that period, 97 percent will be in the global South. Currently, half the world's population growth occurs in just six countries—India, China, Pakistan, Nigeria, Bangladesh, and Indonesia. Among the world's poorest countries, population is expected to triple in the next 50 years, whereas many rich countries will see population shrinkage in that period.[35]

---

[35] UNFPA data. See United Nations, *World Population Prospects: The 2000 Revision* (NY: UN, 2001).

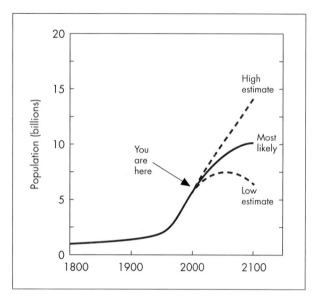

Figure 13.3 World Population Trends and Projections

Source: Based on data from the UN Population Office.

Forecasting beyond 25 years is difficult. When today's children grow up, the number of children they bear will be affected by their incomes (because of the "demographic transition," discussed shortly). To the extent that countries of the global South accumulate wealth—a subject that was taken up in Chapter 12— their population growth will likely slow. A second factor affecting the rate of population growth will be government policies regarding women's rights and birth control.

Because of these two uncertainties, projections beyond a few decades have a range of uncertainty (see Figure 13.3). By 2050, world population will probably be over 9 billion, with a final levelling out around 10 billion in the next 200 years. In the 1980s the decline in birthrates stalled in a number of countries and economic growth in the global South fell below expectations, pushing population projections up. However, successes in regions of the South outside Africa—in raising incomes and lowering birthrates in the 1990s—brought projections downward again. New data in 2002 showed that higher women's status and literacy are reducing population growth more than expected in large, poor countries.[36] The actions of states and IOs *now* will determine the earth's population in 200 years.

Two hundred years ago, British writer *Thomas Malthus* warned that population tends to increase faster than food supply and predicted that population growth would limit itself through famine and disease. Today, experts and officials who warn against world over-population are sometimes called *Malthusian*. Critics point out that technology has kept pace with population in the past, allowing more food and other resources to be extracted from the environment even as population keeps growing.

However, leaders of most states in the global South now recognize that unrestrained population growth drags down per capita income. But actions taken to slow population growth tend to have short-term costs and long-term benefits, and can sometimes be very coercive, especially when directed at controlling women and men's reproductive choices. Doing nothing is the cheapest and often most politically acceptable course in the short run—and the most expensive in the long run.

The Demographic Transition

Population growth results from a difference between rates of birth (per 1000 people) and rates of death. In agrarian (pre-industrial) societies, both birthrates and death rates are high. Population growth is thus slow—even negative at times when death rates exceed birthrates (during a famine or plague, for instance).

The process of economic development—of industrialization and the accumulation of wealth on a per capita basis—brings about a change in birth and death rates that follows a fairly universal pattern called the **demographic transition** (see Figure 13.4). First, death rates fall as food supplies increase and access to health care expands. Later, birthrates fall as people become educated, more secure, and more urbanized, and as the status of women in society rises. At the end of the transition, as at the beginning, birthrates and death rates

demographic transition
The pattern of falling death rates, followed by falling birthrates, that generally accompanies *industrialization* and *economic development*.

---

[36] Shiro Horiuchi, "Stagnation in the Decline of the World Population Growth Rate during the 1980s," *Science* 257 (7 Aug. 1992): 761–65. Barbara Crossette, "Population Estimates Fall as Women Assert Control," *New York Times* 10 March 2002.

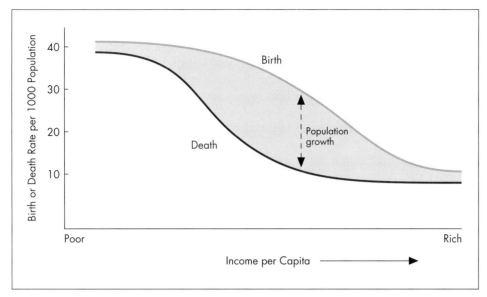

Figure 13.4
The Demographic Transition

As income rises, first death rates and then birthrates fall. The gap between the two is the population growth rate. Early in the transition, the population contains a large proportion of children; later it contains a large proportion of elderly people.

are fairly close to each other, and population growth is limited. But during the transition, when death rates have fallen more than birthrates, population grows rapidly.

One reason poor people tend to have many children is that under harsh poverty a child's survival is not assured. Disease, malnutrition, or violence may claim the lives of many children, leaving parents with no one to look after them in their old age. Having many children helps ensure that some survive. (The collective goods problem appears again, because each family wants more children but when all pursue this strategy the economic development of the whole community or state is held back.)

As a state makes the demographic transition, the structure of its population changes dramatically. At the beginning and middle of the process, most of the population is young. Families have many children, and adults do not have a long life expectancy. Because children are not very productive economically, the large number of children in poor countries tends to slow down the accumulation of wealth. But by the end of the demographic transition, because adults live longer and families have fewer children, the average age of the population is much older. Eventually a substantial section of the population is elderly—a different nonproductive population that the economy must support.

The industrialized countries have been through the demographic transition and now have slow population growth—even negative growth in a few states.[37] Most countries of the global South are in the middle of the transition and have rapid population growth.

The dilemma of the demographic transition is this: rapid population growth and a child-heavy population are powerful forces lowering per capita income. Yet the best way to slow population growth is to raise per capita income.

Population growth thus contributes to a vicious cycle in many poor states. Where population rises at the same rate as overall wealth, the average person is no better off over time. Even when the economy grows faster than population, so that the *average* income rises, the total *number* of poor people may increase. From 1987 to 1998, according to the World Bank, the *proportion* of people living in dire poverty (under a dollar per day) dropped from 29 to 24 percent worldwide. But the actual *number* of people living in poverty increased from just below to just above 1.2 billion.

---

[37] Carlo M. Cipolla, *The Economic History of World Population* (Harmondsworth, UK: Penguin, 1979).

The demographic transition tends to widen international disparities of wealth. States that manage to raise incomes a bit enter an upward spiral—as population growth slows, income levels per capita rise more, which further slows population growth, and so forth. Meanwhile, states that do not raise incomes have unabated population growth; per capita incomes stay low, which fuels more population growth—a downward spiral.

Globally, this disparity contributes to the gap in wealth between the North and South (see Chapter 11). Within the South disparities are also sharpened, as a few countries manage to slow population growth and raise incomes while others fail to do so. Even within a single country, the demographic transition sharpens disparities. Cities, richer classes, richer ethnic groups, and richer provinces tend to have low birthrates compared to the countryside and the poorer classes, ethnic groups, and provinces. In countries such as France, Israel, and the United States, wealthier ethnic groups (often white) have much slower population growth than poorer ethnic groups (often nonwhite).

In recent decades, countries of the global South seem to be splitting into two groups of states. The first group, including China and India, entered the phase of the demographic transition marked by falling birthrates in the 1970s. But in nearly 70 other poor states, death rates kept falling faster than birthrates, leading to accelerating population growth. These population trends contributed to disparities within the global South that emerged in the 1990s, notably between Africa and Asia.

Although the demographic transition is universal in its outlines, particular changes in birthrates and death rates vary depending on local conditions and government policies.

Population Policies

The policies that governments adopt—not just economic and demographic conditions—influence the birthrate. Among the most important policies are those regarding birth control (contraception). State policies vary widely.

At one extreme, China uses its strong government control to try to enforce a limit of one child per couple. Penalties for having a second child include being charged for services that were free for the first child and being stigmatized at work and in public. Beyond two children, the penalties escalate. Contraceptives and abortions are free, and citizens are educated about them. China's policy has lowered growth rates considerably in the cities but less so in the countryside, where 80 percent of the people live. Still, in a single decade (the 1970s) China's fertility rate fell from 6 children per woman to about 2.5, a dramatic change. (It now stands at 1.6.)

But the Chinese policy has enormous drawbacks. It limits individual freedom in favour of government control. Forced or coerced abortions are widespread. In traditional Chinese society (as in some other countries), sons are valued more than daughters. Couples who have a daughter may keep trying until they have a son. Chinese peasants have reportedly killed newborn daughters so they could try for a son. Simply bribing or paying fines became more common routes around the one-child policy in the 1990s. Most often, parents in China (and some places in India) are using information technology—ultrasound scans—to determine their fetus's gender and abort it if female. China's 2000 census showed the percentage of female births at 0.85 per boy, rather than the normal 0.95, a difference that amounts to a million "missing" girls per year. In the countryside, the sex differential is twice as high as in the cities, reaching 140 men per 100 women in some areas where the one-child policy is strictly enforced. In recent years, hundreds of thousands of young women there have been kidnapped and sold as brides.[38]

---

[38] Celia W. Dugger, "Modern Asia's Anomaly: The Girls Who Don't Get Born," *New York Times* 6 May 2001. Elisabeth Rosenthal, "Harsh Chinese Reality Feeds a Black Market in Women," *New York Times* 25 June 2001: A1.

India's policies are less extreme but have been slower. The birthrate fell from just under 6 per woman to about 4.7 in the 1970s to 2.4 in 2001. India's government, strongly committed to birth control, has tried to make information and means widely available, but as a democracy it does not have China's extreme government control over society. However, India does resort to economic incentives, a practice that was particularly widespread during the 1970s. In this case monetary rewards or livestock were offered to men and women who agreed to be sterilized. Doctors and nurses who convinced patients to undergo the operations were also provided with incentives. Such methods may seem less overtly coercive than China's approach, but using incentives to persuade people to be sterilized is also considered a coercive approach to birth control and family planning.

Countries with somewhat higher incomes than India or China can succeed more easily. Mexico's strong but noncoercive family-planning program, adopted in 1974, cut birth rates in half over 15 years, to 2.7 per woman (and to 2.3 in 2001).[39]

Family planning programs have had at best a mixed history, and many have been accused of very questionable practices. International NGOs such as the International Planned Parenthood Federation had their early origins in eugenicist movements—organizations aimed at the "betterment" of the races through selective breeding. Although that connection no longer exists, family planning is sometimes still viewed with suspicion by many people around the world. In addition to incentive programs, birth control programs also sometimes recommended unsafe or unproven methods of birth control. For a long time the injectable contraceptive Depo-Provera was not approved for use in the United States or Canada, for example, but was widely available in countries of the global South.[40]

At the other extreme from China are governments that encourage or force childbearing, and outlaw or limit access to contraception. Such a policy is called **pronatalist** (pro-birth). Traditionally, many governments have adopted such policies because population was seen as an element of national power. More babies today meant more soldiers later. Recall (from p. 57) that the major difference in potential power between Iraq and Iran was population—Iran's being three times larger. On the battlefield, this power played out as "human wave" assaults of Iranian men and boys (who were slaughtered by the tens of thousands), which ultimately wore the Iraqis down.

Communist countries, including the Soviet Union, often adopted pronatalist policies. They gave awards for mothers who produced large numbers of children for the fatherland—an extension of the factory quota system of centrally planned production.

Today, only a few governments have strongly pronatalist policies, but many do not make birth control or sex education available to women. In some such states, population is not considered a problem (and may even be seen as an asset); in other states, the government simply cannot afford effective measures to lower birthrates. (Again, birth control has short-term costs and long-term benefits.) According to the UNFPA, 300 million women do not have access to effective contraception.

Industrialized states have provided financial assistance for family planning programs in poor countries. One reason the drop in birthrates slowed in the 1980s is that international financial assistance slowed dramatically. The U.S. government, providing more than a quarter of the voluntary contributions that finance the UNFPA's annual budget of US$225 million, terminated contributions in 1976 after U.S. antiabortion activists protested that some UNFPA funds were financing abortions. The United States did the same to the

pronatalist policy A government policy that encourages or forces childbearing, and outlaws or limits access to contraception.

---

[39] John Ward Anderson, "Six Billion and Counting—But Slower," *Washington Post* 12 Oct. 1999: A1.

[40] Linda Gordon, *The Moral Property of Women: A History of Birth Control Politics in America* (Champaign, IL: U Illinois P, 2002). Betsy Hartmann, *Reproductive Rights and Wrongs: The Global Politics of Population*, rev. ed. (Boston: South End, 1995).

ONE IS ENOUGH

Few governments still promote high birthrates (pronatalism), but states vary widely in their family planning policies. The two most populous countries, China and India, have different approaches to birth control, each with strengths and weaknesses. Both are bringing down birthrates (China's faster), with important long-term implications for world population growth. This bus mural promotes China's one-child policy.

International Planned Parenthood Federation in the 1980s.[41] Some U.S. funding was restored in the 1990s.

Women's Status Perhaps most important, birthrates are influenced by the status of women in society. In cultures that traditionally see women as valuable only in producing babies, great pressures exist against women who stop doing so. Many women do not use birth control because their husbands will not allow them to. These husbands may think that having many children is proof of their manliness. As women's status improves and they can work in various occupations, own property, and vote, women gain the power as well as the education and money necessary to limit the size of their families.

According to the UNFPA, improving the status of women is one of the most important means of controlling world population growth. Government policies about women's status vary from one state to another. International programs and agencies, such as the UN commission on the status of women, are working to address the issue on a global scale. International economic aid programs have been criticized for paying insufficient attention to the status of women, focusing on economic development in isolation from population growth (see "Women in Development" on pp. 429–430).

Mortality and AIDS

Population growth is determined by the death rate as well as the birthrate. In a way, the death rate is more complicated than the birthrate: births have only one source (involving women of childbearing age), whereas people die from many different causes at different ages. In poor countries, people tend to die younger, often from infectious diseases; in richer countries, people live longer and die more often from cancer and heart disease. The proportion of babies who die within their first year is the **infant mortality rate.** This rate is an excellent indicator of overall health, since it reflects a population's access to nutrition, water, shelter, and health care. Infant mortality is 5 percent worldwide, 1 percent or less in rich countries but over 10 percent in the poorest countries and even higher in local pockets of extreme poverty (especially in Africa and in war zones such as Sierra Leone and Afghanistan, with the world's highest at 16 percent).

Although death rates vary greatly from one state or region to another, the overall trends are stable from decade to decade. Wars, droughts, epidemics, and disasters have an

infant mortality rate The proportion of babies who die within their first year of life.

[41] Sandra Whitworth, "Planned Parenthood and the New Right: Onslaught and Opportunity?" *Studies in Political Economy* 35 (Summer 1991): 73–101.

effect locally but hardly matter globally. In the poorest countries, which are just beginning the demographic transition, the death rate declined from nearly 30 deaths per thousand population in 1950 to less than 15 since 1990. In the *industrialized countries*, the death rate bottomed out around 10 per thousand by 1960, and now stands around 7 in the West. However, Russia's death rate *rose* from 11 in 1980 to 15 in 1995 (and rates are high else-where in Eastern Europe and central Asia). In the *midtransition* countries (including China and India), the death rate fell from 25 in 1950 to 10 in 1980 and has equalled the rich countries since then. (Between 1980 and 1995, China's death rate went from 6 to 7; India's fell from 13 to 9.) In this middle group of developing countries, infant mortality is generally much lower than in the poorest countries.[42]

These stable trends in mortality mean that the death rate is not a means by which governments or international agencies can affect population growth—worsening poverty may cause famine and a rising death rate, but this is obviously not a realistic way to con-trol population growth. Nor do wars kill enough people to reduce population growth (short of global nuclear war). Even a major famine or war, one killing a million people, hardly alters world population trends because every year about 75 million people die— 200 000 every day. In short, most of the world is already at or near the end of the trans-ition in *death* rates; the key question is how long birthrates take to complete the transition.

Three mortality factors, however—AIDS, other infectious diseases, and smoking— deserve special attention because they have begun to exact very high costs even if they do not much affect global population trends. In these cases, actions taken in the short term have long-term and often international consequences, and once again there are short-term costs and long-term benefits.

AIDS In the worldwide AIDS epidemic, one state's success or failure in limiting the spread of HIV (human immunodeficiency virus) affects infections in other states as well. There is a delay of five to ten years after infection by the virus before symptoms appear, and during this period an infected individual can infect others (through sex or blood). AIDS spreads internationally—through business, tourism, migration, and military and peacekeeping operations—reflecting the interdependence of states.

By 2001, an estimated 40 million people were infected with HIV worldwide, two-thirds of them in Africa and half of the rest in South Asia (see Table 13.2). In addition, the epidemic had killed 22 million people and left 13 million orphans. Of the 40 million currently infected, only a small fraction had yet developed AIDS (most did not even know they were infected), so the main costs of the epidemic—human, economic, and political—are yet to be felt. Each year, six million people are newly infected with HIV, and more than two million die from AIDS, including nearly half a million children. About 85 percent of people with AIDS are in the global South. Because of systematic underreporting none of the totals are firm, and other estimates revise them upward.[43]

In Africa, already the world's poorest and most war-torn region, AIDS has emerged as one of several powerful forces driving the region backward into deeper poverty. About 8 percent of adults are infected with HIV, more than half of them women. In the most affected African countries in southern Africa, one in six adults has HIV (one in three for Botswana, the worst case). Infection is also rampant in central African armies, with direct implications for international security in a war-torn zone.

---

[42] Tatyana P. Soubbotina and Katherine Sheram, *Beyond Economic Growth: Meeting the Challenges of Global Development* (Washington, DC: World Bank, 2000).

[43] UN data (see footnote 35 in this chapter). *Washington Post* 24 Nov. 1999: A3. Jonathan Mann, Daniel J. M. Tarantola, and Thomas W. Netter, eds., *AIDS in the World 1992* (Cambridge, MA: Harvard UP, 1992).

Table 13.2 Population and AIDS by World Region

Region[a]	Population (millions)	Growth Rate	HIV Infections (millions)
World	6000	1.4 %	40.0
Global North	1300	0.3	2.5
Global South	4700	1.7	37.5
of which:			
China/East Asia	1300	1.1	1.0
Middle East	500	1.9	0.4
Latin America	500	1.5	1.8
South Asia	1900	1.9	6.1
Africa (sub-Saharan)	500	2.5	28.1

[a]Regions do not exactly match those used elsewhere in this book.

Source: Calculated from United Nations, *World Economic and Social Survey 2001* (UN, 2001). United Nations, *World Population Prospects: The 2000 Revision* (UN, 2001). United Nations, *AIDS Epidemic Update* (UN, 2001).

In North America and other industrialized regions, new drug therapies (which could keep the virus in check for years) dramatically lowered the death rate from AIDS in the late 1990s. But these treatments were too expensive to help much in Africa and other poor regions. India and Brazil began to export cheap generic versions of these drugs, violating patent rights of Western drug companies. The U.S. government threatened to punish South Africa and other countries if they allowed import of these drugs without compensating U.S. corporations holding patents. It filed a complaint against Brazil with the WTO. In response, AIDS activists demonstrated loudly and mobilized public opinion to get these policies changed. The United States withdrew its complaint against Brazil in 2001. Meanwhile drug companies began offering lower prices to poor countries, though many critics claim the costs are still too high for most countries of the global South.

In 2001, during a special UN session on AIDS, Kofi Annan proposed a US$7 to $10 billion per year global budget to combat AIDS (a five-fold increase in funding). The G8 states responded with pledges of US$1.2 billion—"laudable" but "not enough" in Annan's view—and the large funding increase became more even difficult to reach as the global recession unfolded and the war on terrorism absorbed attention and resources.[44] Overall, of worldwide spending on AIDS, less than 10 percent has been in countries of the global South, where more than 80 percent of infected people live. Thus, AIDS has deepened the global North-South division. The 2001 UN session also revealed sharp differences between Western, secular states and a number of Islamic states that objected to any reference to gay people. Catholic authorities worldwide, furthermore, objected to programs that encourage condom use.

States can adopt policies to slow the spread of AIDS. It is primarily a sexually transmitted disease; its transmission can be prevented by using condoms. Drug users and medical personnel can use only new or disinfected needles; hospitals can screen blood. Although there is a massive scientific effort to develop a vaccine, they have not yet pro-

---

[44] Kofi A. Annan, "We Can Beat AIDS," *New York Times* 25 June 2001: A21. David E. Sanger, "Rich Nations Offer a Hand, but the Poor Hope for More," *New York Times* 21 July 2001: A6.

duced a cure. The most effective measures, then, are public education and the distribution of condoms (especially to prostitutes) and clean needles to drug users. All of these are culturally and politically sensitive issues, however.

States have only two means to protect themselves from infection from the outside—a particular concern in countries with current low infection rates, such as China. One way would be to seal themselves off from contact with foreigners or to monitor foreigners on their territory. Considering the benefits of economic exchange (and the realities of interdependence) discussed in Chapter 8, this is not a practical approach. The second way is to cooperate with other states worldwide to try to bring the epidemic under control.

These international efforts are coordinated primarily by WHO and funded mainly by the industrialized countries. But WHO depends on national governments to provide information and carry out policies, and governments have been slow to respond.

Governments falsify statistics to underreport the number of cases (lest tourists be driven away), and many governments are reluctant to condone or sponsor sex education and distribution of condoms because of religious or cultural taboos.

In recent years, HIV has spread rapidly in South Asia, China, and Russia/Eastern Europe, where prostitution and drug use are growing. Thailand was especially vulnerable because of its huge prostitution industry, acceptance of male promiscuity, and large tourism industry. "Sex tours" attract thousands of foreign men each year to visit brothels in Thailand and other Southeast Asian countries. In addition, hundreds of thousands of young women are trafficked across international borders in the growing sex slave trade. However, Thailand was one of the first developing countries to develop an effective anti-AIDS program, which focuses on public education. Condom use among prostitutes went from 20 percent to 90 percent in four years (1988–1992), and cases of sexually transmitted diseases among men (an indicator of HIV spread) dropped by 80 percent. Thailand still faces serious problems with AIDS, but it dramatically lowered the infection rate in the 1990s.[45]

In China, the government has been slow to act, and a stigma still prevents effective identification or treatment of the rapidly growing HIV-positive population. Unscrupulous cash-for-blood businesses, especially in one rural region, caused massive HIV infection. In rural China, medical practice relies heavily on injections—often with poorly sterilized needles—when other forms of treatment would be as effective. As a result, 60 percent of China's population has had hepatitis B, compared with 1 percent in the United States and Japan—a danger sign for the future growth of HIV in China.[46]

The international response to the AIDS epidemic is crucial in determining its ultimate course. AIDS illustrates the transnational linkages that make international borders less meaningful than in the past. Effective international cooperation could save millions of lives and significantly enhance the prospects for economic development in the poorest countries in the coming decades. But there is once again a collective goods problem regarding the allocation of costs and benefits from such efforts. A dollar spent by WHO has the same effect regardless of which country contributed it.

Other Infectious Diseases AIDS is the most severe epidemic of infectious disease in the world, but not the only concern. Tuberculosis (TB), malaria, hepatitis, dengue fever, and cholera have all re-emerged or spread in recent decades, often mutating into

---

[45] Leslie Ann Jeffrey, *Sex and Borders: Gender, National Identity, and Prostitution Policy in Thailand* (Vancouver: U British Columbia P, 2002). Philip Shenon, "Brash and Unabashed, Mr. Condom Takes on Sex Death in Thailand," *New York Times* 20 Dec. 1992. Lawrence K. Altman, "AIDS Surge Is Forecast for China, India, and Eastern Europe," *New York Times*, 4 Nov. 1997.

[46] Elisabeth Rosenthal, "Doctors' Dirty Needles Spreading Disease in China," *New York Times* 20 Aug. 2001: A1.

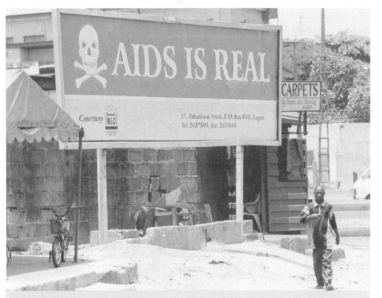

BE CAREFUL OUT THERE

AIDS is spreading rapidly in Southeast Asia and Africa. The worldwide effort to slow AIDS, coordinated by the World Health Organization (WHO), illustrates how global-level problems like AIDS are making IOs like WHO more important. Here is an AIDS poster in Nigeria, 2001.

drug-resistant forms that are increasingly difficult to treat. TB now kills 1.5 million people per year (in addition to AIDS patients who also contract TB). Meanwhile, new and poorly understood diseases have emerged, among them HIV, Ebola virus, hantavirus, SARS, and hepatitis C. Pneumonia, influenza, diarrhea-causing diseases, and measles all continue to be major problems but are not growing or spreading to the same extent. Vaccination programs have reduced the incidence of both polio and measles in recent years. Epidemics among animals have major economic effects. In the late 1990s, Britain lost billions of dollars during an outbreak of mad-cow disease and foot-and-mouth disease among livestock, while diseases shut down Hong Kong's poultry exports and Taiwan's pork exports.[47] Canada's beef exports were also curtailed as a result of a case of mad cow disease in 2003, and poultry on British Columbia farms were slaughtered as a result of avian flu in 2004.

Smoking In the case of smoking, which kills four million people a year, states that fail to curb the spread of nicotine addiction face high future costs in health care—costs that are just beginning to come due in many poor countries. The costs are largely limited to the state itself; its own citizens and economy pay the price. Nonetheless, the tobacco trade makes smoking an international issue. Worldwide, 48 percent of men and 12 percent of women smoke. Tobacco companies' new marketing campaigns targeting women in the global South could produce a huge increase in smokers in that group, according to the World Health Organization. In 2001, tobacco companies with some U.S. support sought to weaken a new proposed treaty, the Framework Convention on Tobacco Control, but in 2003 the U.S. dropped its objections. By mid-2004, the 168 states had signed the treaty, and 25 (excluding Canada and the United States) had ratified it. The treaty will become binding once it receives 40 ratifications.

Population and International Conflict

Population issues are sometimes portrayed as simply too many people using up too little food and natural resources. This is too simplified a picture. In particular, the idea that overpopulation is the cause of hunger in today's world is not really accurate. Poverty and politics more than population are the causes of malnutrition and hunger today (see "World Hunger" on pp. 426–428). There is enough food in the world to feed all the world's people. There is also enough water, enough petroleum, enough land, and so forth—but these are unequally distributed.

---

[47] U.S. Central Intelligence Agency, *The Global Infectious Disease Threat and Its Implications for the United States*, National Intelligence Estimate 99-17D (Washington, DC: CIA, 2000). Laurie Garrett, *The Coming Plague: Newly Emerging Diseases in a World Out of Balance* (NY: Farrar, Straus & Giroux, 1994). See also footnote 35 in this chapter.

Nonetheless, growing populations do put more strain on resources, regionally and globally. Though resources do not usually run out, it costs more to extract them as the quantity needed increases. New agricultural land is less productive than existing plots; new oil or water supplies must come from greater depths; and so on. For example, food production grew more slowly than population in two-thirds of the developing countries in

The Changing World Order
The Return of Smallpox

The world order influences levels of analysis down the ladder—interstate relations, domestic societies, and individuals—as we have seen in previous chapters. Nor does it stop there. The quality of international political cooperation shapes global public health, reaching down to the level of analysis of microscopic viruses and up to the global level of humanity's relationship with the natural environment (e.g., global warming).

The Cold War world order did not put priority on world health. Poor countries became proxy battlegrounds for the superpowers, and political differences dampened cooperation on health issues. For example, the AIDS virus gathered force in Africa (then a zone of great power rivalry for influence) and spread globally before the international community galvanized a credible international response. Nonetheless, a limited regime of international cooperation in health matters—centred on the World Health Organization (WHO)—took form during the Cold War.

One of the greatest achievements of this health regime was wiping out smallpox, a virus that had historically killed about one billion people—in particular, decimating Native American populations after its arrival from Europe. Scientists learned 200 years ago how to inoculate against smallpox (using cowpox), and during the Cold War years the WHO organized a worldwide campaign using modern vaccine. The "baby boom" generation of North Americans still carry small scars on their shoulders where they were vaccinated as children. Today's university students, however, were not vaccinated because in 1980 the WHO declared smallpox eliminated globally, three years after the last case was reported in Somalia.

Since then, smallpox has existed officially in two frozen test tubes in Atlanta and Moscow. An increasing share of the world's population has no immunity to the virus, since vaccinations stopped decades ago. But after the Cold War, defectors revealed that the Soviet Union had secretly developed smallpox for weapons, perhaps genetically modifying it to make vaccination ineffective. These programs have reportedly closed down, but nobody can be sure that no sample of smallpox has made it into other hands. In the wake of the 2001 terrorist attacks, the Canadian and U.S. governments scrambled to begin large-scale production of vaccine again, in case of a terrorist attack with smallpox, which is highly contagious, not treatable, and sometimes fatal. (The vaccine itself causes a few rare deaths, so probably it would not be used until needed.)

The world order that emerged in the 1990s and early 2000s, with its growing interdependence and quickening pace of interactions, is one that allows the rapid spread of viruses and bacteria around the world. Overuse of antibiotics (such as in livestock feed) produced drug-resistant strains of bacteria that threatened to outpace the development of new antibiotics. Meanwhile, the AIDS epidemic defied control by the international community. Viruses cross borders with ease, whereas doctors and vaccines can go only where host governments allow them to be.

Does the world need a stronger form of governance with the power to impose health regulations and interventions globally without regard for national sovereignty? If so, how would it work? If not, how else would you stop global epidemics from ravaging societies and economies?

Smallpox victim, pre-1977.

the 1980s.[48] In the 1960s and 1970s, the "green revolution" increased yields enough to stay ahead of population growth, but had a negative impact on the environment (see "Technology Transfer" on pp. 467–468). Other forms of environmental damage—such as soil erosion and water table depletion—has reduced agricultural productivity in some areas. The faster populations grow, the more pressing will be world food problems.

Growing populations exacerbate all the international conflicts over natural resources discussed earlier. Conflicts over water, which are very serious in several regions, become worse as populations grow. So do a range of issues such as overfishing, deforestation, and the loss of agricultural land to urban sprawl. Although it does not cause these problems, population growth affects how severe they become and how quickly they develop.

There is not a simple linear relationship between the number of people in a state and its need for resources. Rather, as an economy develops, population growth slows but the demand for resources continues to rise. The resources are then needed for raising incomes (industrialization) rather than just feeding more mouths. The type of resources needed also changes—less food and more petroleum—as the state's technological needs evolve. But overall, while more states moving through the demographic transition more quickly will slow population growth, it will not decrease the quantity of resources they use or the environmental damage they cause. More likely the opposite is true.

If population growth can be limited at lower income levels—shifting the demographic curve by using government policies to encourage lower birthrates—strains on the environment will be less. A country would then not only increase its per capita income sooner and faster but would do so at lower total population levels. This outcome would reduce the load on the environment and resources as compared with industrializing at a higher level of population. Presumably, international conflicts would also be reduced.

Some IR scholars have argued that population growth leads states to expand outwardly in search of resources (the theory of lateral pressure mentioned on p. 170). During the rise of Germany from the mid-nineteenth century through World War II, a consistent theme of German expansionists was the need for "living space" for the growing German population. This need was as much psychological as physical, but it was used to justify German territorial expansion, imperialism, and aggression.

Another source of international conflict connected with demographics is migration from poor states with high population growth to rich states with low population growth. For example, illegal immigration from Mexico to the United States is an irritant in U.S.-Mexican relations. Refugees are a recurrent source of interstate conflict as well. Migration and refugees are population issues, but are discussed in Chapter 11 (pp. 431–434) in the context of North-South relations.

Thus, population pressures are not a simple explanation for the world's problems but contribute in various ways to international conflicts. Demographic and environmental factors are playing a larger role and receiving more attention from IR scholars.

As we have seen, the implications of population issues differ greatly in the world's North and South. Strains on the environment and on natural resources are global in scope, yet in the North they arise from industrialization (growing GDP per capita), whereas in the South they are more affected by growing populations.

These differences in environmental impacts are by no means the only such North-South difference. In many ways the world seems to be splitting in two, with different realities in the rich and poor regions—a trend running contrary to the integration theme of the previous few chapters.

---

[48] See footnote 35 in this chapter.

Thinking Critically

1. Given the collective goods problem in managing environmental issues—heightened by the participation of large numbers of actors—what new international organizations or agreements could be created in the coming years to help solve this problem? Are there ways to reduce the number of actors participating in the management of global problems like ozone depletion? What problems might your proposals run into regarding issues such as state sovereignty?

2. Few effective international agreements have been reached to solve the problem of global warming. Given the several difficulties associated with managing this problem, what creative international solutions can you think of? What would be the strengths and weaknesses of your solutions in the short term and in the long term?

3. Does the record of the international community on environmental management reflect the views of mercantilists, of liberals, or critical theorists? In what ways?

4. Some politicians call for the Western industrialized countries to be more self-sufficient in energy resources in order to reduce dependence on oil imports from the Middle East. In light of the overall world energy picture and the economics of international trade, what are the pros and cons of such a proposal?

5. Dozens of poor states appear to be stuck midway through the demographic transition; death rates have fallen, birthrates remain high, and per capita incomes are not increasing. How do you think these states, with or without foreign assistance, can best get unstuck and complete the demographic transition?

Chapter Summary

*   Environmental problems are an example of international interdependence and often create collective goods problems for the states involved. The large numbers of actors involved in global environmental problems make them more difficult to solve.

*   To resolve such collective goods problems, states have used international regimes and IOs, and have in some cases extended state sovereignty (notably over territorial waters) to make management a national rather than an international matter.

*   International efforts to solve environmental problems aim to bring about sustainable economic development. This was the theme of the 1992 UN Earth Summit.

*   Global warming results from burning fossil fuels—the basis of industrial economies today. The industrialized states are much more responsible for the problem than are global South states. Solutions are difficult to reach because costs are substantial and dangers are somewhat distant and uncertain.

*   Damage to the earth's ozone layer results from the use of specific chemicals, which are now being phased out under international agreements. Unlike global warming, the costs of solutions are much lower and the problem is better understood.

*   Many species are threatened with extinction due to loss of habitats such as rain forests. An international treaty on biodiversity and an agreement on forests aim to reduce the destruction of local ecosystems, with costs spread among states.

*   The UN Convention on the Law of the Sea (UNCLOS) establishes an ocean regime that puts most commercial fisheries and offshore oil under control of states as territorial waters. The United States signed the treaty after a decade's delay.

- Pollution—including acid rain, water and air pollution, and toxic and nuclear waste—tends to be more localized than global and has been addressed mainly through unilateral, bilateral, and regional measures rather than global ones.

- The economies of the industrialized West depend on fossil fuels. Overall, these economies import energy resources, mostly oil, whereas the other world regions export them. Oil prices rose dramatically in the 1970s but declined in the 1980s as the world economy adjusted by increasing supply and reducing demand. After spiking around 1991 and again around 2000, prices dropped again. Such fluctuations undermine world economic stability.

- The most important source of oil traded worldwide is the Persian Gulf area of the Middle East. Consequently, this area has long been a focal point of international political conflict, including the 1991 Gulf War.

- States need other raw materials such as minerals, but no such materials have assumed the importance or political status of oil. Water resources are a growing source of local international conflicts, however.

- War and other military activities cause considerable environmental damage—sometimes deliberately inflicted as part of a war strategy.

- World population—now at 6.2 billion—will reach 7 to 8 billion within 25 years and may eventually level out around 10 billion. Virtually all of the increase will come in the global South.

- Future world population growth will be largely driven by the demographic transition. Death rates have fallen throughout the world, but birthrates will fall proportionally only as per capita incomes go up. The faster the economies of poor states develop, the sooner their populations will level out.

- The demographic transition sharpens disparities of wealth globally and locally. High per capita incomes and low population growth make rich states or groups richer, whereas low incomes and high population growth reinforce each other to keep poor states and groups poor.

- Within the overall shape of the demographic transition, government policies can reduce birthrates somewhat at a given level of per capita income. Effective policies are those that improve access to birth control and raise the status of women in society. Actual policies vary, from China's very strict rules on childbearing to pronatalist governments that encourage maximum birthrates and outlaw birth control.

- Death rates are stable and little affected in the large picture by wars, famines, and other disasters. Raising the death rate is not a feasible way to limit population growth.

- Although the global AIDS epidemic may not greatly slow world population growth, it will impose huge costs on many poor states in the coming years. Currently 36 million people are infected with HIV, and 22 million more have died. Most are in Africa, and new infections are growing rapidly in Asia.

- AIDS demonstrates that growing international interdependence—the shrinking world—has costs and not just benefits. Because states cannot wall themselves off from the outside world, international cooperation in addition to unilateral state actions will be necessary to contain AIDS.

- Population pressures do not cause, but do contribute to, a variety of international conflicts including ethnic conflicts, economic competition, and territorial disputes.

Key Terms

tragedy of the commons   490
enclosure of the commons   490
epistemic communities   491
carrying capacity   492
Commission on Sustainable Development   493
global warming   495
fossil fuels   496
greenhouse gases   496
UN Environment Programme (UNEP)   498
ozone layer   498
Montreal Protocol   498

biodiversity   499
International Whaling Commission   500
high seas   502
UN Convention on the Law of the Sea (UNCLOS)   502
Antarctic Treaty of 1959   505
acid rain   505
Chernobyl   507
oil shocks   510
demographic transition   516
pronatalist   519
infant mortality rate   520

Weblinks

The following is a small sampling of the many sites devoted to the environment and population:

Amazon Watch:
 http://www.amazonwatch.org

Environment Canada:
http://www.ec.gc.ca/envhome.html

Greenpeace:
http://www.greenpeace.org/homepage

United Nations Environment Program:
http://www.unep.org

United Nations Population Fund:
http://www.unfpa.org

World Wildlife Fund:
http://www.panda.org

Soldier and child, Sarajevo, 1993.

Ultimately the conflicts and dramas of international relations are little different from those of other spheres of political and social life. The problems of IR are the problems of human society—struggles for power and wealth, efforts to cooperate despite differences, social dilemmas and collective goods problems, the balance between freedom and order, the costs of efficiency versus equity and of long-term versus short-term outcomes. These themes are inescapable in human society, from the smallest groups to the world community. The subject of international relations is in this sense an extension of everyday life and a reflection of the choices of individual human beings. IR belongs to all of us—North and South, women and men, citizens and leaders—who live together on this planet.

Technological development is just one aspect of the profound, yet incremental, changes taking place in international relations. New actors are gaining power, long-standing principles are becoming less effective, and new challenges are arising for states, groups, and individuals alike. The post–Cold War era, just over a decade old, remains undefined. Will it, like past "postwar" eras, lapse slowly into the next "prewar" era, or will it lead to a robust and lasting "permanent peace"?

Consider a few aspects of these changes that this book has discussed. One major theme of the book was the nature of the international system, which for some observers operated on a well-developed set of rules based on state sovereignty, territoriality, and "anarchy"—a lack of central government. Yet, others argued that the international system was far more complex, more nuanced, and more interconnected with other aspects of planetary society, and this complexity is becoming ever more apparent. State sovereignty is challenged by the principle of self-determination. International norms have begun to limit the right of government to rule a population by force against its will and to violate human rights. Territorial integrity is also problematic, since national borders do not stop information, environmental changes, or missiles. Information allows actors—state, substate, and supranational—to know what is going on everywhere in the world to coordinate actions globally.

Technology is also profoundly changing the utility and role of military force. The power of defensive weaponry makes successful attacks more difficult, and the power of offensive weaponry makes retaliation an extremely potent threat to deter an attack. The twentieth-century superpowers could not attack each other without destroying themselves, and a large force cannot reliably defeat a small one (or, to be more accurate, the costs of doing so are too high), as demonstrated in Vietnam, Afghanistan, and now Iraq. Nonmilitary forms of leverage, particularly economic rewards, have become much more important power capabilities.

In IPE, we see simultaneous trends toward integration and disintegration among states. People continue to speak their own language, to fly their own flag, to use their own currency with its pictures and emblems. Nationalism continues to be an important force. At the same time, however, although people identify with their state, they also now hold competing identities based on ethnic ties, gender, and sometimes region. In international trade, liberal economics prevails but sometimes at great cost to those on the periphery of the global political economy. States have learned that in order to survive they must help, not impede, the creation of wealth by MNCs and other economic actors, which means sometimes siding with foreign economic interests over local citizens.

North-South relations meanwhile are moving to the centre of world politics. Demographic and economic trends are sharpening the global North-South gap, with the North continuing to accumulate wealth while much of the South lingers in great poverty. Ultimately, the North will bear a high cost for failing to address the economic development of the South. Perhaps, by using computerization and biotechnology innovations, poor states can develop their economies much more efficiently than did Europe or North America.

Environmental damage may become the single greatest obstacle to sustained economic growth in both the North and South. Because of high costs, the large number of actors, and collective goods problems, international bargaining over the environment is difficult. However, the 1992 Earth Summit's call for sustainable economic growth that does not deplete resources and destroy ecosystems may be supported by new technology that moves information, instead of materials, to accomplish the same goals. The traditional technological style of industrialization cannot be sustained environmentally on the giant scale of countries like China and India.

The future is unknowable now, but as it unfolds you can compare it—at mileposts along the way—to the worlds that you desire and expect. The comparison of alternative futures may be facilitated by examining a variety of possible branch points where alternative paths diverge. For example, you could ask questions such as the following (asking yourself, for each one, why you answer the way you do for your desired future and expected future):

1. Will state sovereignty be eroded by supranational authority?
2. Will norms of human rights and democracy become global?
3. Will the UN evolve into a quasi-government for the world?
4. Will the UN be restructured?
5. Will World Court and International Criminal Court judgments become enforceable?
6. Will the number of states increase?
7. Will China become democratic? Will it become rich?
8. What effects will information technologies have on IR?
9. Will military leverage become obsolete?
10. Will weapons of mass destruction proliferate?
11. Will disarmament occur?
12. Will women participate more fully in IR? With what effect?
13. Will there be a single world currency?
14. Will there be a global free trade regime?
15. Will nationalism fade out or continue to be strong?
16. Will many people develop a global identity?
17. Will world culture become more homogeneous or more pluralistic?
18. Will the EU or other regional IOs achieve political union?
19. Will global environmental destruction be severe? How soon?
20. Will new technologies avert environmental constraints?
21. Will global problems create stronger or weaker world order?
22. Will population growth level out? If so, when and at what level?
23. Will the poorest countries accumulate wealth? How soon?
24. What role will NGOs play in the South's development?

The choices you make and actions you take will ultimately affect, in some way, the world you live in. You cannot opt out of involvement in international relations. You are involved, and year by year the information revolution and other aspects of interdependence are drawing you more closely into contact with the rest of the world. You can act in many ways, large and small, to bring the world you expect more into line with the world you desire. You can empower yourself by finding the actions and choices that define your place in international relations.

Now that you have completed the studies covered in this book, don't stop here. Keep learning about the world beyond your country's borders. Keep thinking about the world that might exist. Be a part of the changes that will carry this world through the coming decades. It's your world: study it, care for it, make it your own.

Glossary

acid rain Caused by air pollution, it damages trees and often crosses borders. Limiting acid rain (via limiting nitrogen oxide emissions) has been the subject of several regional agreements.   (*p. 505*)

airspace The space above a state that is considered its territory, in contrast to outer space, which is considered international territory.   (*p. 168*)

alliance cohesion The ease with which the members hold together an alliance; it tends to be high when national interests converge and when cooperation among allies becomes institutionalized.   (*p. 243*)

Amnesty International An influential nongovernmental organization that operates globally to monitor and try to rectify glaring abuses of political (not economic or social) human rights.   (*p. 289*)

anarchy In IR theory, the term implies not complete chaos but the lack of a central government that can enforce rules.   (*p. 71*)

Antarctic Treaty of 1959 One of the first multilateral treaties concerning the environment, it forbids military activity in Antarctica as well as the presence of nuclear weapons or the dumping of nuclear waste there, sets aside territorial claims on the continent for future resolution, and establishes a regime for the conduct of scientific research.   (*p. 505*)

Anti-Ballistic Missile (ABM) Treaty Treaty that prohibited either the United States or the Soviet Union from using a ballistic missile defense as a shield, which would have undermined mutually assured destruction and the basis of deterrence.   (*p. 273*) See also *mutually assured destruction (MAD)* and *Strategic Defence Initiative (SDI)*.

arms race A reciprocal process in which two (or more) states build up military capabilities in response to each other.   (*p. 66*)

autarky (self-reliance) A policy of avoiding or minimizing trade and trying to produce everything one needs (or the most vital things) by oneself.   (*p. 311*)

authoritarian (government) A government that rules without the need to stand for free elections, respect civil and political rights, allow freedom of the press, and so forth.   (*p. 150*)

balance of payments A summary of all the flows of money in and out of a country. It includes three types of international transactions: the current account (including the merchandise trade balance), flows of capital, and changes in reserves.   (*p. 344*)

balance of power The general concept of one or more states' power being used to balance that of another state or group of states. The term can refer to (1) any ratio of power capabilities between states or alliances, (2) a relatively equal ratio, or (3) the process by which counter-balancing coalitions have repeatedly formed to prevent one state from conquering an entire region.   (*p. 74*)

balance of trade The value of a state's exports relative to its imports.   (*p. 308*)

ballistic missiles The major strategic delivery vehicles for nuclear weapons; they carry a warhead along a trajectory (typically rising at least 80 kilometres high) and let it drop on the target.   (*p. 221*) See also *intercontinental ballistic missiles (ICBMs)*.

bargaining Tacit or direct communication that is used in an attempt to reach agreement on an exchange of value.   (*p. 61*)

basic human needs The fundamental needs of people for adequate food, shelter, health care, sanitation, and education. Meeting such needs may be thought of as both a moral imperative and a form of investment in "human capital" essential for economic growth.   (*p. 423*)

bilateral aid Government assistance that goes directly to the global South governments as state-to-state aid.   (*p. 475*)

biodiversity The tremendous diversity of plant and animal species making up the earth's (global, regional, and local) ecosystems.   (*p. 499*)

Biological Weapons Convention Treaty that prohibits the development, production, and possession of biological weapons, but makes no provision for inspections.   (*p. 224*)

blue helmets The UN peacekeeping forces, so called because they wear helmets or berets in the UN colour, blue, with UN insignia.   (*p. 260*)

bourgeoisie In Marxist terminology, the class of owners of capital—people who make money from their investments rather than from their labour.   (*p. 411*) See also *proletariat*.

brain drain Poor countries' loss of skilled workers to rich countries.   (*p. 467*)

Bretton Woods system A post–World War II arrangement for managing the world economy, established at a meeting in Bretton Woods, New Hampshire, in 1944. Its main institutional components are the World Bank and the International Monetary Fund (IMF).   (*p. 341*)

burden sharing The distribution of the costs of an alliance among members; the term also refers to the conflicts that may arise over such distribution.   (*p. 243*)

bureaucratic politics model A decision-making model that sees foreign policy decisions as flowing from a bargaining process among various government agencies that have somewhat divergent interests in the outcome ("where you stand depends on where you sit"). Also called the *government bargaining model*.   (*p. 137*)

capital accumulation The creation of standing wealth (capital) such as buildings, roads, factories, and so forth; such accumulation depends on investment and the creation of an economic surplus. *(p. 406)*

capitalism An economic system based on private ownership of capital and the means of production (standing wealth and other forms of property). *(p. 408)* See also *socialism*.

carrying capacity The limits of the planetary ecosystem's ability to absorb continual growth of population, industry, energy use, and extraction of natural resources. *(p. 492)*

cartel An association of producers or consumers (or both) of a certain product, formed for the purpose of manipulating its price on the world market. *(p. 459)*

cash crops Agricultural goods produced as commodities for export to world markets. *(p. 427)*

central bank An institution common in industrialized countries whose major tasks are to maintain the value of the state's currency and to control inflation. *(p. 340)*

centrally planned (or command) economy An economy in which political authorities set prices and decide on quotas for production and consumption of each commodity according to a long-term plan. *(p. 304)*

Chemical Weapons Convention Treaty that bans the production and possession of chemical weapons, and includes strict verification provisions and the threat of sanctions against violators, including nonparticipants in the treaty. *(p. 224)*

Chernobyl A city in Ukraine that was the site of a 1986 meltdown at a Soviet nuclear power plant. *(p. 507)*

civil war A war between factions within a state trying to create, or prevent, a new government for the entire state or some territorial part of it. *(p. 188)*

class struggle The process in which the more powerful classes oppress and exploit the less powerful by denying them their fair share of the surplus they create, and the oppressed classes try to gain power, to rebel, and to organize in order to seize more of the economic surplus for themselves. *(p. 410)*

Cold War The hostile relations—punctuated by occasional periods of improvement, or détente—between the two superpowers, the U.S. and the U.S.S.R., from 1945 to 1990. *(p. 38)*

collective goods problem A collective good is a tangible or intangible good, created by the members of a group, that is available to all group members regardless of their individual contributions; participants can gain by lowering their own contribution to the collective good, yet if too many participants do so, the good cannot be provided. *(p. 91)* See also *free riders*.

collective security The formation of a broad alliance of most major actors in an international system for the purpose of jointly opposing aggression by any actor; sometimes seen as presupposing the existence of a universal organization (such as the United Nations) to which both the aggressor and its opponents belong. *(p. 95)* See also *League of Nations*.

Commission on Sustainable Development An organization established at the 1992 UN Earth Summit that monitors states' compliance with their promises and hears evidence from environmental *nongovernmental organizations* (NGOs). *(p. 493)*

Common Agricultural Policy (CAP) A European Union policy based on the principle that a subsidy extended to farmers in any member country should be extended to farmers in all member countries. *(p. 373)*

common market A zone in which labour and capital (as well as goods) flow freely across borders. *(p. 373)*

Commonwealth of Independent States (CIS) The loose coordinating structure linking the former republics of the Soviet Union (except the Baltic states) since 1991. *(p. 43)*

comparative advantage The principle that states should specialize in trading those goods which they produce with the greatest relative efficiency and at the lowest relative cost (relative, that is, to other goods produced by the same state). *(p. 300)*

compellence The use of force to make another actor take some action (rather than, as in *deterrence*, refrain from taking an action). *(p. 66)*

Comprehensive Test Ban Treaty (CTBT) It bans all nuclear weapons testing, thereby broadening the ban on atmospheric testing negotiated in 1963. *(p. 274)*

conditionality See *IMF conditionality*.

conflict A difference in preferred outcomes in a bargaining situation. *(p. 156)*

conflict resolution The development and implementation of peaceful strategies for settling conflicts. *(p. 98)*

constructivism A movement in IR theory that examines how changing international norms help shape the content of state interests and the character of international institutions. *(p. 123)*

consumption goods Goods whose consumption does not contribute directly to production of other goods and services, unlike some forms of investment. *(p. 408)*

containment A policy adopted in the late 1940s by which the United States sought to halt the global expansion of Soviet influence on several levels—military, political, ideological, and economic. *(p. 38)*

Conventional Forces in Europe (CFE) Treaty A U.S.-Soviet agreement that provided for asymmetrical reductions in Soviet forces in Europe and limited those of both sides. *(p. 275)*

convertible currency The guarantee that the holder of a particular currency can exchange it for another currency. Some states' currencies are nonconvertible. *(p. 334)* See also *hard currency*.

core The manufacturing regions of the world-system. (*p. 414*)

cost-benefit analysis A calculation of the costs incurred by a possible action and the benefits it is likely to bring. (*p. 68*)

Council of the European Union (Formerly known as the Council of Ministers.) The Council is the main legislative and decision-making body in the European Union and comprises relevant ministers (foreign, economic, agriculture, finance, etc.) from the 25 member countries. When a meeting takes place among the state leaders it is called the "European Council." (*p. 375*) See also *European Commission*.

counterinsurgency An effort to combat guerrilla armies, often including programs to "win the hearts and minds" of rural populations so that they stop sheltering guerrillas. (*p. 189*)

coup d'état French for "blow against the state," it refers to the seizure of political power by domestic military forces—that is, a change of political power outside the state's constitutional order. (*p. 208*)

crimes against humanity A category of legal offences created at the Nuremberg trials after World War II to encompass genocide and other acts committed by the political and military leaders of the Third Reich (Nazi Germany). (*p. 288*) See also *dehumanization* and *genocide*.

critical theory Theory that questions the very framework (the very world) that problem-solving theory takes for granted, and that is concerned with relations of inequality and the issues that are unexplored or made invisible within more mainstream approaches to IR. (*p. 107*)

cruise missile A small winged missile that can navigate across thousands of kilometres of previously mapped terrain to reach a particular target; it can carry either a nuclear or a conventional warhead. (*p. 223*)

Cuban Missile Crisis A superpower crisis, sparked by the Soviet Union's installation of medium-range nuclear missiles in Cuba, that marks the moment when the United States and the Soviet Union came closest to nuclear war. (*p. 40*)

cultural imperialism A critical term for Western (especially U.S.) dominance of the emerging global culture. (*p. 394*)

customs union A common external tariff adopted by members of a free trade area; that is, participating states adopt a unified set of tariffs with regard to goods coming in from outside. (*p. 373*) See also *free trade area*.

debt renegotiation A reworking of the terms on which a loan will be repaid; frequently negotiated by global South debtor governments in order to avoid default. (*p. 469*)

debt service An obligation to make regular interest payments and repay the principal of a loan according to its terms, which is a drain on many economies of the global South. (*p. 468*)

default The failure to make scheduled debt payments. (*p. 469*)

dehumanization Stigmatization of enemies as subhuman or nonhuman, leading frequently to widespread massacres or, in the worst cases, destruction of entire populations. (*p. 176*) See also *crimes against humanity* and *genocide*.

democracy A government of "the people," usually through elected representatives, and usually with a respect for individual rights in society (especially rights to hold political ideas differing from those of the government). (*p. 150*)

democratic peace The proposition, strongly supported by empirical evidence, that democracies almost never fight wars against each other (although they do fight against authoritarian states). (*p. 152*)

demographic transition The pattern of falling death rates, followed by falling birthrates, that generally accompanies *industrialization* and *economic development*. (*p. 516*)

dependency theory A Marxist-oriented theory that explains the lack of capital accumulation in the global South as a result of the interplay between domestic class relations and the forces of foreign capital. (*p. 421*) See also *enclave economy*.

deterrence The threat to punish another actor if it takes a certain negative action (especially attacking one's own state or one's allies). The term has a somewhat more specific meaning in the context of the nuclear balance between the superpowers during the Cold War. (*p. 66*) See also *mutually assured destruction (MAD)*.

devaluation A unilateral move to reduce the value of a currency by changing a fixed or official exchange rate. (*p. 339*) See also *exchange rate*.

developing countries States in the global South, the poorest regions of the world—also called Third World countries, less-developed countries, and undeveloped countries. (*p. 403*)

Development Assistance Committee (DAC) A committee whose members—consisting of states from Western Europe, North America, and Japan/Pacific—provide 95 percent of official development assistance to countries of the global South. (*p. 475*) See also *foreign assistance*.

diplomatic immunity Refers to diplomats' activity being outside the jurisdiction of the host country's national courts. (*p. 281*)

diplomatic recognition The process by which the status of embassies and that of an ambassador as an official state representative are explicitly defined. (*p. 281*)

direct foreign investment See *foreign direct investment*.

disaster relief The provision of short-term relief in the form of food, water, shelter, clothing, and other essentials to people facing natural disasters. (*p. 478*)

discount rate The interest rate charged by governments when they lend money to private banks. The discount rate (called the bank rate in Canada) is set by countries' central banks.   *(p. 340)*

dumping The sale of products in foreign markets at prices below the minimum level necessary to make a profit (or below cost).   *(p. 313)*

economic base A society's mode of production, such as slavery, feudalism, or capitalism.   *(p. 412)*

economic class A categorization of individuals based on economic status (which for Marxists is determined by one's relationship to the means of production, for example, as either owners of capital or workers).   *(p. 410)*

economic conversion The use of former military facilities and industries for new civilian production.   *(p. 200)*

economic development The combined processes of capital accumulation, rising per capita incomes (with consequent falling birthrates), the increasing of skills in the population, the adoption of new technological styles, and other related social and economic changes.   *(p. 444)*

economic liberalism An approach to IPE that emphasizes the gains that can be made through trade and which, in practice, is committed to free trade, free capital flows, and an "open" world economy.   *(p. 295)* See also *mercantilism* and *neoliberalism*.

economic surplus Made by investing money in productive capital rather than using it for consumption.   *(p. 406)*

electronic warfare The use of the electromagnetic spectrum (radio waves, radar, infrared, etc.) in war, such as employing electromagnetic signals for one's own benefit while denying their use to an enemy.   *(p. 215)*

elite model (with a more critical variant called instrumental Marxism). Elite theorists and instrumental Marxists argue that decision-makers within governments or state agencies share a common business or class background, and that their decisions will reflect their business or class interests.   *(p. 147)*

empowerment In the development context, it refers to the grassroots efforts of poor people to gain power over their situation and meet their basic needs.   *(p. 483)*

enclave economy An historically important form of dependency in which foreign capital is invested in a global South country to extract a particular raw material in a particular place—usually a mine, oil well, or plantation. *(p. 421)* See also *dependency theory*.

enclosure of the commons The splitting of a common area or good into privately owned pieces, giving individual owners an incentive to manage resources responsibly. *(p. 490)*

epistemic communities Transnational communities of experts who help structure the way states manage environmental and other issues.   *(p. 491)*

ethnic cleansing Forced displacement of an ethnic group or groups from a particular territory, accompanied by massacres and other human rights violations; it has occurred after the breakup of multinational states, notably in the former Yugoslavia.   *(p. 164)*

ethnic groups Large groups of people who share ancestral, language, cultural, or religious ties and a common identity.   *(p. 173)*

ethnocentrism The tendency to see one's own group (in-group) in favourable terms and an out-group in unfavourable terms.   *(p. 176)*

Euratom Created in the Treaty of Rome in 1957 to coordinate nuclear power development by pooling research, investment, and management in Europe.   *(p. 373)*

euro Also called the *ECU (European currency unit)*, the euro is a single European currency used by 12 members of the *European Union (EU)*.   *(p. 379)*

European Commission A European Union body whose members, while appointed by states, are supposed to represent EU interests. Supported by a multinational civil service in Brussels, the Commission's role is to identify problems and propose solutions to the Council of the European Union.   *(p. 375)* See also *Council of the European Union*.

European Court of Justice A judicial arm of the European Union, based in Luxembourg. The Court has actively established its jurisdiction and its right to overrule national law when it conflicts with EU law.   *(p. 376)*

European Parliament A quasi-legislative body of the European Union that operates mainly as a watchdog over the *European Commission* and has little real legislative power.   *(p. 376)*

European Union (EU) The official term for the European Community (formerly the European Economic Community) and associated treaty organizations. The EU has 25 member states and is negotiating with other states that have applied for membership.   *(p. 371)* See also *Maastricht Treaty*.

exchange rate The rate at which one state's currency can be exchanged for the currency of another state. Since 1973, the international monetary system has depended mainly on flexible (or floating) rather than fixed exchange rates.   *(p. 333)* See also *convertibility; fixed exchange rates; Exchange Rate Mechanism (ERM);* and *managed float*.

Exchange Rate Mechanism (ERM) A system that established nearly fixed exchange rates among European currencies while letting them all float freely relative to the rest of the world.   *(p. 337)*

export-led growth An economic development strategy that seeks to develop industries capable of competing in specific niches in the world economy.   *(p. 456)*

fiscal policy A government's decisions about spending and taxation, and one of the two major tools of macroeconomic policy-making (the other being *monetary policy*).   *(p. 347)*

fissionable material The elements uranium-235 and plutonium, whose atoms split apart and release energy via a chain reaction when an atomic bomb explodes. *(p. 218)* See also *fusion weapons*.

fixed exchange rates The official rates of exchange for currencies set by governments; not a dominant mechanism in the international monetary system since 1973. *(p. 335)* See also *floating exchange rates*.

floating exchange rates The rates determined by global currency markets, in which private investors and governments alike buy and sell currencies. *(p. 335)* See also *fixed exchange rates*.

foreign assistance Money or other aid made available to developing countries to help them speed up economic development or meet humanitarian needs. Most foreign assistance is provided by governments and is called official development assistance (ODA). *(p. 474)* See also *Development Assistance Committee (DAC)*.

foreign direct investment The acquisition by residents of one country of control over a new or existing business in another country. Also called direct foreign investment. *(p. 345)*

foreign policy process The process by which foreign policies are arrived at and implemented. *(p. 129)*

fossil fuels Oil, coal, and natural gas, burnt to run factories, cars, tractors, furnaces, electrical generating plants, and other things that drive an industrial economy. *(p. 496)*

"four tigers"/"four dragons" The most successful newly industrialized areas of East Asia: South Korea, Taiwan, Hong Kong, and Singapore. *(p. 447)*

free economic zones The southern coastal provinces of China that were opened to foreign investment and run on capitalist principles with export-oriented industries, in the 1980s and 1990s. *(p. 450)*

free riders Those who benefit from someone else's provision of a collective good without paying their share of costs. *(p. 91)* See also *collective goods problem*.

free trade The flow of goods and services across national boundaries unimpeded by tariffs or other restrictions; in principle (if not always in practice), free trade was a key aspect of Britain's policy after 1846 and of U.S. and Canadian policy after 1945. *(p. 32)*

free trade area A zone in which there are no tariffs or other restrictions on the movement of goods and services across borders. *(p. 373)* See also *customs union*.

fusion weapons Extremely destructive, expensive, and technologically sophisticated weapons in which two small atoms fuse together into a larger atom, releasing energy. Also referred to as "thermonuclear weapons" or "hydrogen bombs." *(p. 217)* See also *fissionable material*.

G7 See *Group of 7*.

G20 See *Group of 20*.

game theory A branch of mathematics concerned with predicting bargaining outcomes. Games such as Prisoner's Dilemma and Chicken have been used to analyze various sorts of international interactions. *(p. 69)*

gender gap Refers to polls showing women lower than men on average in their support for military actions (as well as for various other issues and candidates). *(p. 114)*

General Agreement on Tariffs and Trade (GATT) A world organization established in 1947 to work for freer trade on a multilateral basis; the GATT has been more of a negotiating framework than an administrative institution. It became the World Trade Organization (WTO) in 1995. *(p. 323)*

General Assembly See *UN General Assembly*.

Generalized System of Preferences (GSP) A mechanism by which some industrialized states began in the 1970s to give tariff concessions to global South states on certain imports; an exception to the most-favoured nation (MFN) principle. *(p. 324)* See also *most-favoured nation (MFN) concept*.

genocide The intentional and systematic attempt to destroy a national, ethnic, racial, or religious group, in whole or part. It was confirmed as a crime under international law by the UN Genocide Convention (1948). *(p. 37)* See also *crimes against humanity* and *dehumanization*.

geopolitics The use of geography as an element of power, and the ideas about it held by political leaders and scholars. *(p. 60)*

global culture Worldwide cultural integration based on a massive increase in satellite television, radio, and internet communication. *(p. 393)*

globalization The increasing integration of the world in terms of communications, culture, and economics; may also refer to changing subjective experiences of space and time accompanying this process. *(p. 297)*

global social movements Non-state groups that organize transnationally, usually to protest around an issue or event (such as the environment, peace, women's issues, human rights, globalization). *(p. 11)*

global warming A slow, long-term rise in the average world temperature caused by the emission of greenhouse gases produced by burning fossil fuels—oil, coal, and natural gas. *(p. 495)* See also *greenhouse gases*.

gold standard A system in international monetary relations, prominent for a century before the 1970s, in which the value of national currencies was pegged to the value of gold or other precious metals. *(p. 333)*

great powers Generally, the half dozen or so most powerful states; the great-power club was exclusively European until the twentieth century. *(p. 76)* See also *middle powers*.

greenhouse gases Carbon dioxide and other gases that, when concentrated in the atmosphere, act like the glass in a greenhouse, holding energy in and leading to *global warming*. (p. 496)

green revolution The massive transfer of agricultural technology, such as high-yield seeds and tractors, to countries of the global South that began in the 1960s. *(p. 467)*

gross domestic product (GDP) The size of a state's total annual economic activity. *(p. 9)*

Group of 7 (G7) The world's seven largest industrial market economies: the United States, Japan, Germany, France, Britain, Italy, and Canada. The leaders of G7 countries meet in annual summits, and the finance ministers of G7 countries meet several times a year. When the group includes Russia, as it has done at summits since 1998, it is called the G8. On some issues, particularly monetary matters, the G7 acts without Russia (primarily because Russia's currency is not convertible).   *(p. 336)*

Group of 20 (G20) The G20 comprises the G7, Australia, Argentina, Brazil, China, India, Indonesia, Mexico, Korea, Russia, Saudi Arabia, South Africa, and Turkey, along with the European Union, International Monetary Fund, and World Bank. Members of the G7 realized that even acting together, they were not sufficient in number to manage world financial markets.   *(p. 349)*

groupthink The tendency of individual members of a group to go along with ideas they think other group members support, leading to the adoption of decisions that conform to group sentiment but not necessarily to the available evidence (and in extreme cases, that contravene legal or ethical norms)   *(p. 139)*

guerrilla war Warfare without front lines and with irregular forces operating in the midst of, and often hidden or protected by, civilian populations.   *(p. 188)*

hard currency Money that can be readily converted to leading world currencies.   *(p. 334)* See also *convertibility (of currency)*.

hegemonic stability theory The argument that regimes are most effective when power in the international system is most concentrated.   *(p. 93)* See also *hegemony*.

hegemonic war War for control of the entire world order—the rules of the international system as a whole. Also known as world war, global war, general war, or systemic war.   *(p. 187)*

hegemony The holding by one state of a preponderance of power in the international system, so that it can single-handedly dominate the rules and arrangements by which international political and economic relations are conducted.   *(p. 80)* See also *hegemonic stability theory*.

high seas That portion of the oceans considered common territory, not under any kind of exclusive state jurisdiction.   *(p. 502)* See also *territorial waters*.

home country The state where a *multinational corporation (MNC)* has its headquarters.   *(p. 360)* See also *host country*.

host country A state in which a foreign *multinational corporation (MNC)* operates.   *(p. 360)* See also *home country*.

Human Development Index (HDI) An alternative measure of development to the gross domestic product (GDP) alone. It measures a country's achievements in the areas of: life expectancy at birth (as a measure of a long and healthy life); knowledge (including adult literacy and enrolment levels in primary, secondary, and tertiary education); and standard of living, based on per capita GDP.   *(p. 445)*

human rights Rights of all persons to be free from abuses such as torture or imprisonment for their political beliefs (political and civil rights), and to enjoy certain minimum economic and social protections (economic and social rights).   *(p. 288)*

human security Expands the notion of security away from a focus on states to one that examines all of the complex ways in which people are made secure, including through human rights protections; access to education, food, and shelter; availability of health services; and an environmentally sustainable environment.   *(p. 97)*

humanitarian intervention Armed intrusion into a state, without its consent, to prevent or alleviate widespread or severe human rights violations.   *(p. 240)*

hyperinflation An extremely rapid, uncontrolled rise in prices, such as occurred in Germany in the 1920s and some global South countries more recently.   *(p. 334)*

idealism An approach that emphasizes international law, morality, and international organization, rather than power alone, as key influences on international relations.   *(p. 54)* See also *realism*.

IMF conditionality An agreement to loan IMF funds on the condition that certain government policies are adopted. Dozens of global South states have entered into such agreements with the IMF in the past two decades.   *(p. 471)* See also *International Monetary Fund (IMF)*.

immigration law National laws that establish the conditions under which foreigners may travel and visit within a state's territory, work within the state, and sometimes become citizens of the state (naturalization).   *(p. 280)*

imperialism The acquisition of colonies by conquest or otherwise. Lenin's theory of imperialism argued that European capitalists were investing in colonies where they could earn big profits, and then using part of those profits to buy off portions of the working class at home.   *(p. 412)*

import substitution A strategy of developing local industries, often conducted behind protectionist barriers, to produce items that a country had been importing.   *(p. 456)*

industrialization The use of fossil-fuel energy to drive machinery and the accumulation of such machinery along with the products created by it.   *(p. 32)*

industrial policy The strategies by which a government works actively with industries to promote their growth and tailor trade policy to their needs.   *(p. 316)*

infant mortality rate The proportion of babies who die within their first year of life.   *(p. 520)*

infantry Foot soldiers who use assault rifles and other light weapons (mines, machine guns, and the like).   *(p. 212)*

informal sector Those modes of business, such as shadow markets and street vendors, operating beyond state control; some scholars see this sector as the core of a new development strategy.   *(p. 458)*

information screens The subconscious or unconscious filters through which people put the information coming in about the world around them.   *(p. 134)* See also *misperceptions* and *selective perceptions*.

instrumental Marxism See *elite model*.

intellectual property rights The legal protection of the original works of inventors, authors, creators, and performers under patent, copyright, and trademark law. Such rights became a contentious area of trade negotiations in the 1990s.   (p. 317)

intercontinental ballistic missiles (ICBMs) The longest-range ballistic missiles, able to travel 8000 kilometres. (p. 221) See also *ballistic missiles*.

interdependence A political and economic situation in which two or more states are simultaneously dependent on each other for their well-being. The degree of interdependence is sometimes designated in terms of "sensitivity" or "vulnerability."   (p. 309)

interest groups Coalitions of people who share a common interest in the outcome of some political issue and who organize themselves to try to influence the outcome. (p. 143)

intergovernmental organizations (IGOs) Organizations (such as the United Nations and its agencies) whose members are state governments.   (p. 11)

Intermediate Nuclear Forces (INF) Treaty Treaty that banned an entire class of missiles that both the Soviet Union and the United States had deployed in Europe. (p. 274)

International Committee of the Red Cross (ICRC) An organization based in Geneva Switzerland that provides practical support, such as medical care, food, and letters from home, to civilians caught in wars and to *prisoners of war (POWs)*. The ICRC works with national societies of the Red Cross or Red Crescent in providing that support. Exchanges of POWs are usually negotiated through the ICRC.   (p. 285)

International Court of Justice See *World Court*.

International Criminal Court (ICC) Permanent tribunal for war crimes and crimes against humanity.   (p. 283)

international integration The process by which supranational institutions come to replace national ones; the gradual shifting upward of some sovereignty from the state to regional or global structures.   (p. 369)

International Monetary Fund (IMF) An *intergovernmental organization (IGO)* that coordinates international currency exchange, the balance of international payments, and national accounts. Along with the *World Bank*, it is a pillar of the international financial system.   (p. 341) See also *conditionality*.

international norms The expectations held by participants about normal relations among states.   (p. 238)

international organizations (IOs) Institutions including *intergovernmental organizations (IGOs)* such as the UN, and *nongovernmental organizations (NGOs)* such as Médecins sans Frontières or Amnesty International.   (p. 240)

international political economy (IPE) The study of the politics of trade, monetary, and other economic relations among nations, and their connection to other transnational forces. (p. 3)

international regime A set of rules, norms, and procedures around which the expectations of actors converge in a certain international issue area (such as oceans or monetary policy).   (p. 92)

international relations (IR) The relationships among the world's state governments and the connection of those relationships with other actors (such as the United Nations, multinational corporations, and individuals), with other social relationships (including economics, culture, and domestic politics), and with geographic and historical influences. (p. 1)

international security A subfield of *international relations (IR)* that focuses on questions of war and peace. (p. 3)

international system The set of relationships among the world's states, structured by certain rules and patterns of interaction.   (p. 8)

International Whaling Commission An *intergovernmental organization (IGO)* that sets quotas for hunting certain whale species; states' participation is voluntary. (p. 500)

investment Putting surplus wealth into capital-producing activities rather than consuming it, to produce long-term benefits.   (p. 408)

irredentism A form of nationalism whose goal is the regaining of territory lost to another state; it can lead directly to violent interstate conflicts.   (p. 161)

Islam/Muslims A broad and diverse world religion whose divergent populations include Sunni Muslims, Shiite Muslims, and many smaller branches and sects, practised by Muslims, from Nigeria to Indonesia, centred in the Middle East.   (p. 179)

just war doctrine A branch of international law and political theory that defines when wars can be justly started (*jus ad bellum*) and how they can be justly fought (*jus in bello*).   (p. 287) See also *war crimes*.

Keynesian economics The principles articulated by British economist John Maynard Keynes, used successfully in the Great Depression of the 1930s, including the view that governments should sometimes use deficit spending to stimulate economic growth.   (p. 347)

land mines Concealed explosive devices, often left behind by irregular armies, which kill or maim civilians after wars end. Such mines number more than 100 million, primarily in Angola, Bosnia, Afghanistan, and Cambodia. A movement to ban land mines is underway; nearly 100 states have agreed to do so.   (p. 212)

land reform Policies that aim to break up large land holdings and redistribute land to poor peasants for use in *subsistence farming*.   (p. 428)

lateral pressure Theory that holds that the economic and population growth of states fuels geographic expansion as they seek natural resources beyond their borders, which in turn leads to conflicts and sometimes to war. (p. 170)

League of Nations Established after World War I and a fore-runner of today's United Nations, the organization achieved certain humanitarian and other successes but was weakened by the absence of U.S. membership and by its own lack of effectiveness in ensuring collective security. *(p. 36)* See also *collective security*.

liberal feminism A strand of feminism that emphasizes gender equality and views the "essential" differences in men's and women's abilities or perspectives as trivial or nonexistent. *(p. 110)*

liberalism See *economic liberalism*.

limited war Military actions that seek objectives short of the surrender and occupation of the enemy. *(p. 188)*

London Club See *Paris Club*.

Maastricht Treaty Signed in the Dutch city of Maastricht and ratified in 1992, the treaty commits the European Union to monetary union (a single currency and European Central Bank) and to a common foreign policy. *(p. 377)* See also *European Union (EU)*.

malnutrition The lack of needed foods including protein and vitamins; about 10 million children die each year from malnutrition-related causes. *(p. 426)* See also *undernourishment*.

managed float A system of occasional multinational government interventions in currency markets to manage otherwise free-floating currency rates. *(p. 336)*

Marxism A theoretical and political approach that views capitalism as exploitative and emphasizes class struggle; includes both socialism and communism and other approaches to social transformation. *(p. 409)* See also *socialism*.

mediation The use of a third party (or parties) in *conflict resolution*. *(p. 99)*

mercantilism An economic theory and a political ideology opposed to free trade; it shares with *realism* the belief that each state must protect its own interests without seeking mutual gains through international organizations. *(p. 83)* See also *liberalism*.

microcredit The use of very small loans to small groups of individuals, often women, to stimulate economic development. *(p. 458)*

middle powers States that rank somewhat below the great powers in terms of their influence on world affairs (for example, Canada, Brazil, and India). *(p. 78)* See also *great powers*.

migration Movement between states, usually emigration from the old state and immigration to the new state. *(p. 431)*

militarism The glorification of war, military force, and violence. *(p. 101)*

military governments States in which military forces control the government; most common in global South countries, where the military may be the only large modern institution. *(p. 208)*

military-industrial complex A huge interlocking network of governmental agencies, industrial corporations, and research institutes, all working together to promote and benefit from military spending. *(p. 148)*

misperceptions and selective perceptions The selective or mistaken processing of the available information about a decision; one of several ways—along with affective and cognitive bias—in which individual decision-making diverges from the *rational actor model*. *(p. 134)* See also *information screens*.

Missile Technology Control Regime A set of agreements through which industrialized states try to limit the flow of missile-relevant technology to global South states. *(p. 229)*

mixed economies Economies such as those in the industrialized West that contain both some government control and some private ownership. *(p. 305)*

monetary policy A government's decisions about printing and circulating money, and one of the two major tools of macroeconomic policy making (the other being *fiscal policy*). *(p. 347)*

Montreal Protocol (1987) An agreement on protection of the ozone layer in which states pledged to reduce and then eliminate use of chlorofluorocarbons (CFCs). It is the most successful environmental treaty to date. *(p. 498)*

most-favoured nation (MFN) concept The principle that one state, by granting another state MFN status, promises to give it the same treatment given to the first state's most-favoured trading partner. *(p. 324)* See also *Generalized System of Preferences (GSP)*.

multilateral aid Government foreign aid from several states that goes through a third party, such as the UN or another agency. *(p. 475)*

multinational corporations (MNCs) Companies based in one state with affiliated branches or subsidiaries operating in other states. *(p. 356)* See also *home country* and *host country*.

multipolar system An international system with typically five or six centres of power that are not grouped into alliances. *(p. 79)*

Munich Agreement A symbol of the failed policy of appeasement, this agreement, signed in 1938, allowed Nazi Germany to occupy a part of Czechoslovakia. Rather than appease German aspirations, it was followed by further German expansions, which triggered World War II. *(p. 36)*

mutually assured destruction (MAD) The possession of second-strike nuclear capabilities, which ensures that neither of two adversaries could prevent the other from destroying it in an all-out war. *(p. 231)* See also *deterrence*.

national debt The amount a government owes in debt as a result of deficit spending. *(p. 348)* national interest The interests of a state overall (as opposed to particular parties or factions within the state). *(p. 67)*

nationalism The identification with and devotion to the interests of one's nation. It usually involves a large group of people who share a national identity and often a language, culture, or ancestry. *(p. 30)*

nation-states States whose populations share a sense of national identity, usually including a language and culture. *(p. 8)*

negotiation The process of formal bargaining, usually with the parties talking back and forth across a table. *(p. 62)*

neocolonialism The continuation, in a former colony, of colonial exploitation without formal political control. *(p. 421)*

neofunctionalism The theory which holds that economic integration (functionalism) generates a "spillover" effect, resulting in increased political integration. *(p. 370)*

neoliberalism Shorthand for "neoliberal institutionalism," an approach that stresses the importance of international institutions in reducing the inherent conflict that realists assume in an international system; the reasoning is based on the core liberal idea that seeking long-term mutual gains is often more rational than maximizing individual short-term gains. *(p. 90)* See also *liberalism*.

neorealism A version of realist theory that emphasizes the influence on state behaviour of the system's structure, especially the international distribution of power. *(p. 79)* See also *realism*.

New International Economic Order (NIEO) A global South effort begun in the mid-1970s, mainly conducted in UN forums, to advocate restructuring of the world economy so as to make North-South economic transactions less unfavourable to the South. *(p. 474)*

newly industrializing countries (NICs) States of the global South that have achieved self-sustaining capital accumulation, with impressive economic growth. *(p. 447)*

nonaligned movement Movement of mostly global South states, led by India and the former Yugoslavia, that attempted to stand apart from the U.S.-Soviet rivalry during the Cold War. *(p. 248)*

nongovernmental organizations (NGOs) Transnational groups or entities (such as the Catholic Church, Greenpeace, and the International Olympic Committee) that interact with states, multinational corporations (MNCs), other NGOs and intergovernmental organizations (IGOs). *(p. 10)*

Non-Proliferation Treaty (NPT) Treaty that created a framework for controlling the spread of nuclear materials and expertise, including the International Atomic Energy Agency (IAEA), a UN agency based in Vienna that is charged with inspecting the nuclear power industry in NPT member states to prevent secret military diversions of nuclear materials. *(p. 228)*

nonstate actors Actors other than state governments that operate either below the level of the state (that is, within states) or across state borders. *(p. 10)*

nontariff barriers Forms of restricting imports other than tariffs, such as quotas (ceilings on how many goods of a certain kind can be imported). *(p. 314)*

nonviolence/pacifism A philosophy based on a unilateral commitment to refrain from using any violent forms of leverage. More specifically, *pacifism* refers to a principled opposition to war in general rather than simply to particular wars. *(p. 106)*

normative bias The personal norms and values that IR scholars bring to their studies, such as a preference for peace rather than war. *(p. 98)*

norms (of behaviour) The shared expectations about what behaviour is considered proper. *(p. 72)*

North American Aerospace Defense Command (NORAD) An agreement (not a formal treaty) between Canada and the United States signed in 1958. Both countries agreed to work together to monitor and defend North American airspace. *(p. 246)*

North American Free Trade Agreement (NAFTA) A free trade zone encompassing the United States, Canada, and Mexico since 1994. *(p. 321)*

North American Monetary Union (NAMU) A proposed currency union between Canada and the U.S. The NAMU has become a regular feature in some policy discussions but has never been endorsed by a federal political party. *(p. 383)*

North Atlantic Treaty Organization (NATO) A U.S.-led military alliance, formed in 1949 with mainly West European members, to oppose and deter Soviet power in Europe. It has recently expanded into the former Soviet bloc. *(p. 243)* See also *Warsaw Pact*.

North-South gap The disparity in resources (income, wealth, and power) between the industrialized, relatively rich countries of the West (and the former East) and the poorer countries of Africa, the Middle East, and much of Asia and Latin America. *(p. 14)*

oil shocks The two sharp rises in the world price of oil that occurred in 1973–1974 and 1979. *(p. 510)*

optimizing Picking the very best option; contrasts with *satisficing*, or finding a satisfactory but less than best solution to a problem. The model of "bounded rationality" postulates that decision-makers generally "satisfice" rather than optimize. *(p. 135)*

organizational process model A decision-making model in which policy-makers or lower-level officials rely largely on standardized responses or standard operating procedures. *(p. 136)*

Organization of Petroleum Exporting Countries (OPEC) The most prominent cartel in the international economy; its members control over half the world's total oil exports, enough to significantly affect the world price of oil. *(p. 459)*

ozone layer The part of the atmosphere that screens out harmful unltraviolet rays from the sun. Certain chemicals used by some industries, in particular chlorofluorocarbons (CFCs), break the ozone layer down. *(p. 498)*

Paris Club A group of global North governments that have loaned money to global South governments; it meets periodically to work out terms of debt renegotiations. Private creditors meet as the **London Club**. *(p. 470)*

peace movements Movements against specific wars or against war and militarism in general, usually involving large numbers of people and forms of direct action such as street protests. *(p. 104)*

periphery The global South regions of the world-system that mostly extract raw materials from their area. *(p. 414)*

positive peace A peace that resolves the underlying reasons for war; not just a ceasefire but a transformation of relationships, including elimination or reduction of economic exploitation and political oppression. *(p. 103)* See also *structural violence*.

postmodernism An approach that denies the existence of a single fixed reality, and pays special attention to texts and to discourses—that is, to how people write and talk about a subject. *(p. 118)*

post-positivist feminism An effort to combine feminist and postmodernist perspectives with the aim of uncovering the hidden influences of gender in IR and showing how arbitrary the construction of gender roles is. *(p. 110)*

power The ability or potential to influence others' behaviour, as measured by the possession of certain tangible and intangible characteristics. (p. 56)

power projection The ability to use military force in areas far from a country's region or sphere of influence. *(p. 213)*

prisoners of war (POWs) Soldiers who are captured or have surrendered (and who thereby receive special status under the laws of war). *(p. 285)*

problem-solving theory Approach that takes the world as it finds it, and attempts to make institutions and relationships work more smoothly within that given framework. Problem-solving theory is usually contrasted with critical theory, which stands apart from the prevailing order of the world and asks how that order came about. *(p. 107)*

proletariat In Marxist terminology, the class of workers who must sell their labour power to capitalists in order to survive and whose labour is needed to produce surplus value; more specifically, industrial factory workers. It was considered the class that would spearhead the socialist revolution. *(p. 411)* See also *bourgeoisie*.

proliferation The spread of weapons of mass destruction (nuclear, chemical, or biological weapons) into the hands of more actors. *(p. 226)*

pronatalist policy A government policy that encourages or forces childbearing, and outlaws or limits access to contraception. *(p. 519)*

protectionism The protection of domestic industries against international competition, by trade tariffs and other means. *(p. 311)*

proxy wars Wars in the global South—often civil wars—in which the United States and the Soviet Union jockeyed for position by supplying and advising opposing factions. *(p. 40)*

public opinion In IR, the range of views on foreign policy issues held by the citizens of a state. *(p. 144)*

rally 'round the flag syndrome The public's increased support for government leaders during wartime, at least in the short term. *(p. 147)*

rational actors Actors conceived as single entities that can "think" about their actions coherently, make choices, identify their interests, and rank the interests in terms of priority. *(p. 67)*

rational actor model A model in which decision-makers calculate the costs and benefits of each possible course of action, then choose the one with the highest benefits and lowest costs. *(p. 130)*

realism (political realism) A broad intellectual tradition that explains international relations mainly in terms of power. *(p. 54)* See also *idealism* and *neorealism*.

reciprocity A response in kind to another's actions; a strategy of reciprocity uses positive forms of leverage to promise rewards and negative forms of leverage to threaten punishment. *(p. 65)*

refugees People fleeing their countries to find refuge from war, natural disaster, or political persecution. International law distinguishes them from migrants. *(p. 431)*

reserves Hard-currency stockpiles kept by states. *(p. 335)*

risk assessment The preinvestment efforts by corporations (especially banks) to determine how likely it is that future political conditions in the target country will change so radically as to disrupt the flow of income. *(p. 362)*

satisficing The act of finding a satisfactory or "good enough" solution to a problem. *(p. 135)* See also *optimizing*.

Secretariat See *UN Secretariat*.

secular (state) A state created apart from religious establishments and in which there is a high degree of separation between religious and political organizations. *(p. 179)*

security community A situation in which low expectations of interstate violence permit a high degree of political cooperation—as, for example, among NATO members. *(p. 370)*

Security Council See *UN Security Council*.

security dilemma A situation in which states' actions taken to assure their own security (such as deploying more military forces) are perceived as threats to the security of other states. *(p. 74)*

semiperiphery The area in the world-system in which some manufacturing occurs and some capital concentrates, but not to the extent of the core areas. *(p. 414)*

service sector The part of an economy that concerns services (as opposed to the production of tangible goods); the key focus in international trade negotiations is on banking, insurance, and related financial services.   *(p. 317)*

settlement The outcome of a bargaining process.   *(p. 156)*

Single European Act Treaty that set a target date of the end of 1992 for the creation of a *true common market* (free cross-border movement of goods, capital, people, and services) in the European Community (EC).   *(p. 377)*

Sino-Soviet split A rift in the 1960s between the communist powers of the Soviet Union and China, fuelled by China's opposition to Soviet moves toward peaceful coexistence with the United States.   *(p. 38)*

socialism A term encompassing many political movements, parties, economic theories, and ideologies, historical and present-day. With its idea that workers should have political power (or a larger share of power), socialism favours the redistribution of wealth toward the workers who produce it. In economic policy, socialists have favoured different combinations of planning and reliance on market forces, as well as various patterns of ownership.   *(p. 409)* See also *capitalism* and *Marxism*.

sovereignty A state's right, at least in principle, to do whatever it wants within its own territory; traditionally sovereignty is the most important international norm.   *(p. 72)*

Special Drawing Right (SDR) A world currency created by the *International Monetary Fund (IMF)* to replace gold as a world standard. Valued by a "basket" of national currencies, the SDR has been called "paper gold."   *(p. 343)*

Stalinism The system that prevailed during Stalin's rule in the Soviet Union (1924–1953), which was marked by totalitarian state control under the Communist party and the ruthless elimination of the regime's opponents on a massive scale.   *(p. 410)*

standpoint feminism A strand of feminism that believes gender differences are not just socially constructed and that views women as inherently less warlike than men.   *(p. 109)*

state An inhabited territorial entity controlled by a government that exercises sovereignty on its territory.   *(p. 7)*

state-owned industries Industries such as oil-production companies and airlines that are owned wholly or partly by the state because they are thought to be vital to the national economy.   *(p. 305)*

state-sponsored terrorism The use of terrorist groups by states, usually under control of a state's intelligence agency, to achieve political aims.   *(p. 192)*

stealth technology The use of special radar-absorbent materials and unusual shapes in the design of aircraft, missiles, and ships to scatter enemy radar.   *(p. 216)*

Strategic Arms Limitation Treaties (SALT) SALT I (1972) and SALT II (1979) put formal ceilings on the growth of U.S. and Soviet strategic weapons. SALT II was never ratified by the U.S. Senate (due to the subsequent Soviet invasion of Afghanistan).   *(p. 274)*

Strategic Arms Reduction Treaties (START) START I (1991) called for reducing the superpowers' strategic arsenals by about 30 percent. START II (1992) proposes to cut the remaining weapons by more than half in the next decade. START III is under discussion.   *(p. 274)*

Strategic Defense Initiative (SDI) A U.S. effort, also known as "star wars," to develop defences that could shoot down incoming ballistic missiles, spurred by President Ronald Reagan in 1983. Critics call it an expensive failure that would violate the ABM Treaty.   *(p. 232)* See also *Antiballistic Missile (ABM) Treaty*.

structural violence A term used by some scholars to refer to poverty, hunger, oppression, and other social and economic sources of conflict.   *(p. 103)* See also *positive peace*.

subsistence farming Rural communities growing food mainly for their own consumption rather than for sale in local or world markets.   *(p. 427)*

subtext Meanings that are implicit or hidden in a text rather than explicitly addressed.   *(p. 119)* See also *postmodernism*.

summit meeting A meeting between heads of state, often referring to leaders of great powers, as in the Cold War superpower summits between the United States and the Soviet Union or today's meetings of the Group of Eight on economic coordination.   *(p. 40)*

superstructure In Marxist terminology, the forms of politics and culture that are shaped by the economic base or mode of production (slavery, feudalism, capitalism).   *(p. 412)*

supranationalism The subordination of state authority or national identity to larger institutions and groupings, such as the European Union.   *(p. 368)*

tariff A duty or tax levied on certain types of imports (usually as a percentage of their value) as they enter a country.   *(p. 313)*

technology transfer Global south states' acquisition of technology (knowledge, skills, methods, designs, specialized equipment, etc.) from foreign sources, usually in conjunction with *direct foreign investment* or similar business operations.   *(p. 467)*

terms of trade The overall relationship between prices of imported and exported goods.   *(p. 457)*

territorial waters The waters near states' shores generally treated as part of national territory. The UN Convention on the Law of the Sea provides for a 12-nautical mile territorial sea (exclusive national jurisdiction over shipping and navigation) and a 200-nautical mile exclusive economic zone (EEZ) covering exclusive fishing and mineral rights (but allowing for free navigation by all).   *(p. 167)* See also *high seas* and *UN Convention on the Law of the Sea (UNCLOS)*.

Third World countries See *less-developed countries*.

tit for tat A strategy of strict reciprocity (matching the other player's response) after an initial cooperative move; it can bring about mutual cooperation in a repeated Prisoner's Dilemma game, since it ensures that defection will not pay.   *(p. 90)*

total war Warfare by one state waged to conquer and occupy another; modern total war originated in the Napoleonic Wars, which relied upon conscription on a mass scale. *(p. 187)*

tragedy of the commons A collective goods dilemma that is created when common environmental assets (such as the world's fisheries) are depleted or degraded through the failure of states to cooperate effectively. One solution is the *enclosure of the commons* (splitting them into individually owned pieces); international regimes can also be a (partial) solution.   *(p. 490)*

transitional economies Countries in Russia and Eastern Europe that are trying to convert from communism to capitalism, with various degrees of success.   *(p. 305)*

Treaty of Rome The founding document of the European Economic Community (EEC) or Common Market, now subsumed by the European Union.   *(p. 373)*

United Nations (UN) An organization of nearly all world states, created after World War II to promote collective security.   *(p. 7)*

UN Charter The founding document of the United Nations; it is based on the principles that states are equal, have *sovereignty* over their own affairs, enjoy independence and territorial integrity, and must fulfill international obligations. The Charter also lays out the structure and methods of the UN.   *(p. 249)*

UN Conference on Trade and Development (UNCTAD) A structure established in 1964 to promote global South development through various trade proposals.   *(p. 269)*

UN Convention on the Law of the Sea (UNCLOS) A world treaty (1982) governing use of the oceans. The UNCLOS treaty established rules on territorial waters and a 200-nautical mile exclusive economic zone (EEZ).   *(p. 502)* See also *territorial waters*.

UN Development Programme (UNDP) UN agency that coordinates the flow of multilateral development assistance and manages 5000 projects at once around the world (focusing especially on technical development assistance).   *(p. 478)*

UN Environment Programme (UNEP) UN agency that monitors environmental conditions and, among other activities, works with the World Meteorological Organization to measure changes in global climate. *(p. 498)*

UN General Assembly Comprised of representatives of all states, it allocates UN funds, passes nonbinding resolutions, and coordinates global South development programs and various autonomous agencies through the Economic and Social Council (ECOSOC).   *(p. 249)*

UN Secretariat The UN's executive branch, led by the secretary-general.   *(p. 251)*

UN Security Council A body of five great powers (which can veto resolutions) and ten rotating member states, which makes decisions about international peace and security, including the dispatch of UN peacekeeping forces.   *(p. 251)*

undernourishment The lack of needed foods; a lack of calories.   *(p. 426)*

urbanization A shift of population from the countryside to the cities that typically accompanies economic development and is augmented by displacement of peasants from *subsistence farming*.   *(p. 428)*

Uruguay Round A series of negotiations under the *General Agreement on Tariffs and Trade (GATT)* that began in Uruguay in 1986, and concluded in 1994 with agreement to create the World Trade Organization. The Uruguay Round followed earlier GATT negotiations such as the Kennedy Round and the Tokyo Round. *(p. 325)* See also *World Trade Organization (WTO)*.

U.S.-Japanese Security Treaty A bilateral alliance between the United States and Japan, created in 1951 against the potential Soviet threat to Japan. The United States maintains troops in Japan and is committed to defend Japan if attacked, and Japan pays the United States to offset about half the cost of maintaining the troops. *(p. 245)*

war crimes Violations of the law governing the conduct of warfare, such as by mistreating prisoners of war or unnecessarily targeting civilians.   *(p. 283)* See also *just war doctrine*.

Warsaw Pact A Soviet-led Eastern European military alliance, founded in 1955 and disbanded in 1991. It opposed the NATO alliance. See also *North Atlantic Treaty Organization (NATO)*.   *(p. 244)*

weapons of mass destruction Nuclear, chemical, and biological weapons, all distinguished from conventional weapons by their enormous potential lethality, and by their relative lack of discrimination in whom they kill. *(p. 217)*

World Bank Formally the International Bank for Reconstruction and Development (IBRD), it was established in 1944 as a source of loans to help reconstruct the European economies. Later, the main borrowers were global South countries and, in the 1990s, Eastern European ones.   *(p. 341)*

World Court (International Court of Justice) The judicial arm of the UN; located in The Hague, it hears only cases between states.   *(p. 276)*

world government A centralized world governing body with strong enforcement powers.   *(p. 104)*

World Health Organization (WHO) Based in Geneva, it provides technical assistance to improve health conditions in the global South and conducts major immunization campaigns.   *(p. 269)*

world-system theory A view of the world in terms of regional class divisions, with industrialized countries as the *core*, poorest global South countries as the *periphery*, and other areas (for example, some of the newly industrializing countries) as the *semiperiphery*.   (*p. 413*)

World Trade Organization (WTO) An organization begun in 1995 that expanded the GATT's traditional focus on manufactured goods, and created monitoring and enforcement mechanisms.   (*p. 323*) See also *General Agreement on Tariffs and Trade (GATT)* and *Uruguay Round*.

World University Service of Canada (WUSC) Agency involved in development assistance projects in over 50 countries that also coordinates professional and volunteer positions in many of those projects.   (*p. 477*)

zero-sum games A situation in which one actor's gain is by definition equal to the other's loss, as opposed to a non-zero-sum game, in which it is possible for both actors to gain (or lose).   (*p. 69*)

Photo Credits

Author Index

Subject Index

REFERENCE MAPS

North America

Scale 1:38,700,000

Lambert Conformal Conic Projection,
standard parallels 37° N and 65° N

0   500 Kilometres
0   500 Nautical Miles

Boundary representation is
not necessarily authoritative.

802374 (B01267) 5-95

Central America and the Caribbean

South America

Africa

Scale 1:67,000,000

Azimuthal Equal-Area Projection

0   500   1000 Kilometres

0   500   1000 Nautical Miles

Boundary representation is not necessarily authoritative.

802380 (R00475) 5-95

Northern Africa and the Middle East

North Atlantic Ocean

Azores (PORT.)

Madeira Islands (PORT.)

Canary Islands (SP.)

PORTUGAL
Lisbon

SPAIN
Madrid

GIBRALTAR (U.K.)

MOROCCO
Rabat

El Aaiún

Western Sahara

MAURITANIA
Nouakchott

SENEGAL
Dakar

THE GAMBIA
Banjul

GUINEA-BISSAU

GUINEA
Conakry

SIERRA LEONE
Freetown

Monrovia
LIBERIA

CÔTE D'IVOIRE
Yamoussoukro

MALI
Bamako

Niger

BURKINA
Ouagadougou

GHANA
Accra

TOGO
Lomé

BENIN
Porto-Novo

Niamey

NIGER

NIGERIA
Abuja

CAMEROON
Yaoundé

Malabo
EQUATORIAL GUINEA

SAO TOME AND PRINCIPE
São Tomé

Gulf of Guinea

Libreville
GABON

CONGO

DEMOCRATIC CONGO

Bangui
CENTRAL AFRICAN REPUBLIC

N'Djamena
CHAD

ALGERIA
Algiers

TUNISIA
Tunis

Tripoli
LIBYA

Balearic Islands

Corsica

Sardinia

Sicily

FRANCE

ITALY
Rome

MALTA
Valletta

Mediterranean Sea

Tirané
ALBANIA

SLO
CRO
Zagreb
Belgrade
Sarajevo
Podgorica
MNE
Skopje
BULGARIA
Sofia
ROMANIA
Bucharest

Tropic of Cancer

Crete

GREECE
Athens

TURKEY
Ankara

Black Sea

UKRAINE

CYPRUS
Nicosia

LEBANON
Beirut
Damascus
SYRIA
ISRAEL
Jerusalem
Amman
JORDAN

Cairo
EGYPT

Nile

Red Sea

SUDAN
Khartoum

White Nile

Blue Nile

UGANDA
Kampala

Lake Victoria

KENYA

ETHIOPIA
Addis Ababa

ERITREA
Asmara

DJIBOUTI
Djibouti

SOMALIA
Mogadishu

Gulf of Aden

Socotra (YEMEN)

YEMEN
Sanaa

SAUDI ARABIA
Riyadh

Red Sea

KUWAIT
Kuwait

BAHRAIN
Manama
QATAR
Doha
Abu Dhabi
U.A.E.

Muscat
OMAN
Gulf of Oman

Persian Gulf

Caspian Sea

IRAQ
Baghdad

Tigris

Euphrates

Tbilisi
GEORGIA
ARMENIA
Yerevan
AZERBAIJAN
Baku

RUSSIA

KAZAKHSTAN

TURKMENISTAN
Ashgabat

UZBEKISTAN

TAJIKISTAN
Dushanbe

AFGHANISTAN
Kabul

PAKISTAN

IRAN
Tehran

Indian Ocean

Equator

Boundary representation is not necessarily authoritative.

Scale 1:42,300,000

0   500 Kilometres
0   500 Nautical Miles

Azimuthal Equal-Area Projection

Europe

Serbia and Montenegro have asserted the formation of a joint independent state, but this entity has not been formally recognized as a state by the United States.

Scale 1:19,500,000

Lambert Conformal Conic Projection, standard parallels 40°N and 56°N

0   300 Kilometres

0   300 Nautical Miles

Asia